THE ROUTLEDGE HANDBOOK OF SOCIAL EPISTEMOLOGY

Edited by an international team of leading scholars, *The Routledge Handbook of Social Epistemology* is the first major reference work devoted to this growing field. The *Handbook*'s 46 chapters, written by philosophers and social theorists from around the world and appearing in print here for the first time, are organized into eight main parts:

    I. Historical Backgrounds to Social Epistemology
    II. The Epistemology of Testimony
    III. Disagreement, Diversity, and Relativism
    IV. Science and Social Epistemology
    V. The Epistemology of Groups
    VI. Feminist Epistemology
    VII. The Epistemology of Democracy
    VIII. Further Horizons for Social Epistemology

    With lists of references after each chapter and a comprehensive index, this volume will prove to be the definitive guide to the burgeoning interdisciplinary field of social epistemology.

Miranda Fricker is presidential professor of philosophy at The Graduate Center, City University of New York. Her research is primarily in ethics and social epistemology with a special interest in virtue and feminist perspectives. She is the author of *Epistemic Injustice: Power and the Ethics of Knowing* (2007); co-author of *Reading Ethics: Selected Texts with Interactive Commentary* (2009); and co-editor of a number of edited collections, the most recent of which is *The Epistemic Life of Groups: Essays in the Epistemology of Collectives* (2016). She is an associate editor of the *Journal of the American Philosophical Association* and a fellow of the British Academy.

Peter J. Graham is professor of philosophy and linguistics at the University of California, Riverside, where he also served as associate dean for arts and humanities. He specializes in epistemology and related areas in the philosophies of psychology, biology, and the social sciences. He is associate editor of the *Journal of the American Philosophical Association* and the co-editor of *Epistemic Entitlement* (2019).

David Henderson is Robert R. Chambers distinguished professor of philosophy at the University of Nebraska, Lincoln. He teaches and writes primarily in the fields of epistemology and the philosophy of the social sciences. He is the co-author, with Terry Horgan, of *The Epistemological Spectrum: At the Interface of Cognitive Science and Conceptual Analysis* (2011) and co-editor, with John Greco, of *Epistemic Evaluation: Point and Purpose in Epistemology* (2015).

Nikolaj J. L. L. Pedersen is associate professor of philosophy at Underwood International College, Yonsei University, and is the founding director of the Veritas Research Center, also at Yonsei University. He is co-editor of *New Waves in Truth* (2010), *Truth and Pluralism: Current Debates* (2013), *Epistemic Pluralism* (2017), and *Epistemic Entitlement* (2019).

ROUTLEDGE HANDBOOKS IN PHILOSOPHY

Routledge Handbooks in Philosophy are state-of-the-art surveys of emerging, newly refreshed, and important fields in philosophy, providing accessible yet thorough assessments of key problems, themes, thinkers, and recent developments in research.

All chapters for each volume are specially commissioned, and written by leading scholars in the field. Carefully edited and organized, *Routledge Handbooks in Philosophy* provide indispensable reference tools for students and researchers seeking a comprehensive overview of new and exciting topics in philosophy.

They are also valuable teaching resources as accompaniments to textbooks, anthologies, and research-orientated publications.

Also available:

The Routledge Handbook of Virtue Epistemology
Edited by Heather Battaly

The Routledge Handbook of Moral Epistemology
Edited by Karen Jones, Mark Timmons, and Aaron Zimmerman

The Routledge Handbook of Love in Philosophy
Edited by Adrienne M. Martin

The Routledge Handbook of the Philosophy and Psychology of Luck
Edited by Ian M. Church and Robert J. Hartman

The Routledge Handbook of Emergence
Edited by Sophie Gibb, Robin Hendry, and Tom Lancaster

The Routledge Handbook of the Philosophy of Evil
Edited by Thomas Nys and Stephen de Wijze

The Routledge Handbook of Social Epistemology
Edited by Miranda Fricker, Peter J. Graham, Nikolaj J. L. L. Pedersen, David Henderson

For more information about this series, please visit: www.routledge.com/Routledge-Handbooks-in-Philosophy/book-series/RHP

THE ROUTLEDGE HANDBOOK OF SOCIAL EPISTEMOLOGY

Edited by Miranda Fricker, Peter J. Graham, David Henderson, and Nikolaj J. L. L. Pedersen

Routledge
Taylor & Francis Group
New York London

First published 2020
by Routledge
605 Third Avenue, New York, NY 10017

and by Routledge
2 Park Square, Milton Park, Abingdon, Oxon, OX14 4RN

First issued in paperback 2021

Routledge is an imprint of the Taylor & Francis Group, an informa business

© 2020 Taylor & Francis

The right of Miranda Fricker, Peter J. Graham, David Henderson, and Nikolaj J.L.L. Pedersen to be identified as the authors of the editorial material, and of the authors for their individual chapters, has been asserted in accordance with sections 77 and 78 of the Copyright, Designs and Patents Act 1988.

Publisher's Note
The publisher has gone to great lengths to ensure the quality of this reprint but points out that some imperfections in the original copies may be apparent.

Library of Congress Cataloging-in-Publication Data
A catalog record for this title has been requested

ISBN 13: 978-1-03-209098-6 (pbk)
ISBN 13: 978-1-138-85851-0 (hbk)

Typeset in Bembo
by Swales & Willis, Exeter, Devon, UK

CONTENTS

Contents

CONTRIBUTORS

Kristoffer Ahlstrom-Vij is a reader in philosophy at Birkbeck College, University of London. He works on social epistemology and epistemic normativity, and has been published in, among other places, *Noûs, Philosophy and Phenomenological Research, Episteme, Philosophical Quarterly*, and *Philosophical Studies*. His books include *Epistemic Consequentialism* (2018), co-edited with Jeffrey Dunn, and *Epistemic Paternalism: A Defense* (2013).

Linda Martín Alcoff is professor of philosophy at Hunter College and the Graduate Center, CUNY. She is a past President of the American Philosophical Association, Eastern Division. Her recent books include *Visible Identities: Race, Gender and the Self* (2006), *The Future of Whiteness* (2015), and *Rape and Resistance* (2018).

Zachary Bachman is currently visiting assistant professor of philosophy at Sam Houston State University. His main areas of research include the nature of normativity, both practical and epistemic, with a focus on constitutivist approaches, and applied ethics, especially climate ethics.

Jason Baehr is professor of philosophy at Loyola Marymount University. His main research areas are epistemology and virtue theory, especially virtue epistemology. He is the author of *The Inquiring Mind: On Intellectual Virtues and Virtue Epistemology* (2011) and editor of *Intellectual Virtues and Education: Essays in Applied Virtue Epistemology* (2016). He recently directed the *Intellectual Virtues and Education Project* (sponsored by the John Templeton Foundation).

Matthew A. Benton is assistant professor in philosophy at Seattle Pacific University. Previously he was a postdoctoral research fellow at the University of Notre Dame, and a junior research fellow at the University of Oxford. He writes primarily in epistemology, philosophy of language, and philosophy of religion.

Alexander Bird is Peter Sowerby professor of philosophy and medicine at King's College London. His research covers the philosophy of science and medicine, metaphysics, and epistemology. He is author of the books, *Thomas Kuhn* (2000) and *Nature's Metaphysics: Laws and Properties* (2007).

Allen Buchanan is professor of philosophy in the Department of Philosophy and Freedom Center at the University of Arizona. He served as staff philosophy for the President's Commission on Medical Ethics in 1983, and from 1996 to 2000 he served on the advisory council for the National Human Genome Research Institute. His books include *Justice, Legitimacy and Self-Determination* (2003), *Better than Human* (2011), *Beyond Humanity* (2011), *The Heart of Human*

Rights (2013), and *The Evolution of Moral Progress: A Biocultural Theory* (2018), co-authored with Russell Powell.

Laura Frances Callahan is assistant professor of philosophy at the University of Notre Dame. She works on responsibility and rational belief. She has published essays in epistemology, medical ethics, and the philosophy of religion. She is the co-editor, with Timothy O'Connor, of *Religious Faith and Intellectual Virtue* (2014).

J. Adam Carter is lecturer of philosophy at the University of Glasgow. His main research interests are epistemology and social epistemology. His monographs include *Metaepistemology and Relativism* (2016) and, with C. Littlejohn, *This Is Epistemology* (Forthcoming). He has published in journals such as *Noûs, Philosophy and Phenomenological Research, Philosophical Studies,* and *Analysis.*

David Coady is senior lecturer in philosophy and gender studies in the School of Humanities at the University of Tasmania. His research covers a wide variety of philosophical topics, including rumour, conspiracy theory, the blogosphere, expertise, and democratic theory. He has also published on the metaphysics of causation, the philosophy of law, climate change, cricket ethics, police ethics, and the ethics of horror films. He is the author of *What to Believe Now: Applying Epistemology to Contemporary Issues* (2012), the co-author of *The Climate Change Debate: an Epistemic and Ethical Enquiry* (2013), the editor of *Conspiracy Theories: the Philosophical Debate* (2006), and a co-editor of *A Companion to Applied Philosophy* (2016).

Finn Collin is emeritus professor of philosophy at the University of Copenhagen and adjunct professor at the University of Aalborg Copenhagen. His writings are mainly in philosophy of science, focusing upon the social sciences and humanities. His chief publications in English are *Theory and Understanding* (1985), *Social Reality* (1993), and *Science Studies as Naturalized Philosophy* (2011).

Sharon Crasnow is professor emerita, Norco College. She co-edits the Lexington Books series *Feminist Strategies.* Recent publications include "Feminist Standpoint Theory" in *Philosophy of Social Science: A New Introduction,* edited by Nancy Cartwright and Eleonora Montuschi (2014).

Nancy Daukas is professor of philosophy and contributing faculty in women's, gender, and sexuality studies at Guilford College in Greensboro, North Carolina. Her research interests focus on feminist epistemology, social epistemology, and virtue epistemology.

Shannon Dea is associate professor of philosophy at University of Waterloo, where she also teaches women's studies, and was formerly the director of the women's studies program. She is the author of a number of articles on Peirce and pragmatism, and the book *Beyond the Binary: Thinking About Sex and Gender* (2016).

Franz Dietrich is research professor at Paris School of Economics and CNRS, working on economics and philosophy. He primarily addresses foundational and methodological questions about decisions, both at the individual level and the group level, and from both formal and philosophical perspectives. In particular, he works on the reason-based foundations of choice, preference change, and the aggregation of judgments, probabilistic beliefs, and preferences.

Igor Douven is CNRS research director at Science, Normes, Décision (Sorbonne University). He works in cognitive science and philosophy. His publications appeared in such journals as *Analysis, British Journal for the Philosophy of Science, Cognition, Cognitive Psychology, Cognitive Science, Journal of Philosophy, Mind, Nous, Philosophical Review, Philosophy and Phenomenological Research, Philosophy of Science, Psychonomic Bulletin and Review,* and *Thinking and Reasoning.* He is the author of *The Epistemology of Indicative Conditionals* (2016).

Peter van Elswyk is assistant professor of philosophy at the University of Wisconsin, Milwaukee. His research focuses on topics in the philosophy of language, and in semantics and pragmatics. He has recently published on these topics in *Philosophical Studies* and *The Philosophical Quarterly*.

Eva Erman is professor at the Department of Political Science, Stockholm University. She works in the field of political philosophy. She has published numerous articles and books, most recently the monograph *The Practical Turn in Political Theory* (2018). Erman is also the editor-in-chief of the journal *Ethics & Global Politics*.

Filippo Ferrari is a research fellow in philosophy at the University of Bonn. His research focuses primarily on normative aspects of enquiry and disagreement and on topics surrounding the nature of truth, including deflationism, relativism and pluralism. He has published essays in *Analysis, Mind, Synthese, The Philosophical Quarterly*, and other leading journals.

Miranda Fricker is presidential professor of philosophy at The Graduate Center, CUNY. Her work is primarily in ethics and social epistemology with a special interest in virtue and feminist perspectives. She is the author of *Epistemic Injustice: Power and the Ethics of Knowing* (2009), co-author of *Reading Ethics: Selected Texts with Interactive Commentary* (2009), and co-editor of a number of edited collections. She is an associate editor of the *Journal of the APA*, and a fellow of the British Academy.

Michael Fuerstein is associate professor of philosophy at St. Olaf College in Northfield, Minnesota. His research interests are in social/political philosophy, social epistemology, American pragmatism (especially Dewey), and business ethics. His current research focuses on the epistemic aspects of liberalism and democracy. He has published in *Episteme, Social Theory and Practice*, and the *Journal of Political Philosophy*, among other venues.

Sanford C. Goldberg is professor of philosophy at Northwestern University. He works in epistemology, social epistemology, philosophy of language, and philosophy of mind. His books include *Anti-Individualism* (2007), *Relying on Others* (2010), *Assertion* (2015), and *To the Best of Our Knowledge* (2018), as well as being editor of the forthcoming *Oxford Handbook on Assertion*, among other edited works. He is editor-in-chief of *Oxford Handbooks Online*, and series co-editor of *Cambridge Studies in Philosophy*. He is the founder and inaugural director of the Social Epistemology Network.

Alvin I. Goldman is board of governors professor of philosophy and cognitive science, emeritus, at Rutgers University, New Brunswick. He has made seminal contributions in epistemology, social epistemology, cognitive science, philosophy of mind, and philosophy of action. Much of his later work has focused on the development of social epistemology. His many books include *Epistemology and Cognition* (1986), *Pathways to Knowledge: Public and Private* (2004), *Simulating Minds* (2006), *Reliabilism and Contemporary Epistemology* (2012), and *Joint Ventures: Mindreading, Mirroring, and Embodied Cognition* (2014). His book *Knowledge in a Social World* (1999) is a landmark publication in contemporary analytic social epistemology. He is also co-editor, with Dennis Whitcomb, of *Social Epistemology: Essential Readings* (2011).

Peter J. Graham is professor of philosophy and linguistics, and former associate dean of arts & humanities, at the University of California, Riverside. He is currently a fellow at the Institute for Advanced Study in the Humanities at the University of Edinburgh. He works primarily on the epistemology of testimony, the role of functions in the analysis of epistemic warrant and epistemic goods, and the role of social norms in epistemology and the philosophy of language. Along with Nikolaj J. L. L. Pedersen, he is co-editor of *Epistemic Entitlement* (2019).

Heidi Grasswick is the George Nye and Anne Walker Boardman professor of mental and moral science in the Department of Philosophy at Middlebury College and an affiliate of the gender, sexuality, and feminist studies program. Her research interests span questions of feminist epistemology, philosophy of science, and social epistemology more generally, including questions concerning the relationship between the epistemic and the ethical, the epistemic role of trust, and relations between individual knowers and their communities. She is the editor of *Feminist Epistemology and Philosophy of Science: Power in Knowledge* (2011).

David Henderson is Robert R. Chambers distinguished professor of philosophy at the University of Nebraska, Lincoln. He teaches and writes primarily in epistemology and the philosophy of the social sciences. Recent work brings together these interests, as he has come to focus on social norms, and epistemic norms as social norms. He is the co-author, with Terry Horgan, of *The Epistemological Spectrum: At the Interface of Cognitive Science and Conceptual Analysis* (2011), and co-editor, with John Greco, of *Epistemic Evaluation: Point and Purpose in Epistemology* (2015).

Jules Holroyd is a vice-chancellor's fellow in philosophy at the University of Sheffield, pursuing research on topics in moral psychology, social philosophy and feminist philosophy. In particular, she researches the ways that our cognitions are influenced by, and complicit in, injustices that track social identity, such as gender and race.

Klemens Kappel is professor of philosophy and director of the Social Epistemology Research Group (SERG) at the Department of Media, Cognition and Communication, University of Copenhagen. His main research area is social epistemology.

Eric Kerr is lecturer and research fellow at the National University of Singapore. He is associate editor at *Social Epistemology* and writes at the intersection of social epistemology and the philosophy of science and technology.

Melissa A. Koenig is the director of the Early Language and Experience Lab and a professor at the Institute of Child Development in the College of Education and Human Development at the University of Minnesota. She specializes in early language development and theory of mind. Her recent research focuses on children's evaluation of testimony, the bases upon which they credit knowledge to others, and the epistemic significance of doubt. She also explores the importance of credible and accurate advertising to young children, and the ways in which adults can expand children's critical thinking abilities.

Jaakko Kuorikoski is associate professor of new social research at the University of Tampere. His main areas of specialization are philosophy of economics and philosophy of social sciences, and he has published on scientific explanation, modeling, simulation and causal reasoning.

Michael E. Lynch is professor emeritus in the Department of Science & Technology Studies at Cornell University. His research focuses on discourse, visual representation, and practical action in research laboratories, clinical settings, and legal tribunals. His books include *Scientific Practice and Ordinary Action* (1993), and *Truth Machine: The Contentious History of DNA Fingerprinting* (with Simon Cole, Ruth McNally, and Kathleen Jordan, 2008). From 2002 until 2012, he was editor of the journal *Social Studies of Science*, and in 2007–09 he was president of the Society for Social Studies of Science.

Michael Patrick Lynch is board of trustees distinguished professor of philosophy and director of the Humanities Institute at the University of Connecticut. He is the author of *True to Life* (1998), *Truth as One and Many* (2009), *In Praise of Reason* (2012), and *The Internet of Us* (2016).

Carlo Martini is assistant professor at Vita-Salute San Raffaele University in Milan and visiting associate researcher at the TINT Centre for Philosophy of Social Science. He works in philosophy of science and social epistemology and has published on disagreement, expertise, economic methodology, and science-policy.

Benjamin McMyler is associate professor of philosophy at Texas A&M University. He works in epistemology and philosophy of mind, broadly construed. He is particularly interested in issues concerning the nature and significance of various forms of social influence on thought and action, issues lying at the intersection of epistemology, philosophy of mind, moral psychology, philosophy of language, and social and political philosophy. He is the author of *Testimony, Trust, and Authority* (2011).

Boaz Miller is senior lecturer at the Department of Community Information Systems at Zefat Academic College. His research interests include testimony, science and values, consensus and dissent, and the epistemology of digital technologies. He has published articles in *Episteme, Social Epistemology, Studies in the History and Philosophy of Science, Synthese, The Philosophical Quarterly*, and other journals.

Niklas Möller is associate professor at the Division of Philosophy, Royal Institute of Technology (KTH). He works in the field of moral and political philosophy. He has published numerous articles in peer reviewed journals as well as, with Eva Erman, the monograph *The Practical Turn in Political Theory* (2018).

Philip J. Nickel specializes on philosophical aspects of our reliance on others, including trust, consent, and testimonial belief. Some of his research is in the domain of biomedical ethics, focusing on issues of consent and the mediation of care through technology and data. He is associate professor in the Philosophy and Ethics Group in the Department of Industrial Engineering and Innovation Sciences at the Eindhoven University of Technology.

Gloria Origgi is senior researcher at the Institut Jean Nicod, CNRS Paris. He research focuses on topics in social epistemology, philosophy of social science, and the study of social cognition. Her books include *Reputation: What It Is and Why It Matters* (2018).

Nikolaj J. L. L. Pedersen is associate professor of philosophy and founding director of the Veritas Research Center and UIC Research Institute at Underwood International College, Yonsei University. His main research areas are truth, epistemology (including social epistemology), and metaphysics. He has published in journals such as *Noûs, Philosophical Issues, Philosophical Quarterly, Analysis, Synthese, Erkenntnis*, and *The Monist*. His co-edited volumes include *Truth and Pluralism* (2013), *Epistemic Pluralism* (2017), and *Epistemic Entitlement* (2019).

Katherine Puddifoot is assistant professor of philosophy at Durham University. She recently worked as a research fellow on the ERC-funded Project PERFECT at the University of Birmingham. Her current research is at the intersection of social epistemology and philosophy of psychology, addressing issues relating to memory, stereotyping and implicit bias.

Samuli Reijula is a postdoctoral researcher at the University of Tampere. He is also a member of the TINT Centre for the Philosophy of Social Science at the University of Helsinki. His current research focuses on the social epistemology of science and on philosophical questions in evidence-based policy.

Kristina Rolin is research fellow at Helsinki Collegium for Advanced Studies and the university lecturer in research ethics at Tampere University. Her publications can be found in *Philosophy of Science, Studies in History and Philosophy of Science, Philosophy of the Social Sciences, Perspectives on Science, Social Epistemology, Episteme*, and *Hypatia*.

Joseph Shieber is professor of philosophy at Lafayette College. He is the author of *Testimony: A Philosophical Introduction* (2015). He works in epistemology, philosophy of language, the history of modern philosophy, and the history of 20th century analytic philosophy.

Matthew Silk has a PhD in philosophy from the University of Waterloo, Canada. He has published on the history of pragmatism and logical empiricism.

Kai Spiekermann is associate professor of political philosophy at the London School of Economics. Among his research interests are normative and positive political theory, philosophy of the social sciences, social epistemology and environmental change. He is particularly interested in applying formal methods, computational simulations, and experiments to problems in political philosophy.

Robert B. Talisse is W. Alton Jones professor of philosophy at Vanderbilt University. He specializes in contemporary political philosophy, with particular interest in democratic theory and liberalism. His most recent work engages issues at the intersection of political philosophy and epistemology. His books include *Democracy After Liberalism* (2007), *A Pragmatist Philosophy of Democracy* (2007), *Democracy and Moral Conflict* (Cambridge UP, 2009), *Pluralism and Liberal Politics* (2012), and *Engaging Political Philosophy* (2016).

Alessandra Tanesini is professor of philosophy at Cardiff University. She is the author of *An Introduction to Feminist Epistemologies* (1999), of *Wittgenstein: A Feminist Interpretation* (2004), and of several articles in feminist philosophy, the philosophy of mind and language, epistemology, and on Nietzsche. Her current work lies at the intersection of ethics and epistemology, and focuses on epistemic vice, prejudice, and ignorance.

Deborah Perron Tollefsen is a professor of philosophy and associate dean of the College of Arts and Sciences at the University of Memphis. Her research and teaching interests include philosophy of mind, social epistemology, and social ontology. She has published research articles on group testimony, collective moral responsibility, joint action, co-authorship, and group knowledge, and the book *Groups as Agents* (2015).

Stephen Turner is distinguished university professor of philosophy at the University of South Florida. His books include *The Social Theory of Practices: Tacit Knowledge and Presuppositions* (1994), *Brains/Practices/Relativism: Social Theory after Cognitive Science* (2002), *Liberal Democracy 3.0: Civil Society in an Age of Experts* (2003), *Explaining the Normative* (2012), *The Politics of Expertise* (2013), *Understanding the Tacit* (2014), and *Cognitive Science and the Social: A Primer* (2018)

Lani Watson works in epistemology and the philosophy of education. Her research focuses on the role that the practice of questioning, and the intellectual virtues of curiosity and inquisitiveness, play in everyday life. She held a postdoctoral fellowship at the Institute for the Study of Human Flourishing and is currently a Leverhulme early career fellow at the University of Edinburgh.

K. Brad Wray works at the Centre for Science Studies at Aarhus University in Denmark. His research addresses issues in the social epistemology of science, Kuhn's philosophy of science, and the anti-realism/realism debate in philosophy of science. His books include *Kuhn's Evolutionary Social Epistemology* (2011) and *Resisting Scientific Realism* (2018). He has also published on scientific authorship and collaborative research in science.

Chase Wrenn is professor of philosophy at the University of Alabama. His research centers on problems epistemic normativity and the nature and value of truth. His most recent book is *Truth* (2015).

Julie Zahle is a research fellow in the Department of Philosophy, University of Bergen, and a visiting research fellow at the TINT Centre of Excellence in the philosophy of the social sciences, Department of Political and Economic Studies, at University of Helsinki. Her main area of research is the philosophy of the social sciences.

INTRODUCTION

Social epistemology is the interdisciplinary inquiry into the myriad ways humans socially acquire, create, construct, transmit, store, represent, revise, and review knowledge, information, belief, and judgment. Though social epistemology has its roots in the history and philosophy of science and the sociology of science (think here of Thomas Kuhn and Robert Merton, among many others), social epistemology really took off as a field of inquiry in its own right after two figures (though with very different intellectual orientations and backgrounds) published landmark books: Steve Fuller and Alvin Goldman.

Fuller published the first edition of *Social Epistemology* in 1988 (with a second edition in 2002). The year before he founded the journal *Social Epistemology: A Journal of Knowledge, Culture and Policy*. Fuller's decades-long work developing and advancing social epistemology is now systematically expounded in the recently published *Knowing Humanity in the Social World: The Path of Steve Fuller's Social Epistemology*, by Francis X. Remedio and Val Dusek (2018).

Goldman published *Knowledge in a Social World* a decade later in 1999. Though published in 1999, Goldman first addressed questions of social epistemology in the late 1970s, and even planned to address "social epistemics" in his widely influential book of individual epistemology, *Epistemology and Cognition* (1986). He subsequently published important essays in social epistemology in his 1992 book, *Liaisons: Philosophy Meets the Cognitive and Social Sciences*. Goldman's 1999 book complemented two earlier influential books by analytic philosophers that also played a large role in the explosion of interest in social epistemology, C.A.J. Coady's *Testimony: A Philosophical Study* (1992), and Philip Kitcher's *The Advancement of Science* (1993). But Goldman's book more than complemented Coady's book on testimony and Kitcher's book on science, as Goldman took up a number of other topics, including many now addressed in the *Handbook* you now have in your hands.

Another journal of social epistemology, *Episteme*, was founded by Leslie Marsh and Christian Onof in 2004, with articles by Alvin Goldman and Steve Fuller in the inaugural issue. Alvin Goldman soon took his turn as editor of *Episteme*. Though *Episteme*, now edited by Jennifer Lackey, has taken on a wider remit, it continues to be a leading contributor to social epistemology.

Fuller's brand of social epistemology is sometimes called *critical* social epistemology—more revisionary or even revolutionary in its intent—and Goldman's brand is sometimes called *analytic* social epistemology—equally normative though perhaps more descriptive in its implementation. Some of the chapters in Part I address these two brands, and the extent to which they represent different fields or just different orientations. In putting this *Handbook* together, we chose to address topics instead of orientations, though the *Handbook* as a whole will strike many as having a stronger analytic, as opposed to critical, orientation.

As you read through the *Handbook*, you'll find a number of authors who would identify themselves as belonging to one or the other brand, but just as many who probably don't care to identify themselves with one or the other, or perhaps even to think about the labels. We see this diversity as a good thing, as social epistemology as an interdisciplinary field thrives on differences and disagreements, as well as continual cross-fertilization, as one theorist takes up an interest in topics and methods from one or another area of social epistemology.

We invited an intellectually diverse group of experts in their respective fields to contribute state-of-the-art essays. Our experts include some of the most distinguished practitioners of social epistemology as well as some of the most exciting new contributors to the field. We are sure that you will learn as much as we have from reading their contributions to the *Handbook*.

The *Handbook* has over 40 chapters divided into eight parts. Part I—*Historical Background to Social Epistemology*—includes chapters from David Henderson, Alvin I. Goldman, Finn Collin, Stephen Turner, K. Brad Wray, and Chase Wrenn. These chapters cover a good deal of the intellectual terrain and intellectual history we just alluded to, including the differing orientations of various practitioners.

One useful distinction Goldman makes in his chapter is worth highlighting here. When we talk of social epistemology, though we may mean many things, we often focus on one of three areas of inquiry: the way individuals may acquire knowledge from others; the way groups may acquire knowledge; and the way various institutions that themselves may not have beliefs, but are made of individuals or groups that do, influence the creation and transmission of knowledge. Goldman calls the first "interpersonal social epistemology", the second "collective social epistemology", and the third "institutional social epistemology". When reading a chapter or even an entire section, you might find it helpful to ask yourself whether the focus is on interpersonal, collective, or institutional epistemology, a combination of two, or all three at once.

Part II—*The Epistemology of Testimony*—clearly falls under interpersonal social epistemology. The various chapters address the knowledge and beliefs individuals acquire through communication, typically from other individuals. Epistemology from Descartes largely focused on the individual knower in isolation from others. But surely most of what we know we learn from relying on others. In early modern philosophy, David Hume drew our attention to this fact, partly relying on some remarks from John Locke on the topic. Thomas Reid paid the issue special attention. But then the issue largely fell again to the wayside. For most of the twentieth century, epistemology was predominantly concerned with the problems of perception and induction. Coady's 1992 book put testimony back on the agenda. Since the late 1990s, interest has continued to grow, with a fascinating broadening of issues that fall within the epistemology of testimony.

With chapters from Peter J. Graham, Zachary Bachman, Gloria Origgi, Joseph Shieber, Phillip J. Nickel, Melissa A. Koenig, Benjamin McMyler, Carlo Martini, Laura Frances Callahan, and Peter van Elswyk, Part II discusses a wide range of topics that fall within the epistemology of testimony: knowledge transmission; trust, reputation, and other mechanisms by which we "filter" communication; the way testimonial knowledge relies on a broader scheme of knowledge distributed across social networks; the nature of assurance as a speech act, its interpersonal dimension, and the ongoing debate as to its special role in testimonial knowledge; how we identify and rely on experts when deciding what to believe; special questions about moral testimony in particular—believing others about right and wrong; and the often overlooked role that evidentials—parts of speech that are grammatically mandatory in some languages that purport to identify how we know something when we pass on our knowledge to others—play when intersecting with the epistemology of testimony.

Part III—*Disagreement, Diversity, and Relativism*—focuses on a cluster of interrelated issues in interpersonal and collective social epistemology: what is the epistemic significance of diversity, within and across cultures and communities? What, if any, are the connections between diversity, disagreement, and epistemic relativism? Does the epistemic significance of disagreement correlate in interesting ways with subject-matter (whether, e.g., the disagreement concerns religion, ethics, or physics)? What is the significance of disagreement between parties that regard each other as epistemic peers?

J. Adam Carter examines a variety of arguments in favor of epistemic relativism. These appeal to different kinds of epistemic diversity, typically as they manifest themselves in disagreements (e.g., disagreements underwritten by diverging epistemic frameworks or conceptions of what qualifies as good evidence). Michael Patrick Lynch (the professor of philosophy) likewise discusses arguments in favor of epistemic relativism, with an emphasis on the idea the best explanation of intractable disagreements is that statements of the form "the belief that *p* is justified" are justified only relative to epistemic systems. Lynch considers several ways to call this idea into question. Filippo Ferrari and Nikolaj J. L. L. Pedersen continue the discussion of disagreement, but switch the focus from relativism to *peer disagreement.* The massive interest in perceived peer disagreement derives from the idea that this type of disagreement allows us to isolate the significance of the disagreement *itself.* This contrasts with cases in which the disagreeing parties regard each other as enjoying unequal epistemic standings. In such cases deference on part of the perceived epistemic inferior would seem natural—something that is explained by the disagreement *together with* the perceived difference in epistemic status. Ferrari and Pedersen review conformism and non-conformism—the two main views concerning peer disagreement—as well as several alternatives. Matthew A. Benton's contribution first offers a presentation of general ideas and principles of relevance to the disagreement debate and then proceeds to zoom in on religious disagreement. Religious disagreements are of particular interest, as they serve to bring to life several key issues in epistemology: what counts as evidence? What paths, if any, might there be to religious knowledge? Could testimony be such a path, or perception (or something like it)? Kristina Rolin and Eric T. Kerr discuss the epistemic significance of diversity. Rolin focuses on cognitive diversity *within* scientific communities, while Kerr investigates diversity *across* cultures. Rolin argues that cognitive diversity promotes the epistemic goals of science under certain—but not all—circumstances, and that cognitive diversity can be epistemically beneficial for a variety of reasons. It promotes a distribution of research efforts; it is a source of critical perspectives; it is a source of scientific creativity; and it can help counter epistemic injustice. Kerr examines the issue of diversity of epistemic intuitions across cultures—one example being the alleged cross-cultural variation in intuitions about whether knowledge is compatible with epistemic luck. Collection of data concerning epistemic intuition and analysis of that data are the bread and butter of experimentally oriented epistemology. Kerr critically examines experimental work in epistemology within the tradition of analytic philosophy. He suggests that a more fruitful and significant approach to cross-cultural epistemology would ensue if, instead of focusing narrowly on epistemology within analytic philosophy, a whole range of epistemological traditions were to be engaged.

Part IV—*Science and Social Epistemology*—represents a turn from interpersonal social epistemology to collective and institutional social epistemology. The chapter from Michael E. Lynch (the professor of science and technology studies) reviews a good deal of the history of the sociology of science, from Karl Mannheim through Robert Merton to David Bloor, among others, to the fizzling out of the "science wars" of the 1990s. As Lynch explains, a central branch of the history and sociology of science was resistant to thinking of practices and results in terms that could readily serve as measures of epistemic success. This was at the heart of the science wars. On such normatively neutered approaches, groups sometimes do produce a consensus, and one can study the processes making for such a consensus. However, epistemologists will want to ask when a consensus is the result of group processes that are adequately truth-conducive (and thus to be normatively prescribed). This general question is reflected in all the chapters in this part of the *Handbook.* Chapters from Boaz Miller, Samuli

Reijula, and Jaakko Kuorikoski take up a set of issues surrounding how groups may be structured so as to be relatively productive in epistemic terms. Miller notes that both societal features of groups may be significant here (features such as norms for critical practices among the group) as well as cognitive features to which members are sensitive. Reijula and Kuorikoski survey the recent literature attempting to deploy the tools of modeling found in various scientific disciplines to understand the epistemic consequences of various features at the level of groups. This literature takes its departure from Philip Kitcher's recognition that a community may get epistemcally farther if it distributes research problems across members and subgroups in fitting ways. But what kinds of cues are available to agents within communities that allow the fitting distribution of epistemic efforts, and what community norms encourage a fitting distribution. Work by feminist philosophers of science have contributed important insights and illustrations concerning how community norms, practices, and structure have far reaching social epistemological significance. Sharon Crasnow's chapter surveys this literature.

Part V—*The Epistemology of Groups*—takes up puzzling questions focused within collective epistemology. What is it for a group to believe and then to know something, especially if that doesn't simply consist in the beliefs or knowledge of a privileged subset of members of the group? If, in everyday life, we take groups such as juries or governments to have beliefs or indeed to know things—as we hope they often will!—then we need to understand what inner structure may be required for this to be so. Deborah Perron Tollefson's chapter provides an informative guide to the growing interest and literature on this topic, with connections to questions of social ontology and issues of extended cognition, with the possibility that reflection on group epistemology might reveal important limitations in individual epistemology. Some finer-grained debates in the ontology and epistemology of group belief and knowledge are further explored in Alexander Bird's chapter, in which he considers certain advantages and disadvantages of commitment models of collective epistemic states as contrasted with distributed models. Allen Buchanan's chapter then raises a fundamental question in social moral epistemology: how do conditions of social discrimination constrain the ability of a discriminated against group from coming to know their own interests? The way various social facts influence and epistemically distort beliefs concerning our interests then has important ramifications for fundamental debates about the scope and justification for human rights.

Part VI—*Feminist Epistemology*—contains six chapters from Heidi Grasswick, Linda Martín Alcoff, Jules Holroyd and Katherine Puddifoot, Nancy Daukas, Alessandra Tanesini, Shannon Dea and Matthew Silk. In Grasswick's overview we gain a sense not only of the range of interests that come under the purview of feminist epistemology—as one might anticipate if one proceeds from an intersectionally understood idea of gender—but also its historical development. Feminist epistemology helped form social epistemology as we know it in a range of ways, most notably its rejection of epistemic atomism in favor of epistemic relationality and dependence; its critique of the idea of the asocial knowing subject in favor of the idea of 'situated knowing'; and the development of the idea that our epistemic relations are a domain in which concepts of justice and injustice apply. The notion of situated knowing is at the fore in Alessandra Tanesini's chapter, which focuses on standpoint theory considered as a research program, not only in social epistemology but also in the social sciences where it has led to some significant successes. Growing from early Marxist insights and adapted to fit the politics of gender more than class, standpoint theory has evolved greatly and still has a role to play today. One of the themes internal to standpoint theory is that of epistemic privilege as implicitly contrasted with epistemic ignorance of false consciousness. This kind of structural ignorance is explored in a new way as a central theme of Linda Martín Alcoff's chapter on race in feminist philosophy. Looking at ignorance, and in particular the willful ignorance of white privilege in the U.S., Alcoff endorses a conception of race as a social kind that influences social meanings, often distorting them and creating radically stereotypical thinking. It can easily have a deleterious effect on actual patterns of knowledge and ignorance, so that the real social relations that constitute a shared social world are actively obscured. These biases may be explicit and represented in beliefs, or again they may be implicit. In the chapter co-authored by Jules Holroyd and Katherine Puddifoot, the terrain of implicit bias is mapped out. Some biases might be epistemically advantageous, but others not; and the possibilities of de-biasing our thinking are explored. But the question is also raised how far empirical findings can and should influence our thinking in philosophy, and the suggestion is made that they should at least not be allowed to displace efforts to pay closer attention to the explicit narratives of lived experience offered by those living marginalized lives. This idea of the narratives of marginalized lives puts us in mind of the general question of the justice or injustice of our epistemic relations, and in Nancy Daukas's chapter she explores different contributions to the literature on epistemic injustice. Whether in the form of prejudice or diverse forms of epistemic marginalization, epistemic injustices distort the social-epistemic landscape so that knowledge and other epistemic goods do not flow as they should, with the result that objectivity is the loser, whether in science, or social science or just in our everyday knowledge of the social world. Correcting for these distortions, Daukas argues, will involve not only theoretical work but also sustained and focused activism to change the functioning of those institutions involved in the production of knowledge. This practical stance is taken up, as part of a historical thread, in the essay co-authored by Shannon Dea and Matthew Silk on classic pragmatist thought, with a special focus on the figure of Jane Addams. Her central commitments—that perspective makes a difference to knowledge, and that it is possible to gain understanding of others' perspectives—could not be more central in feminist social epistemology. Sister notions of epistemic standpoint and of socially situated knowledge find early expression in all but name here in this explicitly pragmatist frame, whose commitment to the social, collective and practical nature of inquiry no doubt helps explain the strong feminist interest in American pragmatist thought quite generally. This, together with the pragmatist commitment to the democratic idea of a community of inquirers of many different perspectives coming together effectively in inquiry, remain key notes in feminist epistemology as it has developed over the decades.

Part VII—*The Epistemology of Democracy*—consists of six chapters. Robert B. Talisse's contribution provides an overview of the debate, taking as his starting point the fundamental tension between the epistemic ideals of democracy (including free speech and informed, reason-based decision-making) and real-life democracy. The epistemic ideals of democracy may enable demagogues, propagandists, and epistemic opportunists to manipulate democratic citizens and thereby undermine the proper realization of those very ideals. Yet, there is a long-standing, venerable tradition of arguing in favor of democracy on epistemic grounds, as represented by the works of Jean-Jacques Rousseau, Marquis de Condorcet, and John Stuart Mill. John Dewey paved the way for a broadening of epistemic pro-democracy considerations by conceiving democracy as a way of life rather than purely as a form of government. On the contemporary scene deliberative democracy has been the paradigm in democratic theory. Talisse highlights three key issues pertaining to deliberative democracy: the epistemic character and capabilities of groups, the epistemic vulnerability of group deliberation, and the epistemic nature and character of public discourse. Some theorists argue that, under certain conditions, diverse groups outperform even experts (Scott Page and Helene Landemore are notable examples). This type of epistemic pro-democracy argument is countered by data that suggest that group deliberation is fragile, as people are individually subject to a wide variety of biases and, collectively, to socio-psychological phenomena such as belief polarization. These data make salient the third key issue: the epistemic nature and character of public discourse, especially as it occurs in actual societies. In order for democracy to be inclusive and epistemically beneficial, public discourse must be conducted in such a way that it can succeed or do reasonably well in real life.

According to Condorcet's jury theorem, majority voting on a yes/no question tends towards infallibility as the number of voters goes towards infinity, provided that certain conditions hold. This result has been—and often is—touted as supporting the *wisdom of the crowds*. In particular, the result has been taken to support the wisdom of *democratic* crowds—and, hence, not surprisingly has played a central role in epistemological discussions of democracy. Franz Dietrich and Kai Spiekermann's contribution offers a survey and discussion of various jury theorems. A common objection to the original version of Condorcet's jury theorem is that it rests on two controversial assumptions—that voters are independent and that each of them has a probability better than chance (0.5) of getting the right answer. Dietrich and Spiekermann deem implausible strong jury theorems formulated in terms of infallibility, at least as results that could be of relevance to the epistemic aspects of real democracies. Instead the discussion should be focused on jury theorems that attribute merely growing—but less than infallible—reliability to majority-voting groups of increasing size, and Dietrich and Spiekermann discuss whether theorems of this kind can be established without reliance on implausible assumptions.

The contribution by Eva Erman and Niklas Möller introduces and discusses three kinds of pragmatist approaches to epistemic aspects of democracy—the common pragmatist denominator being the conception of democracy as being tied to social, everyday practices such as problem-solving and enquiry. Michael Fuerstein discusses epistemic proceduralism.

Pure *epistemic* arguments seek to show that democracy likely leads to epistemically good outcomes. Pure *procedural* arguments seek to show that democratic procedures—regardless of their outcomes—are fair and egalitarian and, for this reason, morally good procedures for decision-making. Epistemic proceduralism combines these two types of arguments, David Estlund being a prominent proponent of the view.

While equality is one of the core values of democracy, it is nonetheless also widely thought that certain views should carry extra weight or enjoy a privileged epistemic status within democracies. In particular, it is widely thought that experts—and, in particular, scientists—should play a special epistemic role in democracies. Klemens Kappel and Julie Zahle investigate this issue. They present criticisms of the idea that science should occupy a privileged epistemic position and likewise examine what can be said in its defense.

Kristoffer Ahlstrom-Vij offers a critical assessment of the epistemic benefits of democracy. His chief focus is voter ignorance. Since democracy is the rule of the people, voter ignorance should be a major concern for friends of the epistemic benefits of democracy. Ahlstrom-Vij points out that, rather than alleviate concerns about voter ignorance, Condorcet's jury theorem *presupposes* that the majority of the electorate is not ignorant. Ahlstrom-Vij presents reasons for thinking that liberal and deliberative models of democracy are not well equipped to assuage concerns about voter ignorance either. In light of these critical conclusions Ahlstrom-Vij briefly examines the alternative approach of expert rule, exemplified by respectively Plato and Mill's work, and the question whether such rule might qualify as (politically) legitimate.

Part VIII—*Further Horizons of Social Epistemology*—takes up various issues that connect with earlier topics in the *Handbook* but also take social epistemology in new directions. Sanford C. Goldberg's chapter addresses issues arising from the "critical" vs. "analytic" social epistemology debate and advances his own perspective on where social epistemology is going. The chapter by David Henderson and Peter J. Graham connects with earlier chapters on the sociology of science and then raises further questions about the nature of norms that govern the discovery, creation, and transmission of knowledge. Though no sociologist would doubt that the norms of science identified by Merton are epistemic norms, Henderson and Graham ask to what extent epistemic norms in general are social norms. The chapters by Lani Watson and Jason Baehr draw out connections between social epistemology, the philosophy of education, the structure of educational institutions, democracy, and intellectual virtue. Igor Douven's chapter on computational modeling in social epistemology usefully shows how one of the tools of the social scientist's tool-box—agent-based models—fruitfully applies to various topics in social epistemology, and more importantly can be used to help engineer social institutions towards epistemic ends. The *Handbook* ends with an engaging chapter by David Coady on perhaps the most pressing issue of our time: climate change. Coady's chapter also argues against two prevalent ideas within our culture, that testimony is second-rate and that scientists make their discoveries largely independently of one another. Coady's chapter touches on a number of issues raised throughout the *Handbook*—the evidence of testimony and the role of experts, group belief and knowledge, the sociology of science, disagreement, and the aspiration that social epistemology might make a difference to the great issues of the day—and so it is appropriate that we conclude our *Handbook* with Coady's essay.

As you can see from this overview of the various chapters that comprise *The Routledge Handbook of Social Epistemology*, social epistemology is a wide-ranging interdisciplinary field, both within philosophy and without. We see this *Handbook* as a state-of-the-art contribution to the ongoing development of the field. We opened this introduction with a brief review of the influence of Steve Fuller and Alvin Goldman. We are pleased to report that in addition to all of the work reviewed in this *Handbook*, conferences continue to be held on various topics within epistemology, collections and edited anthologies continue to be published, and searches for academic positions in social epistemology are now even beginning to appear in professional circles. Two other recent developments are noteworthy. James H. Collier, the current editor of *Social Epistemology: A Journal of Knowledge, Culture and Policy*, founded a flourishing online offshoot in 2011: the *Social Epistemology Review and Reply Collective*. And then just two years ago, Sanford C. Goldberg helped launch the international *Social Epistemology Network*, which held its first international conference at the University of Oslo, in the spring of 2018. Nikolaj J. L. L. Pedersen hosted the second conference at Yonsei University's Underwood International College in June of 2019 in South Korea. We see a bright future for social epistemology. We trust *The Routledge Handbook of Social Epistemology* will prove to play an important role

References

Coady, C.A.J. (1992) *Testimony: A Philosophical Study* (Oxford, UK: Clarendon Press).

Fuller, Steve (1988) *Social Epistemology* (Bloomington, IN: Indiana University Press, First Edition).

Goldman, Alvin (1986) *Epistemology and Cognition* (Cambridge, MA: Harvard University Press).

Goldman, Alvin (1992) *Liaisons: Philosophy Meets the Cognitive and Social Sciences* (Cambridge, MA: The MIT Press).

Goldman, Alvin (1999) *Knowledge in a Social World* (Oxford, UK: Oxford University Press).

Kitcher, Philip (1993) *The Advancement of Science* (Oxford, UK: Oxford University Press).

Remedios, Francis X and Dusek, Val (2018) *Knowing Humanity in the Social World: The Path of Steve Fuller's Social Epistemology* (London, UK: Palgrave Macmillan).

PART I

Historical Backgrounds to Social Epistemology

1

ON THE BACKGROUND OF SOCIAL EPISTEMOLOGY

David Henderson

The contributions to this section commonly survey wide literatures, reflecting big, interrelated issues. They seek to provide overviews of lines of development within philosophy and in related fields that afford background and perspective for contemporary social epistemology.

Work in both the sociology and history of science has prompted, encouraged, and reinforced the realization among many philosophers that there is a need for a social turn within epistemology—that epistemologists need to take account of processes at various social scales in which beliefs came to be formed and transmitted, and in which epistemic sensibilities or norms took form and were transmitted and enforced. Taking account of such processes would afford at least an important complement to traditional, narrowly individualistic epistemology. For example, work in the history of science by Thomas Kuhn (1957, 1962, 1977) and others focused on the practices within disciplines that had produced many of our most cherished exemplars of knowledge. Such work made evident that developments in those disciplines commonly turned on social processes within a community with shifting sensibilities. Communities of investigators seem to coalesce around notable work—which then serves as models for ongoing practice. It was in communities that scientists commonly came to share understandings of what made for the successes represented by such notable or exemplary work—which then served as the normative take away to which community members aspired, and insisted on. It was in view of the shared results of conforming practice that community members developed and refined a sense for promising or favored lines of further inquiry. In this, social processes involving ongoing public evaluation and exchange were significant. Such processes shaped the evaluation of extant results and conditioned the parameters of evaluation (reinforcing or revising those parameters). These social processes also made for an ongoing regulation of the practices of individual investigators and groups of investigators—as community standards informed the practices of making and evaluating observations, and of weighing the implications of their results for their general understandings. Thus, work by Kuhn and others historians presented epistemologists with a compelling case: if one were serious about understanding how best to form beliefs, it seems one would need to attend to community-level processes—to what were the features of such processes that furthered or hindered scientific practice and epistemic practice generally. At the very least, one needed to add a social leg or two to epistemology. In this handbook, K. Brad Wray discusses the work of Thomas Kuhn and the related historical study of science—and he traces some of the associated work in the philosophy of science that responded to the history of science.

In his contribution to this handbook, Stephen Turner discusses the philosophical roots of the sociology of science. He focuses on the lines of thought that ultimately issued in the sociology of science of Karl Mannheim ([1929] 1954): German Idealism and the body of social theory that begins with Henri de Saint-Simon and extends through Marx and his followers. This is, admittedly, not standard fare for contemporary epistemologists. However, Turner's discussion makes recognizable various antecedents of concerns that are both sociological and philosophical. This serves as background for understanding more contemporary sociological and historical treatments of science. Turner's entry can be combined with Michael E. Lynch's contribution, "The Sociology of Science of Social Constructivism," (in the Science and Social Epistemology section of this handbook). Together, these make for a sustained treatment of the sociology of science and its philosophical roots. Lynch traces the sociological thread forward from where Turner leaves off, beginning with Robert Merton's (1973) sociology of science, and follows it into subsequent sociological approaches, notably the strong programme in the sociology of science (Barnes and Bloor, 1982; Bloor, 1976). Wray's chapter also discusses the Strong Programme and the uptake of Kuhn's work in the sociology of science. Obviously, these discussions must cover a lot of ground and literature; in so doing they provide a glimpse of fields that are important when thinking about our life situated within a community of interdependent epistemic agents. They raise questions about the advantages and limitations endemic to even in the most sophisticated of our epistemic practices and communities—advantages and limitations that result from our cultural and intellectual interdependencies. One might fruitfully compare the concerns highlighted with the issues pursued by the philosopher of science Philip Kitcher in his article, "The Naturalists Return." (1992).

Let us turn to the contributions in this part of the handbook that focus on background work within philosophy. In "The Twin Roots and Branches of Social Epistemology," Finn Collin provides a particularly broad perspective. One root is traditional analytic epistemology—and here the development of naturalistic and reliabilist approaches loom large. The second root is work in the philosophy of science—particularly that prompted by work in the history of science such as that by Kuhn. Collin characterizes several branches coming off of each major branch. Branches arising out of the philosophy of science includes work labeled "critical social epistemology." This set of work is associated with the writings of Steve Fuller and with the journal *Social Epistemology* that Fuller founded. Critical social epistemology seeks comparatively less continuity with traditional epistemology than is sought in most work within social epistemology.

Collin traces the way in which contemporary analytic epistemology came to be concerned with the social production and (particularly recently) the social distribution of knowledge. Here, the writings of Alvin Goldman (for example, 1967, 1972, 1986, 1992, 1999) represent several notable junctures in the development of a distinctively social focus within epistemology. Traditional analytic epistemology focused pretty exclusively on matters that were internal to the mental life of individual epistemic agents—several central evaluative statuses of interest were taken to turn on internal states of the individual agent—the agent's perceptions, beliefs, and inferences. Such epistemology is termed *internalist*. Goldman and others (Alston, 1985, 1989; Harman, 1986, for example) advanced influential arguments for a reorientation of epistemology beyond merely matters to which the individual agent has internal access. *Externalist* epistemology—epistemology that is not simply *internalist*—is now prominent in mainstream epistemology. Goldman's suggestion was that, even when an agent could not access justificatory reasons supporting a given belief, that belief might yet be justified as a result of being generated by a reliable cognitive process. Beliefs could be so justified even though the agent did not have independent internal resources for certifying the reliability of the generating process. Thus, attention comes to focus on the reliability of the processes by which agents form their beliefs.

The development of externalist, commonly reliabilist, epistemology opened the space for a social turn. After all, some of the relevant processes by which agents gain reliable belief extend beyond the individual agent and include wider social processes and exchanges—thus social epistemology. Processes at the level of the group may be more (or less) reliable than the processes employed by the members individually. As the resulting social epistemology is part of a piece with wider (commonly externalist and reliabilist) developments within analytic epistemology, Collin labels this branch Analytic Social Epistemology (ASE). He traced its development using Goldman's influential writings as representative.

In his discussion of ASE, Collin notes the important work of Miranda Fricker, who argues that undervaluing the epistemic capacities and contributions of members of various groups—such as women—yields a form of *epistemic injustice* that is harmful both to the agents and to the epistemic results in the community (Fricker, 2007).

As Collin indicates, the socially focused literature in analytic epistemology has developed so as to remain very much of a piece with the literature in analytic epistemology generally. Somewhat surprisingly, this has proceeded with only occasional attention to a separate social epistemological literature: that arising out of the philosophy of science. At least it is safe to say that the two branches of social epistemology have not been ideally integrated. As Collin notes, the sciences constitute "an especially eminent example of social cognition"—so it is fitting that epistemological reflections on the sciences have generated a social epistemological literature. Perhaps analytic epistemologists have been hesitant to draw on the philosophy of science in part because that tradition confronts concerns that seem to make problematic the idea of the accretion or accumulation of a socially shared body of knowledge. Those concerns are represented by (at least some readings of) the work initiated by Thomas Kuhn, and responding to these concerns has been important within the philosophy of science. Some epistemologists have been content to leave such issue largely to philosophers of science.

Philip Kitcher had developed a position in the philosophy of science that has real social epistemological meat. As Collin discusses (Chapter 3 of this volume), Kitcher has sought a "sociologically realistic analysis of science"—one that can provide "a robust sense for the notion of scientific progress" and the growth of knowledge, while acknowledging the complexities to which the history and sociology of science have directed attention. As Collin also notes, Kitcher's work has significant continuity with Goldman's—for example, in its occasional use of micro-economic models (Kitcher, 1993). Perhaps we should add that Kitcher's general epistemological bearings are reliabilist, and that Kitcher (1992) as well as Goldman adhere to a program of naturalizing epistemology along lines suggested in Quine's classic (1969) "Epistemology Naturalized." To naturalize epistemology is to pursue it in a way that draws freely on scientific results. One might think of this as a scientifically informed engineering of our pursuit of truth. It is safe to say that quite generally naturalizing epistemology has loomed large in externalist epistemology and in social epistemology in particular. (More on naturalizing epistemology later; it is the subject of Chase Wrenn's contribution to this volume.)

Of course, science as a social phenomenon will inherit various biases and limits from the social groups in which it is practiced. Consequently, in reflecting on science as an epistemically important, paradigmatic, form of social organization in the production of knowledge, one will want to come to terms with such biases and foibles. In engineering our scientific pursuit of truth, it will be important to limit the distortions or biases occasioned. Again, one finds such concerns in Kitcher's work. They are also doggedly pursued in the work of a set of feminist philosophers of science and epistemologists. Representatives of this work include the writings of Sandra Harding (1991), and Lorraine Code (1991). Collin's chapter focuses on the work of Helen Longino (1990, 2002).

Longino wanted to salvage scientific objectivity while making science more sensitive to social concerns, among which feminism had her special interest. She buttressed her critique of traditional science with detailed studies of biological theorizing in particular, demonstrating gender bias of various sorts. Still, Longino wanted to show that science as such is not inherently biased against women or other particular groups. The task was to devise a conception of science that would have room for a plurality of social concerns.

(Collin, this volume)

Indeed, one might say that the responsiveness to "a plurality of social concerns" is central in Longino's social epistemology—as such it is thought to vitiate bias and provide gains in ultimate objectivity. It does this by allowing all qualified parties to bring to bear relevant information so as to subject candidate positions to scrutiny (see also Wylie and Hankinson, 2007). (Much relevant discussion is also to be found in Sharon Crasnow's "Feminist Philosophy of Science as Social Epistemology", later in this handbook.)

Finally, Collin discusses Critical Social Epistemology (CSE)—a tradition in science studies associated with the journal *Social Epistemology: A Journal of Knowledge, Culture and Policy* founded by Steve Fuller. He notes that, unlike those approaches previously discussed that also focus on science, "Fuller [and CSE] does not try to work out a compromise between analytic philosophy of science and its various critics of the 1970s and 1980s." While CSE is commonly viewed as pursuing a science-debunking agenda (also associated with the Science and Technology Studies program), Collin argues that this reading may be overdrawn. He suggests that Fuller's position comprises a set of views held by philosophers of science—each being a minority position in that field. However, this set of minority views is not espoused in combination by those working outside the CSE approach. Collin provides a balanced overview of the main outlines of Fuller's thought. In so doing, he allows one to understand how this form of social epistemology (CSE) relates to the more widespread variants such as: (a) ASE as represented by Goldman and many others; (b) the kind of social philosophy of science represented by Philip Kitcher; and (c) important work by feminist philosophers of science and epistemologists.

As noted already, externalist epistemology afforded the opening for social epistemology. Epistemology had to do with the class of processes by which folk ought to form and maintain their beliefs or understandings, and these were taken to be those with some fitting balance of reliability and power or fecundity. Now, insofar as matters such as: (a) the reliability, tractability or implementability, and productive power of belief forming processes are concerns central to epistemology; and (b) processes at the social level can significantly enhance or diminish such features, epistemologists would need to attend to social processes. They must consider how social organization and more or less tractable forms of cooperative belief formation and transmission can contribute to reliability and veritistic productivity. But, from the philosophical armchair, one cannot get far gauging the reliability and veritistic productivity of belief-producing and belief-transmitting processes at either the social level or at the level of individual cognitive processes. For example, some armchair attractive processes may not be tractable or implementable within human cognitive architectures, or within human communities. Further, some features of individual and social processes may be needed in order to guard against pitfalls or biases that are characteristic of human cognitive or social life. These are matters about which decidedly empirical work provides crucial information. Thus, it would seem that a fitting social epistemology ought to "permeable to"—informed by—empirical understandings of groups as well as empirical understandings of human cognition.

The consequence just bruited is in keeping with an important trend in some contemporary analytic philosophy: its being *naturalized*—its being pursued as a branch of applied science. If externalist epistemology (exemplified by reliabilist epistemology) constitutes one leg of a general stance enabling social epistemology, another leg is naturalized epistemology. Chase Wrenn's contribution to this handbook focuses on epistemological naturalism. As Wrenn explains:

> Epistemology is "naturalized" to the extent it is informed by and continuous with empirical science. Naturalized epistemology contrasts with what we can call, somewhat misleadingly, "traditional" epistemology, an approach that aims to answer epistemological questions independently of contingent or empirical considerations.

At the same time, Wrenn continues, quoting Rysiew (2016) "epistemological naturalism is more a family of related theories and methods than a unified philosophical doctrine." Presumably this results from (a) differences in the implications different writers find in various bodies of scientific results, and (b) different misgivings regarding what can be taken from traditional *aprioristic* philosophy. For example, naturalistic epistemologists may vary in the extent to which they find conceptual analysis of evaluative epistemic concepts uninformative. Those who find little light or constraint to be gotten via "analysis," will tend to advance accounts that are relatively revisionary. They will ask why one should conform to some extant evaluative concepts, when better-informed engineering concepts might be fashioned in their place. Further, they will feel the need for empirical information about both human cognizers' cognitive capacities and limits, and about the epistemic gains and losses that come by way of human social-epistemological interdependencies. They may note that much traditional philosophical reflection has been concerned only with an individual epistemic agent—and, further, it has drawn on little information about the cognitive capacities of real agents.

As Wrenn explains, Quine himself (1969) was driven to recommend naturalizing epistemology because he was convinced of the bankruptcy of conceptual analysis and was deeply skeptical of those claiming to discern significant *a priori* bearings for epistemology. If conceptual truths do not provide important epistemic bearings, we do better engaging in an unabashedly empirically informed engineering of our pursuit of truth. Kitcher (1992, 1993) shares these motivations—as well a philosopher of biology's healthy appreciation for the kinds of messy human critters one might seek to fashion into good epistemic agents and to organize into epistemic communities. He advocates a "meliorative epistemology" that amounts to a kind of cognitive and social engineering. Alternatively, Kornblith (2002) argues that epistemic concepts such as *knowledge* should be natural-kind concepts, thus that the nature of such states is a wholly empirical matter—as it is with other natural kinds. The meliorative engineering approach and the science of epistemic natural kinds approach constitute two rather distinct flavors of naturalism. If *knowledge*, for example, is a natural kind concept, then there are truths about the kind—knowledge—to discover empirically, while what is discoverable from the armchair is very thin. Compare: from the armchair we can discover that "water" refers to stuff of the same theoretically significant kind as the stuff in the samples—but the nature of the stuff, what makes some stuff water, can only be ascertained empirically. In contrast, if evaluative epistemic concepts are concepts that we *develop* and deploy in a project of ameliorating our practice, such evaluative concepts need not pick out antecedently existing "natures." Rather, such epistemic evaluative concepts may reflect evolving normative sensibilities around which folk pragmatically/emotively coordinate in their individual and joint pursuit of truth or understanding. What would be important would be whether the evaluative concepts or sensibilities we have do indeed, as a matter of fact, coordinate folk in epistemically productive ways. If they do not, so much the worse for the sensibilities. We are in the neighborhood of some big issues here. Some have to do with whether epistemology is a normative discipline—and whether normative concepts (knowledge, justified/unjustified, good/bad, etc.) can be natural kinds.

Perhaps we should note also that some philosophers do find a place for philosophical reflection within a naturalized epistemology. They suggest that philosophical reflection on our epistemic evaluative concepts may yield some substantive results, and yet find the concepts themselves to call for a kind of responsiveness to information of an empirical sort—so that conceptual reflection, such as it can be, itself leads us to naturalize epistemology. Some (but not all) reliabilists think of reliability as a conceptually grounded necessary condition for objective justification—while allowing that it is an empirical matter which cognitive and social processes are thus demanded. For example, Henderson and Horgan (2011) argue that reflection leads to the conclusion that various forms of reliability are necessary for objectively justified belief, and for knowledge. At the same time, the relevant forms of reliability turn on the way in which processes can undergo ongoing refinement (they write of "modulational control") in light of wider information. Think, for example, of the ways in which one fashions and refines measurement processes in light of information regarding pitfalls and alternative measurement technologies. If objective epistemic justification requires responsiveness to empirical information concerning cognitive and social processes, epistemology must be naturalized.

In any case, as Wrenn indicates, there are multiple ways in which one might naturalize epistemology. Still, in all variants, empirical information is important for a fitting epistemology. In all versions, it would seem that an important class of empirical information would have to do with the pitfalls and the opportunities that come with our interdependencies in epistemic communities. Such information would be needed to engineer, tailor, or modulate our epistemic lives together. In thinking about such matters, we are motivated to adopt a perspective on our practice that considers agents with various cognitive practices being embedded in communities and environments. Thus we find motivation for pursuing an externalist social epistemology. Of course, some of the relevant information about our lives in epistemic communities will come from our historical and sociological (and other social scientific) reflection on some our epistemic communities.

One encounters references to the work of Alvin I. Goldman repeatedly in chapters found in this Part I of this handbook. Clearly, Goldman has from early on been an influential and steady contributor to naturalized epistemology, reliablist epistemology, and social epistemology. In his chapter in this volume, "The What, Why, and How of Social Epistemology," he provides a survey of the issues and approaches that have come to characterize social epistemology. He distinguishes three broad variants.

- *Interpersonal* social epistemology takes its departure from the deep interdependencies that characterize individual epistemic agents within an epistemic community. These interdependencies turn on the ways in which beliefs are produced drawing on the beliefs of others, often in cooperative groups, and then shared. Of course, much that an individual agent holds is then beholden to the sharing of others. Interpersonal social eipstemology is concerned with what individual epistemic agents can do by way of acquiring and deploying beliefs gotten by and with others.
- *Collective* social epistemology supposes that various groups or institutions can themselves be agents—perhaps with beliefs and minds of their own, and at least with commitments that are analogous. What is then sought is a normative epistemology for such agents—for juries, committees, and fact-finding bodies, corporations, governmental and corporate departments, clubs, and so on.
- *Institutional* social epistemology focuses on "large" entities that do not qualify as doxastic agents themselves. These institutions (networks, markets, ongoing organized groups or communities insofar as they do not constitute agents with doxastic states themselves) have members, or constituents, whose norms or shared sensibilities make for their organization and epistemically relevant processes. One can seek a descriptive understanding of various norms and organizational characteristics of such organizations, and one can seek a normative epistemology concerning how organizational features can serve to produce epistemically good results for their members.

Goldman provides an overview of central questions within each of these approaches to social epistemology. As his title suggests, he draws certain lessons regarding methods in social epistemology. Notably, given the diversity of the approaches, he does not advocate a single unified epistemology for social epistemology. Rather, after discussing compelling questions that seem raised in each form of social epistemology, and after discussing a variety of samples of social epistemology associated with the various approaches, he suggests that while there are methods fitting to each, and while there are significant connections between work in each, the fitting methods are diverse. They can, in the fashion of naturalized epistemology, draw on work in the various social and psychological sciences, and on related work in mathematics and in biology.

References

Alston, W. (1985). Concepts of epistemic justification. *Monist: An International Quarterly Journal of General Philosophical Inquiry*, *62*, pp. 57–89.

Alston, W. (1989). *Epistemic justification: essays in the theory of knowledge*. Ithaca, NY: Cornell University Press.

Barnes, B. and Bloor, D. (1982). Relativism, rationalism, and the sociology of knowledge. In: M. Hollis and S. Lukes, eds., *Rationality and relativism*. Cambridge, MA: MIT Press, pp. 21–47.

Bloor, D. (1976). *Knowledge and social imagery*. London: Routledge & Kegan Paul.

Code, L. (1991). *What can she know?* Ithaca, NY: Cornell University Press.

Fricker, M. (2007). *Epistemic injustice: power and the ethics of knowing*. Oxford: Oxford University Press.

Goldman, A. (1967). A causal theory of knowing. *Journal of Philosophy*, *64*(12), pp. 355–372.

Goldman, A. (1972). What is justified belief. In: G. Pappas, ed., *Justification and knowledge*. Dordrecht: Reidel, pp. 1–23.

Goldman, A. (1986). *Epistemology and cognition*. Cambridge, MA: Harvard University Press.

Goldman, A. (1992). *Liaisons: philosophy meets the cognitive and social sciences*. Cambridge, MA: MIT Press.

Goldman, A. (1999). *Knowledge in a social world*. Oxford: Oxford University Press.

Harding, S. (1991). *Whose science? whose knowledge? thinking from women's lives*. Ithaca, NY: Cornell University Press.

Harman, G. (1986). *Change in view: principles of reasoning*. Cambridge, MA: MIT Press.

Henderson, D. and Horgan, T. (2011). *The epistemological spectrum: at the interface of cognitive science and conceptual analysis*. Oxford: Oxford University Press.

Kitcher, P. (1992). The naturalists return. *Philosophical Review*, *101*(1), pp. 53–114.

Kitcher, P. (1993). *the advancement of science: science without legend, objectivity without illusions*. New York, NY: Oxford University Press.

Kornblith, H. (2002). *Knowledge and its place in nature*. Oxford: Clarendon Press.

Kuhn, T. (1957). *The copernican revolution; planetary astronomy in the development of western thought*. Cambridge: Harvard University Press.

Kuhn, T. (1962). *The structure of scientific revolutions*. Chicago, IL: University of Chicago Press.

Kuhn, T. (1977). *The essential tension: selected studies in scientific tradition and change*. Chicago: University of Chicago Press.

Longino, H. (1990). *Science as social knowledge: values and objectivity in scientific inquiry*. Princeton, NJ: Princeton University Press.

Longino, H. (2002). *The fate of knowledge*. Princeton, NJ: Princeton University Press.

Mannheim, K. ([1929] 1954). *Ideology and Utopia: An Introduction to the Sociology of Knowledge*, trans. L. Wirth and E. Shils. New York: Harcourt Brace & Company. Available at: https://archive.org/details/ideologyutopiain00mann (accessed 5 February 2016).

Merton, R. K. (1973). *The sociology of science*. Chicago, IL: University of Chicago Press.

Quine, W. V. (1969). Epistemology naturalized. In: *Ontological relativity, and other essays*. New York, NY: Columbia University Press, pp. 69–90.

Rysiew, P. (2016) Naturalism in epistemology. In: E. N. Zalta ed., *Stanford Encyclopedia of Philosophy*. Available at: http://plato.stanford.edu/archives/sum2016/entries/epistemology-naturalized/ (accessed 13 August 2016).

Wylie, A. and Hankinson, N. (2007). Coming to terms with the values of science: insights from feminist science scholarship. In: J. Kincaid and A. Wylie, eds., *Value free science: ideal or illusion?* Oxford: Oxford University Press, pp. 58–86.

2

THE WHAT, WHY, AND HOW OF SOCIAL EPISTEMOLOGY

Alvin I. Goldman

This chapter addresses three central questions concerning social epistemology: the "what" question, the "why" question, and the "how" question. The first part of the chapter tackles the straightforward question: what *is* social epistemology? What makes it *social* and what makes it *epistemological*? How does it differ from traditional epistemology, on the one hand, and from other forms of social theory such as social constructivism? The second part of the chapter asks why we need this new branch of epistemology. Is there something missing in the old variety, and if so, how does social epistemology aim to fill this gap? What varieties of social epistemology emerge from this project? The third part of the chapter examines some *methods* or *models* that have been or might be used by social epistemologists to tackle the problems of interest. Some of these methods are continuous (even identical) with those of traditional epistemology, and others are divergent.

What Is Social Epistemology?

Social epistemology is a branch of epistemology. So what is epistemology? As a starter, epistemology may be characterized as the science or study of *knowledge*. The root of the term is the Greek word "episteme," usually translated as "knowledge." A core question of the field is simply stated, "What *is* knowledge?" It is commonly said that knowledge consists, minimally, of a person's *believing* a *true proposition*. You cannot know that the sun has twelve planets unless you believe it has twelve planets and this is true. But you don't know something simply because you believe it and by chance it happens to be true. If you ask where the roulette wheel will stop on its next roll, and you confidently select a number that turns out to be right, this doesn't imply that you *knew* where it would stop. Saying what qualifies as knowledge is a tricky matter.

Traditional epistemology is not interested exclusively in knowledge. It is also interested in how one can arrive at beliefs or opinions to which one is intellectually entitled. If one is entitled to believe P, epistemologists say that the belief is "justified" or "rational." These terms of "epistemic" appraisal are also used in evaluating cognitive or intellectual activity. Traditional epistemology studies what confers justification and/or rationality in part because it seeks to guide people in forming better beliefs. A common view is that you have a better prospect of forming *true* beliefs if you form them in ways that generate justification or rationality. Believing truths and avoiding errors are epistemic "goods," and epistemology tries to help us attain such goods.

With these introductory remarks behind us, let us next ask how social epistemology is distinguished from its traditional form. Traditional epistemology focuses on the intellectual behavior of *individual* persons rather than groups. By contrast, social epistemology (at least in one of its varieties) is also concerned with *collective* epistemic agents, i.e., teams, juries, committees, corporations, and other kinds of collectivities that can plausibly be viewed as epistemic agents. Assuming that such groups possess beliefs, social epistemology asks how these group beliefs are justified, rational, or constitutive of knowledge.

Individual cognizers are also studied by social epistemology, however. They can be the subjects of social epistemology if and when they take account of other people's statements (or thoughts) when deciding what to believe. Traditional epistemology was centered on a person's use of his own perceptual systems and reasoning systems to decide what and when to believe.

René Descartes (1569–1650) embodied the image of a skeptical inquirer, doubting whatever he could doubt, accepting only what was beyond doubt. He argued that the starting-point for knowledge is the contents of one's own mind. All further inquiry must begin from that egocentric position. Many philosophers in the ensuing centuries embraced Descartes' starting point, centering the investigation on (an initially) self-focused methodology. This was the motivating template for much of the epistemology that followed. Social epistemology contrasts with this ego-centric focus by asking how cognitive agents should proceed (intellectually) through discourse and debate with others. How does such inter-personal activity bear on one's prospects for justified belief and knowledge?

The rise of contemporary social epistemology has a somewhat odd history. It was preceded by an intellectual movement that flourished between the 1960s and 1980s. The movement went under such titles as "post-modernism," "social constructivism," "social studies of science (and technology)," and the like. It sought to critique ideas such as truth, rationality, or reliability – deflating them and by implication deflating the subject-matter of epistemology. In this sense the movement threatened to debunk epistemology as a whole.

Among the leaders of the movement were Michel Foucault, Thomas Kuhn, Bruno Latour, Barry Barnes, David Bloor, Steven Shapin, and Richard Rorty. They sought to undercut many of the basic working assumptions that characterize science and philosophy (especially epistemology). First, there was the assumption that (for many propositions) there are truths of the matter. Second, there was the assumption that certain modes of reasoning are more rational and truth-conducive than others, and can lead to the discovery or recognition of *objective* facts. The debunkers, by contrast, challenged the very notions of truth, rationality, and objectivity. In addition, there was the novel theme that what is *thought* to be true and/or objective is largely a result of *social practices*. Everything previously thought to be a matter of truth and/or rational discovery was now attributed, with the help of sociological analysis, to social forces (read "power" and "politics"). Here are a few statements of such debunking theses.

1 "[T]here are no context-free or super-cultural norms of rationality." (Barnes and Bloor 1982: 27)
2 "'True' is merely a compliment we pay to statements we find good to believe. Truth is not a property possessed by beliefs in virtue of some relation they bear to 'worldly' facts that stand outside of discursive practices." (Rorty 1991: 24)
3 "[In] effect [Kuhn] showed that all of natural science was located inside social history ... [Any] theory can always be retained as long as its defenders hold enough institutional power to explain away potential threats to it." (Harding 1992: 582)

During the foregoing periods of post-modernism and social constructivism, very few epistemologists subscribed to these attempts to debunk epistemology or science. Although they may not have agreed about how to respond to these theoretical assaults, few were convinced. Beginning in the late 1980s and 1990s, however, epistemologists and philosophers of science began to make sustained responses to the debunkers, but also to accept one central idea of the debunkers, namely, that social factors must play a role (or several roles) in any minimally satisfactory epistemology. Epistemologists and philosophers of science like Goldman (1987, 1999), Kitcher (1990, 1993), Michael P. Lynch (2004), and Paul Boghossian (2006) took aim at the truth-deniers. Both Kitcher and Goldman provided samples of how epistemology and philosophy of science could be substantially socialized without abandoning traditional epistemic standards. The results were some blueprints, or at least sketches, of systematic programs for social epistemology.

What does epistemology look like when it embraces an important role for social perspectives on knowledge? As indicated above, we can distinguish three types of epistemic scenarios that incorporate important social factors. The first type of scenario – briefly discussed earlier – is where an individual epistemic subject makes use of the beliefs or assertions of others to form or revise his/her view on a certain question. This type of social epistemology (SE) might be called *interpersonal* SE.

According to a second branch of social epistemology, *collective* SE, there are groups or collective agents, such as juries, committees, and fact-finding bodies that have beliefs or credences. It's an ontological assumption that these collective entities have beliefs or doxastic states. But when epistemologists seek to evaluate the rationality or justifiedness of group beliefs, they are working in (social-) epistemological territory.

A third type of social epistemology involves large entities but not ones that qualify as doxastic agents. These are institutions, networks, markets, etc. which do not themselves have belief-like states but do have members, or constituents, with such states. A question can then be raised: how do these assemblages or institutions influence the flow of information among its members? Call this *institutional* social epistemology.

Why Is Interpersonal Social Epistemology Needed?

The foregoing three species of social epistemology provide a good partial answer to the question "What *is* social epistemology?" Now let us comment on our second general question, the *why* question: why do we need social epistemology? What work can it do for us? There are two rather different types of "help" or "assistance" epistemological theories might provide. First, they might offer answers to theoretical problems that theorists (in the relevant sub-fields) would like to have. Second, it might provide principles that can guide people (not just theorists but ordinary folks) in their day-to-day belief-forming practices.

A major component of interpersonal SE is devoted to the question of when it is advisable for a person to trust the assertions and claims of others. After all, from toddler-hood through the rest of our lives, we hear and/or read umpteen statements from others. And very often we are persuaded by what they say, or take it as obvious that their word should be heeded. But when, exactly, should another person's words be trusted and accepted? Some have said that one needs to have evidence of another person's veracity (or the veracity of people in general) before trusting them. Others say that one has a default entitlement (= justification) to believe others, an entitlement that holds unless one has contrary evidence.[1]

An off-shoot of this problem is now one of the liveliest issues in social epistemology: the problem of "peer disagreement" (Feldman 2007). Imagine a case in which one person, S, has some evidence for proposition P and proceeds to believe it. She now runs into her old friend S★, whom she regards as an intellectual equal of hers. To her surprise, it turns out that S★ has exactly the same evidence with respect to P as S does. But, even more surprising, S★ believes the *denial* of P rather than P. Once S learns about S★'s contrary opinion with respect to P, should she revise her own credence? Should she "conciliate" with S★, "moderating" her degree of belief in S★'s direction?

How could SE be helpful in connection with problems of peer disagreement? One way to help, as suggested above, is to offer a general theoretical approach to the problem that delineates the "proper" solution to it. Second, it might provide principles that could actually be applied (at least in favorable cases) by people who find themselves in a peer-disagreement situation. There are at least two ways that this might lead to (epistemically) "good" results. First, it might give instructions to the epistemic agent to modify her belief so as to increase the probability of having a true belief. Second, it might give instructions to the epistemic agent to take doxastic steps that produce a justified or rational belief given her circumstances (whether or not it's true).

Another problem to which social epistemology can contribute is the identification of experts. How to select a trustworthy expert is not merely a "possible" problem (like the peer-disagreement case) but a problem that ordinary people regularly confront. Whether in matters of financial investment, choosing a doctor for diagnosis or surgery, getting advice on the choice of a college, etc., people often seek advice from others who are better informed. But if you are ignorant on a given subject, how can you even select which advisor to rely upon? Experts often disagree. How can you, who by hypothesis is under-informed on the subject in question, identify the superior expert when confronted with a pair of opposing experts? Call this the "novice/two-experts problem" (Goldman 2001; Coady 2012, Chap. 2).

A solution to this kind of problem is often elusive. Does a diploma or an employment history tell a layperson how well trained or capable a self-professed expert is? Can one extract from academic degrees or other credentials which of two alleged experts is really superior? Can one identify the superior expert by listening to them debate with one another? It is questionable whether a layperson can reliably identify from a debate which expert is superior. Doesn't that depend on having a prior body of knowledge, precisely what is lacking in the hypothesized situation? What about determining an expert's skill by checking his past track-record and seeing how often he was right? An obvious problem here is that a layperson or novice may lack access to past track-records. Even if they can determine what a given expert said on past occasions, how can the layperson apply this information unless he already knows whether what E said on those occasions was true or false? But this is just what laypersons are unlikely to know.

At this point debunkers of expertise (and of social epistemology) might enter the fray. Appealing to the foregoing considerations (or the like), they might contend that there is no such thing as genuine expertise. According to some debunkers, there are only people who make *claims* to expertise and have been given a privileged status by their community, team, or culture. But there isn't *really* any such thing as expertise in which some people genuinely know the facts and others do not. There are only social hierarchies, no independent reality of truths, facts, and genuine (truth-linked) knowledge.

This is a challenge – or set of challenges – that social epistemology should take on. Why? In most societies people regularly rely on claims to expertise. If people are deluded about there being any such legitimate claims, this is an important thing to know. If they are not deluded, that is also important to know. Social epistemology can play a valuable role in setting these issues straight.

Expertise isn't the only arena in which social epistemology might usefully enter the fray. In many societies people are advised not to believe in *rumors*. If you hear something that's a mere rumor, rather than something that comes from an "authenticated" source, don't believe it. This is a rule of epistemic conduct; but is it sound? Social epistemology may weigh in on this topic. One social epistemologist, David Coady (2012), takes issue with the principle. Rumors may be characterized as unofficial communications; they lack a certain kind of institutional endorsement. Does this mean that believing them is always or typically unjustified, or that we should adopt an attitude of prima facie skepticism toward them? Whether rumors are more or less subject to inaccuracy than formal modes of transmission will depend on what the available formal modes of transmission are. For example, in the Soviet Union in 1953, a study showed that the majority of people believed that official information was less reliable than "word-of-mouth communication," and this was particularly widespread among the better-educated classes (Coady 2012: 97). Sixty-five years later it may well turn out that government-supplied information in the United States is more likely to feature "fake news" than word-of-mouth communications. So the social-epistemological study of how much credence to place in what you hear – and from what channel you hear it – has work to do. And society needs good work in this territory.

How Important Is Collective Social Epistemology?

There are many reasons, then, to go beyond purely individual epistemology by studying interpersonal SE. What about the other two types of SE we have identified: collective and institutional SE? Do we need to study them? Why? What benefits might they bring?

For the sake of clarity, we must draw a sharp distinction between the *metaphysical* thesis that there are collective agents (i.e., doxastic agents whose members are other doxastic agents) and any *epistemological* thesis concerning such agents. That there are "groups with minds of their own" (borrowing a title from Pettit (2003)) is a metaphysical or ontological thesis, not an epistemological one. We concede the truth of this ontological thesis for present purposes. The distinctive epistemological question that can then be posed is: "For any collective agent, what makes its beliefs *justified* or *unjustified*?" To address this question is to engage in *collective* SE.

In everyday life it is common to speak of collective entities. In the run-up and aftermath to the American-led war against Iraq, it was routinely said that the U.S. government *thought* (believed) that Saddam Hussein had weapons of mass destruction. Critics questioned whether the Bush Administration was *justified* in defending this charge, but they didn't (generally) deny that the Administration *held* the belief. And it was therefore in order to ask whether the belief was justified. This is how questions about the epistemology of collective entities enter the picture.

Another such example can be drawn from scientific literature on climate change. The Intergovernmental Panel on Climate Change (IPCC) presents itself as a body that has beliefs or belief-like "positions," which they often articulate in terms of "levels of confidence." Given the research on which their reports are based, one expects these positions to be regarded as justified rather than unjustified. But what exactly makes a *group* belief justified? Is it a matter of the justificational statuses of its *members*? Just how do the members' J-statuses affect the group's J-status? This is an issue for collective social epistemology.

These problems are currently receiving a good bit of attention. To be precise, there are two distinct problems. The first is how the belief of a collective entity is determined by the beliefs of its assorted members? (And do different members' beliefs count for more than other members' beliefs?) The second is how the epistemic status of a collective entity's beliefs is determined by the epistemic statuses of its members' beliefs?

As concerns the first problem, quite a few proposals have been made. For example, Margaret Gilbert (1989: 306) and Fred Schmitt (1994: 262) hold the following:

> A group G believes that p just in case the members of G jointly accept p, where the latter obtains just in case each member openly expresses a willingness to let p stand as the view of G, or openly expresses a commitment jointly to accept that p, conditional on a like open expression of commitment by other members of G.

This joint commitment requirement threatens to be both too strong and too weak. It seems too strong to require that *all* members of G must express this commitment. And is it sufficient that they make this verbal commitment – even if they don't really accept that p?

Rejecting this "commitment model" of group belief and justification, Alexander Bird (2010, 2014; also see Hutchins 1995) instead defends what he calls the "distributed model":

We talk as if we are committed to social epistemic states. We use locutions such as "it is now known that Kepler's conjecture is true," "we know that smoking causes cancer," "North Korea knows how to build a nuclear weapon," and so forth. Such locutions are not reducible to claims about individuals .... For example, it is unlikely that any individual North Korean knows how to build a nuclear weapon .... For any entity that has parts there must be something that unites those parts .... For most physical objects that unity is mechanical – the parts will be physically joined to one another. For social entities, the principle of composition will not be like this. We ought to bear in mind that there might be different ways in which individuals can form social entities and that the resulting different kinds of entity may differ in their existence conditions .... So we may wish to consider that the principal of composition for a social *epistemic* subject ought to be one that plays some part in explaining how that resulting entity can be the possessor of epistemic states.

(Bird 2014: 51–53)

If Bird is right then especially in the case of ("wide") science the epistemologist has good reasons to say that the social entity or collectivity typically knows things that are not known by each individual scientist. It isn't feasible for every individual member to know what the group knows. In other cases of collective knowledge or justified belief, however, there is an additional factor. Society may want the judgment-making entity to be a collective body rather than a personal one. This holds especially for legal judgments. Society does not want defendants to be rendered guilty by individual jurors; it wants them to be judged guilty (or innocent) by a *court*, an *impersonal* agent. The social epistemology of legal judgment should support the anonymity of such judgments. One hopes that judicial deliberations can make sense of the idea that courts render judgments, not individual jurors. This is an additional reason *why* we would like to have an appropriate theory of collective justification.[2]

The theory of collective justification also runs into significant issues of a formal, or technical, nature. These have been well set out by Philip Pettit and Christian List (List and Pettit 2002, 2011; Pettit 2003; List 2005). In order to study the justification or rationality of a group (or collective), it is useful to introduce the notion of an aggregation procedure. An aggregation procedure is a mechanism by which a group can generate collectively endorsed beliefs or judgments on the basis of the group members' individual beliefs and judgments. A simple example is majority voting, whereby a group judges a given proposition to be true whenever a majority of group members judges it to be true. What properties should a group's aggregation procedure have to meet the rationality challenge, that is, to generate consistent collective judgments over a range of cases whenever the group members are individually consistent? Troubles arise because of the "discursive dilemma" (List 2005; reprinted in Goldman and Whitcomb 2011).

Suppose that a group has to form collectively endorsed beliefs on certain propositions. Can it ensure consistency or rationality? Consider an expert committee that has to prepare a report on the health consequences of air pollution in a big city. The experts have to make judgments on the following propositions.

(P) The average particle pollution level exceeds 50 micrograms per cubic meter of air. (Premise 1)

(P → Q) If the average particular pollution level exceeds 50 micrograms per cubic meter of air, then residents have a significantly increased risk of respiratory disease. (Premise 2)

(Q) = Residents have a significantly increased risk of respiratory disease. (Conclusion)

Suppose the experts use majority voting as their aggregation procedure, so that the collective judgment on each proposition is the majority judgment on that proposition by the members. Finally, suppose that a majority of experts judge P to be true, a majority judge P → Q to be true, and a majority judge Q to be false. Then, using the majoritarian principle, the committee as a whole will judge P to be true, P → Q to be true, and Q to be false. This yields an inconsistent collective set of judgments. The committee fails to meet the rationality challenge in this case.

It might not seem so serious that an appealing aggregation procedure like majority rule some-times allows inconsistencies to arise. Things become more worrisome when one learns about the following "impossibility theorem" (List and Pettit 2002; cf. List 2011, in Goldman and Whitcomb 2011: 226):

> There exists no aggregation procedure generating complete and consistent collective judgments that satisfies the following three [initially compelling] conditions simultan-eously: universal domain, anonymity, and systematicity.

In short, it is not only majority voting that incurs inconsistency problems, but any aggregation procedure whatever that satisfies the foregoing plausible conditions. How should a theorist of collective rationality respond to this dilemma? That problem must be confronted by social epistemologists.

Like many other investigators, List and Pettit focus on *rationality* as the primary term of epistemic appraisal. But now let us revisit the other term of epistemic appraisal so prevalent in epistemology, viz. *justification*. An account of collective justification has been advanced by Goldman that closely parallels process reliabilism for individual justification. It might be prom-ising if accounts with substantially similar components could work for both individual and col-lective justification. Since talk of collective beliefs and their justification have already been found to have an important place in society, it would be helpful if such talk could be ratified by a defensible account of group justification. This is where social epistemology has an import-ant role to play.

The core idea of individual process reliabilism (Goldman 1979) is that an individual's belief is justified just in case it is produced by a reliable belief-forming process (or sequence of processes) in the agent's psychological history. It is left vague precisely how reliable this must be; but it needn't be 100 percent reliable. The theory also distinguishes between conditional and uncondi-tional reliability. A process is unconditionally reliable if and only if the ratio of true beliefs to total beliefs that it produces is very high. This is the appropriate standard for processes like perception. For processes like inference or memory, however, the appropriate standard is condi-tional reliability. A given inference type might generate a lot of false conclusions but still confer justification, because it tends to produce a high percentage of true beliefs *when its input beliefs are true*. In addition to this requirement on processes, the input beliefs to the process must also be justified if the output belief is to be justified.

The foregoing themes are now extended from *individual* process reliabilism to *social* process reliabilism (Goldman 2014). The core idea is that the justification-status (J-status) of a group-belief B_G is determined by the J-statuses of group G's members' beliefs that are operative in gen-erating B_G. The "processes" in cases of social aggregation are not psychological processes. Rather they are functions that get implemented by some sort of organizational processes. For conveni-ence think of the prototypical process as a balloting process that occurs at a meeting of the group. The group belief so formed is then available for use by the group. If a large enough proportion of the members' beliefs that generate B_G are themselves justified, and if the aggrega-tion function (from member beliefs to group beliefs) has a high enough conditional reliability, then the group belief B_G is also justified.

What we have presented here is merely a sketch of social process reliabilism. Numerous details and problems need to be worked out. A number of serious challenges for the account are pre-sented in Lackey (2016). The main point, however, is that a successful approach in this general territory would support the integrity of classifying group beliefs as justified or unjustified.

How Useful Is Institutional Social Epistemology?

We turn now from the prospects of *collective* social epistemology to the prospects of *institutional* social epistemology. Let us remind ourselves what "institutional SE" deals with. It deals with cases in which a social institution has a significant influence on the beliefs of its members but does not qualify as a collective entity with a mind of its own.

A criminal law system may be viewed as an institution with truth-linked goals, and its operation is largely designed to produce verdicts that accord with the facts. Some sectors of a criminal law system – e.g., juries – can be regarded as collective agents. But the present section does not focus on juries, but rather on legal *systems*, which are not collective agents that themselves have beliefs. What, then, are legal systems "about"? Here is an account given by Larry Laudan, a philosopher of science turned legal theorist (Laudan 2006, 2011).

> If we look closely at the criminal justice system in the United States (or almost anywhere else for that matter), it soon becomes evident that there are three distinct families of basic aims or values driving such systems. [Only two of these are discussed here.] One of these core aims is to find out the truth about a crime and thus avoid false verdicts, what I will call the role of *error reduction*. A second is premised on the recognition that, however much one tries to avoid them, errors will occur from time to time. This goal addresses the question of which sort of error, a false acquittal or a false conviction, is more serious and is thus more earnestly to be avoided. In short, the worry here is with how the errors distribute themselves .... A whole body of doctrine and practices has grown up in the common law about how to conduct trials so as to make it more likely that, when an error does occur, it will be a false acquittal rather than a false conviction.
>
> *(Laudan 2011: 271–272)*

The institution of the common law, then, includes precepts aimed at generating certain kinds of truth-linked outcomes. This aim is right up the alley of the practice of social epistemology. To be sure, most people involved in shaping the common law never thought of themselves as "epistemologists." Nonetheless, they were engaged in what we are here calling (one aspect of) social epistemology, viz. the creation of institutional arrangements dedicated toward "epistemic" ends. Of course, pure epistemologists, who have never devoted much attention to the law, might not be great contributors to this endeavor. In principle, though, they could focus their attention on providing analyses that fit within this framework. This is what Laudan's work aims to do. In short, this strand of social epistemology, which might be labeled "applied social epistemology," is a specialty that ideally should involve collaboration between legal scholars and (philosophical) epistemologists. That social epistemologists can usefully contribute in this fashion is another example of "why" social epistemology is a worthwhile enterprise.

The Methods of Social Epistemology: Present and Future

In the two previous parts, we have sought to explain what social epistemology is and why anyone should be interested in it. In the process, we have provided a wide variety of samples of social epistemology. What can be said in general, then, about the *methods* of social epistemology? Do the methods of social epistemology differ from those of individual epistemology? It should be obvious that many methods used by individual epistemology – including appeals to intuition, applications of logic, probability theory, and mathematics – are present in both individual and social epistemology. However, since the role of mathematics has received only slight attention here thus far, let me provide a more lively illustration of this, focusing on the area of philosophy of science.

The question of resource allocation in science has been treated in a mathematical fashion by at least three philosophers: Charles Saunders Peirce (1958), Philip Kitcher (1990, 1993) and Michael Strevens (2003). Strevens explains the problem as follows:

> The problem of resource allocation is the problem of distributing limited resources among different [research] programs so as to maximize the return to society …. [I]t is not in general true that the optimal allocation devotes all resources to the program with the greatest intrinsic potential; the problem, then, is not trivial.
>
> *(2003: 61)*

To keep things abbreviated and simple, only a portion of Strevens' extended treatment is quoted below:

> I investigate the optimal allocation [of resources] for the additive case in the remainder of this section …. You have a limited number N of resources – say, worker hours – to distribute between two research programs. You goal is to maximize the total expected return. The programs' benefits are additive. Assuming that additional worker hours always improve a program's chances of success, you will distribute all N worker hours available, n to one program and $N\text{-}n$ to the other. Your return, then, is
>
> $$V_1 s_1(n) \; + \; v_2 s_2(N - n)$$
>
> The problem is to find the value of n that maximizes this return.
>
> *(Strevens 2003: 62)*

This is a straightforward application of a mathematical technique, typical especially of economics. But it also functions as a social-epistemological approach to science, in which the question is: what practice of distributing credit to scientists is (epistemically) optimal for the institution of science?

Here is a second example of exploiting an economics-inspired model for epistemic purposes. The field of economics, of course, has long been entranced with the notion of a "market." Economists have long applauded free markets as devices that optimize certain economic consequences. In thinking about what social systems are best from the perspective of information generation (a crucial epistemic matter), the idea of open debate has long been prized as a desirable system. In a recent paper, however, Cass Sunstein (2011) has promoted a certain variant of free markets – i.e., *prediction markets* – as a superior way for groups to generate more and better information. Sunstein writes as follows:

> [A] market creates strong incentives for revelation of whatever information people actually hold. And indeed, prediction markets have been found not to amplify individual errors but to eliminate them; the prices that result from trading prove reliable even if many individual traders err. In recent years, prediction markets have done more than to provide valuable information. In countless domains, their forecasts have proved extremely accurate. The most dramatic finding is that prices generally operate as probabilities. When prices suggest that events are likely to occur with 90 percent probability, they occur 90 percent of the time.
>
> *(Sunstein 2011: 320–330)*

A very different example shows how social epistemologists might profit from models of group behavior in non-human animals, a field that is enjoying a surge of interesting research, including a paper by Christian List and Adrian Vermeule (2014). There is a long history of humans using tricks of design from other species. In applied sciences such as engineering aerodynamics, "biomimicry" exploits designs used from animals. For example, the shape of the Mercedes Benz bionic car mimics the box-fish to maximize aerodynamic efficiency. Is it possible that humans can improve their informational exchange processes and decision-making processes to improve their group performance? Recent research suggests that insect colonies make collective decisions very well, and through striking procedures. Drawing partly on work by Thomas Seeley (1995), List and Vermeule argue that homo sapiens can learn from these procedures. Not everything of interest in this territory, of course, involves *epistemic* matters, which is the central concern of social epistemologists. But there may be enough material of epistemic interest.

The main lesson from the hive for epistemic decision-making, argue List and Vermeule, is to balance the procedures of independence and interdependence. In the area of voting and group decision-making, the Condorcet Jury Theorem (which dates to 1785) has long been taken to show that a group's epistemic goals are best secured through the avoidance of interdependence. Theorists working in this Condorcetian tradition have tended to see interdependence as a risk. But bees utilize a mixed procedure, behaving interdependently in their epistemic "agenda" and independently in deciding whether to "vote" for any given option. List and Vermeule suggest that a mixed procedure may also be optimal for humans. There is much to be learned from the processes that evolution has deposited in a variety of species. Future work in social epistemology may find it instructive to explore this territory with the aim of finding the best collective-epistemic procedures available to homo sapiens.

Notes

1 Among the early contributions to this literature are Coady (1992), Fricker (1995), Burge (1993), and Lackey (2008).
2 Other contributors to this arena of investigation include Mathiesen (2006) and Tollefsen (2007).

References

Barnes, B. and Bloor, D. (1982). Relativism, rationalism, and the sociology of knowledge. In: M. Hollis and S. Lukes, eds., *Rationality and relativism*, Cambridge: MIT Press, pp. 21–47.

Bird, A. (2010). Social knowing. *Philosophical Perspectives* 24, pp. 23–56.

Bird, A. (2014). When is there a group that knows? In: J. Lackey, ed., *Essays in collective epistemology*, Oxford: Oxford University Press, pp. 42–63.

Boghossian, P. (2006). *Fear of knowledge, against relativism and constructivism*. Oxford: Clarendon Press.

Burge, T. (1993). Content preservation. *Philosophical Review* 102, pp. 457–488.

Coady, C. (1992). *Testimony: a philosophical study*. Oxford: Clarendon Press.

Coady, D. (2012). *What to believe now: applying epistemology to contemporary issues*. Malden, MA: Wiley-Blackwell.

Feldman, R. (2007). Reasonable, religious disagreement. In: L. Antony, ed., *Philosophers without God*, Oxford: Oxford University Press, pp. 194–214.

Fricker, E. (1995). Telling and trusting: reductionism and anti-reductionism in the epistemology of testimony. *Mind* 104, pp. 393–411.

Gilbert, M. (1989). *On social facts*. London: Routledge.

Goldman, A. (1979). What is justified belief? In: G. Pappas, ed., *Justification and knowledge*, Dordrecht: Reidel, pp. 1–23.

Goldman, A. (1987). Foundations of social epistemics. *Synthese* 73, pp. 109–144.

Goldman, A. (1999). *Knowledge in a social world*. Oxford: Oxford University Press.

Goldman, A. (2001). Experts: which ones should you trust? *Philosophy and Phenomenological Research* 63(1), pp. 85–110.

Goldman, A. (2014). Social process reliabilism. In: J. Lackey, ed., *Essays in collective epistemology*, Oxford: Oxford University Press, pp. 11–41.

Goldman, A. and Whitcomb, D. eds. (2011). *Social epistemology: essential readings*. Oxford: Oxford University Press.

Harding, S. (1992). After the neutral ideal: science, politics, and "strong objectivity." *Social Research* 59, pp. 567–587.

Hutchins, E. (1995). *Cognition in the wild*. Cambridge, MA: MIT Press.

Kitcher, P. (1990). The division of cognitive labor. *Journal of Philosophy* 87, pp. 5–22.

Kitcher, P. (1993). *The advancement of science*. New York: Oxford University Press.

Lackey, J. (2008). *Learning from words*. Oxford: Oxford University Press.

Lackey, J. (2016). What is justified group belief? *Philosophical Review* 125(3), pp. 341–396.

Laudan, L. (2006). *Truth, error, and the criminal law*. Cambridge: Cambridge University Press.

Laudan, L. (2011). Thinking about error in the law. In: A. Goldman and D. Whitcomb, eds., *Social epistemology, essential readings*, Oxford: Oxford University Press, pp. 271–296.

List, C. (2005). Group knowledge and group rationality: a judgment aggregation perspective *Episteme: A Journal of Social Epistemology* 2(1), pp. 25–38.

List, C. and Pettit, P. (2002). Aggregating sets of judgments: an impossibility result. *Economics and Philosophy* 18, pp. 89–110.

List, C. and Pettit, P. (2011). *Group agency: the possibility, design, and status of corporate agents*. Oxford: Oxford University Press.

List, C. and Vermeule, A. (2014). Independence and interdependence: lessons from the hive *Rationality and Society* 26(2), pp. 170–207.

Lynch, M. P. (2004). *True to life: why truth matters*. Cambridge, MA: MIT Press.

Mathiesen, K. (2006). The epistemic features of group belief. *Episteme* 2(3), pp. 161–176.

Peirce, C. (1958). Note on the theory of the economy of research. In: A. Burks, ed., *Collected papers of Charles Saunders Peirce, vol. 7*, Cambridge, MA: Harvard University Press, pp. 76–83.

Pettit, P. (2003). Groups with minds of their own. In: F. Schmitt, ed., *Socializing metaphysics*, Lanham, MD: Rowman and Littlefield, pp. 257–287.

Rorty, R. (1991). Solidarity or objectivity. In: R. Rorty, ed., *Objectivity, relativism, and truth*, New York: Cambridge University Press, pp. 21–34.

Schmitt, F. (1994). The justification of group beliefs. In: F. Schmitt, ed., *Socializing epistemology: the social dimensions of knowledge*, Lanham, MD: Rowman & Littlefield, pp. 257–287.

Seeley, T. (1995). *The wisdom of the hive: the social physiology of honey bee colonies*. Cambridge, MA: Harvard University Press.

Strevens, M. (2003). The role of the priority rule in science. *Journal of Philosophy* 100(2), pp. 55–79.

Sunstein, C. (2011). Deliberating groups versus prediction markets (or Hayek's challenge to Habermas). In: A. Goldman and D. Whitcomb, eds., *Social epistemology, essential readings*, New York: Oxford University Press, pp. 314–337.

Tollefsen, D. (2007). Group testimony. *Social Epistemology* 21, pp. 299–311.

3

THE TWIN ROOTS AND BRANCHES OF SOCIAL EPISTEMOLOGY

Finn Collin

Social epistemology is a field of research within Anglo-American philosophy that has emerged over the last decades in the borderland between epistemology and philosophy of science. Breaking with an ancient philosophical tradition, social epistemology adopts a *social* perspective upon knowledge, construing it as a phenomenon of the public sphere rather than as an individual, or even private or "mental", possession. Knowledge is generated by, and attributed to, not only individuals but also collective entities such as groups, businesses, public institutions and entire societies. Like traditional epistemology, social epistemology is a *normative* enterprise, but whereas traditional epistemology typically contents itself with laying down abstract principles for the justification of knowledge while taking little interest in their practical implementation, social epistemology is concerned to provide directions for the improvement of our collective epistemic practices and institutions. In pursuing this agenda, social epistemology adopts a *naturalistic* stance, in the recognition that conceptual analysis will not get us very far in identifying the conditions for effective knowledge generation on a societal scale. We must adopt an empirical approach, drawing on disciplines such as psychology, sociology, anthropology and economics.

The above tenets are agreed upon by most current philosophers who label themselves as social epistemologists. However, behind this consensus lurks considerable divergence. Social epistemology (SE) comprises two roughly demarcated lines of development, one being an extension of classical analytic epistemology while the other is inspired mainly by philosophy of science. This difference in pedigree brings a couple of significant divergences with it. On both sides there is some amount of organization and joint efforts, in the form of journal publication and similar academic manifestations, often involving some critical attention to the activities of the other branch; still there are many independents and borderline figures in the field. In the following, we shall look at both branches.

Analytic Social Epistemology: The Naturalist and Reliabilist Turns

We start with the branch emerging out of classical epistemology, often labeled Analytic Social Epistemology (ASE). ASE is a descendant of classical epistemology, which defined itself by the task of defeating the *radical sceptic*. If we accept the rules of play proposed by the radical (Cartesian) sceptic, all we have to work with epistemically are our own subjective experiences ("ideas"). The result is epistemic solipsism: the very existence of the external world becomes moot and, *a forteriori*, so does the existence of other human beings with whom one might have shared the task of gaining knowledge about that world. This radically individualist and subjectivist perspective would be retained even after 20th-century epistemology made its celebrated "linguistic turn", replacing Cartesian talk of mental operations upon "ideas" with the analysis of evidential relations between propositions (or sentences). The individualist-subjectivist stance would survive in the principle that all the human knower has to work with are first-person observation sentences and their ilk.

Analytic epistemology would eventually break with this individualist tradition and produce a social offshoot, but the move was made by small and cautious steps, and along an indirect route. First came a break with the *a priori* approach and a turn towards an alternative, *naturalistic* conception of human knowledge, i.e. the empirical examination of how human cognition actually functions. This idea had been proposed by Willard Quine in a celebrated article entitled "Epistemology Naturalized" (Quine 1969), but its implementation had to await the pioneering work of Alvin Goldman, the founding father and central figure of analytic social epistemology. Goldman developed the naturalistic conception in a series of texts of the 1970s and 1980s, culminating with Goldman (1986).

The empirical turn would seem to abandon traditional epistemology's normative agenda, which aims to lay down the – formal and idealized – conditions for a belief to be justified by the evidence, and takes little interest in the actual, invariably error-prone, workings of the human mind. Goldman found a way, however, to salvage normativity by devising an alternative to the traditional "internalist" models of justification, where a belief is warranted by the evidence the believer can cite on its behalf. On the novel, *externalist* view proposed by Goldman, we can grant to a belief the status of knowledge even if unsupported by premises known to the believer, as long as the cognitive process through which it was generated is generally a reliable deliverer of truth. It does not matter if this process consists in purely neuro-physiological goings-on, the nature of which is unknown to the believer, as is, for example, the case in vision. Goldman arrived at this theory through a series of steps. Early on, he adopted a causal theory of (empirical) knowledge, in order to circumvent certain familiar counter-examples to the standard analysis of knowledge as justified true belief (Goldman 1967). According to Goldman, this analysis could be amended by adding the condition that the fact known be causally connected to the belief about it. In subsequent articles, Goldman would address the problem that not just any causal connection would do; it had to be of an epistemically "appropriate" kind. This requirement was resolved by a general condition to the effect that the causal mechanism in question be a *reliable producer of truth* under the given circumstances, i.e. that it would generate true beliefs in a high proportion of cases (Goldman 1972).

There was some vacillation in Goldman's early presentations with respect to the nature of his enterprise: Was this a case of conceptual analysis of notions such as "justification" and "knowledge", or was it an attempt to naturalistically *explain* the philosophical intuitions that we draw on in such an analysis, hence a case of second-order naturalism (Goldman 1972)? Be that as it may, Goldman's commitment to first-order naturalism (naturalism with respect to empirical beliefs) was firm, and he would explore this approach in a monograph that offered a comprehensive review of contemporary empirical research into individual human cognition in psychology and cognitive science (Goldman 1986). An important task of normative epistemology would henceforth be to determine which cognitive processes are reliable producers of truth.

Analytic Social Epistemology: The Social Turn

Next, Goldman expanded externalism and reliabilism to encompass even the social components of the cognizer's environment, thereby finally extending analytic epistemology into the social realm (Goldman 1987, 1999). His first steps were cautious. The point of socializing epistemology is to legitimize the immense increase in each individual's knowledge that ensues if we accept the testimony of others. But, given epistemology's classical sceptical roots, this immediately raises a number of problems: Under which conditions can we trust other people's testimony? And is such trust an autonomous mode of validation, or must it be backed up by other, independently recognized types of evidence? Moreover, our informants sometimes contradict each other. How can we rationally handle such disagreement? These questions already arise in everyday contexts, but recur in pointed versions in the sciences: How can lay people identify trustworthy scientific experts, and how should they react when experts disagree?

Such questions were among the first to be treated by analytic social epistemologists, using the familiar tool of thought experiment. They constituted key topics of discussion in the journal founded by Goldman in 2004, *Episteme: A Journal of Social and Individual Epistemology*. In large part, the aim was to overcome resistance from traditional individualist epistemologists who argued that social epistemology is not real epistemology. Later, when the conceptual ground-works were secured and interest turned from person-to-person testimony to larger societal institutions of knowledge production and dissemination, ASE adopted a more naturalistic stance (Goldman 1999). Topics of investigation were institutions such as law, science and the media. This effort had an empirical and a theoretical side, of which the former consisted in examining actual epistemic practices for their "veritistic" merits, i.e. their reliability as truth-producers. This aspect has to this day remained somewhat programmatic, and has largely relied on data collected by other disciplines for other, more local or specific purposes.

ASE has put more effort into the development of theory. ASE's preferred theoretical models are typically formal and abstract, with micro-economics being a particularly popular source of inspiration. Such models adopt the stance of methodological individualism by anchoring all societal phenomena in individuals, their deeds and their cognitive proclivities, and ASE's penchant for this approach is no doubt a remnant of the individualism of classical epistemology. ASEers have also devised models of their own making, less closely tied to micro-economic paradigms. Thus, Goldman and collaborators have developed models based upon Bayesian probability theory (Goldman and Shaked 1991).

Proponents of ASE are aware that the institutions of knowledge production have vast and sometimes invidious social implications, and also grant that knowledge maximisation is not the sole goal of social epistemology; other concerns are at play as well, such as social equality. But ASE holds that the exploration of such broader normative issues belongs to political philosophy rather than social epistemology (Goldman 2004). ASE has gradually moved in the direction of a broader ethico-political perspective, however, although again, these developments have been piecemeal and cautious. Miranda Fricker's work is a pioneering effort in this direction, demonstrating the existence of a specific, epistemic type of injustice that constitutes a legitimate topic for epistemology (Fricker 2007). It is perpetrated, e.g. when somebody's testimony is neglected because of prejudices concerning that person's gender, race or lowly social status. Such neglect impugns a person's status as a knower, thereby negating a crucial aspect of our humanity. Fricker is not unaware of the more mundane, material fruits of possessing knowledge; nevertheless, she is unwilling to make issues concerning the societal distribution of knowledge part of the ambit of social epistemology. Instead, it is a subject for political philosophy or ethics.

The reluctance of ASE to address broader issues of distributive fairness may be a carry-over from the strong focus in traditional epistemology on the "production" side of knowledge, to the neglect of its "consumption": The aim was to lay down the conditions for *generating* knowledge – "generating" to be understood in the highly etiolated sense of "furnishing beliefs with adequate evidence". ASE has long since embraced the idea, however, that knowledge can be encapsulated in more tangible vessels than minds, such as books, computers, measuring instruments, university disciplines, educational programs, etc.; this is implicit in the externalist turn. It is a natural next step to start addressing issues of the ethics and politics of the distribution of such embodiments. And indeed, that process is underway. An example is Sanford Goldberg, whose most recent work contains a program for the development of ASE in the direction of addressing general normative issues (Goldberg 2016).

Science-Oriented Social Epistemology

We now turn to the other branch of SE, which has philosophy of science, rather than epistemology, as its most important progenitor. This discipline deals with an especially eminent example of social cognition, science; thus a social perspective on knowledge was inherent in it from the very start. Thus, while much ASE work still revolves around the legitimacy of the very step from individualism to collectivism, the other branch rests confidently in its collectivist stance. Moreover, philosophy of science typically is not much concerned with securing indubitable evidence for beliefs already held, but has a more dynamic goal, i.e. promoting the progress or "growth" of science, and this stance is inherited by its academic descendant.

The notion of scientific progress had come under pressure through Kuhn's work, however. Kuhn granted that science progresses in the direction of ever higher "puzzle-solving" power, but denied that this implies an ever closer correspondence to the fundamental structure of reality (Kuhn 1962/1970). Kuhn's revolutionary and sociologized conception of science inspired a spate of empirical investigations of science. This effort, known as Science and Technology Studies (STS), was instigated by the work of David Bloor and his collaborators in the so-called Edinburgh School (Bloor 1976/1991), while a more recent and highly influential contribution was made by Bruno Latour (Latour 1987, 1999). In its turn, STS influenced developments within science-oriented social epistemology, in particular Steve Fuller's program.

The science-oriented social epistemologists form a highly diverse and loosely connected group, not a collective organized around a common project; although, as we shall see, there are pockets of more organized efforts within this branch. Hence, any brief survey will involve huge simplifications. In the following, the representatives of science-oriented social epistemology are treated in an order of increasing divergence from ASE.

First, Philip Kitcher will receive brief mention. Kitcher is primarily a philosopher of science trying to work out a more sociologically realistic analysis of science, following the debunking that idealized positivistic models had suffered at the hands of Kuhn, while still saving science's rational status. In particular, Kitcher wanted to secure a robust sense for the notion of scientific progress, rebutting Kuhn's dismissal of that idea (Kitcher 1993).

What earns Kitcher the epithet of a "social epistemologist" is, first, his treatment of science as not a world onto itself, to be grasped only in its own sui generis categories, but as a mode of the general category of societal knowledge production. He emphasizes that the optimal strategies for achieving truth and other epistemic goals, even individual goals, will involve coordination of effort with others (Kitcher 1992). In this spirit, he analyzes science in theoretical terms with general application to social systems, such as "consensus practices" and "organization of cognitive labor". Moreover, in his more recent work, he explicitly addresses political and ethical aspects of scientific organization and the role of science in society (Kitcher 2011).

Methodologically, Kitcher's work shows considerable affinity with that of Alvin Goldman and ASE, using formal models similar to those of microeconomics. This combination of features defines Kitcher's views as something like a midway position between the two wings of social epistemology.

Social Epistemology and the "New Social Movements"

Among another group of philosophers of the post-Kuhnian era, the issue of science's social and political role was in focus from the start. During the 1970s and 1980s, many philosophers of science were disappointed with science's stance on various key social and ideological issues of that era. It was felt that science tended to support conservative agendas and neglected such current challenges as the erosion of the environment, militarism, racism, gay rights and gender inequality, issues raised by the so-called "new social movements". The issue of gender discrimination played a special role, and it is hardly an accident that many of the philosophers involved were female. Several of them had a background in analytic philosophy, and their agenda did not call for the outright rejection of science, as was the aim of certain radical feminists, but rather to work out a compromise position. Representatives of this effort are Helen Longino (Longino 1990, 2002), Sandra Harding (Harding 1991) and Lorraine Code (Code 1991), each of them with a different balance between the twin, somewhat contrary aims of reconstructing science and defending it against more radical criticisms. Obviously, the agenda of a political critique of science would also be shared by some male philosophers, such as Joseph Rouse (Rouse 1987). All these authors regarded science as a model of human knowledge in general and saw its flaws as those of human thinking as such, only writ large; hence they deserve the epithet of social epistemologists.

There is no room for discussion of all these authors, so I choose Helen Longino as a good representative. Longino wanted to salvage scientific objectivity while making science more sensitive to social concerns, among which feminism had her special interest. She buttressed her critique of traditional science with detailed studies of biological theorizing in particular, demonstrating gender bias of various sorts. Still, Longino wanted to show that science as such is not inherently biased against women or other particular groups. The task was to devise a conception of science that would have room for a plurality of social concerns. She articulated this as the need to eliminate the division between the rational and the social in our understanding of science.

Longino's analysis starts from the insight that science does not proceed by generalizing induction on observations that are cleansed of all theoretical bias, as logical positivists would have it, but uses more complex patterns of reasoning (later to be known as "inference to the best explanation"). Such complex patterns typically involve deep background assumptions of a metaphysical nature needed to bridge the gap between evidence and theoretical conclusion. This is known as the "underdetermination of theory by data" and is normally seen as a weakness of scientific method, especially since those background assumptions often encode societal and ideological values that make science subject to normative bias.

Longino argues rather to the contrary, however, viz. that underdetermination makes room for the input of ideological and valuational concerns into the scientific process in a way that does not invalidate that process, thus safeguarding the societal relevance of science. It is crucial, however, that such interests not be allowed to determine the course of research in a covert manner. To secure transparency, the theories at play must be subjected to an open process of discussion and criticism. (Here, her theory shows a clear and acknowledged affinity with Popper's criticist methodology of science.) Longino stresses, however, that the scientific process cannot be guaranteed to produce a single winner: The result may instead be a multiplicity of different theories representing different perspectives upon reality. This pluralism is generated by differences in topics addressed, methodology, instrumentation, research interests, etc., which contribute to the *contextual* nature of the scientific process.

Longino's position, which she calls "critical contextual empiricism", shares important traits with instrumentalism, from which it is however distinguished by Longino's acceptance of truth as one of the goals of science. Still, the notion of "truth" is not the best to capture science's essential tie to reality, according to Longino. She prefers what she calls "conformity", which also comprises the relationship of resemblance between a scientific model and reality. Moreover, while Longino grants the legitimacy of the traditional striving for unification in science, the viability of this goal cannot be demonstrated by metaphysical argument, nor is its accomplishment guaranteed by methodology. Longino emphasizes that this does not represent a simple relativism, but rather pluralism. Pluralism is an epistemic value and is pernicious only from the point of view of a dogmatic metaphysical monism, and reductivism.

To Longino, individual knowledge has the same structure as scientific knowledge, i.e. it is a matter of advancing a claim and defending it against relevant objections (sometimes referred to as the "default and challenge"-structure of knowledge). This means that knowledge, scientific or everyday, is inherently social as it is defined not only by its conformity to reality, but also by its normative legitimacy in the context of discourse, which in the case of science may encompass all of society.

Such social legitimacy must be earned: In the societal process of validating a piece of scientific knowledge, equality must be preserved, in the sense that all qualified voices must be heard, regardless of gender, race or social status. To Longino, this principle safeguards both the validity of scientific results, and the ideal of social equality.

Critical Social Epistemology

Next, we turn to a segment of the science-oriented branch of social epistemology that presents itself as an organized effort, communicating through a journal founded by Steve Fuller in 1987 named *Social Epistemology* and subtitled *A Journal of Knowledge, Culture and Policy*. This branch is sometimes referred to as Critical Social Epistemology (CSE), a term signaling its keen interest in the ethics and politics of societal knowledge production. The name also marks a distinction to Goldman's ASE with which CSE has enjoyed a somewhat troubled relationship. CSE is a collective effort, and among its other key figures is James Collier, long-time editor of *Social Epistemology*. Still, the development of CSE is still largely shaped by the twists and turns of the thought of its founder, Steve Fuller. In the following, for lack of space, I shall deal with Fuller's work only.

Unlike Longino and others, Fuller does not try to work out a compromise between analytic philosophy of science and its various critics of the 1970s and 1980s. He takes for granted that the traditional philosophical project of developing a logic of theory choice is defunct; instead, we must turn to social science for an understanding of science. Moreover, he takes it as a mere truism that knowledge seeking is a social enterprise, that science is the most important manifestation of this collective effort, and that science is therefore a model of human cognition as such. Finally, a concern with the social role of science, the politics of knowledge production and the fairness of its societal distribution was in focus for CSE from the start. Thus, Fuller sets out from largely the position that ASE has eventually come to occupy by small and cautious steps. Moreover, he has absorbed many of the lessons of Science and Technology Studies and puts them to use in his work – albeit not uncritically. These foundational points of CSE were laid down by Fuller in an early work simply entitled *Social Epistemology* (Fuller 1988/2002).

In ASE writings, Fuller is often depicted as a radical (CSE is called "radical social epistemology" by Goldman), and his project is thought to be continuous with the supposed science-debunking agenda of Science and Technology Studies. This interpretation of Fuller's work should be disputed; as a matter of fact, there is no single element in Fuller's position on key epistemological issues that is not embraced by one or another prominent epistemologist or philosopher of science in the analytic tradition. The radical air springs rather from the fact that Fuller combines a handsome number of such minority views. Add to this a somewhat polemical style and a desire to provoke, including by a controversial intervention in the debates about creationism (Fuller 2008), and Fuller's reputation as a radical readily follows.

Among Fuller's minority views is an epistemic constructivism (which is shared, for example, with Bas van Fraassen and his "constructive empiricism"), and instrumentalism (shared with Larry Laudan). Fuller's position is somewhat eclectic, however, in combining constructivism in natural science with realism in social science. Moreover, contrary to the conception of some ASE critics, Fuller is not averse to characterizing science as the pursuit of *truth* (Fuller 2012b), although not necessarily in the sense of one comprehensive theoretical system. This stance puts him in the company of such notables of analytic philosophy of science as Ronald Giere.

Fuller's work resists simple summary because of his somewhat unsystematic style of writing. Moreover, he likes to embed his discussion of general philosophical topics within historical narratives that add an extra dimension of complexity to his writings. Here I shall try to connect the most important dots that define Fuller's version of social epistemology.

Elements of Fuller's Social Epistemology

The sociological framework in terms of which Fuller understands science is, at the highest level, a macro-sociological one of great abstractness. To Fuller, "science" is a socio-functionalist term, referring to whatever mode of thought is socially dominant and authoritative in a given society (Fuller 1997). The institution that we refer to as "science" in our culture is only one particular realization of this function, while magical or religious modes of thought have fulfilled a similar role in non-Western societies and among our own historical ancestors.

While Fuller's view of science is thus nominally relativist, this characterization would be misleading in conflating Fuller's broader, functionalist concept of science and our accustomed one. With respect to science in its standard sense, he is a non-relativist and universalist, albeit in a somewhat unorthodox sense: he insists that such knowledge should be useful to everyone. He distances himself from the "standpoint epistemology" advocated by some feminist epistemologists because it tends to promote knowledge that is of value only to a limited societal segment. Instead, science, to which every member of society contributes resources in one way or another, should aim at producing knowledge accepted by and useful to everyone (he refers to this as the "proletarianization" of science production, cf. Fuller 1993). This aim can be achieved only by looking for scientific knowledge of universal scope, generated through procedures acceptable to everyone. Fuller's universalism is thus ideologically based, rather than metaphysical or methodological.

Like ASE, Fuller is a naturalist with respect to uncovering the principles for organizing societal knowledge production: We have to go about this empirically. Fuller is a dedicated interdisciplinarian, drawing broadly upon sociology, psychology, rhetoric, economics, law and history. Methodologically, he insists on a top-down holistic approach that takes society as the starting point, in contrast to a bottom-up, individualist methodology that starts with individuals and constructs the social as the aggregation of their actions. Fuller is critical of ASE's penchant for models of the latter kind, especially if they duplicate the tendency of micro-economic models towards a priorism and over-abstraction. Fuller's insistence that a holistic approach is needed for a genuinely *social* epistemology does not mean, however, that he eschews empirical research into the cognitive powers of individuals. On the contrary, Fuller advocates the development of an experimental "psychology of science". He constantly stresses the point, however, that human beings are essentially flawed as cognizers, even when they appear in the garb of scientists (Fuller 1989/1993); flaws that can only be neutralized by embedding individuals in larger cognitive communities. Thus, a psychology of science, and indeed cognitive psychology in general, must be a social psychology.

Fuller's catholicity with respect to input from the social sciences raises a problem of methodology: Currently an enormous body of experimental data is being generated in social psychology, cognitive psychology and related areas, much of it with links to the booming field of brain research and neuroscience. It is difficult to get an overview, and even harder to merge these results with overarching sociological theories. Fuller's methodological preference would clearly be to integrate such particular findings "upwards" into a holistic conception of man and society, but he does not appear to have a clear strategy for how this should be achieved – or at least nothing matching in clarity ASE's opposite strategy of methodological individualism, using formalized models based upon the notion of a rational agent.

Fuller's apparent insouciance on this point may reflect his subscription to what he calls a "realizationist" conception of science itself, according to which we can largely shape it as we like without relying too heavily upon theoretical guidance (Fuller 2012b). This is tied up with his adoption of a "shallow" conception of science (Fuller 1993), which denies that science possesses a unique deep structure: It is not a "social kind" with a distinctive socio-cognitive essence to be unearthed empirically. Instead, it is a fairly superficial organizational phenomenon, its virtues being largely the same as those that make industrial production superior to the crafts; that is, rather elementary features of the mass organization of (cognitive) labor. To Fuller, science is basically a matter of communication and information sharing, hence he looks to *rhetoric* as a key tool for the improvement of science (Fuller 1993). Rhetorical interventions can serve to counteract the tendency of scientists to form disciplinary fiefdoms, rationalized by reference to "paradigms" and "incommensurability". Fuller sees these and attendant Kuhnian notions as largely fictions designed to protect academic turf.

Fuller does not view the current shift towards industrial-style knowledge production in universities and research institutions as a great threat since he basically shares the instrumentalist premise of current science policy: Science is a tool for the production of societal goods, in the broadest sense. We should not try to roll back this development but to control it, which involves *inter alia* ensuring that the epistemic goods are evenly distributed. Fuller's overall normative stance with respect to science may thus justly be called utilitarian, but with an egalitarian constraint: It is a matter of creating the maximum good for a maximum of people, and with a fair distribution. Moreover, people should not only enjoy the fruits of science on equal terms but also have a say about which ones to produce. Thus, Fuller's normative model is borrowed from political philosophy – that is, the ideals of egalitarian democracy – just as much as from welfare economics. He advocates that knowledge be made available as a public good, so that no-one can use epistemic advantage to exploit or dominate others.

Fuller is not oblivious of the tension between the material and the politico-ideological functions of science, and that the current managerial mode of organization poses potential threats to the vital freedom of research. In this spirit, he has written extensively about the formal safeguards of academic freedom in research institutions, and has proposed detailed prescriptions for how this freedom can be legally protected (Fuller 2000). He adopts the term "republicanism" for his preferred mode of organization in which the scientist has a right to investigate whatever he pleases and to communicate his findings without fear of losing his livelihood. Here, we see another manifestation of Fuller's "realizationism" with respect to science: Science is something we can freely create, and sustain, by the establishment of appropriate institutional structures and legal instruments.

In the most recent work, Fuller has radicalized his agenda of employing scientific results to make science more productive: We should take the daring step of genetically modifying man himself, to make him (among other things) a more reliable cognizer and eventually a new and superior human species, *Homo 2.0*. Fuller is aware of the perils of this high-risk strategy; still he endorses it in view of the "proactionary principle" (the opposite of the precautionary principle) and what he terms *superutilitarianism*, which is basically utilitarianism with a very long time perspective, allowing that ills inflicted upon current generations are outbalanced by increased welfare for future ones (Fuller 2012a). Here, finally, emerges a truly radical element in Fuller's thought, shifting it out of epistemology and into politics and ideology; his critics would no doubt say, science fiction.

In Conclusion

The relationship between ASE and CSE has been needlessly antagonistic, with both sides tending to overstate their mutual differences. Here, I have pointed to similarities, captured in the picture of the two schools as moving in roughly the same direction, only with CSE having started out from a point farther along the common route. Recent work on the ASE side that narrows the gap between the two branches, such as that by Sanford Goldberg, supports this view. Still, as we have seen, there are genuine and substantial differences between the methodological preferences of the two branches; moreover, each side takes detours and byways from the common direction that the other would shun. Furthermore, the conservative and cautious intellectual temper of ASE contrasts strongly with the reformist tendency of CSE. This is related to a difference in organizational structure: Whereas ASE is a purely academic effort operating through traditional academic channels such as book and journal publication, CSE has a somewhat broader agenda and a more diversified modus operandi. Its communication platform includes an internet-based discussion forum that invites contributions from a more extensive group of interested parties. The ambition is that this broader basis will secure CSE an audience even outside of narrow academic circles. Finally, add to this Fuller's recent venture into transhumanism where ASE is unlikely to tread, and the conclusion must be that the two main organized efforts within social epistemology will remain distinct also in the future.

There is likely to be a more accurate recognition in both branches of the other side's agenda, however, and a more constructive interchange between the two. Finally, a substantial number of social epistemologists will remain noncommittal with respect to the two organized efforts within the discipline, offering an independent breeding ground for new ideas and developments.

References

Bloor, D. (1976/1991). *Knowledge and Social Imagery*. 2nd ed. London; Chicago, IL: Routledge & Kegan Paul; University of Chicago Press.

Code, L. (1991). *What Can She Know?* Ithaca, NY: Cornell University Press.

Fricker, M. (2007). *Epistemic Injustice*. Oxford: Oxford University Press.

Fuller, S. (1988/2002). *Social Epistemology*. Bloomington, ID: Indiana University Press.

Fuller, S. (1989/1993). *Philosophy of Science and its Discontents*. 2nd ed. New York: The Guilford Press.

Fuller, S. (1993). *Philosophy, Rhetoric and the End of Knowledge*. Madison, WI: University of Wisconsin Press.

Fuller, S. (1997). *Science*. Minneapolis, MN: University of Minnesota Press.

Fuller, S. (2000). *The Governance of Science*. Buckingham: Open University Press.

Fuller, S. (2008). *Dissent over Descent: Intelligent Design's Challenge to Darwinism*. Thriplow, Cambridgeshire: Icon.

Fuller, S. (2012a). *Preparing for Life in Humanity 2.0*. London: Palgrave Macmillan.

Fuller, S. (2012b). Social Epistemology: A Quarter-Century Itinerary. *Social Epistemology: A Journal of Knowledge, Culture and Policy*, 26, pp. 3–4.

Goldberg, S. (2016). A Proposed Research Program for Social Epistemology. In: P. Reider, ed., *Social Epistemology and Epistemic Agency: Decentralizing the Epistemic Agent*. London: Rowman and Littlefield, pp. 3–20.

Goldman, A. (1967). A Causal Theory of Knowing. *Journal of Philosophy*, 64(12), pp. 355–372.

Goldman, A. (1972). What is Justified Belief? In: G. Pappas, ed., *Justification and Knowledge*. Dordrecht: D. Reidel, pp. 1–23.

Goldman, A. (1986). *Epistemology and Cognition*. Cambridge, MA: Harvard University Press.

Goldman, A. (1987). Foundations of Social Epistemics. *Synthese*, 73(1), pp. 109–144.

Goldman, A. (1999). *Knowledge in a Social World*. Oxford: Oxford University Press.

Goldman, A. (2004). The Need for Social Epistemology. In: B. Leiter, ed., *The Future of Philosophy*. Oxford: Oxford University Press, pp. 182–207.

Goldman, A. and Shaked, M. (1991). An Economic Model of Scientific Activity and Truth Acquisition. *Philosophical Studies*, 63, pp. 31–55.

Harding, S. (1991). *Whose Science? Whose Knowledge?* Ithaca, NY: Cornell University Press.

Kitcher, P. (1992). The Naturalists Return. *The Philosophical Review*, 101, p. 1.

Kitcher, P. (1993). *The Advancement of Science*. Oxford: Oxford University Press.

Kitcher, P. (2011). *Science in a Democratic Society*. Amherst, NY: Prometheus Books.

Kuhn, T. (1962/1970). *The Structure of Scientific Revolutions*. Chicago, IL: University of Chicago Press.

Latour, B. (1987). *Science in Action*. Cambridge, MA: Harvard University Press.

Latour, B. (1999). *Pandora's Hope*. Cambridge, MA: Harvard University Press.

Longino, H. (1990). *Science as Social Knowledge: Values and Objectivity in Scientific Inquiry*. Princeton, NJ: Princeton University Press.

Longino, H. (2002). *The Fate of Knowledge*. Princeton, NJ: Princeton University Press.

Quine, W. (1969). Epistemology Naturalized. In: W. Quine, ed., *Ontological Relativity and Other Essays*. New York: Columbia University Press, pp. 69–90.

Rouse, J. (1987). *Knowledge and Power: Towards a Political Philosophy of Science*. Ithaca, NY: Cornell University Press.

Further Reading

Collin, F. (2013). Two Kinds of Social Epistemology. *Social Epistemology Review and Reply Collective*, 2(8), pp. 79–104.

Goldman, A. (2003). Pathways to Knowledge: Private and Public. *Oxford Scholarship Online*.

Haddock, A., Millar, A. and Pritchard, D., eds. (2010). *Social Epistemology*. Oxford: Oxford University Press.

Pritchard, D. and Hendricks, V., eds. (2014). *Social Epistemology: 5 Questions*. Automatic Press/VIP.

4

THE PHILOSOPHICAL ORIGINS OF CLASSICAL SOCIOLOGY OF KNOWLEDGE

Stephen Turner

The philosophical origins of "classical" sociology of knowledge, which for my purposes here will consist of the writings of Karl Mannheim (Mannheim [1929] 1954), are in two contemporaneous bodies of thought: German Idealism and the body of social theory that begins with Henri de Saint-Simon and extends through Marx and his followers. Interacting with these sources is the distinct history of the term "ideology" itself, which figures in complex ways in this history. As I will show, the background ideas are deeply rooted in the history of philosophy, and interact with it in complex ways. In what follows I will reconstruct the elements out of which later sociology of knowledge was constructed.

The term "ideology" is central to this discussion, and is both contested and used in a variety of conflicting ways. The term itself is normally traced to Destutt de Tracy, who employs it in a way unlike the subsequent literature to mean "moral and social science" ([1801] 1817). However, de Tracy is still relevant: he was an error theorist, who pointed to two sources of intellectual error: the insufficiency of evidence and anterior judgments which are mistakenly attached to our present judgments. Error comes from interpreting something wrongly because of what one already thinks, or prejudice. These errors are not the sorts of errors that a person would normally be aware of or be able to correct: the error produced by attachment to the prior element is built into the judgment itself. This account thus already contains the germ of the idea of a tacit and inaccessible contribution to cognition, as well as the idea of a false ideology as a system of mutually dependent ideas which transform our judgments.

De Tracy's discussion of error is psychological, causal, and individual. There is another important feature: for de Tracy, the contrast between truth and error is a contrast between the "scientific" and something else, such as prejudice or popular belief. This way of thinking shapes much of what follows in the analysis of social ideologies, by problematizing everyday beliefs, or common beliefs of a particular kind, especially those that can be said to be interconnected.

The term took on different associations very early. By the 1840s Marx is writing about "the German Ideology" ([1846] 1947) meaning something like a philosophical worldview, and the term also acquires the pejorative sense of describing ideas and representations which are "more or less conscious disguises of the real nature of a situation, the true recognition of which would not be in accord with his interests," as Karl Mannheim put it. It was the free use of this kind of reductive analysis, associated especially with Marxism, during the Weimar Republic that motivated Mannheim's *Ideology and Utopia*. The classical sociology of knowledge is an attempt to construct a neutral account of ideology and related concepts. The obstacle to doing this, as Mannheim understood, was that what was an ideology from one perspective was commonsense from its own perspective: a form of the occlusion de Tracy noted. This was a problem Mannheim did not solve, and which runs through this literature: whatever viewpoint we choose to analyze an ideology from can be understood as itself ideological.

Saint-Simon: Social Theory vs. "Reason"

Saint-Simon and his followers supply a key addition to the idea of interconnectedness, the idea of organic unity, but at the level of historical epochs rather than individual thought. Saint-Simon's social theory was a cyclical theory of change: he distinguished revolutionary or "critical" from "organic" periods, which followed one another in history. The prime example of an organic period was the medieval period, in which religion, political ideology, and forms of the division of labor and authority fit together as a whole and in which the intellectual aspects of social life justified and explained the social order, which was a productive order and division of labor. Ancient Rome was another. In contrast, the French Revolution and the Enlightenment, continuing into Saint-Simon's own post-revolutionary Restoration period represented critical periods, in which ideas and the division of labor were in turmoil, and the technology of production had changed or was changing.

This new account depended on a new conception of the nature of ideas and the social role of ideas. The ideas for the Saint-Simonians were responses to "the dual problem which mankind has always posed," namely, "What is man's destiny in relation to his fellow man and in relation to the universe?" Answers to these questions obviously vary historically. But there is some sort of commonality in particular societies at particular periods, and this is especially true for social and political ideas, those involving "man's destiny in relation to his fellowman." The Saint-Simonians thought of these dominant ideas as "solutions," and also argued that "All organic epochs have been at least temporary solutions of these problems." These "solutions" sound like worldviews. But they have a pragmatic aspect, and this aspect drives change: "soon the progress achieved with the help of these solutions, and sheltered by social institutions based on these solutions, makes even them insufficient and new solutions are called for" (Saint-Simonians [1829] 1958: 52).

This reasoning accounts for beliefs with a rudimentary social theory: beliefs had a functional or pragmatic role for which they came in time to be insufficient, and a role especially in relation to the social order, for which they were both a base and an aid in its progress. The ideas tended to persist and become outdated because they were "sheltered," by the inertia of customary adherence to the institutions, which allows them to persist when they are no longer "sufficient." This amounts to an error theory, but of an unusual kind. It goes to the heart of the problem that later concerned the neo-Kantians, validity, and described the conditions of validity in terms of the coherence of the social order and division of labor that defined it.

> During organic periods, the goal of activity is clearly defined. We have said that all efforts are dedicated to achieving this goal, toward which man is continuously directed by education and legislation during his entire life. If general relations are fixed, individual relations are modeled on them and are also fixed. The goal that society intends to attain is revealed to all hearts and all intellects. It becomes easy to recognize the men of capacity most suited to further this trend, and the truly superior are, of course, in possession of power. Legitimacy, sovereignty, and authority exist in the real meaning of these words. Harmony rules in social relationships.
>
> *(Saint-Simonians [1829] 1958: 53)*

The "real meaning of these words" was to be found where they were valid for the people who used them, and where hearts and intellects recognized and responded to "the goal of society."

The basic thought was that the inherited medieval social institutions had ceased to function in the original "organic" manner, producing, after centuries of decay, a revolutionary period. But although the Saint-Simonians had, along with many thinkers of the century, Romantics, Christians, and socialists, nostalgia for the "organic" Middle Ages, they also believed that there was no going back. Instead, Saint-Simon predicted that a new division of labor and authority, and a new doctrine, would arise, leading to new organic period organized around industry and science. Their capacities for anticipating this new order, they thought, were limited by their own historical situation. But understanding this situation was not a matter of Enlightenment-style public discussion and evident reason: it was a matter that needed to be approached scientifically and empirically. And the empirical evidence was historical.

The idea that thinking was itself organically related to some sort of unified whole, and that the future organic whole had itself to emerge organically as part of the historical process, amounted to a radical shift. The original notion of ideology had been individual. Saint-Simon, with his notion of the organic, and of systems of ideas as historically temporary "solutions" to the problems of relating to the world and to others, took a step toward a fully social collective subject: it was assumed that people of a given era would accept the ruling ideas, and that the relation between the ruling ideas and the social situation validated the ruling ideas, because they represented a socially pragmatic truth—real legitimacy grounded in the common understanding of the goals of society. When this relationship no longer held, the ideas and the institutions they had justified were invalidated and properly subject to critique.

The epistemological implications of this line of argument were not worked out by Saint-Simon, but in a different way by his one-time secretary August Comte, and by Karl Marx in a related way. Saint-Simon and the Saint-Simonians relativized the notion of validity or truth to historical periods, and were holists about "organic" periods. At the same time they had an account of the decay, through pragmatic failure, of these organic unities. This was not unlike Kuhn's notion of paradigms which decay through the accumulation of anomalies, and are replaced by new holistic paradigms. Both were open to the charge of relativism. Comte and Marx responded to this problem, but by positing a universal end of history. For Comte, the claim was that human thought, and each of the sciences, went through three stages: the theological, the metaphysical, and the positive. There was no stage beyond the positive: this was a stage of final truth. For Marx, the triumph of the proletariat was the final and universal stage. But each combined this with a holistic analysis of the preceding stages.

German Idealism

Aparallel to these developments, with which they ultimately merge, is found in German Idealism. The starting point preceded Saint-Simon: the dispute between Kant and Herder over history, in which Herder emphasized the pervasive fact of variation in cultural traditions rather than universality. This conflict took on a sharp edge during the Napoleonic occupation of Prussia and reform of the German principalities in the early 19th century. A reaction, in the form of German cultural and linguistic nationalism, took place, especially within German philosophy, in the hands of such people as Fichte. Rationalization came to be associated with French "civilization." At the same time, ironically, these thinkers translated French political ideas into Kantian language, radically transforming it, particularly by the use of the concept of will in relation to collective facts, such as the law, producing the will-theory of law.

Hegel plays a crucial role in the development of two ideas: the idea of a collective subject and the idea of false consciousness, by identifying objective *Geist* with a collective process in which individuals are vehicles for the unfolding of *Geist*, so that this process is one of self-discovery of the collective subject, and by treating individual *Geist* as a false and partial approximation of it. Schiller had made the suggestion that false society produced false consciousness, and Hegel himself, in such places as the discussion of the master–slave relation, treats social relations as a kind of cause of false consciousness. But these accounts are essentially accounts of error, which presuppose not only a correct view but in the case of Hegel a novel collective or objective ideal object, namely objective spirit or *Geist*, to be wrong about. This is idealism, but Hegel also hints that the full unfolding of *Geist* requires some transformation of social conditions, and this is implicit in Schiller as well.

Johann Gustav Droysen and Karl Marx, in parallel ways, develop these ideas, but differ in key respects that lead them in different directions. One takeaway from Kant was the distinction between constitutive principles, those which postulate some object, and regulative principles, those which prescribe a goal. As Beiser points out, the neo-Kantians later did much to efface this distinction (Beiser 2013: 123). The way this was done is exemplified in Droysen, who preceded the movement. Droysen, who was influenced by the Young Hegelians, argued, against "positivism" and Ranke, that history as a discipline was concerned with both the actual and the moral, and that genuine understanding in history involved understanding it *as* the realization of ideals. As he puts it,

§ 77 All movement in the historical world goes on in this way: Thought, which is the ideal counterpart of things as they really exist, develops itself as things ought to be.

(Droysen 1893: 45–46; quoted in Mannheim [1929] 1954: 179)

He understood this in a cyclical manner, precisely reminiscent of Saint-Simon, which implied that thoughts produced change in conditions, at first, then became fixed, and then retrograde:

§ 78 Thoughts constitute the criticism of that which is and yet is not as it should be. Inasmuch as they may bring conditions to their level, then broaden out and harden themselves into accord with custom, conservatism, and obstinacy, new criticism is demanded, and thus on and on.

(Droysen 1893: 45–46; quoted in Mannheim [1929] 1954: 179)

But he also argued "That out of the already given conditions, new thoughts arise and out of the thoughts new conditions—this is the work of men" (Droysen 1893: 45–46; quoted in Mannheim [1929] 1954: 179–180). This, as we will see, is also the core thought of Marx. Droysen, however, applied it reflexively to the thought of the historian. As Beiser puts it, for Droysen, "The necessity of perspective was not the historian's limitation but his opportunity" (Beiser 2011: 306). He thus accepted a kind of relativism: "I want to appear to have nothing more—but also nothing less—than the relative truth of the standpoint bequeathed to me by my fatherland, and political and religious convictions, my earnest study" (Droysen quoted in MacLean 1982: 361). For Droysen, then, the source of his specific standpoint is partly collective or national, and partly personal: "my fatherland, and political and religious convictions, my earnest study" (quoted in MacLean 1982: 361). Indeed, it was part of his historiography to insist on the value of personality in historical writing.

Despite the clarity of Droysen's affirmation of the relative truth of his and all historical standpoints, he drew different epistemic conclusions, for he did not abandon the idea of universal truth, but instead argued that the path to the universal was through the particular. Epistemic validation, in the universal sense, was possible, but only through a collective universalizing historical developmental process, which he understood in an intellectualist way as the development of consciousness: this was the remnant of his Hegelianism. This way of dealing with the problem of universality was typical of German Idealism. These teleologies are problematic: as the example of

Hegel shows, one can only construct a universalizing teleology from within a perspective. The teleological element, however, is critical: it is a way to talk about error with respect to perspectives or standpoints themselves. And not surprisingly it recurs in the literature, especially in relation to the notion of false consciousness.

Marx

If the teleological view of the development of universal consciousness is eliminated from these accounts, we are still left with something important: the idea that thought arises out of conditions, meaning local conditions, and the idea of relative standpoints. But this seemingly simple and highly persuasive idea of "arising" turns out to be extremely difficult to make sense of. This becomes apparent when we turn to Marx, who had already addressed some of these issues in his private and unpublished writings of the early 1840s, stimulated by some of the same Young Hegelian sources, but also by another source: Feuerbach's critique of religion. Marx substitutes "materialism" for idealism, and introduces the idea that at the basis of perspectives there are not mere culture-like presuppositions of thought, but "real premises," meaning particular kinds of facts with a special relation to thought.

> The premises from which we begin are not arbitrary ones, not dogmas, but real premises from which abstraction can only be made in the imagination. These "real premises" are the real individuals, their activity and the material conditions under which they live, both those which they find already existing and those produced by their activity. These premises can thus be verified in a purely empirical way.
>
> *(Marx and Engels [1846] 1947: Part I: Feuerbach First Premises of Materialist Method: 42)*

Materialism thus amounts to asserting the explanatory priority of a certain set of facts, namely "definite individuals who are productively active in a definite way [who] enter into … definite social and political relations." It is because of "the connection of the social and political structure with production," i.e., the relation of this material base and the ideational superstructure of society, that the subject can be treated empirically (Marx and Engels [1846] 1947: Part I: Feuerbach First Premises of Materialist Method: 46).

All of the issues over the mechanism of the relation between conditions and thought reappear in Mannheim, so we may delay further consideration of them temporarily. The takeaway from Marx, however, is this: "material" conditions are the relevant causal conditions of consciousness, and this means the explanatory primacy of "practice"; the forms of thought produced by this process are illusions, often inversions of reality, which perhaps can only be seen as such from the perspective of the rising class at a later stage of a particular epoch defined by a particular class struggle. This last consideration implies that it is the "practice" of the revolutionary struggle of this class that reveals reality and dispels the illusions produced by the dominant but historically doomed class it is struggling against. The epistemic significance of this argument is an almost accidental consequence of the social theory: perspectives are the product of material forces in history; the only true and universal perspective is that of the final revolution, because this revolution ends class struggle and therefore history.

Neo-Kantianism

The fourth and crucial source is neo-Kantianism, which figures in several forms. The German neo-Kantians were divided, roughly, into two groups, one deriving from Kuno Fischer and Wilhelm Windelband, the other from Hermann Cohen. Cohen turned Kant upside down, in the sense that he started from the "*faktum der Wissenschaft*," the fact of a successful science, and tried to reconstruct its presuppositions or transcendental conditions.

The enduring achievement of the neo-Kantians was the taking of what they called the transcendental method from its narrow context in Kant. In their hands it became a transposable intellectual strategy that could be applied of virtually anything with intellectual content, and which allowed them to infer its "presuppositions." The effect of this line of reasoning in social contexts was to invert the theory of the Überbau and replace it with the idea of society constituted by presuppositions. But this thinking agreed with Marxism in one respect. It affirmed the collectivization of the subject. The Kantian distinction between logical and psychological played a particular role here: it allowed the neo-Kantians to evade causal questions about how these presuppositions arose, how a collective order of thinking operated in individual minds, and so forth. Instead, the existence of a body of ideas with a certain degree of intellectual uniformity or a "perspective" was sufficient. One could then inquire into the "presuppositions" of this body of ideas, and reason transcendentally about them.

The oddity or flaw in this reasoning was this. Imagine a case in which I failed to bring an umbrella with me on a rainy day. My failure might be made comprehensible by saying that I presupposed or assumed that there would be no rain. But the causal explanation might be that I simply forgot or was unaware that it would be raining. Presuppositional reasoning of this kind thus tells us nothing about psychological, causal, fact. But claims about actual communities as collective subjects are difficult to construe as being about anything but the contents of some sort of mind. So this presuppositional way of thinking about social differences in belief and practice became ingrained in many fields, to the extent that Foucault could say "we are all neo-Kantians now" (Foucault 1994, vol. I: 546; quoted in Han 2002: 3).

Mannheim's Synthesis

Karl Mannheim was the inventor of the field of sociology of knowledge, and his major work, *Ideology and Utopia*, is the most systematic attempt to think through its problems. It represented a turn from epistemology in the philosophical sense, which was concerned with the problem of validity, which was solved by the neo-Kantians with the idea of starting with a *faktum der Wissenschaft*, that is to say an established science, which could be assumed to have validity, and inferring the premises that were the conditions for the possibility of this science, which guaranteed their validity through their necessity to the science in question. Mannheim explicitly disavowed this kind of epistemology, and replaced it with what he styled as an "empirical" inquiry. His argument was nevertheless an attempt to clarify several issues with epistemic implications. The first involves error and the term ideology. The problem with associating the term ideology with error was that "ideology" referred to two different sets of facts: one was the kind of viewpoint that one encountered in politics or cultural life which differed from one's own and which one could see obscured or distorted reality: "the ideas and representations advanced by our opponent … [that] are regarded as more or less conscious disguises of the real nature of a situation, the true recognition of which would not be in accord with his interests" (Mannheim [1929] 1954: 49). Mannheim solves the problem of the relation between the two sets of facts by calling these "partial ideologies," to distinguish from total ideologies, "the ideology of an age or of a concrete historico-social group, e.g., of a class" (Mannheim [1929] 1954: 49).

This distinction was not a model of clarity, but its point can be better understood in terms of another distinction Mannheim adds to it, between ideology and utopia. This usage is itself confusing. Mannheim uses the term ideology in a specific way, unlike its later use, and uses the term "utopia" for what would normally be called ideology. Mannheim distinguishes utopia and ideology by saying that ideologies are *concrete*: in fact they are a lot like practices, or *habitus*. Ideologies, like a habitus, tend to become obsolete in relation to developing practice: this is the same pragmatic point made by the Saint-Simonians. Utopias, in contrast, are not concrete, but are forward-looking regulative ideals. Utopias are thus like imaginaries—they emphasize certain aspects of present situations, as in the case of the bourgeois idea of a free society, and treat others as not yet achieved, and ignore others which conflict with the imaginary.

The difference corresponds to the Kantian distinction between the constitutive and the regulative, but like the neo-Kantians, Mannheim runs the two together in an epistemically relevant way. His account of the utopian element, which one would have thought was a regulative ideal, emphasizes that it is a "wish" that fundamentally shapes experience itself:

> It is the utopian element—i.e. the nature of the dominant wish—which determines the sequence, order, and evaluation of single experiences. This wish is the organizing principle which even moulds the way in which we experience time. The form in which events are ordered and the unconsciously emphatic rhythm, which the individual in his spontaneous observation of events imposes upon the flux of time, appears in the utopia as an immediately perceptible picture, or at least a directly intelligible set of meanings.
>
> *([1929] 1954: 188)*

The shaping of experience is pervasive and is the source of its meaning: "Bare facts set themselves in perspective, and emphasis in meaning are distributed and apportioned to individual happenings in accordance with the fundamental directions in which the personality strives" (Mannheim [1929] 1954: 189).

This formulation avoids the neo-Kantian problem of the relation between constitutive and regulative by building a causal substitute for the regulative aspect into the concept, as "wish." But we are still faced with the problem of where the wishes come from, a question which presumably is to be answered by reference to "the 'connectedness to existence' (*Seinsverbundenheit*), and the 'situational determination' (*Situationsgebundenheit*) of thinking" (Mannheim *Mensch und Gesellschaft* 1935: 164–165; quoted in Kettler and Meja 1995: 194–195). This notion was a problem for Marx, and the question of how this worked remained a problem for Mannheim, and the issue was seized on by his critics, who noted that Mannheim had multiple inconsistent formulations, which, as with Marx, promised more than they delivered. This problem led to the temporary death of the sociology of knowledge, which was particularly relevant to the sociology of science, a topic taken up in other chapters. The coup de grace was administered in a long, lacerating essay on Mannheim by Robert K. Merton, who was to turn the sociological study of science into a largely institutional direction. Merton proceeded by listing a large number of pseudo-explanatory usages found in Mannheim. The following is a sort selection: the idea that perspectives "follow inevitably and unwittingly from certain *causal determinants*"; that they are "*bound up with and grow out of* a certain social reality"; that they are "*in harmony with it*"; that they are "rooted in a definite *Weltanschauung* and has progressed *in close connection with* definite political interests"; or that they are "transformed *in close conjunction with* social forces" such that "It is *never by accident* that they appear at given moments in the social process" (Merton [1941] 1968: 553). The Marxian lineage of these phrases is clear, and the issues are similar: the causal mechanism is not clear, and therefore the relation with the supposed social causes is not clear.

The insight that remains from Mannheim, if we ignore the confusing "causal" claims about social determination and interests, was already there, but obscured, in neo-Kantianism. Structures of presuppositions are associated with bodies of knowledge that are produced and reproduced in communities of practice. But the neo-Kantians avoided thinking of sciences as communities. So they were also able to avoid the obvious conclusion: rather than relativize fundamental presuppositions to what was shared by actual communities, which led straight to relativism, they went through endless contortions to avoid this implication and conceal its significance. Mannheim did the same thing, but with a different strategy: his desire to avoid not only relativism but the self-undermining reflexive application of his own arguments led him to the idea of the free-floating intellectual, free from interests and therefore social determination.

Mannheim wanted an empirical sociology of knowledge that was neutral between perspectives and also that avoided epistemological claims. The issue of reflexivity was central to this: it was characteristic of Weimar era discourse in Germany to engage in a kind of *Ideologikritik* that exposed the presuppositions of a standpoint and associated it with class interests. To reflexively absolve oneself of interests, by reference to an empirical theory of ideology, was to assure that this project was not merely another ideology conditioned on unacknowledged and hidden social causes and interests. This amounted to attaining an epistemic end by empirical means: to use the means of causal analysis, or what passed for it, to warrant an exemption from this kind of reductive critique. Mannheim's moral purpose for his own project, however, was irenic. He thought of it as a way to overcome the conflicts between worldviews of the Weimar setting. In his later work he envisioned a future planned society in which values themselves would be planned.

Mannheim's solution to the problem of reflexivity was to provide an empirically based exemption from the considerations he applied to ideologies and utopias rather than a philosophical one, which would have been challenged for the groundlessness of its presuppositions. Not surprisingly, his empirical approach was itself criticized for the groundlessness of its presuppositions (Arendt [1930] 1990). He also exempted mathematics and science. The latter exemption was challenged by the "Strong Programme in the Sociology of Science" discussed in another chapter, and had been previously rejected by Marxist historians of science (Turner 2008). The reflexivity problem persisted. The basic ideas of Mannheim were taken over by feminist standpoint theory, and appear in claims about "positionality," but with a rejection of the possibility of a "view from nowhere" or an exemption of the sort Mannheim envisioned. These uses of ideas from the sociology of knowledge, however, were associated with positive epistemological arguments about the superiority of certain standpoints and the possibility of strengthened objectivity through this kind of analysis (Harding 1992), or, in a vein similar to Mannheim's original irenic intent, arguments for the importance for community processes in science of epistemic diversity rooted in differences in position, such as the differences resulting from gender (Longino 1993). Some of these arguments were indebted to Quinean notions of underdetermination, which allowed for the possibility that theories from different standpoints would each be consistent with the data.

References

Arendt, H. ([1930] 1990). Philosophy and Sociology. In: M. Volker Meja and S. Nico, eds., *Knowledge and Politics: The Sociology of Knowledge Dispute*. London and New York: Routledge, pp. 196–208.

Beiser, F. (2011). *The German Historicist Tradition*. Oxford: Oxford University Press.

Beiser, F. (2013). Weimar Philosophy and the Fate of Neo-Kantianism. In: J. McCormick and P. Gordon, eds., *Weimar Thought: A Contested Legacy*. Princeton, NJ: Princeton University Press, pp. 115–132.

de Tracy, A. ([1801] 1817). *Elements of Ideology*. Edited by T. Jefferson. Georgetown, DC: J. Milligan.

Droysen, T. G. (1893). *Outline of the Principles of History*. Translated by E. Benjamin. Boston, MA: Ginn and Company.

Han, B. (2002). *Foucault's Critical Project: Between the Transcendental and the Historical*. Translated by E. Pile. Stanford, CA: Stanford University Press.

Harding, S. (1992). Rethinking Epistemology: What Is Strong Objectivity. *The Centennial Review* 36(3), pp. 437–470.

Kettler, D., and Meja, V. (1995). *Karl Mannheim and the Crisis of Liberalism: The Secret of These New Times*. New Brunswick, NJ and London: Transaction.

Longino, H. (1993). Subjects, Power, and Knowledge: Description and Prescription. In: L. Alcoff and E. Potter, eds., *Feminist Philosophies of Science in Feminist Epistemologies*. New York: Routledge, pp. 101–120.

MacLean, M. (1982). Johann Gustav Droysen and the Development of Historical Hermeneutics. *History and Theory* 21(3), pp. 347–365.

Mannheim, K. ([1929] 1954). *Ideology and Utopia: An Introduction to the Sociology of Knowledge.* Translated by L. Wirth and E. Shils. New York: Harcourt Brace & Company. Available at https://archive.org/details/ideologyutopiain00mann [Accessed 3 February 2016].

Marx, K. and Engels, F. ([1846] 1947). *The German Ideology: Part One.* Edited by C. J. Arthur. New York: International Publishers. Available at www.marxists.org/archive/marx/works/1845/germanideology/ch01a.htm.

Merton, R. ([1941] 1968). Karl Mannheim and the Sociology of Knowledge. In: *Social Theory and Social Structure.* Rev. and Enl. Glencoe, IL: Free Press, pp. 543–562.

Saint-Simonians. ([1829] 1958). Conception, Method, and Historical Classification. In: *The Doctrine of Saint-Simon: An Exposition; First Year, 1828–1829.* Translated by G. Iggers. Boston, MA: Beacon Press, pp. 41–57.

Turner, S. (2008). The Social Study of Science before Kuhn. In: E. J. Hackett, O. Amsterdamska, M. Lynch, and J. Wajcman, eds., *The Handbook of Science and Technology Studies,* 3rd edn. Cambridge, MA: MIT Press, pp. 33–62.

Additional Readings

Mannheim, K. ([1925] 1986). *Conservatism: A Contribution to the Sociology of Knowledge.* Edited by D. Kettler, V. Meja, and N. Stehr. London: Routledge & Kegan Paul.

Mannheim, K. (1982). *Structures of Thinking.* Edited by D. Kettler, V. Meja, and N. Stehr; Translated by J. Shapiro and S. W. Nicholson. London, Boston, MA: Routledge & Kegan Paul.

Meja, V. and Stehr, N., eds. (1990). *Knowledge and Politics: The Sociology of Knowledge Dispute.* London and New York: Routledge.

Scharff, R. C. (1996). *Comte after Positivism.* New York: Cambridge University Press.

Stark, W. (1958). *The Sociology of Knowledge: An Essay in Aid of a Deeper Understanding of the History of Ideas.* London: Routledge & Kegan Paul.

Woldring, Henk E. S. (1986). *Karl Mannheim: The Development of His Thought: Philosophy, Sociology and Social Ethics.* Assen: Van Gorcum.

5

KUHN AND THE HISTORY OF SCIENCE

K. Brad Wray

This article examines Thomas Kuhn's work in the history of science with special attention to its relevance to subsequent developments in social epistemology. I will focus narrowly on the social epistemology of science as Kuhn has had a negligible influence on general social epistemology. The article will begin with a discussion of Kuhn's historical work, and then examine the so-called historical school in philosophy of science. Then I will examine Kuhn's views on textbook science. This will be followed by an analysis of Kuhn's views on the relations between the history of science and the philosophy of science, followed by a discussion of what Kuhn calls "the historical perspective." Then I will discuss Kuhn's contributions to our understanding of the social dimensions of science and scientific inquiry. Finally, I will discuss his influences, direct and indirect, on the social epistemology of science and the sociology of science.

Kuhn's Historical Work

Kuhn was educated at Harvard, completing an undergraduate degree and a Ph.D. in physics. During his graduate program he began to work as a teaching assistant with James B. Conant, the President of Harvard, in a General Education Science course designed for non-science majors. It was then that he had his famous Aristotle epiphany. As he prepared a lecture for the class, he wondered why Aristotle was such a poor physicist. Kuhn ultimately realized that Aristotle's concerns were not the same as Newton's, and consequently it was fruitless to evaluate Aristotle's achievements by the same standards one might evaluate Newton's. "Aristotle's subject was change-of-quality in general," rather than mechanics (see Kuhn 1977, xi). Kuhn realized that Aristotle and Newton were working with radically different conceptual schemes. And in order to understand Aristotle's physics one has to look at the world from within Aristotle's conceptual framework. By the time Kuhn completed his Ph.D. he was set on retraining as a historian of science, and he did so as a junior fellow in the Harvard Society of Fellows, with the support of Conant.

Not surprisingly, Kuhn's early publications were in the history of science. In "Energy Conservation as an Example of Simultaneous Discovery," Kuhn examines the discovery of energy conservation, a discovery that can be traced to 12 scientists working between the 1830s and the 1850s (see Kuhn 1959/1977). Though Kuhn identifies three key factors that led to the discovery of energy conservation in the early to mid-1800s, he was struck by the range of ways in which the various scientists came to make the discovery.

The culmination of Kuhn's historical work was his book, *Black-Body Theory and the Quantum Discontinuity, 1894–1912*. Part of Kuhn's aim in this book was to set the historical record straight by showing that Max Planck has mistakenly been attributed with making a significant contribution to Quantum Mechanics with his work on the Black-Body Problem (see Kuhn 1978). As Kuhn notes, in Planck's efforts to solve the Black-Body Problem, he assumed that the radiation in a heated body was in discrete cells, an assumption he made in order to make the problem mathematically tractable. At that time, though, Planck did not believe that radiation was really emitted in discrete units. Rather, he believed that radiation was emitted continuously. It was only the subsequent work of other physicists that led to the reification of Planck's assumption, and the realization that in fact radiation is emitted in discrete units rather than continuously, that led to the Quantum Revolution. Typical of Kuhn's historical work, this book aims to take the reader inside the minds of the historical agents, and see how they saw things. Kuhn provides an apt description of his method and goals in historical research: "my historical [papers] … start with the isolation of passages which, as usually read, don't make sense, and they conclude by producing a reading which gets rid of apparent textual anomalies and presumably recovers the author's intent" (see MC.0240, Box 20, Folder 40). This process would often lead to myth-busting, as we see with the case of Planck and his alleged contribution to Quantum Theory.

Interestingly, Kuhn's historical work has had a negligible effect on the history of science (see Wade 1977). In fact, Lorraine Daston has recently argued that *Structure* does not meet the standards of contemporary scholarship in the history of science (see Daston 2016, 119–121). She also argues that the notion of structure, which figures centrally in the book, is at odds with the contemporary focus in the history of science on "irreducibly local details and contingencies" that defy generalization (Daston 2016, 122). In addition, it appears that Kuhn's work on Planck did not affect scientists' own understanding of their field, as the Planck myth persists in physics textbooks (see Brush 2000).

The Historical School of Philosophy of Science

Kuhn's influence in philosophy of science, on the other hand, has been quite significant. Kuhn is part of the Historical School in philosophy of science, which included Paul Feyerabend, Norwood Russell Hanson, Mary Hesse, and others. In the late 1950s and early 1960s these philosophers looked to the history of science as a source of data in their theorizing about science. The proponents of the Historical School felt that our philosophy of science should be developed with an eye to how science actually works (see Kuhn 1991/2000, 95). This was a reaction against the rational reconstructions of the history of science, the sorts of histories written by their predecessors, specifically, Karl Popper and the logical positivists and empiricists.

Kuhn's *Structure of Scientific Revolutions* was a key contribution to the Historical School. From an examination of the history of science Kuhn was led to believe that scientists do not discard theories when they encounter anomalies or recalcitrant experiences (see Kuhn 1962/2012, 145–146). Thus, contrary to what Popper claims, unexpected observations are not counted as falsifying instances. Instead, scientists often try to modify and develop their theories until they can reconcile them with the observations. There is nothing unscientific or irrational about this practice, Kuhn argued. Kuhn also argued that the commonly held view that scientific knowledge grows by more or less constant accumulation of new knowledge cannot be reconciled with the historical record. Instead what we find is that periods of normal science, which are characterized by the steady accumulation of knowledge, are interrupted by periods of revolutionary theory change. The successor theories, though, often make radically different assumptions about reality than did the theories they replaced. This dynamic, Kuhn argues, undermines the standard view of scientific progress.

This historical approach to the philosophy of science has been quite influential. But one of the most common criticisms against the Historical School is that it is concerned merely with the descriptive enterprise of providing an account of how scientists behave. It thus fails to address the philosophical issues which are essentially normative (see, for example, Feyerabend 1970/1974, 198–199). The critics claim that an account of scientific rationality is about how scientists ought to behave, and a study of how they in fact behave is largely beside the point. Contrary to what these critics claim, Kuhn believes that in order to effectively embark upon the normative task one must first embark upon the descriptive task. Until we know how science works, we cannot begin to prescribe changes.

The History of Science in Science Textbooks

In *Structure*, Kuhn made another important observation about the history of science. He notes that the natural sciences are taught with very little attention to the history of the disciplines. There is no equivalent of the canon, as there is in disciplines like Philosophy and Literature. Instead, students learn from textbooks specifically written for students of science. Philosophy students, on the other hand, read classics like Hume's *Enquiry* and Plato's *Republic*, books that were not explicitly written for students, and certainly not for 21st Century students.

What little history there is in science textbooks is distorted. It is selective, and emphasizes the continuities between past scientists and contemporary science. For example, only those aspects of Newton's physical theory that are more or less continuous with contemporary physics are discussed. And there is no mention of Newton's preoccupations with alchemy and theology, even though Newton spent a considerable amount of time on them and saw these activities as continuous with his scientific research (see Dobbs 1983). Kuhn also notes that after a revolutionary change of theory text books are rewritten. He compares this practice to the rewriting of history in George Orwell's *1984*. The new history of the discipline selectively recasts the past in a manner that emphasizes its relationship to the new reigning theory, erasing those parts of the past that do not contribute to this narrative of continuity and growth.

The importance of this for our purposes is to note that history of science as written for science students serves the function of preserving the image that scientific knowledge is growing continuously, with no significant ruptures or setbacks. Such histories thus play an important role in the socialization of young scientists-in-training. These histories perpetuate an image of science that is agreeable to scientists and to scientists' self-understanding.

Relations between History and Philosophy of Science

Over the course of his career, but especially in the 1970s, Kuhn wrote a number of pieces discussing the relevance of the history of science to the philosophy of science. Kuhn's views about the relationship between the two fields was informed, to a large extent, by his experience teaching students from both fields in the History and Philosophy of Science Program at Princeton. He felt he was teaching two radically different audiences who had little understanding of each other.

Kuhn believes that the two fields are distinct, and have very different goals (see Kuhn 1976a/1977, 4–5). Whereas the goal of the historian is to develop a plausible narrative usually about a specific episode in the history of science, the goal of the philosopher is to develop a general theory about science and scientific change. On the one hand, Kuhn thinks that historians of science have little to learn from the philosophy of science (see Kuhn 1976a/1977, 11). That is, philosophy of science offers no new or important insights relevant to the historian's research. On the other hand, he believes that philosophers would profit from a familiarity with the history of science (1976a/1977, 12). Familiarity with the history of science can give philosophers a familiarity with the actual practice of science, which would rein in much of their rather abstract (and misleading) theorizing about science. But Kuhn felt that a philosopher could acquire a familiarity with the practice of science in other ways, for example, by learning contemporary science (see Kuhn 1976a/1977, 13). Still, Kuhn insists that "history of science provides the most practical and available among several possible methods by which the philosopher might more closely acquaint himself with science" (1976a/1977, 13). An insightful philosophy of science, Kuhn argues, must be built on an understanding of actual scientific practice.

The Historical or Evolutionary Perspective

Kuhn later developed a different attitude about the relevance of the history of science to the philosophy of science. Rather than seeing the history of science as a source of data from which to build a philosophy of science, he thought that the key insight philosophers could gain from the history of science is a particular perspective, the historical or evolutionary perspective (Kuhn 1992/2000, 112). This involves seeing science as a process underway. Scientists do not choose between two competing theories from a neutral standpoint. Instead, they confront the choice between competing theories already accepting a theory, that is, from within a theoretical framework. This profoundly affects how scientists go about evaluating competing theories. When scientists evaluate competing theories they ask which theory is superior, not which theory is true. It is a comparative evaluation, not a categorical evaluation.

This orientation toward the study of science that Kuhn recommends has had little influence on philosophers of science, though it is commonplace among sociologists of science. For example, this orientation is captured in Bruno Latour's plea to examine "*science in action*" rather than just focusing on "*ready made science*," the finished products of research (see Latour 1987, 2–6). Similarly, Stephen Cole argues that in order to understand how scientific research works we need to examine both (i) the *core knowledge* in a scientific field, that is, accepted theories, and (ii) *the research frontier*, where there is often no consensus on key issues (see Cole 1992, 15–17). But Kuhn is not the source of this orientation in the sociology of science.

The Social Dimensions of Science

Most relevant to our concerns here is the way in which Kuhn drew philosophers' attention to the social dimensions of science.

The theory of scientific change in *Structure*—the cycle from a period of normal science to crisis, from crisis to revolution, and then to a new period of normal science—is described by Kuhn as involving significant shifts in the social structure of the specialty community. For example, in periods of normal science, scientists take many things for granted, as the accepted theory is assumed to supply scientists with the conceptual resources they need to solve the research problems they address. As a field enters a crisis stage, the specialty community becomes more tolerant of different interpretations of the accepted theory. The norms governing the research community are relaxed considerably during periods of crisis, as scientists scramble to resolve the outstanding anomalies that led the field into crisis. They even become open to considering new theories. When a new contender emerges, the field is susceptible to a revolutionary change of theory. Kuhn takes the comparison between scientific revolutions and political revolutions very seriously (see Kuhn 1962/2012, Chapter IX, Wray 2011, Chapters 1 and 2). Like a political revolution, the change of theory that threatens to occur during a scientific revolution is not sanctioned by the long-accepted theory. And if the new theory prevails the community settles into a new normal science tradition.

Kuhn claims that in times of crisis, scientists' individual differences influence their decision-making and evaluations of competing theories. Rather than seeing this as an impediment to science, or a sign of irrationality, Kuhn regards it as key to understanding why science is so successful. When scientists are influenced by such subjective factors different scientists will be led to work with different theories. Kuhn claims this is "the community's way of distributing risk and assuring the long-term success of its enterprise" (see Kuhn 1969/2012, 186; see also D'Agostino 2004).

Also in his discussions of scientific education, Kuhn emphasized how young scientists-in-training are *socialized* into the community, taught to make the same sorts of discriminations among the phenomena that their peers make (see Kuhn 1974/1977; also Andersen *et al.* 2006, especially Chapter 2). The ways scientists see the world are not the "natural" ways to see the world. Rather, one needs to be trained to reason and observe as scientists reason and observe. Kuhn compares this training process to the process by which a young child learns to discriminate between different types of birds (see Kuhn 1974/1977).

Kuhn periodically reflected on the development of new specialties in science, noting that this process was an integral part of scientific change (see Kuhn 1969/2012, 176–177, 1976b/1977). In his later writings, Kuhn developed these ideas further, arguing that some crises in science are resolved, not by the replacement of a long-accepted theory by a revolutionary new theory, but by the creation of a new scientific specialty (see Kuhn 1991/2000, 97–99, 1992/2000, 116–118). The specialty community thus divides, with each of the two parts taking responsibility for different research questions. The parent field continues on in a more restricted domain, having relinquished responsibility for the recalcitrant phenomena that led the field into crisis in the first place. And the new field takes responsibility for the recalcitrant phenomena, but with the aid of new conceptual resources designed to address the research problem that gave rise to the crisis in the first place. K. Brad Wray discusses examples of this process in detail, specifically, the creation of virology as a field of study separate from bacteriology, and the creation of endocrinology as a field of study separate from physiology (Wray 2011, Chapter 7). This is an important insight from Kuhn's later work, but one that has yet to make a larger impact on the social epistemology of science.

In general, Kuhn has shown that changes and progress in science often involve a reconfiguration of the social groups responsible for the field of study, and these reconfigurations are not incidental to the growth of science.

Kuhn's Influence on the Social Epistemology of Science

In addressing Kuhn's influence on the social epistemology of science, I want to draw distinctions between (i) his indirect influence on the field, (ii) his influence on the sociology of science, and (iii) his direct influence on recent work in the social epistemology of science. I will discuss each of these in order.

Anyone working in the philosophy of science since the 1970s has encountered Kuhn's *Structure*. The book has sold over a million copies, and it is highly cited in many fields of study. As a result, it should come as no surprise that philosophers working in the social epistemology of science have been influenced by Kuhn. The influence though is most often quite indirect. There is now far greater attention to the social dimensions of science and scientific change than there was before 1962, when *Structure* was first published. The Society for Philosophy of Science in Practice (SPSP) is an offspring of Kuhn's work, and his insistence on studying the actual practice of science. The influence of Kuhn's work is evident in the work of Hanne Andersen (2016), Hasok Chang (2012), and others working in this interdisciplinary research program. Even the rather abstract and formal studies of the social dimensions of science that employ the resources of game theory and the like owe some debt to Kuhn (see, for example, Zollman 2007; Weisberg & Muldoon 2009). But direct engagements with Kuhn's ideas are far less common in the social epistemology of science literature published in the last 30 years.

Matters are quite different in the sociology of science. In the 1970s, the Mertonians, the sociologists of science working in the broad framework initially developed by Robert K. Merton, were superseded by a new school, the Strong Programme in the Sociology of Scientific Knowledge (SSK). These sociologists, initially based in Britain, claimed to be building on Kuhn's work (see especially Barnes 1982; also Barnes *et al.* 1996, Chapter 3). Central to their programme was a desire to provide *social* explanations for all beliefs, that is, both true and false beliefs. Traditionally, it was assumed that whereas true beliefs could be explained by scientists getting at the structure of nature, only false beliefs had social causes. The sociology of science was thus construed as the sociology of error (see, for example, Laudan 1977, 198–204). The sociologist was to step in when no rational explanation was available to explain the outcome of some scientific dispute. The proponents of the Strong Programme reject this view.

Much of their work involves developing detailed historical case studies and studies of particular laboratories. Their detailed studies seek to identify various contingencies that have affected the resolution of scientific disputes. They thus seek to show that, contrary to the traditional view, even true beliefs have social causes. This approach to the sociology of science attracted harsh criticism from philosophers as it was associated with relativism, a view that is anathema to those working in the epistemology of science. Further, the rise of the Strong Programme reinforced a relativist reading of Kuhn's *Structure* among philosophers (see Laudan 1984, 16–19). This, no doubt, has weakened the impact of Kuhn on the philosophy of science.

Kuhn went to great lengths to distance himself from the Strong Programme. He describes their claims about science as "an example of deconstruction gone mad" (Kuhn 1992/2000, 110). Most importantly, he felt that their focus on negotiation left no role for nature to play in determining what scientists believe (see 1992/2000, 110). Sociology of science, though, does seem relevant to our theorizing about science. If we take W. V. Quine's (1969) call to naturalize epistemology seriously, we should realize that there is also a need to sociologize epistemology. Science is conducted by social groups of a very specific sort. Sociologists, it seems, could offer insight into the nature and structure of such groups. Kuhn admits this much (see Kuhn 1969/2012; Wray 2015).

Recently, there have been some more direct engagements with Kuhn's work in the social epistemology of science. Steve Fuller, for example, has read Kuhn's *Structure* as providing a social epistemology of science (see Fuller 2004). Fuller, though, is quite critical of Kuhn, arguing that his view is socially reactionary, emphasizing the role of tradition in normal science. In contrast, Fuller argues that Popper's critical rationalism is a more progressive social epistemology, emphasizing the demand for reasons and evidence in support of our views, and permitting no beliefs to be shielding from critical scrutiny. Fuller traces Kuhn's conservatism to his working in the Cold War era, when scientists were being called upon by governments to support military and war efforts (see Fuller 2000). Fuller argues that Kuhn's *Structure* provided an image of the scientist that fit well with how scientists *wanted* to see themselves, shielded from the sometimes unsavory applications of their "pure" research. This image was comforting as many scientists tried to distance themselves from the Manhattan Project, which led to the development of the atomic bomb.

More recently, especially with the passing of the 50th anniversary of the publication of *Structure*, philosophers have been giving Kuhn's work more serious consideration. As a result there are some who suggest that Kuhn's work, even his largely neglected later work, can provide valuable resources for developing a social epistemology of science. Wray's *Kuhn's Evolutionary Social Epistemology* provides a thorough assessment of Kuhn's work and its relevance to the epistemology of science (see Wray 2011). Wray draws attention to Kuhn's insightful remarks about specialization in science, an aspect of science that deserves the attention of the social epistemologist of science.

Wray points out that specialization narrows the domain scientists seek to model, and this enables scientists to develop more accurate models and theories.

Fred D'Agostino (2004) has discussed and defended Kuhn's risk-spreading argument, mentioned above. Some of the behaviors of individual scientists that may initially seem irrational will be seen to contribute to the success of science when we look at science from the perspective of the research community as a whole. Various subjective factors, for example, play a crucial role in times of crisis, encouraging different scientists to pursue different theories. The net result is that the research community as a whole is in a better position to determine which of the competing hypotheses is superior. And Rogier De Langhe (2014) has used formal models to test and illustrate a variety of Kuhn's claims about how scientific research communities behave and should be structured.

Kuhn's legacy to social epistemology is to shift the focus of philosophers of science from the study of the logic of science to a consideration of the social dimensions of science. Studies of the logic of science are by no means a thing of the past. Rather, these new studies of the social dimensions of science supplement them, giving us a richer picture of science, and reminding us of the practice of science.

Acknowledgements

Much of the work on this article was done while I was a Visiting Scholar in the Department of Linguistics and Philosophy at the Massachusetts Institute of Technology in Fall 2015. I thank MIT for providing a comfortable atmosphere in which to work, including access to the Thomas S. Kuhn Papers in the Institute Archives at MIT. I also thank the State University of New York, Oswego, for my sabbatical leave in the 2015–2016 academic year.

References

Andersen, H. (2016). Collaboration, Interdisciplinarity, and the Epistemology of Contemporary Science. *Studies in History and Philosophy of Science*, 56, pp. 1–10.

Andersen, H., P. Barker, and X. Chen. (2006). *The Cognitive Structure of Scientific Revolutions*. Cambridge: Cambridge University Press.

Barnes, B. (1982). *T. S. Kuhn and Social Science*. New York: Columbia University Press.

Barnes, B., D. Bloor, and J. Henry. (1996). *Scientific Knowledge: A Sociological Analysis*. Chicago: University of Chicago Press.

Brush, S. G. (2000). Thomas Kuhn as a Historian of Science. *Science & Education*, 9, pp. 39–58.

Chang, H. (2012). *Is Water H₂O?: Evidence, Realism and Pluralism*. Dordrecht: Springer.

Cole, S. (1992). *Making Science: Between Nature and Society*. Cambridge, MA: Harvard University Press.

D'Agostino, F. (2004). Kuhn's Risk-Spreading Argument and the Organization of Scientific Communities. *Episteme*, 1(3), pp. 201–209.

Daston, L. (2016). History of Science without Structure. In R. J. Richards and L. Daston, eds., *Kuhn's Structure of Scientific Revolutions at Fifty: Reflections on a Science Classic*. Chicago: University of Chicago Press, pp. 115–132.

De Langhe, R. (2014). A Comparison of Two Models of Scientific Progress. *Studies in History and Philosophy of Science*, 46, pp. 94–99.

Dobbs, B. J. T. (1983). *The Foundation of Newton's Alchemy: or 'The Hunting of the Greene Lyon'*. Cambridge: Cambridge University Press.

Feyerabend, P. K. (1970/1974). Consolations for the Specialist. In I. Lakatos and A. Musgrave, eds., *Criticism and the Growth of Knowledge: Proceedings of the International Colloquium in the Philosophy of Science, London, 1965, vol. 4*, Reprinted with corrections. Cambridge: Cambridge University Press, pp. 197–230.

Fuller, S. (2000). *Thomas Kuhn: A Philosophical History for Our Times*. Chicago: University of Chicago Press.

Fuller, S. (2004). *Kuhn vs. Popper: The Struggle for the Soul of Science*. New York: Columbia University Press.

Kuhn, T. S. (1959/1977). Energy Conservation as an Example of Simultaneous Discovery. In T. S. Kuhn, ed., *The Essential Tension: Selected Studies in Scientific Tradition and Change*. Chicago: University of Chicago Press, pp. 66–104.

Kuhn, T. S. (1962/2012). *Structure of Scientific Revolutions*, 4th ed. Chicago: University of Chicago Press.

Kuhn, T. S. (1969/2012). Postscript — 1969. In *Structure of Scientific Revolutions*, 4th ed. Chicago: University of Chicago Press.

Kuhn, T. S. (1974/1977). Second Thoughts on Paradigms. In T. S. Kuhn, ed., *The Essential Tension: Selected Studies in Scientific Tradition and Change*. Chicago: University of Chicago Press, pp. 293–319.

Kuhn, T. S. (1976a/1977). The Relations between the History and the Philosophy of Science. In T. S. Kuhn, ed., *The Essential Tension: Selected Studies in Scientific Tradition and Change*. Chicago: University of Chicago Press, pp. 3–20.

Kuhn, T. S. (1976b/1977). Mathematical versus Experimental Traditions in the Development of Physical Science. In T. S. Kuhn, ed., *The Essential Tension: Selected Studies in Scientific Tradition and Change*. Chicago: University of Chicago Press, pp. 31–65.

Kuhn, T. S. (1977). Preface. In T. S. Kuhn, ed., *The Essential Tension: Selected Studies in Scientific Tradition and Change*. Chicago: University of Chicago Press, pp. ix–xxiii.

Kuhn, T. S. (1978). *Black-Body Theory and the Quantum Discontinuity, 1894–1912*. Chicago: University of Chicago Press.

Kuhn, T. S. (1991/2000). The Road since *Structure*. In T. S. Kuhn, ed., *The Road since* Structure*: Philosophical Essays, 1970–1993, with an Autobiographical Interview*, edited by J. Conant and J. Haugeland. Chicago: University of Chicago Press, pp. 90–104.

Kuhn, T. S. (1992/2000). The Trouble with the Historical Philosophy of Science. In T. S. Kuhn, ed., *The Road since Structure: Philosophical Essays, 1970–1993, with an Autobiographical Interview*, edited by J. Conant and J. Haugeland. Chicago: University of Chicago Press, pp. 105–120.

Latour, B. (1987). *Science in Action: How to Follow Scientists and Engineers through Society*. Cambridge, MA: Harvard University Press.

Laudan, L. (1977). *Progress and its Problems: Towards a Theory of Scientific Growth*. Berkeley and Los Angeles: University of California Press.

Laudan, L. (1984). *Science and Values: The Aims of Science and their Role in Scientific Debate*. Berkeley and Los Angeles: University of California Press.

Quine, W. V. (1969). Epistemology Naturalized. In W. V. Quine, ed., *Ontological Relativity and Other Essays*. New York: Columbia University Press, pp. 69–90.

Wade, N. (1977). Thomas S. Kuhn: Revolutionary Theorist of Science. *Science*, 197 (8 July 1977), pp. 143–145.

Weisberg, M., and R. Muldoon. (2009). Epistemic Landscapes and the Division of Cognitive Labor. *Philosophy of Science*, 76(2), pp. 225–252.

Wray, K. B. (2011). *Kuhn's Evolutionary Social Epistemology*. Cambridge: Cambridge University Press.

Wray, K. B. (2015). Kuhn's Social Epistemology and the Sociology of Science. In *Kuhn's* Structure of Scientific Revolutions *50 Years On*, W. J. Devlin and A. Bokulich, eds., *Boston Studies in the Philosophy of Science*, Vol. 311. Dordrecht: Springer, pp. 167–183.

Zollman, K. J. S. (2007). The Communication Structure of Epistemic Communities. *Philosophy of Science*, 74 (5), pp. 574–587.

Archival Material

Thomas S. Kuhn Papers, MC.0240, Box 20. Massachusetts Institute of Technology, Institute Archives and Special Collections, Cambridge, Massachusetts.

Further Reading

The best way into this topic is to read Kuhn's own work. *Structure of Scientific Revolutions* is still essential reading for those interested in Kuhn's philosophy of science. Though his views changed, *Structure* provides useful insight into his use of history of science for philosophical ends. Kuhn's essay "The Relations between the History and the Philosophy of Science" is very insightful on the relevance of the history of science to the philosophy of science. It is published as Essay 1 in

Essential Tension. "The Trouble with the Historical Philosophy of Science" is the single best paper from his later writings that discusses his changing views on the relevance of history to the philosophy of science. This paper is reprinted in *The Road since Structure*, an edited volume of his papers published after his death. K. Brad Wray's *Kuhn's Evolutionary Social Epistemology* provides a wide-ranging assessment of Kuhn's contributions and continuing relevance to the social epistemology of science. Fred D'Agostino's paper, "Kuhn's Risk-Spreading Argument and the Organization of Scientific Communities," is also useful and speaks directly to one important aspect of Kuhn's social epistemology. It is published in the journal *Episteme.*

6

THE NATURALIZED TURN IN EPISTEMOLOGY

Engineering for Truth-Seeking

Chase Wrenn

Introduction

Epistemology is "naturalized" to the extent it is informed by and continuous with empirical science. Naturalized epistemology contrasts with what we can call, somewhat misleadingly, "traditional" epistemology, an approach that aims to answer epistemological questions independently of contingent or empirical considerations. Though there are other, and earlier, naturalized programs in epistemology, this chapter examines the wave of epistemological naturalism that traces itself to W. V. Quine's seminal call for epistemology to "fall into place as a chapter of psychology" in "Epistemology Naturalized" (1969), which has deeply influenced much work in social epistemology (see Collin, this volume).

The idea that epistemology should—or even could—be naturalized is controversial. Advocates of naturalizing epistemology are epistemological naturalists, and we can call those who oppose it traditionalists. An important point of contention is the relevance of science to epistemology's distinctively normative issues. For example, epistemology aims to tell us what makes beliefs justified or not, and it aims to tell us about what we ought or ought not to believe. Naturalism's critics often contend empirical science is irrelevant to such issues or incapable of addressing them. Naturalists often reply that such issues are really engineering problems about how best, individually and collectively, to pursue cognitive goals such as acquiring or preserving significant, true beliefs. As questions about how to cause certain desirable effects, they are amenable to scientific investigation.

This chapter contrasts naturalized epistemology to traditional epistemology and outlines some reasons naturalists have offered in favor of their approach. It also explores some ways naturalistic treatments of normative questions in epistemology reflect the idea of epistemology as engineering. The chapter aims not to be a comprehensive survey, but only to give a good impression of naturalism's motivation and a sense of how some naturalists have addressed normative issues. Other good overviews of naturalized epistemology are Rysiew (2016), Kappel (2011), Wrenn (2016), and Goldman (1994). Kornblith (1994) is a good sample of work from the first 20 years of recent naturalized epistemology, and excellent exemplars of naturalized social epistemology include Goldman (1992, 1999, 2002a, 2009) and Kitcher (1990, 1993: Ch. 8).

As Rysiew (2016) points out, epistemological naturalism is more a family of related theories and methods than a unified philosophical doctrine. Its contrast with traditional epistemology is often more a matter of degree and emphasis than disagreement over particular claims. Here,

I have sometimes omitted nuances or details of views in order to highlight the contrast between naturalism and traditionalism.

Naturalized vs. Traditional Epistemology

We can distinguish naturalism from traditionalism both *substantively* and *methodologically* (see Goldman 1994). Substantively, naturalists and traditionalists differ in the contents of their theories and in what they take the principal point of an epistemological theory to be. Methodologically, they differ in the relevance they assign to empirical information in framing and defending epistemological theories.

The starkest substantive difference between naturalism and traditionalism concerns what they take to be the fundamental target of epistemic appraisal. Naturalists are interested in epistemically significant states of organisms or groups of organisms. They see knowledge and justified belief as products of organisms' causal interactions with their physical and social environments, and they frame their theories in terms of those interactions. What qualifies a belief as "justified" or "know-ledge" is primarily a matter of the causal properties of the processes through which it is formed and sustained. A good example of this view is the process reliabilist theory of justified belief, which says beliefs are justified exactly when they are the outputs of cognitive processes with suitably reliable tendencies to output true beliefs (Goldman 1979).

Traditionalists, in contrast, are interested in abstract relations of evidential support among propositions or sentences. For a belief to be justified is for its contents to be supported by the contents of the beliefs and/or sensory experiences on which it is based. Such support is to be understood independently of the empirical details of how the belief is formed or sustained. A fine example of traditionalism is Richard Feldman and Earl Conee's "evidentialism," which says believing a given proposition is justified if and only if one's evidence favors believing it over disbelieving it or withholding judgment, where "favoring" is to be understood as an abstract relation among contents (Conee & Feldman 2004).

The main methodological difference between naturalism and traditionalism concerns the relevance of empirical science to epistemology. Naturalists think "epistemology should either consist in, or at least be informed and beholden to, the results of scientific disciplines" (Goldman 1994: 305). For example, science tells us it would take longer than the age of the universe for us to check all our beliefs for truth-functional consistency. Such naturalists as Christopher Cherniak (1994) conclude that such checking thus could not be a requirement for justified believing.

Traditionalists think we should pursue epistemology without relying on the particular results of empirical science. Their view has three chief motives. First, they think epistemology is properly seen as *prior to* science. Since epistemology tells us the difference between justified and unjustified scientific theories, it would be viciously circular to rely on science in framing and defending epistemological theories. Second, they often think of epistemic standards as rules that guide responsible or blameless thinking. Such guidance would require standards accessible independently of any particular empirical information, including information about the operations of one's cognitive apparatus. Third, they think epistemology should characterize essential features of knowledge and justified belief, which are invariant across possible worlds. If our epistemology leans too heavily on contingent information from science, it is liable to give wrong accounts of what non-actual subjects know or are justified in believing, or else to be unacceptably limited or parochial—a theory of *knowledge as it occurs in beings like us in worlds like ours*, rather than a theory of knowledge as such.

One of epistemology's tasks is to clarify our epistemic concepts, such as the concept of justification or of knowledge. A traditional methodology for that is to introspect about cases and counterexamples, trying to formulate a set of conditions that are necessary and sufficient for the target concept to apply. A naturalist, in contrast, might note that psychologists have abandoned the idea that concepts are sets of necessary and sufficient conditions. To study concepts, psychologists examine patterns among people's judgments, including not only what judgments they make, but such other factors as how long it takes to make them and the influence of priming. Naturalists inspired by this approach are apt to avoid introspection and counterexamples, and to offer psychologically informed theories of epistemic concepts instead (Goldman 1993, Nichols *et al.* 2003).

Why Naturalize Epistemology?

Some empirical matters of fact are obviously relevant to epistemology, naturalized or not. For example, it is an empirical fact that we have perceptual experiences, and so it is at least partly an empirical question whether our perceptual judgments are justified. Naturalists see a more central place for empirical science in epistemology, though. Not only do we need empirical information in order to apply epistemological theories to the real world, but, naturalists say, the theories themselves should answer to empirical considerations and treat knowledge and justified belief as natural, physical, causal phenomena. Increasingly, they also emphasize our epistemic interdependence and the social dimension of knowledge and justified belief (Goldberg 2016).

Naturalism has two prominent motivations, one negative and one positive. The negative motivation derives from various failures of traditionalist epistemology. The positive motivation derives from confidence that naturalized epistemology can help us in the pursuit of our cognitive goals.

Quine thought the alternatives to naturalized epistemology were hopeless. They aimed, he thought, to validate our empirical knowledge on grounds that are independent of our scientific theories. The most salient such approaches are rationalist and empiricist foundationalism. Rationalists sought foundations in substantive *a priori* certainties, such as Descartes' *Cogito*, but Quine argued that there are no such *a priori* certainties to be had (Gibson 1988: 26, Quine 1969, 1980). Empiricists sought foundations in sensory experiences, by trying to show either that our knowledge is deducible or rationally reconstructible from them. Quine objects that the deductive project cannot succeed because experience gives no logical guarantee that the external world is any particular way, or even that it exists (Quine 1969: 71–72). Nor can "rational reconstruction" succeed, because it would require correlating individual beliefs with the experiences that count for or against them, but whether any given experience counts for or against any given belief depends crucially on what other empirical beliefs we take for granted (Gibson 1988: 27–28, Quine 1969, 1980).

In Quine's view, there is no extra-scientific validation of science. Rather than draw the skeptical conclusion that our scientific beliefs are unfounded, though, Quine envisioned epistemology "in a new setting and a clarified status," as part of psychology (1969: 82). We want to know how we build our theories in response to sensory experience, and we want to know how much our overall view of the world transcends the available evidence. The only reason to pursue those questions *without* drawing freely on science was the hope of grounding science in something outside itself. Abandoning such hope frees epistemology to draw on all available information.

Another motivation for naturalizing epistemology is distrust of traditional epistemology's methods, especially introspection and thought experiments testing proposed necessary and sufficient conditions for applying epistemic concepts, such as *knowledge* or *justified belief*. Traditionalism assumes such methods yield insight on the contents of those concepts and, correlatively, on the natures of the categories the concepts designate.

The traditional approach remains popular. Richard Feldman's textbook, for example, embraces it explicitly (Feldman 2003). Naturalists have serious concerns about it, though. Empirical psychology has taught us that concepts typically aren't sets of necessary and sufficient conditions, even when they are concepts such as *odd number* for which such conditions can be given. Studying epistemic concepts by looking for such conditions might be misguided from the very start (Goldman 1993). Naturalists have also raised doubts about the reliability of philosophers' intuitions as guides to the nature of epistemic categories. What convergence there is among philosophers' intuitive judgments might be more the product of demographic homogeneity than of the good calibration of their intuitions to mind-independent facts (Nichols *et al.* 2003). Still other naturalists (e.g. Kornblith 2002) have argued that our *concept* of knowledge can't tell us any more about what knowledge is than our concept of water can tell us what water is. Rather than reflecting on concepts, Kornblith thinks epistemologists should attend to what science tells us about knowledge as a natural phenomenon.

The second, more positive stream of motivation for epistemological naturalism is confidence that it can provide good guidance in our pursuit of our cognitive ends. For naturalists, the central question of epistemology is often: How best can we, individually and collectively, find answers to the questions that interest us?

Many naturalists have pointed to the need for empirical information in answering that question. Alvin Goldman identifies several dimensions of evaluation that matter to us. We care not only about the *reliability* of our ways of finding answers, but also about such things as their *problem-solving power, speed,* and *efficiency* (Goldman 1986: Ch. 6). Richard Boyd (1980) and Larry Laudan (1984) have likewise argued that resolving methodological disputes in science often requires drawing on empirical details of the methods in question; they cannot be settled on purely *a priori* grounds.

Goldman has also indicated ways empirical research can help answer epistemological questions that, at first, appear to be matters for introspection. A case in point is belief based on memory. What features of memory cues are indicators of reliability? Goldman cites empirical research on features that tend to differ as a function of whether the memory derives from perception or imagination. Such research can give advice about how and when to rely on memory, of a sort we might not be able to get from purely *a priori* or introspective investigations of memory (Goldman 2002b).

Michael Bishop and J. D. Trout (2005) draw on the idea that epistemology should give us good problem-solving advice both in criticizing traditionalism and arguing for their style of naturalism. Traditionalism, they say, has produced little useful guidance on how to reason. In contrast, empirically informed work has yielded advice whose effectiveness and reliability can be quite surprising —such as the advice to favor the predictions of statistical rules over expert judgments when they disagree (2005: 12–13), and the advice to reason about medical test results in terms of frequencies rather than mathematically equivalent probabilities (2005: 139–142).

Engineering and Normativity

On at least one natural understanding of the field, epistemology is about distinguishing what is worthy of belief from what is unworthy. It deals with a special sort of reasons—purely intellectual reasons to believe or disbelieve propositions. As such, epistemology is as normative as ethics. While ethics is about how we (morally) ought to behave, epistemology is about how we (intellectually) ought to think (Berker 2013, Kim 2008).

That understanding of epistemology's normative subject matter has often motivated objections to naturalism. In its simplest form, the worry is that science is always descriptive and never normative. Science can tell us how our minds *do* work or how we *do* think, but not how our minds *ought* to work or how we *ought* to think. So, science is only tangentially relevant to epistemology's central questions.

Wilfrid Sellars mooted a version of this objection, in anticipation of the coming wave of naturalism. He contended "knowledge" is not an empirical description of a belief, but rather the name for a status beliefs can have in "the space of justifying and being able to justify what one says" (Sellars 2000: 248, §36). Sellars's idea was an important influence on both Richard Rorty (1979) and Robert Brandom (1994). Morton White (1998) pressed Quine to address the problem, and Jaegwon Kim (2008) develops a version aimed specifically at Quine's call for naturalizing epistemology.

Quine expresses the idea of the most common answer to the normativity challenge in his reply to White:

> Naturalization of epistemology does not jettison the normative and settle for the indiscriminate description of ongoing procedures. For me normative epistemology is a branch of engineering. It is the technology of truth-seeking, or, in a more cautiously epistemological term, prediction. ... There is no question here of ultimate value, as in morals; it is a matter of efficacy for an ulterior end, truth or prediction.
>
> *(1998: 664–665)*

Quine addresses the simplest version of the normativity challenge, which assumes science has nothing to say about good, bad, right, or wrong, and so scientific epistemology has nothing to say about good, bad, right, and wrong in our thinking (see Wrenn 2006). As Quine points out, that assumption is false. By examining the causal connections between means and ends, science has plenty to say about good, bad, right, and wrong *in relation to those ends*. Getting true beliefs is one of the ends we care about, and naturalized epistemology addresses how we might best pursue that end.

The spirit of the engineering reply is already present in the second line of motivation for naturalizing epistemology discussed above. If epistemology's central problems really are about what one should believe from a purely intellectual perspective, and epistemology really is supposed to guide us in pursuit of answers to our questions, then its central problems have an inescapably causal dimension: what processes or methods of inquiry are best suited to realizing such goals as acquiring, preserving, or transmitting true beliefs? What systems of social organization and distribution of cognitive labor best promote those goals?

The precise commitments of an engineering approach to epistemology are not entirely clear. At the very least, it involves understanding epistemic normativity in goal-directed terms. Such an approach is aptly characterized as "teleological" or "hypothetical," in contrast to "deontological" or "categorical" approaches (Berker 2013, Wrenn 2004). The latter would evaluate our cognitive performance by appeal to standards thought to be prior to the pursuit of any cognitive goals whatsoever, or standards whose bindingness on us is partly constitutive of having a mind at all (Berker 2013).

An engineering approach to epistemology might or might not commit itself to analyzing traditional normative epistemic categories, such as justification, evidence, rationality, or knowledge. When it does, it is committed to accounting for their normativity in goal-directed terms. For example, traditionalists might try to derive claims about what constitutes good cognitive performance by reflecting on the concept of *being a thinker*. Naturalists, in contrast, might instead consider empirical information on the efficacy of problem-solving strategies.

Engineering Epistemology in Practice

Many naturalists have taken up the engineering approach to normative issues. Sometimes, they are explicit in citing Quine's proposal that normative epistemology is a chapter of engineering. Other times, the approach is manifest in their emphasis on cognitive ends and questions about how best to achieve them. Some exemplars can illustrate how the engineering approach works in practice.

In Quine's normative epistemology, the main problem is how to best achieve the epistemic aim of true belief or, at least, accurate prediction of future sensory experience. This is an engineering problem because the "best" way is the way most likely to succeed, given our available resources. We address it not by speculating about the concept of evidence, but by doing applied science and mathematics.

In his last two books, Quine gives a fuller picture of what he has in mind on epistemology's normative dimension. It includes applying science to derive practical advice about what sources of information to trust: for example, science tells us there is no ESP, so we should not believe soothsayers (Quine 1992: 19–20). It addresses the engineering problem of how best to conjecture new theories (1992: 20, 1995: 49–50), and it aims to expose and correct erroneous or unreliable patterns in our thinking, such as the gambler's fallacy (1995: 50).

Alvin Goldman has endorsed a "moderate naturalism" that does not treat epistemology as a branch of empirical science. He thinks epistemology addresses distinctively philosophical questions that no branch of empirical science addresses directly. Nor does Goldman reject the idea of *a priori* justification altogether, as Quine appears to. Rather, Goldman's moderate naturalism combines two theses. First, the epistemic justification of a belief is "a function of the *processes that produce or preserve*" it. Second, epistemology "needs help" from empirical science—for example, to tell us what processes produce and sustain our beliefs and to tell us how reliable those processes are, under what kinds of circumstances (2002b: 19).

To address normative questions about our intellectual lives, Goldman thinks epistemology needs help from the cognitive and social sciences. He calls the resulting interdisciplinary pursuit, which includes both individual and social dimensions, "epistemics."

Individual epistemics primarily addresses mental processes, structures, and mechanisms. It evaluates them along such dimensions as reliability, problem-solving power, and speed. It addresses epistemological questions about the justification of perceptual beliefs, memory, or inductive inference, for example, by looking at what cognitive science tells us about the processes underlying such beliefs and their reliability (see Goldman 1986: Chh. 9, 10, and 14).

Social epistemics addresses the broad constellation of social influences and factors relevant to our intellectual lives. It considers the ways we rely on the testimony of others and identify experts, for the purpose of deciding what we as individuals should believe (Goldman 2001). It also addresses and epistemically evaluates social institutions and systems, from courtrooms and legal procedures (1999: Ch. 9) to classrooms and educational curricula (1999: Ch. 11).

Although Goldman does not draw the analogy with engineering explicitly, his program of epistemics certainly manifests the spirit of epistemology as engineering. For Goldman, true belief is the fundamental epistemic good, and epistemic value is to be understood in terms of promotion or conduciveness to that end. He sees the normative problems of epistemology, individual and social, as empirical problems about producing, preserving, and maintaining true beliefs, within the limits of our available resources.

Like Goldman, Louise Antony endorses a naturalistic epistemology that has room for the *a priori* and is generally reliabilist (Antony 2004). Like Quine, she emphasizes the unity of epistemology with science and the holism of our web of belief. She argues that that holism makes bias inescapable in inquiry: inquirers always have background beliefs and values that influence how they respond to new information and data. The effects of those commitments and values are not necessarily bad, though. Although some may reduce our chances at getting to the truth, others may actually *improve* them. Antony argues that androcentric bias in particular is deleterious to the pursuit of truth, but feminist values are often truth-conducive (1993).

Antony's approach also exemplifies the pursuit of epistemology as engineering. Epistemologists have often supposed any intrusion of background values—and especially political values—into one's interpretation of the evidence is epistemically bad. From the naturalized, engineering perspective, though, two considerations are especially salient. First, if we take seriously the way our values-commitments ramify through the rest of our lives, the idea of inquiry in which background values have *no* influence is quite likely a pipe dream. Second, what matters to the epistemic status of biases is the same as anything else: how much does it impede or promote the goal of truth? Biases are not epistemically objectionable *per se*. Their goodness or badness depends on their reliability or truth-conduciveness, which are an empirical matter (1993: 215).

Philip Kitcher has argued that a naturalistic perspective brings with it the insight that our beliefs are partly the products of historical, social processes. We can thus consider not only cognitive optimality for an individual, with respect to her personal epistemic ends, but also optimality for a community, with respect to its collective intellectual progress or attainment of the cognitive good (1992: 110–111). For Kitcher, social epistemology aims to identify the properties of epistemically well-designed social systems. He pursues that aim by applying modeling methods from the social sciences, especially economics (1993: Ch. 8).

A striking result of Kitcher's work is that *epistemic diversity* is desirable at the collective level. In an epistemically well-designed community, individuals differ in the weight they give different lines of evidence and the importance they assign different questions. The reasoning of some is, from the perspective of others, not rational, but that is more conducive to progress than uniform adherence to common standards would be. This casts doubt, naturally, on the idea that there is any single standard of rationality individuals ought to adhere to (Kitcher 1990).

David Henderson and Terence Horgan have recently articulated a version of naturalized epistemology that includes a range of different kinds of inquiry, which they refer to as the "E-spectrum." The *E* is deliberately ambiguous between *epistemology* and *engineering*, for they endorse Quine's claim that the normativity of naturalized epistemology should be understood along the lines of the normative evaluations found in engineering and applied science.

In at least one respect, Henderson and Horgan may take the analogy with engineering more seriously even than Quine does. They see the normative part of epistemology as aimed at laying out *"design specifications* for an effective truth-seeking cognitive agent: principles of design to which such an agent should largely conform, in its belief-forming cognitive process" (Henderson & Horgan 2011: 164). One aspect of their naturalism is a conviction that purely *a priori* methods cannot reveal those design specifications completely and in full detail. For that, cognitive science is needed (2011: 165).

At one end of the E-spectrum are "low-grade *a priori*" inquiries that look very much like traditional conceptual analysis, aimed at clarifying such epistemological concepts as *knowledge* and *justified belief*. As in much traditional epistemology, the method at this end of the spectrum is to reflect on judgments concerning the concepts' applicability to particular cases and to project a theory that systematizes those judgments, preserving as many as possible while perhaps discounting some as the result of "performance error." The naturalism in this part of the project is in Henderson and Horgan's view that even at this stage, the projection of the theory from our intuitions is an inference to the best explanation, ultimately constrained by an array of empirical considerations (2011: Ch. 2).

At the other end of the E-spectrum are empirical, scientific investigations of cognition and its neural basis. Even cognitive-science-as-usual, Henderson and Horgan contend, has a normative, engineering dimension (2011: 166). A theory of primate vision, for example, is not a historical account of what *has happened* in the eyes and nervous systems of primates. Rather, it is a theory that distinguishes better from worse functioning of the visual system, by way of constructing, in response to the empirical evidence, a view of the system's design specifications and overall function.

There is, of course, a range of other inquiries between the two ends of Henderson and Horgan's E-spectrum. Methodological issues often come up in the practice of science, and they can rarely be settled on purely *a priori* grounds (e.g., see Laudan 1984: Ch. 2). Philosophers consider problems about the justification of testimonial beliefs and inductive or statistical inference. On Henderson and Horgan's view, even if those problems are closer to the *a priori* end of the range, they still cannot be addressed in isolation from what science tells us about the mind's operation and what cognitive competence amounts to for human beings.

Conclusion

Naturalistic epistemology has two main distinctive features. First, its theories tend to be framed in terms of the interactions between thinking organisms or groups of them and the physical/social world. It focuses on belief-states and the causal (often social) processes that produce them, in the first instance, rather than starting with analyses of quasi-formal support relations among propositions. Second, it works in concert with empirical science, paying close attention to empirical details, rather than proceeding in a purely *a priori* fashion in hopes of discovering non-empirical standards by which to evaluate our empirical beliefs. Naturalists tend to see the core, normative issues of epistemology as engineering problems or problems for applied science. The key question is: What are the best ways, given the resources available, to pursue our cognitive ends? In most of the cases discussed here, the "cognitive end" in question is true belief, but some avowed naturalists have argued for others (Laudan 1984, Stich 1990).

As Finn Collin (this volume) outlines, naturalism has been central to the development of social epistemology. It is a matter of empirical fact that many of our pathways to knowledge involve other people, on whom we rely as sources of information and as collaborators in inquiry. Among the normative questions epistemology must address, then, are questions about what social practices and institutions best promote the epistemic good not only at the individual level, but collectively as well.

Related Topics

The other chapters in Parts I and IV of *The Routledge Companion to Social Epistemology* are all useful to persons interested in naturalized epistemology. Additional chapters of interest are "Anthropology and Epistemology" (Part III, Chapter 8), "Prejudice and Implicit Bias" (Part VI, Chapter 4), and "Economic Experiments and Game Theory," (Part IX, Chapter 3).

References

Antony, L.M. (1993). Quine As Feminist: The Radical Import of Naturalized Epistemology. In L.M. Antony & C. Witt, eds., *A Mind of One's Own: Feminist Essays on Reason and Objectivity*. Westview Press, Boulder, CO, pp. 110–153.

Antony, L.M. (2004). A Naturalized Approach to the A Priori. *Philosophical Issues*, 14(1), pp. 1–17.

Berker, S. (2013). Epistemic Teleology and the Separateness of Propositions. *Philosophical Review*. 122(3), pp. 337–393.

Bishop, M.A. & Trout, J.D. (2005). *Epistemology and the Psychology of Human Judgment*. Oxford University Press, New York, NY.

Boyd, R. (1980). Scientific Realism and Naturalistic Epistemology. In P.D. Asquith & R.N. Giere, eds., *PSA: Proceedings of the Biennial Meeting of the Philosophy of Science Association*, pp. 613–662.

Brandom, R. (1994). *Making It Explicit: Reasoning, Representing, and Discursive Commitment*. Harvard University Press, Cambridge, MA.

Cherniak, C. (1994). Computational Complexity and the Universal Acceptance of Logic. In H. Kornblith, ed., *Naturalizing Epistemology*. MIT Press, Cambridge, MA, pp. 239–260.

Conee, E.B. & Feldman, R. (2004). Evidentialism. In *Evidentialism: Essays in Epistemology*. Oxford University Press, New York, NY, pp. 83–101.

Feldman, R. (2003). *Epistemology*. Prentice Hall, Upper Saddle River, NJ.

Gibson, R.F. (1988). *Enlightened Empiricism: An Examination of W. V. Quine's Theory of Knowledge*. University of South Florida Press, Gainesville, FL.

Goldberg, S. (2016) A Proposed Research Program for Social Epistemology. In P. Reider ed., *Social Epistemology and Epistemic Agency: Decentralizing Epistemic Agency*. Rowman and Littlefield, pp. 3–20.

Goldman, A.I. (1979). What Is Justified Belief? In *Justification and Knowledge*. Springer Netherlands, pp. 1–23.

Goldman, A.I. (1986). *Epistemology and Cognition*. Harvard University Press, Cambridge, MA.

Goldman, A.I. (1992). Foundations of Social Epistemics. In *Liaisons: Philosophy Meets the Cognitive and Social Sciences*. MIT Press, Cambridge, MA, pp. 179–207.

Goldman, A.I. (1993). Epistemic Folkways and Scientific Epistemology. *Philosophical Issues*, 3, pp. 271–285.

Goldman, A.I. (1994). Naturalistic Epistemology and Reliabilism. *Midwest Studies in philosophy*, 19(1), pp. 301–320.

Goldman, A.I. (1999). *Knowledge in a Social World*. Oxford University Press, New York, NY.

Goldman, A.I. (2001). Experts: Which Ones Should You Trust? *Philosophy and Phenomenological Research*, 63 (1), pp. 85–110.

Goldman, A.I. (2002a). *Pathways to Knowledge: Private and Public*. Oxford University Press, New York, NY.

Goldman, A.I. (2002b). A Priori Warrant and Naturalistic Epistemology. In *Pathways to Knowledge: Private and Public*. Oxford University Press, New York, NY, pp. 24–50.

Goldman, A.I. (2009). Social Epistemology: Theory and Applications. *Royal Institute of Philosophy Supplement*. 64, pp. 1–18.

Henderson, D. & Horgan, T. (2011). *The Epistemological Spectrum: At the Interface of Cognitive Science and Conceptual Analysis*. Oxford University Press, Oxford, UK.

Kappel, K. (2011). Naturalistic Epistemology. In S. Bernecker & D. Pritchard, eds., *The Routledge Companion to Epistemology*. Taylor & Francis, London, pp. 836–847.

Kim, J. (2008). What is "Naturalized Epistemology?". In E. Sosa, J. Kim, J. Fantl & M. McGrath, eds., *Epistemology: An Anthology*. Blackwell Publishing, Malden, MA, pp. 538–551.

Kitcher, P. (1990). The Division of Cognitive Labor. *The Journal of Philosophy* 87(1), pp. 5–22.

Kitcher, P. (1992). The Naturalists Return. *The Philosophical Review*, 101(1), pp. 53–114.

Kitcher, P. (1993). *The Advancement of Science*. Oxford University Press, New York, NY.

Kornblith, H. ed. (1994). *Naturalizing Epistemology*. MIT Press, Cambridge, MA.

Kornblith, H. (2002). *Knowledge and Its Place in Nature*. Oxford University Press, New York, NY.

Laudan, L. (1984). *Science and Values: The Aims of Science and Their Role in Scientific Debate*. University of California Press, Berkeley, CA.

Nichols, S., Stich, S. & Weinberg, J., (2003). Metaskepticism: Meditations in Ethno-epistemology. *The Skeptics*, pp. 227–247.

Quine, W.V. (1969). Epistemology Naturalized. In *Ontological Relativity, and Other Essays*. Columbia University Press, New York, NY, pp. 69–90.

Quine, W.V. (1980). Two Dogmas of Empiricism. In *From a Logical Point of View: Nine Logico-philosophical Essays*. Harvard University Press, pp. 20–46.

Quine, W.V. (1992). *Pursuit of Truth*. Harvard University Press, Cambridge, MA.

Quine, W.V. (1995). *From Stimulus to Science*. Harvard University Press, Cambridge, MA.

Quine, W.V. (1998). Reply to Morton White. In L.E. Hahn & P.A. Schilpp, eds., *The Philosophy of W. V. Quine*. Open Court, La Salle, IL., pp. 663–665.

Rorty, R. (1979). *Philosophy and the Mirror of Nature*. Princeton University Press, Princeton, NJ.

Rysiew, P. (2016). Naturalism in Epistemology. In E.N. Zalta, ed., *Stanford Encyclopedia of Philosophy*. Available at: http://plato.stanford.edu/archives/sum2016/entries/epistemology-naturalized/ [accessed 13 August, 2016].

Sellars, W. (2000). Empiricism and the Philosophy of Mind. In W.A. DeVries & T. Triplett, eds., *Knowledge, Mind, and the Given*. Hackett Publishing, Indianapolis, IN, pp. 205–276.

Stich, S.P. (1990). *The Fragmentation of Reason: Preface to a Pragmatic Theory of Cognitive Evaluation*. MIT Press, Cambridge, MA.

White, M. (1998). Normative Ethics, Normative Epistemology, and Quine's Holism. In P.A. Schilpp & L.E. Hahn, eds., *The Philosophy of W.V. Quine*. Open Court, Chicago, IL, pp. 649–665.

Wrenn, C.B. (2004). Hypothetical and Categorical Epistemic Normativity. *The Southern Journal of Philosophy*, 42(2), pp. 273–290.

Wrenn, C.B. (2006). Epistemology As Engineering? *Theoria*, 72(1), pp. 60–79.

Wrenn, C.B. (2016). Naturalistic Epistemology. In *Internet Encyclopedia of Philosophy*. Available at: www.iep.utm.edu/ [Accessed 13 August, 2016].

Further Reading

Clough, S. (2004). Having It All: Naturalized Normativity in Feminist Science Studies. *Hypatia*, 19(1), pp. 102–118. (An argument for a style of naturalism in feminist science studies that is less individualistic than Quine's.)

Dretske, F.I. (1981). *Knowledge and the Flow of Information*. MIT Press, Cambridge, MA. (A classic, scientifically informed theory of knowledge and cognition.)

Jenkins, C.S. (2007). Epistemic Norms and Natural Facts. *American Philosophical Quarterly*, 44(3), pp. 259–272. (A defense of the view that normative epistemological claims and certain naturalistic descriptive claims pick out the same facts without necessarily meaning the same thing.)

Kornblith, H. (2014). *A Naturalistic Epistemology: Selected Papers*. Oxford University Press, New York, NY. (A collection of papers working out details of Kornblith's naturalistic program in epistemology.)

Millikan, R.G. (1984). *Language, Thought, and Other Biological Categories: New Foundations for Realism*. MIT Press, Cambridge, MA. (An approach to epistemology, philosophy of mind, and philosophy of language as inquiries continuous with biological theory.)

PART II

The Epistemology of Testimony

7

COUNTEREXAMPLES TO TESTIMONIAL TRANSMISSION

Peter J. Graham and Zachary Bachman

It is natural to think that we learn (come to know) many things by believing what other people tell us. This is a perfectly ordinary way to learn new things. If we don't already know ourselves, it must be that we learn *because* the speaker has the knowledge we're after. Testimonial knowledge is then knowledge arrived through believing another's testimony because the sender had knowledge to transmit. *Testimonial* knowledge is *transmitted* knowledge.

From these ordinary observations, two highly plausible principles follow. First, modulo certain qualifications, when a recipient believes a sender's testimony that P, if the sender knows that P, then the recipient comes to know—or is in a position to come to know—that P as well. The sender's knowledge *suffices* for the recipient's knowledge, much like when you run up a tab at a bar but don't have any money and someone else kindly offers to pay. Call this **sufficiency**.

Second, when a recipient believes a sender's testimony that P, if the sender doesn't know that P, then there is no way the recipient can come to know that P through believing the sender. That would be like relying on someone to pay your tab, but they are just as broke as you are. That's no way to pay your bill. Call this **necessity**.

Here are some authors endorsing **necessity**. Michael Dummett says testimonial knowledge "is the transmission from one individual to another of knowledge." He goes on to say that the "original purveyor ... —the first link in the chain of transmission—must himself have known it ... or it cannot be knowledge for any of those who derived it ultimately from him" (1994: 264). Angus Ross writes "your telling me that P can only be said to provide me with knowledge if you know that P" (1986: 62). Michael Welbourne writes "it is necessary, if there is to be a successful process of testimonial transmission, that the speaker have knowledge to communicate" (1994: 302). And Robert Audi says, "my testimony cannot give you testimonially grounded knowledge that P without my knowing that P. ... Testimony transmits knowledge but does not, as such, generate it" (1997: 410).

Here are some authors endorsing **sufficiency**. C.A.J. Coady says,

> if S knows that P then (given the satisfaction of certain conditions relating to S's sincerity, the willingness of S's audience to accept what S says as an honest expression of what he knows etc.) S can bring his listeners to know that P by telling them that P.
>
> *(1992: 224)*

Elizabeth Fricker says when

> a belief of S's gives rise to an utterance by him, which utterance produces in his audience H a belief with the same content; and all this happens in such a way that, if S's belief is knowledge, then we may allow that title to H's belief too.
>
> *(1987: 57)*

One can also find endorsements hedged with the expression "normally" or qualified in other ways. For example, Timothy Williamson writes "in normal circumstances, a speaker who asserts that P thereby puts a hearer in a position to know that P if (and only if) the speaker knows that P" (1996: 520). Robert Audi writes

> concerning knowledge, we might say that at least normally, a belief that P based on testimony constitutes knowledge ... provided that the attester knows that P and the believer has no reason to doubt either P or the attester's credibility concerning it.
>
> *(1997: 412)*

Tyler Burge writes "if one has acquired one's belief from others in a normal way, and if the others know the proposition, one acquires knowledge" (1993: 477, fn. 16). And Gareth Evans claims

> if the speaker S has knowledge of x to the effect that it is F, and in consequence utters a sentence in which he refers to x, and says of it that it is F, and if his audience A hears and understands the utterance, and accept it as true (and there are no defeating conditions), then A himself comes to know of x that it is F.
>
> *(1982: 310)*

Given the obvious pull of our two principles and their widespread endorsement, they must form a part of our intuitive, folk epistemology. And our "folk epistemology," Fricker writes, "cuts our epistemic situation at its true joints" (2015: 194).

Even so, various thinkers have concocted prima facie counterexamples to both. Our purpose in this chapter is to catalog many of these cases. We find them interesting in their own right, not only because they challenge what might otherwise appear to be the orthodox view of testimonial knowledge as transmitted knowledge, but because reflection on these cases holds out the promise of discovering deeper principles that explain why our two folk principles seem so compelling, and exactly why and when they might fail. We will point in the direction of some of this work to date as we conclude, but for the most part our goal here is to categorize and catalog the counterexamples. We will not, regrettably, consider other grounds for challenging the orthodox view. We hope readers find this chapter a useful resource as they engage in further philosophical detective work on their own, whether primarily case-based or based on other considerations.

Counterexamples to Sufficiency

In a counterexample to **sufficiency**, a sender knows that P but the recipient does not come to know that P; knowledge does not transmit. We isolate three categories of counterexamples to **sufficiency**, three categories of cases of transmission failure:

- Cases where the cause of failure *resides in the sender*;
- Cases where the cause of failure *resides in the environment*;
- Cases where the cause of failure *resides in the recipient*.

Transmission Failure Due to the Sender

We begin with a case from Fred Dretske:

Dretske's Drinker

George ... is especially fond of [Bordeaux wines] from the Medoc region of Bordeaux. He ... unerringly identifies a genuine Medoc as a Bordeaux, and specifically as a Medoc, when he tastes one. Strangely ... George is confused about Chianti. He has no trouble distinguishing a Chianti from a Medoc ... or in identifying a Chianti as a Chianti, but he thinks Chianti is a Bordeaux wine. He has never studied the labels very carefully, but he has the vague idea that "Tuscany" is the name of a wine-growing region in southern Bordeaux ... [At a dinner party he has a Medoc wine. He tells his friend the next day that he had Bordeaux at the party].

(From Dretske 1982: 109–110. Discussed by Welbourne 1983; Coady 1992: 224–230; Adler 1996: 104–105; and Graham 2000b: 136–138)

Dretske takes this case to show that even if a speaker knows that P when asserting that P, it does not follow that the recipient can learn that P from believing that P on the basis of understanding and accepting the speaker's assertion. In this example, the problem is that the speaker has a false background belief, that Tuscany is a region of Southern France (the way many people think that New York is a part of New England). This belief does not rob his knowledge that the wine he drank was a Bordeaux, for just as one can know that Vermont is in New England without knowing that New York is not, one can know that Medocs are from Bordeaux without knowing that Chiantis are not. That's why George would easily say that the wine is a Bordeaux, even when it is not. And that's why Dretske thought you can't learn from George's testimony, even if he speaks from knowledge.

We now turn to a different kind of case from Jennifer Lackey.

Almost a Liar 1

Phil ... trusts those whom he has good reason to trust—or at least those whom he has no clear reason to distrust—and distrusts those whom he has good reason to distrust. Yesterday ... Phil ran into Jill ... and she ... told him that she had seen an orca whale while boating ... Phil, having acquired very good reasons for trusting ... her, ... accepted her testimony... Jill did in fact see an orca. [She] is very reliable [about whales] ... [and] Phil has no reason to doubt [her]. However, in order to promote a whale watching business ..., she would have reported ... that she had seen an orca whale even if she hadn't.

(From Lackey 2006: 91, 2008: 69)

In this example the speaker, we can stipulate, *speaks from her knowledge* (she says what she does because she knows), but it is also clear that *she would easily assert that she saw an orca even if she did not*. She would easily assert that P even if not P. Here is a related example from Christopher Peacocke:

Astrologist

Mary sometimes comes to believe that it is raining by looking, and sometimes by deduction from astrological principles. [When she looks], she knows it is raining; [When she "reads the stars"], she does not. ... [So] if she tells her friend that it is raining [even when she looks], he does not come to know that it is raining.

(From Peacocke 1986: 149–150. Endorsed by McDowell 1994: 222, fn. 33. Endorsed by Graham 2000b: 149, fn. 20; Graham 2016: 175–176)

We can describe this case the same way, where Mary speaks from her knowledge on the occasion but often, nevertheless, does not; she would easily assert that it is raining even when she does not know it is.

Nozick's case of a grandmother in a hospital can be framed as an analogue of these cases. The first two sentences are from Nozick (1981: 179). The rest concocts the analogue:

Grandmother's Call

A grandmother sees her grandson is well when he comes to visit; but if he were sick or dead, others would tell her he was well to spare her upset. In the former case, when she tells her friends on the phone that her grandson is well, she speaks from her knowledge. But in the latter case, when she tells her friends on the phone that her grandson is well, she speaks from what she thinks is knowledge, but is not. She would easily tell her friends that her grandson is fine when he is not.

Compare also Graham (2016: 175). We turn to a similar, but even so different kind of case:

Almost a Liar 2

A speaker knows that p and tells a listener that p. However, the speaker says that p not because she knows that p but because having the listener believe that p is in the speaker's interests. So even if the speaker didn't know that p, or even didn't believe that p, she would still have told the listener that p. The listener comes to believe that p by taking the speaker's word for it.

(This example is from Wright 2016: 69. See also Wright 2018, ch. 7)

Wright says his example is just Lackey's example, above. However, "Almost a Liar 2" differs from "Almost a Liar 1." In Lackey's case, we stipulate that the speaker speaks from her knowledge. In Wright's case, the speaker does not speak from her knowledge. So the proximal causes differ in the two cases. Wright himself would argue that this difference makes a difference. We simply hereby *note* the difference.

Here is a summary of the underlying causes of transmission failure due to the sender:

- "Dretske's Drinker": Though the speaker speaks from knowledge, *because of the speaker's relevant false background belief*, the speaker would easily assert that P even if not P.

- "Almost a Liar 1": Though the speaker speaks from knowledge, she would easily assert that P even if not P *because of a background motive to deceive.*
- "Astrologist," "Grandmother's Call": Though the speaker speaks form knowledge, she would easily assert that P even if not P *because of nearby, unreliable, but unused belief-forming methods.*
- "Almost a Liar 2": Though the speaker knows, *the speaker does not speak from knowledge but instead because of her operative motive to deceive* in asserting that P, and would also thereby easily assert that P even if not P.

We now turn to putative counterexamples caused by features of the recipient's local environment.

Transmission Failure Due to the Local Environment

Newspaper

A political leader is assassinated. His associates, fearing a coup, decide to pretend that the bullet hit someone else. On nationwide television they announce that an assassination attempt has failed ... However, before the announcement is made, an enterprising reporter on the scene telephones the real story to his newspaper, which has included the story in its final edition. Jill ... reads the story of the assassination. ... Jill has justified true belief ... . But she does not know that the ... leader has been assassinated. For everyone else has heard about the televised announcement.

(From Harman 1973: 143–144)

Harman thinks the recipient does not acquire knowledge; a speaker's knowledge can fail to transmit to the hearer because the hearer lacks "accessible" but misleading evidence that would defeat her justification. Take away the misleading evidence, and knowledge transmits. The problem is with the environment.

Lycan (1977) is a classic reply to Harman; Lycan thinks the recipient acquires knowledge. For further discussion as the case applies to testimony, see Adler (1996: 100).

Reflecting on Harman's newspaper case, Graham devised a variant that he says is structurally similar to Alvin Goldman's thermometer case (Goldman 1986: 45–46, Graham 2000b: 148, n. 15). In Goldman's case, someone reaches in to a box of thermometers and grabs the only working thermometer. All the rest are broken and would read 98°F regardless. When the agent uses the one working thermometer, it reads 98°F. Can the agent learn that his temperature is 98°F in such a case? Goldman thinks not. Here is Graham's analogous case:

Assassination

The military of a small country hopes to stage a successful coup and threatens all of the reporters in the country to report that the President has been assassinated regardless of what happens ... . All but one of the reporters gives in. Adler will report what really happens, no matter what. ... [The] assassination is successful and Adler is the only eyewitness. The other reporters ... simply report that the President was assassinated. When Harman walks down the street and just happens

---

> to read Adler's newspaper among all the others on the stand, Harman does not learn (come to know) that the President was assassinated, for Harman would easily rely on the other newspapers.
> (From Graham 2000b: 134–136, Graham 2016: 179)

The speaker knows; would not assert that P unless she knows; would not assert that P unless P; but even so the hearer does not acquire knowledge. The presence of the other unreliable but (on this occasion) accurate newspapers undermines knowledge, for Harman would easily rely on an unreliable newspaper. (The case where Harman would only read Adler's report is a different case.) But take away the surrounding unreliable reports in the other newspapers, and knowledge transmits. The problem is with the local environment.

We now turn to a case somewhat like "Assassination," except that the other "reporters" would say something false:

A Lucky Choice

[I]n Chicago for the first time, Pierre asks the closest passerby ..., Zoe, for directions to the Sears Tower and she reports that it is six blocks east. ... Zoe knows that this is the case, and Pierre has no reason to doubt ... her ... [But] she is the only reliable speaker in this part of Chicago, completely surrounded by incompetents and liars. Because of this, the fact that Pierre chooses a reliable testifier ... is entirely ... good luck.

(From Lackey 2008: 68. See also her structurally similar Case #5 Lackey 2003: 714–715 involving Marvin who travels to a town full of villagers hostile to outsiders and luckily talks to the one villager willing to help outsiders)

In both of Lackey's cases the speaker speaks from her knowledge, would not easily not speak from her knowledge, would not assert that P unless P, but even so the hearer does not acquire knowledge. Remove the surrounding incompetents and hostile villagers and knowledge transmits. Again, the problem is the local environment.

Transmission Failure Due to the Recipient

We now turn to a case from Lackey that purports to isolate the case of transmission failure in the recipient:

Compulsively Trusting

Bill is ... compulsively trusting ... [of] [Sue] ... ... He is incapable of distrusting her when he has very good reason [not to]. ... [W]hen he has ... overwhelming evidence for believing that she is ... deceitful, Bill cannot come to believe this ... . Yesterday ... Bill ran into [Sue], and she told him that she had seen an orca whale ... that day. [Sue] ... did in fact see an orca ... [and] she is very reliable [and] Bill has no reason to doubt [her] testimony. Given his compulsively trusting nature with respect to [Sue], however, even if he had had massive amounts of evidence available to him indicating, for instance, that [she] did not see an orca whale, that she is an unreliable epistemic agent, that she is an unreliable testifier, that orca whales do not live in this part of the country, and so on, Bill would have just as readily accepted [her] testimony.

> (From Lackey 2006: 88–89; Lackey 2008: 66–68. See also Lackey 2003: 711 for a structurally similar case involving someone who would ignore defeating evidence of a sender's testimony because the recipient is so "good-natured")

One might doubt that this case undermines **sufficiency** insofar as proponents of **sufficiency** hold that irrational uptake blocks knowledge transfer. (Proponents don't, after all, generally think knowledge transfers when a recipient's other evidential grounds rationally defeat acceptance.) In this case, though lacking defeaters for the sender's testimony, the recipient is still prone to irrationality when relying on this recipient. So though knowledge does not transfer, that's no objection to the underlying motivation for **sufficiency**.

Counterexamples to Necessity

We now turn to putative counterexamples to **necessity**. In a counterexample to **necessity**, the sender does not know that P, but the recipient comes to know that P nonetheless. Knowledge is thereby generated. We isolate five categories, five types of cases of knowledge generation:

1   Cases where generation is due to a "gap" in belief;
2   Cases where generation is due to defeated belief in sender;
3   Cases where generation results from partial support from the recipient;
4   Cases where generation is due to features of the environment;
5   Cases where generation is due to content inversion.

Generation Due to a "Gap" in Belief

> #### Creationist Teacher
>
> Suppose that a Catholic elementary school requires ... teachers to include ... evolutionary theory in their science classes and to ... conceal their own personal beliefs [on evolution]. Mrs. Smith, a teacher at the school ..., researches [evolution] from reliable sources ... and develops a set of reliable lecture notes ... Mrs. Smith is ... a devout creationist and ... does not believe ... evolutionary theory, but ... none the less follows the requirement to teach [it]. ... [I]n this case it seems reasonable to assume that Mrs. Smith's students can come to have knowledge via her testimony, despite the fact that she [does not believe evolutionary theory] and hence does not [know] it. ... [S]he can give to her students what she does not have ... ... I take it that similar considerations apply in cases where a Kantian teaches utilitarianism, a dualist teaches physicalism, an atheist teaches Christianity, and so on.
> (From Lackey 1999: 477, 2008: 48–53)

Paul Faulkner independently suggested cases like these:

> Suppose a teacher propounds a theory he does not believe. The teacher's rejection of the theory seems to imply that he does not have knowledge of it. However, if the theory is known, then it seems likely that the students could be in a position to acquire this knowledge.
> *(Faulkner 2000: 595)*

For discussion of schoolteacher-type cases, see Audi (2006), Fricker (2006), Graham (2006), Lackey (2008), Kletzl (2011), Burge (2013) and Wright (2016). Graham argues that the case does not undermine **necessity**, for there is knowledge of evolutionary theory in the chain of sources. Knowledge is not generated by the chain, but only skips a link in the chain. This point is also made by Faulkner (2000: 595, 2011: 61, 73). It was also anticipated by Burge (1993).

To get around this obstacle, Graham imagined the following variant:

Fossil

Mr. Jones, a devout creationist, teaches second grade ... [and is] required to [teach evolution]. He [keeps] his personal views to himself. He develops a reliable set of notes ... and even ... a sophisticated understanding of fossils and the fossil record ... . He "accepts" the theory for the purposes of teaching his students, fulfilling his duty to the schoolboard ... [On] a field trip ... he discovers a fossil. [He] rightly deduces that the fossil is of a creature now long extinct, and tells his students that the extinct creature once lived right where they are, millions of years ago. Given his understanding of the theory, and his commitment to teach evolution ..., he would not easily say that the extinct creature lived there millions of years ago ... if it did not. But he does not believe it, in part because he does not believe the earth is a million years old, among other things. The children accept his report, and come to believe that the creatures once lived right where they are, millions of years ago ... [The] children learn (come to know) by accepting Mr. Jones' report.

(From Graham 2000a: 377. This version is from Graham 2006: 112. See also Graham 2016: 176)

In "Fossil," the teacher is the first link in the chain of communication regarding the particular fact in question. If anyone is the first to know the fact, it is the children, for the teacher does not believe it. For some critical discussion, see Burge (2013: 256–258). Burge argues that knowledge is dispersed in the chain—different parts of the chain have different pieces of knowledge. This explains the recipient's knowledge. The point is anticipated by Graham (2006: 111, n. 4): collaborative work in the sciences often involves distributed knowledge.

Other cases followed on the heels of these two. Adam Carter and Philip Nickel worry that "Fossil" is not strong enough, for "Mr. Jones is not a practicing scientist and does not follow valid scientific methods" (2014: 148, n. 9). They propose a new case ("Grant Scholars") involving scientists with world-class training and expertise who are, nonetheless, religiously committed to the denial of a certain finding. Even so, when they make the discovery, they share it with the world, privately suspending judgment (Carter and Nickel 2014: 150–151).

Once you see how a commitment to creationism can create a "gap in belief" where a scientist "accepts" a proposition well-supported by the evidence but does not believe the proposition (so does not know the proposition), "schoolteacher"-type cases are easy. You should also see how "belief-gap" cases might generalize. Here is another example:

Distraught Doctor

A doctor understands that all of the scientific evidence indicates that there is no connection between vaccines and autism. However, after his child was diagnosed with autism shortly after receiving her vaccines, the doctor's grief causes him to abandon his belief that there's no connection between

---

vaccines and autism. When asked by one of his patients, however, about whether or not there's a connection between vaccines and autism, the doctor tells her that there is [no] connection. He does this because he realizes that this is what the evidence best supports and takes himself to have a duty to say whatever the evidence best supports.

(From Lackey 2008: 110–111)

Belief-gap cases are straightforward cases where the speaker has what she needs to know—and so it is no surprise that a hearer can learn from her testimony—but the speaker does not form the required belief, and so the speaker does not have *knowledge* to pass along. For criticism, see Audi (2006). For extended discussion, see Wright (2018, chs. 2 and 7).

Generation Due to Defeated Belief in the Sender

Lackey has offered a number of cases where the speaker would otherwise have knowledge to transmit but for a defeater. In her examples the defeater is a believed undercutting defeater that the relevant belief-forming mechanism is unreliable, or insufficient for knowledge. Rationality would then ordinarily lead to suspension of judgment. But the sender does not suspend judgement (and so believes anyway, on what turns out to be reliable mechanisms, ordinarily sufficient for knowledge) and goes on to assert what she believes. The recipient (ignorant about the sender's irrationality) thereby comes to know what the speaker asserts. But the speaker does not know, for the speaker's warrant or justification for her belief is defeated by the undercutting defeater. Hence the recipient acquires knowledge, even though the sender does not have knowledge to transmit.

Persistent Believer

Millicent in fact possesses her normal visual powers, but she has cogent reasons to believe that these powers are temporarily deranged. She is the subject of a neurosurgeon's experiments, and the surgeon falsely tells her that some implants are causing malfunction in her visual cortex. While she is persuaded that her present visual appearances are an entirely unreliable guide to reality, she continues to place credence in her visual appearances. She ignores her well-supported belief in the incapacitation of her visual faculty; she persists in believing, on the basis of her visual experiences, that a chair is before her, that the neurosurgeon is smiling, and so on. These beliefs are all, in fact, true and they are formed by the usual, quite reliable, perceptual processes. As Millicent is walking out of the neurosurgeon's office, she is the only person to see a badger in Big Bear Field. On the basis of this visual experience, she forms the corresponding true belief that there was a badger in this field, and then later reports this fact to her friend Bradley without communicating the neurosurgeon's testimony to him. Bradley, who has ample reason to trust Millicent from their past interaction as friends, forms the corresponding true belief solely on the basis of her testimony.

(From Lackey 2008: 59, cp. Goldman 1986: 53–54. See her structurally similar case in Lackey 1999: 487, and her 2003: 710)

In cases like these, the speaker has what she needs for knowledge, but for a defeater. She can't pass along what she doesn't have (knowledge), but for all that she has what the hearer needs to come to know.

Generation Due to Partial Support by the Recipient

Both Lackey and Graham imagine cases where a sender does not know that P because there is a relevant alternative possibility in the environment (think of fake barn alternatives that the sender cannot rule out (that is why the sender does not know)). On the other hand, the recipient has background knowledge that the relevant alternative possibility does not obtain. So when the sender truly asserts P on good evidence, the sender does not know because of the relevant alternative possibility that Q, incompatible with P. But the recipient knows that not-Q. Even though the recipient need not bring this background knowledge to consciousness, this background knowledge explains why the recipient learns (comes to know) when the recipient believes the senders' assertion. That's the "partial support." Lackey's example is from Lackey (1999: 487–488). Here is Graham's example:

Judy and Trudy

Judy and Trudy are clumsy twins who work in a library. Almost everyone in the library ... can tell them apart. Susan works in a section of the library with Judy. Though Trudy sometimes works in Susan's section of the library, Susan has not met Trudy, nor does she know or even believe that there is someone named "Trudy" who works in the library ... . If Susan were confronted with Trudy, she would mistake her for Judy. Bill also works in the library ... One afternoon both Judy and Trudy are at work in adjacent sections of the library re-shelving books. Judy is in plain sight of Susan and Trudy is in plain sight of Bill. Judy knocks over a statue in plain sight of Susan. After hearing the crash, Bill calls Susan and asks what happened. Susan tells him that Judy knocked over a statue ... . In the circumstances, Trudy might have very well knocked over the statue if Judy had not [for Trudy just walked past this section for the first time, while re-shelving books herself]. [Susan thus does not know it was Judy ... But from Susan's testimony, Bill knows it was Judy. For he] knows that it was not Trudy. He was looking right at her when he heard the crash [and can easily tell the twins apart].
(From Graham 2000a: 371–372. For some discussion of this case, see Keren 2007: 370–371)

In these kinds of cases, the sender does not have enough to know the target proposition herself, but the hearer's "partial support" makes up for that. So when the hearer relies on the speaker, the hearer has enough to know, even though the speaker doesn't.

Generation Due to Features of the Environment

Sanford Goldberg (2005) concocted a case where a recipient comes to know that P by believing a sender who does not know that P, where the recipient's knowledge is due to support of the recipient's belief by another agent in the environment. Here's the case:

Milk

Frank [has] a strange habit. Every morning at 7:30 ... he ... dumps out whatever [milk is] left [in the fridge], but places the empty [opaque, cardboard] carton back in the fridge ... [He remains in the kitchen until noon], as that is where he [works] [He then throws away] the ... empty ... carton ... [His friend] Mary is unaware of Frank's milk dumping practice. One morning, having spent the prior evening at Frank's house with Frank and her son Sonny, she awakens at 7:40 and goes to the kitchen

---

with Sonny. Upon entering (Frank is already there) she [opens the fridge and] casually observes a small carton of milk. She [tells] Sonny ... there is milk in the fridge. As luck would have it, there is indeed milk in the carton on this day (Frank failed to remember that he had bought milk yesterday). When Frank observes Mary's testimony, he realizes that he forgot to dump the milk; when Sonny observes her testimony, he forms the belief that there is milk in the fridge.

(This is from Goldberg 2005: 302–304)

Goldberg goes on: if there had been no milk, Frank would have spoken up and thereby stopped Sonny from believing milk is in the fridge. Hence, Goldberg argues, Sonny's belief that there is milk in the fridge is both sensitive and safe. So it is intuitive and theoretically plausible that Sonny learns there is milk in the fridge, although Mary doesn't know.

This case involves a number of tricky temporal factors. At the time of her assertion, Mary does not know there is milk in the fridge (very easily there is no milk in the fridge). At the time of first hearing the assertion, Sonny might form a belief that falls short of knowledge. But then at the time Frank would intervene but doesn't (for he recalls there is milk in the fridge), both Mary and Sonny come to know, for Frank's counterfactual intervention makes a difference not only to Sonny, but Mary as well. For extensive discussion of the case, see Lackey (2008: 79–91), Pelling (2013: 210–213) and Wright (2018, ch. 7).

Here's another example emphasizing environmental features:

Territorial Farmer

Farmer Fred is highly territorial. He worries continually that Randy may be trespassing on his land. Fred hears a rustle in the bushes. In his agitated state of mind, he jumps straight to the conclusion that it was Randy who made the rustle. On that basis, Fred shouts "Randy, you're trespassing on my land". Although the rustle might easily have been made by something else (there are many wild animals in the area), it so happens that Randy did make the rustle and he is indeed trespassing on Fred's land. On hearing Fred's words, Randy comes to believe that he is trespassing on Fred's land.

(From Charlie Pelling 2013: 213)

Pelling argues that Fred's belief is not safe (he's easily wrong on his evidence), but Randy's belief is safe, for he would only easily form the belief that he's on Fred's land through testimony when he's on Fred's land. Another case of knowledge generation, but this time due to environmental factors.

These cases are importantly different from the first three kinds cataloged so far. In these cases, the speaker is not in a position to know, for the speaker doesn't have what is required for knowledge, never mind a gap of belief or the possession of a defeater. And it is not obvious that the hearer relies on additional information in his possession.

Generation Due to Content Inversion in the Channel

We now turn to even less prosaic cases that involve two stages of content inversion along the information channel: from the relevant fact to the sender's cognitive system, to the sender's assertion, and then to the recipient's comprehension and uptake. The first stage takes an accurate representation and forms an inaccurate one. The second stage then inverts the inaccurate representation back to an accurate one. Accuracy (reliability) flows through the information channel, just as it does in normal, non-inversion cases. We will present three content inversion cases.

Consistent Liar

Bertha ... suffered a head injury ... and ... became ... prone to telling lies ... about her perceptual experiences involving wild animals. ... [Her] parents became ... distressed and ... took her to ... a neurosurgeon, Dr. Jones. ... Dr. Jones [diagnosed] a lesion in Bertha's brain [as] the cause of her behavior, and [decided upon surgery]. Unfortunately, Dr. Jones discovered during the surgery that he couldn't repair the lesion—instead, he decided to ... create another one so that her pattern of lying would be extremely consistent and would combine in a very precise way with a pattern of consistent perceptual unreliability. Dr. Jones [kept] the procedure that he performed on Bertha completely to himself.

[After the surgery], nearly every time [Bertha] sees a deer, she believes ... it is a horse; nearly every time she sees a giraffe, she believes that it is an elephant; nearly every time she sees an owl, she believes that it is a hawk, and so on. At the same time, however, Bertha is also [a] radically insincere, yet highly consistent, testifier of this information. For instance, nearly every time she sees a deer and believes that it is a horse, she insincerely reports to others that she saw a deer; nearly every time she sees a giraffe and believes that it is an elephant, she insincerely reports to others that she saw a giraffe, and so on. ... Yesterday, Bertha ... insincerely though correctly [told Henry] that she saw a deer ... nearby ... . Henry ... accepted her testimony.

(From Lackey 2006: 82–83. See also Lackey 2008: 53–58. It is structurally similar to an earlier case from Lackey involving color inversion and pathological lying Lackey 1999: 480–481)

In Lackey's inversion cases the speaker does not believe P but reliably asserts that P. It's the reliability of the assertion, Lackey argues, that explains why the recipient, in coming to believe that P, acquires testimonial knowledge through believing the speaker. Graham offers two kinds of inversion cases. Here is the first:

Inverted Alan

Alan lives in Malibu Beach, California. Eddie is a good friend from college who lives in Chicago. Eddie regularly calls Alan on weekends and asks about the weather. "Blue skies for miles" Alan reports. But Alan is not an ordinary perceiver and reporter. Alan's color experience, color concepts, and color words are inverted. When he looks out the window from his Malibu Beach apartment, the sky looks yellow to him and he believes it is yellow. But when he reports the color, he says it is "blue" (meaning, and so asserting, that it is yellow). Alan has no idea that he's any different from anyone else. Alan does not know the skies are blue (he believes they are yellow). He does not mean that they are blue (he means they are yellow), and so does not state (assert) that they are blue. Eddie relies on (his representation of) Alan's assertion, and so comes to believe that the sky in Malibu is blue. Though Alan does not know that the skies are blue, they are, and Eddie would not take him to state they are blue unless they are.

(From Graham 2016: 180. See also Graham 2000a: 379–381)

In "Consistent Liar" the speaker asserts P and the hearer rightly takes the speaker to have asserted that P, and thereby comes to believe that P. In "Inverted Alan," the sender does not assert that P and the hearer wrongly takes the speaker to have asserted that P, but nevertheless comes to believe that P, exactly as if the speaker had asserted that P. So believing, Graham argues, the hearer even so comes to know that P. The hearer is in exactly the same position vis-à-vis relying on a reliable channel as if everything were as ordinary as could be. But since the speaker does not know (for he does not believe) that the skies are blue, but the hearer comes to know that they are, knowledge is generated through the communication channel.

In "Consistent Liar" the canceled-out inversion occurs within the mind of the sender; a false belief is canceled out by a lie. In "Inverted Alan," there is inversion within the mind of the sender that is canceled out by the inversion at the stage of the utterance. Graham's (2016: 179–180) second case is modeled on "Consistent Liar" where there is inversion in the sender that is then canceled out by inversion in the recipient. We can call his case "Consistent Miscomprehension." You should be able to easily imagine how it would go.

Some Critical Reactions

Having categorized and cataloged a number of the putative counterexamples to the commonsense view that testimonial knowledge is transmitted knowledge, we now conclude with a brief summary of some of the better-known responses to these cases.

There has been little explicit discussion of the counterexamples to **sufficiency**. Perhaps that is not so surprising, as there are a number of things that might go wrong in the transfer from sender to receiver. But if the counterexamples go through, the falsity of **sufficiency** suggests the possible falsity of **necessity**. For if something *more* than the speaker's knowledge is required for the recipient to come to know, then perhaps that something more *supplants* the need for the speaker to have knowledge in the first place. In other words, perhaps something *other* than the speaker's knowledge explains testimonial knowledge. So if one's critical reaction to the putative counterexamples to **necessity** is to deny them, one might also need to deny the putative counterexamples to **sufficiency**.

We now turn to critical responses to the counterexamples to **necessity**. Here we find that there has been a good deal of discussion of these cases.

We begin with a critical reaction to those counterexamples that, though once common, now seems to have fallen out of favor. This reaction is to deny all of the counterexamples on the grounds that the orthodox view already allows for cases where a hearer observes an assertion that P, comes to know that P as a result, but the speaker did not know that P. These are cases where the hearer has sufficient background knowledge to reason as follows: S asserted that P; S's assertions are reliable guides to reality; hence P. In these cases, the hearer's background knowledge does not refer to the speaker's knowledge. Here the hearer has correlated the speaker's assertions with reality, like the way one might learn to correlate an animal's behavior with a pending change in the weather. And so here the hearer simply treats the speaker's assertion as a reliable sign of the reality it represents. In these cases, it clearly does not matter whether the speaker knows that P. In these cases, the hearer need not believe, or even be disposed to believe, that the speaker knows that P. In fact, the hearer may even believe that the speaker does not know that P. Just as long as the speaker's reports correlate with reality, and the hearer has figured that out, the hearer can come to know something from a speaker's report, regardless of the speaker's state of mind when making that report. The counterexamples, then, are not really counterexamples. In those cases, the hearer isn't really relying on the *speaker* for knowledge. Rather the hearer is just treating the speaker's assertion as a *reliable sign*. The counterexamples are then not cases of testimonial knowledge, knowledge where we rely on another person for knowledge. For this reply, see Audi (2006), Fricker (2006) and Wright (2018). This reply was anticipated in Graham (2000a, 2000b).

Those offering the counterexamples reply as follows (e.g. Graham 2000a: 372–373, 2006: 114–115, 2016: 77–178, Lackey 2008). Sure, there are cases where a hearer does not rely on the speaker, but only *makes use* of the speaker's report as one might make use of an animal's behavior to predict the weather. But both sides agree that there are cases where the hearer lacks such background beliefs and the hearer indeed relies on the speaker—when the hearer takes the speaker's assertion at face value, and relies on the information channel, not on background beliefs about the channel. Those offering the counterexamples argue that in the cases they imagined, the hearer indeed relies on the speaker. Consider a case where the hearer relies on the speaker, and the speaker believes and knows what she is asserting. Then imagine a psychological duplicate of that hearer. The duplicate is then also relying on the speaker. But change the speaker. The speaker, for example, might be Mr. Jones as in "Fossil." Changing the psychology of the speaker does not ipso facto change the psychology of the hearer. The first reaction is thereby blocked. The cases really are cases of testimonial knowledge, of knowledge through reliance on the speaker, not on background knowledge about the channel.

The second critical reaction goes as follows. Sure, the putative counterexamples to **necessity** are cases where the hearer relies on the speaker and not on background knowledge about the channel. And yes, in some of the cases, knowledge is generated. But even so they are not cases of *testimonial* knowledge, for the phrase "testimonial knowledge" just means knowledge from someone else's knowledge, knowledge that is transmitted through testimony. So if the hearer learns (comes to know), but the speaker did not have knowledge to transmit, then as far as the meaning of the phrase "testimonial knowledge" goes, the hearer's knowledge is *not* testimonial knowledge. Maybe it is knowledge *through* testimony (knowledge *through reliance* on the channel and not through background knowledge about the channel), but for all that it is not *testimonial knowledge*. Semantics immunizes **necessity** to counterexample.

Some readers will find this reply compelling. Some will find it uninteresting. Lackey (2008: 101–102) provides an interesting response: Why not group so-called *testimonial knowledge* and *knowledge from testimony* into the same epistemological category? If we can provide a unified account of both kinds, then all else being equal, we should treat them as just one epistemological kind.

A third critical response has been to deny the counterexamples on theoretical grounds. Fricker (2006) and Faulkner (2011) argue that since the "no false lemmas" theory of knowledge is correct, and since to rely on a speaker to believe P when the speaker asserts that P entails believing that the speaker knows that P, it follows that the recipient cannot acquire knowledge if the speaker does not know that P. The recipient falsely believes the sender knows that P, and this robs the recipient of knowledge that P.

One reply is to deny the no false lemmas theory. After all, it has its problems. Furthermore, it currently does not count as a leading proposal in the debate about the analysis of knowledge. Second, there seem to be clear cases where one can come to know through believing a falsehood (Warfield 2005, Klein 2008, cp. Graham 2000a: 390–391). There is clear evidence against the theory.

A fourth critical response was already hinted at. This response grants the counterexamples, but aims to restrict their force, as they do not show that the spirit behind **necessity** is mistaken. One need only weaken the principle while retaining the core insight that it is knowledge, or the materials required for knowledge, in the chain of sources, which explains why recipients acquire knowledge through reliance on that chain.

One version of this idea says that the hearer can acquire testimonial knowledge that P only if the speaker is in a position to know that P. Surely the various teachers in the belief-gap cases are in a position to know that P (they have all the warrants and evidence they need to know). And surely someone who already knows is in a position to know.

Another version of this idea says that the hearer can acquire propositional knowledge that P only if the speaker has propositional justification for the belief that P (even if the speaker does not believe P or does not believe P on that basis). In all the belief-gap cases, for example, it does clearly seem that the speaker has propositional (even if not doxastic) justification for the belief that P. Stephen Wright (2016, 2018), for one, argues for this analysis of these cases. Wright argues that if the sender has a propositional justification to believe P, and asserts on the basis of that justification, then that justification transfers to the recipient. The recipient knows because the sender has knowledge supporting justification for believing that P, even if the sender does not know that P. And for Wright, justification transmission is the main issue, for he sees it as more fundamental than knowledge transmission.

A third version of this idea says that the hearer can acquire testimonial knowledge that P only if knowledge supporting P (perhaps of other propositions that support P) is in the chain of sources, where the supporting knowledge might be distributed across the chain of sources. In "Fossil," for example, others know what fossils show. Mr. Jones can "read" the fossil because of that knowledge, and so knows what evolutionary theory would say about the fossil. All of that knowledge combined supports the knowledge that the children acquire. The children learn that P because sufficient supporting knowledge of other propositions exists in the chain. Tyler Burge (2013) suggests this reply in his discussion of "Fossil." It should also be obvious that all three versions of this idea would say similar things about the partial support cases, and maybe even the defeated speaker's belief cases.

A possible shortcoming of this approach is that it does not easily cover all the cases, especially the environmental case "Territorial Farmer" and the inversion case "Inverted Alan." The "Consistent Liar" and "Consistent Miscomprehension" cases provide challenges as well. Wright (2016) is aware of this issue.

One critical response we haven't mentioned to "Inverted Alan" and "Consistent Miscomprehension" argues that these are not cases of testimonial knowledge that P because in these cases the speaker does not testify (does not assert) that P. Testimonial knowledge that P, this reply asserts, is knowledge that P from *testimony* that P. Since the senders in these cases did not *testify* that P, the recipient's knowledge that P cannot be *testimonial* knowledge that P. Again, semantics to the rescue.

Graham is aware of this issue (2000a: 380, 2015, 2016: 181–182). One may categorize testimonial knowledge this way, if one chooses. But if psychologically the recipient in these cases is no different from a "normal" case where the sender did assert P, why insist that there are two different epistemological kinds? Compare: color perception, shape perception, and auditory perception are all different kinds. But they all fall within the same epistemological category: perceptual knowledge. If the recipient in "Inverted Alan" is psychologically identical to another recipient talking to a "normal" sender about the weather, and both know for both receive what they need for knowledge, why not categorize them as both possessing the same type of knowledge? Paraphrasing Lackey (2008: 102), why not prefer a *unified* account?

Lackey and Graham reacted differently to the counterexamples to **sufficiency** and **necessity**. Independently, they both took them to show that what matters for testimonial knowledge is not the sender's knowledge (or position to know, or propositional justification), but rather the reliability of the information channel. Lackey focused on the reliability of the speaker's statement (viz. assertion) that P (1999, 2006, 2008) and Graham (2000a, 2000b, 2006, 2016) focused on the reliability of the hearer's state (or event) of comprehending the speaker's assertion. Lackey shifted focus from the speaker's state of belief and whether it measured up to knowledge to the speaker's assertion and whether it provided the goods required for the hearer's knowledge.

Graham shifted the focus further, from the speaker's assertion to the hearer's representation of the speaker's assertion, and whether it provided the goods required for the hearer's knowledge. Lackey (2008) labels the traditional view the "Belief View of Testimony" and calls her view the "Statement View of Testimony." Following her nomenclature, we might call Graham's view the "Comprehension View of Testimony." Despite her appeal to unity when defending her Statement View, Lackey would reject Graham's view, which classifies "Inverted Alan," "Consistent Miscomprehension" and "Consistent Liar" together as all cases of the same epistemic kind. For Lackey, the speakers in "Inverted Alan" and "Consistent Miscomprehension" do not *testify* that P, so the hearer's knowledge that P is not *testimonial* knowledge that P.

Elizabeth Fricker is perhaps the best-known defender of the orthodox view. Not only has she argued that the speaker must know for the recipient to know (compare also Faulkner), she has offered cases of her own designed to establish that the reliability of the speaker's assertion, when not backed by knowledge, isn't enough for the recipient to come to know. She has set out, in other words, to turn the tables on analyses like Lackey's and Graham's (Fricker 2015, 2016). We invite the interested reader to follow up on her cases on their own.

Acknowledgement

We are grateful to Stephen Wright for very helpful comments on the penultimate draft.

References

Adler, Jonathan (1996) "Transmitting Knowledge" *Nous* 30: 99–111.
Audi, Robert (1997) "The Place of Testimony in the Fabric of Knowledge and Justification" *American Philosophical Quarterly* 34: 405–422.
Audi, Robert (2006) "Testimony, Credulity, and Veracity" in J. Lackey & E. Sosa (eds.) *The Epistemology of Testimony* (Oxford: Oxford University Press): 25–49.
Burge, Tyler (1993) "Content Preservation" *The Philosophical Review* 102: 457–488.
Burge, Tyler (2013) "Postscript: Content Preservation" in his *Cognition through Understanding* (Oxford: Oxford University Press): 254–284.
Carter, J. Adam & Philip Nickel (2014) "On Testimony and Transmission" *Episteme* 11: 145–155.
Coady, C.A.J. (1992) *Testimony: A Philosophical Study* (Oxford: Clarendon Press).
Dretske, Fred (1982) "A Cognitive Cul-de-sac" *Mind* 91(361): 109–111.
Dummett, Michael (1994) "Testimony and Memory" in B.K. Matilal & A. Chakrabarti (eds.) *Knowing from Words* (Dordrecht: Kluwer Academic): 251–272.
Evans, Gareth (1982) *The Varieties of Reference* (Oxford: Oxford University Press).
Faulkner, Paul (2000) "On the Social Character of Testimonial Knowledge" *Journal of Philosophy* 97: 581–601.
Faulkner, Paul (2011) *Knowledge on Trust* (Oxford: Oxford University Press).
Fricker, Elizabeth (1987) "The Epistemology of Testimony" *Proceedings of the Aristotelian Society* 61: 57–84.
Fricker, Elizabeth (2006) "Second Hand Knowledge" *Philosophy and Phenomenological Research* 73: 592–618.
Fricker, Elizabeth (2015) "How to Make Invidious Distinctions Amongst Reliable Testifiers" *Episteme* 12: 173–202.
Fricker, Elizabeth (2016) "Unreliable Testimony" in B. McLaughlin & H. Kornblith (eds.) *Goldman and His Critics* (Chichester, UK: Wiley Blackwell): 88–124.
Goldberg, Sanford (2005) "Testimonial Knowledge through Unsafe Testimony" *Analysis* 65: 302–311.
Goldman, Alvin (1986) *Epistemology and Cognition* (Cambridge, MA: Harvard University Press).
Graham, Peter J. (2000a) "Conveying Information" *Synthese* 123: 365–392.
Graham, Peter J. (2000b) "Transferring Knowledge" *Nous* 34: 131–152.
Graham, Peter J. (2006) "Can Testimony Generate Knowledge?" *Philosophica* 78: 105–127.
Graham, Peter J. (2015) "Testimony as Speech Act, Testimony as Source" in M. Mi, M. Slote & E. Sosa (eds.) *Moral and Intellectual Virtues in Western and Chinese Philosophy: The Turn toward Virtue* (New York: Routledge): 121–144.
Graham, Peter J. (2016) "Testimonial Knowledge: A Unified Account" *Philosophical Issues* 26: 172–186.
Harman, Gilbert (1973) *Thought* (Princeton, NJ: Princeton University Press).

Keren, Arnon (2007) "On the Alleged Perversity of the Evidential View of Testimony" *Analysis* 72: 700–707.

Klein, Peter (2008) "Useful Falsehoods" in Q. Smith (ed.) *Epistemology: New Essays* (Oxford: Oxford University Press): 25–62.

Kletzl, Sebastian (2011) "Somebody Has to Know: Jennifer Lackey on the Transmission of Epistemic Properties" in C. Jaeger & W. Loeffler (eds.), *Epistemology: Contexts, Values, Disagreement. Contributions of the 34th International Wittgenstein Symposium*: 140–141.

Lackey, Jennifer (1999) "Testimonial Knowledge and Transmission" *The Philosophical Quarterly* 49: 471–490.

Lackey, Jennifer (2003) "A Minimal Expression of Non-Reductionism in the Epistemology of Testimony" *Nous* 37: 706–723.

Lackey, Jennifer (2006) "Learning from Words" *Philosophy and Phenomenological Research* 73: 77–101.

Lackey, Jennifer (2008) *Learning from Words: Testimony as a Source of Knowledge* (Oxford: Oxford University Press).

Lycan, William (1977) "Evidence One Does Not Possess" *Australasian Journal of Philosophy* 55: 114–126.

McDowell, John (1994) "Knowledge by Hearsay" in B.K. Matilal & A. Chakrabarti (eds.) *Knowing from Words* (Dordrecht: Kluwer Academic): 195–224.

Nozick, Robert (1981) *Philosophical Explanations* (Cambridge, MA: Harvard University Press).

Peacocke, Christopher (1986) *Thoughts: An Essay on Content* (Oxford: Basil Blackwell).

Pelling, Charlie (2013) "Testimony, Testimonial Belief, and Safety" *Philosophical Studies* 164: 205–217.

Ross, Angus (1986) "Why Do We Believe What We Are Told?" *Ratio* 38: 69–88.

Warfield, Ted (2005) "Knowledge from Falsehoods" *Philosophical Perspectives* 19: 405–416.

Welbourne, Michael (1983) "A Cognitive Thoroughfare" *Mind* 92: 410–412.

Welbourne, Michael (1994) "Testimony, Knowledge, and Belief" in B.K. Matilal & A. Chakrabarti (eds.) *Knowing from Words* (Dordrecht: Kluwer Academic): 297–314.

Williamson, Timothy (1996) "Knowing and Assertion" *The Philosophical Review* 105: 489–523.

Wright, Stephen (2016) "The Transmission of Knowledge and Justification" *Synthese* 193: 293–311.

Wright, Stephen (2018) *Knowledge Transmission* (London: Routledge).

8

TRUST AND REPUTATION AS FILTERING MECHANISMS OF KNOWLEDGE

Gloria Origgi

Introduction: The Social Sciences Strike Back

After many decades of triumphant individualistic approaches to human behavior, cognition and reasoning, over the last twenty years we have witnessed a rise of *social approaches* to our epistemic practices: social cognition, collective intelligence, social networks and social neuroscience. *Social epistemology* falls squarely among these new approaches. Social epistemology is the study of the influence of social mechanisms and social institutions in the production, diffusion and legitimization of knowledge. These are all new fields tackling the social dimension of our cognitive life.

The social sciences thrived through most of the 20th century. We saw the founding of anthropology, sociology, social anthropology, and the growing influence of structuralist approaches to human thought.[1] A period of skepticism towards social explanations of human behavior, however, soon emerged. For rational choice-based individualism and *homo economicus* took on a hegemonic status in the behavioral sciences. This skepticism coincided with the rise of cognitive science in the 1980s and 1990s and the computational model of the mind. But this skepticism is residing, as the social sciences are now striking back.

Epistemology has been deeply transformed by this comeback of the social sciences and today *social epistemology* is one of the most lively fields of research in philosophy of knowledge, which encompasses a variety of perspectives and traditions, from formal epistemology to critical theory, in order to understand how society filters, biases, distorts and (sometimes) improve our epistemic capacities.

This new "social turn" is due to many factors:

1 A number of major technological transformations of the information society that the rise of the Internet and the World Wide Web provoked, like new algorithms to "evaluate" information and new techniques of collective construction of knowledge.

2 A more specific deep change in the production and transmission of *science*, that is, that portion of knowledge that is considered as a common good of a society and whose reliability is legitimated through specific procedures. Today, what we may call the "industrialization" of knowledge production, based on the competitive model of cumulating *peer-reviewed* publications and on a system of incentives that is geared toward productivity and "prestige", has deeply changed the perception of science as a disinterested activity by provoking the "crisis of trust" in science so typical of our times.[2]

3   The massive use of social networks and other web-based systems for the circulation of various kinds of information, which provoked a revolution in the traditional filtering mechanisms of knowledge and a claim for a sort of "epistemic anarchism" in which all opinions are equivalent.[3]

4   A bundle of hopes and fears around the possibility of *collective knowledge*, that is, of having better epistemic results *collectively* than *individualistically*, fostered by results in collective knowledge production systems that suggested that the wisdom of the many could overcome experts' knowledge in many domains.[4]

All these factors have contributed to a general rethinking of the filtering mechanisms of knowledge and the role that both our cognitive processes and the social systems in which our cognition is embedded play in our epistemic life.

In this chapter, I would like to focus on two main filtering mechanisms: *trust*[5] and *reputation*.[6]

Coming from the *toolbox* of social sciences, trust and reputation have become major tools for navigating knowledge in *information-dense societies* such as our late modern societies. Who trusts what, who is expert on what, what other people whom I esteem believe about this and that, all these have become constitutive aspects of our knowledge forming processes. Paradoxically, in a society in which information becomes more and more accessible and grows exponentially, the weight of trust in other people's reputations becomes an essential ingredient of our epistemic practices. From the lay man who wants to get a well-founded opinion about climate change, to the scientist who needs to trust her colleague's data sets to conduct her own experiment, we are all epistemically dependent on each other.

In what follows, I will sketch an approach to trust and reputation as constitutive elements of our coming to know. I will argue that these two notions are to be integrated into a broader epistemological analysis on how we come to believe and how we justify our knowledge. Knowledge is a complex social practice that involves cognitive abilities, communicative skills and social roles. As Steven Shapin points out: "Knowledge is a common good". The cognitive order of a society, that is, its way of producing, transmitting and legitimatizing knowledge, is intimately related to its social order, that is, how a society is organized and which trust relations are assured among its members.[7]

How Do We Trust?

Much of the recent literature on the epistemology of trust relates the issue of trust to that of *testimonial knowledge*. "Trust enables knowledge via testimony" write Paul Faulkner and Thomas Simpson in a recent introduction to the *Philosophy of Trust*.[8] It is a blatant truth that our cognitive life is a permanent immersion in other people's beliefs and points of views: most of what we come to know is based on the words of others. The *epistemology of testimony* asks on what conditions we are justified in acquiring information from others. There are various attempts in past and present philosophy to justify our reliance on others, a feature of our cognitive life that *prima facie* contradicts the intellectual autonomy that is required for acquiring justified beliefs. Reductionist,[9] say, Humean approaches, reduce the assessment of the reliability of testimonial reports to that of any other kind of evidence, that is, an inductive inference on the probability of its truth. Antireductionist approaches see trust in testimony as a basic channel for acquiring information, not reducible to more fundamental mechanisms such as perception or inference, and ground it in some innate psychological bias (as a *principle of credulity* invoked by Thomas Reid, that would dispose us to believe what other people say, and that is optimistically coupled by Reid with a *principle of veracity*, that is, a disposition to speak the truth) or structural properties of language. Antireductionism has been reintroduced in the contemporary philosophical debate by the philosopher Antony Coady, who, in his 1992 book, *Testimony*, argued that testimony is nowadays too fundamental a source of knowledge acquisition to be relegated to a secondary mechanism: we must have some *a priori* warrant to believe what other people say that depends on how language is structured. Yet, as Paul Faulkner and other authors[10] have rightly pointed out, trust is much more than just believing in testimony: it is a complex affective attitude that implies a degree of cognitive vulnerability and creates normative commitments in our informants. Trust is more than just coming to believe: it is a two-sided relation based on reciprocal commitments, personal attachments and cognitive dependences. So how do we trust? Why? Is it possible to pry apart situations in which our trust is justified from those in which our trust is irrational?

In the following, I shall distinguish different mechanisms, both social and cognitive, that are at the basis of our trust in others[11] and then try to illustrate how they can be adjusted in communicative settings to maximize our acquisition of knowledge from others. But let me detail this list of mechanisms:

1   Inferences regarding the reliability of the speaker
2   Inferences regarding the reliability of the informational content
3   Internalized social norms of deference to authority
4   Socially distributed reputational cues
5   Robust signals
6   Emotional reactions
7   Moral commitments

These mechanisms are not sealed off from each other: it is impossible to distinguish them completely one from the other. They often overlap and combine within the heuristics that we use to navigate the social world. In the same way, although it is not possible to distinguish clearly mechanisms that are "reliable" from those that are not, there are ecological conditions for the success of each of these mechanisms that have to do with the *pragmatic* dimension of epistemic trust. Trust as an epistemic relation always implies a communicative context in which these heuristics are employed by following a number of pragmatic rules. But let's present first the different mechanisms.

Inferences about the Reliability of the Speaker

Amongst the heuristics we commonly use to trust someone, there are the numerous inferences and fleeting perceptions regarding the reliability of the speaker. Some signs of reliability are contextual: for instance, the *best epistemic position* of a speaker in a given context. I call my sister in Milan to know the weather there. It isn't that she is an expert in meteorology, but the simple fact that she lives in Milan confers on her an epistemic superiority over me about the matter, since I live in Paris and have no direct access to the temperature in Milan. Of course I could look it up on the Web, and the fact that I trust my sister more than a weather website could be based on the prejudices and biases that tend to influence my thinking. I can follow the events in Syria through the tweets of a local informer, a blogger whose name I know and who seems to me to be well informed. Again, I may be wrong. My sister could simply look out of the window and tell me that it is good weather because she saw a sunbeam, whereas if I had gone online I would have found much more detailed information about the storm predicted for the late afternoon. The Syrian blogger could reveal himself to be biased and select information that supports his faction.

Nevertheless, however mistaken I may be, these trust strategies are part of my thinking; they guide, at least at first glance, my relation to information and they bear upon the trust I have in my interlocutors.

Trust evidently depends also on the information we already have regarding our interlocutors. *Prejudices*, for instance, are a kind of information that is *a priori* concentrated into social stereotypes. We could not be rational without managing the social information around us and classifying it into a series of "mental files". The process of categorizing essentially consists in generalizing specific cases, classifying them according to their being *types* or *kinds*. The problem of stereotypes is that the categories of social types into which we classify information are usually tendentious, contingent, and influenced by local cultures and traditions.

Sometimes, to evaluate the reliability of a speaker, we need to attribute *expertise* to him or her. The evaluation of the expertise of others, albeit with all its tendencies and biases, is always present within our epistemic practices: it creates expectations regarding the credibility of the speaker that inflect how we interpret what we are being told.

Inferences about the Content of Information

What people say and how they say it tells us something about their credibility. Trust has a very rich pragmatic dimension, one that hasn't been much studied: why do we trust a potential tenant on Airbnb and not another one? Or a comment on TripAdvisor? Sometimes it seems that we trust "in the dark", on the basis of a simple exchange of messages or of a writing style that reassures us. The content and form of the message certainly play a role in determining our trust in it. In the case of Twitter, one of the social networks where the reliability of information counts most, the quality of the tweet in terms of linguistic coherence and structure influences its circulation. The *argumentative theory of reasoning*, recently developed by the cognitive scientists Hugo Mercier and Dan Sperber,[12] maintains that the logical structure of arguments is an indicator of their reliability. On this, the content of a message is not only evaluated according to the factual sources at our disposal: its credibility is also evaluated according to its structure and coherence. An argument that is logically coherent has a higher probability of being judged as true than one that is badly constructed. Of course, in this case too one is exposed to the risk of a tendentious selection of information. For instance, information that confirms what we already know or that is similar to our way of expressing ourselves is accepted more easily: in this way, it suffices that our potential tenant on Airbnb be clever enough to understand what is the "right" tone to use with us to be trusted more than someone who doesn't say anything wrong but whose mode of expression and argument is too distant from our own.

Social Norms of Deference to Authority

But in how we choose to trust, what is most fundamental, profound, and hard to control is deference – often implicit and unconscious – to norms we have internalized over the course of our life: a series of "acts of faith" that surreptitiously condition our beliefs, making it difficult for us to question some forms of "epistemic loyalties". The life of the mind is inhabited by a great number of thoughts and beliefs that we only partly understand. However, they structure our common sense, and we are loath to dispute them. Most often, these are beliefs that we have adopted at a time of our lives when deference to others was the best way to learn something, that is, our childhood; or within a relationship with authority that we aren't able to question, unless we find ourselves excluded from the group we belong to or would like to belong to.

In a book about reliability and truth, the historian of science Steven Shapin tells of his first experiences as a researcher in a genetics laboratory. He was entrusted with confirming the following scientific statement: "DNA contains cytosine".[13]

> Here is what I did: I was given some pieces of rat liver which I then minced and froze in liquid nitrogen; I ground the frozen tissue and suspended it in digestion buffer; I incubated the sample at 50°C for 16 hours in a tightly capped tube; [many other operations follow] I went on to hydrolize the sample and to perform a chemical test confirming the presence of nucleotide cytosine. This was DNA: I had it in my hand; I had verified the facts of its composition.
>
> *(Shapin 1994, p. 18)*

Although this is a scientific experiment, the direct nature of the knowledge obtained is arguable. The entirety of the information at Shapin's disposal to realize this experiment and the correlation between the result and the truth of the statement in question are based on acts of trust with respect to the validity of laboratory practices, of the experts/leaders/teachers who have transmitted this knowledge and on the colleagues who provide the materials necessary for the experiment. The *validity* of the scientific statement in question could not be established independently of the networks of trust that guarantee its emission. It is interesting to note that the Latin root of the word *validity* means power (*validus* means strong, potent, someone who has authority). One cannot learn how to navigate a field of knowledge without deferring to others, to practices, teachers, common sense, in short to everything that structures the epistemic landscape of that field. Common sense is nothing but that feeling of legitimacy in putting our trust in a discourse that has authority in our eyes. It contains within itself beliefs that have a special authority: the untouchable authority of tradition.

Socially Distributed Reputational Cues

A social setting in which we learn something new is one in which we can establish a well-made association between a number of ideas that are new to us and the social configuration of epistemic authority that we have been able to map out thanks to a variety of cues.

Reputational cues, to which I will come back later in this chapter, make up the social information present in the environment. Social information can be picked up in an informal way, or it can be highly organized and structured to be easily legible. We will see in the section of this chapter dedicated to reputation how these differences matter for epistemology.

Robust Signals

The reputational signs I have described above are signals: they show the presence or absence in an individual, idea or object of a certain quality, proper to them and not directly observable. The problem is that signals are often indirect, filtered by the gazes of others, deformed by speech: it is the authorities we give our trust to who turn these signals into something more robust. A signal thus has a two-fold problem: how can one trust an authority to send us back a reliable reading of the signals emitted by the individual, objects or ideas we are evaluating? What are the robust signals, and which the weaker ones? How reliable is a classification, a comment on TripAdvisor, a disparaging gaze upon a dress or a bottle of wine? According to *Signaling Theory*,[14] robust signals are those that are harder to fake. An algorithm on the Web that classifies the best car dealing websites is more reliable than a list drawn up by a group of experts, because the results of the algorithm are harder to falsify. We are keen to trust robust signals although sometimes we may be fooled about their robustness because our experience of their robustness is indirect.

Emotional Reactions and Moral Commitments

Our "sense of others" is constructed through a mix of rationality and emotion. A leap in the dark that commits us for life in the absence of crucial information about the other is sometimes easier to make than a step that is well thought through. Trust can precede risk calculation. The feeling of security that accompanies this kind of "motivational" trust depends on the suspension of doubt and of suspicion regarding the intentions of the other, a sort of emotional solace one could describe in these terms: "I don't know anything about you but I feel safe, with you I feel calm". One could define the emotional dimension of our trust as an *optimistic* attitude regarding the kindness and competence of others.

The psychological disposition to trust the other can be determined by emotional, non-reasoned reactions. Well-known experiments by Janine Willis and Alexander Todorov show that we evaluate the reliability of others on the basis of extremely fleeting judgments in turn based on the assessment of facial expressions. These judgments are at once quick and lasting: acquiring more information about the persons in question won't affect our initial judgment.[15] Trust can thus be immediately established out of a first impression. The heuristics that are solicited in this case are perceptual and based on a series of implicit biases that lead us to connect certain emotional reactions to certain facial features. Of course, nothing assures us in this case that the person in question will indeed be kind to us. This poses the problem, in more general terms, of the moral commitments that arise out of relations of trust. We sometimes feel obliged to trust certain people. And obversely, we feel that those we have trusted are constrained to have moral obligations to us.

Virginia Woolf talked of *unreal loyalties* that ruin our existence and drive us to make bad choices. We think we owe something to someone, we care about what our mother or boss believes is right for us, we feel guilty when our judgment grows apart from that of our reference group. But there is no necessary link between our emotional commitment within a relation of trust and the moral/epistemological implications of that relation. It is true that our trust is often based on emotions and commitments that we are not capable of putting in question very easily, but this does not always legitimate normative expectations on our part in exchange for our acts of trust.

All these heuristics play some role in our trust relations and, I argue, also in the thick relational exchanges that characterize our epistemic relations. Each time we trust others in order to come to believe something, we undergo a series of inferential steps that calibrate our trust along our interpretation of what is said to us and end up in a reasonable pairing of a level of trust with a certain plausible interpretation. It is within the communicative dimension of acquiring beliefs from others that our heuristics of trust are calibrated. I call this dynamics of adjusting trust and interpretation a *pragmatics of trust*.[16]

The Pragmatics of Trust

It is within the rich inferential process of communication that we come to believe what other people say. Our almost permanent immersion in talks and direct or indirect conversations is the major source of cognitive vulnerability to other people's beliefs and reports, even when the exchange is not particularly focused on knowledge acquisition.[17] Communication is a voluntary act. Each time we speak we are intentionally seeking the attention of our interlocutors and thus presenting what we have to say as potentially relevant for them.[18] Each time we listen, we intentionally engage in an interpretation of what has been said, and expand our cognitive effort to make sense of what our interlocutor had in mind. It is remarkable how effortless and natural this process is: we don't seem to make a series of heavy assumptions on the rationality of speakers, their commitments to shared norms of truth etc., rather we infer what they say in the context of our own thoughts and sometimes we gain new insights about reality and may update or revise our beliefs. We search for relevant information rather than for truths: that is a general trait of our cognitive life. Communication is a special cognitive activity in which the search of relevant information is guided by our interlocutor. The simple fact that someone intentionally tries to attract our attention elicits a presumption of trust in the relevance of what she or he says.

So, to adopt a stance of trust in our interlocutors means to accept a degree of cognitive vulnerability to share with them a great number of assumptions, representations and hypotheses that are elicited "for the sake of the conversation". We do not trust our interlocutors to provide us with knowledge. This seems an unrealistic epistemic aim and implies a too restrictive view of linguistic communication as a matter of information transfer. We happen to acquire knowledge through communication by reworking what we're being told in the context of our own thoughts and epistemic objectives, as in the example I have discussed above. Appropriateness and credibility vary from one context of communication to another, and may shift within the same conversational setting. The heuristics I have detailed above enter at this point: to calibrate the plausibility of the hypotheses that we are sharing with our interlocutors for the sake of the conversation, and come to believe some of them. We need to pry apart the assumptions that we share in a contingent social situation of information exchange from the information actually transferred from the sender and believed by the receiver.

We trust other people to provide us with relevant information, and adjust our epistemic requirements according to the context in which the interpretation takes place. We exercise our *epistemic vigilance* during our interpretation by adopting a stance of trust that our interlocutors will provide relevant information for us.[19] This stance of trust is guided by imperfect heuristics, but given that the main aim of our epistemic effort is to extract relevant information, the use of these heuristics is optimized. Any departure from the satisfaction of our expectations of relevance may result in a revision or a withdrawal of our default trust.

Let us turn now to the second mechanism of social filtering of information which I have already mentioned in describing some of the trust heuristics above, that is, *reputation*.

Reputation as an Epistemic Tool

People do not share information. They share evaluated and classified information that creates a "reputational stream" of shared judgments. The epistemological implications of the massive use of shared ratings in networked societies are significant. Relying on other people's judgments and authority has become a customary epistemological practice in our information-dense societies. Each social interaction leaves an informational track, a pattern of reciprocal judgments, an evaluated image of ourselves in the eyes of others. This evaluative dimension of social interaction, this generation of opinions on each other is what I call here reputation.

Reputation serves the cognitive purpose of making us navigate among things and people whose value is opaque for us because we do not know enough about them. We use seals, scales, grades, indexes and classifications not only to evaluate them, but also to create valuable categories that allow us to classify reality. The very act of classifying entities orders them according to the reputational rankings that sometimes are already available in our culture, sometimes are *ad hoc* artifacts that organize a space of discrimination. Let us start with the timeline of "classification" and "evaluation". When we think about categorization, we commonly view taxonomies as cognitive tools that describe objective relations and properties between classes and objects. Taxonomies, then, provide an ontological structure for a domain. Evaluative tools come afterwards to impose a ranking on these items. Contrasting this classical picture of knowledge organization, I would like to argue that reputation is prior to classification. In many epistemic practices, we use rating systems to categorize and classify items. Our capacity of organizing our thoughts about how the world is structured and conceiving appropriate institutions would be much more limited without the contribution of the preferences already aggregated in the past by others. In this sense, cultural representations help reduce cognitive complexity. Another important aspect of reputational and rating systems is that they combine two types of information for the sake of knowledge organization and evaluation: 1) information about the fact of the matter (e.g. perceptual information about the taste of wine, factual information about the wine region) and 2) *social* information about people and past interactions, that is, what people have said about a particular product and how the cultural representations of that product are conveyed in a series of labels, signs and received discourses (as for example, the cultural representations of a particular wine that we may infer from its label on a bottle). One of the examples I have analyzed elsewhere of the interplay between reputation and classification is the system of *classification of wines*.[20]

The presence of these "reputational devices", that is the complex socio-cultural mechanisms that organize social information, is a necessary condition for any acquisition of information: the unbiased interaction with the external world, an image so dear to the traditional epistemology, is an unrealistic limit-case of a subject in contact with a reality not filtered by others. Without the presence of filters, of already existing evaluations that shape a corpus of knowledge we would face the impossible task of *Bouvard et Pécuchet*, the two heroes of Flaubert who decided to retire and to go through every known discipline without, in the end, being able to learn anything.[21]

Preferences, conventions and values that others have expressed thus play a central epistemic role in the making of knowledge: they shape the reputational landscape that we use to organize our own heuristics to extract information and provide a – sometimes reliable and sometimes too biased – shortcut to what is worth keeping, remembering and preserving as knowledge. The epistemological inquiry I am advocating here implies that reputation and rating systems are an *essential ingredient* of knowledge. Reputation *is* a rational criterion of information extraction, a fundamental shortcut for cumulating knowledge in processes of collective wisdom and an ineludible filter to access facts. In an environment where sources are in constant competition to get attention and the option of the direct verification of the information is simply not available at reasonable costs, evaluation and rankings are epistemic tools and cognitive practices that provide an inevitable shortcut to information. This is especially striking in contemporary informationally overloaded societies, but it may also be considered as a permanent feature of any extraction of information from a corpus of knowledge. There is no ideal knowledge that we can adjudicate without the access to previous evaluations and adjudications of others, no Robinson Crusoe minds that investigate and manipulate the world in a perfect solitude. The higher the uncertainty on the content of information, the stronger the weight of the opinions of others to establish the quality of this content.

Conclusions

Among the many social mechanisms that filter our access to knowledge and contribute to the very construction and maintenance of our knowledge institutions, I have focused on *trust* and *reputation*. I think these mechanisms are at the core of our epistemic practices. The way in which they participate to the knowledge process helps to explain our deep vulnerabilities and fears in coping with knowledge. We face knowledge in social contexts that are highly structured and can be difficult to understand. Good management of our way of trusting others and assessing their reputation may empower us as knowers in a social world.

Notes

1 I use the broad category of *Structuralism* to refer to a 20th-century central intellectual approach to the human sciences with profound effects on linguistics, sociology, anthropology and philosophy, that attempts to analyze a specific field as a complex system of interconnected parts. Roughly speaking, Structuralism holds that all human activity and its products, even perception and thought itself, are constructed – and not natural – within an organized "language-like" system in which we operate.

2 On the "crisis of trust" in science, cf. O. O'Neill (2002) *Reith Lectures on Trust and Public Life*, www.bbc.co.uk/radio4/reith2002/ and M. A. Edwards and S. Roy (2017) "Academic Research in the 21st Century: Maintaining Scientific Integrity in a Climate of Perverse Incentives and Hypercompetition", *Environmental Engineering Science*, 34:1, 51–61. https://doi.org/10.1089/ees.2016.0223.

3 Cf. on this point: R. Rini (2017) "Fake News and Partisan Epistemology", *Kennedy Institute of Ethics Journal*, 27:2, 43–64.

4 For a review of the topic, see J. Lackey (eds) (2014) *Essays in Collective Epistemology*, Oxford: Oxford University Press; M. Brady and M. Fricker (eds) (2016) *The Epistemic Life of Groups*, Oxford: Oxford University Press.

5 For an overview of the literature on the role of trust in knowledge see: P. Faulkner and T. Simpson (eds) (2017) *The Philosophy of Trust*, Oxford: Oxford University Press; J. Simon (ed) (forthcoming) *Routledge Handbook of Trust and Philosophy*, London: Routledge.

6 On the notion of reputation see F. Giardini and R. Wittek (eds) (2019) *Oxford Handbook of Gossip and Reputation*, Oxford: Oxford University Press; and G. Origgi (2018) *Reputation: What It Is and Why It Matters*, London: Princeton University Press.

7 See Steven Shapin (1994) *A Social History of Truth*, Cambridge: Cambridge University Press.

8 Cf. Faulkner, Simpson *cit.*, p. 3.

9 This debate is reconstructed in a variety of introductory texts to social epistemology. See Faulkner and Simpson (*cit.*) and J. Lackey and E. Sosa (eds) (2006) *The Epistemology of Testimony*, Oxford: Oxford University Press.

10 Cf. P. Faulkner (2011) *Knowledge on Trust*, Oxford: Oxford University Press; R. Moran (2006) "Getting Told and Being Believed" in J. Lackey and E. Sosa (eds) *The Epistemology of Testimony*, (*cit.*) pp. 272–306.

11 I have already presented these heuristics of trust in G. Origgi (2012) "Epistemic Injustice and Epistemic Trust", *Social Epistemology: A Journal of Knowledge, Culture and Policy*, 26:2, 221–235; and in chapter 5 of G. Origgi (2018) *Reputation: What It Is and Why It Matters*, London: Princeton University Press.

12 See H. Mercier and D. Sperber (2017) *The Enigma of Reason*, Cambridge: Harvard University Press.

13 See Shapin (1994), p. 18.

14 For an introduction to *Signaling Theory*, see D. Gambetta (2010) "Signaling Theory" in P. Hedström and P. Bearman (eds) (2009) *Oxford Handbook of Analytical Sociology*, Oxford: Oxford University Press, pp. 168–194.

15 Cf. J. Willis and A. Todorov (2006) "First Impressions: Making Up Your Mind after a 100-ms Exposure to a Face", *Psychological Science*, 17: 592–598.

16 I have sketched the idea of a « pragmatics of trust » in other works. See G. Origgi (2004) "Is Trust an Epistemological Notion?", *Episteme*, 1:1, 61–72; G. Origgi (2005) "What Does It Mean to Trust in Epistemic Authority?", *Columbia Working Papers*, online at: https://academiccommons.columbia.edu/catalog/ac%3A130569.

17 On the fortuitous character of a lot of our knowledge, cf. R. Hardin (2003) "If It Rained Knowledge", *Philosophy of the Social Sciences*, 33, 3–24; J. Lackey (1999) "Testimonial Knowledge and Transmission", *The Philosophical Quarterly*, 49:197, 490, 199.

18 I here adopt the notion of *relevance* developed by D. Sperber and D. Wilson (1986) *Relevance: Communication and Cognition*, Oxford: Basil Blackwell.

19 For the notion of *epistemic vigilance*, see D. Sperber, G. Origgi *et al.* (2010) "Epistemic Vigilance", *Mind and Language*, 25, 359–393.

20 Cf. G. Origgi (2007) "Wine Epistemology: The Role of Reputation and Rankings in the World of Wine" in B. Smith (ed.) *Questions of Taste*, Oxford: Oxford University Press, pp. 183–198; G. Origgi (2018) ch. 8: "Experts and Connoisseurs: The Reputation of Wine" in *Reputation*, Princeton, NJ: Princeton University Press, pp. 191–210.

21 Cf. G. Flaubert (1880/1999) *Bouvard et Pécuchet*, Paris: Gallimard, Folio.

9

SOCIALLY DISTRIBUTED COGNITION AND THE EPISTEMOLOGY OF TESTIMONY

Joseph Shieber

Introduction

Much of what we know is not based on our own immediate experience, but is based on the knowledge or experience of others. If I know of something as trivial as a recent victory for some sports team in the town where I grew up, far away from where I now reside, or as momentous as the killing of an innocent, unarmed person by law enforcement personnel in that same town, I know it because I read about it, or heard about it, or saw a report about it on television or the internet.

At the risk of oversimplifying, we can group all of these routes to the acquisition of information from others under the heading of "testimony". If the observations in the preceding paragraph are correct, this would suggest that we can at least sometimes know by acquiring information through testimony.

To say that we have knowledge, however, is to say more than merely that we have acquired information. Rather, to say that we have knowledge is to say that we satisfy certain conditions over and above the mere acquisition of information. To say, then, that we can at least sometimes know by acquiring information through testimony, is to say that we can—at least sometimes— both satisfy whatever conditions are required for knowledge and do so by means of acquiring through testimony the information that forms the content of that knowledge.

Given this, a central task for an epistemology of testimony is to address how it is that we can simultaneously satisfy the conditions required for knowledge while acquiring information via testimony. Traditional attempts at accomplishing this task have focused on individuals—individual recipients of information and individual providers of that information—and have tried to account for how the capacities and actions of those individuals might result in the satisfaction of the conditions for knowledge in testimonial interactions. In what follows here, however, we will explore the possibility that it might well be productive for the epistemology of testimony to alter the focus from individuals in testimonial exchanges to consider the dynamics of information flow in groups.

The Personalist Requirement

We can characterize the personalist requirement (PR) in terms of two conditions, corresponding to the two types of participants in testimonial interactions: transmitters of information and recipients of information. With respect to transmitters of information, this component of the personalist requirement PR1 holds that it is the characteristics of the persons who are the transmitters of testimonial information that are salient in determining whether or not that information is a candidate for knowledge. With respect to recipients of information, this component of the personalist requirement PR2 holds that it is the characteristics of persons who are the recipients of testimonial information that are salient in determining whether or not that information is a candidate for knowledge.

More precisely, we may express PR1 and PR2 as follows. Let us say that, for any given testimonial exchange E, the parties involved in E are individual persons: a transmitter of information, T, and a recipient of information, R. Given this, then, we have:

PR1 A necessary condition for R to be in a position to gain knowledge on the basis of E involves properties or attributes of T—e.g., T's competence and/or honesty.

PR2 A necessary condition for R to be in a position to gain knowledge on the basis of E involves properties or attributes of R—e.g., R's faculties for reliably assessing T's competence and/or honesty.

Note that PR1 and PR2 are independent of each other. One may maintain either of them while denying the other, or one may espouse both simultaneously. Thus, e.g., Lackey and Sosa (2006; Lackey 2008) rejects PR1 while embracing PR2, arguably Burge (1993) rejects PR2 while embracing PR1, and a number of authors embrace both PR1 and PR2 (including Adler 2002, Faulkner 2011, Fricker 2006, 2007—but not M. Fricker 2012, Goldberg 2007—but notably not, Goldberg 2010).

Problems with a Focus on Personal Pathways of Testimonial Transmission

There is one central problem with a focus on personal pathways of testimonial transmission—namely, that the link between a given episode of testimony and the truth of the matter might have little to do with the personal qualities of the individual person that recipients identify as the issuer of that testimony.

Consider the following case. Due to a health scare, you go to a local hospital at which doctors run a series of tests. At a follow-up visit with your family doctor, part of the same health network that includes the hospital to which you went as well as a number of laboratories for collecting and analyzing samples and running diagnostic tests, you go over the test results. Your doctor punches some keys on her computer and says, "I'm looking at your CAT scan results and everything looks fine here." Not able to see her computer screen, you think that she is actually looking at images from your CAT scan and performing a diagnosis. You believe her and are reassured.

What you don't see is that what your doctor was actually looking at was a report produced by the unit that performed the CAT scan: about six or seven sentences, one of which even includes the words, "everything looks fine". While you were operating on the tacit assumption that the professional judgment on which you were relying to be reassured about your health was that of your personal physician, in fact your professional physician was just acting as a spokesperson for a network of health professionals, unknown to you, who conducted and analyzed your medical tests.

Note that, in many instances, it may well be better, from the standpoint of receiving reliable health information, to rely on a specialist team than any single doctor (cf., for example, Epstein 2014). Certainly, this would especially seem to be the case when one considers that a personal physician may encounter a few examples of a particular medical condition over the course of her career, while a specialist in that sort of condition would likely encounter many more instances, lending the specialist an expertise—and the specialist's judgment a level of reliability—that the personal physician lacks. It doesn't seem plausible to suppose that a misplaced tacit assumption on your part—namely, that the judgment you received in your personal physician's office was her own, rather than that of a specialist medical team—should rule out the possibility that your belief in the information conveyed in that judgment could count as knowledge.

Indeed, when one considers the wide range of multi-person teams that are engaged in the discovery, storage, retrieval, and transmission of information, it quickly becomes clear that much of what we know is a product of such teams. Examples of such teams include, but are not limited to scientific research groups; multi-person journalistic investigative teams; news reporting organizations with data analysts, journalists, editors, etc.; think tanks; large-scale industrial research groups; and governmental research organizations, with their hierarchies of bureaucrats, chief scientists, bench scientists, technicians, and public information officers. Often, the information that we receive from such groups comes to us through a spokesperson, but the spokesperson in such cases is a mere transmitter of the information produced by the team as a whole, of which we are largely unaware (cf. Brown and Duguid 2000: 126–7).

Lack of Sensitivity to the Properties and Attributes of Transmitters of Testimony

There are two problems with a focus on personal pathways of testimonial reception. First, if one assumes that the personal properties and attributes of transmitters of testimony are of importance, it turns out that recipients of testimony are not reliably sensitive to those properties and attributes. Second, if one allows that the properties and attributes of socially distributed systems of information transmission are of importance, it is pretty clear that recipients of testimony are not reliably sensitive to those properties and attributes either. We will consider the first problem in this section, and turn to the second problem in the next section.

Since social psychologists have, for the better part of half a century, acquired a great deal of experimental data on the mechanisms by which subjects form beliefs on the basis of communications with others, it would behoove us to subject our armchair evidence-gathering to the crucible of actual empirical investigation. Unfortunately, a growing amount of social psychological literature on trustworthiness and deceit would suggest that, even if there are traits signaling trustworthiness or deceptiveness, subjects aren't reliably sensitive to those traits. Indeed, the preponderance of evidence from the social psychological literature is that we are terribly unreliable at responding to indicators of trustworthiness or deceit (for more detail on this, cf. Shieber 2012, 2015).

For one example of this, consider the studies by Chaiken (1979) and Chaiken and Eagley (1983) to the effect that subjects determine trustworthiness of their interlocutors on the basis of the interlocutors' attractiveness and likeability. As ought to be obvious, there is little reason to think that subjects relying on attractiveness or likeability are in fact responding sensitively to actual trustworthiness. Or consider eye contact. Though we do in fact rely on eye contact as an indicator of sincerity, taking sustained eye contact to be a sign of trustworthiness, this is indeed problematic, as eye contact has consistently been shown not to be a reliable indicator of sincerity. As Sitton and Griffin (1981) demonstrate, deceivers in fact maintain more sustained levels of eye contact than truth tellers. Or, to consider another intuitively held belief regarding sincere interlocutors, that they have no problem "keeping a straight face" when communicating, evidence suggests that liars produce no more nervous smiles than sincere interlocutors; in fact, studies suggest that liars smile somewhat less often (Bond et al. 1985). Nor are education and expertise of recipients of testimony effective inoculations against the effects of charisma, appearance, and presentation (cf. Naftulin et al. 1973).

We might hope that, although we are not particularly good at recognizing signs of trustworthiness, we are good at deception detection. Unfortunately, however, there is no empirical support for the notion that subjects are reliable deception detectors. Rather, as Ekman and O'Sullivan note, "in every study reported, people have not been very accurate in judging when someone is lying. … Average accuracy in detecting deceit has rarely been above 60% (with chance being 50%), and some groups have done worse than chance" (Ekman and O'Sullivan 1991: 913). These results have been demonstrated even for professionals whose jobs presumably depend on their ability to detect deception—customs officials (Kraut and Poe 1980), federal law enforcement officers (DePaulo and Pfeifer 1986), and police officers (Kohnken 1987). Apparently, the ability to deceive without being detected is acquired early, as recent studies have shown that adults are no better at detecting deception in children than they are at detecting deception in adult subjects (Crossman and Lewis 2006).

Even the few research results that have found some groups capable of detecting deception at a rate better than chance serve in fact to underscore the challenges involved in reliably responding to lying. Thus, though Ekman et al.were able to demonstrate that two law-enforcement groups and a group of clinical psychologists were highly accurate in detecting deception, the results were equivocal enough that the researchers concluded that "it is unlikely that judging deception from demeanor will ever be sufficiently accurate to be admissible in the courtroom," and that "most of us would do well to entertain some skepticism about our ability to detect deception from demeanor" (1999: 265).

Even limiting our consideration to the possibility of deception detection in interactions with subjects with whom we are familiar, there is reason to doubt whether subjects' abilities at detecting deception improve over repeated exposure to—and increased familiarity with—particular interlocutors. The difficulty is that, in such interactions, just as potential detectors of deception gain experience from repeated exposure to their interlocutors, potential deceivers should also become more adept at tailoring their performance to their audience. Thus, Buller and Burgoon suggest that "deceivers in interactive contexts should display increasing immediacy and involvement, pleasantness, composure, fluency, and smooth turn taking over the course of the interaction" (1996: 220). This would seem to be borne out by the evidence. For example, as McCornack and Parks (1986) demonstrate, though intimate partners have greater confidence in their ability to detect deception, they are in fact poorer at detecting deception in their partners than in other interlocutors. Indeed, research by Dunbar et al. (2003) suggests that interactive deception differs from non-interactive deception and that the interactive situation gives the upper hand to deceptive communicators rather than to deception detectors (cf. Millar and Millar 1995).

Even this cursory review of the available evidence, then, would quite strongly indicate that the empirical evidence does not in fact support the appeal to a faculty of testimonial sensitivity in the formulation of a workable epistemology of testimony. For, though the evidence supports philosophers' claims that our experience of testimonial situations involves our sensitivity to properties of our interlocutors—e.g., likeability or eye contact, to cite two commonly cited properties —the evidence is equally clear that such sensitivity does not sufficiently improve our reliability in detecting testifier honesty or trustworthiness to a level that would confer epistemic license. Indeed, the evidence suggests that we are little better than chance.

Lack of Sensitivity to the Properties and Attributes of Socially Distributed Systems of Information Transmission

There are at least two features integral to socially distributed systems of information transmission that are incompatible with the reliable sensitivity of recipients of testimony to the epistemically relevant properties and attributes of those socially distributed systems. Following Shieber (2013, 2015), we may consider these under the two features of non-locality of expertise and opacity.

The non-locality of expertise within socially distributed cognitive systems involves the way in which such systems often evolve so that even non-experts working within the system can perform complicated tasks and generate valuable information. As Norman describes one sort of socially distributed cognitive system, such systems enable "decision making and action [to] take place within the context established by the physical environment, where the structures can often act as a distributed intelligence, taking some of the memory and computational burden off the human" (1993: 146–7).

The problem that such non-locality poses for recipients of testimony from non-experts embedded within such socially distributed cognitive systems is that most recipients have no way at all of assessing the expertise of the socially distributed system. Recall the case of the patient interacting with her personal physician. The patient has no knowledge of which lab performed the analysis of her CAT scan, how generally reliable that lab is, or how it handles such analyses —indeed, in the case described, the patient mistakenly takes it for granted that her personal physician has analyzed the results. Nevertheless, it seems plausible that the patient could acquire knowledge about the state of her health by receiving information produced by the lab and transmitted by her personal physician.

The second feature of socially distributed cognitive systems is opacity: the fact that the epistemically relevant features of those systems are often opaque both to participants within the systems and to those who interact with them. It should be obvious that, if socially distributed cognitive systems display opacity, as described, this attribute would be incompatible with the reliable sensitivity of recipients of testimony to the epistemically relevant properties and attributes of those systems.

There are three attributes of socially distributed systems that contribute to the opacity of those systems. First, tasks within the system are local, removing the requirement that any one participant have an overview of the system as a whole. Second, the skills needed to perform those local tasks are limited and often unrelated to those skills that would be needed to analyze the system as a whole. Third, the evolution of socially distributed cognitive systems means that current participants in those systems often are unfamiliar with the developmental history of such systems, and thus unaware of the adaptive pressures in response to which features of those systems arose. We will briefly examine each of these attributes.

The first attribute is the embeddedness of tasks in discrete regions of the socially distributed cognitive system, obviating the need for performers of those tasks to have knowledge of the entire system. It should be apparent why such a feature of socially distributed systems would be of advantage: local embeddedness reduces the cognitive load on participants within the system. The downside from the point of view of the epistemology of such systems, however, is that the epistemically relevant features of the system become inextricable to those not within the system. As Brown and Duguid describe it, "become a member of a community, engage in its practices, and you can acquire and make use of its knowledge and information. Remain an outsider, and these will remain indigestible" (2000: 126).

The second attribute contributing to opacity is that the skills necessary to participate in a socially distributed system are seldom those that would be necessary to analyze the features of that system. This should be obvious. Take again the example of a large medical laboratory. The skills necessary to participate in such a laboratory would involve the ability to operate the medical equipment, analyze data, or generate and communicate reports based on the data, not the ability to trace the network linking the members of the lab or to analyze the sociology of the employees. Indeed, a growing body of research suggests that participants in socially distributed cognitive systems often fail to recognize even basic features of the procedures they follow (Miyake 1986), or how to optimize the performance of the system (cf. Ilgen et al. 2005, Knorr Cetina 1999: 293, Mesmer-Magnus et al. 2009). Indeed, one of the challenges posed by analyzing such systems, even for experts, is that "it isn't always obvious just which parts are critical to the social, distributed nature of the task, which are irrelevant or detrimental" (Norman 1993: 145).

Finally, the third attribute that leads to opacity is the evolutionary nature of the development of socially distributed cognitive systems. As Norman notes, socially distributed cognitive systems often evolve over many years, through a process of small, incremental changes, in "a process of natural evolution [that] can lead to remarkably efficient results, even if nobody is in charge, even if nobody is aware of the process" (1993: 145). Given that the time-frame for such changes will often vastly exceed the tenure of any of the participants within the system, it is unsurprising that the attributes of the system resulting from such evolutionary development will remain opaque to the participants. And given the complexity involved in understanding any sort of evolutionary process, it is equally unsurprising that such attributes will often also remain opaque to those interacting with such systems from outside the system.

One Way of Overcoming the Personalist Requirement: Abandoning the Individual as Knowledge-Bearer

Given the difficulties posed by maintaining an allegiance to the personalist requirement in either of its forms, one might be tempted to abandon the very idea that it is individuals who are the primary loci of epistemic evaluation, the bearers of states like belief or knowledge. Rather, one might hold instead, it is communities as a whole that are the bearers of states like belief and knowledge. In this way, one would no longer have to account for the fact that individual persons are not the sole transmitters of testimonial information, nor are individual believers seemingly capable of assessing the transmitters of information—whether individual persons or socially distributed cognitive systems—with respect to their epistemically relevant attributes.

One example of a philosopher who seems to feel this temptation is Hardwig, who, in discussing a large-scale physics experiment similar in scope to those discussed by Knorr-Cetina, comes to the conclusion that

> Perhaps [in cases in which the conclusion that p is arrived at on the basis of a large-scale scientific endeavor] that p is known, not by any one person, but by the community ... Perhaps [individual members of the community] are not entitled to say, "I know that p," but only, "We know that p." This community is not reducible to a class of individuals, for no one individual and no one individually knows that p. If we take this tack, we could retain the idea that the knower must ... have evidence for the truth of what he knows, but in doing so we deny that the knower is always an individual or even a class of individuals.
>
> *(1985: 349; cf. Kusch 2002, Welbourne 1981, Tollefsen 2002)*

Certainly, this would allow Hardwig to avoid the problems faced by the personalist requirement. Since belief and knowledge would not, in this view, be properties of individuals, the fact that individuals do not comport with either PR1 or PR2 would pose no challenge for the actual bearers of beliefs and knowledge—namely, groups.

There is a vast literature concerning the ontology of groups—including on the question of whether properties of groups are reducible to properties of their constituents. Of particular relevance to the discussion here, there is an active debate on the question of whether we might attribute states like belief and knowledge to groups, and the relation of those group-level attributions to the attributions of such states to the constituents of those groups. However, it would be worth investigating if there is some way to avoid the problems posed for PR1 and PR2 without invoking potentially questionable phenomena like group-level beliefs or knowledge. In the next section, we'll sketch a way that relies on the notion of group-level processes, culminating in person-level beliefs and knowledge.

Modest Social Epistemology

If the problems presented so far for PR1 and PR2 are indeed as pressing as they seem, then, if the processes involved in the testimonial transmission and reception of information are solely understood in terms of individual cognitive processes, it would seem that there is no way that we can understand those processes to be reliable, at least in a wide range of very common situations involving social information acquisition. If we are to treat such testimonial transmission and reception processes as species of warranted belief, however, it would seem that we must understand such processes as reliably conducing to the formation of true beliefs.

In contemporary epistemology, the standard understanding of the notion of a reliable true belief-forming process, is in fact a personalist one. To take one very influential example, Alvin Goldman suggests that such processes involve "how a cognizer deals with his cognitive input, i.e., ... the operations that register and transform ... [by means of] 'information-processing' equipment internal to the organism ... the stimulation that reaches him" (1986: 116) If this is true, however, then what is required is a different understanding of process, one that includes—pace Goldman—socially distributed cognitive processes (cf. Evans's 1982 discussion of "social informational systems").

In particular, it would seem that our discussion of socially distributed cognitive systems and their place in the transmission of information would suggest that epistemological analyses of testimony require more general ways of understanding the notion of social belief-forming processes. Despite Goldman's influential reliabilist formulation of processes along personalist lines, there is in fact no obstacle preventing us from adopting a reliabilist framework for such a more general understanding—a standard reliabilist framework with one modification. We might term such a framework, following Shieber (2013, 2015) a *modest social epistemology* (cf. Kitcher 1993: 113), allowing that:

1   Individuals are the primary bearers of belief; and
2   Some individual S has adequate grounds for her belief that p just in case S's belief that p was produced by a process that reliably produces true beliefs, where
3   Such processes may include the properties and actions of agents other than S as well as properties of the environment (i.e., instruments, etc.).

In other words, this is a standard reliabilist account of knowledge, with one significant change: a broadening of the notion of process to include genuinely social belief-forming processes.

This social epistemology is a modest one in that it avoids the strategy pursued by Hardwig, Kusch, and others of abandoning or weakening the commitment to individuals as the bearers of belief and knowledge that is so firmly anchored in traditional epistemology. Furthermore, this epistemology occupies a moderate position with respect to the phenomenon of the extended mind (cf. Clark and Chalmers 1998; for criticism, see, e.g., Adams and Aizawa 2008). According to the extended mind hypothesis,

> if, as we confront some task, a part of the world functions as a process which, were it done in the head, we would have no hesitation in recognizing as part of the cognitive process, then that part of the world is ... part of the cognitive process.
>
> *(Clark and Chalmers 1998: 29)*

Modest social epistemology, however, does not require any commitment to the idea that the socially distributed belief-forming process is a cognitive process of the believer. Rather, it is that the belief-forming process that results in a believer's belief need not be limited to the cognitive processes of the believer alone. Instead, these processes may include socially distributed processes, where what makes the processes socially distributed is precisely that they are external to the minds of the individual persons whose beliefs come about as a result of those processes.

References

Adams, F., and Aizawa, K. (2008). *The Bounds of Cognition*. Chichester: Wiley.

Adler, J. (2002). *Belief's Own Ethics*. Cambridge, MA: MIT Press.

Bond, C. F., Kahler, K. N., and Paolicelli, L. M. (1985). The Miscommunication of Deception: An Adaptive Perspective. *Journal of Experimental Social Psychology*, 21(4), pp. 331–345.

Brown, J. S., and Duguid, P. (2000). *The Social Life of Information*. Boston, MA: Harvard Business School Press.

Buller, D. B., and Burgoon, J. K. (1996). Interpersonal Deception Theory. *Communication Theory*, 3, pp. 203–242.

Burge, T. (1993). Content Preservation. *The Philosophical Review*, 102(4), pp. 457–488.

Chaiken, S. (1979). Communicator Physical Attractiveness and Persuasion. *Journal of Personality and Social Psychology*, 37, pp. 1387–1397.

Chaiken, S., and Eagley, A. H. (1983). Communication Modality as a Determinant of Persuasion: The Role of Communicator Salience. *Journal of Personality and Social Psychology*, 45, pp. 241–256.

Clark, A., and Chalmers, D. (1998). The Extended Mind. *Analysis*, 58(1), pp. 7–19.

Crossman, A. M., and Lewis, M. (2006). Adults' Ability to Detect Children's Lying. *Behavioral Sciences and the Law*, 24, pp. 703–715.

DePaulo, B. M., and Pfeifer, R. L. (1986). On-the-Job Experience and Skill at Detecting Deception. *Journal of Applied Social Psychology*, 16, pp. 249–267.

Dunbar, N. E., Ramirez, A., and Burgoon, J. K. (2003). The Effects of Participation on the Ability to Judge Deceit. *Communication Reports*, 16(1), pp. 23–33.

Ekman, P., and O'Sullivan, M. (1991). Who Can Catch a Liar? *American Psychologist*, 46(9), pp. 913–920.

Ekman, P., O'Sullivan, M., and Frank, M. G. (1999). A Few Can Catch a Liar. *Psychological Science*, 10, pp. 263–266.

Epstein, N. E. (2014). Multidisciplinary In-Hospital Teams Improve Patient Outcomes: A Review. *Surgical Neurology International*, 5(Suppl 7), pp. 295–303.

Evans, G. (1982). *The Varieties of Reference*. Oxford: Clarendon Press.

Faulkner, P. (2011). *Knowledge on Trust*. New York: Oxford University Press.

Fricker, E. (2006). Testimony and Epistemic Autonomy. In Lackey, J. and Sosa, E. eds., *The Epistemology of Testimony*. Oxford: Oxford University Press., pp. 225–251.

Fricker, M. (2007). *Epistemic Injustice*. Oxford: Oxford University Press.

Fricker, M. (2012). Group Testimony: The Making of a Collective Good Informant. *Philosophy and Phenomenological Research*, 84, pp. 249–276.

Goldberg, S. (2007). *Anti-Individualism: Mind and Language, Knowledge and Justification*. Cambridge: Cambridge University Press.

Goldberg, S. (2010). *Relying on Others*. Oxford: Oxford University Press.

Goldman, A. (1986). *Epistemology and Cognition*. Cambridge, MA: Harvard University Press.

Hardwig, J. (1985). Epistemic Dependence. *Journal of Philosophy*, 82(7), pp. 335–349.

Ilgen, D.R., Hollenbeck, J.R., Johnson, M. and Jundt, D. (2005). Teams in Organizations: From Input-Process-Output Models to IMOI Models. *Annual Review of Psychology*, 56(1), pp. 517–543.

Kitcher, P. (1993). *The Advancement of Science: Science Without Legend, Objectivity Without Illusion*. New York: Oxford University Press.

Knorr Cetina, K. (1999). *Epistemic Cultures: How the Sciences Make Knowledge*. Cambridge, MA: Harvard University Press.

Kohnken, G. (1987). Training Police Officers to Detect Deceptive Eyewitness Statements: Does it Work? *Social Behaviour*, 2, pp. 1–17.

Kraut, R. E., and Poe, D. (1980). On the Line: The Deception Judgments of Customs Inspectors and Laymen. *Journal of Personality and Social Psychology*, 39, pp. 784–798.

Kusch, M. (2002). *Knowledge by Agreement: The Programme of Communitarian Epistemology*. Oxford: Oxford University Press.

Lackey, J. (2008). *Knowing from Words*. New York: Oxford University Press.

Lackey, J. and Sosa, E. eds. (2006). It takes Two to Tango. In Lackey, J. and Sosa, E. eds., *The Epistemology of Testimony*. Oxford: Oxford University Press, pp. 160–189.

McCornack, S. A., and Parks, M. R. (1986). Deception Detection and Relationship Development: The Other Side of Trust. *Annals of the International Communication Association, Communication Yearbook*, 9(1), pp. 377–389.

Mesmer-Magnus, J.R., and DeChurch, L.A. (2009). Information Sharing and Team Performance: A Meta-Analysis. *Journal of Applied Psychology*, 94(2), pp. 535–546.

Millar, M., and Millar, K. (1995). Detection of Deception in Familiar and Unfamiliar Persons: The Effects of Information Restriction. *Journal of Nonverbal Behavior*, 19, pp. 69–84.

Miyake, N. (1986). Constructive Iteration and the Iterative Process of Understanding. *Cognitive Science*, 10, pp. 151–177.

Naftulin, D. H., Ware, J. E., and Donnelly, F. A. (1973). The Dr. Fox Lecture: A Paradigm of Educational Seduction. *Journal of Medical Education*, 48, pp. 630–635.

Norman, D. (1993). *Things that Make Us Smart*. Reading, MA: Addison-Wesley.

Shieber, J. (2012). Against Credibility. *Australasian Journal of Philosophy*, 90(1), pp. 1–18.

Shieber, J. (2013). Toward a Truly Social Epistemology: Babbage, The Division of Mental Labor, and the Possibility of Socially Distributed Warrant. *Philosophy and Phenomenological Research*, 86(2), pp. 266–294.

Shieber, J. (2015). *Testimony: A Philosophical Introduction*. New York: Routledge.

Sitton, S. C. and Griffin, S. T. (1981). Detection of Deception From Clients' Eye Contact Patterns. *Journal of Counseling Psychology*, 28, pp. 269–271.

Tollefsen, D. (2002). Organizations as True Believers. *Journal of Social Philosophy*, 33(3), pp. 395–411.

Welbourne, M. (1981). The Community of Knowledge. *Philosophical Quarterly*, 31, pp. 302–314.

10

ASSURANCE VIEWS OF TESTIMONY

Philip J. Nickel

In this chapter, I describe the assurance view of testimonial knowledge and warrant and consider a significant challenge to the view. Excellent critical discussions of some earlier versions of the assurance view can be found in Lackey (2008, ch. 8) and Schmitt (2010). Here, I will emphasize literature that has appeared since 2010. Other recent critical discussions may be found in Shieber (2015, ch. 5) and Gelfert (2014, ch. 8).

What Is the Assurance View?

The assurance view is an epistemological position regarding testimonial knowledge and warrant. It holds that I can acquire knowledge from other people in virtue of the fact that when they tell me things, they thereby assure me that what they say is true, and in so doing provide me with an entitlement to rely on their authority. Suppose I am wondering whether Shakespeare's diaries are in the library, my friend Frost tells me that they are not (without further explanation), and I think I come to have knowledge of this fact as a result. On the assurance view, in such cases we may speak of a distinctively testimonial kind of *epistemic warrant*, based on the interpersonal act of assurance by which a speaker takes responsibility for the truth of what she says. Two theses are definitive of the assurance view: (I) acts of assurance are an important feature of testimony in our communicative practices; and (II) the practice of assurance allows for a distinctive and valid kind of epistemic warrant, and this is sometimes adequate to provide me with knowledge. A significant strand of scholarship, going back to an early moment in the revival of philosophical interest in the topic of testimony, has argued for similar claims (Ross 1986; Welbourne 1979).

A central goal of the assurance view is to provide an account of what is distinctive about testimonial warrant and knowledge. This is sometimes expressed as the aim of drawing a distinction between the way we normally treat *testimony that p* as supporting *p*, and the way we treat *evidence that p* as supporting *p*. If I believe Frost, I do not take his claim as a form of *evidence* that Shakespeare's diaries are not in the library, to be weighed in light of other evidence and experience. In this way, the assurance view is fundamentally opposed to reductive accounts of testimony which ground it fundamentally in personal experience and/or inference.

An important but infrequently discussed variant of the assurance view holds that assurance is closely tied to assertion itself and the norms governing assertion. Many philosophers hold that when we make an assertion, we invoke epistemic norms such as the norm that a person must only assert what she knows or has sufficient reason to believe (Goldberg 2015). This seems to generate a sort of norm-based entitlement in the hearer of testimony to believe what is said (Faulkner 2011; Goldberg 2011, 2015; Nickel 2013). Such views could be called *norms of assertion* views. By contrast, a more frequently discussed type of assurance view holds that assurances are a recognizable subspecies of assertion, similar to a promise, in which one makes a real commitment that backs up the warrant (cf. Schmitt 2010: 220–221). I will call these *real commitment* views.

One of the key arguments for both norms of assertion and real commitment versions of the assurance view is based on the remarkable fact that if a person has formed a belief on the basis of an assurance and his belief is challenged by a third party, he may "pass the buck" by holding the *original speaker* responsible for the truth and justification of the belief.[1] For example, if Macy challenges me to show that Shakespeare's diaries are not in the library, I don't necessarily have to look for my own evidence for this claim (e.g., in the card catalogue or the library stacks). I can respond to her challenge by saying that I believe it because Frost told me so, passing the justificatory buck to Frost. This shows both that the act of responsibility-taking is often assumed as part of our conversational practices, supporting (I), and also that this has an epistemic aspect (since the "buck" being passed is the onus of providing an epistemic justification sufficient for one's claim to be maintained in the face of a challenge), supporting (II). It is also claimed that reductive accounts of testimony cannot explain epistemic buck-passing, because these accounts imply that the audience is fundamentally personally responsible for how (s)he treats testimony as evidence for a belief she acquires.

The epistemic import of buck-passing is not immediately clear, but it can be understood such a way that it supports the warrant for the audience's belief in what a speaker says. The support for (II) could be further worked out as follows. Since the speaker and the audience know about assurance and buck-passing, the speaker will be aware that the audience may hold her accountable for the epistemic reasons for her claim, and (s)he will try to make sure only to make statements that are well-justified. This increases the reliability of what the speaker says, and the audience can grasp this fact by thinking about the situation, giving them an extra epistemic warrant to believe what is said (Faulkner 2011, ch. 6; Goldberg 2015, chs. 2–3). We can call this phenomenon "dependence-responsiveness" (Nickel 2012).

Some assertions seem to involve no act of responsibility-taking, or generate no actionable rights. For example, when a student makes an assertion on a written exam, or proposes an answer to a question posed in a classroom, (s)he is not generally supposing that others will use these assertions as definitive answers to open questions, no matter how much confidence (s)he has when answering. Many versions of the assurance view hold that assurance is different in kind from mere assertion (Welbourne 1979: 5). It is sometimes thought of as similar to a promise in that it has a specific recipient or recipients who come to have certain actionable rights as a result.

There are two ways in which the real commitment variant of the assurance view can explicate an idea of assurance distinct from assertion. The first corresponds to the *content* of the assurance, and the second to the *parties* whom the assurance relates. First, we can distinguish a particular mode of epistemic responsibility-taking that is characteristic of assurance, in the sense that the content of what one takes responsibility for is epistemic. Second, we can develop the idea that assurance has a distinctly second-personal character, so that, like promising, it relates specific persons. It is given to a specific person or persons, the audience, who are to be distinguished from others, mere bystanders or eavesdroppers, who are not proper objects of the assurance and may not take advantage of it for knowledge and justification in the same way. In the next two sections, I discuss these two ways of developing the real commitment view.

Assurance as Epistemic Responsibility-Taking

Krista Lawlor (2013) develops an account of assurance that is helpful in understanding what its particular character might be, as contrasted with ordinary assertion.[2] She uses *assurance* to refer to cases in which one communicates "I *know* P" instead of merely asserting P. On her account, this is associated with a commitment by the speaker to "guarantee against reasonable alternatives" (10) in a way that is "good enough for anyone" (13) and is meant to end inquiry, at least provisionally.[3] Mere assertions, by contrast, cover cases in which the speaker expects disagreement, such as when the committee chair states that "The federal stimulus package will reduce unemployment" (ibid.). We might also add the cases of assertions made by students on an exam or in a classroom, discussed above. Mere assertion is not meant to end inquiry or decide a question, and it issues no guarantee against reasonable alternatives.

On this view, the distinctive epistemic properties of assurance make it suitable for the transmission of knowledge via testimony[4]: assurance is distinctive in that it makes a claim to knowledge. The point is *not* that one must have knowledge in order to transmit it. That point, if it is even defensible,[5] would give no special role to assurance in securing transmission. For the assurance view, a role must be given to the assurance itself—as Lawlor understands it, the *claim* to knowledge—in the practice of testimony, and this role must be sufficient, under the right conditions, to provide knowledge in the audience. For that we need a further explanation of how this is supposed to create epistemic warrant in the audience.

A speaker's adding a *mere* verbal guarantee does not put the hearer in a better epistemic position, for the speaker could be lying, careless or incompetent. It is only when the guarantee goes along with a particular epistemic and practical state in the speaker that the guarantee makes the hearer better off epistemically. Consider an example from Lawlor, in which Henrik looks in the refrigerator and wonders if the leftovers there are still edible, and Serena assures him that they are (Lawlor 2013: 19). How can Henrik know on this basis that the leftovers are still edible (assuming he cannot verify the matter without taking a bite—perhaps his sense of smell is impaired)?

Intuitively, it seems that for Henrik to get knowledge from Serena, he must also have *reason to trust* her, so that lies and incompetence are ruled out. Accounts of assurance are frequently paired with accounts of trust (Faulkner 2011; Hinchman 2005; McMyler 2011). There are two dimensions of the reasons for trusting somebody, corresponding to "external" and "internal" aspects of the trust relation. The first dimension is that Serena is *trustworthy*, so that Henrik's trust correctly represents real dispositions and capacities of Serena, which *back up* his trust. The second dimension is that Henrik grasps or has access to reasons to believe or expect that Serena is trustworthy, so that his trust is suitably *well-founded*.

Some accounts of trust and its epistemology play up the internal aspect of reasons for trust, emphasizing that the audience should have sufficient positive reason to set aside reasonable doubts about the motives and competence of the speaker. This is helpful for allowing audience greater control and (shared) responsibility, in terms of what beliefs they do or do not acquire through testimony. The underlying idea is that trust should not be blind. However, the grasp of reasons for trust must not then require unrealistic intellectual capacities. Is this a realistic requirement on reasons for trust?

Perhaps something like the following story would make this a realistic requirement. In normal conditions, humans are sometimes capable of accurately representing the interests and practical reasons that would lead others to be trustworthy, and thus less prone to lie or be careless with the truth. People are often highly sensitive to whether the interests of others are coincident or non-coincident with their own. This is bound up with the ability to construct a mental model of the intentional behavior of others in terms of their goals and interests, which is required for interpretive and predictive purposes in a social world. (In everyday contexts we try not to rely too much on the assurances of those about whose interests we can make no such model.) For those who are not equipped with such representational capacities, it may also be plausible to adopt a double standard about the basing dimension of trust in some contexts. For example, one could hold that young children who trust their parents need not have a grasp of positive reasons for doing so in order for them to take advantage of the assurances their parents give. But sophisticated adults in a professional environment might be required to have such a grasp in order for their trust to be suitably based.

On such a view, it seems as if the engine of testimonial justification is trust and trustworthiness, rather than assurance. But in fact, the two elements work together, in a way broadly suggested by Hinchman (2012, 2014). Consider a far-fetched variant of the case we have been considering which illustrates the point that without assurance, trust and trustworthiness alone are not sufficient for testimonial warrant. Suppose that Henrik trusts Serena on an adequate basis, and that Serena is sufficiently trustworthy in the domain of their shared interactions. Henrik has a technologically advanced brain-wave detector that can tell him some of Serena's occurrent beliefs, and the detector now tells him accurately that her occurrent belief while looking at the leftovers is that they are still edible. Reading Serena's occurent beliefs is surely different from hearing Serena make an *assurance* that the leftovers are still edible. For if Henrik just reads Serena's brain waves, he might *not* be able to reasonably conclude that the leftovers are really still edible. Because of his different context or history, he might have different standards from Serena, either of edibility or what counts as sufficient evidence for edibility. (Maybe he recently had food poisoning!) But if Serena *attunes her assurances to his standards*, which often happens in ordinary talk, this barrier can be overcome. The underlying idea is that when Serena provides an assurance, she is not merely reporting an occurrent belief. She is representing herself "as helping him to know in the context of his epistemic needs, not merely in the context of her own" (Hinchman 2013: 618, pronouns changed). This is, presumably, part of the commitment or responsibility she undertakes in assurance. Conversely, this implies that even when Serena does not believe something herself, she can still rightfully assure Henrik of it, because she knows that it meets his standards. In such a case, reading Serena's brainwaves would not serve Henrik's epistemic needs.

To sum up: the real commitment view can be specified, in part, by explicating the distinctive content of epistemic responsibility-taking made in an assurance. Lawlor (op cit.) describes this as a commitment by the speaker to defend the testimonial claim against reasonable alternatives, and thereby to provide conclusive backing for a testimonial belief in the audience. Such a commitment is of questionable value to an audience if they have no trust in the speaker; accounts of trust are, for this reason, often given alongside accounts of assurance. However, these accounts may threaten to make the role of assurance as a distinctive form of commitment-taking epistemically extraneous, because it is trust and the reasons for it, rather than a special kind of guarantee, that make it reasonable to believe what somebody else says. Hinchman's (op cit.) account of how assurance plays a distinctive role in providing warrant—on which a speaker takes responsibility for adjusting what is assured to the epistemic context of the audience—helps respond to this worry.

Assurance as Person-to-Person Responsibility-Taking

Some philosophers see a crucial role for assurance, not merely in the distinctive kind of knowledge claim that it makes or in the way that it can be attuned to the epistemic context of the audience, but rather in the fact that assurance is a *person-to-person* act of responsibility-taking. This "second-personal" view of assurance, set out in detail by McMyler (2011), holds that assurance is expressed in an interpersonal speech act, *telling*, with an intended recipient. This type of view, building on the work of Welbourne (1979), Ross (1986), Moran (2006), and Hinchman (2005), is the one perhaps most often associated with the label "assurance view of testimony."

The second-personal character of assurance, according to McMyler, is to be explained in terms of the speaker's act of assuming responsibility in relation to a specific audience. McMyler, applying Darwall's (2006) account of second personal reasons, claims that a second-personal reason only has its force by being *given by A to B and recognized by B as such, where A takes responsibility for giving the reason and is recognized by B as having the authority to do so* (McMyler 2011: 145). Applied to testimony, second-personality captures what is distinctive about testimonial justification. Testimonial assurance is given to a specific person or persons, the audience, who must recognize it as being given to them. Just as those who have merely overheard a promise are not in a position to demand its fulfillment, mere bystanders and eavesdroppers do not have the same warrant as the intended audience of an act of assurance, because they are not the ones to whom the relevant reason is given. Whereas *evidence* is the kind of thing that is available to anybody who observes it as a reason for belief, testimonial assurance is only available to those to whom it is offered. Others who witness the assurance but are not its intended audience may treat it as evidence, but they cannot treat it in the way it is offered to the intended audience, as expressing *authority*.

To see why this conception of assurance is attractive, let us briefly recapitulate the main argument for the assurance view. The essence of testimonial warrant and knowledge lies in the fact that in testifying we offer an assurance to the audience. This assurance consists of taking responsibility for the truth of what is said, which is to be understood in terms of one's taking on the burden of having appropriate reasons for what one says, and being willing to produce or defend what is said when challenged. The justificatory role of assurance is thus conceptually linked with the phenomenon of epistemic buck-passing. When I acquire a belief by relying on Frost's testimony, and this belief is reasonably called into question, it seems appropriate to question or criticize Frost and not only me. If Frost can't produce the goods when challenged, he is to be criticized for speaking insincerely or without sufficient evidence. In this way, the "buck" of justification is passed to Frost and stops with him, unless of course he obtained his own information through testimony, in which case the call for justification may be carried back still further.

McMyler's theory suggests that only a view on which second-personal epistemic authority is offered and accepted can adequately explain the phenomenon of epistemic buck-passing. If testimonial authority were reason-giving but not second-personal, it would have to be in virtue of the evidence it provided for what was testified. But in that case, the audience would be responsible for gathering this evidence itself. Then it would also make sense for them to defend their testimonial beliefs themselves. Epistemic buck-passing would be difficult to explain or justify. It is only in virtue of the act of responsibility-taking by the speaker, and the recognition of this by the audience, that transmitting requests for justification to the speaker becomes legitimate. Reductive or evidential views of testimony cannot explain this phenomenon.

As I see it, however, this important point need not imply that mere bystanders have no right to take up offers of testimonial authority, or to demand justification from the speaker if there are doubts about the statements made on the basis of that authority.[6]

The Challenge to Assurance Views

A persistent challenge for assurance views is that although they may capture in a satisfying way some key aspects of the phenomenology of relying on testimony, the fact that testifiers assume responsibility for what they say does not provide an adequate warrant for testimonial belief. Put another way: even if the speaker's assurance gives the audience the entitlement to believe what is testified from a conversational or moral point of view, this is far from adequately ensuring that the audience comes to have knowledge in so doing. Issuing such a guarantee is compatible with many plausible, non-hyperbolic scenarios on which the belief is false.

Joseph Shieber describes this as a failure to satisfy a fundamental epistemic requirement, which he calls the "Adequacy Goal": the goal of "maximiz[ing] the likelihood that the recipient believes a proposition only if that proposition is true" (2015: 5). The assurance view seems to license belief-adoption that it should not license from this austerely epistemological point of view. On the other hand, most beliefs, and certainly most testimonial beliefs, carry a non-zero risk of being false. Testimony adds a source of risk—other people—that can only be avoided completely by kicking away reliance on testimony completely. This makes it clear that the best way of satisfying Shieber's Adequacy Goal is to maintain *no testimonial beliefs whatsoever*. This is absurd as a core principle of guidance in an epistemology of testimony. A more adequate Adequacy Goal would start by acknowledging that I *must* form and maintain many of my beliefs on the basis of testimony, and that I should do so, if possible, in ways that reliably produce true beliefs.[7] The more relevant form of the challenge, then, is this: assurance views, by licensing us to rely on assurances (at least in situations where we have reason to trust the speaker) on the basis of the speaker's fundamental authority, endorse a form of testimonial belief-formation that does not reliably produce true beliefs.

A concrete case helps to bring out the implications of the view more forcefully. In 2011, the Dutch social psychologist Diederik Stapel, Dean of the School of Social and Behavioral Sciences at his faculty, was determined to have based much of his scientific work on fraudulent data (Bhattacharjee 2013). Colleagues and Ph.D. students who had not themselves participated in the fraud had nonetheless collaborated with him on various studies and (prior to the revelations about him) plainly believed many of his statements on testimony, without performing independent checks sufficient to reveal discrepancies in his account. After all, he satisfied reasonable criteria for trustworthiness: he was highly trained and experienced, his work had been vetted by scientific journals, and he had a reputation to defend. His assurances had an excellent pedigree.

Assurance views seem to tolerate or even endorse Stapel's colleagues' acceptance of his assurances, prior to the revelation of fraud. But more importantly, they seem committed to the claim that any adequate account of testimony and testimonial belief *must* endorse such cases of acceptance. If epistemologists require independent checks and verification in order to restrain testimonial belief and epistemic authority so that such reliance counts as epistemically unreasonable, this is equivalent to rejecting testimonial belief itself from the point of view of epistemology. This seems to be a problematic commitment of the assurance view. It seems more attractive to adopt a more modest view of the appropriate role of authority in testimonial belief, one on which warranted reliance on testimony in high-standards contexts (such as the modern practice of science) *requires*—and therefore must allow for—substantial independent checks and reasoning that would greatly diminish the role of assurance in our practices.

Notes

1 It could be that the meaning of buck-passing is a bit misunderstood. Harry S. Truman famously had a placard on his desk that said "The buck stops here," and he explained it in terms of the fact that he was ultimately the one who had to make difficult and uncertain decisions, rather than the fact that he possessed epistemic authority or had to provide a compelling justification after the fact. The "buck" in poker is said to point to that person whose turn it is to deal the cards, not who has to pay. As Truman explained, "The President—whoever he is—has to decide. He can't pass the buck to anybody. No one else can do the deciding for him. That's his job." Farewell address, January 1953, as quoted at "'The Buck Stops Here' Desk Sign," Harry S. Truman Library & Museum, www.trumanlibrary.org/buckstop .htm, accessed 21 May 2016.
2 Nb. Lawlor's interest is in developing the idea of assurance, rather than advancing the assurance view of testimony. She remains agnostic about the latter.

3 Here a *reasonable alternative* is, approximately, a possible state of affairs that would falsify the statement, is not obviously incompatible with the observed evidence, and is salient to reasonable people in the context. Ruling out reasonable alternatives is often held as a condition on knowledge.

4 When I talk about "transmission" here, I am referring to a general phenomenon in which the speaker conveys knowledge to a hearer, not a rigid principle according to which testimonial knowledge always originates from a source who has knowledge (cf. Lackey 2008, ch. 2).

5 Well-known challenges to this sort of idea can be found in Graham (2006: 112–113), Lackey (2008, ch. 2).

6 McMyler appeals to the intuition that mere bystanders and eavesdroppers do not have the right of buck-passing, to support the restriction of assurance-based warrant to the intended audience. Lawlor disputes this, holding that mere bystanders and eavesdroppers have the same rights of challenge as the intended audience (Lawlor 2013: 22). There is some empirical evidence for the hypothesis that mere bystanders and eavesdroppers are not ordinarily attributed the right of buck-passing (Turri 2015). However, one might explain this hypothesis in terms of privacy norms rather than epistemic factors: demanding justification from somebody who wasn't speaking to you violates informational privacy (Nickel 2013). It doesn't have to do with warrant.

7 This is obviously different from a criterion for assessing whether a person has knowledge or conclusive warrant for a belief.

References

Bhattacharjee, Y. (2013). The Mind of a Con Man. *New York Times Magazine*, April 26.

Darwall, S. (2006). *The Second Person Standpoint*. Cambridge, Mass.: Harvard University Press.

Faulkner, P. (2011). *Knowledge on Trust*. Oxford: Oxford University Press.

Gelfert, A. (2014). *A Critical Introduction to Testimony*. London: Bloomsbury Academic.

Goldberg, S. (2011). Putting the Norm of Assertion to Work: The Case of Testimony. In J. Brown & H. Cappelen, eds., *Assertion: New Philosophical Essays*. Oxford: Oxford University Press, pp. 175–195.

Goldberg, S. (2015). *Assertion: On the Philosophical Significance of Assertoric Speech*. Oxford: Oxford University Press.

Graham, P. (2006). Can Testimony Generate Knowledge? *Philosophica* 78, pp. 105–127.

Hinchman, E. S. (2005). Telling as Inviting to Trust. *Philosophy and Phenomenological Research* 70(3), pp. 562–587.

Hinchman, E. S. (2012). Can Trust Itself Ground a Reason to Believe the Trusted? In *A Symposium on Paul Faulkner's Knowledge on Trust*. *Abstracta*, Special Issue VI, pp. 47–83.

Hinchman, E. S. (2013). Assertion, Sincerity, and Knowledge. *Noûs* 47(4), pp. 613–646.

Hinchman, E. S. (2014). Assurance and Warrant. *Philosophers' Imprint* 14(17), pp. 1–58.

Lackey, J. (2008). *Learning from Words*. Oxford: Oxford University Press.

Lawlor, K. (2013). *Assurance: An Austinian View of Knowledge and Knowledge Claims*. Oxford: Oxford University Press.

McMyler, B. (2011). *Testimony, Trust, and Authority*. Oxford: Oxford University Press.

Moran, R. (2006). Getting Told and Being Believed. In J. Lackey & E. Sosa, eds., *The Epistemology of Testimony*. Oxford: Oxford University Press, pp. 272–306.

Nickel, P. J. (2012). Trust and Testimony. *Pacific Philosophical Quarterly* 93(3), pp. 301–316.

Nickel, P. J. (2013). Testimonial Entitlement, Norms of Assertion, and Privacy. *Episteme* 10(2), pp. 207–217.

Ross, A. (1986). Why Do We Believe What We Are Told? *Ratio* 1, pp. 69–88.

Schmitt, F. F. (2010). The Assurance View of Testimony. In A. Haddock, A. Millar & D. Pritchard, eds., *Social Epistemology*. Oxford: Oxford University Press, pp. 216–242.

Shieber, J. (2015). *Testimony: A Philosophical Introduction*. London: Routledge.

Turri, J. (2015). Assertion and Assurance: Some Empirical Evidence. *Philosophy and Phenomenological Research* 90(1), pp. 214–222.

Welbourne, M. (1979). The Transmission of Knowledge. *The Philosophical Quarterly* 29(114), pp. 1–9.

11

TESTIMONIAL KNOWLEDGE

Understanding the Evidential, Uncovering the Interpersonal

Melissa A. Koenig and Benjamin McMyler

"One can often believe other people's testimony more than one can believe one's own experience."
(Kant)

Introduction

One remarkable thing about testimony is that any claim can be passed on – testimony is a promiscuous source of knowledge, one that does not discriminate among the kinds of content it conveys. This promiscuity underscores the vast range of information that speakers testify to and discuss, but it can also *mask* the different kinds of reasoning that hearers engage, and the ways in which hearers can treat a speaker's testimony as having different kinds of rational significance. Here we draw on the philosophical and empirical literatures to argue for two basic types of reasoning that operate jointly but distinctly in our evaluations of testimony, and that appeal to different kinds of considerations: what we refer to as "evidential" considerations (indications of a speaker's competence and sincerity, their positional advantages, the hearer's background knowledge), and more robustly "interpersonal" considerations (a speaker's responsiveness to the listener, the responsibility they accept, the hearer's rights of complaint). By characterizing these two distinct types of reasoning, and reviewing evidence that children engage both types of considerations in their testimonial reasoning, we challenge accounts that treat children as narrowly monitoring only evidential considerations (Mercier, 2011; Sobel & Kushnir, 2013; Sperber, Clément, Heintz, Mascaro, Mercier, Origgi, & Wilson, 2010) or as having no epistemic standards at all (i.e., Fricker, 1995; Williams, 2002).

Our aims are twofold: First, to argue that not only do children appeal to important categories of protection or vigilance early on, but that the types of reasons or considerations they respond to are much broader than most epistemological accounts recognize, be they reductionist or anti-reductionist. Second, by considering more carefully the case of child learners, theoretical and philosophical accounts of testimonial knowledge are pushed to more clearly indicate what constitutes legitimate bases of acceptance and rejection, as well as illegitimate bases of acceptance (e.g., gullibility) and rejection (e.g., prejudice). Many scholars working on testimony typically think in terms of two primary sources of risk or error – namely, deception and incompetence. This focus on risk leads to accounts that frame the problem as either (a) requiring positive reasons on behalf of a source's competence or sincerity to minimize one's risk for error; or (b) requiring sensitivity to incompetence and insincerity as sources of defeat, because testimony brings its own warrant. Here, in contrast, we argue that children are responsive to a much wider range of considerations than just competence and sincerity, at least as these are typically understood. They are also responsive to signs of mutual regard, commitment, a speaker's responsiveness, and other characteristics of human nature that go beyond mere accuracy and the expression of what one believes. Thus, in this chapter, we discuss two distinct kinds of consideration that feature early in development – the evidential and the interpersonal.

Many in psychology and philosophy treat testimony as a species of evidence, testimonial acceptance and rejection as evidence-based decisions, and the speakers who provide it as mere instruments of transmission (Hume, 1999; Lackey, 2006; Locke, 1979; Shafto, Eaves, Navarro, & Perfors, 2012; Sobel & Kushnir, 2013; Sperber, Clément, Heintz, Mascaro, Mercier, Origgi, & Wilson, 2010). While we don't deny that we *can* indeed take an evidential stance toward what we are told and an instrumental stance toward sources of information, we argue that evidential views fail to capture the fact that when speakers offer their testimony to others, and implicitly commit or vouch for it, they offer learners a distinct kind of reason, and something other than mere inductive evidence. Consider Kant's observation above that one often believes other's testimony more than one's own experience (1900). Kant is pointing to the contingent empirical nature of all experience, including testimony, and that respect is due to rational agents when they report on their experiences. He argues that testimony allows us to advance and revise our beliefs, not by simply collecting further probabilistic evidence, but by taking speakers at their word, and trusting them (Gelfert, 2006; see also Anscombe, 2008a; Moran, 2005). In believing someone, we presuppose that they are the author of their report, that they believe what they report, and that they report what is the case (Anscombe, 2008b). These presumptive obligations to take seriously what others tell us are not solely epistemic obligations but interpersonally moral ones. Thus, in turning the spotlight on children's use of interpersonal considerations, we examine the moral reasons at play in order to illustrate central but less-understood aspects of our testimonial practices: that communication is not only in the service of transmitting information, but allows people to intentionally offer up their ideas, make simple commitments to each other, clarify their agreements and disagreements, jointly reason to specific conclusions, all in virtue of their mutual regard for each other.

In line with long-standing scholarship and common intuition, we could begin a chapter on children's use of testimony with a discontinuity thesis: a proposal that children must begin their lives with a "simple trust" (Fricker, 1995) or "primitive trust" (Williams, 2002) in what they are told. After all, upon reflection, children are often agreeable despite contrary perceptual evidence (Jaswal, 2004; Jaswal & Markman, 2007), and they can be found believing things that adults do not (or at least, would never admit to) (Clark, 1998; Harris & Koenig, 2006; Shtulman & Carey, 2007; Woolley, Phelps, Davis, & Mandell, 1999). Indeed, many argue that it must be that children have to first acquire some working knowledge of a human language in order to tap into this testimonial system of knowledge in the first place (Coady, 1992; Davidson, 1984; Quine & Ullian, 1970; Wittgenstein, 1972). On the evidential view, a primitive simple trust might seem necessary since it's only after children acquire a sufficient amount of linguistic knowledge "on trust" that they can begin to measure claims against what they know.

These ideas have intuitive merit but carry with them important limits. First, to characterize any learner as unthinking, uncritical, or as simply accepting (or rejecting) all information, including what other people say, is to characterize that learner as failing to meet basic epistemic requirements that we think hold for knowledge acquisition. Second, the question of whether children's testimonial learning represents a discontinuous shift from one type of reasoning to another involves two separate questions: open, empirical hypotheses that concern how children reason, as well as normative hypotheses that concern the kinds of reasons that may be required when gaining knowledge from testimony. Below, we argue that when we assume that testimonial learners begin with an early blind trust, we risk treating testimony narrowly as inductive evidence and fail to account for the greater stock of reasons that children, and all learners, have access to. Even more importantly, we fail to substantiate what it means to trust someone, and thereby neglect the role trust can play in testimonial learning.

Several scholars have appealed to the developmental literature to deny a blind trust thesis (e.g., Clément, 2010; Sperber, Clément, Heintz, Mascaro, Mercier, Origgi, & Wilson, 2010; Stephens, Suarez, & Koenig, 2015). By pointing to early-emerging mechanisms of epistemic vigilance (Clément, 2010; Sperber, Clément, Heintz, Mascaro, Mercier, Origgi, & Wilson, 2010), cognitive "filters" that learners use to check for inconsistencies in content (Mercier & Sperber, 2011), or cues to speaker trustworthiness (Stephens, Suarez, & Koenig, 2015), scholars clarify that children have recourse to some of the same forms of epistemic vigilance as adults. However, by treating testimony as a species of evidence, such accounts run into two kinds of problems. First, by stressing children's sensitivity to evidence, such accounts can only push for modified descriptive claims regarding when blind trust ends, and when children's evidential monitoring begins in ontogeny. Such arguments do not defeat claims of blind trust; rather, they simply push them back to earlier developmental periods. A second problem is that such accounts do not clarify the interpersonal grounds that listeners, including children, have for trusting others and taking them at their word. In other words, when children's testimonial knowledge is tied to evidence only, to the ability to detect risk, and to suspend belief without sufficient evidence, the result is that testimonial reasoning no longer involves trusting others at all. Rather, it involves making a probabilistic inference based on the evidence. So, instead of treating speakers as sources of goodwill and mutual regard, an arguably necessary condition for trusting others, evidentialist accounts construe speakers as variably good instruments for gathering and transmitting evidence.

Here we wish to defend a different thesis: that child learners treat a host of reasons – interpersonal and evidential – as legitimate reasons to seriously consider a claim. Our hope is that this does better justice to the problem that faces any testimonial learner, and better justice to the bases of testimonial knowledge. Our testimonial decisions are responsive to considerations that speak to a speaker's knowledge or competence, but also to indications that testimony is intentionally and freely given, often in response to a listener's epistemic and practical needs. Thus, learning from testimony depends not only upon monitoring for signs of insincerity, knowledge or competence, but also involves an operation of our mutual understanding, recognizing those who tie their experiences with my own, who make evident their interests and ideas, their willingness to cooperate, and who make good on their commitments. In all cases in which we trust others, we are protected not only by our appeals to speaker knowledge, but also by the responsibilities that speakers assume toward us, either by way of contingent interpersonal practices, secure relationships or by the assurances we make clear in communication.

Testimony as Evidence

A speaker's telling a hearer that p provides the hearer with an epistemic reason for believing that p. Depending on the circumstances, the speaker's testimony might not be a good reason to believe that p. If p is very improbable given the hearer's other beliefs, if the speaker isn't competent to pronounce on whether p is the case, or if there is reason to believe that the speaker isn't speaking sincerely, then the speaker's testimony might not provide the hearer with an epistemic reason that is sufficient to justify them in believing that p. Nevertheless, a speaker's testimony often is broadly consistent with a hearer's other beliefs, a hearer often does have good reason to believe (or at least no reason to doubt) that a speaker is competent concerning what they testify, and a hearer often does have good reason to believe (or at least no reason to doubt) that a speaker is sincerely expressing their own beliefs. In such cases, a speaker's testimony can provide a hearer with a good reason for believing that p.

In these respects, testimony is very much like other forms of evidence on which knowledge and justified belief can be based. Just as a fingerprint left at the scene of a crime can, in the right circumstances, give one a very good reason for believing that so-and-so was the perpetrator, so a speaker's testimony that so-and-so committed the crime can, in the right circumstances, give one a very good reason for believing that this is the case. The epistemic task for the hearer is one of determining whether the circumstances are right, whether the fingerprint or the testimony is sufficient reason to believe that this person committed the crime. In the case of testimony, this will require determining the competence and sincerity of the speaker as well as the extent to which the testimony is consistent with the hearer's other beliefs. The hearer's task is one of determining whether the evidence provided by the speaker is reliable.

On this general way of construing the epistemic import of testimony, the fact that testimony is a social act in which one person actively purports to give an epistemic reason to another is largely inconsequential. A hearer's task is to determine whether the evidence they confront is reliable, and while the fact that this particular evidence takes the form of an intentional communicative act might matter for how one goes about determining its reliability, the hearer's reasoning about this evidence is not different in kind from their reasoning about other non-testimonial forms of evidence. The fact that testimony is a social act aimed at communicating information might make determining its reliability particularly difficult – other agents can deliberately lie and mislead in a way that fingerprints and footprints cannot – but this does not make the hearer's task in evaluating the evidence different in kind. The hearer must simply be attuned to the particular kinds of considerations of competence and sincerity that are relevant to assessing the reliability of such social acts.

If one thinks about the epistemic import of testimony in this way, then it will be natural to think of the developmental task facing young children as one of developing the appropriate responsiveness to conditions of competence and sincerity that is required for assessing the reliability of testimonial evidence. Again, this might be more difficult than learning to assess the reliability of other kinds of non-personal evidence in that it requires learning to identify dimensions of competence in speakers and social cues of sincerity, but the learning problem itself is not different in kind from that pertaining to other kinds of evidence. On evidential accounts, children evaluate testimony in much the same way that they evaluate things like footprints in the snow. They learn to distinguish the circumstances in which such things amount to reliable evidence for believing a proposition.

This evidential construal of the epistemic import of testimony has been the dominant one among philosophers and psychologists. Among philosophers, this is most clearly the case for reductionists about testimony who by and large construe testimony as a species of ordinary inductive evidence (Fricker, 1987, 1995; Hume, 1999; Locke, 1979; Stevenson, 1993), but it is also true of many non-reductionist positions that model the epistemology of testimony on other non-inferential sources of knowledge like perception or memory (Burge, 1993; Coady, 1992; Reid, 1997). Among psychologists, this understanding of testimony is tacitly at play in work that aims to identify the forms of epistemic vigilance that children employ in testimonial learning (Koenig & Harris, 2005; Mercier, 2011; Sobel & Kushnir, 2013; Sperber, Clément, Heintz, Mascaro, Mercier, Origgi, & Wilson, 2010, Stephens, Suarez, & Koenig, 2015). On the evidential route, children are understood to recruit their prior knowledge along with a suite of protective cognitive mechanisms – in source memory and attention (Baltazar, Shutts, & Kinzler, 2012; Bjorklund & Sellers, 2013; Hoff, 2016; Kinzler & Shutts, 2008), source monitoring (Corriveau & Harris, 2009; Gopnik & Graf, 1988; Johnson, Hashtroudi, & Lindsay, 1993), and metacognition (Begus & Southgate, 2012; Flavell, 1999; Stephens & Koenig, 2015) – in ways that are continuous with adults (Baumeister, Bratslavsky, Finkenauer, & Vohs, 2001; Buchner, Bell, Mehl, & Musch, 2009; Goldsmith & Koriat, 2007).

Children indeed monitor the evidence: they monitor the reliability of informants (Jaswal & Neely, 2006; Koenig & Harris, 2005; Stephens & Koenig, 2015), their arguments or reasons for belief (Baum, Danovitch & Keil, 2008; Corriveau & Kurkul, 2014; Koenig, 2012), their domain-specific expertise (Aguiar, Stoess, & Taylor, 2012; Kushnir, Vredenburgh, & Schneider, 2013; Koenig & Jaswal, 2011; Lutz & Keil, 2002), and their access to information (Chow, Poulin-Dubois & Lewis, 2008; Kondrad & Jaswal, 2012; O'Neill, 1996). On the evidential route, a speaker's prior reliability constitutes relevant evidence, along with other information, that can be used to assess the truth of a current claim. Prior inaccuracy can be treated as one type of information that features in a stock of relevant considerations – some that may favor the speaker, and others that speak against them. It is always up to the listener to come to their own conclusions about how a speaker's prior behavior relates to the validity of their current claims, whether any given claim is likely to be true and how much confidence to have in it. A speaker's prior reliability relates probabilistically (not deterministically) to the validity of their future claims, and a child's interpretation of the reliability depends upon what contextual factors might explain the behavior (Corriveau, Kinzler & Harris, 2013; Kondrad & Jaswal, 2012; Stephens & Koenig, 2015). By monitoring speaker reliability, for example, children show their concern for one type of relevant, and probabilistic, evidence (see Sobel & Kushnir, 2013, for an analogy between children's reasoning about testimony and other forms of probabilistic data).

Testimony Provides Interpersonal Reasons for Belief

While it is true that we can treat a speaker's testimony as ordinary inductive evidence, there is good reason to think that we do not always treat testimony as such, that the status of testimony as a social act, intentionally aimed at communicating information, makes human testimony very different from a footprint in the snow or a fingerprint left at the scene of a crime. If I believe that there is a deer in the vicinity on the basis of observing some footprints in the snow, it would be odd for me to say that I believe this because I trust the footprints. I might be said to *trust that* the footprints are reliable indicators of the presence of deer, but this sense of trust seems very different from the sense in which we trust other persons, a sense that appears to involve estimating the other's goodwill towards us, among other things (Baier, 1994; Faulkner, 2011; Holton, 1994; Jones, 1996). This more robustly interpersonal sense of trust does seem to characterize many instances of reliance on testimony, however. If I believe that p on the basis of a speaker's telling me that p, it might be perfectly natural for me to say that I believe that p because I trusted the speaker. In believing a speaker, I am *trusting that speaker* for the truth (Anscombe, 2008b), and the sense in which I trust a speaker seems quite different from the sense in which I might be said to trust that other forms of non-personal evidence are reliable indicators of the facts.

Several theorists have thus recently proposed that testimony can provide a distinctively interpersonal kind of reason for belief, one that derives from the dynamics of the person-to-person transaction involved in a speaker's telling a hearer that p and the hearer's taking the speaker's word (Brandom, 1994; Faulkner, 2011; Hinchman, 2005, 2014; McMyler, 2011; Moran, 2005; Ross, 1986; Zagzebski, 2012). If one thinks of the epistemic import of testimony in this interpersonal way, then the developmental task facing children will be categorically different from that involved in learning to appreciate the various factors affecting the reliability of impersonal evidence. The developmental task will instead involve learning to appreciate interpersonal dynamics involved in the way in which testimony is addressed from one person to another. These include such things as a speaker's responsiveness to the addressee's epistemic needs (Hinchman, 2014), committing themselves to the truth of what they say (Moran, 2005), and assuming epistemic responsibility for the addressee's belief (McMyler, 2011). Far from starting with a form of "simple" or "primitive" trust, children are here in the position of developing an increasingly sophisticated interpersonal understanding that is never left behind, but modulated as they participate in various exchanges through childhood and into adulthood. On this analysis, to the extent that testimony is freely, fluently, and intentionally given to another person, this counts against its value as evidence (Moran, 2005), and in favor of its value as a sign of our regard for another person (McMyler, 2011). Below, we begin our empirical review by discussing evidence that children appreciate the mutual regard inherent in their earliest exchanges.

Mutual Regard or Responsiveness

Infants' entry into communication is marked not by the exchange of words, but by the exchange of gestures, points, emotional displays and "showing" behaviors that accompany ostensive communication. Liszowski and colleagues (2006; 2008) have argued that a species-specific adaptation that sets human communication apart from non-human signaling systems can be seen in a human child's early-emerging motivation to show and share with others their interest, emotions, and objects-of-attention, using declarative pointing gestures across varied cultural contexts by 10 to 13 months (Callaghan, Moll, Rakozcy, Warneken, Liszkowski, Behne, & Tomasello, 2011; Liszkowski, Brown, Callaghan, Takada, & de Vos, 2012). Note that infants' earliest ostensive bids succeed in specifying their content, inform listeners of their intention to communicate, and not only draw attention to their own interests but offer information to those who need it (Liszkowski, Brown, Callaghan, Takada, & de Vos, 2012; Liszkowski, Carpenter, & Tomasello, 2008). When infants exchange information with variably responsive others (Gergely & Watson, 1999; Hobson, 2002; Rochat, 2001), they monitor these exchanges for "good responsivity," prove upset when others fail to be mutually responsive (Hobson, 2002; Rochat & Striano, 1999; Trevarthen, 1979), and do various things to re-engage a recalcitrant adult (Ross & Lollis, 1987; Warneken & Tomasello, 2007). Even as third-party observers, infants expect receivers to give speakers the objects they indicate (Martin, Onishi, & Vouloumanos, 2012), and to execute their preferred actions (Vouloumanos, Onishi, & Pogue, 2012). Thus before they can monitor an exchange for truth or accuracy, infants evaluate their own and others' exchanges for mutual responsiveness, and show that they have an emotional stake in these exchanges going well.

We take this as suggestive evidence that from a very early age, children show an early responsiveness to other persons – a distinctively social attunement that may be a distinguishing aspect of human ontogeny. Rather than reflecting a form of blind trust, children's responsiveness to the contingent and mutual dimension of our interactions provides a window into their own interpersonal expectations and standards for others at this age.

Complaint

Contemporary epistemologists argue that listeners who accept a speaker's claim, acquire a suite of rights: rights to hold speakers accountable, rights of complaint, rights to demand an apology, rights to forgive, rights to release the speaker from their obligations, and so on (Feinberg, 1970; Gilbert, 1992; Hinchman, 2005; McMyler, 2011). In fact, if you ignore a speaker's testimony in the spirit in which it was given, and insist on treating claims only as evidence with some probabilistic value, you give up many of your rights to hold speakers accountable. As Hinchman puts it, "You can only hold me to my word, if you accepted my word in the first place" (2005).

Next, we review developmental evidence of children's *complaint*, in response to agents who violate different aspects of testimonial exchanges.

Using various methodologies, researchers have examined infants' reactions to speakers who misname common objects (Begus & Southgate, 2012; Grassmann & Tomasello, 2010; Koenig & Echols, 2003; Pea 1982) or who present difficult or anomalous requests (e.g, "Can you bring me the refrigerator?"; Grosse, Behne, Carpenter and Tomasello, 2010; Shwe & Markman, 1997; Wellman, Song, & Peskin-Shephard, 2019). Overall, the general finding is that even infants actively correct speakers who make mistakes, with the specific conditions of each investigation adding further information about what their corrections reveal. Koenig and Echols (2003) found that 16-month-old infants directed more of their attention to persons who misnamed objects, than to the objects they misnamed. In three subsequent studies, infants did not exhibit this pattern when labels emanated from an audio speaker (not a person) or when the person was turned away from the objects and looked elsewhere. In fact, when a person with access to the objects was responsible for the mistake, 15 out of 16 infants "corrected" that speaker by stating the correct name; a rate of correction that did not obtain toward audio speakers (6/16) or toward speakers who looked elsewhere (8/16). Second, infants showed a tendency to cry or become distressed in response to speakers who falsely addressed them (Koenig & Echols, 2003). Importantly, work by Rakoczy and colleagues clarifies that infants' objections are not only directed at deviant speakers, but at non-cooperative listeners too. For example, Rakoczy and Tomasello (2009) showed 2- and 3-year-old children a series of successful and failed third-party interactions, some involved non-fulfilled imperatives, others involved failed assertions. Children not only actively complained or protested against speakers who failed to describe a scene accurately, but also against agents who failed to fulfill the commands of a speaker (Rakoczy & Tomasello, 2009). Finally, infants' corrections show that their desire is to *be understood*, over and above achieving instrumental goals. Grosse, Behne, Carpenter and Tomasello (2010) created situations that would provoke children to point at some desirable object, and in response, the adult provided the requested item, either accidentally or deliberately. In the crucial "happy accident" condition, the adult accidentally bumped a requested object closer to the child while referencing an out-of-reach non-requested object, "Oh, you want this". In cases like this, the child is misunderstood yet still receives their requested object. By 18 months, infants showed that they want their request *understood* over and above merely getting the object. For example, when a ball was delivered accidentally by a speaker who said, "Oh, you want this paper," toddlers re-pointed to the received object and said things like, "No – ball," while referring to the ball already in their hands. This work clarifies that infants' corrections are not aimed solely at securing their own aims, but at securing a common understanding with a speaker who failed to understand their efforts at communication (Gross, Behne, Carpenter, & Tomasello, 2010; see also Liszkowski, Carpenter, Henning, Striano, & Tomasello, 2004; Liszkowski, Carpenter, Striano, & Tomasello, 2006).

Such an interpretation gains support from further work on children's partner choice. When speakers signal their unwillingness to share information, children seem to give such omissions a moral interpretation (e.g., as failing to provide help), not simply an instrumental one (e.g., as failing to provide information), and prefer to share information with more cooperative and responsive partners (Dunfield, Kuhlmeier, & Murphy, 2013). Consistent with this idea, toddlers selectively provided help to an adult who attempted to share with them, even if they were unsuccessful and never provided a toy (Dunfield & Kuhlmeier, 2010). Young children often prefer partners who showcase interpersonal virtues, like friendship (Ruble & Dweck, 1995), and later in development, become more inclined to consider partners based on skill or competence.

Early complaints, repairs or corrections are typically understood as efforts to instrumentally repair communication, raising long-standing questions about whether early repairs are primarily meant to influence behavior (Csibra & Gergely, 2009; Moore & Corkum, 1994; Shatz & O'Reilly,

1990; Shwe & Markman, 1997) or mental states (Golinkoff, 1993; Liszkowski, Carpenter, & Tomasello, 2008). Our focus here is different. Regardless of whether children represent a given miscommunication as a behavioral failing or a mentalistic one (or both), our suggestion is that such failings may carry moral significance for children. That is, it is important to consider the conceptual possibility that infants' complaints occur in response to the harm that inaccurate speakers risk doing to their listeners, and to the harm that incredulous or reticent listeners do to speakers who address them. Thus, children's objections and sustained attention to such speakers may not only reflect their own abilities to manage and repair informational exchanges, but may also reflect their response to the interpersonal harm that problematic speakers and listeners can do.

Significance of Moral Information

Information about a person's goodwill can be as important, if not more important, than competence information in adults' evaluations of others. Adults report greater interest in moral traits than competence traits when forming an impression of someone (for review, see Fiske, Cuddy, & Glick, 2007, Wojciszke, Dowhyluk, & Jaworski, 1998). Adults respond faster to person cues from the moral than the competence domain, respond more quickly to moral terms with negative than positive valence ("disloyal", "cruel", "deceitful"), and judge trustworthiness in a face more quickly and accurately than competence in a face (Willis & Todorov, 2006; Ybarra, Chan, & Park, 2001). Recent work on children's person perception found greater consensus among 3- to 10-year-old children in response to trustworthy faces than to competent or dominant faces (Cogsdill, Todorov, Spelke, & Banaji, 2014). It could be that as soon as we see a face, we automatically estimate how much to trust it. In fact, automatic assessments to trust or mistrust may be part of what leads us to make judgments about individuals even when our information about them is scant and inadequate (e.g., prejudice) (Adolphs, Tranel, & Damasio, 1998; Stanley, Sokol-Hessner, Banaji, & Phelps, 2011)

Moral information about a source may be as important, if not more important, than competence information to children. In work by Landrum, Mills, and Johnston (2013), children endorsed claims made by morally trustworthy speakers despite their explicit lack of knowledge, and did so over unkind or antisocial speakers who possessed the right knowledge. Similarly, when a speaker's accuracy and niceness were put into conflict, children wrongly attributed accuracy to inaccurate informants said to be "always nice", "to share things … and care about others feelings" (Johnston, Mills & Landrum, 2015). Interestingly, when children are deciding whom to believe, and place greater weight on signs of benevolence, one could argue that it simply reflects a premium placed on a certain kind of inductive evidence that counts for or against a speaker's sincerity. However, young children typically struggle to reject information from overtly deceptive speakers who previously deceived them on repeated occasions (Couillard & Woodward, 1999; Jaswal, Croft, Setia, & Cole, 2010; Peskin, 1992; Sher, Koenig, & Rustichini, 2014; Vanderbilt, Liu, & Heyman, 2011). Heyman, Sritanyaratana, and Vanderbilt (2013) argue that children find it especially difficult to reject deceptive information when they perceive it as being intentionally offered to them, much like advice that is offered by one person to another. We agree with this emphasis, and would further underscore that children's trust (and perhaps that of any of learner) in situations like this may be more directly based in the optimism they have about the good intentions and responsibilities that people make evident in conversation, and less directly based in positive estimates of speaker's knowledge and beliefs.

To sum, our empirical review aimed to highlight: First, that infants attend to the responsiveness of other persons – an early mutual regard that is reflected in their own responses to human exchanges. Second, children treat testimonial transactions as implicating distinctively interpersonal commitments and responsibilities; commitments and responsibilities that can swamp more purely evidential considerations of prior accuracy and reliability. Third, children treat moral or interpersonal considerations of helpfulness and trustworthiness as sometimes more significant than more purely evidential considerations.

Conclusion – The Philosophical Import of Child Learners

If children's early learning begins in testimonial exchanges characterized by mutual responsiveness, with abilities to detect interpersonal violations and to issue complaints to those responsible, as well as a capacity for weighing indications of people's good intentions, then any account that argues that testimonial knowledge involves some process of leaving a form of trust behind so that mature reasoning can emerge needs to be reconsidered, in favor of accounts that (1) characterize the interpersonal reasoning that children showcase in their decisions to trust, in concert with (2) the evidential reasoning that increasingly constrains children's decisions to accept and reject information. Accounts that appeal to an early "blind" trust in order to secure the acceptance of information, not only fail specifically to describe the considerations that factor into the decisions of the youngest and perhaps earliest cultural learners; such accounts fail more generally by falling short in providing a comprehensive account for what constitutes the range of legitimate reasons we have for forming testimonial beliefs, and gaining knowledge from others.

References

Adolphs, R., Tranel, D., & Damasio, A. R. (1998). The human amygdala in social judgment. *Nature, 393* (6684), pp. 470–474.

Aguiar, N. R., Stoess, C., & Taylor, M. (2012). The development of children's ability to fill the gaps in their knowledge by consulting experts. *Child Development*, 83(4), pp. 1368–1381.

Anscombe, E. (2008a). Faith. In M. Geach and L. Gormally, eds., *Faith in a Hard Ground: Essays on Religion, Philosophy and Ethics*. Charlottesville, VA: Imprint Academic, pp. 11–19.

Anscombe, E. (2008b). What is it to believe someone? In M. Geach and L. Gormally, eds., *Faith in a Hard Ground: Essays on Religion, Philosophy and Ethics*. Charlottesville, VA: Imprint Academic, pp. 1–10.

Baier, A. (1994). Trust and antitrust. In *Moral Prejudices*. Cambridge, MA: Harvard University Press, pp. 95–129.

Baltazar, N. C., Shutts, K., & Kinzler, K. D. (2012). Children show heightened memory for threatening social actions. *Journal of Experimental Child Psychology*, 112(1), pp. 102–110.

Baum, L. A., Danovitch, J. H., & Keil, F. C. (2008). Children's sensitivity to circular explanations. *Journal of Experimental Child Psychology*, 100(2), pp. 146–155.

Baumeister, R. F., Bratslavsky, E., Finkenauer, C., & Vohs, K. D. (2001). Bad is stronger than good. *Review of General Psychology*, 5(4), p. 323.

Begus, K., & Southgate, V. (2012). Infant pointing serves an interrogative function. *Developmental Science*, 15(5), pp. 611–617.

Bjorklund, D. F., & Sellers, P. D. (2013). Memory development in evolutionary perspective. *The Wiley Handbook on the Development of Children's Memory*, 1, pp. 126–156.

Brandom, R. (1994). *Making It Explicit*. Cambridge, MA: Harvard University Press.

Buchner, A., Bell, R., Mehl, B., & Musch, J. (2009). No enhanced recognition memory, but better source memory for faces of cheaters. *Evolution and Human Behavior*, 30(3), pp. 212–224.

Burge, T. (1993). Content preservation. *The Philosophical Review*, 102(4), pp. 457–488.

Callaghan, T., Moll, H., Rakoczy, H., Warneken, F., Liszkowski, U., Behne, T., & Tomasello, M. (2011). *Early Social Cognition in Three Cultural Contexts*. Hoboken, NJ: Wiley-Blackwell.

Chow, V., Poulin-Dubois, D., & Lewis, J. (2008). To see or not to see: Infants prefer to follow the gaze of a reliable looker. *Developmental science*, 11(5), pp. 761–770.

Clark, C. D. (1998). *Flights of Fancy, Leaps of Faith: Children's Myths in Contemporary America*. Chicago, IL: University of Chicago Press.

Clément, F. (2010). To trust or not to trust? Children's social epistemology. *Review of Philosophy and Psychology*, 1(4), pp. 531–549.

Coady, C. (1992). *Testimony: A Philosophical Study*. Oxford: Oxford University Press.

Cogsdill, E. J., Todorov, A. T., Spelke, E. S., & Banaji, M. R. (2014). Inferring character from faces a developmental study. *Psychological Science*, 25(5), pp. 1132–1139.

Corriveau, K., & Harris, P. L. (2009). Choosing your informant: Weighing familiarity and recent accuracy. *Developmental Science*, 12(3), pp. 426–437.

Corriveau, K. H., Kinzler, K. D., & Harris, P. L. (2013). Accuracy trumps accent in children's endorsement of object labels. *Developmental Psychology*, 49(3), pp. 470–479.

Corriveau, K., & Kurkul, K. (2014). "Why does rain fall?" Children prefer to learn from an informant who uses noncircular explanations. *Child Development*, 85, 1827–1835.

Couillard, N. L., & Woodward, A. L. (1999). Children's comprehension of deceptive points. *British Journal of Developmental Psychology*, 17(4), pp. 515–521.

Csibra, G., & Gergely, G. (2009). Natural pedagogy. *Trends in Cognitive Sciences*, 13(4), pp. 148–153.

Davidson, D. (1984). *Inquiries into Truth and Interpretation*. New York: Oxford University Press.

Dunfield, K. A., & Kuhlmeier, V. A. (2010). Intention-mediated selective helping in infancy. *Psychological Science*, 21(4), pp. 523–527.

Dunfield, K. A., Kuhlmeier, V. A., & Murphy, L. (2013). Children's use of communicative intent in the selection of cooperative partners. *PloS One*, 8(4), pp. e61804.

Faulkner, P. (2011). *Knowledge on Trust*. Oxford: Oxford University Press.

Feinberg, J. (1970). *Doing & Deserving; Essays in the Theory of Responsibility*. Princeton, NJ: Princeton University Press.

Fiske, S. T., Cuddy, A. J., & Glick, P. (2007). Universal dimensions of social cognition: Warmth and competence. *Trends in Cognitive Sciences*, 11(2), pp. 77–83.

Flavell, J. H. (1999). Cognitive development: Children's knowledge about the mind. *Annual Review of Psychology*, 50(1), pp. 21–45.

Fricker, E. (1987). The epistemology of testimony. *Proceedings of the Aristotelian Society Supplement*, 61, pp. 57–83.

Fricker, E. (1995). Telling and trusting: reductionism and anti-reductionism in the epistemology of testimony. *Mind*, 104(414), pp. 393–411.

Gelfert, A. (2006). Kant on testimony. *British Journal for the History of Philosophy*, 14(4), pp. 627–652.

Gergely, G., & Watson, J. S. (1999). In P. Rochat (Ed.), Early socio-emotional development: Contingency perception and the social-biofeedback model. In *Early Social Cognition: Understanding Others in the First Months of Life*, Vol. 60, New York: Psychology Press, pp. 101–136.

Gilbert, M. (1992). *On Social Facts*. Princeton, NJ: Princeton University Press.

Goldsmith, M., & Koriat, A. (2007). The strategic regulation of memory accuracy and informativeness. In A. S. Benjamin (Ed.), *Psychology of Learning and Motivation*, Vol. 48. Amsterdam: Academic Press, pp. 1–60.

Golinkoff, R. M. (1993). When is communication a 'meeting of minds'? *Journal of Child Language*, 20(01), pp. 199–207.

Gopnik, A., & Graf, P. (1988). Knowing how you know: Young children's ability to identify and remember the sources of their beliefs. *Child Development*, 59(5), pp. 1366–1371.

Grassmann, S., & Tomasello, M. (2010). Young children follow pointing over words in interpreting acts of reference. *Developmental Science*, 13(1), pp. 252–263.

Grosse, G., Behne, T., Carpenter, M., & Tomasello, M. (2010). Infants communicate in order to be understood. *Developmental Psychology*, 46(6), p. 1710.

Harris, P. L., & Koenig, M. A. (2006). Trust in testimony: How children learn about science and religion. *Child Development*, 77(3), pp. 505–524.

Heyman, G. D., Sritanyaratana, L., & Vanderbilt, K. E. (2013). Young children's trust in overtly misleading advice. *Cognitive Science*, 37(4), pp. 646–667.

Hinchman, E. (2005). Telling as inviting to trust. *Philosophy and Phenomenological Research*, 70(3), pp. 562–587.

Hinchman, E. (2014). Assurance and warrant. *Philosopher's Imprint*, 14(17), pp. 1–58.

Hobson, P. (2002). *The Cradle of Thought: Exploring the Origins of Thinking*. London: Pan Macmillan.

Hoff, E. (2016). *Young Children's Source Monitoring and Selective Learning from Problematic Individuals*. Dissertation Thesis. The University of Minnesota Libraries.

Holton, R. (1994). Deciding to trust, coming to believe. *Australasian Journal of Philosophy*, 72(1), pp. 63–76.

Hume, D. (1999). *An Enquiry Concerning Human Understanding*. Oxford: Oxford University Press.

Jaswal, V. K. (2004). Don't believe everything you hear: Preschoolers' sensitivity to speaker intent in category induction. *Child Development*, 75(6), pp. 1871–1885.

Jaswal, V. K., Croft, A. C., Setia, A. R., & Cole, C. A. (2010). Young children have a specific, highly robust bias to trust testimony. *Psychological Science*, 21(10), pp. 1541–1547.

Jaswal, V. K., & Markman, E. M. (2007). Looks aren't everything: 24-month-olds' willingness to accept unexpected labels. *Journal of Cognition and Development*, 8(1), pp. 93–111.

Jaswal, V. K., & Neely, L. A. (2006). Adults don't always know best: preschoolers use past reliability over age when learning new words. *Psychological Science*, 17(9), pp. 757–758.

Johnson, M. K., Hashtroudi, S., & Lindsay, D. S. (1993). Source monitoring. *Psychological Bulletin*, 114 (1), p. 3.

Johnston, A. M., Mills, C. M., & Landrum, A. R. (2015). How do children weigh competence and benevolence when deciding whom to trust? *Cognition*, 144, pp. 76–90.

Jones, K. (1996). Trust as an affective attitude. *Ethics*, 107(1), pp. 4–25.

Kant, I. (1900). *Kant's Gesammelte Schriften, (Academy Edition)*, Berlin: V. von Georg Reimer, W. de Gruyter.

Kinzler, K. D., & Shutts, K. (2008). Memory for "mean" over "nice": The influence of threat on children's face memory. *Cognition*, 107(2), pp. 775–783.

Koenig, M. A. (2012). Beyond semantic accuracy: Preschoolers evaluate a speaker's reasons. *Child Development*, 83(3), pp. 1051–1063.

Koenig, M. A., & Echols, C. H. (2003). Infants' understanding of false labeling events: The referential roles of words and the speakers who use them. *Cognition*, 87(3), pp. 179–208.

Koenig, M. A., & Harris, P. L. (2005). Preschoolers mistrust ignorant and inaccurate speakers. *Child Development*, 76(6), pp. 1261–1277.

Koenig, M. A., & Jaswal, V. K. (2011). Characterizing children's expectations about expertise and incompetence: Halo or pitchfork effects? *Child Development*, 82(5), pp. 1634–1647.

Kondrad, R. L., & Jaswal, V. K. (2012). Explaining the errors away: Young children forgive understandable semantic mistakes. *Cognitive Development*, 27(2), pp. 125–135.

Kushnir, T., Vredenburgh, C., & Schneider, L. A. (2013). "Who can help me fix this toy?" The distinction between causal knowledge and word knowledge guides preschoolers' selective requests for information. *Developmental Psychology*, 49(3), pp. 446–453. doi: 10.1037/a0031649.

Lackey, J. (2006). Learning from words. *Philosophy and Phenomenological Research*, 73(1), pp. 77–101.

Landrum, A. R., Mills, C. M., & Johnston, A. M. (2013). When do children trust the expert? Benevolence information influences children's trust more than expertise. *Developmental Science*, 16(4), pp. 622–638.

Liszkowski, U., Brown, P., Callaghan, T., Takada, A., & de Vos, C. (2012). A prelinguistic gestural universal of human communication. *Cognitive Science*, 36(4), pp. 698–713.

Liszkowski, U., Carpenter, M., Henning, A., Striano, T., & Tomasello, M. (2004). Twelve-month-olds point to share attention and interest. *Developmental Science*, 7(3), pp. 297–307.

Liszkowski, U., Carpenter, M., Striano, T., & Tomasello, M. (2006). 12-and 18-month-olds point to provide information for others. *Journal of Cognition and Development*, 7(2), pp. 173–187.

Liszkowski, U., Carpenter, M., & Tomasello, M. (2008). Twelve-month-olds communicate helpfully and appropriately for knowledgeable and ignorant partners. *Cognition*, 108(3), pp. 732–739.

Locke, J. (1979). *An Essay Concerning Human Understanding*. Oxford: Clarendon Press.

Lutz, D. J., & Keil, F. C. (2002). Early understanding of the division of cognitive labor. *Child Development*, 73 (4), pp. 1073–1084.

Martin, A., Onishi, K. H., & Vouloumanos, A. (2012). Understanding the abstract role of speech in communication at 12months. *Cognition*, 123(1), pp. 50–60.

McMyler, B. (2011). *Testimony, Trust, and Authority*. New York: Oxford University Press.

Mercier, H. (2011). Reasoning serves argumentation in children. *Cognitive Development*, 26(3), pp. 177–191.

Mercier, H., & Sperber, D. (2011). Why do humans reason? Arguments for an argumentative theory. *Behavioral and Brain Sciences*, 34(02), pp. 57–74.

Moore, C., & Corkum, V. (1994). Social understanding at the end of the first year of life. *Developmental Review*, 14(4), pp. 349–372.

Moran, R. (2005). Getting told, being believed. *Philosopher's Imprint*, 5(5), pp. 1–29.

O'Neill, D. K. (1996). Two-year-old children's sensitivity to a parent's knowledge state when making requests. *Child Development*, 67(2), pp. 659–677.

Pea, R. D. (1982). Origins of verbal logic: Spontaneous denials by two-and three-year olds. *Journal of Child Language*, 9(03), pp. 597–626.

Peskin, J. (1992). Ruse and representations: on children's ability to conceal information. *Developmental Psychology*, 28(1), p. 84.

Quine, W. & Ullian J. (1970). *The Web of Belief*. New York: Random House.

Rakoczy, H., & Tomasello, M. (2009). Done wrong or said wrong? Young children understand the normative directions of fit of different speech acts. *Cognition*, 113(2), pp. 205–212.

Reid, T. (1997). *An Inquiry into the Human Mind*. University Park: Penn State University Press.

Rochat, P., & Striano, T. (1999). Emerging self-exploration by 2-month-old infants. *Developmental Science*, 2(2), pp. 206–218.

Rochat, P. R. (2001). Social contingency detection and infant development. *Bulletin of the Menninger Clinic*, 65(3), p. 347.

Ross, A. (1986). Why do we believe what we are told? *Ratio*, 27(1), pp. 69–88.

Ross, H. S., & Lollis, S. P. (1987). Communication within infant social games. *Developmental Psychology*, 23(2), p. 241.

Ruble, D. N., & Dweck, C. S. (1995). Self-conceptions, person conceptions, and their development. In: N. Eisenberg ed., *Review of Personality and Social Psychology: Vol. 15. Social Development*. Thousand Oaks, CA: Sage, pp. 109–139.

Shafto, P., Eaves, B., Navarro, D. J., & Perfors, A. (2012). Epistemic trust: Modeling children's reasoning about others' knowledge and intent. *Developmental Science*, 15(3), pp. 436–447.

Shatz, M., & O'Reilly, A. W. (1990). Conversational or communicative skill? A reassessment of two-year-olds' behavior in miscommunication episodes. *Journal of Child Language*, 17(01), pp. 131–146.

Sher, I., Koenig, M., & Rustichini, A. (2014). Children's strategic theory of mind. *Proceedings of the National Academy of Sciences*, 111(37), pp. 13307–13312.

Shtulman, A., & Carey, S. (2007). Improbable or impossible? How children reason about the possibility of extraordinary events. *Child Development*, 78(3), pp. 1015–1032.

Shwe, H. I., & Markman, E. M. (1997). Young children's appreciation of the mental impact of their communicative signals. *Developmental Psychology*, 33(4), p. 630.

Sobel, D. M., & Kushnir, T. (2013). Knowledge matters: How children evaluate the reliability of testimony as a process of rational inference. *Psychological Review*, 120(4), p. 779.

Sperber, D., Clément, F., Heintz, C., Mascaro, O., Mercier, H., Origgi, G., & Wilson, D. (2010). Epistemic vigilance. *Mind & Language*, 25(4), pp. 359–393.

Stanley, D. A., Sokol-Hessner, P., Banaji, M. R., & Phelps, E. A. (2011). Implicit race attitudes predict trustworthiness judgments and economic trust decisions. *Proceedings of the National Academy of Sciences*, 108(19), pp. 7710–7715.

Stephens, E., Suarez, S., & Koenig, M. (2015). Chapter five-early testimonial learning: Monitoring speech acts and speakers. *Advances in Child Development and Behavior*, 48, pp. 151–183.

Stephens, E. C., & Koenig, M. A. (2015). Varieties of testimony: Children's selective learning in semantic versus episodic domains. *Cognition*, 137, pp. 182–188.

Stevenson, L. (1993). Why believe what people say? *Synthese*, 94, pp. 429–451.

Trevarthen, C. (1979). Instincts for human understanding and for cultural cooperation: Their development in infancy. In M. von Cranach, K. Foppa, W. Lepenies, & D. Ploog (Eds.), *Human Ethology: Claims and Limits of a New Discipline*. Cambridge, UK: Cambridge University Press, pp. 530–571.

Vanderbilt, K. E., Liu, D., & Heyman, G. D. (2011). The development of distrust. *Child Development*, 82(5), pp. 1372–1380.

Vouloumanos, A., Onishi, K. H., & Pogue, A. (2012). Twelve-month-old infants recognize that speech can communicate unobservable intentions. *Proceedings of the National Academy of Sciences*, 109(32), pp. 12933–12937.

Warneken, F., & Tomasello, M. (2007). Helping and cooperation at 14 months of age. *Infancy*, 11(3), pp. 271–294.

Wellman, H., Song, J.,& Peskin-Shephard, H. (2019). Children's awareness of understanding as evident in their spontaneous corrections of speech errors. *Child Development*, 90(1), 196–209.

Williams, B. (2002). *Truth and Truthfulness*. Princeton: Princeton University Press.

Willis, J., & Todorov, A. (2006). First impressions making up your mind after a 100-ms exposure to a face. *Psychological Science*, 17(7), pp. 592–598.

Wittgenstein, L. (1972). *On Certainty*. New York: Harper and Row.

Wojciszke, B., Dowhyluk, M., & Jaworski, M. (1998). Moral competence-related traits: how do they differ? *Polish Psychological Bulletin*, 29(4), pp.283–294.

Woolley, J. D., Phelps, K. E., Davis, D. L., & Mandell, D. J. (1999). Where theories of mind meet magic: The development of children's beliefs about wishing. *Child Development*, 70(3), pp. 571–587.

Ybarra, O., Chan, E., & Park, D. (2001). Young and old adults' concerns about morality and competence. *Motivation and Emotion*, 25(2), pp. 85–100.

Zagzebski, L. (2012). *Epistemic Authority: A Theory of Trust, Authority, and Autonomy in Belief*. New York: Oxford University Press.

12

THE EPISTEMOLOGY OF EXPERTISE

Carlo Martini

Introduction

As social animals, humans typically rely on others to do things for them. In exchange, they usually accept that they will have to do things for others as well. So the baker may provide bread to the banker, while the banker administers the baker's finances. Both of them will probably live in houses built by the mason, while the mason received both bread and financial help from the baker and the banker. Reliance on one another among humans is both material and intellectual. We rely on one another for things we need, but we also rely on one another for information. Reliance on information and knowledge from experts is a special kind of mutual epistemic support among humans: we rely on those whom we think are epistemically better placed than us on a certain subject. We usually call "experts" those who have excellent skills at a given task, or in a given field. These are usually people who have gained the experience and competence we lack through training and personal capacities.

"Expert" is a relative term. It is relative to a layperson. In this chapter we are mostly interested in epistemic experts and epistemic laypeople. Epistemic experts (just "experts", henceforth) are people who are in a superior epistemic position with respect to a group of laypeople. They may be in such a position as a result of superior cognitive abilities, more extended training, greater learning, or simply because of the contingencies of their epistemic status, for example when a witness can testify with their first-hand experience about a murder.

Some epistemologists have claimed that reliance on experts is ubiquitous. Elizabeth Fricker (2006), claims that without epistemic reliance on others we could not trust electricians to wire our home, or doctors to prescribe a medicine for us. Similarly, John Hardwig (1991) portrays a picture of science in which scientists doing research have to constantly rely on the innumerable theses, proofs, and facts and methods already established by other scientists.

In science, experts are usually those who have achieved a high level of competence and experience in their own field. Expertise is typically disciplinary and often sub-disciplinary; but it can also be found outside disciplinary boundaries (see Collins and Evans 2002). Whether there can be interdisciplinary expertise is a matter of debate, but there can be expertise in communicating between disciplines (see Collins and Evans 2008).

Imagine the following situation, in which most people have probably occasionally found themselves: We start feeling a pain in our body; we are looking for a solution to the problem and we would like to know what causes the pain and what could be done about it. The first question we might ask is "can we find the information we seek ourselves, or should we rely on someone else?" The ease with which we usually do not pay much mind to such a question, and with which we immediately assume that, when in pain, we ought to seek professional help, is only revealing of how pressing the question is in a number of less common circumstances. First, it is not always the case that we can rely on someone else; for instance, doctors are not always available in some parts of the world. Second, when it comes to more arcane fields of knowledge, there may not be recognized expertise in that field. In those two cases just mentioned, and in many more, the question "can we gain knowledge from someone else, or should we instead seek knowledge by our own means?" is a pressing one.

But let us assume that, from time to time, we can and ought to seek knowledge from others. Even then, a second problem is likely to arise: How do we know who is and who is not an expert, say, in pain matters? This question is not as easily dismissed as the one we asked before, if only because frauds and impostors are numerous, and compete for authority in all fields of knowledge. Even in the relatively unproblematic field of medical knowledge we still need to know that doctors are usually more qualified than spiritual healers or voodoo priests in pain matters. A further problem is that we may be able to recognize the general field of expertise, but unable to discriminate among competing experts in the same field. To stick to the example at hand (pain), the problem may arise when a physiotherapist gives us advice that conflicts with other information we have received from a surgeon. Telling experts apart from laypeople, and judging among conflicting expert judgments, are problems that we are likely to encounter in many everyday situations, and not just interesting philosophical puzzles.

We can then formulate the three questions that will lead the next sections of this chapter. These are key epistemological questions about expertise.

1 Can we gain knowledge from experts?
2 How do we recognize experts?
3 Is there private expertise? That is, is expertise possessed individually, or is it a relational property?

Experts and Testimonial Knowledge

John Locke considered reliance on authority a fallacy in reasonable argumentation. In his *Essay Concerning Human Understanding* he denies that we can claim to know something on the grounds that it is the opinion of "men, whose parts, learning, eminency, power, or some other cause has gained a name, and settled their reputation in the common esteem with some kind of authority" (see Locke 1689/1999: Chapter XVII). Can we claim to know something because we have received information from an expert? The question is part of a more general family of problems related to testimonial knowledge. While we cannot address those problems in this chapter, we note that it is a generally accepted principle that we can rely on testimony to gain knowledge about the world. This is sometimes called the "default rule on testimony": "If the speaker S asserts that p to the hearer H, then, under normal conditions, it is correct for H to accept (believe) S's assertion, unless H has special reason to object" (Adler 2015).

Despite Locke's skepticism towards authority, reliance on authority is widespread. We read newspapers to learn about exotic countries, and we consult manuals to learn how to use a tool, or how to build furniture. These are examples of how reliant people are on testimonial knowledge, and, solving the epistemological problem of testimony would be a major achievement towards securing knowledge in a social world. Fricker claims that

> The epistemically autonomous individual could not trust an electrician to wire her [...] house for her, since she would not accept his testimony about what he was going to

do, and that it would work safely; nor her doctor to prescribe medicines; nor would she try skiing because her friends [...] told her it was fun.

(2006: 228)

How ubiquitous is really *epistemic* reliance on expert authority? It is debatable whether taking a medicine always requires that we know that the medicine works, or whether scientists are always interested in knowledge, per se, rather than practical applications of their science. We do not rely on electricians to know whether the electrical wiring in our house or office is safe. In fact, we often do not know, or are not interested in knowing, whether it is safe. Let us imagine that someone asked us the question: Do you trust that the building you work in is unlikely to catch fire due to a short circuit? The question might give us pause, but we might answer that we trust city officials to enforce safety regulations; we also trust the legislators to have worked out the law as to give us the safest possible environment, etc. The chain of trust might, at some point, lead us to a matter of testimonial knowledge, but for the most part we live our lives in epistemic darkness.

That is not to say that we never seek knowledge from experts. Sometimes we are genuinely interested in knowing the cause of our illness, or the risk associated with an investment we have made. These are facts we usually do not have direct access to, but which require the competence of an expert, a highly knowledgeable and competent person in the relevant field. Often we are in a situation that Alvin Goldman (2001) has named the "novice/two-expert problem": We want to know whom to trust among a group (two or more) of experts who disagree on the matter we seek knowledge about. Other times, we are in the "novice/expert problem", where a novice is looking for information and has to recognize the expert in a mixed crowd of laypeople, false experts, and true experts.

Both problems are significant and ubiquitous. Suppose we wanted to know whether the fish we are eating is polluted by hazardous chemicals present in fishing waters. There is academic research on ocean and water pollution, but such research is conducted by NGOs and think tanks as well. Then there are environmental organizations, public speakers, journalists, science commentators, conspiracy theorists, and a number of other parties claiming expertise on ocean and water pollution. It is hard to separate the wheat from the chaff, and the trove of potential information we can find freely available makes it hard to find valuable expert judgment that we can rely on. Suppose instead that we wanted to know whether the back pain we are feeling ought to be treated with surgery or physiotherapy. We consult with two doctors and while one of them suggests physiotherapy, the other tells us we should undergo surgery. How do we decide among competing experts?

As we will explain in the next section, deciding who is an expert and who is not is a matter of discriminating among a number of markers of expertise.

Recognizing Expertise

Defining expertise is not the same as recognizing it when we find it. Definitions allow us to identify something, but in practice, identification is not always straightforward. We might have a clue that somebody is an expert, without being able to look, as it were, into the DNA of expertise. Some might like to know what the DNA of expertise is but, if that were possible at all, we will have to leave this intellectual task for another time. In the space of this chapter, we can only point to two fundamental traits of expertise: experience and competence. These are the backward-looking and forward-looking characteristics of an expert. Experts have experience in their field of expertise, and are competent in applying their knowledge and experience to new problems.

Martini (2015a) explains why we cannot detect experience and competence directly. On the one hand, the problem with experience is that we cannot quantify it adequately without first deciding what is relevant and irrelevant experience. On the other hand, the problem with competence is that we cannot know directly whether someone is a competent expert for a new problem or situation, just like we cannot know whether an algorithm that is parametrized on past data will perform well in predicting future data. While we cannot detect experience and competence directly, we can identify a number of indicators (traits) that point to them; that is, we can identify a number of directly observable traits that under normal circumstances are associated with expertise. For example, an extensive track record of successfully solved problems would be a good indicator of an expert's ability to solve similar problems in the area in which the record was tracked, hence fallibly indicating competence.

From the previous paragraph, however, it follows that we can never detect expertise on a certain domain *D* with full certainty. In this section, we will see why recognizing experts is a fallible activity: we can only rely on proxies for expertise, but we cannot detect expertise directly, at least not if we define expertise as the possession of experience and competence.

In the previous section we identified two problems: the novice/expert problem and the novice/ two-experts problem. In the former problem, we want to know whether there is any expertise at all, as when we have a pain and are looking for a doctor in a crowd of laypeople. In the latter, we are trying to find out where there is more expertise, as in the case when two or more experts give us conflicting opinions. We will see that even in the former case we are really only looking at whether there is more expertise in anyone else around us than there is in ourselves, but we can leave those details for the next section. What are then, the individual or group traits that tell us that there is expertise? We can turn the question around, and ask "when can we trust the judgment of a putative expert?" A putative expert is a social construct: putative experts are officially called experts in a given social setting, because of qualifications, reputation, or social standing; but they do not always display the kind of judgment that we should trust. For example, doctors are putative experts on health, but when they prescribe medicines in collusion with interested pharmaceutical companies they cannot be held in high trust by their patients.

In the following, we will list a number of criteria for expertise, each of which will give us some grounds for trusting a putative expert's judgment. We may say that each of the criteria identifies a "proxy" for expertise; that is, a trait which, under normal conditions and in most cases, is correlated with a high level of competence and/or experience. Philosophers, scholars, sociologists and psychologists have provided and discussed several criteria of expertise. The list below provides useful summaries, for more complete reviews see Martini (2014) and Shanteau et al. (2002). Roughly, we can divide proxies for expertise in internal and external ones. An expert's accreditation—for instance, her titles, certificates, and anything that might go into an official curriculum vitae—are external proxies for expertise. In principle, there can be any number of external factors pointing towards the presence of expertise without real expertise. An expert's consistency in judgment, or her self-confidence, on the other hand, are internal proxies for expertise (see Shanteau et al. 2002). It is debatable whether there can be any combination of internal or external proxies for expertise without any real expertise, but arguably it would be rather odd to find in a putative expert a number of internal and external traits that are typically associated with expertise without any real expertise; that is, without any experience and competence.

The following list is by no means a comprehensive and complete list of every proxy for expertise. There can be numerous markers that correlate one way or another with true expertise, and it is in large part an empirical matter to decide which proxies correlate with expertise on a certain subject rather than another. Nonetheless, the following list can serve as a review of some of the traits that are usually associated with expertise.

> *Objectivity.* Experts back their judgments with arguments, and present evidence in support of their opinions. See Walton (1989), Colander (1994), Cooke and Goossens (2000), Goldman (2001), Reiss (2008).

Track-record. Experts have credentials, usually as a track-record of their experience in the relevant field. See Shanteau (1992), Goldman (2001).

Pertinence (domain-specificity). Experts give judgments within their field of competence, they do not judge without qualifications on matters that are not in their field of expertise. See Walton (1989), Shanteau (1992), Reiss (2008).

Proportionality (social acclamation). Experts enjoy a certain degree of consensus in their field. See Hume (1748/2007), Goldman (2001), Shanteau (2000).

Unbiasedness. Experts should not be biased. See Hume (1748/2007), Colander (1994), Cooke and Goossens (2000), Goldman (2001), Reiss (2008).

Content-knowledge. Experts possess content-knowledge; that is, information specific to the field in which they possess expertise. See Shanteau (1992).

Meta-knowledge. Experts know how much they know and how much they do not know. Meta-knowledge comes as good calibration, and the ability to manage the uncertainty related to a problem. See LaBarge (1997), Steve (1982).

Consistency. Experts give judgments that are internally consistent. See Shanteau et al. (2002).

Discrimination ability. Experts are able to discriminate between very similar but not completely equivalent cases. See Hammond (1996), Shanteau et al. (2002).

It must be noted that none of the proxies listed above are fool-proof. True expertise can be correlated with many combinations of the traits above, and there are arguably other traits that may be correlated with true expertise understood as experience and competence. But it is unlikely that true expertise will exist in the complete absence of any of the traits above. That might sound unsatisfying to someone looking for a more precise account of how to identify expertise. Some might desire a set of necessary and sufficient conditions for expertise; but that would not work in the empirical framework of this account. We must accept that finding expertise, and comparing "expertises" are empirical matters, and therefore open to skeptical attacks. The alternative however, that is, to make expertise an easily and precisely definable notion, would trivialize the concept of expertise, rendering it inadequate for any applied epistemological purpose.

To better track expertise, Shanteau et al. (2002) propose a ratio that combines discrimination ability and consistency. The index, they claim, is empirically more successful at tracking expertise (see also Weiss and Shanteau 2004). We recognize that the effort of finding a combination of proxies that better track true expertise empirically is valuable. Nonetheless, in the next section, we will explain why the project of finding the most empirically adequate combination of traits that correlates with expertise is flawed in the long-run. We will argue that expertise cannot be detected, or measured, in the same way as we would perhaps measure the weight of a sphere, or the area of a building. Expertise is a social concept, and measuring expertise is more like measuring a country's wealth, or an individual's happiness: a measuring process that must be constantly updated and corrected.

Social Epistemology of Expertise

In the previous sections, we have identified the main traits of expertise as experience and competence. Even though we cannot detect either of them directly, we can identify a number of internal and external proxies that under normal circumstances correlate with expertise. We could still imagine, however, an ideal world in which we could identify with high empirical precision the traits that correspond to the highest amount of experience and competence. In this ideal world, expertise would be a property of individuals: a certain person would either be or not be an expert or a layperson, given a certain threshold. After all, this is usually how we identify things: flowers are identified by their color, number of petals, shape of the leaf, habitat in which they grow, and so on. In this section we will show that that is not the case for experts. To be an expert is not to possess a more or less fixed number of traits, but to stand in a relation with someone else, namely, a layperson. In this sense, the epistemology of expertise can only be social epistemology, because expertise can only exist in a relational (i.e. social) context.

Let's imagine we could define expertise as being able to perform a set of tasks. For example, an expert violinist is a person who can play the violin. That surely won't do, we'd say; anyone can "play the violin", as long as they can draw the bow over the strings to generate sound. Although that wouldn't be considered "playing the violin", but rather just making noise with the violin, where is the difference between making noise with the bow and strings of a violin and playing the violin? The novice violin player, giving her very bad interpretation of Vivaldi, may receive the same negative judgment from the professional violinist who thinks she is really just making noise, not really playing. Is one year of conservatory school enough to go from "making noise", to playing? Is one week, or ten years, enough? Being an expert violin player is a social fact, not a private one.

Of course we could define experts in a way that would make expertise a private fact. We could define an expert economist as someone who can solve non-linear differential equations, and knows the formulas for at least half of the major economic models produced between the years 1900 and 2000. These definitions are trivial, though, and we would not want to rely on experts whose credentials are established on such flimsy grounds. Imagine a standardized test for college admission that tested students on the number of dictionary words they can define, or the number of math problems they can solve. Or imagine a standardized test for language competence that tested subjects on the number of dictionary words they can translate from one language to another. We would most likely find those tests highly fallible in detecting language competence or academic potential. Both standardized tests and minimal achievement levels may be useful to detect expertise (see the previous section) but they cannot determine who is and who is not an expert.

An even more challenging question is whether there can be expertise outside a social context. Imagine a Robinson Crusoe, stranded on a desert island, who became an accomplished hut builder. Would we call him an expert in hut building? By the social standards he left behind when he shipwrecked on the island, we might well call him so, but in the loneliness of his desert island Crusoe would not feel himself to be an expert in construction; rather, he would just know how to build masterly crafted huts. It is not just that we cannot define expertise as the acquisition of a fixed set of competences, or a fixed record of experiences. The problem is that the concept of expert does not seem to make sense other than in opposition to the concept of the layperson, and, as we argued above, it would be arbitrary to decide at which point a layperson becomes an expert outside of a social context.

Knowledge and skills grow and decline from one society to another, and vary both across time and across geographical locations. What was considered expertise in the early 20th century might be the skills of a layperson today, and a lost skill that any layperson once possessed may be in the bag of tricks of only a few experts today. There is no private fact of the matter whether we are experts or not, so, unlike knowledge—assuming we either know or do not know something—expertise is a social fact. For comparison with this account, the interested reader might examine Elizabeth Fricker's account of expertise, according to which expertise is also a community-relative concept (see Fricker 2006). We can conclude here that epistemology of expertise is therefore social epistemology, in the sense that there cannot be an epistemology of expertise that does not take the social world into account.

A corollary of the previous considerations is that the two problems listed above, which, for simplicity, we classified as the laymen/expert problem, and the layman/two-experts problem, are one and the same problem. Both in the laymen/two-experts and in the layman/expert problems we are comparing levels of expertise in a number of putative experts. If we have two putative experts giving us conflicting opinions, we'll be comparing their expertise relative to one another, but also relative to our own expertise. If, instead, we are to tell the expert apart from a group of laypeople, we are looking for someone who has more expertise than we ourselves do. In other words, we are always comparing ourselves to an expert, even when we are looking for expertise in a world of laypersons, because we always have some expertise, albeit minimal, on the subject matter for which we seek help. Recognizing we need expertise is the first step towards acquiring expertise.

Conclusion

In this chapter we asked three main questions: (a) Can we gain knowledge from experts? (b) How do we recognize experts? (c) Is there private expertise? The first answer is that we can rely on experts just as long as our epistemology allows us to rely on testimonial knowledge. While we cannot tackle the problem of testimonial knowledge in the short space of this chapter, it is usually accepted that much of our knowledge comes from testimony. However, we also pointed out that when we rely on experts we are not so epistemically dependent on other individuals as some commentators have pointed out. Often times we simply rely on expertise in the context of social institutions, and our epistemic status is as good as the social epistemology of the institutions we live in.

The answer to the second question is that we can use a number of fallible proxies for expertise, like social accreditation, or cognitive capacities, but we cannot detect expertise directly, at least if give a non-trivial definition of expertise as experience and competence. Detecting expertise in a given field is an empirical task, and as such highly fallible. The answer to the third question is that expertise is a social concept, and a community-related one. We cannot detect expertise once and for all, because the knowledge and abilities of experts change with the community in which they are embedded. For that reason, the epistemology of expertise is essentially social epistemology.

References

Adler, J. (2015). Epistemological problems of testimony. In: E. Zalta ed., *The Stanford Encyclopedia of Philosophy (Summer 2015 Edition)*, http://plato.stanford.edu/archives/sum2015/entries/testimony-episprob/.

Colander, D. (1994). The art of economics by the numbers. In: R. Backhouse ed., *New Directions in Economic Methodology*, London: Taylor & Francis, pp. 35–49.

Collins, H. and Evans, R. (2002). The third wave of science studies of expertise and experience. *Social Studies of Science*, 32(2), pp. 235–296.

Collins, H. and Evans, R. (2008). *Rethinking Expertise*. Chicago: University of Chicago Press.

Cooke, R. and Goossens, L. (2000). Procedures guide for structural expert judgement in accident consequence modelling. *Radiation Protection Dosimetry*, 90, pp. 303–309.

Fricker, E. (2006). Testimony and epistemic authority. In: J. Lackey and E. Sosa eds., *The Epistemology of Testimony*, Oxford: Oxford University Press, pp. 225–252.

Goldman, A. (2001). Experts: which ones should you trust? *Philosophy and Phenomenological Research*, 63(1), pp. 85–110.

Hammond, K. R. (1996). *Human Judgment and Social Policy*. New York: Oxford University Press.

Hardwig, J. (1991). The role of trust in knowledge. *The Journal of Philosophy*, 88(12), pp. 693–708.

Hume, D. (1748/2007). *An Enquiry Concerning Human Understanding, and Other Writings*. Cambridge: Cambridge University Press.

LaBarge, S. (1997). Socrates and the recognition of experts. *Apeiron*, 30(4), pp. 51–62.

Locke, J. (1698/1999). *An Essay Concerning Human Understanding (Clarendon Edition of the Works of John Locke)*. Oxford: Oxford University Press.

Martini, C. (2014). Experts in science: a view from the trenches. *Synthese*, 191, pp. 3–15.

Martini, C. (2015a). The paradox of proof and scientific expertise. *Humana Mente: Journal of Philosophical Studies*, 28(3-4), pp. 1–16.

Martini, C. (2015b). Expertise and institutional design in economic committees. *Journal of Economic Methodology*, 22(3), pp. 391–409.

Reiss, J. (2008). *Error in Economics: Towards a More Evidence-based Methodology*. New York, NY: Routledge.

Shanteau, J. (1992). The psychology of experts an alternative view. In: G. Wright and F. Bolger eds., *Expertise and Decision Support*, NY: Plenum Press, pp. 11–23.

Shanteau, J. (2000). 'Why do experts disagree?' In: Green, B., Cressy, R., Delmar, F., Eisenberg, T., Howcroft, B., Lewis, M., Schoenmaker, D., Shanteau, J., & Vivian, R. eds., *Risk behaviour and Risk Management in Business Life*. Dordrecht, The Netherlands: Kluwer Academic Press, pp. 186–196.

Shanteau, J. et al. (2002). Performance-based assessment of expertise: how to decide if someone is an expert or not. *European Journal of Operational Research*, 136(2), pp. 253–263.

Steve, C. (1982). Expert judgments under uncertainty: some evidence and suggestions. *Social Science Quarterly*, 63(3), pp. 428–444.

Walton, N. (1989). Reasoned use of expertise in argumentation. *Argumentation*, 3, pp. 59–73.

Weiss, D. and Shanteau, J. (2004). The vice of consensus and the virtue of consistency. In: K. Smith, J. Shanteau and P. Johnson eds., *Psychological Investigations of Competence in Decision Making*, Cambridge: Cambridge University Press, pp. 226–240.

13

MORAL TESTIMONY

Laura Frances Callahan

Introduction

Testimony is a fabulous and fundamental thing. Without the ability to learn and gain knowledge from others by simply taking their word, we would be severely cognitively impoverished. But as it is, by identifying appropriate experts, we can learn truths both useful and erudite. The age of a star, the market value of an old car, the details of human exploits millennia in the past – all can be learned via testimony, if only one can find qualified testifiers. Indeed, epistemologists thinking about testimony tend to treat any proposition as a possible object of such learning. We argue about when and why it is appropriate to believe testimony that '*p,*' where this is understood to range over an unrestricted domain of propositions.

But are there limits to testimony? Are there things one can't – or shouldn't – come to believe by identifying a reliable, knowledgeable expert and deferring to her opinions? Many think some propositions with moral content constitute such an exception.[1] Consider the following scenarios in which adults acquire beliefs via testimony:

1   ALEC doesn't know whether out of pocket expenses for charitable work (e.g., ingredients used to bake for a fundraiser) can be deducted from her taxable income, so she consults a tax expert she trusts to be competent in figuring taxes. The tax expert tells her that yes, in general out of pocket expenses for charitable work can be deducted, which doesn't sound totally crazy, so Alec accepts this.
2   BILL doesn't know whether exclusionary detailing (lying by omission) generally counts as morally wrong. So he consults a person he trusts to be competent in judging these kinds of moral issues. The moral expert tells him it is generally wrong to lie by omission, which doesn't sound totally crazy. So Bill accepts this.

Intuitively, Alec in (1) enhances her knowledge of the tax code, via a perfectly good, untroubling method.[2] But (2) is not so straightforward. If Bill truly has not thought the matter through for himself or *felt* the wrongness of lying by omission, does he really do well, epistemically and/or morally, to simply add 'exclusionary detailing is generally wrong' to his stock of other beliefs? Philosophers have claimed cases like (2) seem 'off-putting' or 'odd' or 'problematic' or 'fishy.' There is a felt *asymmetry* between the two cases.

Why should this be so? Burgeoning literature on 'moral testimony' has produced a number of potential explanations.[3] While this central question is interesting in its own right, what is perhaps most striking about this literature is the way various attempts to accommodate our intuitions about 'off-puttingness' accept sweeping implications for the nature of morality, epistemic normativity, and the epistemology of testimony. The oddness of these cases of moral testimony deserves attention because it can be seen as a spanner in the works of any number of attractive positions – notably moral realism, optimism about the ability of testimony to transmit valuable epistemic states, and the thesis that epistemic normativity generalizes across content of any sort.

My project here is simply to describe and clarify current debates over moral testimony. First, I propose a definition of moral testimony. Then I outline three sources of controversy over the scope of the problem with moral testimony, which seem to be in the background of the more specific debate about the right explanation of moral testimony's seeming fishiness. Lastly, I detail some of these specific explanations and briefly discuss objections.

What Is Moral Testimony?

Some incredulity, on being told there is a funny issue with moral testimony, would be under-standable. After all, people do seem to learn about morality from each other all the time, and legitimately so. Friends ask other friends for advice on moral matters and incorporate their judg-ments as well as their proffered reasons into wider critical reflection. Whole communities and nations are influenced by moral leaders. And we often need expert guidance on non-moral matters to enable our moral judgments. All of this can seem perfectly un-fishy, and there is a very natural sense in which all of it *ought* to count as 'moral testimony.' But parties to debates over moral testimony have in mind something much more specific.

Moral testimony, as generally discussed in this literature and as I will use the term in what follows, has two crucial features. Let a speaker (S) assert a proposition (*p*) to a hearer (H). This will be a case of moral testimony iff

i H *defers* to S on the matter whether *p*,

and

ii *p* has *strong moral content*.

I will discuss each condition in turn.

Deference

Not every hearer who comes to believe a proposition she is told *defers* to the speaker on that occasion.[4] I find it helpful to think of deference in contrast with what Alan Gibbard termed 'Socratic Influence' (1990), wherein a speaker's ideas and suggestions convince a hearer to draw conclusions for herself that are similar to the speaker's own. Foley (2001: p. 85) nicely contrasts what he calls 'authority' with Gibbard's Socratic Influence, claiming that the differ-ence between the two is that 'between my taking your word for something and my not doing so.'

It seems deference occurs (on the part of the hearer) just when 'authority' – in Foley's sense – is exercised (on the part of the speaker), or just when a hearer 'takes a speaker's word.' Note how Hills (2009) also distinguishes deference as one of two 'responses' to moral testimony. You may 'trust or defer to moral testimony, where you simply believe what is said to you' (p. 122). On the other hand, you might 'treat the testimony as moral advice, which you subject to critical scrutiny, and you decide whether or not to accept, on its own merits' (p. 123). Similarly, McGrath (2011) defines cases of deference as those in which 'one holds a view solely because another person holds that view' (p. 113), in contrast to cases in which reasons why the view is true play some role in our adopting it.[5]

The idea is that there is a deferent way of accepting the testimony of others – the way, e.g., Alec and Bill both proceed in our opening examples – that is something like taking a box from them and placing it on one's own shelf, with nothing more than a glimpse inside (a 'not-crazy' check). Having identified a reliable source, one accepts the content of his/her testimony without significant reflection, on his/her word. Now, one might have excellent reason for thinking the testifier reliable and sincere, and hence, in some sense, have excellent reason to believe the testified content. Deference needn't be blind or careless. But, necessarily, one's acceptance in deference cases is not based on any reasons one sees for oneself *bearing on the testified content*. As parties to this debate use the term 'moral testimony,' deference is a necessary component; other instances of learning about morality by way of 'Socratic Influence' are generally set aside as cases of 'moral advice' (see, e.g., Hills 2009: p. 123; see also Nickel 2001: p. 255 on varieties of dependence).[6]

Strong Moral Content

Secondly, in order for a case of deference to count as *moral* testimony, it obviously needs to be deference with respect to a moral matter. Thus it is common for those defending the robust oddity of moral testimony to distance it from testimony about non-moral matters that enables one to make moral judgments.

However, gesturing at a class of moral propositions seems still too vague. *Some* statements employing moral concepts strike us as the kind of thing to which we ought not to say, 'Sure – I trust you – whatever you say.' This is what makes moral testimony an interesting topic. But it seems not all such statements do, or at least not to the same degree. Consider the following:

> *Lying by omission is generally wrong.*
> *Failing to acknowledge advisors when attempting to publish is generally wrong.*
> *Stalin was a cruel person.*
> *Private Smith, who fought in the Hundred Years War, was a brave person.*
> *Gay people should have the right to marry.*
> *Only sovereign states should have the right to print currency.*
> *Mrs. C did the right thing in divorcing her husband for infidelity.*
> *Mrs. C always did the right thing in her dealings in foreign investments as a hedge fund manager.*

When I imagine someone accepting each of these in turn, by way of deferring to another's testimony, my own sense of fishiness varies significantly. And, unfortunately, I see no clear way of splitting off worrisome cases from those less worrisome – for example, it seems we cannot just separate propositions stating principles from claims about individuals.

Here I can only acknowledge the difficulty in giving an informative analysis of the category. Propositions with 'strong moral content' will be provisionally defined ostensively, by reference to cases like Bill's: i.e., propositions with strong moral content will be just those that initially seem highly off-putting when we consider hearers deferring to speakers for their truth. I take it that it is a desideratum for any attempt to explain moral testimony, that the explanation shed light on why *just this* set of propositions strikes us as so odd. In other words, theories of moral testimony should include (and be partly evaluated on) theories of strong moral content.

How Bad Is Moral Testimony?

Having specified the kind of case at issue in this debate, I will now consider three sources of controversy over the scope of the problem with moral testimony, which may illuminate some divergence among positions philosophers find attractive.

i   First, there may be genuine, significant variation in the cases different people classify as seeming fishy vs. not: e.g., a Catholic might see nothing even *prima facie* worrisome about deference to the Church on certain moral matters, whereas Protestants might think that something more is required from individuals if they are to have an unproblematic grasp of the issues at hand. Philosophers who similarly perceive different sets of cases to be explained may understandably be attracted to different explanantia.[7]

ii   Second, for the cases that *do* strike us as fishy, should we take this fishiness to indicate a real *defect* in these testimonial exchanges? And how severe a defect – how bad *is* it to defer on certain moral matters? I take it that controversy over the severity of the defect is roughly what Hopkins (2007) had in mind in making his influential distinction between 'optimists' and 'pessimists' about moral testimony. Roughly, optimists think there is nothing especially bad about learning by moral testimony, while pessimists think it is quite bad and ought not to be done except in certain, exceptional cases.

However, it seems many authors in this literature fit neither characterization and instead fall somewhere in between. Even the most 'pessimistic' may be more approving of moral testimony than one would suppose. Hills (2009: p. 98) famously thinks we have 'strong reasons neither to trust moral testimony nor to defer to moral experts.' And Nickel (2001) suggests that in deferring we violate moral requirements. But even these authors admit that the general prohibition against believing on moral testimony can be overridden in many cases. Parties to the moral testimony debate generally *agree* that common circumstances like the exigencies of time in making moral decisions or 'blind spots' in one's moral education or psychological makeup can render one permitted or even required to accept (or solicit) moral testimony. It seems that strong pessimistic language may then be misleading; perhaps we should not set up a firm rule we fully expect and want people often to be breaking.

The idea that learning by moral testimony is *pro tanto* wrong or bad may be more plausible.[8] On such a view, the defectiveness of moral testimony is just one factor that must be taken into account in assessing whether it is permissible (or even required[9]) for one to learn via moral testimony on a particular occasion, all things considered. Accepting moral testimony, then, would be the sort of option that is always at least somewhat defective, but might still be the best (even morally best) option on offer in given circumstances. A seemingly very similar position holds that moral testimony is merely 'suboptimal.'[10]

Finally, of course, one might deny that our fishiness intuitions latch onto any real defect at all. (One might be wholly 'optimistic' in Hopkins's sense.) The optimist needn't think that *all* cases of moral testimony are kosher. Particular cases might be problematic for any number of moral or epistemic reasons – but, so the thought goes, none of these reasons would stem from the case *simply* being a case of moral testimony. Or, the optimist might say, there is no *in principle* problem with learning a moral proposition via testimony. Moreover, she would want to claim, many actual cases of moral testimony are entirely legitimate.

iii   The third broad source of controversy I have in mind applies only to those who take there to be some real kind of defect in moral testimony. What *kind* of a defect is this – moral or epistemic – and what is the bearer of the defect – the testimonial belief itself, the solicitation or acceptance of the testimony, actions based on the testimonial belief, or the agent receiving the moral testimony?

Multiple combinations are possible here. Hills, I take it, thinks *moral* defects in both the agent and her potential actions also generate *epistemic* defectiveness in the deferring agent (2010: pp. 169–214). On the other hand, Howell (2014), for example, thinks that epistemic defectiveness in testimonial moral beliefs is implausible, and he maintains instead that the defect is moral and borne specifically by the agent or her character.

The relationship between moral and epistemic normativity is, of course, controversial. Many people think that epistemic values can generate moral demands – e.g., the moral demand that we combat epistemic injustice. Perhaps moral values can also generate epistemic demands.[11] Underlying Hills's diagnosis of the defect is her commitment to the idea that what is morally important about moral beliefs *sets the conditions* for epistemic rationality for those very beliefs (2010: pp. 178–179, 213–214). For one holding a highly interrelated view of epistemic and moral normativity, distinguishing between moral and epistemic defects in moral testimony may be a more difficult and less necessary project.

The kind of defect we think is fundamentally at issue in cases of moral testimony will determine the kind of primary norm we need to posit in order to vindicate our judgments (or the primary kind of dis-value[12]). If there is an epistemic defect in moral testimonial beliefs, then presumably some epistemic norm instructs us (*ceteris paribus*) not to have them. On the other hand, if there is a moral defect either in the moral testimonial beliefs themselves, in acting on the basis of those beliefs, or in being an agent with moral testimonial beliefs, presumably some moral norm instructs us (again, *ceteris paribus*) not to believe such propositions, or do such actions, or be such people.

Allow me to recap. So far I have noted that there are some fishy-seeming cases of moral testimony and tried to focus us on the class of these defined by deference and strong moral content. I have also sketched 'background' controversies as to the size of this class, the severity of the defect we should ascribe in such cases, and the nature of any said defect – moral or epistemic, in what bearer. I hope that these distinctions may provide a useful map for comparing particular explanations of moral testimony. Now I turn to examining a few of these explanations in greater detail.

'Dismissive' Explanations

Several putative norms governing the acquisition of beliefs via testimony, or of moral beliefs, might seem to explain moral testimony's seeming fishiness. In this section I want to consider three such norms that underlie 'dismissive' explanations of moral testimony's fishiness, so-called because optimists have appealed to them in attempting to show that there is no in principle problem with moral testimony. (See discussion of such explanations in Hills 2009: pp. 96–97.) For example, Sliwa (2012) appeals to both (a) and (c) below, in the course of offering a piecemeal diagnosis of fishy-seeming cases of moral testimony.

Despite the fact that none of these explanations entail an in principle problem with moral testimony, note that they *need not* be paired with full-blooded optimism about moral testimony. One might think such explanations go a long way in accounting for the fishiness of moral testimony but that they still need supplementing by one of the proposals I will discuss subsequently. Or, even if one thought some dismissive explanation(s) sufficient, one might not count as an optimist if one thought that, in practice, moral testimony *is* always particularly problematic for one or more of the reasons given below. (Though there may be no 'in principle' problem with moral testimony, it might in practice be particularly problematic.)

Moral Disagreement

'One shouldn't take claims in a controversial domain on testimony.'

It seems clear that disagreement among testifiers can sometimes make trusting any one of them inappropriate, including in moral cases. However, moral disagreement may seem unpromising as a complete and general explanation of the seeming fishiness of moral testimony, for a number of reasons.

First, there is not obviously more disagreement in morality than in other domains where testimony does not feel fishy (e.g., dinosaur science). Second, the norm appealed to is contentious among epistemologists of testimony. Can we really never learn any propositions in controversial domains from reliable testifiers? (Surely this would have unacceptably broad consequences?) Finally, it is not as though all particular moral claims are terribly controversial. I think I can perfectly well imagine cases where every last trace of controversy has been stipulated away (Bill does not have any good reason to think that the rough status of lying by omission is controversial, and in fact it is not.) The problem – i.e., the seeming fishiness – seems robust.[13]

Moral Expertise

'One shouldn't take claims on testimony from individuals one cannot reliably identify as experts.'

Plausibly, testifiers do need to have some superior epistemic status that their hearers can detect, if hearers are going to learn anything legitimately via a testimonial exchange. Conceivably, there could be a domain where no one would meet this condition – either because no one had the requisite superior epistemic status, or because those who did were so rare or hard to identify that in practice learning by testimony in a legitimate way would be impossible.

This, it has been suggested, is the state of morality. Some have claimed that there simply are no moral experts.[14] It has also been argued that moral experts are very difficult to identify. There would seem at least sometimes to be a circularity involved in assessing which individuals often make correct, relevantly similar moral judgments, when one is lacking a piece of specifically moral knowledge.[15]

But the non-existence of any moral experts may seem hard to swallow. Plausibly, some people really are better than others at making moral judgments, at least when it comes to particular kinds of issues.[16] And the general difficulty of identifying moral experts seems to explain only some cases of fishy moral testimony – in others, identification of an expert seems clearly not to be the problem.[17] As with disagreement above, we can stipulate away any difficulties in identifying a moral expert, in imagining particular cases. And here too, the fishiness seems robust. There is neither widespread disagreement over the general wrongness of lying by omission, nor (we are assuming) any problem with Bill taking his testifier to be a reliable source on this particular sort of issue. Even taken together, problems with disagreement and expertise do not seem to explain the full range of fishy-seeming cases.

Moral Ignorance

'One shouldn't be ignorant of simple moral truths.'

This norm differs from the previous two, in that it does not purport to apply to all cases of testimony, but rather to all cases of moral belief, testimonial or otherwise.[18]

Sliwa (2012: pp. 184–186) appeals to something like this norm as underlying our fishiness intuitions in certain cases where the hearer's very need for information is, intuitively, morally problematic. Indeed, precisely those cases that are not plausibly explained by issues with moral disagreement will often be ones where the hearer's very need for the information strikes us as off-putting, even morally bad.

However, note that in cases where one is problematically morally ignorant, it would seem good to remedy one's ignorance in certain ways (e.g., reasoning to a moral conclusion, coming to see a moral truth via immersive, practice-based learning in a community) but odd or off-putting to remedy it simply by deferring to a reliable source. It is not *only* Bill's ignorance that strikes us as problematic; it is also the means by which he addresses it.

Now, it seems undeniable that some or all of the norms in (a) to (c) create 'noise' in many actual cases of moral testimony. Moral testimony is often worrisome for some of the same reasons that other testimony can be, and perhaps also for the reason that having basic moral beliefs in place is so morally important. My sense, though, is that a fishy odor would remain even if we could strip away all these reasons to worry about particular cases. To admit as much seems to require admitting that moral testimony is rather a tricky problem, in that other available explanations – such as the next three I will consider – seem rather more controversial and revisionary for our ways of thinking about epistemology and/or ethics.

'Ambitious' Explanations

The following explanations, which appeal to more controversial and hence more 'ambitious' norms, have all generally been associated with pessimism about moral testimony. However, note that these proposals are compatible with quite a weak view of the norms in question. The 'in principle' problems with moral testimony these explanations posit need not be viewed as *big* problems that would strictly forbid actually deferring across circumstances.

Moral 'Truth'

'One shouldn't take [purely expressive, or otherwise non-cognitive] claims on testimony.'

Some authors have argued that only moral realists, or especially moral realists, have trouble accounting for the fishiness of moral testimony. (See McGrath 2011.) If moral claims actually differ semantically in important ways from other, straightforwardly cognitive claims about objective matters, we might positively *expect* there to be special problems in communicating those claims via testimony.

This explanation obviously will be unappealing to those who take themselves to have strong, independent reason to adopt moral realism. But note too that it is far from clear whether particular non-cognitivist or non-realist positions of the sort that currently hold sway will be able to offer easy, satisfying explanations of the fishiness of moral testimony. Most contemporary non-cognitivists and constructivists want to vindicate (much) intersubjective discourse about morality, including the way moral claims often seem to function as though they were 'realist' in nature.[19]

Seeing moral testimony as a challenge to moral realism may be under-motivated. It remains unclear whether other plausible metaethical positions fare better. Moreover, if there is some other attractive explanation of the phenomenon compatible with moral realism, moral realists might adopt it without much cost.

Autonomy

'One should make moral judgments for oneself.'[20]

The thought that drawing moral conclusions or making moral judgments is simply a kind of cognitive work one should do for oneself derives some plausibility both from the nature of moral responsibility and from particular, substantive theses in ethics.

Claiming, 'Janie told me to do it,' does not absolve one's bad behavior (or not entirely, or at least not all of the time). Perhaps, 'Janie told me it was all right to do it,' should not absolve bad moral beliefs (or not entirely, or at least not all of the time). A feature of beliefs acquired through deference is the tendency of the believer to refer to the testimonial source when asked for justification.[21] But perhaps, if an agent is to take moral responsibility for the moral beliefs she holds, she may not pass the burden of justification onto even a reasonably trusted other.

Moreover, some Kantians, for example, may be committed to the idea that it is part of the nature of a right moral belief that one hold it on the basis of one's own *rational reflection*. Anscombe considers (but ultimately wants to reject and revise) this view:

> This view [that there is something essentially less teachable about morals than other subjects] might be maintained in connection with that autonomy of the will about which Kant wrote. To take one's morality from someone else – that, it might be held, would make it not morality at all; if one takes it from someone else, that turns it into a bastard sort of morality, marked by heteronomy.
>
> *(45, brackets mine)*

Not only does the basic norm stated above have some *prima facie* plausibility, it also seems straightforwardly to deliver the verdict that there is something non-ideal or *pro tanto* bad about cases of moral testimony as such. Those who defer to another on certain moral matters (like Bill in our opening example) are 'outsourcing' moral judgments, which, according to this explanation, ought not to be done.

The most convincing objections to the strategy under consideration seem to be (i) that the norm is implausible as stated and misrepresentative of any true requirements of autonomy, or (ii) that explanations appealing to autonomy are incomplete.

Driver (2006: p. 636) and Zagzebski (2012: pp. 166–170) have both argued that deference to testimony needn't be in tension with autonomy. Their contention, roughly, is that we exercise autonomy in the relevant, plausibly required, sense when we *choose* whom to trust as a moral testifier:

> A decision is made at a higher level – a higher legislative level, if you will – to trust the judgment of a person one has good reason to trust. The trust is not blind, it is not faith. Thus the agent exhibits both independence of mind and responsiveness to reasons.
>
> *(Driver 2006: p. 636)*

In response, the autonomy explanation proponent might maintain that such choosing is insufficient for important autonomy and that the actual making of moral judgments – the drawing of moral conclusions on the basis of the reasons that ground their truth – is something each agent should do for herself. Perhaps it is just true that, as Coady has it, in moral matters '… the agent has a special adjudicatory task that he cannot abdicate' (1994: p. 72). If there is something problematic about leaning on another's judgment in the moral realm, choosing well with respect to the one trusted will not help matters in any obvious way.

A more convincing objection to the autonomy explanation, to my mind, is the charge that it is *incomplete*, or that a lack of autonomy is only *part* of what makes cases of moral testimony seem fishy. After all – as long as we are working with a relatively 'thin' notion of autonomy – we can conceive of cases where moral judgments are made autonomously, where still the resulting moral beliefs are fishy and problematic. A deluded or vicious person might autonomously make all her moral judgments on the basis of whims, or of 'reading' tea leaves. In such cases, part of what seems fishy or problematic about these beliefs seems to be a lack of understanding of the reasons why moral propositions are true. But this kind of understanding of one's beliefs *also* seems to be in tension with deference to *testimony*, or so many authors in this literature have argued.

In practice, very recent literature on moral testimony has blurred the lines between appeals to the importance of autonomy and appeals to the importance of understanding (which I will consider next). Advocates of the understanding explanation generally *agree* that it is important to make moral judgments for oneself; however, they think there is an additional requirement that is intuitively important: that one hold one's beliefs in a certain *way*, involving an appropriate grasp of the reasons why they are true. Indeed, it is because accomplishing this kind of hold on a moral belief can generally only be done by the individual who comes to hold it, that some version of the autonomy requirement comes along 'for free,' as it were, once we require agents to have understanding. However, note that, whereas autonomy explanations tend to locate the root of the fishiness of moral testimony immediately in a hearer's deference, appeals to understanding have largely cast the fishiness as stemming from extrinsic problems with deference (e.g., tension with acting with full moral worth.) For this reason at least, autonomy explanations deserve separate mention and consideration.

Understanding

'One should have *understanding* of one's moral beliefs.'

Now, while in principle one could have a different view of the sort of 'understanding' important for moral beliefs, I will focus in this section on an influential view of understanding propounded by, for example, Nickel (2001), Riggs (2003), and Hills (2009). The rough idea is that having understanding that *p* involves grasping the status of other propositions one believes as reasons for *p*, and, more generally, rational support relations among some cluster of relevant other propositions. So, having understanding that *p* includes appreciating some reasons why *p* is true, as well as appreciating some things that follow from *p*. According to Hills (2009: pp. 102–103), understanding that *p* involves various abilities – e.g., to follow and also give explanations why *p*, or to draw similar conclusions consistent with one's reasoning in similar cases.

The contention underlying this explanation of the fishiness of moral testimony is that having understanding, of this sort, is both (i) especially or distinctively important in the moral domain, and (ii) in tension with deferring to testimony.

Hills (2009) and Nickel (2001) both argue that understanding is particularly important in the moral domain. First, such understanding, when moral, seems to have a distinctive instrumental importance given the essentially practical nature of many moral propositions. The thought is that it is crucially important for agents to have, for themselves, a mastery of moral reasons, if they would form additional correct moral beliefs and act rightly in particular, novel situations.

Second, understanding might be thought to have a distinctive final importance in the moral domain, or at least to be partly constitutive of actions or traits with final value. Some hold that only actions undertaken for the reasons that make those actions morally required or permitted are morally worthy (see Nickel (2001); see also recent discussions of moral worth in, e.g., Markovits (2010).) Understanding, construed as appreciating reasons for moral judgments, may then be a pre-requisite for morally worthy action.[22] It has also been argued that this kind of understanding in the moral domain is simply a component of moral virtue, that agents are morally better for having it (see Howell (2014).)

Finally, it is argued that deference to testimony is in tension with acquiring understanding. Certainly it seems that one who defers to a testifier for her belief does not to come to any *automatic* appreciation of the reasons why it is true. And Hills (2009, 2013) has argued for the much stronger thesis that acquiring understanding via deference is impossible.

In objecting to the understanding explanation, one might first question whether the instrumental practical importance of understanding why moral propositions are true is in general greater than the instrumental importance of understanding why many other propositions are true. One might also worry that this proposal will only be able to explain the fishiness of moral testimony on matters relevant to action.[23] If one explains the importance of moral understanding by reference to its impact on the quality of one's actions and character, one may be at a loss to explain the fishiness of relatively un-actionable moral propositions with strong moral content. Moreover, one might question whether deferring to testimony really is sufficiently in *tension* with achieving understanding of moral propositions, to explain our fishiness intuitions.

But I suspect that the most important reasons to worry about this explanation, as in the case of the autonomy explanation, stem from its incompleteness. Understanding moral propositions, in the sense of seeing reasons for them and things that follow from them, hardly *guarantees* us a good relationship with moral truth. We might have such understanding and yet still (problematically) lack appropriate *emotions* and/or *motivations*. But such emotions and motivations may *also* seem to be difficult to acquire via testimonial deference.[24] It may be necessary, for a full explanation of the fishiness of moral testimony, to also appeal to norms requiring us to have appropriate moral sentiments (Fletcher 2016) or requiring us to develop moral virtue (Howell 2014).

Conclusion

I have just suggested that the seeming fishiness of moral testimony may well motivate the recognition of special norms or values governing moral belief acquisition, stemming from the distinctive (moral and/or epistemic) importance of autonomous judgment, understanding, and perhaps further elements (such as emotion and motivation) in the moral domain. Recalling earlier discussion of these fishiness intuitions, note that it would add to the appeal of such an explanation if proponents of the explanation could come up with a principled theory of strong moral content. To offer guidance on the proper place of moral testimony in our communal life, proponents would also need to specify the strength and nature they take the norms posited by their explanations to have.

Pressing, further questions I have not had space to consider here concern the relationship between moral testimony's seeming fishiness and other, plausibly related phenomena. Do our conclusions about moral testimony apply in any straightforward way to, for example, religious testimony? What about other seemingly 'fishy' kinds of testimony – e.g., aesthetic or expert testimony (see note 1)? Should we in fact see moral testimony as one instance of some broader class that is problematic, and how should our diagnosis of the specific problem with moral testimony relate to our diagnosis of the problematic nature of that broader class?

The issues raised by debates over moral testimony are important and far-reaching. I take it that the recent explosion in literature on this topic is fully warranted, and in fact there is much more work to be done understanding the implications of simple cases like Bill's.

Notes

1 See also Lackey (2011, 2013) for discussion of cases of 'expert' and 'aesthetic' testimony that seem to be 'deficient' as well. Within the moral testimony literature there is also discussion of other problematic types of testimony. See, e.g., Driver (2006), Enoch (2014), Groll and Decker (2014), and Fletcher (2016).

2 These cases were inspired by McGrath (2011: 111), who writes, 'There is something off-putting about the idea of arriving at one's moral views by simply deferring to an expert. By contrast, there is no problem with deferring to a tax specialist about one's taxes.'

3 See, for example, Roger Crisp's (2014) 'Moral Testimony Pessimism: A Defence,' Julia Driver's (2006) 'Autonomy and the Asymmetry Problem for Moral Expertise,' David Enoch's (2014) 'A Defense of Moral

Deference,' Guy Fletcher's (2016) 'Moral Testimony: Once More with Feeling,' Daniel Groll's and Jason Decker's (2014) 'Moral Testimony: One of These Things is Just Like the Others,' Alison Hills's (2009) 'Moral Testimony and Moral Epistemology' and (2013) 'Moral Testimony,' Robert Hopkins's (2007) 'What is Wrong with Moral Testimony?' Robert Howell's (2014) 'Google Morals, Virtue, and the Asymmetry of Deference,' Karen Jones's (1999) 'Second-Hand Moral Knowledge,' Hallvard Lillehammer's (Lillehammer 2014) 'Moral Testimony, Moral Virtue, and the Value of Autonomy,' Sarah McGrath's (2009) 'The Puzzle of Pure Moral Deference' and (2011) 'Skepticism about moral expertise as a puzzle for moral realism,' Andres Mogensen's (2017) 'Moral Testimony Pessimism and the Uncertain Value of Authenticity,' Philip Nickel's (2001) 'Moral Testimony and Its Authority,' Paulina Sliwa's (2012) 'In defense of moral testimony.'

4 It may or may not be that deference is a feature of every strictly *testimonial* exchange, properly so-called. I sometimes follow others' usage of 'testimony' in a looser, broader sense, but I mean to take no stand on this issue.

5 As I've sketched it, deference seems to be distinguished by both (i) its disregard for content, in its exclusive sensitivity to the 'higher order' evidence that so-and-so believes *p*, and (ii) the decisive *weight* one gives this higher-order evidence. But perhaps fishiness intuitions may be generated in cases where one only 'defers' in the sense of (i) – where one alters one's moral beliefs to any degree purely in the light of such higher-order evidence. If this is correct, debates over moral testimony may have even greater implications for the correct response to moral *disagreement*.

6 McGrath (2011) notes that deference is actually a more general phenomenon than testimony. We can defer to another's belief whenever we learn of it, even if this does not happen by way of receiving their testimony. And, she thinks, non-testimonial deference on moral matters is also off-putting. Hence, McGrath eschews talk of moral testimony in favor of considering moral *deference*. Similarly, Howell (2014: 390) notes that one might defer to one's past or future self, in a way that also seems problematic in the moral domain.

Still, there is reason to continue discussing moral testimony in particular. Testimony is not only the most common way for us to learn about each other's moral opinions – it is a practice that epistemologists have considered at length. We have complex, subtle theories about when and why it is appropriate to believe the testimony of another. Moral testimony is interesting, in part, because it seems to throw those off.

7 Robust data on the degree and types of variation in fishiness intuitions across individuals and cultures would seem highly useful for theorizing about moral testimony. Significant variation might favor explanations of moral testimony's fishiness that appealed to more controversial norms of moral belief formation – norms accepted only by some individuals, or cultures.

8 See especially Crisp (2014).

9 See especially Enoch (2014).

10 See, e.g., Howell (2014).

11 Consider requirements to avoid culpable ignorance, or the call to satisfy epistemic conditions on acting with moral worth.

12 I will primarily discuss moral and epistemic *norms* in what follows. But everything I say should be easily translatable for those who would prefer axiological explanations.

13 See, e.g., Hopkins (2007: 620–621).

14 See, e.g., Williams (1995: 205). See also McGrath (2009) for extended discussion of 'egalitarian' (roughly, expert-denying) responses to moral testimony.

15 See especially McGrath (2009: 332–335).

16 See, e.g., Jones (1999), Singer (1972), and Hills (2009: 96–97).

17 See, e.g., Zagzebski (2012: 164); Hills (2009: 96–97); Hopkins (2007: 623–626).

18 Groll and Decker (2014) defend a similar norm applying to all 'normal knowledge' – knowledge the lack of which is evidence of a kind of dysfunction.

19 See McGrath (2011: fn. 11).

20 It is an interesting question how closely appeals to the value of autonomy are related to appeals to the value of authenticity (Mogensen 2017). It seems the accounts will face similar challenges.

21 See, e.g., McMyler (2011).

22 However, it is not clear that mere *knowledge* of moral reasons and action on the basis of those would be insufficient for moral worth. See Sliwa (2016).

23 See McGrath (2011: 135–136).

24 See especially Fletcher (2016). Even Zagzebski, who defends substantial deference to testimony on moral matters, worries about the limitations of deference precisely to engage hearers' emotions:

In contemporary epistemology testimony is typically treated on a simple model of a propositional belief acquired on the say-so of another. Once the believer accepts the proposition, she can then use it the same way she uses any other belief. But the ability to act on a moral belief acquired by testimony is limited by the fact that a moral judgment needs to engage the motivations of the believer …

(2012: 170)

References

Coady, J. A. (1994). *Testimony: A philosophical study*. Oxford: Oxford University Press.

Crisp, R. (2014). Moral testimony pessimism: A defence. *Aristotelian Society: Supplementary Volume*, 88(1), pp. 129–143.

Driver, J. (2006). Autonomy and the asymmetry problem for moral expertise. *Philosophical Studies*, 128(3), pp. 619–644.

Enoch, D. (2014). A defense of moral deference. *Journal of Philosophy*, 111(5), pp. 229–258.

Fletcher, G. (2016). Moral testimony: Once more with feeling. In: R. Shafer-Landau, ed., *Oxford studies in metaethics*. Volume 11 Oxford, UK: Oxford University Press, pp. 45–73.

Foley, R. (2001). *Intellectual trust in oneself and others*. New York: Cambridge University Press.

Gibbard, A. (1990). *Wise choices, apt feelings*. Cambridge, MA: Harvard University Press.

Groll, D., & Decker, J. (2014). Moral testimony: One of these things is just like the others. *Analytic Philosophy*, 55(1), pp. 54–74.

Hills, A. (2009). Moral testimony and moral epistemology. *Ethics: An International Journal of Social, Political, and Legal Philosophy*, 120(1), pp. 94–127.

Hills, A. (2010). *The beloved self*. Oxford: Oxford University Press.

Hills, A. (2013). Moral testimony. *Philosophy Compass*, 8(6), pp. 552–559.

Hopkins, R. (2007). What is wrong with moral testimony? *Philosophy and Phenomenological Research*, 74(3), pp. 611–634.

Howell, R. J. (2014). Google morals, virtue, and the asymmetry of deference. *Noûs*, 48(3), pp. 389–415.

Jones, K. (1999). Second-hand moral knowledge. *The Journal of Philosophy*, 96(2), pp. 55.

Lackey, J. (2011). Assertion and isolated second-hand knowledge. In: J. Brown, and H. Cappelen, eds., *Assertion*. Oxford: Oxford University Press, pp. 251–275.

Lackey, J. (2013). Deficient testimonial knowledge. In: T. Henning, and D. Schweikard, eds., *Knowledge, virtue, and action: Putting epistemic virtues to work*. New York: Routledge, pp. 30–52.

Lillehammer, H. (2014). Moral testimony, moral virtue, and the value of autonomy. *Aristotelian Society: Supplementary Volume*, 88(1), pp. 111–127.

Markovits, J. (2010). Acting for the right reasons. *Philosophical Review*, 119(2), pp. 201–242.

McGrath, S. (2009). The puzzle of pure moral deference. *Nous-Supplement: Philosophical Perspectives*, 23(1), pp. 321–344.

McGrath, S. (2011). Skepticism about moral expertise as a puzzle for moral realism. *Journal of Philosophy*, 108 (3), pp. 111–137.

McMyler, B. (2011). *Testimony, trust, and authority*. Oxford: Oxford University Press.

Mogensen, A. (2017). Moral testimony pessimism and the uncertain value of authenticity. *Philosophy and Phenomenological Research*, 92(2): pp. 261–284.

Nickel, P. (2001). Moral testimony and its authority. *Ethical Theory and Moral Practice*, 4(3), pp. 253–266.

Riggs, W. D. (2003). Understanding 'virtue' and the virtue of understanding. In: M. DePaul, and L. T. Zagzebski, eds., *Intellectual virtue: Perspectives from ethics and epistemology*. Oxford: Oxford University Press, pp. 203–226.

Singer, P. (1972). Moral experts. *Analysis*, 32(4), pp. 115–117.

Sliwa, P. (2012). In defense of moral testimony. *Philosophical Studies*, 158(2), pp. 175–195.

Sliwa, P. (2016). Moral worth and moral knowledge. *Philosophy and Phenomenological Research*, 93(2): pp. 393–418.

Williams, B. (1995). *Making sense of humanity*. Cambridge: Cambridge University Press.

Zagzebski, L. (2012). *Epistemic authority: A theory of trust, authority, and autonomy in belief*. New York: Oxford University Press.

14

TESTIMONY AND GRAMMATICAL EVIDENTIALS

Peter van Elswyk

Introduction

Testimony is a social practice in which a speaker presents a proposition to a hearer who becomes positioned to accept that proposition because it was presented. At the center of a typical interaction is a declarative sentence.[1] A speaker provides testimony by using a declarative.[2] That declarative then expresses the proposition that a hearer may decide to accept.

But declaratives differ from one language to the next. Some contain tense, Mandarin declaratives do not. Some contain dedicated expressions that mark the sentence as declarative, English declaratives do not. Faced with variety, we should ask two questions.

(q₁) Do the linguistic properties of a language's declarative make a difference to how testimony is socially practiced?

(q₂) If so, are such differences in social practice relevant to the epistemology of testimony?

In this chapter, I answer both questions positively to show how cross-linguistic considerations are relevant to the epistemology of testimony. Unlike other sources of evidence like perception and memory, testimony is intimately related to language. That intimacy cannot be overlooked.

I make my case with declaratives containing evidentials. These are grammatical elements found in 25 percent of the world's languages that specify the source of evidence for a proposition expressed by a declarative (Aikhenvald, 2004). After explaining in the second section how testimony is practiced differently in languages with evidentials, I illustrate in the third and fourth how these differences matter to the epistemology of testimony.[3] My illustration has a negative and a positive part. For the negative part, it is argued that some definitions of testimony are mistaken because they do not apply to testimony offered by a declarative containing an evidential. The positive component discusses a new puzzle noted by McCready (2015) that evidentials raise about the justificatory status of testimony-based beliefs. I conclude in the final section.

Evidentiality

The most basic unit of meaning is a morpheme. Some morphemes are words, some are not. For example, *impossible* consists of two morphemes: the word *possible* and the prefix *-im*. Evidentials are morphemes that specify a source of evidence. Consider an example in Cheyenne with an English translation from Murray (2010, 46).

(1) É-némene-sėstse Sandy.
     Sandy sang, I hear(d).

The evidential in the Cheyenne sentence is *sėstse*. It appears as a suffix on the verb for singing. What it specifies is that the speaker has hearsay evidence for the proposition that Sandy sang.

Importantly, not all expressions about evidence source are evidentials. Though most languages have expressions about evidence, languages only have evidentials when their grammar contains evidentiality as a category (Aikhenvald, 2004; Speas, 2008). For example, English has adverbs like *allegedly* and parenthetical verbs like *I heard*, but these expressions are not evidentials. An apt parallel is tense. Though most languages have expressions to specify the time at which an event occurs, not all languages contain tense.

That evidentials belong to a grammatical category is significant. Morphemes belonging to a grammatical category can sometimes be obligatory. Consider tense again. Declaratives are ungrammatical in English without a tense morpheme specifying the time at which the verb's event occurs. Compare *Pim smile* and *Pim smiled*. The first is uninterpretable but the second is interpretable because it contains the past tense morpheme -*d*. In some languages with evidentiality, a declarative is similarly ungrammatical when it lacks an evidential. As Aikhenvald (2004, 1–2) notes:

> Tariana, an Arawak language spoken in the multilingual area of the Vaupé's in northwest Amazonia, has an even more complex system. In this language, one cannot simply say 'José played football'. Just like in all other indigenous languages from the same area, speakers have to specify whether they saw the event happen, or heard it, or know about it because somebody else told them, etc. This is achieved through a set of evidential markers fused with tense. Omitting an evidential results in an ungrammatical and highly unnatural sentence.

The significance of evidentials to testimonial practice is therefore immediate. In languages with obligatory evidentials, speakers are not capable of providing testimony by using a declarative without disclosing the source of their information. Merely stating how things are is grammatically impossible.

But how does a declarative with an evidential convey the speaker's evidence source? Taking the tense parallel too seriously tempts the conclusion that languages with obligatory evidentials limit speakers to only saying propositions about their evidence sources. Tense places limits on what can be said, after all. But evidentials are different. A use of a declarative can express many propositions because of the expressions it contains. An expressed proposition is at-issue when it is the sentence's main point or primary contribution. Being at-issue contrasts with being not-at-issue which is the status content has when it is expressed but backgrounded. Examples of not-at-issue content include presuppositions triggered by verbs like *stopped* and conventional implicatures conveyed by expressions like *therefore*.[4] Evidentials are similar in that they contribute not-at-issue content distinct from that expressed by the declarative's main clause.[5] Reconsider (1). It expresses two propositions: that Sandy sang, the proposition associated with the main clause, and that the speaker heard that Sandy sang, the proposition contributed by the evidential.

To illustrate, an important diagnostic for being at-issue is being directly challengeable with replies like *That's false* (Tonhauser, 2012). But the contribution of an evidential is never directly challengeable. Korotkova (2016, 66) observes that "Based on the data from available studies of evidentiality … the non-challengeability of the [evidential's contribution] is a *universal* property of morphological evidentials." The only proposition targetable is the one contributed by the main clause. Here are some examples in Cuzco Quechua from Faller (2006, 157–158) where the demonstrative *that* is used to target different propositions with varying success.

(2) Inés-qa qaynunchay ñaña-n-ta-s watuka-sga.
    At-issue: Inés visited her sister today.
    Not-at-issue: Speaker was told that Inés visited her sister today

(3) Mana-n chiqaq-chu. Manta-n-ta-lla-n watuku-rqa-n.
    That's not true. She only visited her mother.

(4) Mana-n chiqaq-chu. #Mana-n chay-ta willa-rqa-sunki-chu.
    That's not true. #You were not told this.

(3) and (4) are replies to (2). The reply in (3) is acceptable. *That* targets the at-issue proposition while the speaker disagrees that Ine´s visited her sister. In contrast, (4) is not acceptable because it attempts to target the not-at-issue proposition to disagree that the speaker heard as much.

Standardly, evidentials are categorized according to whether they specify that the speaker has direct or indirect evidence for the at-issue proposition. Direct evidentials specify that the speaker has perceptual evidence (*e.g.* sight, sound) while indirect evidentials specify that the speaker's evidence is mediated (*e.g.* inferred, hearsay). Cross-linguistic variation is found in the number of evidentials a language has and which sources receive a dedicated evidential (Willett, 1988; Aikhenvald, 2004). Some like Cherokee only have evidentials coarsely marking whether the source is direct or indirect (Pulte, 1985). Others have a more fine-grained system. Tariana has direct evidentials for information sourced visually or non-visually and indirect evidentials for information that was inferred, assumed, or reported (Aikhenvald, 2004).

Speakers of many languages with evidentials consider some sources to be weaker or less reliable than others. As Givón (2005, 169) puts it, "evidential markers code primarily the evidential source that can back up an assertion and … indirectly, the strength or reliability of that evidence."[6] To explain speaker judgements about strength, scales like Figure 14.1 are frequently found in the linguistics literature.[7]

Fundamental facts about the nature of evidence may not be reflected in Figure 14.1. However, what Figure 14.1 does reflect is that an evidential can sometimes determine the strength with which the at-issue proposition is recommended by a speaker.[8] For example, perception licenses the use of both a direct evidential and an inferential evidential because a speaker can draw inferences about her experience. In choosing which to use, speakers often base their selection based on how forcefully they want to stand behind the at-issue proposition. A speaker choosing to stand behind a proposition less uses an inferential evidential. Otherwise, she uses a perceptual evidential.

We can observe the difference that evidentials make to strength by considering what happens when a speaker follows the presentation of an at-issue proposition with a disavowal of belief in that proposition. In English, disavowing belief in the at-issue proposition expressed by an unqualified declarative is Moorean paradoxical (Moore, 1962).

(5) Pim smiled, but I don't believe it.

Declaratives with evidentials specifying a source that is considered strong are similarly infelicitous. However, evidentials specifying a source that is considered weak can be followed by

Figure 14.1 Scale of speaker judgements

a disavowal in some languages. Hearsay evidentials are the prime example. Below is another illustration in Cuzco Quechua from Faller (2002, 194).

(6) Para-sha-n-si, ichaqa mana crei-ni-chu.
     It is raining (I heard), but I don't believe it.

The speaker in (6) presents the at-issue proposition that it is raining and specifies that her evidence is hearsay. Then she immediately states without infelicity that she does not believe what she overheard.

Evidentials therefore influence testimonial practice in another striking way. Depending on the evidence source that is specified, the strength with which the speaker recommends the at-issue proposition varies. Testimony sourced directly in the speaker's own experience is regarded as stronger than testimony sourced indirectly.[9] Consequently, how a hearer is positioned to respond to testimony varies with the oomph of the speaker's recommendation. Hearers offered only testimony backed by hearsay, for example, may want to suspend judgment until they receive testimony backed by a stronger source.

Altogether, I have identified two major ways in which testimonial interactions are distinct because of evidentiality. The first is that a speaker always conveys a not-at-issue proposition about her evidence for the at-issue proposition. The second is that the strength of the testimony varies depending on which source is specified by the not-at-issue proposition. Atop these features of testimonial practice other conventions and norms take shape. To pick one example, evidentiality informs how trustworthiness is determined. A speaker's reliability can be measured by whether she accurately uses evidentials or not. As a consequence, speakers whose native language has obligatory evidentials often mistrust what other speakers say in another language that does not have obligatory evidentials. Aikhenvald (2004, 343) reports, for example, that "Indians of the Vaupés area complain that when non-Indians speak Portuguese they are not explicit enough and often 'lie.'"

Testimony as Source

Having seen how testimonial practice is different in languages with evidentials, we turn to its epistemology.[10] Most theorizing about testimony is informed by cases where it is offered by speakers using unqualified declaratives like *Pim smiled*. Let's call testimony offered by an unqualified declarative UNQUALIFIED TESTIMONY and use EVIDENTIAL TESTIMONY to name testimony that a speaker offers by using a declarative with a grammatically obligatory evidential. In this section, I show how considering only unqualified testimony has produced mistakes in how some demarcate testimony as a source.

Definitions of testimony are either broad, narrow, or somewhere in the middle (Lackey, 2008). Having few conditions on what testimony is, broad definitions count many acts as sources of testimony. Narrow definitions countenance fewer acts as testimony by having more conditions. Common to various moderate and narrow definitions is what I call an offering condition. An offering condition requires that a speaker's saying a proposition is presented as evidence for that proposition. The condition is explicit in the first condition of the narrow definition provided by Coady (1992, 42).

(c_1) S stating that p is evidence that p and is offered as evidence that p.

It is also explicit in the first condition of a weaker definition that Graham (1997, 227) offers.

(g_1) S's stating that p is offered as evidence that p.

The condition is implicit in many understandings of testimony as well. When Burge (1993, 467) glosses testimony as an act where a proposition is "presented as true" by a rational speaker, he appears to assume that the speaker's expressing *p* is regarded as evidence for *p*. Similarly, Moran (2005, 15) does not offer outright a definition of testimony, but he says that what separates testimony from other linguistic acts is that, in testimony, the speaker is "presenting his utterance as a reason to believe" a proposition.

The problem with an offering condition is that it does not apply to all instances of evidential testimony. In the second section, we learned that an evidential declarative expresses an at-issue proposition (call it *p*) and a not-at-issue proposition about the speaker's source of evidence for the at-issue proposition (call it *q*). That means the speaker is always offering *q* as evidence for *p* in evidential testimony. As a result, we can distinguish two ways that a speaker can support a proposition through an act of testimony.

DOUBLE-BARRELED SUPPORT
Both *S*'s stating that *p* and *S*'s stating that *q* are evidence for *p*.

SINGLE-BARRELED SUPPORT
Only *S*'s stating that *q* is evidence for *p*.

What double-barreled and single-barreled support have in common is that *q* is offered as evidence for *p*. But they differ on whether the speaker's stating that *p* is also offered as evidence for *p*. Since only *q* is offered as evidence for *p* with single-barreled support, an offering condition cannot apply to evidential testimony backed with single-barreled support.

Let's consider a concrete example. In some languages with grammatical evidentials, they can appear in interrogatives as well as declaratives (Aikhenvald, 2004; Speas, 2008). When they appear in interrogatives, the evidential does not specify the speaker's source of evidence. Instead, the evidential constrains what evidence source the hearer can specify in an answer. Here is an example in Cheyenne from Murray (2017, 87).

(7) Tósa'e é-hoé-sėstse
     Given what you heard, where does Annie live?

As a result of the evidential, (7) cannot be sincerely answered by a hearer unless she can support her answer with hearsay evidence. With this feature of evidentials in view, consider the following hypothetical situation between two speakers of Cheyenne.

HESITANT CHELSEA
Chelsea has no beliefs about where Annie lives. She is skeptical of propositions for which she does not have direct evidence and her only evidence concerning Annie's residence is hearsay that she lives on George Street. So Chelsea is suspending judgment until her epistemic position improves. But Rebecca, a mutual friend, asks Chelsea to state where Annie lives given what she heard. Chelsea would not normally volunteer such information because she does not believe it. Still, she cooperates with Rebecca's request by answering that she heard (*sėstse*) that Annie lives on George Street. To ensure that Rebecca knows her own attitude on the question, Chelsea quickly follows her answer by disavowing belief.

In such a case, Chelsea is not offering her statement that Annie lives on George Street as evidence. Murray (2017, 72) describes *sėstse*, the hearsay evidential, as not "commit[ting] the speaker at all to the truth or the possibility of the at-issue proposition" expressed by a declarative. So

Chelsea cannot be understood as supporting the proposition that Annie lives on George Street. Her disavowal of belief underscores her lack of support. Nevertheless, Chelsea still testifies that Annie lives on George Street. By disclosing that she has hearsay evidence, Chelsea enables Rebecca to make up her own mind. If she is less skeptical about hearsay evidence than Chelsea, Rebecca could come to believe that Annie lives on George Street on the basis of Chelsea's answer.

The particular lesson to learn is that definitions of testimony cannot possess an offering condition. Though such a condition may aptly characterize unqualified testimony, it does not apply to evidential testimony with single-barreled support. So broader characterizations of testimony are better suited to apply to evidential and unqualified testimony alike. The definition in Fricker (1994, 396) of testimony as "tellings generally" will do, but so will less broad definitions that lack an offering condition.[11] The general lesson to learn is methodological. Mistakes about testimony will be made if we are not attentive to practice differences caused by language.

Testimony-Based Beliefs

Once testimony has been demarcated as a source, the natural epistemological question to ask is how beliefs based upon testimony are justified. On one side, there are REDUCTIONISTS. They maintain a hearer's testimony-based beliefs are justified only through other sources available to the hearer (*e.g.* memory, perception, induction).[12] On the other side, NON-REDUCTIONISTS maintain that testimony- based beliefs have independent justification.[13] A proposition's being testified is sufficient justification for a hearer's belief. In between reductionism and anti-reductionism are various hybrid positions.[14] This section motivates that evidential testimony presents new considerations relevant to understanding the justificatory status of testimony-based beliefs.

Depending on one's view, different advice will be given about how to respond to testimony. Reductionists and hybrid views will provide you with a checklist to resolve before you accept what is testified. For example, they may want to know whether the speaker providing the testimony is reliable in your experience. Non- reductionists will not present you with a checklist. As long you do not have prior reasons for not accepting what was testified, you are justified in accepting the testified proposition. Let's distill this advice as the following principle inspired by Burge (1993).

> Acceptance principle (AP)
> We are justified in accepting anything that we are told unless there is positive evidence
>   against accepting what we are told.

Importantly, AP is not limited to the at-issue proposition expressed by the declarative used to offer testimony. Nor should it be. A sentence can express many propositions and a hearer is just as positioned to accept one as she is to accept any other. That one proposition is at-issue while the others are not does not make a difference to a hearer's ability to learn.

But most not-at-issue content is not about the at-issue content. Presuppositions are not, for example. So evidential testimony is unique. It puts the hearer in a position where she can learn about the epistemic status of the at-issue proposition from the not-at-issue proposition contributed by the evidential. What the hearer learns might then influence whether she decides to accept the at-issue proposition. That can lead to situations where a hearer both has reason to accept and not to accept the at-issue proposition. McCready, one of the few to consider the epistemological significance of evidentiality, observes that evidential testimony generates that paradoxical situation when an unreliable source is specified (2015, 260–261).

Suppose that the speaker has a choice between asserting *Dirφ* and *Repφ* (from some direct evidential *Dir* and hearsay evidential *Rep*). *Repφ* requires a weaker justification than *Dirφ*

and is likely to be less reliable. Thus, given that the speaker asserted *Repφ* rather than *Dirφ*, we can conclude ... that she was not sufficiently confident in her justification to assert *Dirφ* ... But then ... it does not appear to be reasonable for the hearer to add φ to her stock of beliefs. But ... the Acceptance Principle tells us that φ should be accepted, given that there are no confounders. Thus the fact that the speaker proffers φ will be enough to justify the hearer coming to believe that φ.

Let's call this the ACCEPTANCE PUZZLE. Those favoring reductionist or hybrid theories of testimonial justification have an easy solution. They will deny AP because more is needed for justification than what AP requires. But what solutions are available to the non-reductionist?

One option is to restrict AP only to propositions for which the speaker has direct evidence. McCready (forthcoming) proposes such a solution by endorsing a principle we can reconstruct as AP_r.

Acceptance principle restricted (AP_r)
We are justified in accepting anything the speaker says that she acquired directly unless
    there is positive evidence against accepting what we are told.

Supplanting AP with AP_r solves the acceptance puzzle. That is because AP_r does not justify a hearer in accepting φ on the basis of testimony taking the form *Repφ*. We are only justified in believing φ on the basis of testimony when the speaker's source of evidence for φ is direct.

But this solution comes with a steep cost. It renders a huge swathe of testimony-based beliefs unjustified. As Martini (forthcoming) notes, beliefs based in hearsay include those developed in response to oral history, those students learn from what teacher report from textbooks, those formed by young children about the meanings of words, those about the distant past, and more. Though some non-reductionists may be willing to rid many testimony-based beliefs of their justification, I doubt most will want to. Reductionism is frequently criticized on the grounds that it cannot justify enough testimony-based beliefs (Coady, 1992; Adler, 2002; Lackey, 2008). Non-reductionists wary of underjustifying many of our beliefs should similarly not favor AP_r.

Denying that hearsay evidence is weak might seem to be the most straightforward solution available to the non-reductionist. If non-reductionism is true, after all, the speaker's source of evidence is irrelevant to testimonial justification. That the testified proposition is backed by hearsay arguably provides extra justification as well. It means that the belief is supported by a chorus of testifiers who have checked it against their own knowledge.

A cost accompanies this solution as well. Though the view that hearsay evidence is weak is not unique to languages with evidentials, evidentiality integrates the view into language in a unique way.[15] As we learned in the second section, the weakness of hearsay follows from the strength scale of Figure 14.1 that reflects speaker judgments. So maintaining that testimony backed by hearsay is strong as opposed to weak entails that speakers of languages with evidentials systematically err. I did not take a side in the second section on whether information about the strength of an evidence source was part of the semantic content of an evidential or a pragmatic inference made by hearers.[16] But suppose it is semantic such that part of the not-at-issue content contributed by an evidential is that the source specified is weak. Then the non-reductionist must conclude that speakers cannot specify that they have hearsay evidence without saying something false. They may truthfully say *Repφ*, but they falsely say that *Rep* is weak.

That cost snowballs into another. Many non-reductionists begin by identifying what our testimonial practices are and then finish by explaining why those practices are epistemically responsible (Coady, 1992; Graham, 2000). For example, acceptance is the default response to unqualified testimony if a hearer does not have prior reason to doubt the speaker. A principle like AP accounts for why that response is not irresponsible. But we have seen that evidential testimony with a hearsay evidential is not associated with the same defaults. The testimonial practices are different in languages with evidentials. So to hold that speakers of languages with evidentials systematically err betrays the methodology. A non-reductionist wanting to be consistent in this methodology will therefore need to somehow accommodate that hearsay is weak.

Let's consider one final response. The non-reductionist might argue that there is no puzzle in the first place. AP states that acceptance is justified unless there is positive evidence against accepting what we are told. So maybe evidential testimony is just unusual in that the positive evidence against accepting the at-issue proposition can be learned from the not-at-issue proposition expressed in that very act of testimony. In other words, the situation McCready describes is not paradoxical because the hearer can accept the not-at-issue proposition that the speaker has hearsay evidence, as advised by AP, but not accept the at-issue proposition because she now has positive evidence that the speaker's evidence for the at-issue proposition is weak.

Nevertheless, there remains good reason for thinking that the non-reductionist is confronted with a puzzle. Consider what the hearer does not learn from the not-at-issue proposition. She does not learn that the at-issue proposition is false or that speaker has evidence that it is false. She does not learn that the speaker is untrustworthy, deceptive, or confused. Instead, what she learns is that the speaker learned the at-issue proposition through testimony. That is not positive evidence against accepting what was said. It is exactly the opposite. If the speaker learned the at-issue proposition through testimony, then, given AP, the speaker was justified in accepting the at-issue proposition. The hearer should likewise be justified in accepting that proposition. And yet, the fact that the speaker used a hearsay evidential as opposed to a direct evidential signals that the speaker does not have stronger evidence with which to support the at-issue proposition. As a result, the hearer has reason to not accept the at-issue proposition in this situation. In the words of McCready (2015, 261), "we now have two inferential chains which lead to contradictory conclusions."

Perhaps the non-reductionist can do better than the three responses I have considered.[17] My aim in discussing the puzzle was not to argue against non- reductionism. It was to showcase how evidential testimony raises new issues in the epistemology of testimony. What we have seen is that evidential testimony supported by hearsay does exactly that. It generates a puzzle that does not have an easy solution.

Conclusion

In showing how evidentiality in particular makes a difference to how testimony can be understood, I have only scratched the surface. There are many more questions about testimony that are raised by evidentials. Still, this chapter has made a case for the importance of cross-linguistic considerations to the epistemology of testimony. Like many corners of philosophy, theorizing about testimony often treats English as the lingua franca. But that assumption can only get us so far. If we want to understand testimony as an act and source available in every language, we need to attend to how it is practiced differently in some societies because of the language spoken.

Notes

1 By *declarative*, I mean the sentence type with a proposition for its meaning that contrasts with the interrogative and imperative types (Sadock and Zwicky, 1985; König and Siemund, 2007). Some mean by *indicative* in the literature on testimony what I mean by *declarative*. But *indicative* has another use identifying a syntactic configuration that contrasts with a subjunctive configuration. To avoid confusion, I stick with *declarative*.

2 In what follows, I forego discussion of the interplay between testimony and speech acts. Usually, though, testimony is characterized as being the product of an assertion and an assertion is what is performed by the use of a declarative. My reason for omission is that evidentials raise just as many questions about assertion as they do about testimony. For some discussion, see Faller (2002), Chung (2010), Velleman (2014), Murray (2017), and van Elswyk (2018).

3 The explanation of evidentiality that I provide is tailored to highlight its significance to testimony. For more expansive introductions, I recommend the reader begins with Aikhenvald (2004), Speas (2008), and Murray (2017).

4 Potts (2004), Tonhauser et al. (2013), and Horn (2016) provide taxonomies of not-at-issue content. See Simons et al. (2010), Murray (2014, 2017), Syrett and Koev (2015), Hunter and Asher (2016), and Frazier et al. (2017) for theories of the (not-)at-issue distinction.

5 See Murray (2010, 2014, 2017), Izvorski (1997), Faller (2002), Matthewson et al. (2007), and Krawczyk (2009).

6 It is an open question how evidentials are associated with judgments about the reliability of an evidence source. That association could be coded into the meaning of evidentials or it could be the result of a pragmatic inference. For various perspectives on this issue, consult Faller (2012), Krawczyk (2009), Davis et al. (2007), Northrup (2014), McCready and Ogata (2007), McCready (2015), and Murray (2017).

7 See Givón (1982, 2005), Barnes (1984), Willett (1988), Chafe and Nichols (1996), Faller (2002, 2012), and Davis et al. (2007).

8 I hedge with *sometimes* because not every language with evidentiality as a grammatical category allows their use to influence strength or force. Aikhenvald (2004, 6, *fn*.1) notes that it depends on the size of an evidential system and the number of expressions within that system. The examples given in this paper are from languages where fieldwork has confirmed that evidentials do influence strength.

9 Hedges like *Pim smiled, I heard* behave similarly in English. See Benton and van Elswyk (2018) for discussion.

10 My discussion of testimony is limited to showcase the significance of evidentiality to its epistemology. For more thorough introductions, see Lackey (2010), Adler (2015), Gelfert (2014), and citations therein.

11 Definitions that fit this description include those given by Lackey (2008) and Cullison (2010).

12 Reductionism has its roots in David Hume. The leading defender is Fricker (1994).

13 An early non-reductionist was Thomas Reid. Among others, contemporary defenses of non-reductionism are offered by Coady (1992), Burge (1993), Moran (2005), and Graham (2010).

14 Prominent hybrid positions are found in Lackey (2008) and Faulkner (2011).

15 Consider, for example, the hearsay evidence rule found in many legal systems. For some discussion of the rule, see Coady (1992) and Gelfert (2014).

16 See *fn*.6.

17 McCready (2015) offers another solution that I do not discuss for reasons of space. That solution comes in the form of a dynamic semantics for evidentials. One may wonder, though, whether an epistemic puzzle can be solved with semantics.

References

Jonathan Adler. *Belief's Own Ethics*. Cambridge, MA: MIT Press, 2002.

Jonathan Adler. Epistemological problems of testimony. *The Stanford Encyclopedia of Philosophy*, 2015. Available at: https://plato.stanford.edu/entries/testimony-episprob/.

Alexandra Aikhenvald. *Evidentiality*. Oxford: Oxford University Press, 2004.

Janet Barnes. Evidentials in the Tuyuca verb. *International Journal of American Linguistics*, 50: 255–271, 1984.

Mathew Benton and Peter van Elswyk. Hedged assertion. In Sandy Goldberg, editor, *Oxford Handbook of Assertion*. Oxford University Press, 2019.

Tyler Burge. Content preservation. *The Philosophical Review*, 102(4): 457–488, 1993.

W. Chafe and J. Nichols. *Evidentiality: The Linguisitic Coding of Epistemology*. Norwood, NJ: Ablex, 1996.

Kyung-Sook Chung. Korean evidentials and assertion. *Lingua*, 120(4): 932–952, 2010.

C.A.J. Coady. *Testimony: A Philosophical Study*. Oxford University Press, 1992.

Andrew Cullison. On the nature of testimony. *Episteme*, 7(2): 114–127, 2010.

Christopher Davis, Christopher Potts, and Peggy Speas. The pragmatic values of evidential sentences. *Proceedings of SALT*, 17: 72–88, 2007.

M. Faller. Evidentiality below and above speech acts, 2006.

Martina Faller. *Semantics and Pragmatics of Evidentials in Cuzco uechua*. PhD thesis, Stanford University, 2002.

Martina Faller. Evidential scalar implicatures. *Linguistics and Philosophy*, 35(4): 285–312, 2012.

Paul Faulkner. *Knowledge on Trust*. Oxford, UK: Oxford University Press, 2011.

Lyn Frazier, Brian Dillon, and Charles Clifton. Together they stand: Interpreting not-at-issue content. *Language and Speech*, 2018, pp. 199–226.

Elizabeth Fricker. Against gullibility. In A. Chakrabarti and Bimal Krishna Matilal, editors, *Knowing from Words*. Dordrecht: Kluwer, 1994, pp. 125–162.

Axel Gelfert. *A Critical Introduction to Testimony*. Bloomsbury Critical Introductions to Contemporary Epistemology. London: Bloomsbury, 2014.

T. Givón. Evidentiality and epistemic space. *Studies in Language*, 6(1), 1982, pp. 23–49.

T. Givón. *Context as Other Minds: The Pragmatics of Sociality, Cognition and Communication*. Amsterdam: John Benjamins, 2005.

Peter J. Graham. What is testimony? *Philosophical Quarterly*, 187: 227–232, 1997.

Peter J. Graham. The reliability of testimony. *Philosophy and Phenomenological Research*, 61(3):695–709, 2000.

Peter J. Graham. Testimonial entitlement and the function of comprehension. In Alan Millar and Adrian Haddock, editors, *Social Epistemology*. Oxford, UK: Oxford University Press, 2010, pp. 148–174.

Larry Horn. Information structure and the landscape of (not-)at-issue meaning. In Caroline Fery and Shinichiro Ishihara, editors, *Oxford Handbook of Information Structure*. Oxford, UK: Oxford University Press, 2016, pp. 108–127.

Julie Hunter and Nicholas Asher. Shapes of conversation and at-issue content. *Semantics and Linguistics Theory*, 26: 1022–1042, 2016.

Roumyana Izvorski. The present perfect as an epistemic modal. *Proceedings of SALT 12*, 222–239, 1997.

E. König and P. Siemund. Speech act distinctions in grammar. In T. Shopen, editor, *Language Typology and Syntactic Description*, 1. Cambridge, UK: Cambridge University Press, 2007, pp. 276–324.

Natalia Korotkova. Disagreement with evidentials: A call for subjectivity. In Julie Hunter, Mandy Simons, and Matthew Stone, editors, *JerSem: The 20th Workshop in the Semantics and Pragmatics of Dialogue*, New Brunswick, NJ: Rutgers University Press, 2016, pp. 65–75.

Elizabeth Krawczyk. Do you have evidence for that evidential? In Corinne Hutchinson and Elizabeth Krawczyk, editors, *Theoretical Approaches to Understudied Languages*, Washington, DC: Georgetown University Department of Linguistics, 7, 2009.

Jennifer Lackey. *Learning from Words: Testimony as a Source of Knowledge*. Oxford, UK: Oxford University Press, 2008.

Jennifer Lackey. Testimony: Acquiring knowledge from others. In Alvin Goldman and Dennis Whitcomb, editors, *Social Epistemology: Essential Readings*. Oxford, UK: Oxford University Press, 2010.

Francesco Martini. Hearsay viewed through the lens of trust, reputation and coherence. *Synthese*, forthcoming.

Lisa Matthewson, Hotze Rullmann, and Henry Davis. Evidentials as epistemic modals. *The Linguistic Variation Yearbook*, 7: 201–254, 2007.

Elin McCready. *Reliability in Pragmatics*. Oxford: Oxford University Press, 2015.

Elin McCready. Testimony, trust, and evidentials. In Chung-Min Lee and Jinho Park, editors, *Evidentials and Modals*. Leiden: Brill, forthcoming.

Elin McCready and N. Ogata. Evidentiality, modality, and probability. *Linguistics and Philosophy*, 30(2): 147–206, 2007.

G.E. Moore. *Commonplace Book: 1919-1953*. London: George Allen and Unwin, 1962.

Richard Moran. Getting told and being believed. *Philosophers' Imprint*, 5(5): 1–29, 2005.

Sarah Murray. *Evidentiality and the Structure of Speech Acts*. PhD thesis, Rutgers University, New Brunswick, 2010.

Sarah Murray. Varieties of update. *Semantics and Pragmatics*, 7: 1–53, 2014.

Sarah Murray. *The Semantics of Evidentials*. Oxford: Oxford University Press, 2017.

Oliver Northrup. *Grounds for Commitment*. PhD thesis, UC Santa Cruz, 2014.

Christopher Potts. *The Logic of Conventional Implicatures*. Oxford, UK: Oxford University Press, 2004.

W. Pulte. The experienced and nonexperienced past in cherokee. *International Journal of American Linguistics*, 51: 543–544, 1985.

Jerrold Sadock and Arnold Zwicky. Speech act distinctions in syntax. In Timothy Shopen, editor, *Language Typology and Syntactic Description*, 155–196. Cambridge, UK: Cambridge University Press, 1985.

Mandy Simons, Judith Tonhauser, David Beaver, and Craige Roberts. What projects and why. *Proceedings of SALT 20*, 309–327, 2010.

Margaret Speas. On the syntax and semantics of evidentials. *Language and Linguistics Compass*, 2: 940–965, 2008.

Kristen Syrett and Todor Koev. Experimental evidence for the truth conditional contribution and shifting informational status of appositives. *Journal of Semantics*, 32(3): 525–577, 2015.

Judith Tonhauser. Diagnosing (not-)at-issue content. *Proceedings of Semantics of Under-Represented Languages of the Americas*, 6: 239–254, 2012.

Judith Tonhauser, David Beaver, Craige Roberts, and Mandy Simon. Toward a taxonomy of projective content. *Language*, 89(1): 66–109, 2013.

Peter van Elswyk. *Un/qualified declaratives*. PhD thesis, Rutgers University, New Brunswick, 2018.

J. David Velleman. Doables. *Philosophical Explorations*, 17(1): 1–16, 2014.

Thomas Willett. A cross-linguistic survey of the grammaticization of evidentiality. *Studies in Language*, 12 (1):51–97, 1988.

PART III

Disagreement, Diversity, and Relativism

15

EPISTEMIC DISAGREEMENT, DIVERSITY AND RELATIVISM

J. Adam Carter

From Diversity to Disagreement to Relativism: Ethics and Epistemology

Diversity often gives rise to disagreement. Consider a straightforward non-epistemic example, described by Herodotus in the *Histories*, concerning funerary customs.[1] The custom of the ancient Greeks was always to bury their dead; eating them would have been appalling. The Callatians on the other hand honoured the dead by eating them; burying them would have been out of the question. As Herodotus noted, each thought the other custom was not merely different, but *obviously wrong*. Their differing funerary codes accordingly led to a disagreement, overseen by King Darius of Persia, about the right way to honour the dead. And it's unclear what, if anything, could have settled such a disagreement.

Perhaps, in such circumstances, mutual tolerance is the way forward. Here's a slogan that is often trotted out: burying the dead is right for the Greeks, eating them is right for Callatians. And there's no 'culture-independent' sense in which either is right or wrong. (Compare with an epistemic analogue: Western science is right for you, Azande witchcraft is right for me, and there's no 'culture-independent' sense in which either of us is right or wrong.)

As James Rachels (2003, 16) puts it, this kind of diversity-to-relativism thinking, abstracted from the Greeks vs. Callations case and applied more generally in the domain of morality, can be framed as the Cultural Differences Argument.

Cultural Differences Argument

1 Different cultures have different moral codes.
2 Therefore, there is no objective 'truth' in morality. Right and wrong are only matters of opinion, and opinions vary from culture to culture.

Even if the conclusion is true, the Cultural Differences Argument is not a promising argument. And that's the case even though its premise is obviously true. For starters, the argument is not valid without an additional premise to the effect that *if* different cultures have different moral codes, then there's no objective or culture-independent truth about morality. But this premise is open to various kinds of well-worn objections.[2]

Interestingly, in his critique of the Cultural Differences Argument, Rachels challenges this implicit premise on the grounds that, among other things, *even if* different cultures have different moral codes, there are nonetheless

> [...] some moral rules that *all* societies will have in common, because those rules are necessary for society to exist [...] Cultures may differ in what they regard as legitimate exceptions to the rules, but this disagreement exists against a background of agreement on the larger issues.
>
> *(2003, 22)*

Here, Rachels is expressing the idea that at least one way to block the move from diversity to relativism is to highlight the very fact of a *shared background* of at least some minimal universal moral agreement. Examples he gives of universally shared values include a general norm of truth-telling and a prohibition on murder. As he puts it, 'Not *every* moral rule can vary from society to society'.[3]

Those sympathetic to Rachels' reply here might be optimistic that a similar kind of 'anti-relativistic' move can be made in *epistemology*, and indeed, such a move has been pursued in recent work by Howard Sankey (2010).[4] Cultural disagreements about (for example) what justifies what, what counts as knowledge, must exist against a shared background of agreement about fundamental epistemic norms.

However, this kind of move is perhaps too quick. For one thing, *contra* Rachels, it's not entirely clear how the 'shared background' rejoinder is supposed to work even in the moral case where he is explicitly applying it. Consider that on the hypothesis that moral relativism is *true*, a shared background would be entirely possible. On such a scenario, the particular moral claims constituting the shared background would fail to be candidates for objective moral truths, despite their popularity. In fact, one very influential argument for such a possibility owes to the latter Wittgenstein, as developed in his posthumous *On Certainty* (1969). Wittgenstein effectively subverts Rachels' appeal to a shared background, as a means to establishing objectivity, by arguing that a shared background is exactly the sort of thing that cannot *itself* be critically appraised one way or another.[5]

Wittgenstein's position about the status of our shared background beliefs is unsurprisingly a controversial one.[6] But even if one is unsympathetic to the Wittgensteinian rejoinder to Rachels, there's another important reason to be suspicious that we can very easily diffuse (moral or epistemic) variants on the Cultural Differences Argument by simply by pointing—as it is tempting to do—to examples of minimal cross-cultural agreement. This second line of argument owes to none other than Rachels himself.

According to Rachels, the '*fundamental mistake* in the Cultural Differences Argument is that it attempts to derive a substantive conclusion about a subject (morality) from the mere fact that people disagree about it'.[7] This is a compelling point. But a corollary of this idea is that it is fallacious to derive a substantive conclusion about a subject (morality) from facts about what people *agree* about, including the fact that most cultures agree on certain basic moral truths. If disagreement is irrelevant to what's actually true of the status of moral claims, then so is agreement.

The upshot, in the case of epistemic as opposed to moral disagreements, is that *even if* it turns out that all cultures accept some basic epistemic norms,[8] we *can't simply appeal to this fact* in order to decisively conclude the epistemic relativism is false. Some further argument is needed.

Granted, this is not so much a problem in the face of the Cultural Differences Argument. This is because the implicit premise of that argument is subject to a barrage of other well-known objections.[9] However—and this will be important in what follows—there are other more subtle ways to reason from facts about diversity, broadly speaking, to the conclusion that epistemic relativism is true—i.e., subtler than the Culture Differences Argument's insistence that diversity of opinion *itself* is a consideration in favour of truth of epistemic relativism.

Given that the mere fact of a shared minimal background is ineffectual in principle as an anti-relativistic response, rejoinders to more subtle moves from diversity to relativism will require other kinds of responses.

Here is the plan. In what follows, I will canvass three styles of argument for epistemic relativism which take considerations to do with diversity and disagreement as a motivating premise. I engage with argument strategies for epistemic relativism on the basis of considerations to do with non-neutrality. I then move on to arguments for epistemic relativism which highlight how diverse starting points can lead to relativism by way of epistemic circularity. I close by contrasting these forms of argument with a newer, semantic approach to epistemic relativism, wherein diversity plays a very different kind of motivating role.

'No Neutrality, Therefore Relativism'[10]

In *Philosophy and the Mirror of Nature*, Richard Rorty (1979) recounts a famous dispute between Galileo and Cardinal Bellarmine, concerning the truth of geocentrism, the doctrine that the earth is the orbital centre of the universe. One piece of evidence Galileo had proffered against the geocentric model is that moons were spotted orbiting Jupiter. This is evidence he acquired through his telescope, and which counted against the prevailing thought that the earth was the only centre of motion. However, as Cardinal Bellarmine saw it, revealed scripture indicates that geocentrism is correct, and so *ipso facto* the telescope must not be a good source of evidence about the heavens.[11]

Perhaps unsurprisingly, neither party was successful in persuading the other. As Steven D. Hales (2014) has noted, in circumstances like these—where it appears that interlocutors can't agree on even the most basic epistemic norms—the relativist option can look attractive. And this was Rorty's (1979) own take on the matter: both Galileo and Bellarmine were right relative to their own epistemic 'grid', and there's nothing further to say.

Harvey Siegel (2011, 205–6) helpfully summarises how the kind dialectical impasse resulting from such diverse starting points has provided fuel for the relativist:[12]

> Not only did the two parties disagree as to the truth of the relevant claim—Galileo affirmed the existence of the moons, while his opponents denied it—they also disagreed about the relevant standards (telescopic observation? naked eye observation? Scripture? Aristotle?) to which appeal should be made in order to resolve their disagreement.

And from this position, the move to relativism proceeds as follows:

> The relativist here claims that there can be no non-relative resolution of the dispute concerning the existence of the moons, precisely because there is no neutral, non-question-begging way to resolve the dispute concerning the standards. Any proposed meta-standard that favors regarding naked eye observation, Scripture, or the writings of Aristotle as the relevant standard by which to evaluate "the moons exist" will be judged by Galileo as unfairly favoring his opponents since he thinks he has good reasons to reject the epistemic authority of all these proposed standards; likewise, any proposed meta-standard that favors Galileo's preferred standard, telescopic observation, will be judged to be unfair by his opponents, who claim to have good reasons to reject that proposed standard. In this way, the absence of neutral (meta-) standards seems to make the case for relativism.[13]
>
> *(2011, 205–6)*

We can characterise the key steps of this argument as follows:

No-neutrality, Therefore Relativism

1   There can be a non-relative resolution of the dispute concerning the existence of the moons, only if there is available to the interlocutors an appropriately neutral epistemic meta-norm.
2   In the context of the dispute between Galileo and Bellarmine, no such appropriately neutral meta-norm is available.
3   Therefore, it's not the case that there can be a non-relative resolution of the dispute concerning the existence of the moons.
4   Therefore, epistemic relativism is true.[14]

This piece of reasoning makes a seemingly wild leap from (5) to (6). What's responsible for this leap is (3), the premise that there can be a non-relative resolution to the dispute concerning the existence of the moons, *only if* there is available to the interlocutors an appropriately neutral epistemic meta-norm.

We can generate a counterexample to (3) by simply following Sextus Empiricus: Sextus, in *Outlines of Pyrrhonism* thought that in the face of *equipollence*, or a seemingly irresolvable dialectical standpoint—the appropriate move is to simply *withhold judgment*, a move compatible with the falsity of relativism.[15] If withholding judgment is a viable option, then (3) is false, and the move to relativism between (5) and (6) is illicit.[16]

Interestingly, a further potential problem with this argument is (4), the claim that, in the context of the dispute between Galileo and Bellarmine, no such appropriately neutral meta-norm is available to the interlocutors. Is this really true? For one thing, surely Bellarmine and Galileo could agree upon some very basic epistemic norms. Take, for example, the law of non-contradiction.[17]

However, even if one finds an appropriately *neutral* meta-norm, it's hardly obvious that mutual acceptance of such a norm would be of any *use* to Bellarmine and Galileo for the purposes of navigating out of their deadlock. Consider, for example, this tautological epistemic norm: Infer $A \rightarrow A$. Suppose Bellarmine and Galileo both (happily) accept this. The state of play becomes:

Is this new position more promising than their previous one—viz., their dialectical position prior to realising that they're both happy to infer $A \rightarrow A$? While the tautologous meta-norm is certainly *neutral* enough, it plausibly fails to be appropriately *discriminatory*; it is so neutral that it would plausibly fail to afford either party any 'Archimedean' point from which rational adjudication (one way or another) would be possible.[18] The sort of epistemic meta-norm that would seem to be needed to facilitate rational navigation out of the deadlock would have to be both appropriately neutral *and* appropriately discriminatory.

Of course, it is a matter of historical record whether in the case of Galileo and Bellarmine, there really *was* such a meta-norm, appropriately neutral and appropriately discriminatory, available to both parties. However, a moment's reflection here should generate some philosophical

	Galileo	Bellarmine
Telescopic Evidence	Accept	Reject
Scriptural Revelation	Reject	Accept
Tautologous meta-norm	Accept	Accept

discomfort: the 'No Neutrality, Therefore Relativism' argument seems to have led us down a path where the matter of whether relativism is true would appear to turn importantly on biographical contingencies to do with some particular dispute. More generally, what might rightly seem odd is that the matter of whether epistemic relativism is true should hang in the balance of what shape any *actual* debate takes or has taken.

But perhaps the relativist has a perfectly sensible way to diffuse this concern. The relativist can grant their critic that the matter of whether epistemic relativism is *true* does not depend on any biographical contingencies of particular arguments (i.e., whether any particular historical interlocutors, such as Bellarmine and Galileo, were or were not able to locate appropriately neutral and discriminatory meta-norms). The relativist can proceed to tell us that, while such actual historical arguments are useful reference points, all that's really needed is that there *could* be situations in the neighbourhood of Bellarmine v. Galileo where no appropriately neutral and discriminatory meta-norm is available. And so, on this line, the historical Bellarmine v. Gallileo debate is as irrelevant as any other actual historical dispute. Call this kind of reply *possibilism*. Let's now consider this strategy more closely.

A 'Possibilist' Variation

One way to motivate a possibilist variation on the 'No Neutrality, Therefore Relativism' argument is to simply come up with an imagined case where all the relevant features hold—viz., where two interlocutors are such that, in the context of their disagreement, no appropriately neutral or discriminatory meta-norm is available.

In recent work, Steven Hales (2014) offers just such a case, featuring two characters—Jack and Diane—who are engaged in what Hales describes as an irreconcilable disagreement over the matter of whether there is a soul that animates the human body (call this 'P').[19] Jack's primary source of evidence is Jaegwon Kim's analytic philosophy of mind; Diane's is the Catechism of the Catholic Church. Hales writes:

> In the present example, Jack and Diane have a genuine irreconcilable difference; they disagree over proposition 'P', they disagree over what evidence is relevant to establishing to truth or falsity of 'P', and they have no additional means of settling their debate about the relevant evidence. Jack and Diane cannot discover any mutually agreeable meta-evidence which would allow them to settle their dispute over first-order evidence ... we might regard a persistent failure to agree about even the meta-evidence for a claim as a good reason to conclude that there is no such thing as the right kind of first-order evidence. In such a case, provided we are not tempted by scepticism, *relativism appears to be our last option*. The dispute between Jack and Diane is resolved by determining that 'P' is both true and false. 'P' is true relative to Diane's perspective, a perspective which includes as an epistemological component the methodology of appeal to revelation, the Bible, and its expert interpreters as a source of noninferential beliefs. 'P' is false relative to Jack's perspective, the epistemology of which includes analytic rationalism.
>
> *(2014, 78–80, my italics)*

Hales' move from irreconcilable disagreement to relativism doesn't (like the version of the argument noted in the previous section) depend on any historical facts about how any actual disagreements proceeded. Rather, it reasons from facts about how a non-actual disagreement could go, to the conclusion that epistemic relativism is true. In this respect, it seems like an improvement. However, as I've argued elsewhere, a dilemma arises for the proponent of a possibilist strategy.[20]

To appreciate the dilemma, first consider that, once we retreat to possible disagreements, we can conceive of individuals, Jack$_{Math}$ and Diane$_{Math}$ who rely on math books, and the Catechism$_{Math}$—a possible religious text that includes revealed mathematical dogma—respectively, to reach an analogous dialectical position as Jack and Diane do in Hales' case. If possibilism is assumed, it looks as though the case of Jack and Diane motivates epistemic relativism only if the case of Jack$_{Math}$ and Diane$_{Math}$ motivates mathematical relativism.

The first horn of the dilemma for the possibilist is to accept *global* relativism; after all, the possible dispute between Jack$_{Math}$ and Diane$_{Math}$ is such that we can replace 'Math' with any 'X' whatsoever. But global relativism is a very difficult pill to swallow.[21] The 'possibilist' proponent of the 'No Neutrality Therefore Relativism' argument who wishes to avoid global relativism can opt for the second horn: explain why the unavailability of an appropriately neutral and discriminatory meta-norm is supposed to motivate a relativist conclusion when the lack of such a meta-norm is a property of a possible disagreement between Jack and Diane, but not when it's a property of a possible disagreement between other possible disputants, such as Jack$_{Math}$ and Diane$_{Math}$. Opting for the second horn would appear to be unacceptably arbitrary. Opting for the first incurs the baggage of global relativism.

Suppose for a moment that the foregoing dilemma could somehow be avoided entirely. There is yet another kind of issue that faces the possibilist strategy no less than the 'actualist' strategy. Recall the sceptical objection to the actualist's premise (3) of the 'No Neutrality, Therefore Relativism' argument. That premise, recall, stated that there can be a non-relative resolution of [Bellarmine and Galileo's] dispute concerning the existence of the moons, only if there is available to the interlocutors an appropriately neutral (and appropriately discriminatory) epistemic meta-norm. The sceptical objection to this premise was (in short) that it effectively begs the question against the sceptic in favour of the relativist. From an apparently irreconcilable standpoint, it's not evident why the relativist conclusion has more to recommend it all-things-considered than does the sceptical response recommended by Sextus. The possibilist, though they don't hang their hat on any historical facts about how any actual disagreements have gone, nonetheless faces this same issue at the last hurdle. Why should possible irreconcilable disagreements (e.g., such as that between Jack and Diane) favour the relativist's conclusion over the sceptic's? It remains for the possibilist who sidesteps the two-horned dilemma to address this point.

Diversity, Framework Circularity and Relativism

The path from diversity to disagreement to relativism traced in the sections above appealed to the seeming *irreconcilability* of certain kinds of disagreements with radically diverse starting points. There is, however, another way to traverse through the diversity—disagreement—relativism sequence which needn't give 'irreconcilability facts' any important role to play in motivating epistemic relativism.

This other strategy proceeds in two parts.[22] Firstly, consider that—at least, outside epistemology classrooms—the activity of attempting to justify one's own system of epistemic principles is typically a pointless exercise. The simple reason is that, very often, our interlocutors already embrace these very same principles. And as a pragmatic point, justifying what is already in the common ground between speakers is, at least outwith purely theoretical interest, without obvious communicative purpose.[23]

However, in cases where diverse groups come into contact with one another, things are different. Epistemic principles taken for granted by each side, respectively, are sometimes in such circumstances not common ground between both parties, and so the provision of a defence of one's own epistemic system can have a kind of relevance it lacks under more epistemically homogeneous (i.e., normal) circumstances.[24]

But just how does one go about establishing that *one's own* epistemic system is justified? This brings us to the next step. Consider here the following often-cited passage from Michael Williams (2007, 94–95), capturing what he calls the 'fundamental argument' for epistemic relativism:

> In determining whether a belief—any belief—is justified, we always rely, implicitly or explicitly, on an epistemic framework: some standards or procedures that separate justified from unjustified convictions. But what about the claims embodied in the framework itself: are they justified? In answering this question, we inevitably apply our own epistemic framework. So, assuming that our framework is coherent and does not undermine itself, the best we can hope for is a justification that is epistemically circular, employing our epistemic framework in support of itself. Since this procedure can be followed by anyone, whatever his epistemic framework, all such frameworks, provided they are coherent, are equally defensible (or indefensible).

Suppose, for example, you encounter the Azande tribe, which regards the Poison Oracle as a fundamental source of truth;[25] in this context, you attempt to justify your own epistemic system, say, 'Western Science', which the Azande reject. In doing so, you naturally apply this very framework in support of itself. The relativist, on Williams' construal of her argument, at this point notes that the justification achieved is circular, and the circular justification achieved is on an even footing with other equally circular justifications of epistemic frameworks—e.g., as if the Azande were to defend their own method of consulting the Poison Oracle by appealing to the Poison Oracle.

There are three key points to register about this particular way of moving from diversity to epistemic relativism. For one thing, note Williams' concession that the ensuing justifications are equally defensible *or indefensible* (*Op. cit.* 95.) In order for the relativist to reason compellingly from the datum that attempts to justify one's own epistemic framework are inevitably circular to the conclusion that epistemic relativism is true, there has to be some positive and non-arbitrary reason to move from the intermediate conclusion that all frameworks are on an equal standing to the relativist's conclusion. However, there is room here for the sceptic to intervene: if the above argument sequence establishes that all attempts to justify epistemic frameworks are circular, then one candidate conclusion to draw is that no one is justified in accepting their own epistemic framework. The relativist must offer some reason to think the intermediate conclusion favours the line that all frameworks are relatively justified to the competing conclusion that no frameworks are justified.

A second and third point to register about the above kind of sequence Williams calls the fundamental argument for epistemic relativism are related. In short, there are potential ways to resist a key premise that this argument depends on: that justifying one's own epistemic system by appealing to epistemic principles within that very system is circular in a way that undermines epistemic justification.

One such route has been developed in work by Paul Boghossian (e.g., 2001). According to Boghossian, certain varieties of epistemic circularity needn't be vicious. Consider, for example, what he calls *rule circularity*, as would be the case if one, in the service of justifying a fundamental rule like *modus ponens*, reasons at least one step in accordance with *modus ponens*.[26] Boghossian concedes that attempting to justify *modus ponens* by reasoning in according with it will leave one in no position to rationally persuade the sceptic, viz., one who antecedently *doubts* this basic inference rule. However, Boghossian maintains that 'something can be a warrant for something even if it is powerless to bring about a determined skeptic'[27] (2001, 38). Applying this idea more generally: the application of principles within one's own epistemic system to support those very principles could potentially leave one with a kind of positive justification 'in spite of the fact that we can produce only rule-circular arguments for them' (2001, 37).

A related route appeals more generally to epistemic *externalism*, according to which it is denied that what justifies one's belief must be accessible by reflection alone.[28] Just suppose, *a la* Williams, that one uses one's own epistemic framework in the service of justifying it. Is the ensuing justification an epistemically acceptable one? Here the epistemic externalist can at least in principle insist that beliefs about our own epistemic systems—no less than perceptual and other kinds of beliefs—attain a positive epistemic status (e.g., epistemic justification) provided the process that issues these beliefs satisfies some externalist condition, e.g., reliability. Of course, externalist approaches such as process reliabilism have been criticised on just this ground—an objection to reliabilism known as 'bootstrapping' (e.g., Vogel 2000).[29] The matter of how and whether this problem can be overcome within a reliabilist framework is a matter of ongoing debate.[30]

A New Argument from Diversity to Relativism

The kinds of epistemological diversity that have been appealed to in order to motivate epistemic relativism in the arguments canvassed above have mostly featured *intercultural epistemic diversity*— viz., as when radically different epistemic frameworks come into contact with one another. There is, however, another kind of diversity which can (but needn't be) entirely *intracultural* and which has nonetheless been argued to have an important bearing on the objectivity of knowledge ascriptions.

This kind of diversity, which can persist within even the most tightly knit epistemic communities, concerns the epistemic standards of individual agents who are assessing knowledge ascriptions (i.e., ascriptions that take the form '*S* knows that *p*') for truth or falsity. According to a kind of epistemic relativism defended in recent work by John MacFarlane (e.g., 2007, 2014), whether a given knowledge-ascribing sentence is true depends on the epistemic standards at play in what he calls the *context of assessment*, which is the context in which the knowledge ascription is being assessed for truth or falsity. These standards can vary across contexts of assessment. For example, the alternatives that are relevant at your context of assessment which must be ruled out might be different from the alternatives that are relevant at my context of assessment.[31] But, because the very same knowledge ascription (e.g., Keith knows that the bank is open) can be assessed for truth or falsity from *indefinitely* many perspectives, knowledge-ascribing sentences do not get their truth values absolutely, but only *relatively*.

This kind of epistemic relativism differs importantly from more familiar forms of context dependence, such as epistemic *contextualism* (e.g., DeRose 1992). According to the contextualist, even though the epistemic standard that is apposite to a given knowledge-ascription is the standard at play in the attributor's context (and different standards can be in operation at different attributor contexts), a given tokening of a knowledge ascription gets its truth value *absolutely*, not relatively. In this respect, MacFarlane's view renders the truth of knowledge attributions relative in a way that contextualism—and for that matter subject-sensitive invariantism (e.g., Hawthorne 2004, Stanley 2005)—does not.

Whether MacFarlane-style epistemic relativism is a viable view is an issue that can be debated on at least two different philosophical fronts. Firstly, MacFarlane's argument strategy consists in a kind of 'costs versus benefits' rationale, according to which his preferred relativist semantics for 'knows' is claimed to better explain our ordinary patterns of using 'knows' than competing semantics (e.g., contextualism, sensitive invariantism and insensitive invariantism).[32] Thus, one natural strategy of critique will be to argue that a competitor's semantics better explains our patterns of use than does MacFarlane's (see here, for example, Stanley 2016).

Given that knowledge is the dominion of epistemology, there is also room to resist MacFarlane-style epistemic relativism on the basis of purely epistemological considerations. One such line of critique is that a relativist semantics about 'knows' couldn't be embraced, within epistemology, without also accepting wholesale epistemic relativism about a range other closely related notions, such as evidence, justification and understanding.[33] A second line of reply, advanced by Carter (2016 Ch. 7), is that a relativist treatment of 'knows' is incompatible with certain kinds of epistemological platitudes, such as the platitude that knowledge excludes luck.[34] Relativism about knowledge attributions is still a young view, and its viability in the philosophy of language and its import in epistemology have largely yet to be explored.

Notes

1 This example, reported in the *Histories* (c. 440 BCE), is often used to introduce the idea of moral relativism. See, for example, Rachels (2003, Ch. 2), who takes this case as a starting point for discussion in the widely used textbook *The Elements of Moral Philosophy*.
2 See, for example, Norris (1996), Siegel (2004) and Seidel (2014). Cf., Baghramian and Carter (2015) for an overview of replies to various kinds of cultural relativism.
3 *Op. cit.* 22. My italics.
4 Sankey refers to this move as a kind of naturalistic rejoinder to epistemic relativism, which he understands to be motivated by the problem of the criterion. See also Sankey (2012) and Sankey (2011). Cf., Carter (2016 Ch. 3) for a critique.
5 For some recent defences of a Wittgenstenian 'hinge' strategy in epistemology, see Pritchard (2015) and Coliva (2015).
6 One crucial dividing line in the contemporary literature on Wittgenstein's epistemology concerns the matter of whether framework, or 'hinge' propositions have other kinds of properties characteristic of typical beliefs, despite their lying beyond what can be rationally supported. For some perspectives on the character of hinge propositions, see for example Coliva (2015), Moyal-Sharrock (2004), Pritchard (2012, 2015) and Stroll (1994).
7 *Op. cit.* 16. My italics.
8 Empirical evidence has become more readily available concerning points of cross-cultural agreement in epistemology, in light of results reported in recent years by experimental philosophers. For example, in an influential study reported by Machery et al. (2015), it was shown that the Gettier intuition is (perhaps surprisingly) robust across cultures.
9 Two such objections are the 'anything goes' objection and the objection from moral progress.
10 This slogan for the piece of reasoning that is under consideration in this section owes to Siegel (2011).
11 See Finocchiaro (1989) for an historical overview of the meeting between Galileo and Bellarmine.
12 For an expanded discussion of this move on behalf of the relativist, see Siegel (2004).
13 Cited also in Carter (2016 Ch. 4).
14 A variation of this argument appears in Carter (2016, 83).
15 See Empiricus et al. (2000) for discussion. Cf., Morison (2014).
16 The relativist might reply, as Hales has, that *ceteris paribus*, scepticism is less motivated than relativism: and so if an irreconcilable dialectical position recommends just relativism or scepticism, relativism is a better option. For a response to this kind of reply, see Carter (2016 Ch. 4).
17 There are some potential issues here, in Bellarmine's case, concerning the doctrine of the trinity, but let's set these aside.
18 For discussion, see Carter (2016, 83).
19 See also Hales (2009) for a detailed defence of various kinds of relativism.
20 To be clear, Hales in virtue of giving the case that he has, isn't committed to possibilism, even though his strategy is compatible with it. This is because Hales could insist that there are *actual* cases like that of Jack and Diane, and that what's relevant to relativism is that there are at least some such actual cases, viz., where an appropriately neutral and appropriately discriminatory meta-norm are unavailable to the interlocutors. However, this interpretation of his case renders it open to the more general kind of problem with 'actualism'; it is deeply perplexing why the truth of a metaphysical thesis such as relativism should hang in the balance of how any actual historical argument proceeded.

21 Plato, in the *Theatetus*, offers a famous refutation of global relativism, of the sort defended by Protagoras. For a charitable reconstruction of this refutation, see Burnyeat (1976). See also Carter (2016 Ch. 2) and Baghramian (2004) for discussion.

22 For a more detailed presentation of this argument strategy, see Carter (2016 Ch. 5).

23 See, for example, Stalnaker (1978, 2002).

24 For an interesting discussion of how encountering radically different perspectives can engender critical intro-spection—in particular, regarding the contingency of certain firmly held beliefs—see Srinivasan (2015).

25 For the details, see Evans-Pritchard (1937).

26 For a related line of discussion, in the case of justifying IBE, see Psillos (1999). For critical discussion, see Carter and Pritchard (2016),

27 On Boghossian's vindication of rule-circular justification, it's argued that one can retain *non-suasive* (i.e., dialectically ineffective) objective grounds for accepting modus ponens. Cf., Wright (2001) for a critique of Boghossian's argument.

28 This is, at least, the externalist position framed as the denial of accessibilist versions of epistemic internal-ism. Externalism, contrasted with mentalist versions of internalism, is the denial of the thesis that justifi-cation supervenes on an individual's mental states. For discussion, see Pappas (2014). For a wider discussion of externalism, which compares epistemic varieties of externalism with content and other forms of externalism, see Carter et al. (2014).

29 For related discussion see Stewart Cohen's (2002) problem of easy knowledge.

30 See, for example, Goldman and Beddor (2015, sec. 4) for an overview of some notable strategies on behalf of the reliabilist in response to bootstrapping and easy-knowledge objections.

31 Although MacFarlane's most recent (2014) articulation of relativism about knowledge attributions unpacks the notion of an epistemic standard in terms of relevant alternatives (e.g., (1996), his earlier formulations of the view do not. See, for example, MacFarlane (2005).

32 A principal argument MacFarlane relies on is that relativism explains disagreement data better than com-petitor views (e.g., MacFarlane 2007). For example, unlike the contextualist, the relativist can explain how disagreements about the truth of knowledge attributions are genuine; and, unlike sensitive invarian-tists, relativists can account for the behaviour of 'knows' under temporal and modal embeddings.

33 For defences of this argument strategy, see Carter (2014).

34 For a defence of this platitude, see for example, Pritchard (2005).

References

Baghramian, M. (2004). *Relativism*. London: Routledge.

Baghramian, M. and Carter, A. (2015). Relativism. In: E. Zalta, ed., *The Stanford Encyclopedia of Philosophy*, http://plato.stanford.edu/entries/relativism/.

Boghossian, P. (2001). How are Objective Epistemic Reasons Possible? *Philosophical Studies*, 106(1), pp. 1–40.

Burnyeat, M. (1976). Protagoras and Self-refutation in Plato's Theaetetus. *The Philosophical Review*, 85(2), pp. 172–195.

Carter, A. (2014). Relativism, Knowledge and Understanding. *Episteme*, 11(1), pp. 35–52.

Carter, A. (2016). *Metaepistemology and Relativism*. London: Palgrave Macmillan.

Carter, A., Kallestrup, J., Palermos, O. and Pritchard, D. (2014). Varieties of Externalism. *Philosophical Issues*, 24 (1), pp. 63–109.

Carter, A. and Pritchard, D. (2016). Inference to the Best Explanation and Epistemic Circularity. In: K. McCain and T. Poston, eds., *Best Explanations: New Essays on Inference to the Best Explanation*, Oxford: Oxford University Press, pp. 133–149.

Cohen, S. (2002). Basic Knowledge and the Problem of Easy Knowledge. *Philosophy and Phenomenological Research*, 65(2), pp. 309–329.

Coliva, A. (2015). *Extended Rationality: A Hinge Epistemology*. London: Palgrave Macmillan.

DeRose, K. (1992). Contextualism and Knowledge Attributions. *Philosophy and Phenomenological Research*, 52 (4), pp. 913–929.

Empiricus, S., Annas, J. and Barnes, J. (2000). *Sextus Empiricus: Outlines of Scepticism*. Cambridge: Cambridge University Press.

Evans-Pritchard, E. (1937). *Witchcraft, Oracles, and Magic Among the Azande*. Oxford: Clarendon Press.

Finocchiaro, M. (1989). *The Galileo Affair: A Documentary History*. Vol. 1. Berkley, CA: University of California Press.

Goldman, A. and Beddor, B. (2015). Reliabilist Epistemology. In: E. Zalta, ed., *The Stanford Encyclopedia of Philosophy*, http://plato.stanford.edu/archives/win2015/entries/reliabilism/.

Hales, S. (2009). *Relativism and the Foundations of Philosophy*. Cambridge, MA: MIT Press.

Hales, S. (2014). Motivations for Relativism as a Solution to Disagreements. *Philosophy*, 89(01), pp. 63–82.

Hawthorne, J. (2004). *Knowledge and Lotteries*. Oxford: Oxford University Press.

MacFarlane, J. (2005). The Assessment Sensitivity of Knowledge Attributions. *Oxford Studies in Epistemology*, 1, pp. 197–233.

MacFarlane, J. (2007). Relativism and Disagreement. *Philosophical Studies*, 132(1), pp. 17–31.

MacFarlane, J. (2014). *Assessment Sensitivity: Relative Truth and Its Applications*. Oxford: Oxford University Press.

Machery, E., Stich, S., Rose, D., Chatterjee, A., Karasawa, K., Struchiner, N., Sirker, S., Usui, N. and Hashimoto, T. (2015). Gettier Across Cultures. *Noûs*, 50(3), pp. 1–20.

Morison, B. (2014). Sextus Empiricus. In: E. Zalta, ed., *The Stanford Encyclopedia of Philosophy*, http://plato.stanford.edu/archives/spr2014/entries/sextus-empiricus/.

Moyal-Sharrock, D. (2004). *Understanding Wittgenstein's on Certainty*. London: Palgrave.

Norris, C. (1996). *Reclaiming Truth: Contribution to a Critique of Cultural Relativism*. Durham, NC: Duke University Press.

Pappas, G. (2014). Internalist Vs. Externalist Conceptions of Epistemic Justification. In: E. Zalta, ed., *The Stanford Encyclopedia of Philosophy*, http://plato.stanford.edu/archives/fall2014/entries/justep-intext/.

Pritchard, D. (2005). *Epistemic Luck*. Oxford: Oxford University Press.

Pritchard, D. (2012). Wittgenstein and the Groundlessness of Our Believing. *Synthese*, 189(2), pp. 255–272.

Pritchard, D. (2015). *Epistemic Angst: Radical Skepticism and the Groundlessness of Our Believing*. Princeton: Princeton University Press.

Psillos, S. (1999). *Scientific Realism: How Science Tracks Truth*. London: Routledge.

Rachels, J. (2003). *The Elements of Moral Philosophy, 4th Edition*. New York: McGraw-Hill.

Rorty, R. (1979). *Philosophy and the Mirror of Nature*. Princeton: Princeton University Press.

Sankey, H. (2010). Witchcraft, Relativism and the Problem of the Criterion. *Erkenntnis*, 72(1), pp. 1–16.

Sankey, H. (2011). Epistemic Relativism and the Problem of the Criterion. *Studies in History and Philosophy of Science Part A*, 42(4), pp. 562–570.

Sankey, H. (2012). Scepticism, Relativism and the Argument from the Criterion. *Studies in History and Philosophy of Science Part A*, 43(1), pp. 182–190.

Seidel, M. (2014). *Epistemic Relativism: A Constructive Critique*. London: Palgrave Macmillan.

Siegel, H. (2004). Relativism. In: M. Sintonen, J. Wolenski and I. Niiniluoto, eds., *Handbook of Epistemology*, Dordrecht: Kluwer, pp. 747–780.

Siegel, H. (2011). Epistemological Relativism: Arguments Pro and Con. In: S. Hales, ed., *A Companion to Relativism*, Oxford: Wiley Blackwell, pp. 199–218.

Srinivasan, A. (2015). The Archimedean Urge. *Philosophical Perspectives*, 29(1), pp. 325–362.

Stalnaker, R. (1978). Assertion. *Syntax and Semantics*, 9, pp. 315–332.

Stalnaker, R. (2002). Common Ground. *Linguistics and Philosophy*, 25(5-6), pp. 701–721.

Stanley, J. (2005). *Knowledge and Practical Interests*. Oxford: Oxford University Press.

Stanley, J. (2016). On a Case for Truth-Relativism. *Philosophy and Phenomenological Research*, 92(1), pp. 179–188.

Stroll, A. (1994). *Moore and Wittgenstein on Certainty*. Oxford: Oxford University Press.

Vogel, J. (2000). Reliabilism Leveled. *The Journal of Philosophy*, 97(11), pp. 602–623.

Williams, M. (2007). Why (Wittgensteinian) Contextualism Is Not Relativism. *Episteme*, 4(1), pp. 93–114.

Wittgenstein, L. (1969). *On Certainty*. Oxford: Blackwell.

Wright, C. (2001). On Basic Logical Knowledge; Reflections on Paul Boghossian's How Are Objective Epistemic Reasons Possible? *Philosophical Studies*, 106(1), pp. 41–85.

Further Reading

Christensen, D. and Lackey, J. (2013). *The Epistemology of Disagreement: New Essays*. Oxford: Oxford University Press.

Feldman, R. and Warfield, T. (2009). *Disagreement*. Oxford: Oxford University Press.

Hales, S. (2006). *Relativism and the Foundations of Philosophy*. Cambridge, MA: MIT Press.

Littlejohn, C. (2013). Disagreement and Defeat. In: D. Machuca, ed., *Disagreement and Skepticism*, London: Routledge, pp. 169–193.

Rovane, C. (2013). *The Metaphysics and Ethics of Relativism*. Cambridge, MA: Harvard University Press.

16

THE EPISTEMIC SIGNIFICANCE OF DIVERSITY

Kristina Rolin

Introduction

Diversity is a property of the social organization of science, including scientific communities and research groups. In order to analyze the epistemic significance of diversity, it is necessary to distinguish between cognitive and social diversity (Page 2007). A community or a group is cognitively diverse when its members have, for example, different research styles and skills, different perspectives on the subject matter of inquiry, or access to different bodies of empirical evidence. A community or a group is socially diverse when its members have different non-epistemic values, such as moral and political values, or different social locations, such as gender, ethnic identity, nationality, and race. Given the cognitive/social distinction, epistemological questions concerning diversity can be brought more sharply into focus: When is cognitive diversity epistemically beneficial and why? Under what conditions does social diversity generate epistemically beneficial cognitive diversity?

While I acknowledge that there is cognitive diversity among scientific communities, in this review essay I focus on cognitive diversity within scientific communities. By scientific communities, I mean specialties where scientists are united by shared concepts, beliefs, epistemic values, or epistemic goals (Wray 2007: 344). Individual scientists can endorse slightly different constellations of these elements, with the consequence that there may not be any unambiguous way to define the boundaries of communities or to distinguish members from non-members. Communities may overlap and individual scientists may belong to several communities either simultaneously or in succession (Kuhn 1996: 178). While many community members pursue similar epistemic goals, communities typically host a diversity of theoretical approaches and methods (Rolin 2011: 473). Communities are also arenas for disagreement and controversy (Solomon 2001: 65). Yet, there is a limit to the amount of cognitive diversity a scientific community can accommodate. This is because communities need to strike a balance between cognitive diversity and the requirement of shared standards. This said, it is important to keep in mind that communities do not form a stable social organization of science. A striking feature of scientific change is that some communities become fragmented or dissolved and new ones emerge (Wray 2011: 117).

When research groups are said to be cognitively diverse, diversity can refer not only to disagreement among group members but also to a diversity of expertise and skills scientists bring to a research collaboration. A diversity of expertise and skills is epistemically productive when it enables a research team to carry out a research project no individual scientist could do on their own (Andersen and Wagenknecht 2013). Diversity in the sense of disagreement can also be epistemically fruitful by generating critical exchanges. Yet, as in the case of scientific communities, there is a limit to the amount of disagreement a research group can tolerate. This is because research groups are under pressure to arrive at a collective view so that they can publish their results in a timely manner. Acknowledging that a pressure to conform may be a problem in research groups, some philosophers have examined how research groups can make use of epistemically fruitful disagreement (Tollefsen 2006; Wray 2014).

The social epistemology of diversity can be mapped by identifying three approaches that emerged in the late 1980s and the early 1990s, and that have been influential from then on: Philip Kitcher's (1990) argument from the distribution of research efforts, Helen Longino's (1990) contextual empiricism, and Sandra Harding's (1986, 1991) feminist standpoint theory. I argue that the three approaches differ in how cognitive diversity and the sources of cognitive diversity are understood.

Distribution of Research Efforts

In Kitcher's article "The Division of Cognitive Labor" (1990), cognitive diversity is understood as a diversity of theories or methods addressing a common problem. Kitcher argues that cognitive diversity is epistemically beneficial in certain phases of inquiry, when it is not yet possible to tell which theory (or theories) will be true or most successful empirically, or which method (or methods) will lead to a breakthrough. When competing theories have different epistemic virtues or when different methods have complementary advantages, it is more reasonable to distribute resources among the theories or the methods than to allocate all available resources to one theory or method. A distribution of research efforts is an efficient solution to the problem of coordinating community wide research activities when the probability that a community will achieve its epistemic aims by means of distribution (in a given time period) is higher than the probability that it will achieve its aims by focusing single-mindedly on one theory or method.

Kitcher's argument is novel in two ways. First, he does not claim merely that disagreement about theories is rational when theory choice is underdetermined by all available evidence and background information. His claim is more radical than this. He claims that a distribution of research efforts can be epistemically desirable even in an instance where it would be rational for all community members to agree that one theory is superior to its rivals. To suggest that a distribution of research efforts is epistemically rational is to suggest that at least some community members should pursue a theory that is widely known to be inferior to the most promising theory. While the pursuit of such a theory is not rational from an individual point of view (given the traditional view that individual rationality is purely epistemic rationality), it can be rational from a community point of view.

Second, Kitcher does not claim merely that disagreement about theories is rational when scientists subscribe to different theoretical virtues. Thus, he departs from Thomas Kuhn (1977) who suggests that rational disagreement is an outcome of scientists' interpreting or weighing theoretical virtues in different ways (see also Longino 1995). Kitcher claims that even in an instance where community members are united in their understanding of theoretical virtues, a distribution of research efforts may be an outcome of scientists' personal interest in credit. Instead of evaluating merely whether a theory is acceptable in light of available evidence and background information, a rational individual makes decisions strategically by anticipating other community members' behavior. If an inferior theory turns out to be true in the end, great credit will be due to the small number of scientists who have risked their careers for it. Choosing to work with a superior theory may not lead to an equal amount of credit even if the theory turns out to be true. This is because the credit will be shared by the large number of scientists who have chosen to work with a low risk theory.

By challenging the traditional view that individual rationality is purely epistemic rationality, Kitcher argues that a community of epistemically "sullied" agents (who are credit-and-truth-seekers) is likely to be more efficient than a community of epistemically "pure" agents (who are merely truth-seekers), because in the former community the agents' desire for recognition will lead some of them to pursue a high risk theory, thereby generating a distribution of research efforts (1993: 310). While personal interest in credit appears to be a non-epistemic factor, it can contribute to the epistemic success of science by generating a distribution of research efforts. In sum, Kitcher suggests that the epistemic benefit of cognitive diversity urges philosophers to (i) modify their traditional conceptions of individual rationality, and (ii) seek to understand collective (or community) rationality by exploring the question: What is an efficient division of cognitive labor?

Kitcher's ideas have been developed further by many philosophers (e.g., Alexander, Himmelreich and Thompson 2015; D'Agostino 2009; Muldoon 2013; Pöyhönen 2017; Strevens 2003; Thoma 2015; Weisberg and Muldoon 2009). Miriam Solomon (1992) argues that epistemically beneficial cognitive diversity can have many sources (see also Kitcher 2011). In her view, a distribution of research efforts does not require that an individual scientist is a credit-seeker. A distribution may take place also in a community of passionate truth-seekers who make use of different cognitive heuristics. For example, scientists may weigh salient and available information more heavily in their decision making than other information. The geological revolution between 1920s and 1960s is an example of scientific change where the phenomena of cognitive bias and belief perseverance played an epistemically positive role by creating a distribution of research efforts. Solomon (2001) suggests also that science policy makers and scientists who are in a position to make funding decisions are responsible for ensuring that scientific controversies are not closed prematurely. Unlike Kitcher (1990), she does not believe that a distribution of research efforts will take place by "an invisible hand of reason" (2001: 95). Solomon concludes that diversity is a "blunt epistemic tool" (2006: 26), by which she means that more than one kind of cognitive diversity can be epistemically beneficial and it is difficult to tell in advance which kind will contribute to epistemic success.

Kevin Zollman (2010) argues that a distribution of research efforts can be maintained by limiting an exchange of information in scientific communities. He emphasizes that an epistemically valuable property of scientific communities is not cognitive diversity as such but rather transient cognitive diversity. By transient cognitive diversity, he refers to a distribution of research efforts that lasts long enough that individuals do not discard theories too quickly, but not so long as to hinder the convergence to one theory. Cognitive diversity has to be transient because the same factors that are responsible for maintaining a distribution of research efforts can also undermine a community's ability to achieve truths.

In a more critical tone, Manuela Fernández Pinto (2016) argues that Kitcher's approach to cognitive diversity does not capture a morally and socially significant phenomenon in the domain of social epistemology. By emphasizing that non-epistemic interests can play an epistemically beneficial role in science, the division of cognitive labor approach overlooks cases where non-epistemic interests play an epistemically harmful role, for instance, by introducing sexist or racist biases into scientific research. As this is one of the concerns in Helen Longino's approach to the social epistemology of diversity, I will turn to it in the next section.

Critical Contextual Empiricism

In contextual empiricism (Longino 1990) – or critical contextual empiricism (Longino 2002) – cognitive diversity is understood as a diversity of perspectives on the subject matter of inquiry. While cognitive diversity does not always go hand-in-hand with social diversity, Longino suggests that in many cases a diversity of perspectives reflects a diversity of non-epistemic values, that is, values that are not justifiable by appealing merely to truth. For example, in the 1970s controversy over human evolution, "man-the-hunter" and "woman-the-gatherer" narratives offered two different perspectives on the anatomical and behavioral development of human species. Neither perspective was apparent in light of empirical evidence. And both perspectives were value-laden in the sense that they assumed the centrality of one sex's behavior in the evolution of the entire species (Longino 1990: 106–8).

Longino's approach to diversity is novel in suggesting that value-laden perspectives are both (i) a source of epistemic problems such as false beliefs or biased accounts of the subject matter of inquiry, and (ii) a solution to these problems. In critical contextual empiricism, cognitive diversity is thought to be epistemically beneficial not only because it generates a distribution of research efforts, but also because it generates critical exchanges in the community. Criticism can improve scientific knowledge in many ways. It can help scientists identify and correct false beliefs or biased accounts of the subject matter of inquiry. And even when criticism does not give scientists a reason to reject a view, it can be epistemically valuable by forcing them to provide better arguments for their view or to communicate their view more clearly and effectively. Criticism can help scientists avoid dogmatism.

Longino suggests that Kitcher's (1993) distinction between epistemically pure and sullied agents is not helpful in understanding value-laden perspectives (2002: 75). The reason for this is that scientific inquiry is often value-laden in ways that elude an individual scientist. Scientists' motivations may not make a difference in an instance where non-epistemic values do not figure explicitly as reasons in an individual scientist's reasoning. Longino suggests that non-epistemic values may be "encoded" in background assumptions that are needed to ensure that evidence is relevant to a particular hypothesis or a theory (1990: 216). Background assumptions are value-laden when they lead scientists to highlight certain morally and socially significant aspects of a phenomenon over others, or when they have morally and socially significant practical consequences, for instance, by promoting one conception of human agency over another (1990: 216–8). Both epistemically pure and sullied agents may end up working with value-laden background assumptions without them being aware of the roles that non-epistemic values play in scientific inquiry or the consequences that value-laden research has for the society.

If Longino is right to suggest that evidential reasoning may involve value-laden background assumptions, then social epistemologists are urged to reflect on the question of how non-epistemic values are kept at bay in scientific inquiry. In response to this problem, Longino proposes that a community practice constrained by the four criteria of publicly recognized venues, uptake of criticism, shared standards, and tempered equality of intellectual authority is needed to ensure objectivity. She argues that the four criteria are epistemically desirable because they facilitate "transformative criticism" (1990: 76).

The fourth criterion is of special interest here because it introduces yet another type of diversity into contextual empiricism. In contextual empiricism, the term "diversity" refers not only to a diversity of perspectives and a diversity of non-epistemic values but also to a diversity of people who participate in scientific communities. The tempered equality criterion requires that a community be inclusive of scientists independently of their race, ethnic identity, nationality, gender, age, and sexual orientation. The criterion invites also outsiders to participate in scientific debates on the condition that they respect the four criteria. Equality of intellectual authority is "tempered" only insofar as human beings differ in domain specific expertise (2002: 132–3). But even when some human beings are more knowledgeable than others in some domains, they all should be treated as equally capable of understanding reasons as well as providing criticisms and alternative points of view. Longino argues that the fourth criterion facilitates transformative criticism in two ways, by disqualifying those communities where certain perspectives dominate because of the political, social, or economic power of their adherents (1990: 78), and by making room for a diversity of perspectives that is likely to generate criticism (2002: 131). In sum, Longino suggests that social diversity is epistemically beneficial because human beings are more likely to identify values that have influenced scientific inquiry when the values in question are different from their own.

Longino's approach to diversity has been well received not only in social epistemology but also in socially engaged philosophy of science. It has been used to strengthen the epistemic rationale for science policy programs that (i) aim to broaden the participation of underrepresented groups in science (Fehr 2011; Intemann 2009), or (ii) encourage scientists to share knowledge or to collaborate with non-scientists (Grasswick 2010; Koskinen 2014; Koskinen and Mäki 2016; Wylie 2015). Yet, some philosophers argue that critical contextual empiricism is in need of further refinement. The challenges come from two directions. Some critics worry that it is not capable of incorporating all the cognitive diversity that is epistemically valuable in science, whereas some other critics worry that it invites the kind of social diversity into science that is problematic from a moral and political point of view.

The first concern, the concern about exclusion, is expressed by Kristen Intemann and Inmaculada de Melo-Martín (2014), who argue that there is a tension between the requirement for tempered equality of intellectual authority and the requirement for shared standards. While the requirement for tempered equality is meant to ensure that scientific communities benefit from a wide range of perspectives, the requirement for shared standards sets constraints for perspectives that can legitimately expect to be heard and taken seriously. The reason for this is that the requirement for shared standards excludes those critics who do not share all or a sufficiently large number of the standards of the scientific community. One question that divides social epistemologists is whether the shared standards criterion should be understood more thickly or thinly (see also Borgerson 2011).

The second concern, the concern about inclusion, is raised by Daniel Hicks (2011), who argues that critical contextual empiricism is not capable of excluding morally and politically problematic views, such as sexist and racist beliefs (see also Intemann 2011; Kourany 2010). While Longino's intention is to ensure that scientific communities are inclusive of social groups that have historically been excluded from scientific education and the scientific profession, the requirement for tempered equality can be abused by sexists and racists to demand not only attention but also resources to scientific theories that are complicit in sexist and racist ideologies. In Hick's view, there is a tension between the egalitarian ethos of critical contextual empiricism and its potentially anti-egalitarian consequences.

In response to the concern about inclusion, Hicks argues that Longino's account of epistemically ideal communities should be understood to include a good faith principle. The principle states that good faith participation in a scientific community aiming to realize the four criteria requires a commitment not only to the epistemic but also to the moral-political values that underwrite and motivate the ideal, including formal egalitarianism and liberal pluralism (2011: 340). By formal egalitarianism, Hicks means the view that "all members of the community enjoy the same formal standing; no individual or subgroup is, as such, given greater privileges or advantages than others" (2011: 342). By liberal pluralism, he means the view that "there is room for reasonable disagreement; two members of the community may disagree substantially without one or both being unreasonable or irrational" (2011: 342). In Hick's view, a diversity of moral-political values cannot include values that threaten to undermine formal egalitarianism and liberal pluralism.

So far we have seen that different approaches to diversity come with different methods and conceptions of epistemic agents. While Kitcher (1990) demonstrates the benefits of cognitive diversity with modelling methods, Longino (1990) develops case studies to illustrate the epistemic benefits of cognitive diversity. And while Kitcher suggests that epistemic agents come in two kinds (epistemically pure or sullied), Longino suggests that they come in many kinds. In Longino's view, a diversity of social locations and a diversity of non-epistemic values explain partly why in many cases there is a diversity of perspectives on the subject matter of inquiry. Yet, Longino, like some other philosophers (e.g., Wylie 2003), acknowledge that social diversity does not automatically give rise to cognitive diversity, nor does cognitive diversity automatically lead to epistemically valuable outcomes. The crucial question is under what conditions social diversity becomes a source of epistemically valuable cognitive diversity. In the next section, I explore this question by introducing feminist standpoint empiricism.

Feminist Standpoint Empiricism

In feminist standpoint theory (Harding 1986, 1991, 2015) – or feminist standpoint empiricism (Intemann 2010; Wylie 2012) – cognitive diversity is understood as a diversity of social experiences that have a bearing on scientific research. When cognitive diversity is understood in this way, it is closely related a diversity of social locations. However, not all social locations are of epistemic interest in all research projects. As standpoint empiricists aim to understand how relations of power interact with the production of knowledge, they are interested especially in those social locations that track systemic relations of power and social inequalities (Wylie 2003, 2011, 2012). Standpoint empiricism has affinities with social epistemologies that emphasize the epistemic benefits of democracy (e.g., Anderson 2006; Bohman 2006; Wylie 2006). In both approaches, a diversity of social locations is seen as an epistemic resource because information that is relevant for understanding complex social phenomena is dispersed across society and distributed asymmetrically depending, among other things, on individuals' social class, occupation, education, gender, race, and ethnic identity.

As Alison Wylie explains, "social location systematically shapes and limits what we know, including tacit, experiential knowledge as well as explicit understanding, what we take knowledge to be as well as specific epistemic content" (2003: 31). Sometimes it is the social location of scientists that is thought to provide them with a critical perspective on their specialty or a particular subject matter of inquiry. For example, scientists who are "outsiders within" are thought to occupy an epistemically significant social location in virtue of having first-hand experience of marginal social locations in the society (Collins 2004). Sometimes social locations matter even when scientists themselves do not have first-hand experience of marginal social locations. It is the social location of their informants or the social location of stakeholders to whom scientists see themselves as being socially responsible that matter epistemically. Ultimately, it is an empirical exercise to find out exactly how social locations shape social experiences in particular contexts, and how these experiences are relevant to particular research projects (Wylie 2003).

Like other social epistemologists, standpoint empiricists believe that cognitive diversity is epistemically valuable when it leads to a distribution of research efforts, critical perspectives, or novel lines of inquiry (Solomon 2009). In addition, standpoint empiricists suggest that a diversity of social experiences brings yet another benefit to scientific communities. Marginal or unprivileged social locations are potentially a source of insight on the way relations of power work in the society as well as in the academic world.

Standpoint empiricists argue also that a marginal or unprivileged social location in and by itself may not have epistemically interesting consequences unless it is developed into a standpoint (Harding 1991: 123). A standpoint differs from a social location in three ways. First, achieving a standpoint requires that one is critically aware of the social conditions under which scientific knowledge is produced (Wylie 2003: 31). Second, participating in the formation of a standpoint requires that one shares some moral-political values with other participants (Harding 1991: 126–127). Third, a standpoint is a collective rather than an individual achievement (Crasnow

2013: 421, 2014: 158). Insofar as there is an epistemic advantage associated with marginal or unprivileged social locations, a sub-community that is part of the larger scientific community, is needed to realize the advantage. I have suggested that such communities can be understood as "scientific/intellectual movements" (Frickel and Gross 2005). Scientific/intellectual movements are epistemically productive when they enable scientists to generate evidence under conditions where relations of power tend to suppress or distort evidence, and they provide scientists with an epistemic community where they can receive fruitful criticism for research that may be ignored in the larger scientific community (Rolin 2016).

Conclusion

Cognitive diversity is not an epistemic virtue intrinsically. But under some circumstances, it promotes the epistemic goals of science when these goals are understood to include significant truth (Kitcher 1993) or empirical success (Solomon 2001). Epistemically beneficial cognitive diversity can come in many kinds – a diversity of theories, methods, perspectives, and social experiences – and it can have many sources. Cognitive diversity is thought to be epistemically beneficial for at least four reasons. One reason is that it generates a distribution of research efforts. As no one is in a position to know in advance which lines of inquiry will be fruitful, scientific communities are better off by distributing their resources on several different and sometimes competing theories and methods. Another reason to value cognitive diversity is that it is a source of critical perspectives that can improve scientific knowledge in many ways. Critical perspectives are needed especially in those cases where scientific research is value-laden. Yet another reason to value cognitive diversity is that it is a source of scientific creativity. It can lead scientists to pursue new lines of inquiry, search for new types of evidence, propose new hypotheses and theories, and develop new methods of inquiry. Finally, cognitive diversity is epistemically beneficial especially in those research projects that aim to produce evidence despite obstacles raised by relations of power and social inequalities.

Acknowledgments

I wish to thank my colleagues at the Academy of Finland Centre of Excellence in the Philosophy of the Social Sciences for comments on an earlier version of the manuscript.

References

Alexander, J., Himmelreich, J., and Thompson, C. (2015). Epistemic Landscapes, Optimal Search, and the Division of Cognitive Labor. *Philosophy of Science*, 82(3), pp. 424–453.

Andersen, H., and Wagenknecht, S. (2013). Epistemic Dependence in Interdisciplinary Groups. *Synthese*, 190 (11), pp. 1881–1898.

Anderson, E. (2006). The Epistemology of Democracy. *Episteme*, 3(1–2), pp. 8–22.

Bohman, J. (2006). Deliberative Democracy and the Epistemic Benefits of Diversity. *Episteme*, 3(3), pp. 175–191.

Borgerson, K. (2011). Amending and Defending Critical Contextual Empiricism. *European Journal for Philosophy of Science*, 1(3), pp. 435–449.

Collins, P. H. (2004). Learning from the outsider within: The sociological significance of black feminist thought. In: S. Harding, ed., *The feminist standpoint theory reader: Intellectual and political controversies*. New York and London: Routledge, pp. 103–126.

Crasnow, S. (2013). Feminist Philosophy of Science: Values and Objectivity. *Philosophy Compass*, 8(4), pp. 413–423.

Crasnow, S. (2014). Feminist standpoint theory. In: N. Cartwright and E. Montuschi, eds., *Philosophy of social science: A new introduction*. Oxford: Oxford University Press, pp. 145–161.

D'Agostino, F. (2009). From the Organization to the Division of Cognitive Labor. *Politics, Philosophy & Economics*, 8(1), pp. 101–129.

Fehr, C. (2011). What is in it for me? The benefits of diversity in scientific communities. In: H. Grasswick, ed., *Feminist epistemology and philosophy of science: Power in knowledge*. Dordrecht: Springer, pp. 133–155.

Frickel, S., and Gross, N. (2005). A General Theory of Scientific/Intellectual Movements. *American Sociological Review*, 70(2), pp. 204–232.

Grasswick, H. (2010). Scientific and Lay Communities: Earning Epistemic Trust through Knowledge Sharing. *Synthese*, 177, pp. 387–409.

Harding, S. (1986). *The science question in feminism*. Ithaca and London: Cornell University Press.

Harding, S. (1991). *Whose science? Whose knowledge? Thinking from women's lives*. Ithaca and London: Cornell University Press.

Harding, S. (2015). *Objectivity and diversity: Another logic of scientific research*. Chicago: The University of Chicago Press.

Hicks, D. (2011). Is Longino's Conception of Objectivity Feminist? *Hypatia*, 26(2), pp. 333–351.

Intemann, K. (2009). Why Diversity Matters: Understanding and Applying the Diversity Component of the NSF's Broader Impacts Criterion. *Social Epistemology*, 23(3–4), pp. 249–266.

Intemann, K. (2010). 25 Years of Feminist Empiricism and Standpoint Theory: Where Are We Now? *Hypatia*, 25(4), pp. 778–796.

Intemann, K. (2011). Diversity and dissent in science: Does democracy always serve feminist aims? In: H. Grasswick, ed., *Feminist epistemology and philosophy of science: Power in knowledge*. Dordrecht: Springer, pp. 111–132.

Intemann, K., and de Melo-Martin, I. (2014). Are There Limits to Scientists' Obligations to Seek and Engage Dissenters? *Synthese*, 191, pp. 2751–2765.

Kitcher, P. (1990). The Division of Cognitive Labor. *The Journal of Philosophy*, 87(1), pp. 5–22.

Kitcher, P. (1993). *The advancement of science: Science without legend, objectivity without illusions*. New York and Oxford: Oxford University Press.

Kitcher, P. (2011). *Science in a democratic society*. New York: Prometheus Books.

Koskinen, I. (2014). Critical Subjects: Participatory Research Needs to Make Room for Debate. *Philosophy of the Social Sciences*, 44(6), pp. 733–751.

Koskinen, I., and Mäki, U. (2016). Extra-academic Transdisciplinarity and Scientific Pluralism: What Might They Learn from One Another? *European Journal for Philosophy of Science*, 6(3), pp. 419–444.

Kourany, J. (2010). *Philosophy of science after feminism*. New York and Oxford: Oxford University Press.

Kuhn, T. (1977). Objectivity, value judgment, and theory choice. In: T. Kuhn, ed., *The essential tension: Selected studies in scientific tradition and change*. Chicago: The University of Chicago Press, pp. 320–339.

Kuhn, T. (1996). *The structure of scientific revolutions*. Chicago: The University of Chicago Press.

Longino, H. (1990). *Science as social knowledge*. Princeton: Princeton University Press.

Longino, H. (1995). Gender, Politics, and the Theoretical Virtues. *Synthese*, 104(3), pp. 383–397.

Longino, H. (2002). *The fate of knowledge*. Princeton: Princeton University Press.

Muldoon, R. (2013). Diversity and the Division of Cognitive Labor. *Philosophy Compass*, 8(2), pp. 117–125.

Page, S. E. (2007). *The difference: How the power of diversity creates better groups, firms, schools, and societies*. Princeton and Oxford: Princeton University Press.

Pinto, M. F. (2016). Economics Imperialism in Social Epistemology: A Critical Assessment. *Philosophy of the Social Sciences*, 46(5), pp. 443–472.

Pöyhönen, S. (2017). The Value of Cognitive Diversity in Science. *Synthese*, 194(11), pp. 4519–4540.

Rolin, K. (2011). Diversity and Dissent in the Social Sciences: The Case of Organization Studies. *Philosophy of the Social Sciences*, 41(4), pp. 470–494.

Rolin, K. (2016). Values, Standpoints, and Scientific/Intellectual Movements. *Studies in History and Philosophy of Science*, 56, pp. 11–19.

Solomon, M. (1992). Scientific Rationality and Human Reasoning. *Philosophy of Science*, 59(3), pp. 439–455.

Solomon, M. (2001). *Social empiricism*. Cambridge: MIT Press.

Solomon, M. (2006). Norms of Epistemic Diversity. *Episteme*, 3(1–2), pp. 23–36.

Solomon, M. (2009). Standpoint and Creativity. *Hypatia*, 24(4), pp. 226–237.

Strevens, M. (2003). The Role of the Priority Rule in Science. *The Journal of Philosophy*, 100(2), pp. 55–79.

Thoma, J. (2015). The Epistemic Division of Labor Revisited. *Philosophy of Science*, 82(3), pp. 454–472.

Tollefsen, D. (2006). Group Deliberation, Social Cohesion, and Scientific Teamwork: Is There Room for Dissent? *Episteme*, 3(1–2), pp. 37–51.

Weisberg, M., and Muldoon, R. (2009). Epistemic Landscapes and the Division of Cognitive Labor. *Philosophy of Science*, 76(2), pp. 225–252.

Wray, K. B. (2007). Who Has Scientific Knowledge? *Social Epistemology*, 21(3), pp. 337–347.

Wray, K. B. (2011). *Kuhn's evolutionary social epistemology*. Cambridge: Cambridge University Press.

Wray, K. B. (2014). Collaborative Research, Deliberation, and Innovation. *Episteme*, 11(3), pp. 291–303.

Wylie, A. (2003). Why standpoint matters. In: R. Figueroa and S. Harding, eds., *Science and other cultures: Issues in philosophies of science and technology*. New York: Routledge, pp. 26–48.

Wylie, A. (2006). Introduction: When Difference Makes a Difference. *Episteme*, 3(1–2), pp. 1–7.

Wylie, A. (2011). What knowers know well: Women, work, and the academy. In: H. Grasswick, ed., *Feminist epistemology and philosophy of science: Power in knowledge*. Dordrecht: Springer, pp. 157–179.

Wylie, A. (2012). Feminist philosophy of science: Standpoint matters. Presidential address delivered at the Annual Meeting of the Pacific Division of the American Philosophical Association.

Wylie, A. (2015). A plurality of pluralisms: Collaborative practice in archaeology. In: F. Padovani, A. Richardson, and J. Y. Tsou, eds., *Objectivity in science: New perspectives from science and technology studies*. Boston Studies in the Philosophy and History of Science, Vol. 310. Dordrecht and London: Springer, pp. 189–210.

Zollman, K. (2010). The Epistemic Benefit of Transient Diversity. *Erkenntnis*, 72, pp. 17–35.

Further reading

Anderson, E. (2015). Feminist epistemology and philosophy of science. In: E. Zalta, ed., *The Stanford encyclopedia of philosophy* (Spring 2017 Edition), https://plato.stanford.edu/archives/spr2017/entries/feminism-epistemology/.

Grasswick, H. (2013). Feminist social epistemology. In: E. Zalta, ed., *The Stanford encyclopedia of philosophy* (Winter 2016 Edition), https://plato.stanford.edu/archives/win2016/entries/feminist-social-epistemology/.

Longino, H. (2015). The social dimensions of scientific knowledge. In: E. Zalta, ed., *The Stanford encyclopedia of philosophy* (Spring 2016 Edition), https://plato.stanford.edu/archives/spr2016/entries/scientific-knowledge-social/.

17

EPISTEMIC RELATIVISM

Michael Patrick Lynch

It sometimes happens that different communities or social groups endorse different standards of justification and evidence. As a result, they can differ over which beliefs are really justified by the evidence. When that happens, a natural question is whether there is an objective fact of the matter about which community, if either is correct—or whether, in some sense, both are correct, relative to their own standards. This latter view is called epistemic relativism. In this chapter, we'll introduce epistemic relativism, discuss one major argument in its favor and how it is particularly pertinent to social epistemology, and canvass some objections against that argument.

What Is Epistemic Relativism?

Broadly speaking, epistemic relativism is the view that knowledge and justification are relative. Barry Barnes and David Bloor, for example, put the view this way:

> For the relativist there is no sense attached to the idea that some standards or beliefs are really rational as distinct from merely locally accepted as such. [The relativist] thinks that there are no context-free or super-cultural norms of rationality …
>
> *(Barnes & Bloor, 1982, p. 27)*

In one sense, it is uncontroversial that epistemic facts are relative—or at least relational. That's because it is more or less uncontroversial that beliefs are justified by evidence and evidence can vary from person to person. For example, two people (S_1 and S_2) can see the same object—a tower, say in the distance—and each can be *prima facie* justified in believing it is a different size and shape simply because they are seeing it from different visual perspectives. In this sense, we assume that justification at a time is itself is relative to the evidence. But that is a position that any epistemologist would presumably accept—even an epistemic absolutist, who holds that epistemic facts are absolute. That's because it could still be an absolute fact that S_1's belief is justified by evidence E_1 and also an absolute fact that S_2's belief is justified by evidence E_2. It is not inconsistent to think that people with different evidence can have equally justified but distinct beliefs.

The kind of epistemic relativism worthy of the name, therefore, holds a further view, namely that *what* justifies *what*—what evidence actually supports what beliefs—is relative to distinct communities' epistemic systems. This is relativism about evidence itself: it is not the banal claim that beliefs can have different epistemic statuses relative to different evidence. It is the controversial claim that beliefs can have different epistemic statuses relative to the same evidence. Following Boghossian (2006, p. 72) therefore, we can say that epistemic relativism is typically the conjunction of three views:

1 Epistemic Non-absolutism: There are no absolute epistemic truths of the form "Belief B is justified by evidence E".
2 Epistemic Pluralism: There is more than one epistemic system.
3 Epistemic Relationalism: All judgments of that form, if they are true at all, are true only relative to an epistemic system.

For the purposes of this chapter, we can take an "epistemic system" to be a network of epistemic principles that describe epistemic norms. Note that they could do so in two specific ways. First, they might, as in (1) above, explicitly state criteria for justification:

(Perceptual): For any perceptual proposition p, if it seems that p to S in normal circumstances D, then S is *prima facie* justified in believing that p.

In addition, epistemic systems may include principles that concern the epistemic reliability of sources as in:

(Sense Perception): Sense perception is a reliable source (to some degree, or within certain constraints) for forming true beliefs about the external world.[1]

Epistemic systems, therefore, are sets of epistemic principles tacitly endorsed by communities whose beliefs are governed by the relevant system. In this way, epistemic principles are just general normative principles similar to general moral principles. But where moral principles tell us what to do, epistemic principles tell us what to believe. They either permit or require the acceptance of particular normative judgments—in the epistemic case, judgments of the form "B is justified by E". Such principles don't have to be explicitly endorsed by communities whose beliefs are governed by the relevant system, any more than moral principles are always explicitly endorsed by communities whose actions are governed by a given a moral system.

Epistemic relativists, as we might put it, believe there can be more than one true epistemic system—differing systems of epistemic principles, such that there is no objective way to choose between them. Consequently, the relativist holds that the particular epistemic judgments one makes in light of those systems can be true only relative to those systems. There is no such thing as an epistemic judgment being true or false period—or absolutely. That, at least is the view. What reason is there for believing it?

The Argument from Epistemic Disagreement

The most well-known argument for relativism of any sort is the argument from disagreement. Where F is a property, the relativist argument from disagreement takes roughly this form:

Argument from Disagreement
i Some judgments about what is F are true.
ii (But) there are fundamental and persisting disagreements about which things are F.
iii There is no rational, objective resolution of these disagreements.
iv The best explanation of these facts is that judgments of the form "x is F" are relatively true if true at all.

This statement of the argument is in "toy" form; clearly not all the details are filled in. Nonetheless, it gives the basic sense of the argument, and we can see how this toy argument might go when the property in question is *being justified by the evidence*:

Argument from Epistemic Disagreement

i Some judgments of the form "B is justified by E" are true.

ii (But) there are fundamental and persisting disagreements about which such judgments are true.

iii There is no rational, objective resolution of these disagreements.

iv The best explanation of these facts is that judgments of the form "B is justified by E" are relatively true if true at all.

The epistemic relativist, therefore, can be seen as offering an abductive argument, or argument from the best explanation of the conjunction of the first three premises.

Of course, whether relativism really is the best explanation depends on (a) whether the premises are true; and (b) the existence of other explanations of those premises. Let's discuss these in turn.

The first premise certainly seems plausible. While in the moral domain, some philosophers are willing to claim that all positive moral judgments are false, most philosophers would be hard pressed to do the same in the case of epistemic judgments. Nonetheless, it is possible (anything is possible in philosophy). But because space is limited, I put aside here. Let's assume that some judgments about what is or isn't justified are true.

More interesting are premises II and III. Why would anybody think that there are fundamental and irresolvable disagreements over what justifies what? The best reason is that there can appear to be such disagreements over fundamental epistemic principles.

Epistemic Incommensurability

Are there irresolvable disagreements over what beliefs are justified as required by the premises of the Argument from Epistemic Disagreement? I'll suggest that the most plausible reason for thinking the answer is "yes" is that there can be disagreements over very fundamental epistemic principles that seem to defy resolution by epistemic reasons.

Let's take an example of how such a debate might arise. In the United States, it sometimes happens that members of a community disagree over what sorts of textbooks to teach in the school. Such cases often occur when the issues concern evolutionary theory or even certain matters regarding the nation's history. In such cases, the disagreement is often not just about the facts, it is about our very standards for determining what the facts are—over what counts as evidence or what sources for producing evidence are reliable—that is, over principles similar to Sense Perception mentioned above

Usually, when we question each other's source principles—as might happen when one doctor questions another about the reliability of a given test—the dispute is settled by an appeal to other, more basic principles. In that way, most disagreements over epistemic principles are relatively shallow. They can be resolved, at least hypothetically, given enough time and so on, by appeal to shared principles.

What I'll call "deep" epistemic disagreements, on the other hand, concern *fundamental* source epistemic principles (FESPs). A FESP is a principle such that it can't be shown to be true without employing the source that the relevant principle endorses as reliable. For this reason, explicit defenses of such principles will always be subject to a charge of what Alston called circularity (Alston, 1986). David Hume (1975) arguably showed that the principle of induction is like this: you can't show that induction is reliable without employing induction. It also seems true of observation or sense perception. It seems difficult, to say the least, to prove that any of the senses are reliable without at some point employing one of the senses.

Induction is plausibly fundamental to everyone's epistemic system; but not every principle that is fundamental to one system need be fundamental to another. Moreover, some principles that are fundamental to a given system will be *comparative*. They give weight, or trumping power, to certain principles over others. Most real epistemic disagreements are over these sorts of principles; they are over the scope of reason, over where to set its limits. Those who wax skeptical about scientific standards of reasonableness, for example, are rarely if ever skeptical about it across the board. Their quarrel is with its use in certain domains. They aren't going to say that we should never use observation, logic and experiment to figure things out. What they will argue is that these methods have a lower priority in some subject matters than others. In some domains, other methods trump. People who think that the Torah or Bible or Koran is a better—not the only—means to the truth about the origin of life on our planet, for example, see the matter in that way.

Thus, so-called "young-earth creationists" typically don't deny induction and abduction (coming up with the best explanation of the data) full stop. They deny that these principles have priority everywhere. Imagine, for example a dispute over these two "source" principles:

(A): Abduction from the fossil and physical record is the *only* reliable source of information about the distant past.

(H): Consultation of the Holy Book is the *most* reliable source of information about the distant past.

It seems possible that a disagreement over these comparative source principles could ground out or become irresolvable. In part, that is because someone who advocates (H) isn't rejecting abduction completely; so we can't just call him out for using it sometimes and not others. Neither can we travel back in time and use observation (another commonly shared method) to settle who is right and who isn't about the distant past. Hence we may get to a point where we can't give an argument for our respective point of view over which sources and methods should take priority that doesn't already presuppose just that way of ranking them. So if I challenge your principles for ranking principles (your "comparative principles") then you can't cite any neutral reason for believing it, and if you challenge my first principles in turn, I'll be in the same boat. Neither of us will be able to offer reasons that the other will recognize from his or her point of view.

This fact is significant because it is plausible that active disagreements can be rationally resolved only when one party could rationally *persuade* the other, where rationally persuading someone means persuading him on the basis of a reason he recognizes as a reason. Of course, someone can be justified in believing something *by a reason* without him *recognizing that it is a reason* for that very belief. Moreover, one can have reasons to believe some proposition that one doesn't give or receive. But that is not what is at issue when we quarrel over principles. In these cases, there is a standing demand to *give a reason to believe, or to defend one's beliefs that can be recognized as a reason by those tending the challenge.*

Given these assumptions, it is not hard to see why it would be difficult to resolve deep epistemic disagreements—especially when we mean, "resolve with epistemic reasons". An epistemic reason for believing a principle is a reason to believe that it is true. Where F is a FESP to which B doesn't believe: A can rationally persuade B to believe F on the basis of an epistemic reason R only if, were B aware of her actual commitments, and reason coherently with them, B would recognize that R is an epistemic reason for F. Yet since F is a fundamental epistemic principle, then any epistemic argument for F—including one involving R—will be epistemically circular. And that of course is the rub. For an epistemically circular argument for a conclusion you don't accept should not, in general, be recognized as an epistemic reason for that conclusion. If I don't trust your basic methods, your reassuring me that they are reliable because employing them informs you that they are really won't impress me—nor should it. In a case where live demands for justification are on the table, we demand reasons we can recognize as such. Epistemically circular arguments are hopeless for doing this. Hence, if B were aware of her principles and reason coherently with them, she would presumably not recognize R as an epistemic reason for F. From which it seems natural to infer that A cannot rationally persuade B to commit to a fundamental epistemic principle (to which B is not committed) on the basis of an epistemic reason.

If this is a plausible argument, then I can't rationally persuade you that my fundamental epistemic principles are true on the basis of epistemic reasons. Epistemic reasons, at least, give out in such a situation. When that happens, we can say that the epistemic principles are incommensurable.[2]

So, to the extent that epistemic incommensurability seems plausible, the first three premises of the relativist argument seem plausible. We now turn to the question of whether epistemic relativism is really the best explanation of those premises.

Alternative Explanations

In order for their argument to succeed, epistemic relativists must not only make it seem likely that epistemic incommensurability sometimes obtains, they must rule out alternative reasonable explanations for epistemic incommensurability. What might these be? Let's briefly run through some options.

One possible explanation comes from the *epistemic expressivist*. On this view (Bar-On & Chrisman, 2009; Chrisman, 2008; Field, 2001) epistemic judgments aren't in the business of describing substantive facts. They don't represent the world and don't ascribe substantive properties to beliefs. If they are true or false at all, they are so only in a minimal sense in which any declarative judgment can be true or false. According to this view, the real function of an epistemic judgment is otherwise—perhaps endorsing it, or urging that inquiry with regard to the relevant belief come to an end. Thus the expressivist might suggest that the best explanation of epistemic incommensurability is not that epistemic judgments are relatively true, but that they aren't in the business of being substantively true (or false) in the first place.

A *skeptic* might claim that the best explanation for epistemic incommensurability is not that there are no objectively true epistemic principles but that we can't *know* which epistemic principles are true. Some of them may well be true; we just can't know which one. Note that this isn't the same as skepticism about the external world—it isn't global skepticism. But, if we assume (a) that particular epistemic judgments are true in virtue of general epistemic principles; and (b) that epistemic principles are either fundamental or epistemically derivative from those that are, then skepticism about epistemic principles might *entail* a global skepticism.

A much less concessive, and arguably more plausible, response draws on externalism about knowledge and justification. Against the skeptic, this view would insist that we *can* know which epistemic principles are true. That's because, according to most externalist views of knowledge, we don't need to be able to *defend* our epistemic principles from challenge in order to know they are true. Knowledge is one thing; rational persuasion is another. Consequently, the externalist will argue that in one sense of "resolve", deep epistemic disagreements can be resolved. They are resolved in favor of the party who knows in the externalist sense of "knows".

Of course, whether these other views in general—and the externalist explanation in particular—are ultimately plausible, depends on weighty issues in substantive epistemology—for example, whether and to what extent, the knowability of a proposition is independent of the ability of agents' to defend that proposition against challenge. But however such weighty debates play out, one possible move that the relativist might make at this point would be to concede to the externalist that it is possible to know—in one externalist sense of "know"—that a given epistemic principle is true, but insist that this fact doesn't actually explain *why* principles can be incommensurable in the first place. The incommensurability stems from indefensibility of the relevant principles. *That* is the fact the relativist will insist must be explained—and that, she may well argue, suggests that at least some epistemic properties (or judgments ascribing those properties) must be relativized. Indeed, she might insist that while a given subject might know that some epistemic principle is true, that fact doesn't itself imply that the principle is absolutely true. It might only be true relative to the knower's community. Thus he might know it is true (relative to his community) without being able to defend it from challenge by a member of another community.

There at least two counter-responses a friend of the externalist explanation might make. First, the externalist could argue that the fact that we can't convince those who challenge our fundamental epistemic principles with epistemic reasons is best explained as a consequence of what "epistemic reasons" and "fundamental epistemic principles" really are. More precisely: once one understands what it means to give an epistemic reason, the fact we can't resolve *deep* epistemic disagreements is just what one should expect. It is a consequence of the human cognitive condition; what Pritchard has memorably called our "epistemic angst".[3] In short, what the fact of epistemic incommensurability shows is that we sometimes can't persuade other people of the truth, even when we know. Hence, there is no call, on this view, to appeal to epistemic relativism.[4]

The founder of externalism, Alvin Goldman (2009) has given another response to the relativist. Goldman's move is to distinguish between first-order beliefs and beliefs about the epistemic status of first-order beliefs. A first-order belief is one like:

(a)   The historical evidence justifies S's belief that the Earth is only four thousand years old.

While a second-order belief is one like:

(b)   S is justified in believing that the historical evidence justifies S's belief that the Earth is only four thousand years old.

Goldman points out that (a) might be objectively or absolutely false (or true) while (b) is true relative to the evidence for her epistemic principles that S has available. Relative to the evidence that S has about her epistemic principles, she is justified in taking them as true. Someone else might be justified, relative to his evidence base, in believing that the historical evidence does not justify S's belief. Relative to his evidence base, (b) is false.

One significant advantage of this suggestion is that, as we noted from the outset, it is uncontroversial that people's beliefs are justified relative to the available evidence. Goldman's insight is that this can be applied to epistemic principles as well as particular propositions. Which epistemic principles you take to be justified may be relative to your epistemic community's over-all context simply because different communities are in different evidential situations with regard to the same epistemic principles. But that fact is completely consistent with those epistemic principles being absolutely true or false.

Goldman's suggestion would seem reasonably well-placed to explain incommensurability. Someone who believes a fundamental principle is in a different evidential situation regarding that principle than one who does not believe that principle. That's because due to the epistemic circularity that always attaches to any fundamental epistemic principle, a fundamental principle P will always be part of the evidence base for the belief that P is true. Thus a person who believes such a principle will be in a different evidential context from a person who does not believe it. Consequently, relative to their different evidential contexts, each party to a deep epistemic disagreement will be justified in believing their fundamental epistemic principles, and there will be no objective way to determine, independent of either evidential context, which epistemic system we are absolutely justified in believing. Consequently there will be no epistemic resolution of the disagreement—no epistemic reason that one side can give the other that will carry the day.

While Goldman's view does offer a reasonable alternative explanation of epistemic incommensurability from that of the relativist, it does make a significant concession to relativism. It concedes that there is no objective epistemic way to resolve the debate. Moreover, it raises a further puzzle, one that the relativist might take as some comfort. If our beliefs about which epistemic principles are justified are only relatively true or false, while the epistemic principles themselves are objectively true or false, then it seems that the objective epistemic facts, as it were, can float free from any resolution of disagreements about such facts. Objectively true epistemic principles are powerless to resolve deep epistemic disagreements. And thus, the relativist might point out, one might wonder what good it really does to hold that there are such facts in the first place.

Notes

1 How distinct these two principles are will depend on the theory of justification encoded in the system and whether it distinguishes between justification (or kinds of justification) and source reliability.
2 For further development of this argument, see Lynch (2010); (Lynch, 2012).
3 See Pritchard, *Epistemic Luck* (Oxford: Oxford University Press, 2005) 245–249.
4 For a related response, see (Pritchard, 2011) and (Boghossian, 2006).

References

Alston, W. P. (1986). Epistemic circularity. *Philosophy and Phenomenological Research*, 47(1), pp. 1–30.
Bar-On, D., & Chrisman, M. (2009). Ethical neo-expressivism. In R. Shafer-Landau, Ed., *Oxford Studies in Metaethics*, 4, pp. 132–165.
Barnes, B., & Bloor, D. (1982). Relativism, Rationalism and the Sociology of Knowledge. In M. Hollis & S. Lukes, Eds., *Rationality and Relativism*. Cambridge, MA: MIT Press, pp. 21–47.
Boghossian, P. (2006). *Fear of Knowledge: Against Relativism and Constructivism*. Oxford: Oxford University Press.
Chrisman, M. (2008). Expressivism, inferentialism, and saving the debate. *Philosophy and Phenomenological Research*, 77(2), pp. 334–358.
Field, H. H. (2001). *Truth and the Absence of Fact*. New York, USA: Oxford University Press.
Goldman, A. (2009). Epistemic Relativism and Reasonable Disagreement. In R. Feldman & T. Warfield, Eds., *Disagreement*. Oxford: Oxford University Press, pp. 187–215.
Hume, D. (1975). *Enquiries Concerning Human Understanding and Concerning the Principles of Morals*. Oxford: Oxford University Press.
Lynch, M. P. (2010). Epistemic Disagreement and Epistemic Incommensurability. In A. Haddock, A. Miller & D. Pritchard, Eds., *Social Epistemology*. Oxford: Oxford University Press, pp. 262–277.
Lynch, M. P. (2012). *In Praise of Reason*. Cambridge, MA: MIT Press.
Pritchard, D. (2011). Epistemic Relativism, Epistemic Incommensurability, and Wittgensteinian Epistemology. In S. Hales, Ed., *A Companion to Relativism*. Wiley-Blackwell, pp. 266–285.

Further Reading

Baghramian, M. (2015). *The Many Faces of Relativism*. London: Routledge.
Carter, J. (2016). *Metaepistemology and Relativism*. Basingstoke: Palgrave Macmillan.
Coliva, A., & Pedersen, N. J. L. L. Eds., (2017). *Epistemic Pluralism*. Basingstoke: Palgrave Macmillan.
Rorty, R. (2009). *Philosophy and the Mirror of Nature*. Princeton, NJ: Princeton University Press.
Wittgenstein, L. (1969). *On Certainty*. Oxford: Basil Blackwell.
Wright, C. (2008). Fear of relativism? *Philosophical Studies*, 141(3), pp. 379–390.

18

EPISTEMIC PEER DISAGREEMENT

Filippo Ferrari and Nikolaj J. L. L. Pedersen[1]

The Epistemic Significance of Perceived Peer Disagreement

Recently the following issue has been widely discussed by epistemologists:

(Significance)
What is the epistemically rational response in the face of mutually recognized disagreement?

(Significance) pertains to what *attitude* an agent is epistemically rational in holding in light of disagreement.

Why should we think that disagreement is of philosophical significance? One reason is that disagreement functions as a sort of litmus paper for detecting the presence of *error* (Christensen 2007: 8, Sidgwick 1907: 342). The exact nature and significance of this error need to be scrutinized. To that end, we introduce three examples of disagreement about different subject matters: ordinary perception, arithmetic, and economic policy.

(Perception)—You and I are traffic cops watching cars pass on Main Street. We are equally good, equally attentive cops, with equally reliable eyesight and regard each other as such. We see a truck pass through the intersection. I think that it ran the red light. You think it got through on yellow. (Vavova 2014: 307)

(Arithmetic)—You and I add a series of ten three digit numbers in our heads. A third party calls out the numbers, one after the other. Each of us keeps a tally, adding the numbers as we go, not attempting to keep track of any particular number in the sequence after it has been added to the running total. Neither I nor you are particularly good at mental arithmetic. We both recognize this and that, when we have played this game in the past, we have made a more or less equal number of mistakes. This time I arrive at the number 5,863 but you think that this is not the right answer.

(Economic policy)—Alberto and Paul are both leading economists who recognize each other as such. They have been engaged in a long debate about economic policy in Europe, exchanging arguments and considerations over an extended period of time. Alberto claims that spending cuts are associated with economic expansions and this is because confidence-inspiring policies will foster and not hamper economic recovery in Europe. Paul, on the other hand, maintains that this confidence leads to disastrous results and that austerity is a self-defeating policy which does great harm to European economies, making their debt grow even faster.

When subjects take each other to be epistemically on a par, they are said to regard each other as *epistemic peers*. The idea of epistemic peerhood can be cashed out as follows (Christensen 2007, 2009, Feldman 2006, 2007, Gutting 1982, Kelly 2005, Lackey 2010a, 2010b):

(Epistemic peers)
S_1 and S_2 are epistemic peers regarding p if and only if

i S_1 and S_2 are cognitive equals, i.e. they are equals with respect to cognitive virtues such as intelligence, thoughtfulness, competence, and freedom from bias, and

ii S_1 and S_2 are evidential equals, i.e. they are equally familiar with the evidence and arguments that concern p and have considered them with equal care.

The first condition pertains to the general cognitive profile of subjects. This impacts how they engage in enquiry—how they deliberate, reason, and how they search for, select, and process evidence. The second condition concerns the relative standing of the subjects *vis-a-vis* evidence pertaining specifically to the question whether p.

The three cases of disagreement just presented raise the following instance of (Significance):

(Significance-Peer)
What is the epistemically rational response in the face of mutually recognized disagreement between subjects who take each other to be epistemic peers?

This is a difficult question. Some cases of disagreement involve a perceived asymmetry: one party takes the other to be epistemically superior, but the converse does not hold. This happens when someone recognized as an expert about a given subject matter disagrees with someone regarded as a novice. In such cases, the rational response would seem for the recognized expert to stick to her initial belief and for the novice to defer to her. However, the three cases just presented do not involve this kind of asymmetry and, thus, seem to be much harder to deal with. For this reason, recognized peer disagreement has been at the heart of the recent epistemological literature on disagreement. Different answers to (Significance-Peer) have been given. We present some prominent answers in the next two sections.[2]

Before proceeding let us note that some epistemologists work within a degree-theoretic framework, representing degrees of beliefs by real numbers in the unit interval (0; 1). Degrees of beliefs behave like subjective probabilities, indicating how likely a subject takes a given proposition to be. Other epistemologists work with three non-graded attitudes: belief, disbelief, and suspension of belief. Disbelieving p is understood as believing not-p, and suspension about whether p is understood as some sort of neutral attitude, contrasting with both believing and disbelieving p (Friedman 2013). Within the degree-theoretic framework, disagreement occurs if two subjects have different degrees of belief. Thus, if Sarah's degree of belief that Paris is in France is 0.95 and Bob's degree of belief in the same proposition is 0.6, Sarah and Bob disagree. Within the framework of full attitudes two subjects disagree if one believes p and the other disbelieves p. Both frameworks are widely used in the discussion of peer disagreement. For this reason we rely on both of them below.

Conformism *Vs.* Non-Conformism

There are two main views on (Significance-Peer): conformism and non-conformism. Conformism is the following view:

(Conformism)
In light of mutually recognized peer disagreement regarding p the epistemically rational response for both parties is to revise their doxastic attitude towards p so it is closer to that of the other party.

Conformism predicts that disagreement with a recognized peer is always epistemically significant. Such disagreement rationally requires both parties to abandon their initial belief (non-degree-theoretic framework) or their initial credence (degree-theoretic framework) and move closer to the other party. Hence the label "conformism" (another commonly used label is "conciliationism").

The perhaps most widely discussed form of conformism is the *equal weight view*—thus called because it requires each view to carry equal weight:

(Conformism$^{\text{ew-full}}$)
In light of mutually recognized peer disagreement regarding p the epistemically rational response for both parties is to suspend belief regarding p (Feldman 2006, 2007).
(Conformism$^{\text{ew-degree}}$)
In light of mutually recognized peer disagreement regarding p the epistemically rational response for both parties is to assign each view equal weight. Put mathematically: if S_1's credence in p is x and S_2's credence is y (where $x \neq y$), the credence of both S_1 and S_2 should equal the average of x and y (Christensen 2007, 2009, Elga 2007).

Within a full belief framework, the two parties' views carry equal weight in the sense that their respective beliefs cancel each other out: they should both suspend belief about p. Within a degree-theoretic framework, recognized disagreement carries equal weight in the sense that the credence of both parties should equal the average of the two initial credences.

All versions of (Conformism) are symmetric in that they require doxastic revision from *both* parties. However, it is compatible with (Conformism) that the parties do not have to revise in the same way—that, e.g., one party should assign 0.8 weight to the other party's view and 0.2 to her own. Note, however, that equal weight versions of conformism are *symmetric* twice over: both parties are rationally required to doxastically revise, *and* they have to do so in the same way. According to (Conformism$^{\text{ew-full}}$), this means that both S_1 and S_2 should suspend belief about p. In (Perception) the disagreeing traffic cops should suspend belief about whether the car ran a red light. The same goes for (Arithmetic) and (Economic policy). According to (Conformism$^{\text{ew-degree}}$) the disagreeing parties should "split the difference" in each case. Suppose that in all three cases the initial degrees of belief of the disagreeing parties are respectively 0.8 and 0.2. Then the degree of belief of both traffic cops in <The car ran a red light> should be 0.5. Similarly, in the arithmetical and the economic policy cases.

Non-conformism is the view that disagreement with a perceived peer does not always rationally mandate doxastic revision. This can happen symmetrically or asymmetrically:

(Non-conformism^{SYM})
In light of mutually recognized peer disagreement regarding p it can be epistemically rational for both parties to maintain their initial doxastic attitude towards p (Foley 2001, Rosen 2001, Wedgwood 2007).
(Non-conformism^{ASYM})
In light of mutually recognized peer disagreement regarding p it can be epistemically rational for one party (but not both) to maintain her initial doxastic attitude towards p (Kelly 2005, Lackey 2010a, 2010b).

To get the full-attitude version of symmetric and asymmetric non-conformism replace "doxastic attitude" with "belief", to get the degree-theoretic version replace it with "credence".

How might (Non-conformism^{SYM}) be supported? Here is a simple argument: suppose that S_1 believes p. The truth of not-p is incompatible with the truth of p. So, when S_1 learns of the disagreement with S_2, from S_1's perspective there is reason to think that S_2 is wrong. Similarly from the perspective of S_2. Thus, both S_1 and S_2 can rationally maintain their initial doxastic attitude.

This line of argument embodies a form of "epistemic egocentrism", as it relies on the idea that the first-person perspective is privileged and epistemically decisive for each subject.[3]

How about (Non-conformism^{ASYM})? Some endorse this form of asymmetric non-conformism by appealing to the so-called "right reasons view" (RRV): in cases of disagreement between recognized peers the party who in fact reasoned correctly from the evidence can rationally maintain her initial doxastic attitude while the other party cannot. This former party has the right reasons supporting her doxastic attitude. E.g., in (Arithmetic) suppose that the sequence of numbers in fact adds up to 5,863, and that this is your claim. In that case you can rationally maintain your initial belief that the sum of the sequence is 5,863 while I should revise my conflicting belief.

Variations

Let us introduce three further views concerning recognized peer disagreement: the total evidence view, the justificationist view, and the reasoning as grounding view. These can be regarded as refinements of conformism or non-conformism.

According to the *total evidence view* (TEV) the body of total evidence determines what response is epistemically rational in the face of recognized peer disagreement. TEV includes both first-order evidence and higher-order evidence, respectively the evidence concerning p considered by the disagreeing parties and information about the disagreement (e.g., the epistemic status of the other party (or parties) and how many people hold the different views; (Kelly 2010), Sect. 4). When a subject's total evidence includes the information that a recognized peer holds a different view, TEV mandates doxastic revision: the subject should be less confident. So, TEV is a conformist view. However, it does not amount to equal weight conformism. The view says that *some*—but not necessarily equal—weight should be accorded to the view of a recognized peer.

Consider the following case:

> (Conjecture)—A mathematician proves a theorem that settles what has long been an open question—say, the Twin Prime Conjecture (i.e. the conjecture that there are infinitely many pairs of primes separated by a difference of two). However, suppose also that the whole mathematical community contests the proof (this case is modeled on Case 6 in Kelly 2010).

TEV predicts that the mathematician should be less confident although she has reasoned correctly and in fact proved the Twin Prime Conjecture. In this respect, TEV is different from the RRV, which would attribute no significance to other members of the mathematical community because they have reasoned incorrectly. However, while conformist in nature, TEV is different from the equal weight view. It is compatible with TEV—but not RRV—that the mathematician can rationally remain quite confident in her initial belief vis-à-vis the disagreement.

According to the *justificationist view* (JV), what counts as epistemically rational responses in the face of recognized peer disagreement is determined by the subjects' degree of justified confidence and, in some cases, certain kinds of information. If a subject has a low degree of justified confidence, then substantial doxastic revision is rationally required in the face of recognized peer disagreement. However, if she has a high degree of justified confidence, she can rationally maintain her initial doxastic attitude just in case she has a *symmetry-breaker*. A symmetry-breaker consists in personal information to the effect that her own epistemic situation is good together with the absence of this kind of information about the other party (Lackey 2010a, 2010b).

JV is a non-conformist view, as it allows for no-revision cases. To see this consider the following case:

(Pasta)—Jen is at the dining table with her flatmate Joe. Joe has a vivid experience as of talking to Sarah, their other flatmate, and as of her eating pasta with great gusto. Jen does not have this kind of experience—she has an experience as of Sarah's *not* being present. Joe says to Jen, "Wow! Sarah is really enjoying the pasta!" Jen responds, "Sarah isn't here." Jen and Joe regard each other as peers with respect to perceptual judgments and have the same kind of evidence, perceptual experience. Jen is justified in believing about herself that she is not drunk; is not under the influence of any drugs; has 20/20 vision; and that she has no history of hallucinating. Furthermore, Jen does *not* have this kind of information about Joe. Jen is having veridical perceptual experiences.

Jen has a high degree of justified confidence that Sarah is not present on the basis of ordinary perception. She also has personal information that provides a symmetry-breaker. For this reason Jen can rationally maintain her initial belief that Sarah is not present (Lackey 2010a). This suffices to show that JV is a brand of non-conformism.

Note that JV delivers doxastic revision verdicts for some cases and provides diagnostics for identifying them. To see this consider (Arithmetic). Since the two subjects are not mathematically gifted, they both have a low degree of justified confidence. Thus, according to JV, when they learn of the disagreement with one another, they are both rationally required to substantially revise their initial doxastic attitude.

Wietmarschen (2013) draws a distinction between well-grounded belief and evidentially supported belief. One thing is to say that evidence *E* supports *S*'s belief that *p*—and thus gives *S* justification *to* believe that *p*; another thing is to say that *S*'s belief that *p* is epistemically well-grounded by *S*'s evidence—and thus that *S* is justified *in* believing that *p*. Wietmarschen defends the *reasoning as grounding view* (RGV)—a form of conformism, understood as a view about well-grounded belief. The distinction between evidentially supported and epistemically well-grounded belief allows for the possibility that a belief that *p* is epistemically supported by evidence *E* without being well-grounded by *E*. By appealing to this distinction one can assuage some of the problematic consequences that other forms of conformism have—in particular, the concern that conformist views seem to make the original evidence on which your belief is based epistemically insignificant (or at least, much less significant than before) once you come to know about the disagreement with your peer (Kelly 2010: 122–25).

To illustrate the mechanics of RGV return to (Conjecture). Initially the mathematician's belief that the Twin Prime Conjecture is true is well-grounded by her evidence, in the form of what she takes to be (and what is in fact) a proof of the conjecture. However, when she learns of the opposition from the mathematical community (including many mathematicians whom she regards as peers), this information provides a potential defeater. RGV predicts that this potential defeater undermines the well-groundedness of the mathematician's belief. Thus she is no longer justified *in* believing the Twin Prime Conjecture and should doxastically revise. However, she still has justification *to* believe the conjecture. This is because her evidence is, in fact, a proof of the conjecture and evidentially supports her belief.

Assessing the Views

In this section, we critically assess some of the views outlined above. The current literature is rich with interesting objections and challenges. However, given limitations of space we confine ourselves to a cursory assessment of a few prominent criticisms of the views presented earlier.

Let us first review the pros and cons of conformism. One general virtue of conformism is that it aligns well with the natural idea that disagreement with someone regarded as a peer provides evidence that one has made a mistake in interpreting the original evidence, and that such evidence should make one less confident. However, conformist proposals have been subject to a variety of criticisms. We will briefly review four of them.

The first criticism puts pressure on the commitment to treat as epistemically irrelevant one's original evidence, once the disagreement with a peer comes to light. This seems highly problematic because it completely disregards the possibility that one of the disagreeing parties might have reasoned impeccably, while the other has reasoned incorrectly (see Kelly 2010: 122–25 for the criticism and Christensen 2011: 4 for a reply).

A second issue with conformism is its seeming self-defeating character. Suppose that as an epistemically well-informed conformist I disagree with an epistemically equally well-informed non-conformist about the epistemic significance of peer disagreement. By my own lights in such a situation I should conciliate by decreasing my confidence in the correctness of my own view (or, working with full attitudes, suspend belief). But this seems absurd since it implies that "your view on disagreement requires you to give up your view on disagreement" (Elga 2010: 179. See also Reining 2016, Weatherson 2013).

A third worry about conformism takes issue with the so-called *Independence Principle*—a key commitment of the view. As Christensen (2009: 758) formulates it:

> In evaluating the epistemic credentials of another person's belief about p, to determine how (if at all) to modify one's own belief about p, one should do so in a way that is independent of the reasoning behind one's own initial belief about p.

Suppose that I am extremely confident not only about the truth of my belief that p but also about the extreme reliability of the reasoning process that led me to believe that p. Let us suppose that I can fully introspect this process and assess its reliability in a way that, on this occasion, I have no reason to doubt is flawed. Moreover, suppose that I lack introspective awareness of the reliability of the other party's reasoning process on this occasion. It would seem that I have reason not to conciliate. It would also seem that I have reason to think that the other party has made a mistake on this particular occasion. However, my reasons for not conciliating and for attributing fault to my opponent are not independent of the reasoning behind my initial belief and reasoning about p. Thus, they would be ruled out as epistemically significant in a conformist framework that incorporates the Independence Principle (Lackey 2010a, Sosa 2010; see Christensen 2011: 9 for a reply and Christensen 2016, Kelly 2013: 37–43, Lord 2014 for a comprehensive discussion of the Independence Principle).

A fourth worry concerns the so-called *Uniqueness Thesis*—the idea that there is a uniquely rational response in the face of disagreement with a perceived peer. Versions of conformism appear to be committed to this thesis. For example, the equal weight view seems to be committed to saying that suspension of belief (Feldman 2006, 2007) or adopting the average of the two initial degrees of belief (Christensen 2007, 2009, Elga 2007) is the uniquely rational response for both parties. Some philosophers raise concerns about uniqueness due to specific cases of disagreement that they take to constitute counterexamples. For example, people who grow up in religious communities and people who grow up among atheists might rationally take the same arguments or body of evidence to support different conclusions (the existence/non-existence of God) due to influences from their different backgrounds (Schoenfield 2014; for a non-case-based argument see Ballantyne and Coffman 2011; for an overview see Kopec and Titelbaum 2016, for defences see Christensen 2016, White 2005).

Let us now turn to a brief discussion of non-conformist views. One general advantage of such views is that they pay due respect to the subject's original evidence, gathered prior to the situation of disagreement. After all, the mere fact that we happen to disagree with a peer should not make all the relevant evidence available to us up to that point epistemically insignificant.

Moreover, non-conformist views support our strong intuition that in many cases where we can have introspective access to the reliability of the reasoning process that led to our opinion on the disputed matter, the fact that it is our own opinion and reasoning process we are considering should make a difference. However, there are also reasons to be skeptical about the general tenability of non-conformist views.

One general worry is that a non-conformist attitude towards situations of recognized peer disagreement seems to encourage dogmatism leading, at its extreme, to the permissibility of a subject's systematically disregarding any unfavorable evidence or contrary opinion (see Pedersen 2018 on strong forms of non-conformism). This seems to clash with the fact that we genuinely regard our opponent as an epistemic peer. And this, of course, would be a rather unwelcome consequence, especially in all those cases where neither subject has reason to believe that the situation is epistemically asymmetrical.

A related, but more specific, worry is discussed by Christensen (2007: 209, 2011: 5). Disagreement with your peer provides new evidence that significantly modifies your epistemic situation compared to your pre-disagreement situation. Non-conformist views seem to seriously downplay the epistemic significance of the presence of disagreement which is clearly a weakness of the view especially in those cases where both disputants regard each other as epistemic peers. After all, the fact that I regard you as an epistemic peer and that you disagree with me about whether p, is a significant piece of evidence that should be factored in in my current epistemic situation—evidence that somehow challenges the good standing of my pre-disagreement epistemic situation.

What these very general criticisms of conformism and non-conformism suggest is that neither of them can be said to successfully provide a wholly general and adequate answer to (Significance-Peer). Non-conformist views seem right—*contra* conformist views—when they insist that the epistemic significance of our initial evidence should not be completely discarded in the face of disagreement with someone regarded as a peer. Conformists have it right—*contra* non-conformists—when they insist that the presence of disagreement with a perceived peer has epistemic significance and changes the epistemic situations of the disputants. The three alternative pictures introduced previously can be seen, roughly, as alternative ways of accommodating the positive features of both conformism and non-conformism while avoiding their respective shortcomings. In this respect, such alternatives represent genuine progress in the debate on peer disagreement.

Disagreement and Varieties of Rationality

We are inclined to think that the peer disagreement debate has been conducted somewhat in isolation from other debates in epistemology. This is unfortunate since the epistemic significance of peer disagreement very much seems to be an issue related to other issues in epistemology. Differences between views on peer disagreement may well reflect—or be traceable to—differences in terms of broader epistemological commitments. To argue this point we draw a distinction between two kinds of rationality and discuss them in relation to the views introduced earlier.

Let us distinguish between internal and external rationality. A belief's being internally rational amounts to its being (i) an appropriate response to phenomenal experiences associated with sensation or perception (being appeared to redly, etc.) or the exercise of memory, a priori reasoning, or introspection (seeming right, etc.), (ii) a member of a coherent belief system, (iii) a trigger of the right inferences when the occasion arises, (iv) a trigger of the right actions when occasion arises, and (v) its being held by a subject who prefers to believe what is true and gather further evidence when called for. A belief's being externally rational amounts to its being based on phenomenal experiences that are the result of properly functioning cognitive capacities or reliable belief-forming processes. (The internal/external rationality distinction drawn here is very much inspired by Plantinga 2000: 110–12. Note, though, that the external rationality part is more liberal.)

Internal rationality tracks whether a given belief is appropriately held given the subject's phenomenal experiences and mental states. It is tied to the subject's perspective—to factors that are internal to the subject. External rationality goes beyond the perspective of the subject. It tracks the epistemic status of the genesis or history of beliefs.

Consider (Pasta★), a case obtained by adding the following information about Joe to (Pasta):

(Pasta★)—Joe is justified in believing about himself that he is not drunk; is not under the influence of any drugs; has 20/20 vision; and that he has no history of hallucinating in the past. Furthermore, Joe does *not* have this kind of information about Jen. Jen is having veridical perceptual experiences. However, unbeknownst to him Joe has been drugged with a hallucinogen. He is in fact hallucinating Sarah's presence although he is not aware that he has been drugged and there are no way that he could discover it through experience, reflection, or introspection.

What is the rational response in the face of the disagreement? Let us consider external and internal rationality in turn.

Jen is externally rational while Joe is not. Her belief that Sarah is not present is based on phenomenal experiences that were brought about by a reliable belief-forming process. Recognizing the disagreement with Joe does nothing to undermine the good epistemic standing of the genealogy of Jen's belief. Joe's belief, on the other hand, is the result of hallucination. Hence, it fails to have the right epistemic pedigree and is not externally rational.[4]

Matters are different when it comes to internal rationality. Jen's belief is an appropriate response to her phenomenal experiences and mental states and integrates in the right way with inference and action. The same goes for Joe's belief. For example, if he believes that Sarah wants to have wine with pasta, he will infer that Sarah wants to drink wine. Furthermore, if Joe always wants to accommodate Sarah's desire to drink wine, he will go fetch a bottle of wine upon forming the belief that Sarah wants to drink wine. For both Jen and Joe pressure to doxastically revise in order to maintain coherence in the face of the disagreement is alleviated by their respective symmetry-breakers (i.e. justified beliefs to the effect that their own epistemic situation is good and the absence of such beliefs about the other party).

These considerations on (Pasta★) suggest that verdicts on specific cases may well depend on what kind of rationality is taken to be relevant to the issue of the epistemic significance of recognized peer disagreement. How do the views considered above relate to the external/internal rationality distinction, and what verdict do they issue regarding (Pasta★)?

Let us start with conformism. The unifying commitment of conformist views is that it is not rational to maintain one's initial doxastic attitude in the face of recognized peer disagreement. This is so on the equal weight view, the total evidence view, and any other conformist view. According to these views, once the disagreement comes within one's purview, doxastic revision is rationally required. Since this demand is driven by the *internalization* of the fact of disagreement, we take the primary focus of conformists to be internal rationality.

How about non-conformist views? Here the picture is more complex. Some non-conformists seem to have in mind external rationality, others internal rationality, and yet others a hybrid kind of rationality.

On the right reasons view the subject who in fact reasoned correctly can rationally maintain her initial doxastic attitude while the other party cannot. What matters is the genealogy of the beliefs of the disagreeing parties: who in fact reasoned correctly from the evidence. This very much suggests an external notion of rationality.

Non-conformists who are moved by the I'm-right-you're-wrong line of reasoning think that each party to the disagreement gets evidence that the other party is wrong upon learning of the disagreement. It is the internalization of the fact of disagreement and the accompanying epistemic "downgrade" of the other party that underwrite the rationality of each party's maintaining their initial doxastic attitude. This points to rationality in the internal sense.

Non-conformists of the justificationist stripe operate with a notion of rationality that is sensitive to both external and internal factors. Recall that two things underwrite rational non-revision on the justificationist view: a high degree of justified confidence and a symmetry-breaker. Jen and Joe both have symmetry-breakers, i.e. justified beliefs to the effect that their own epistemic situation is good and an absence of such beliefs about the other party. However, only Jen has a high degree of justified confidence. This is explained by the genesis of their respective beliefs which involves respectively veridical perception (Jen) and hallucination (Joe). Since Jen has both a high degree of justified confidence and a symmetry-breaker, she can rationally maintain her belief that Sarah is not present. Joe cannot rationally maintain his conflicting belief because he fails to have a high degree of justified confidence. The rationality of Jen's belief is of a mixed kind. It is sensitive to both an external factor and an internal one. Since symmetry-breakers are constituted by beliefs, they are an internal determiner of rationality. However, the epistemic pedigree or history of beliefs is an external matter.

The reasoning as grounding view (RGV) is a form of conformism and is thus concerned with internal rationality. Learning of a disagreement with a perceived peer defeats the well-groundedness of each party's belief and thereby rationally mandates doxastic revision. However, RGV accommodates external rationality as well, at least after a fashion. The view grants that someone who has reasoned correctly to *p* from evidence *E* still has justification *to* believe *p* (although, in the face of disagreement, they are not justified *in* believing *p*). In this sense it is still externally rational to believe *p*.

As just argued, different views on peer disagreement appear to operate with different notions of rationality. It is unfortunate that much of the peer disagreement debate—especially in its early stages—has unfolded somewhat in isolation from broader epistemological issues. For, differences concerning the epistemic significance of peer disagreement may well be interlinked with one's broader epistemological commitments—in particular, one's explicit or implicit commitments regarding the nature of rationality and justification. Hence, being clear about basic commitments concerning the nature of rationality could help clarify the peer disagreement debate.

Our own line on the issue concerning rationality is as follows. Most contributors to the debate implicitly assume that there is a single notion of rationality relevant to addressing the issue of the epistemic significance of recognized peer disagreement. We beg to differ. William Alston (2005) argued that there is a plurality of epistemic desiderata, and that it is futile to try to restrict the focus of epistemology to just one of them (see also Pedersen 2017). Inspired by this kind of pluralist attitude we suggest *pluralism about epistemic rationality* as an interesting, viable option. When it comes to framing the peer disagreement debate, we do not take internal rationality and external rationality to be mutually exclusive. Rather, they are complementary. Internal rationality and external rationality both constitute positive epistemic standings. They are both philosophically interesting species of rationality and, as such, both are relevant to the issue of the epistemic significance of recognized peer disagreement.

Notes

1 Nikolaj J. L. L. Pedersen gratefully acknowledges support from the National Research Foundation of Korea (grants no. 2013S1A2A2035514 and 2016S1A2A2911800). Filippo Ferrari would like to acknowledge the support of the German Research Foundation (DFG—BR 1978/3–1, "Disagreement in Philosophy").

2 (Significance-Peer) is often qualified and framed in terms of (at least) *approximate* epistemic peerhood, as it is very rare that people regard each other as *exact* peers.
3 Foley (2001: 108, 110, 114), Kelly (2005: 179–180). Another argument from epistemic egocentrism can be found in Wedgwood (2007: 261).
4 In saying this we are assuming that the kind of proper functioning or reliability relevant to external rationality is incompatible with hallucination. This is Plantinga's view and shared by many others, including (Burge 2010).

References

Alston, W. (2005). *Beyond 'Justification': Dimensions of Epistemic Evaluation*. Ithaca: Cornell University Press.
Ballantyne, N. and E. J. Coffman. (2011). Uniqueness, evidence, and rationality. *Philosopher's Imprint*, 11, pp. 1–13.
Burge, T. (2010). *The Origins of Objectivity*. Oxford: Oxford University Press.
Christensen, D. (2007). Epistemology of disagreement: The good news. *Philosophical Review*, 116, pp. 187–217.
Christensen, D. (2009). Disagreement as evidence: The epistemology of controversy. *Philosophy Compass*, 4(5), pp. 756–767.
Christensen, D. (2011). Disagreement, question-begging and epistemic self-criticism. *Philosophers' Imprint*, 11 (6), pp. 1–22.
Christensen, D. (2016). Conciliation, uniqueness and rational toxicity. *Noûs*, 50, pp. 584–603.
Elga, A. (2007). Reflection and disagreement. *Noûs*, 41, pp. 478–502.
Feldman, R. (2006). Epistemological puzzles about disagreement. In: S. Hetherington, ed., *Epistemology Futures*. Oxford: Clarendon Press, pp. 216–236.
Feldman, R. (2007). Reasonable religious disagreements. In: L. Anthony, ed., *Philosophers without Gods*. Oxford: Oxford University Press, pp. 194–214.
Foley, R. (2001). *Intellectual Trust in Oneself and Others*. Cambridge: Cambridge University Press.
Friedman, J. (2013). Suspended judgment. *Philosophical Studies*, 162(2), pp. 165–181.
Kelly, T. (2005). The epistemic significance of disagreement. In: J. Hawthorne and T. Gendler, eds., *Oxford Studies in Epistemology* Vol. 1. Oxford: Oxford University Press. pp. 167–196.
Kelly, T. (2010). Peer disagreement and higher-order evidence. In: R. Feldman and T. Warfield, eds., *Disagreement*. Oxford: Oxford University Press, pp. 111–174.
Kopec, M. and M. Titelbaum. (2016). The uniqueness thesis. *Philosophy Compass*, 11, pp. 189–200.
Lackey, J. (2010a). A justificationist view of disagreement's epistemic significance. In: A. Haddock, A. Millar, and D. Pritchard, eds., *Social Epistemology*. Oxford: Oxford University Press, pp. 298–325.
Lackey, J. (2010b). What should we do when we disagree? In: J. Hawthorne and T. Gendler, eds., *Oxford Studies in Epistemology Vol. 3*. Oxford: Oxford University Press. pp. 274–293.
Lord, E. (2014). From independence to conciliationism: An obituary. *Australasian Journal of Philosophy*, 92, pp. 365–377.
Pedersen, N. J. L. L. (2017). Pure epistemic pluralism. In: A. Coliva and N. J. L. L. Pedersen, eds., *Epistemic Pluralism*, London: Palgrave Macmillan, pp. 47–92.
Pedersen, N. J. L. L. (2018). Non-rational action in the face of disagreement: An argument against non-conformism. To appear in *Synthese*.
Plantinga, A. (2000). *Warranted Christian Belief*. New York: Oxford University Press.
Reining, S. (2016). On the supposed dilemma of conciliationism. *Episteme*, 13(3), pp. 305–328.
Rosen, G. (2001). Nominalism, naturalism, epistemic relativism. *Philosophical Perspectives*, 15, pp. 60–91.
Schoenfield, M. (2014). Permission to believe: Why permissivism is true and what it tells us about irrelevant influences on belief. *Noûs*, 48, pp. 193–218.
Sidgwick, H. (1907). *The Methods of Ethics*. London: Palgrave.
Sosa, E. (2010). The epistemology of disagreement. In: A. Haddock, A. Millar, and D. Pritchard, eds., *Social Epistemology*. Oxford: Oxford University Press. pp. 278–297.
Vavova, K. (2014). Confidence, evidence, and disagreement. *Erkenntnis*, 79(S1), pp. 173–183.
Weatherson, B. (2013). Disagreements, philosophical and otherwise. In: D., Christensen and J. Lackey, eds., *The Epistemology of Disagreement: New Essays*. Oxford: Oxford University Press, pp. 54–73.
Wedgwood, R. (2007). *The Nature of Rationality*. Oxford: Oxford University Press.
White, R. (2005). Epistemic permissiveness. *Philosophical Perspectives*, 19, pp. 445–459.
Wietmarschen, H. van. (2013). Peer disagreement, evidence, and well-groundedness. *Philosophical Review*, 122, pp. 395–425.

Further Reading

Cohen, S. (2013). A defense of the (almost) equal weight view. In: D. Christensen and J. Lackey, eds., *The Epistemology of Disagreement: New Essays*. Oxford: Oxford University Press, pp. 98–117.

Enoch, D. (2010). Not just a truthometer: Taking oneself seriously (but not too seriously) in cases of peer disagreement. *Mind*, 119, pp. 953–997.

Feldman, R. (2009). Evidentialism, higher-order evidence, and disagreement. *Episteme*, 6, pp. 294–312.

Hazlett, A. (2013). Entitlement and mutually recognized reasonable disagreement. *Episteme*, 11, pp. 1–25.

Kelly, T. (2013). Disagreement and the burdens of judgment. In: D. Christensen and J. Lackey, eds., *The Epistemology of Disagreement: New Essays*. Oxford: Oxford University Press, pp. 31–53.

Kopec, M. and M. Titelbaum. (2019). When rational reasoners reason differently. In: M. Balcerak-Jackson and B. Balcerak-Jackson, eds., *Reasoning: Essays on Theoretical and Practical Thinking*. Oxford: Oxford University Press, pp. 205–231.

Lackey, J. (2013). Disagreement and belief dependence: Why numbers matter. In: D. Christensen and J. Lackey, eds., *The Epistemology of Disagreement: New Essays*. Oxford: Oxford University Press, pp. 243–268.

Titelbaum, M. (2015). Rationality's fixed point (Or: In defense of right reason). In: T. Gendler and J. Hawthorne, eds., *Oxford Studies in Epistemology Vol. 5*. Oxford: Oxford University Press, pp. 253–294.

Wilson, A. (2010). Disagreement, equal weight and commutativity. *Philosophical Studies*, 149, pp. 321–326.

19

RELIGIOUS DIVERSITY AND DISAGREEMENT

Matthew A. Benton

Introduction

Where liberal societies provide freedoms concerning speech, religious belief, or other matters of personal conscience, disagreement inevitably follows. Yet even where disagreement reigns, there is no shortage of confidence on any side.

To some philosophers, confidence in the face of disagreement is at worst irrational and dubiously dogmatic; and at best, such confidence may only be had by conscientiously reckoning with the fact that a great many highly intelligent and well-read individuals—people whom one would regard as at least one's intellectual peers—have reached opposing conclusions. How one must reckon with such disagreement is hotly debated among epistemologists. I don't intend to settle such matters here. This chapter offers an overview of how philosophers have approached problems of disagreement, with a special focus on religious diversity and disagreement. By the end I shall discuss some novel considerations that seem distinctive of religious inquiry, and which complicate the application of prominent views in the epistemology of disagreement.

Epistemological Puzzles of Disagreement

Disagreement has received a great deal of recent attention in mainstream epistemology.[1] Yet the main questions in the epistemology of disagreement were originally posed by philosophers who had their eyes on the significance of religious disagreement (see Gutting 1982; van Inwagen 1994, 41–46; 1996, 139; Plantinga 1995; Rosen 2001, 83–87). We will first survey some issues raised by disagreement, and then in the next section consider more explicit applications to religious (and atheist) belief.

Why should disagreement matter to how we think about epistemology? First, notice our general tendency to reconsider our beliefs when we discover that others disagree. In particular, when we regard our interlocutors as being our *peers*—those as well-informed as us, and of similar intelligence (and not joking with us)—then learning that they disagree often results in our suspending judgment on the matter. Similar results apply when we move from full *belief, disbelief,* and *suspension* of belief, to finer-grained doxastic states like degrees of belief or subjective probabilities, sometimes called *credences*: if you have a 0.9 credence that it will rain today in our area, whereas I have only 0.3 credence that it will rain today, and we both updated on evidence from what we regard as equally reliable sources about the weather, you will likely lower your credence from 0.9 (and I will likely raise mine from 0.3).[2] Or consider David Christensen's check-splitting case (2007, 193): we go to dinner, and we agreed to split the check evenly, adding a 20% tip. We each mentally calculate our share, and I become highly confident that our shares are $43, whereas you become highly confident that we each owe $45. How should we react to each other's beliefs? Presumably we will each lower our confidence, and rethink our calculations, since either (or both of us) may have made a mistake. Similar cases can be given about perceptual judgments rather than mental reasoning, for example, that you and your friend each see the end of a horse race, from nearly identical viewing points, but you disagree about which horse won (Kelly 2010, 113).

For some philosophers, what we typically do in these disagreements is thought to be indicative of what we *ought* to do if we are to be rational: we ought, in such cases, be conciliatory to our peer by reducing our confidence in our initial conclusion, by suspending judgment or shifting credence toward the peer's. The normative principles behind why we ought to do this, according to these *Strong Conciliationists*, can vary. Some endorse an "Equal Weight" view, according to which one must grant equal evidential weight to my peer's opinion as I do to my own.[3]

Many think that implicit in such views is the idea that a set of evidence only supports one doxastic response.[4] Consider the principle *Uniqueness*:

> **Uniqueness** Given one's total evidence, there is a unique rational doxastic attitude that one can take to any proposition.[5]

If Uniqueness is false, there is room for thinking that there could be reasonable disagreements, even among peers who have the same evidence. Denying Uniqueness amounts to endorsing a permissive view of what rationality requires, such that one's evidence may rationally support more than one doxastic position. Thus one might be what White (2005) calls a *radical* permissivist, by thinking that, at least in some circumstances, one's total evidence can permit either believing that *p* or believing that ~*p*. But if rationality were that permissive, it is hard to see why disagreement would *ever* put pressure on us: for people even with identical evidence could reasonably disagree, on the grounds that said evidence can reasonably support believing either way. Less controversially, one might be a *moderate* permissivist by denying this radical view yet insisting that, at least in some circumstances, one's total evidence can permit, say, either believing that *p* or suspending judgment on *p*. More moderate still would be a view that denies each of the above concerning outright belief and withholding belief, but allows that in some circumstances, one's evidence at least makes rational a (perhaps small) range of credences (Schoenfield 2014).

Perhaps conciliatory pressure is due to the idea that learning of a peer's differing response gives you *new* evidence, higher-order evidence, which bears on how well you handled the initial evidence. Feldman insisted that learning of a peer's reaching a different conclusion, on the basis of the same evidence, amounts to evidence against one's own conclusion because "evidence that there is evidence that *p* is evidence for *p*" (Feldman 2006, 208). Such a principle says that discovering that a peer concludes differently on the basis of the same evidence E provides new higher-order evidence that I have misconstrued what E supports. More specifically, Feldman recently argues for

> **EEE3** If S has evidence, E1, supporting the proposition that there is someone who has evidence that supports *p*, then S has some evidence, E2, that supports *p*.
>
> *(Feldman 2014, 292)*

Such a principle could explain why it often seems we ought to reduce our confidence in such situations. However, EEE3 cannot be correct. Suppose your friend Joe is to guess which one of three objects you are about to put into an empty box: an apple, a ball, or some cheese. Out of his sight, you put in the apple; so you, but not he, know that there is an apple in the box. You then tell Joe that it isn't a ball in the box. Given what Joe knows about the setup, your testimony provides Joe with some evidence there is cheese in the box, because Joe's learning that it's not a ball raises the probability for him that it's cheese in the box. As the antecedent of EEE3 has it, you have evidence (E1) that there is someone (Joe) who has evidence which supports (*p*) that there is cheese in the box; but because you know there is no cheese in the box, your knowing E1 is not, for you, evidence supporting that there is cheese inside. (If it were, then by merely telling Joe that what you put in the box isn't a ball, you thereby would have acquired some additional evidence that you *didn't* put in an apple. But that's absurd.) So EEE3 is false.[6]

Principles like Uniqueness or EEE3 appeal to one's evidence without stipulating exactly what evidence is or what it takes to "have" it.[7] Notice that one's background beliefs (or one's prior probability function), while not typically deemed a part of the relevant evidence, plays a crucial role in how one rationally updates on new evidence to arrive at one's beliefs. For example, if you and I both hear the same testimony from John that he has bought a new sportscar, you might believe him while I—since I also believe it is April Fools' Day—do not believe him, for I take him to be joking. If we don't count my background belief about the date as part of the evidence, then clearly, it can be reasonable for us to have different doxastic responses to the same (testimonial) evidence. Similarly, much depends here on what it takes for us to possess the "same evidence". Suppose we just consider propositions as used in a deductive argument: do two individuals who disagree on what to conclude from it (one infers by *modus ponens*, the other by *modus tollens*) count as "having the same evidence"? Is it possible to have some *p* as evidence when you dismiss it as false? Does one have perceptual evidence when one believes one has just taken a hallucinogen?[8]

Apart from such principles about evidence, some appeal explicitly to the notion of an epistemic *defeater* to suggest that the nature of certain disagreements defeats the justification one might need in order to know, or even acceptably believe, one's views (Goldberg 2013, 2014, 2015). On such an approach, acknowledging that certain peer disagreements are *systematic* presents one with a defeater for the justification one might have for one's belief. Systematic disagreements are (i) widespread, (ii) entrenched, and (iii) non-localized, i.e., involving many related matters rather than the dispute being only over a particular local proposition. Such defeaters are not easily dispensed with (e.g., by defeating them with some other evidence which would defeat the defeater), because such disagreements induce the concern that even those who are believe truly were somehow lucky to arrive at the truth. Given this, systematic disagreements seem to rob one's beliefs of justification.[9]

But matters are rarely as clean-cut as the idealized cases to which Conciliationists appeal. In how many cases do we actually have the exact same evidence as our interlocutor? Or similarly, how often is one's disagreeing interlocutor really thought to be an intellectual peer (King 2012)? These and similar worries have led many to think that there just is nothing general to be said about what one should do when one faces disagreements even with one's peers (see Hawthorne and Srinivasan 2013; Matheson 2014).

Many have criticized the blanket way in which some Conciliationists have aimed to offer a universal principle of rationality which would cover all the relevant cases. A common objection is that (unrestricted) Conciliationism is self-undermining: many philosophers, who presumably regard each other as peers and consider all the same arguments, disagree over the truth of (unrestricted) Conciliationism. So by the (unrestricted) Conciliationist's lights, one should not be very confident in their own view (see Elga 2010; cf. Pittard 2015b for a way out).

Kelly (2005, 2010, 2011) raises several concerns with versions of Conciliationism, even for idealized cases. One worry is that deferring to one's peer by reducing one's confidence amounts to an illicit double-counting of the evidence. Suppose we each begin with the same grounds E bearing on whether *p*; and we disclose that I've concluded *p* whereas you, ~*p*. My treating your contrary belief, reached from *your* evaluation of E, as an added reason to believe ~*p* is to allow E to have additional evidential weight (processed through you) beyond what I've already given it. And somewhat awkwardly, in doing this, I would be treating the fact that you believe ~*p* on the basis of E, as a reason for me to believe ~*p* even though you wouldn't yourself regard your believing that ~*p* as an additional reason—on top of E—for believing ~*p* (Kelly 2005, 187ff.). But if it would be illicit for you to use the fact that you believe it as further reason to believe it, why should it be okay for me to do this?

Another worry is that doing what the Equal Weight view requires can lead one *away* from the rational attitude required by Uniqueness. Suppose there is a fact about the degree to which evidence E supports *p*, namely, that it makes *p* 0.8 probable. Upon evaluating E, your credence in *p* is, quite rightly, 0.8, whereas I quite unreasonably arrive at a credence of 0.2. In such a case you have fulfilled the uniquely rational doxastic attitude given E. But when we meet and discuss our evidence and our conflicting credences, the Equal Weight view requires that you must, to be rational, split the difference with me and we must both then be 0.5 confident in *p*. But to do this would be for you to *depart* from the uniquely rational attitude toward *p* given E. Thus the Equal Weight view results in making the original E irrelevant to the bearing of our new evidence (which includes E but also includes the facts about what credences we had reached upon consulting E) on *p*; the actual evidence bearing on *p* gets completely swamped by psychological facts about what the two of us believe (Kelly 2010, 123–124).

There is something to be said for the idea that the one who has in fact reasoned properly to the conclusion supported by the evidence (even if that conclusion is that the evidence supports suspending judgment), may sometimes remain *steadfast*, and rationally so, in her doxastic position; it is, after all, the one who has made a mistake who should revise their position.[10] If something like this is correct, then what one ought to do in cases of disagreement is not independent of who has rightly handled the evidence. "Steadfasters" like Kelly want to insist that what Conciliationism gets wrong is that each party in a disagreement owes the same belief revision regardless of who is closer to the truth. Indeed, one might draw on the defeater epistemology of disagreement to argue that, in a case of peer disagreement, those who reasoned imperfectly from the evidence are most plausibly the ones whose justification is defeated: for if there is some fact about how they evaluated the evidence that they *should have* understood, which if apprised of would lead them to change their beliefs, that fact seems like a good candidate for generating defeaters.[11]

Though epistemologists working on disagreement have considered abstract and highly idealized cases, the issues they raise provide the backdrop for turning to matters raised by religious disagreement.

Religious Disagreement

Religion is a controversial domain: religions distinguish themselves by making various claims about the supernatural, humanity, and how to live. Even among religious adherents who share certain core religious commitments, there remains much disagreement between sects or denominations over doctrine, worship, spirituality, the afterlife, and so on. Contributing to this diversity are the many non-religious or irreligious, particularly atheists, who think that nearly all positive claims (at least about the existence of the supernatural) are false. For simplicity's sake, we shall focus on the basic positions of the theist,[12] atheist, and agnostic, though it should be clear that the structural issues may extend to diversity between religions (or atheisms).[13]

Complicating matters are concerns about what counts as evidence in the religious domain, whether some forms of evidence are more probative than others, and whether one must grant more weight to public or shared evidence. For example, philosophical arguments often present themselves as publically available and neutral reasoning about, say, whether there is a God, whereas those who appeal to religious experience (Alston 1991) as a kind of evidence for God typically conceive of such evidence as inherently private. Testimony from trusted individuals, or from an entire tradition (cf. Zagzebski 2012), can form another kind of ground for belief or disbelief, and it may be that such testimony can ground religious beliefs even in the midst of religious diversity (Baker-Hytch 2018). But the epistemic force of that testimony may depend on whether the testifier functions as an authority or as a kind of expert advisor (see Lackey 2018). Moreover, most reflective individuals will weight the value of these distinct grounds in different ways. Finally, there is plausibly no dispute-independent standard of the epistemic credentials by which one might be judged a "peer": philosophical atheists may think that only one's capacity for intellectual reasoning matters, whereas certain religious views claim, say, that purity of heart or selfless love for others is a precondition of learning the truth about God (see especially Pittard 2015a, §4). Thus even if there were consensus on what kind of evidence in the religious domain is most probative, there is no dispute-neutral way of assessing which epistemic credentials one must have in order to properly assess that evidence.[14]

Notice that these complications arise even on the assumption that Uniqueness (discussed previously), or some other strong Conciliationist principle, is true. For these complications make it difficult, in matters of religion, to discern what one's total evidence actually is. Even if it is possible to establish in what one's total evidence consists, related complications involve which bits of evidence are most probative and so are to be given most weight, and so what religious propositions that total evidence in fact supports. And even if these matters are settled to everyone's satisfaction, other difficulties loom: for whom is to count as a "peer" or as an epistemic "superior"? And if properly settling the above matters depends on regarding only the right individuals as peers or superiors, then it should be clear that there are many choice-points where things can go wrong, and there will even be disagreement, at each juncture, over which way of settling matters is wrong. As such, reaching agreement over Uniqueness, or between Conciliationists and Steadfasters, will not necessarily help us discern what is required in the face of religious disagreement.

Yet there are some for whom the mere fact of religious disagreement plausibly recommends reconsideration of their position. For the *complacent* theist (or atheist or agnostic), who acquired their view pre-reflectively "at mother's knee" and did not consider the reasons why their position is correct, acknowledging the existence of disagreement should presumably cause them to rethink their position. Rosen (2001) has in mind the complacent theist who takes himself upon reflection to have no positive grounds for his belief: that is, someone who has "no arguments, no compelling authority, and most importantly, nothing that he would regard as direct experience of the divine: a theist who believes simply because he has been immersed in a culture in which God's existence is taken for granted." Though he argues it may be rationally permissible for even such a complacent theist to persist simply as an act of faith, Rosen nevertheless thinks that he "probably should reconsider when he realizes that this commitment is an accident of history," and that "there is something admirable in the choice to reconsider." Though Rosen does not consider the comparably situated atheist or agnostic, presumably similar thoughts apply. But we can go further than Rosen; for there are those who complacently hold their view on the basis of reasons they regard as compelling, though they've never really considered arguments to the contrary. For the (a)theist who thinks they have compelling grounds, but never bothered to consider others' beliefs or the reasons one might think differently, the existence of many who disagree on the basis of different grounds should, if acknowledged, induce one to reconsider. For acknowledging such disagreements involves learning that others have different grounds which one might find compelling, if only one would give them an honest hearing.[15]

Complacency aside, let us focus on those more reflective individuals whose beliefs, at least on matters of religion, were (or are being) formed while engaged with many differing perspectives and arguments. (In virtue of reading this, I shall assume you are one of them.) For reflective individuals, it may be that recognizing the extent of disagreement about religious issues will sometimes put pressure on them to lower their confidence, pushing them toward agnosticism. Indeed, a natural thought is that the greater the diversity, the more one should feel an epistemological problem with holding one's own views.[16] But as noted earlier, whether it does (or must) will depend on specific factors concerning what counts as evidence, how to weigh evidence and expertise more generally, and how charitable one has been to opposing views. Given these complications, and that settling such matters can depend on disputed views in epistemology, I am pessimistic that there can be any general epistemic obligations arising from acknowledging the fact of religious disagreement.

One question that arises is whether the great range of religious diversity, between religions and within religions, provides a kind of support for a particular take on how one's own religious view relates to the others. Hick (2004) contends that such diversity supports a *pluralism* on which a divine being of some kind is the revelatory source of all religions, but where the revelatory process necessarily involves cultural reception which influences how different groups adopt and interpret religious claims. Thus we have different religious perspectives such as Hinduism, Buddhism, Judaism, Christianity, and Islam (among many others) which are geographically and historical situated such that the dominant cultural concepts and social priorities end up influencing how each understands the divine. Looked at one way, Hick's line can seem correct: a pluralist picture, where each religious tradition is accurately (if incompletely) referring to some core features of supernatural reality while also reflecting varying cultural concepts, can look like a better explanation of religious diversity than a particularist exclusivism on which only one religion is the most accurate account of the supernatural. But on the assumption that this pluralist picture is correct, it raises many questions: one such question is why, if pluralism is correct, it is rarely a part of the doctrine of so many religions. If pluralism gains some support from the fact of religious diversity, it also seems at a loss to explain why so few religions have been tolerant enough to allow such diversity.

Plantinga (1995) argues forcefully that the fact of religious diversity, and the pluralist's handling of it, need not make a religious exclusivist suspect that their own religious beliefs suffer from any irrationality or epistemic defect. Yet he allows that acknowledging the diversity of religious perspectives could (though might not) defeat the knowledge which the believer might otherwise have had in the absence of such acknowledgment (1995, 214–215), particularly if it leads one to worry that one believes as one does largely due to the religious culture into which one was born.[17] In this way, knowing more about diversity may lead to less religious knowledge, at least in the short run. Yet again, much will depend on the method by which one gained such knowledge (if knowledge it is) in the first place. If one has in fact gained knowledge of theism by direct acquaintance with the truth of theism (either by apprehending the soundness of an ontological proof, or by perceptual acquaintance with God), it is entirely unclear why acknowledging disagreement must undermine that knowledge.[18]

In what remains, I shall briefly consider two arguments concerning religious agreement and disagreement which I think deserve further attention. The first, discussed by Kelly (2011) and Zagzebski (2012, 185ff.), is the "common consent" (*consensus gentium*) argument for the existence of God. The second argument, put forth by Thurow (2012), is that religious disagreement can actually aid the case for theism, for it might, given an Equal Weight view, rationally require us to end up agreeing on theism. It would seem on a first pass that a theist could not appeal to both arguments on behalf of their view, for one depends on widespread agreement about theism, whereas the other depends on widespread disagreement. But as it happens, these two arguments are not incompatible with each other.

Common consent arguments, in their most modest versions, appeal to the large number of people[19] who believe that *p*, and then suggest that this common consent can at least provide significant evidence for *p*. While our focus so far has been on religious disagreement, the common consent arguer aims to capitalize on the widespread popularity—both currently and historically—of theism, in order to claim that, while not decisive, this fact is at least a reason in favor of theism. While treating common consent as evidence for theism might seem implausible, notice that more generally, broad agreement (even if not unanimous consensus) that p arrived at independently provides some evidence in favor of p. It does so because the truth of p can figure in the best explanation of how broad agreement would have been reached, at least if there are other plausible assumptions about how so many would have arrived at the belief that p.[20] However, where people reach agreement that p in dependent fashion (such that their reaching the same conclusion is due to collaboration or external pressure), most will deny that broad agreement is evidence for p. Note also that *dis*agreement over p, if reached independently, can (if there are sufficiently many on each side) provide reason to suspend judgment: for those who found themselves confident that p (or that not-p), independently reached disagreement offers higher-order evidence that one misjudged the initial evidence. But disagreement similarly loses its force if one learns that such disagreement arose in *dependent* fashion.[21] So common consent arguers for theism will need to make the case for enough independence among those in broad agreement that theism is true.

Thurow (2012) argues that even given an Equal Weight view, there are some cases of peer disagreement over p which rationally require not suspension of judgment, but that the peers come to agreement that p. Such cases can arise when the peers agree on the force of some body of evidence E, but disagree on the force of some larger body of evidence F, where, if they suspend judgment on the force of F, then E justifies belief in p for each of them. If the peers can resolve their more basic disagreement over F first by weighting their judgments about that proposition equally,[22] then they should do so (and continue doing) until their agreed upon evidence supports adopting the same attitude toward p. Thurow then argues that it is possible to apply such insights, in a Bayesian framework, to how experts disagreeing over the evidence for theism ought to proceed: such peers might diverge over the force of the total evidence, but be rationally required to reconcile their dissent by eventually coming to agreement that theism is true, or that theism is false (which one depends on the details). If Thurow's approach to the Equal Weight view is right, then it may turn out that just learning the probability distribution of these experts can rationally require that we work hard to come (after much honest toil) to agreement over the matter of theism.

If a modest common consent argument has something to be said for it, then we should expect to grant some weight to the fact of widespread agreement in favor of theism. If Thurow is right, and it also is the case that disagreement over theism, among experts, boils down largely to which body of evidence those experts think matters for reaching a conclusion about theism, then such experts will only proceed rationally if they work together to resolve those disagreements and reach a consensus. And a theist might argue along both lines, where her hope is that the latter approach should yield a consensus in favor of theism rather than atheism; in this way, the two arguments are in principle compatible with each other.[23]

Yet the prospects for what each argument can accomplish might seem dim. Any modest evidence gained by a common consent appeal is likely to be swamped by the force of other (first-order) evidence for or against theism. And an approach along Thurow's lines seems hampered by the following facts: (i) dissenting experts typically disagree over what a given body of evidence itself supports (and this can be because they find themselves with different prior probability distributions, or different views of what can count as evidence); and (ii) these experts will have personal and professional reasons for avoiding concession and resolution.[24]

Conclusion

Where does all this leave us? We have surveyed the general issues arising from the debates over the epistemology of disagreement, and considered how some of those points carry over to religious epistemology and religious diversity. In doing so, we have had to acknowledge the problems arising from the meta-level disagreements among philosophers over how best to deal with disagreement and the assessment of peer-hood, and over what counts as evidence (of varying strengths) in the religious domain, how easily one could come to know truths concerning matters of religion, and whether testimony or perception or some other method of forming beliefs would put one in an adequate position to believe even while acknowledging disagreements. Even if epistemologists unanimously agreed on some of the broader issues concerning the nature of evidence, how to handle higher-order evidence, or the conditions for acquiring knowledge through testimony, things would only be *slightly* improved; because there would remain disagreement about, for example, how and when those insights apply in religion, about when epistemic humility is a virtue rather than a vice in matters of religion, and how (if at all) moral and spiritual considerations come into play. Learning to live with such disagreement is a part of the challenge.[25]

Notes

1 See especially Feldman and Warfield (2010); Christensen and Lackey (2013), and Chapter 18 in this volume by Ferrari and Pedersen.
2 Hereafter, unless otherwise stated, I shall use "belief" as a catch-all to refer to both full and partial belief, such that "lowering" one's confidence can mean either dropping one's full belief in favor or suspending judgment, or reducing one's credence.
3 See Elga (2007), Christensen (2007), and Cohen (2013).
4 However, see Christensen (2016), who argues that Conciliationism can be motivated even without Uniqueness.
5 White (2005, 445), and Feldman (2007, 205).
6 Note that Feldman's replies to objections to EEE3 (Feldman 2014, 296–299) don't apply to this case. See Fitelson (2012) for a refutation of Feldman's earlier slogan, which also casts doubt on EEE3.
7 As Hawthorne and Srinivasan (2013) point out, if one takes a highly externalist view of evidence, such as Williamson's (2000, Ch. 9) E=K view, the problems concerning disagreement look quite different.
8 For helpful discussion on what it is to provide and have evidence, see Anderson, Forthcoming.
9 Though widely used in epistemology, the viability of defeat in epistemology has come under challenge: see Lasonen-Aarnio (2010), Hawthorne and Srinivasan (2013), and Baker-Hytch and Benton (2015).
10 The trouble, of course, is that from within the disagreer's perspective, one cannot tell who that is.
11 For an account of evidence one should have had, and how it might issue in normative defeaters, see Goldberg (2016); for criticisms, see Benton (2016).
12 By "theist" I mean to be as broad as possible: someone who thinks that an extremely powerful, extremely knowledgeable, and extremely benevolent being exists.
13 For helpful overviews of epistemological issues arising from religious disagreement, see King (2008) and Pittard (2015a); for new essays, see also Benton and Warfield (Forthcoming).
14 This problem may extend to proposals in which having the same evidence does not matter, but rather one should judge another a peer when they are (roughly) as justified, given their evidence, in holding their religious beliefs; see Lackey (2014).
15 What is the status of their beliefs *before* they've acknowledged disagreement in this way? Much depends here on one's theory of knowledge. Some will want to say that their beliefs lack "justification" until they've reckoned with the disagreement and rationally assessed grounds for opposing views; still others will insist that even if "justified" and true, such beliefs aren't yet knowledge. I don't have settled views on this, though I'm enough of an externalist to be open to the idea that such beliefs could be "unreasonable" knowledge in Lasonen-Aarnio's (2010) sense.
16 But see White (2018) for a challenge to the idea that *if* there is an epistemological problem of the diversity of opinion, it only gets worse in a larger universe with more diversity.
17 See White (2010) for related issues.
18 Cf. Bogardus (2013) for similar points. *Mutatis mutandis* if theism is false and it's possible to know, by "seeing" directly, that theism is false. Acknowledging disagreement from theists might not dislodge the atheist's knowledge.
19 At least a strong supermajority. Kelly (2011, 146, n. 18) cites one sociologist (whose avowed goal is to show that non-belief is more prevalent than typically thought) who estimates that around 88% of the global population is theist. A related matter concerns whether considerations from Condorcet's jury theorem would lend support to common consent arguments, since work on jury theorems discuss under what conditions some epistemically significant result can be established. For more on jury theorems, see Part 7 in

this volume on the epistemology of democracy, especially Chapter 38, by Dietrich and Spiekermann (2018).

20 See Kelly (2011) for thoughtful discussion.

21 Suppose one learns that ten people believe *p*, while ten believe not-*p*. But one also learns that their beliefs were formed by each telling the next, one by one, what they believe, and they were lined up in such a way that the next listener was always inclined to distrust and believe the negation of what their informant told them. In such a set-up, the existence of such a balanced disagreement would not lead one to revise one's belief, if one believed that *p*.

22 Perhaps by Thurow's own "Straight Averaging Equal Weight" model (2012, 214), which aims to capture the spirit of the Equal Weight view.

23 Note that someone wanting to use both arguments needn't deny the plausible idea, grounded in the probability calculus, that a proposition *p* is only evidence for some hypothesis H just in case ~*p* is evidence against H. For the common consent argument appeals to widespread agreement among all manner of people, whereas Thurow's Equal Weight view appeals only to the disagreement among various peer experts.

24 And (iii) to undertake the project, one would need a vast sociological study to determine who should be the selected experts, and then what their degrees of belief are concerning (say) the probability that miracles have occurred, or the probability of theism given the horrendous evils in our world.

25 Many thanks to Nathan King, Patrick McDonald, John Pittard, Rebekah Rice, Leland Saunders, and Kelly Weirich for helpful comments.

References

Anderson, Charity. Forthcoming. "On Providing Evidence." *Episteme*.

Alston, William P. 1991. *Perceiving God: The Epistemology of Religious Experience*. Ithaca: Cornell University Press.

Baker-Hytch, Max. 2018. "Testimony Amidst Diversity." In Matthew A. Benton, John Hawthorne, and Dani Rabinowitz (eds.), *Knowledge, Belief, and God: New Insights in Religious Epistemology*. 183–202. Oxford: Oxford University Press.

Baker-Hytch, Max and Matthew A. Benton. 2015. "Defeatism Defeated." *Philosophical Perspectives* 29: 40–66.

Benton, Matthew A. 2016. "Knowledge and Evidence You Should Have Had." *Episteme* 13: 471–479.

Benton, Matthew A. and Ted A. Warfield (eds.). Forthcoming. *Pluralism and Religious Disagreement*. Oxford: Oxford University Press.

Bogardus, Tomas. 2013. "Disagreeing with the (Religious) Skeptic." *International Journal for Philosophy of Religion* 74: 5–17.

Christensen, David. 2007. "Epistemology of Disagreement: The Good News." *The Philosophical Review* 116: 187–217.

Christensen, David. 2016. "Conciliation, Uniqueness, and Rational Toxicity." *Noûs* 50: 584–603.

Christensen, David and Jennifer Lackey, (eds.). 2013. *The Epistemology of Disagreement: New Essays*. Oxford: Oxford University Press.

Cohen, Stewart. 2013. "A Defense of the (Almost) Equal Weight View." In David Christensen and Jennifer Lackey (eds.), *The Epistemology of Disagreement: New Essays*, 98–117. Oxford: Oxford University Press.

Dietrich, Franz and Spiekermann, Kai. (2018). Jury Theorems. In Miranda Fricker, Peter J. Graham, David Henderson, and Nikolaj J. L. L. Pedersen (eds.), *The Routledge Handbook of Social Epistemology*. New York: Routledge/Taylor & Francis.

Elga, Adam. 2007. "Reflection and Disagreement." *Noûs* 48: 478–502.

Elga, Adam. 2010. "How to Disagree about How to Disagree." In Richard Feldman and Ted A. Warfield (eds.), *Disagreement*, 175–186. Oxford: Oxford University Press.

Feldman, Richard. 2006. "Epistemological Puzzles about Disagreement." In Stephen Hetherington (ed.), *Epistemology Futures*. 216–236. Oxford: Oxford University Press.

Feldman, Richard. 2007. "Reasonable Religious Disagreements." In Louise Antony (ed.), *Philosophers without Gods*. Oxford: Oxford University Press.

Feldman, Richard. 2014. "Evidence of Evidence Is Evidence." In Jonathan Matheson and Rico Vitz (eds.), *The Ethics of Belief*, 284–300. Oxford: Oxford University Press.

Feldman, Richard and Ted A. Warfield, (eds.). 2010. *Disagreement*. Oxford: Oxford University Press.

Fitelson, Branden. 2012. "Evidence of Evidence Is Not (Necessarily) Evidence." *Analysis* 72: 85–88.

Goldberg, Sanford C. 2013. "Disagreement, Defeat, and Assertion." In David Christensen and Jennifer Lackey (eds.), *The Epistemology of Disagreement: New Essays*. 167–189. Oxford: Oxford University Press.

Goldberg, Sanford C. 2014. "Does Externalist Epistemology Rationalize Religious Commitment?" In Laura Frances Callahan and Timothy O'Connor (eds.), *Religious Faith and Intellectual Virtue*, 279–298. Oxford: Oxford University Press.

Goldberg, Sanford C. 2015. *Assertion: On the Philosophical Significance of Assertoric Speech.* Oxford: Oxford University Press.

Goldberg, Sanford C. 2016. "On the Epistemic Significance of Evidence You Should Have Had." *Episteme* 13: 449–470.

Gutting, Gary. 1982. *Religious Belief and Religious Skepticism.* Notre Dame: University of Notre Dame Press.

Hawthorne, John and Amia Srinivasan. 2013. "Disagreement without Transparency: Some Bleak Thoughts." In David Christensen and Jennifer Lackey (eds.), *The Epistemology of Disagreement: New Essays*, 9–30. Oxford: Oxford University Press.

Hick, John. 2004. *An Interpretation of Religion: Human Responses to the Transcendent*, 2nd edition. New Haven: Yale University Press.

Kelly, Thomas. 2005. "The Epistemic Significance of Disagreement." In Tamar Szabo Gendler and John Hawthorne (eds.), *Oxford Studies in Epistemology*, volume 1, 167–196. Oxford: Clarendon Press.

Kelly, Thomas. 2010. "Peer Disagreement and Higher-Order Evidence." In Richard Feldman and Ted A. Warfield (eds.), *Disagreement*, 111–174. Oxford: Oxford University Press.

Kelly, Thomas. 2011. "*Consensus Gentium*: Reflections on the 'Common Consent' Argument for the Existence of God." In Kelly James Clark and Raymond J. VanArragon (eds.), *Evidence and Religious Belief*, 135–156. Oxford: Oxford University Press.

King, Nathan L. 2008. "Religious Diversity and Its Challenges to Religious Belief." *Philosophy Compass* 3: 830–853.

King, Nathan L. 2012. "Disagreement: What's the Problem? Or, a Good Peer Is Hard to Find." *Philosophy and Phenomenological Research* 85: 249–272.

Lackey, Jennifer. 2014. "Taking Religious Disagreement Seriously." In Laura Frances Callahan and Timothy O'Connor (eds.), *Religious Faith and Intellectual Virtue*, 299–316. Oxford: Oxford University Press.

Lackey, Jennifer. 2018. "Experts and Peer Disagreement." In Matthew A. Benton, John Hawthorne, and Dani Rabinowitz (eds.), *Knowledge, Belief, and God: New Insights in Religious Epistemology.* 228–245. Oxford: Oxford University Press.

Lasonen-Aarnio, Maria. 2010. "Unreasonable Knowledge." *Philosophical Perspectives* 24: 1–21.

Matheson, Jonathan D. 2014. "Phenomenal Conservatism and Skeptical Theism." In Trent Dougherty and Justin P. McBrayer (eds.), *Skeptical Theism: New Essays*, 3–20. Oxford: Oxford University Press.

Pittard, John. 2015a. "Religious Disagreement." *Internet Encyclopedia of Philosophy*, ISSN 2161–0002, www.iep.utm.edu/rel–disa/.

Pittard, John. 2015b. "Resolute Conciliationism." *Philosophical Quarterly* 65: 442–463.

Plantinga, Alvin. 1995. "Pluralism: A Defense of Religious Exclusivism." In Thomas D. Senor (ed.), *The Rationality of Belief and the Plurality of Faith*, 191–215. Ithaca: Cornell University Press.

Rosen, Gideon. 2001. "Nominalism, Naturalism, and Epistemic Relativism." *Philosophical Perspectives* 15: 69–91.

Schoenfield, Miriam. 2014. "Permission to Believe: Why Permissivism Is True and What It Tells Us about Irrelevant Influences on Belief." *Noûs* 48: 193–218.

Thurow, Joshua C. 2012. "Does Religious Disagreement Actually Aid the Case for Theism?" In Jake Chandler and Victoria S. Harrison (eds.), *Probability in the Philosophy of Religion*, 209–224. Oxford: Oxford University Press.

van Inwagen, Peter. 1994. "Quam Dilecta." In Thomas V. Morris (ed.), *God and the Philosophers*, 31–60. Oxford: Oxford University Press.

van Inwagen, Peter. 1996. "It Is Wrong, Everywhere, Always, and for Anyone, to Believe Anything upon Insufficient Evidence." In Jeff Jordan and Daniel Howard-Snyder (eds.), *Faith, Freedom, and Rationality: Essays in the Philosophy of Religion*, 137–153. Lanham: Rowman and Littlefield.

White, Roger. 2005. "Epistemic Permissiveness." *Philosophical Perspectives* 19: 445–459.

White, Roger. 2010. "You Just Believe That Because…" *Philosophical Perspectives* 24: 573–615.

White, Roger. 2018. "Reasoning with Plenitude." In Matthew A. Benton, John Hawthorne, and Dani Rabinowitz (eds.), *Knowledge, Belief, and God: New Insights in Religious Epistemology.* Oxford: Oxford University Press.

Williamson, Timothy. 2000. *Knowledge and Its Limits.* Oxford: Oxford University Press.

Zagzebski, Linda Trinkaus. 2012. *Epistemic Authority: A Theory of Trust, Authority, and Autonomy in Belief.* Oxford: Oxford University Press.

Further Reading

Audi, Robert. 2014. "Normative Disagreement as a Challenge to Moral Philosophy and Philosophical Theology." In Michael Bergmann and Patrick Kain (eds.), *Challenges to Moral and Religious Belief: Disagreement and Evolution*, 61–79. Oxford: Oxford University Press.

Benton, Matthew A., John Hawthorne, and Dani Rabinowitz (eds.). 2018. *Knowledge, Belief, and God: New Insights in Religious Epistemology*. Oxford: Oxford University Press.

Byrne, Peter. 2004. "It Is Not Reasonable to Believe that Only One Religion Is True." In Michael L. Peterson and Raymond J. VanArragon (eds.), *Contemporary Debates in Philosophy of Religion*, 201–210, 215–217. Malden: Blackwell Publishing.

DeCruz, Helen. 2017. "Religious Disagreement: An Empirical Study among Academic Philosophers." *Episteme* 14: 71–87.

Feldman, Richard. 2003. "Plantinga on Exclusivism." *Faith and Philosophy* 20: 85–90.

Kraft, James. 2012. *The Epistemology of Religious Disagreement: A Better Understanding*. New York: Palgrave Macmillan.

Pittard, John. 2014. "Conciliationism and Religious Disagreement." In Michael Bergmann and Patrick Kain (eds.), *Challenges to Moral and Religious Belief: Disagreement and Evolution*, 80–97. Oxford: Oxford University Press.

van Inwagen, Peter. 2010. "We're Right. They're Wrong." In Richard Feldman and Ted A. Warfield (eds.), *Disagreement*, 10–28. Oxford: Oxford University Press.

Wolterstorff, Nicholas. 2014. "The Significance of Inexplicable Disagreement." In Laura Frances Callahan and Timothy O'Connor (eds.), *Religious Faith and Intellectual Virtue*, 317–330. Oxford: Oxford University Press.

Yandell, Keith E. 2004. "How to Sink in Cognitive Quicksand: Nuancing Religious Pluralism." In Michael L. Peterson and Raymond J. VanArragon (eds.), *Contemporary Debates in Philosophy of Religion*, 191–200, 211–214. Malden: Blackwell Publishing.

20
EPISTEMOLOGY WITHOUT BORDERS

Epistemological Thought Experiments and Intuitions in Cross-Cultural Contexts

Eric Kerr

The Continuity of Epistemological Thought Experiments across Cultures

A   Imagine that we are seeking water on a hot day. We suddenly see water, or so we think. In fact, we are not seeing water but a mirage, but when we reach the spot, we are lucky and find water right there under a rock. (Dharmottara, 8th century,[1] in Dreyfus 1997, p. 293)

B   Looking into a field, S sees an animal only a few yards off that looks, sounds, smells, etc., exactly like a sheep, and S non-inferentially forms the perceptual belief that there is a sheep in a field. Actually the animal is of a different species but has been artfully disguised. Yet there is a sheep in the field – way off in a remote corner of the field, completely hidden behind thick hedges. (Roderick Chisholm 1966[2])

In epistemology, it has been common to refer to the idea that *knowing* something and *only believing* something are not the same.[3] The two cases above are attempts by philosophers to elicit this particular intuition in their readers. In these examples, Dharmottara and Chisholm describe an everyday situation in which a person forms a belief about some matter of fact, using the (typically reliable) everyday methods of belief-formation. What is more, the belief the person forms is true. Yet, they suggest, we should say that this person does not really *know* what she believes. If knowledge is a matter of believing what is true, they both ask, and having the right sort of reasons for believing it, then what is it that prevents us from saying someone knows in cases like this?

   What is intriguing about these cases is that Chisholm was writing in the United States in the 20th century, whilst Dharmottara was writing in 8th century India. The cultures in which these two philosophers were writing were different in uncountable ways and yet both seem to share the intuition that there is something pretty odd about the relationship between knowledge and belief. One can find such examples in philosophical writings from Ancient Greece to 6th century India to 14th century Italy to today's philosophy departments in the US and Europe (see Annex). In other words, across times and places, philosophers have conceived of and considered similar kinds of thought experiments and elicited the same intuitions. Some of these historical examples have been referenced in recent philosophical debate and have become of particular interest to epistemologists because of their potential implications for experimental philosophy and the role of intuition in philosophical argument, especially in arguments against the robustness of such intuitions across cultures (Boyd and Nagel 2014, Seyedsayamdost 2014b).[4] Examples such as (A) and (B) provide a bulwark against the claim that philosophers are stuck in an acultural, ahistorical, detached realm of abstract propositions, referring only to their own specific intuitions, and practising what is pejoratively referred to as 'armchair' philosophy. If such distinctions and conceptual manipulations are so commonly found, they likely refer to something more general than cultural, linguistic or historical contingencies and the armchair is as good a place as any from which to access them.[5]

In this chapter 1 investigate the role experimental epistemology can play in responding to this apparent continuity in intuitions across cultures. I aim to explore the motivations behind experimental epistemology, its successes and failures, and whether cross-cultural epistemology can contribute to motivating further research in both experimental epistemology, with its methodological roots in social psychology, and a more sociohistorical perspective, provided by cross-cultural epistemologists.

Cross-Cultural Epistemology and the Sociohistorical Approach to Variations in Epistemic Intuitions

Cross-cultural philosophy, and cross-cultural epistemology by extension, can mean many things. It is sometimes used simply to denote the study of non-Western philosophical traditions, indigenous philosophy and various theological traditions, sometimes called 'area studies philosophy' despite the Anglocentric bias of this distinction. This is a misnomer as it omits the element of comparison required of cross-cultural studies. The second, more correct, meaning is to equate it to comparative philosophy, the project of comparing and setting in conversation with one another philosophical sources from different cultural, historical, linguistic or geographical lineages. Historically, this has tended to occur more frequently and earlier in Asia than in the West, for example in syncretic religious traditions, but interest in Western philosophy has grown particularly in recent decades (Littlejohn 2016). Lastly, it can be used to refer to the study of philosophical problems across cultural contexts that can come from both philosophical and folk sources. In this chapter I wish to widen the net to include this third kind of cross-cultural epistemology since we are concerned with intuitions that may or may not hold across professional or disciplinary boundaries.

In the latter parts of the 20th century and early 21st century, African (Hallen and Sodipo 1986, Hamminga 2005, Kresse 2007, Òkè 1995, Oruka 1990), Aztec (Maffie 2002), Buddhist and Indo-Tibetan (Hugon 2014, Matilal 1986, Matilal and Evans 1986, Stoltz 2007, 2009, van der Kuijp 2003), Chinese (Ames 1991, Geaney 2002, Hall 2001), Indian and Ancient Indian (Chakrabarti and Matilal 1994, Dasti 2012, Phillips 2012, 2015, Potter 1984, 1991, RamPrasad 2002), Native American (Burkhart 2003, Hester and Cheney 2001, Waters 2003), and Maori (Salmond 1985), to name just a small selection, have been studied through a broadly cross-cultural epistemological lens.[6] Some look at the epistemic practices of people of the particular group studied through philosophical, anthropological, sociological and historical approaches. Some look at what can be called reflective epistemologies: the thoughtful, considered reflections of thinkers, theologians, scientists, and so on. Some have conducted sociologies and histories of philosophers, detailing the practices of historical and living philosophers, often distinguishing them from or comparing them with their Western co-professionals. Ames (1991), for example, investigates the imprecision of translating the Chinese term *chih* (conventionally translated as 'to know') into a Western philosophical vocabulary. Others discuss whether non-Western epistemologies can be framed in terms of justified true belief and others still analyze epistemological concepts such as understanding, testimony, doubt, and belief, to non-Western groups (Chakrabarti and Matilal 1994, Phillips 2012, 2015).

Scholars working in these fields have long argued that we ought to reconsider the legitimacy of a method that involves extrapolating from one's own intuitions, the product of one's own cultural biography, about knowledge to general claims about the nature of knowledge. They have suggested that epistemology ought to look further afield to epistemology practised outside of the Anglophonic world as well as 'folk' epistemology practised outside philosophical institutions and literature. Sometimes, epistemologists have found that non-Western epistemic practices and intuitions, in line with what is found to be the case in the social sciences, seem to be in conflict with contemporary Western ones. Soraj Hongladarom, for example, using the work of the Dutch anthropologist, Neils Mulder, argues Thai folk epistemology is incompatible with veritistic epistemology and the maxim to 'seek truth and avoid error' (Hongladarom 2002, Mulder 2000). Mulder's description of the concept of knowledge in Thailand begins with the influence of Buddhist teachings that emphasize memorization and rote-learning. Knowledge becomes separated from understanding; a

> thing to possess, an arsenal of rules and recipes that are formal and static... a thing to display [that] has primarily a social function. To have relatively more knowledge entitles one to equivalently more respect and position, and, correspondingly, people in higher positions are thought to have knowledge – or at least they are expected to behave as if they know.
>
> *(Mulder 2000, pp. 140–1)*

According to Mulder, truth is not the ultimate goal of epistemic agents in Thailand but instead is 'subordinate to the hierarchical social system where the *phuujaj* [elders] are perceived to be superior *in knowledge* [my emphasis],' even though what they believe is false. Of course, such a claim is highly controversial, especially among analytic epistemologists. Another possible explanation is that there is a distinction to be drawn between social and epistemic norms and that, in this case, the former is overriding the latter. However, we can suppose that, whether or not it is true of Thailand, it is, in Stephen Stich's terms, logically, nominally, and psychologically possible (Stich 1990). What Hongladarom and Mulder succeed in doing is in illustrating how such an alternative society might operate and this is enough to motivate an empirical investigation into cultural variation of epistemic intuitions. Indeed, it may be that seemingly intuitive claims about knowledge are not as widely held as one might initially assume. Whilst Nagel, in a reply to Stich, cites Dharmottara, Sriharsa, and Gangesa as three Indian philosophers who have used the philosophical method of eliciting intuitive responses to thought experiments (Nagel 2013, p. 179), the latter of these arguably contradicts the case for continuity. Matilal's interpretation suggests that Gangesa would have come to the opposite conclusion were he to have read Gettier's paper. That is, he would have said that the subject in Gettier cases *does* know (Matilal, pp. 138–9). It may turn out that whether or not individual folk respond to Gettier-like cases in the same way, even amongst philosophers, we can identify some variation, and many philosophers, anecdotally, report similar experiences when relating the Gettier examples to students part-way through or at the beginning of their philosophical training. It is worth noting further that this continuity is not as well-evidenced as it is sometimes made out to be. One problem is that we do not have data for all philosophers, or even a significantly large number of them, and so there is the chance of selection bias.[7] Philosophers, like any professional group, and individually to a greater or lesser extent, train their intuitions to respond in certain ways and this may reinforce which philosophers form part of the canon and which get consigned to posterity.

Intuitions

Philosophers aim at universality. That is, they aim at a general claim; for example, a claim about knowledge and belief, not about knowledge in 8th century India or belief in 20th century United States. When philosophers write, 'Intuitively, it seems that *p*,' 'It seems to us that *p*,' or 'In such a case, we would surely say that *p*' they do not mean by this that '*I* find *p* intuitive' or that 'We *philosophers* find *p* intuitive at time *t*.' If they did, it would be a rather uninteresting claim. It is instead a shorthand for saying that competent, thoughtful speakers would, given the right conditions, find *p* intuitive (Cullen 2010, p. 4). By this reasoning, if you understand what 'knows' means you also understand that 'knows' is not identical to 'believes'. There may be someone out there who does think that 'knows' is the same as 'believes' (or 'hopes' or 'wishes to be true' or 'heard from *S*') but that would suggest that this person has misunderstood the concepts being manipulated rather than that we should revise our understanding of knowledge to include believing, hoping, wishing to be true, or hearing from someone else. In other words, the claim is meant to be broadly universal, once you understand the concepts being used. This is not to say that all philosophers think of philosophy as the elucidation of ordinary folk discourse. Of course, some take philosophy to be involved with concepts that are uniquely philosophical (see, e.g., Nado 2017). However, those who aim to elicit particular intuitions from an interlocutor, we can assume, have in mind the aforementioned competent speaker.

In the case at hand, examples such as those in the index suggest that the Gettier problem (Gettier 1963) and Gettier-like intuitions have a much longer history than the second-half of the 20th century. Further defence of the armchair is given by Jennifer Nagel who argues that the lexical universality of 'knows' and 'thinks' (read: believes) suggests that the kind of distinction marked by Gettier cases runs deeper than a series of coincidental cultural accidents (Nagel 2013, pp. 185–6). After all, grasping the intuitive support for Gettier cases requires adhering to a distinction between knowing something and merely thinking or believing it. Nagel argues that the kind of distinction Gettier cases are meant to probe are culturally robust, drawing a line between 'superficial' variation and 'deeper structural features of knowledge'. Jennifer Nagel (2013), responding to Stich (2013) and to Alexander and Weinberg (2007), argues that 'intuitions about knowledge typically arise from a basic human capacity that is cross-culturally shared; namely, the capacity for folk psychology or "mindreading."' In other words, humans make sense of the world as thinking and knowing beings. This basic capacity is necessarily reflected in the language we use to talk about each other's mental states.

The Potential for Experimental Contributions to Cross-Cultural Epistemology

The question of whether the intuitions that appear to be similar across quite different cultures – indeed, which might even depend upon deep features of the human condition – really are shared as widely as we might believe is an empirical claim that requires sustained investigation. One approach to this investigation has been taken up by experimental philosophers (henceforth, x-phi). The experimental approach is roughly as follows: As an empirical matter, we witness a great deal of variation in reasoning practices, moral intuitions, semantic intuitions, and the like. Prior to finding out the facts, we should not presume that epistemic intuition is an exception. Since around the start of the 21st century, philosophers and psychologists have been exploring the possibility that many of the assumptions that form the agreed basis of current philosophical and psychological debates might in fact not be generally accepted amongst different populations. Intuitions, previously thought to be beyond empirical investigation, may in fact be a source of disagreement. This new brand of philosophical-psychologist (or psychological-philosopher) argues that relating philosophical questions to actual lived practice is a central part of philosophy and that this requires paying attention to the way people think and reason.[8] They employ the methods of experimental and social psychology, mostly survey-based methods, to understand the different ways in which the judgments people make bear on debates in philosophy (Knobe and Nichols 2007, Nadelhoffer and Nahmias 2007, p. 123, Nichols 2004, p. 154). What is key here is not the observation that human behaviour is contingent and culturally and historically variable. Such a statement is trivially true. The challenge from x-phi is that philosophers should insert their questions into this messy world; that discoveries about how people actually are is relevant to and can inform philosophical theory.

One way in which differences in 'how people actually are' (Knobe and Nichols 2007, p. 3) may be relevant is in their use of intuition to support an argument. It is common practice in philosophy to describe hypothetical cases such as the ones that opened this chapter and to make an appeal to an intuition that is then used to form part of a philosophical argument about the nature of a concept. If one accepts the intuition, the rest ought to follow. If one does not accept the intuition, it is not clear what the next step is beyond adjusting one's intuitions. The available solutions seem to be threefold. The first is to claim that the intuitions of philosophers are no more legitimate than those of non-philosophers and so ensues a battle of contradictory intuitions.[9] The second is to claim that relying on intuitions (whether personal or widely held) at all is illegitimate (Bishop 2009).[10] Lastly, the third claim is that intuitions reported by Western philosophers do not necessarily represent those of the general population (or even those of non-Western philosophers) – that intuitions divide along a wide range of factors including geographical and cultural boundaries – and that this affects their evidentiary status.[11]

One response to the claim that a philosopher's intuitions are no more legitimate than those of non-philosophers is to state that, although intuitions may vary between philosophers and non-philosophers, we ought to rely on the intuitions of philosophers as they are trained in understanding and thinking through the relevant subtleties and nuances in the relevant concepts and cases – call this the expertise defense. Philosophers are, in this sense, expert intuiters when it comes to philosophical arguments (Clark 2013, Lacewing 2013, Williamson 2007, pp. 179–207). Sometimes this argument is posed in the form of an analogy. Just as we do not allow folk judgments in mathematics or physics to undermine the judgments of experts in those disciplines, we should not do so in philosophy either (Rini 2014). Students of philosophy have to learn how to apply technical concepts to specific examples carefully, in the same way that law students have to learn how to analyse hypothetical cases (Williamson 2007, p. 191)

Experimental philosophers have responded to the expertise defence. Alexander and Weinberg, for example, argue that 'experimental evidence seems to point to the unsuitability of intuitions to serve as evidence at all' (2007, p. 63). Williamson (2007, p. 191) points out that it is vital that, in conducting experiments, researchers ensure (or make as likely as possible) that respondents are paying careful attention to the relevant subtleties. This is a problem that presents itself not only to philosophers but it is rather a limitation of the survey methodology upon which, for example, many social psychological experiments rely. His second observation – that disagreement is much lower among philosophers than novices is not surprising but nor is it necessarily a result of the former's expertise in applying concepts to specific examples. It may also be the case that, since philosophers are likely to have a lot else in common aside from their expertise – socio-economic status, ethnicity, education level, and so on – that these may be more significant factors in explaining why they disagree so little. There is also the factor that training in a discipline can serve as a way of unifying attitudes and beliefs and that this is not necessarily co-extensive with expertise either. To get to the facts of the matter, empirical research would need to be undertaken.

This line of argument has its roots in Stephen Stich's work in the late 1980s and early 1990s (Stich 1987, 1990). Stich argued that empirical evidence suggests that there are significant differences in how different people reason about the world. Further, there are significant differences in epistemic intuitions, concepts, judgments, and practices. For Stich, these two hypotheses, if correct, undermine the intuition method. Some have argued that the wide variety of results found in current cross-cultural studies is that intuitions 'are simply not to be trusted.' (Nichols, Stich, and Weinberg 2003, p. 243) Indeed, there is reason to think that the intuitions of Western academic philosophers are particularly suspect since this is a small group who go through extensive training and selection meaning that their intuitions are as much representative of reinforcement and institutional consensus-building as reliable tracking of the truth (Machery, Mallon, Nichols, and Stich 2004, p. 9). Cross-cultural epistemology has been suggested as a corrective since it can illuminate how such consensus-building takes place within a restricted view.

Has Cultural Variation Been Demonstrated by Experimental Epistemology?

One of the earliest studies in experimental epistemology focused on intuitional variation between East Asians, Westerners, and participants from the Indian subcontinent. Weinberg, Nichols, and Stich (2001) found striking results in cross-cultural tests that subsequently spurred a great deal of research. They found that Western participants were more likely than East Asians to attribute knowledge in Truetemp cases,[12] although both were likely to deny knowledge unless the mechanism responsible for the true belief was shared amongst everyone in the community, in which case East Asians were more likely to attribute knowledge. Further, they found that East Asians and participants from the Indian subcontinent were more likely to attribute knowledge in a number of Gettier cases and that participants from the Indian subcontinent were more likely to attribute knowledge in the Cancer Conspiracy case and that East Asians were more likely to attribute knowledge in a Gettier-like case. Their results showed that East Asians did not share the intuition of Euro-Americans that Bob lacked knowledge. Cultural variance in epistemic intuitions has also been discussed in Turri (2012); Starmans and Friedman (2012); and Cullen (2010) who report that Western participants' tendencies to attribute knowledge in Gettier cases differ from non-Western participants. Weinberg et al.'s results have not been replicated in several attempts (e.g. Kim and Yuan 2015, Seyedsayamdost 2012, 2014a, 2014b).

Some research from x-phi has shown certain judgments to be more robust. Beebe, Runya, Wysocki, and Edara (2015) report that Chinese, Polish, and Ecuadorian participants attributed ethical statements in similar patterns. Non-national factors – the participants' strength of opinion about an issue, the level of societal agreement or disagreement, and participants' age – were found to 'significantly affect their inclination to view the truth of an ethical statement as a matter of objective fact'. So whilst there could be some cultural influence, non-cultural factors may play a larger role. Intra-cultural factors – differences within national boundaries, for example, as well as between national groupings – would also have to be studied further to demonstrate that such factors are less influential.

Conclusion

Whether or not experiments conducted in experimental epistemology can ever be shown to be conclusive, it would seem that cross-cultural epistemology has an important role to play. Experiments conducted using surveys suffer from numerous issues. First, many such surveys rely on essentialized metageographies such as 'East Asian' or 'Western'. It is unclear why we should expect the underlying mechanisms giving rise to epistemic intuitions to track these general, quite arbitrary, groupings closely, especially if we are to say that they refer to some deep experience of the species. Such geographical groupings have been roundly debunked in the social sciences and humanities and special pleading for philosophical intuitions have not been made convincingly. Further, when x-phi discusses culture this can mean a number of different things: 'Culture' can be a synonym for place of birth (or place of parent's birth), for the place where one's mother tongue is spoken or for the place where one grows up as a child. It can be very broad, e.g. 'Asian', or more narrow, e.g. 'Glaswegian'. Weinberg et al., for example, conducted experiments in Asia and the United States for some of their experiments but, for others, they used East Asian students studying in the U.S. or first and second generation East Asian immigrants to the United States. The Western participants were 'Americans of European ancestry' (Weinberg et al. 2001, fn. 19). Representatives from all Asian or Western countries can rarely be found and so, for example, Weinberg et al. (2001) rely on Chinese, Japanese, and Korean participants to represent 'East Asia'. In Machery et al., results are extrapolated from Hong Kong undergraduates to represent the East Asian category, whilst U.S. undergraduates represent Westerners (Machery et al. 2004, B2). [14] They use the same ethnic identification questionnaire that Richard Nisbett and his colleagues used in their influential but controversial psychological research into cultural variations in 'systems of thought' (Nisbett 2003). Although they are aware of the issue with these rather crude categories, they argue in a footnote that they still capture the same differences that more nuanced classifications would only reiterate although it is not clear *prima facie* why we should expect that to be the case. (Machery et al. 2004, fn. 9) The assumption that properties of crude categories would hold also for the sub-categories within depends crucially on the premise that these categories are actually good proxies for more fine-grained categories. This seems to beg the question.

A more nuanced approach can instead be offered by cross-cultural epistemology which sets into dialogue distinct, potentially incommensurable, epistemological traditions both among professional or trained philosophers and so-called ordinary folk. This approach brings anthropological, sociological, and historical nuances to the results offered by psychological surveys. By engaging more with their neighbours in the social sciences and humanities, this form of cross-cultural epistemology can hope to address the criticisms above and advance x-phi's own methodology. Through such studies we should come to better understand whether or not our own epistemic intuitions represent our own cultural biographies or something grander.

Annex

A Suppose I close my palm and ask a gambler, 'How many dice do I have in my palm?' The gambler replies, 'Five.' And five it is. (12th century Indian philosopher, Sriharsa, in Matilal 1986, p. 136)

B Socrates: If a man knew the way to Larissa, or any other place you please, and walked there and led others, would he not be a good guide?Meno: Certainly.Socrates: And a person who had the right opinion as to which was the way, but had never been there and did not really know, might also be a good guide, might he not?Meno: Certainly. (Classical Greek philosopher, Plato, Meno 97a–c. Cf. Theaetetus 200d5–201c7)

C Suppose *A* has stolen something, and the police have got the suspect. Now two persons, *B* and *C*, come along to testify. *B*, who does not *know*, tells, simply out of malicious intent, that he has *seen A* in the act. And *C*, who has actually seen *A* in the act, says the same thing. The content of the belief of the police or the judge in both cases would be the same. But if the judge inflicts punishment on the basis of *B*'s testimony rather than *C*'s, we would feel that something has gone wrong. (A re-contextualisation of 6th century Indian philosopher, Candrakirti, in Matilal, p. 104)

D *S* looks at a clock and forms a true belief as to the time of day. *S* has every reason to believe that the clock is working well, but in fact it has stopped. (Scheffler 1965, following 20th century British philosopher, Bertrand Russell 1948)

E Suppose somebody misperceives a cloud of dust as a line of smoke and consequently infers that there is a body of fire in the field beyond. Further suppose there is actually a body of fire there with or without smoke, but the person's inference happens to be based upon a misperception. (Sriharsa in Matilal 1986, p. 136)

F You take your son to the zoo, see several zebras, and, when questioned by your son, tell him they are zebras. Do you know they are zebras? Well, most of us would have little hesitation saying that we did know this. We know what zebras look like, and, besides, this is the city zoo and the animals are in a pen clearly marked 'Zebras.' Yet, something's being a zebra implies that it is not a mule and, in particular, not a mule cleverly disguised by the zoo authorities to look like a zebra. Do you know that these animals are not mules cleverly disguised by the zoo authorities to look like zebras? (Dretske 1970, p. 1015–16. Cf. Kerr and Pritchard 2012, p. 195–7, Weinberg et al. 2001, p. 23 for related formulations)

G You see Plato running right past you. Unfortunately, you mistake him for Socrates and you form the confident belief that Socrates is running, based on what you have seen. As it happens, just at this very moment Socrates *is* running, in a distant city. (14th century Italian philosopher, Peter of Mantua, in Boyd and Nagel, p. 109. Cf. Boh 1985)

H [S]uppose one (correctly) identifies an object at a distance as a cow by looking at a piece of cloth around the neck of the cow and mistaking it for the actual dewlap. (Sriharsa in Matilal 1986, p. 136)

I Mary enters the house and looks into the living room. A familiar appearance greets her from her husband's chair. She thinks, 'My husband is home,' and then walks into the den. But Mary misidentified the man in the chair. It is not her husband, but his brother, whom she had no reason to think was even in the country. However, her husband was seated along the opposite wall of the living room, out of Mary's sight, dozing in a different chair. (Turri 2012, adapted from 20th century American philosopher, Linda Zagzebski, 1996, p. 285–6)

J Alice recently applied for a job. Her boss, who is in charge of hiring the successful applicant, told her that another candidate, Carol, will get the job. Alice forms the (justified) belief that Carol will get the job. She also saw Carol put ten coins in her pocket. She thus (justifiably) forms the belief that 'the successful applicant has ten coins in her pocket.' It turns out that Carol does not get the job, Alice does. As it happens, Alice also, unknowingly and by sheer chance, has ten coins in her pocket. Her belief that 'the successful applicant has ten coins in her pocket' is thus justified and true. (My own paraphrase of 20th century American philosopher, Edmund Gettier, 1963)

Notes

1 Exact dates for many of the historical examples given are not known.

2 For related formulations, see Dretske 1970 and Kerr and Pritchard (2012, p. 195–7).

3 I would like to thank Axel Gelfert, Peter Graham, Nenad Miscevic, Michael Slote, and Malini Sur for their insightful feedback on earlier versions of this paper including a version presented at Soochow University, Taipei.

4 The relevant definition of an intuition is one that has been debated extensively. Goldman and Pust argue that intuitions are judgments whose contents are 'singular classificational propositions, to the effect that [X is a case of C].' (Goldman and Pust 1988, p. 182) Ludwig defines intuition as 'an occurent judgment formed solely on the basis of competence in the concepts involved in response to a question about a scenario, or simply an occurent judgment formed solely on the basis of competence in the concepts involved in it.' (Ludwig 2007, p. 135) Sosa defines intuitions in the following terms: 'S rationally intuits that p if and only if S's intuitive attraction to assent to <p> is explained by a competence (an epistemic ability or virtue) on the part of S to discriminate, among the contents that he understands well enough, the true from the false, in some subfield of the modally strong (the necessarily true or necessarily false), with no reliance on introspection, perception, memory, testimony, or inference (no further reliance, anyhow, than any required for so much as understanding the given proposition.' (Sosa 2007a, p. 61) See also Chudnoff (2013a; 2013b and Williamson 2004) for extended discussions on different accounts of intuition.

5 Stoltz (2007) and Boyd and Nagel (2014, p. 109), for example, make this claim. The question of whether intuitions can be used as evidence in epistemology has generated a substantial and extended debate. See Bealer 1998, Brown 2011, Buckwalter 2012, Cappelen 2012, Cath 2012, Chalmers 2014, Chudnoff 2013a, 2013b, Clark 2013, Deutsch 2010, Earlenbaugh and Molyneux 2009a, 2009b, Goldman 2007, Kornblith 2007, Kuntz and Kuntz 2011, Levin 2004, Liao 2008, Ludwig 2007, 2010, Mizrahi 2012, 2013, Nagel 2007, 2012a, 2012b, 2013, Pust 2000, Seeger 2010, Silva 2013, Sosa 2006, 2007a, 2007b, 2009, Stich

2013, Symons 2008, Tobia, Buckwalter, and Stich 2012, Weatherson 2003, Weinberg 2007, Weinberg, Gonnerman, Buckner, and Alexander 2010, and Williamson 2004.

6 Groupings here are meant only for compactness and are not meant to suggest any internal uniformity or cohesion between texts.

7 The PhilPapers survey – the largest existing survey of professional philosophers' commitments – for example, does not contain a question on Gettier.

8 They are, of course, not the first to have proposed this. The general approach has precursors in the Wittgenstein of the Investigations (Wittgenstein 1953, 116), in Arne Næss' empirical semantics (Chapman 2011), and debates in ordinary language philosophy. A more recent precursor can be found in investigations of folk psychological concepts of belief, e.g. Hewson 1994, Kusch 1997. The precise method deployed by experimental philosophers, however, is newer.

9 Note that, when looked at from a cross-cultural perspective, the same point could be made for the epistemic intuitions of non-Western philosophers. If 8th century Indian philosophers had wildly different intuitions about Gettier-type cases then the argument could be made that, amongst groups of philosophers, the intuitions of one group is no more legitimate than those of another group. Indeed, this happens, although at least in the Gettier case, it is not clear the extent to which these examples are outliers.

10 See, for example, Weinberg et al. 2001, Beebe, Runya, Wysocki, and Endara 2015, Beebe and Undercoffer 2016.

11 Buckwalter (2014) provides an overview of recent debate. For critical reflection on this literature and some experiments testing the assumptions behind it, see Tobia, Buckwalter, and Stich (2012); Weinberg, Gonnerman, Buckner, and Alexander (2010); Schutz, Cokely, and Feltz (2011); and Vaesen, Peterson, and Van Bezooijen (2011). There has since been an explosion in research in experimental epistemology. See Beebe (2012, forthcoming) and Alexander and Weinberg (2007) for overviews. Some key investigations include Beebe and Buckwalter (2010); Beebe and Jensen (2012); Beebe and Shea (2013); Bengson, Moffett, and Wright (2009); Colaço, Buckwalter, Stich, and Machery (2014); Feltz and Zarpentine (2010); Friedman and Turri (2014); May, Sinnott-Armstrong, Hull and Zimmerman (2010); Schaffer and Knobe (2012); Swain, Alexander, and Weinberg (2008); Turri and Friedman (2014); and Turri (2014).

12 The example is due to Keith Lehrer who formulates it as follows: "Suppose a person, whom we shall name Mr. Truetemp, undergoes brain surgery by an experimental surgeon who invents a small device which is both a very accurate thermometer and a computational device capable of generating thoughts. The device, call it a tempucomp, is implanted in Truetemp's head so that the very tip of the device, no larger than the head of a pin, sits unnoticed on his scalp and acts as a sensor to transmit information about the temperature to the computational system of his brain. This device, in turn, sends a message to his brain causing him to think of the temperature recorded by the external sensor. Assume that the tempucomp is very reliable, and so his thoughts are correct temperature thoughts. All told, this is a reliable belief-forming process. Now imagine, finally, that he has no idea that the tempucomp has been inserted in his brain, is only slightly puzzled about why he thinks so obsessively about the temperature, but never checks a thermometer to determine whether these thoughts about the temperature are correct. He accepts them unreflectively, another effect of the tempucomp. Thus, he thinks and accepts that the temperature is 104 degrees. It is. Does he know that it is?" (Lehrer 1990).

References

Alexander, J. and J.M. Weinberg. (2007). Analytic Epistemology and Experimental Philosophy. *Philosophy Compass*, 2(1), pp. 56–80.

Ames, R.T. (1991). Meaning as Imaging: Prolegomena to a Confucian Epistemology. In E. Deutsch, ed., *Culture and Modernity: East-West Philosophic Perspectives*. Honolulu: University of Hawaii Press., pp. 227–244.

Bealer, G. (1998). Intuition and the Autonomy of Philosophy. In M.D.A.W. Ramsey, ed., *Rethinking Intuition: The Psychology of Intuition and Its Role in Philosophical Inquiry*. Lanham: Rowman and Littlefield, pp. 210–240.

Beebe, J.R. (2012). Experimental Epistemology. In A. Cullison, ed., *Companion to Epistemology*. London: Continuum., pp. 248–269.

Beebe, J.R. (2014). *Advances in Experimental Epistemology*. London: Continuum.

Beebe, J.R. and W. Buckwalter. (2010). The Epistemic Side-Effect Effect. *Mind and Language*, 25(4), pp. 474–498.

Beebe, J.R. and M. Jensen. (2012). Surprising Connections between Knowledge and Action: The Robustness of the Epistemic Side-Effect Effect. *Philosophical Psychology*, 25(5), pp. 689–715.

Beebe, J.R., Q. Runya, T. Wysocki, and M.A. Endara. (2015). Moral Objectivism in Cross-Cultural Perspectivism. *Journal of Cognition and Culture*, 15, pp. 386–401.

Beebe, J.R. and J. Shea. (2013). Gettierized Knobe Effects. *Episteme*, 10(3), pp. 219–240.

Beebe, J.R. and R.J. Undercoffer. (2016). Individual and Cross-Cultural Differences in Semantic Intuitions: New Experimental Findings. *Journal of Cognition and Culture* 16(3–3), pp. 322–357.

Bengson, J., M.A. Moffett, and J.C. Wright. (2009). The Folk on Knowing How. *Philosophical Studies*, 142(3), pp. 387–401.

Bishop, M. (2009). Reflections on Cognitive and Epistemic Diversity: Can a Stich in Time Save Quine? In D. Murphy and M.A. Bishop, eds., *Stich and His Critics*. Oxford: Wiley-Blackwell.

Boh, I. (1985). Belief, Justification and Knowledge: Some Late Medieval Epistemic Concerns. *Journal of the Rocky Mountain Medieval and Renaissance Association*, 6, pp. 87–103.

Boyd, K. and J. Nagel. (2014). The Reliability of Epistemic Intuitions. In E. Machery and E. O'Neill, eds., *Current Controversies in Experimental Philosophy*. London: Routledge, pp. 109–127.

Brown, J. (2011). Thought Experiments, Intuitions and Philosophical Evidence. *Dialectica*, 65(4), pp. 493–516.

Buckwalter, W. (2012). Surveying Philosophers: A Response to Kuntz & Kuntz. *Review of Philosophy and Psychology*, 3(4), pp. 515–524.

Buckwalter, W. (2014). Intuition Fail: Philosophical Activity and the Limits of Expertise. *Philosophy and Phenomenological Research*, 89(2), pp. 378–410.

Burkhart, B.Y. (2003). What Coyote and Thales Can Teach Us: An Outline of American Indian Epistemology. In A. Waters, ed., *American Indian Thought*. Oxford: Wiley-Blackwell, pp. 15–26.

Cappelen, H. (2012). *Philosophy without Intuitions*. Oxford: Oxford University Press.

Cath, Y. (2012). Evidence and Intuition. *Episteme*, 9(4), pp. 311–328.

Chakrabarti, A. and B.K. Matilal, eds. 1994. *Knowing from Words: Western and Indian Philosophical Analysis of Understanding and Testimony*. Dordrecht: Kluwer.

Chalmers, D. (2014). Intuitions in Philosophy: A Minimal Defense. *Philosophical Studies*, 171(3), pp. 535–544.

Chapman, S. (2011). Arne Naess and Empirical Semantics. *Inquiry*, 54(1), pp. 18–30.

Chisholm, R. (1966). *Theory of Knowledge*. Englewood Cliffs, NJ: Prentice-Hall.

Chudnoff, E. (2013a). Is Intuition Based on Understanding? *Philosophy and Phenomenological Research*, 86(1), pp. 42–67.

Chudnoff, E. (2013b). *Intuition*. Oxford: Oxford University Press.

Clark, S. (2013). Intuitions as Evidence, Philosophical Expertise and the Developmental Challenge. *Philosophical Papers*, 42(2), pp. 175–207.

Colaço, D., W. Buckwalter, S. Stich, and E. Machery. (2014). Epistemic Intuitions in Fake-Barn Thought Experiments. *Episteme*, 11, pp. 199–212.

Cullen. (2010). Survey-Driven Romanticism. *Review of Philosophy and Psychology*, 1(2), pp. 275–296.

Dasti, M.R. (2012). Parasitism and Disjunctivism in Nyaya Epistemology. *Philosophy East and West*, 62(1), pp. 1–15.

Deutsch, M. (2010). Intuitions, Counter-Examples, and Experimental Philosophy. *Review of Philosophy and Psychology*, 1(3), pp. 447–460.

Dretske, F.I. (1970). Epistemic Operators. *Journal of Philosophy*, 67, pp. 1007–1023.

Dreyfus, G. (1997). *Recognizing Reality: Dharmakirti's Philosophy and Its Tibetan Interpretations*. Albany, NY: SUNY Press.

Earlenbaugh, J. and B. Molyneux. (2009a). Intuitions are Inclinations to Believe. *Philosophical Studies*, 145(1), pp. 89–109.

Earlenbaugh, J. and B. Molyneux. (2009b). If Intuitions Must Be Evidential then Philosophy Is in Big Trouble. *Studia Philosophica Estonica*, 2(2), pp. 35–53.

Feltz, A. and C. Zarpentine. (2010). Do You Know More When It Matters Less? *Philosophical Psychology*, 23 (5), pp. 683–706.

Friedman, O. and J. Turri. (2014). Is Probabilistic Evidence a Source of Knowledge. *Cognitive Science*, 39(5), pp. 1062–1080.

Geaney, J. (2002). *On the Epistemology of the Senses in Early Chinese Thought*. Honolulu: University of Hawaii Press.

Gettier, E. (1963). Is Justified True Belief Knowledge? *Analysis*, 23, pp. 121–123.

Goldman, A. (2007). Philosophical Intuitions: Their Target, Their Source, and Their Epistemic Status. *Grazer Philosophische Studien*, 74(1), pp. 1–26.

Goldman, A. and J. Pust. (1988). Philosophical Theory and Intuitional Evidence. In M. DePaul and W. Ramsey, eds., *Rethinking Intuition: The Psychology of Intuition and its Role in Philosophical Enquiry*. Lanham, MD: Rowman & Littlefield, pp. 179–200.

Hall, D. (2001). Just How Provincial Is Western Philosophy? 'Truth' in Comparative Context. *Social Epistemology*, 15, pp. 285–298.

Hallen, B. and J.O. Sodipo. (1986). *Knowledge, Belief, and Witchcraft*. London: Ethnographica.

Hamminga, B. (2005). Epistemology from the African Point of View. *Poznan Studies in the Philosophy of the Sciences and the Humanities*, 88(1), pp. 57–84.

Hester, L. and J. Cheney. (2001). Truth and Native American Epistemology. *Social Epistemology*, 15, pp. 319–334.

Hewson, C. (1994). Empirical Evidence Regarding the Folk Psychological Concept of Belief. *Proceedings of the Sixteenth Annual Conference of the Cognitive Science Society*. New Jersey. (Atlanta, Georgia). pp. 403–408.

Hongladarom, S. (2002). Cross-Cultural Epistemic Practices. *Social Epistemology*, 16(1), pp. 83–92.

Hugon, P. (2014). Tracing the Early Developments of Tibetan Epistemological Categories in rNgog Blo ldan shes rab's (1059–1109) Concise Guide to the *Nyāyabinduṭīkā*. *Journal of Tibetology*, 9, pp. 194–234.

Kerr, E.T. and D. Pritchard. (2012). Skepticism and Information. In H. Demir, ed., *Luciano Floridi's Philosophy of Technology*. Berlin: Springer, pp. 191–200.

Kim, M. and Y. Yuan. (2015). No Cross-Cultural Differences in Gettier Car Case Intuition: A Replication Study of Weinberg et al. 2001. *Episteme*, 12(3), pp. 355–361.

Knobe, J. and S. Nichols. (2007). An Experimental Philosophy Manifesto. In J. Knobe and S. Nichols, eds., *Experimental Philosophy*. Oxford: Oxford University Press, pp. 3–14.

Kornblith, H. (2007). Naturalism and Intuitions. *Grazer Philosophische Studien*, 74(1), pp. 27–49.

Kresse, K. (2007). *Philosophising in Mombasa*. Edinburgh: Edinburgh University Press.

Kuntz, J.R. and J.R.C. Kuntz. (2011). Surveying Philosophers about Philosophical Intuition. *Review of Philosophy and Psychology*, 2(4), pp. 643–665.

Kusch, M. (1997). The Sociophilosophy of Folk Psychology. *Studies in History and Philosophy of Science A*, 28 (1), pp. 1–25.

Lacewing, M. (2013). Expert Moral Intuition and Its Development: A Guide to the Debate. *Topoi*, 34(2), pp. 1–17.

Lehrer, K. (1990). *Theory of Knowledge*. Boulder, CO: Westview Press., pp. 163–164.

Levin, J. (2004). The Evidential Status of Philosophical Intuition. *Philosophical Studies*, 121(3), pp. 193–224.

Liao, S.M. (2008). A Defense of Intuitions. *Philosophical Studies*, 140(2), pp. 247–262.

Littlejohn, R. (2016). Comparative Philosophy. *Internet Encyclopedia of Philosophy*. ISSN 2161–0002, www.iep.utm.edu/comparat/. Accessed 30 June. 2016.

Ludwig, K. (2007). The Epistemology of Thought Experiments: First Person versus Third Person Approaches. In P.A. French and H.K. Wettstein, eds., *Philosophy and the Empirical*. Oxford: Blackwell Pub. Inc., pp. 128–159.

Ludwig, K. (2010). Intuitions and Relativity. *Philosophical Psychology*, 23, pp. 427–445.

Machery, E., R. Mallon, S. Nichols, and S. Stich. (2004). Semantics, Cross-Cultural Style. *Cognition*, 92, pp. B1–B12.

Maffie, J. (2002). Why Care about Nezahualcoyotl?: Veritism and Nahua Philosophy. *Philosophy of the Social Sciences*, 32, pp. 73–93.

Matilal, B.K. (1986). *Perception: An Essay on Classical Indian Theories of Knowledge*. Oxford: Clarendon Press.

Matilal, B.K. and R.D. Evans, eds. (1986). *Buddhist Logic and Epistemology*. Dordrecht: Kluwer.

May, J., W. Sinnott-Armstrong, J.G. Hull, and A. Zimmerman. (2010). Practical Interests, Relevant Alternatives, and Knowledge Attributions: An Empirical Study. *Review of Philosophy and Psychology*, 1, pp. 265–273.

Mizrahi, M. (2012). Intuition Mongering. *The Reasoner*, 6(11), pp. 169–170.

Mizrahi, M. (2013). More Intuition Mongering. *The Reasoner*, 7(1), pp. 5–6.

Mulder, N. (2000). *Inside Thai Society: An Interpretation of Everyday Life*. Chiang Mai: Silkworm Books.

Nadelhoffer, T. and E. Nahmias. (2007). The past and future of experimental philosophy. *Philosophical Explorations*, 10(2), pp. 123–149.

Nado, J. (2017). Knowledge Second (for Metaphilosophy). In A. Coliva and N.J.L.L. Pedersen, eds., *Epistemic Pluralism*. London: Palgrave Macmillan, pp. 145–170.

Nagel, J. (2007). Epistemic Intuitions. *Philosophy Compass*, 2(6), pp. 792–819.

Nagel, J. (2012a). Intuitions and Experiments: A Defence of the Case Method in Epistemology. *Philosophy and Phenomenological Research*, 85(3), pp. 495–527.

Nagel, J. (2012b). Mindreading in Gettier Cases and Skeptical Pressure Cases. In J. Brown and M. Gerken, eds., *Knowledge Ascriptions*. Oxford: Oxford University Press, pp. 171–191.

Nagel, J. (2013). Defending the Evidential Value of Epistemic Intuitions: A Reply to Stich. *Philosophy and Phenomenological Research*, 86(1), pp. 179–199.

Nichols, S. (2004). *Sentimental Rules: On the Natural Foundations of Moral Judgment*. Oxford: Oxford University Press.

Nichols, S., S. Stich, and J. Weinberg. (2003). Metaskepticism: Meditations in Ethno-epistemology. In S. Luper, ed., *The Skeptics*. Aldershot: Ashgate Publishing., pp. 227–247.

Nisbett, R. (2003). *The Geography of Thought: How Asians and Westerners Think Differently... and Why*. New York: The Free Press.

Òkè, M. (1995). Towards an African (Yoruba) Perspective on Empirical Knowledge. *International Philosophical Quarterly*, 35(2), pp. 205–216.

Oruka, H.O. (1990). *Indigenous Thinkers and Modern Debate in African Philosophy*. Leiden: E.J. Brill.

Phillips, S. (2012). *Epistemology in Classical India: The Knowledge Sources of the Nyāya School*. London: Routledge.

Phillips, S. (2015). Epistemology in Classical Indian Philosophy. [online] *The Stanford Encyclopedia of Philosophy*, E.N. Zalta, ed., Available at http://plato.stanford.edu/archives/spr2015/entries/epistemology-india/ [Accessed Spring 2015].

Potter, K.H. (1984). Does Indian Epistemology Concern Justified True Belief? *Journal of Indian Philosophy*, 12(4), pp. 307–327.

Potter, K.H. (1991). The Commensurability of Indian Epistemological Theories. In E. Deutsch, ed., *Culture and Modernity: East-West Philosophic Perspectives*. Honolulu: University of Hawaii Press., pp. 123–140.

Pust, J. (2000). *Intuitions as Evidence*. London: Routledge.

RamPrasad, C. (2002). *Advaita Epistemology and Metaphysics: An Outline of Indian NonRealism*. London: RoutledgeCurzon.

Rini, R. (2014). Analogies, Moral Intuitions, and the Expertise Defence. *Review of Philosophy and Psychology*, 5(2), pp. 169–181.

Salmond, A. (1985). Maori Epistemologies. In J. Overing, ed., *Reason and Morality*. London: Tavistock, pp. 240–263.

Schaffer, J. and J. Knobe. (2012). Contrastive Knowledge Surveyed. *Noûs*, 46, pp. 675–708.

Schutz, E., E.T. Cokely, and A. Feltz. (2011). Persistent Bias in Expert Judgments about Free Will and Moral Responsibility: A Test of the Expertise Defense. *Consciousness and Cognition*, 20(4), pp. 1722–1731.

Seeger, M. (2010). Experimental Philosophy and the Twin Earth Intuition. *Grazer Philosophische Studien*, 80, pp. 237–244.

Seyedsayamdost, H. (2012). On Normativity and Epistemic Intuitions: Failure to Detect Differences Between Ethnic Groups. Available at: SSRN 2168530.

Seyedsayamdost, H. (2014a). On Gender and Philosophical Intuition: Failure of Replication and Other Negative Results. *Philosophical Psychology*, 28(5), pp. 642–673.

Seyedsayamdost, H. (2014b). On Normativity and Epistemic Intuitions: Further Evidence for Cross-Cultural Uniformity of Epistemic Intuitions – Short Report. Available at SSRN: http://ssrn.com/abstract=2538611

Silva, P. (2013). Epistemically Self-Defeating Arguments and Skepticism About Intuition. *Philosophical Studies*, 164(3), pp. 579–589.

Sosa, D. (2006). Scepticism about Intuition. *Philosophy*, 81(4), pp. 633–648.

Sosa, E. (2007a). Intuitions: Their Nature and Epistemic Efficacy. *Grazer Philosophische Studien*, 74(1), pp. 51–67.

Sosa, E. (2007b). Experimental Philosophy and Philosophical Intuition. *Philosophical Studies*, 132(1), pp. 99–107.

Sosa, E. (2009). A Defense of the Use of Intuitions in Philosophy. In M. Bishop and D. Murphy, eds., *Stich and His Critics*. Oxford: Blackwell, pp. 101–112.

Starmans, C. and O. Friedman. (2012). The Folk Conception of Knowledge. *Cognition*, 124, pp. 272–283.

Stich, S. (1987). Reflective Equilibrium, Analytic Epistemology and the Problem of Cognitive Diversity. *Synthese*, 74(3), pp. 391–413.

Stich, S. (1990). *The Fragmentation of Reason*. Cambridge: MIT Press.

Stich, S. (2013). Do Different Groups Have Different Epistemic Intuitions? A Reply to Jennifer Nagel. *Philosophy and Phenomenological Research*, 87(1), pp. 151–178.

Stoltz, J. (2007). Gettier and Factivity in Indo-Tibetan Epistemology. *Philosophical Quarterly*, 57(228), pp. 394–415.

Stoltz, J. (2009). Buddhist Epistemology: The Study of Pramana. *Religion Compass*, 3(4), pp. 537–548.

Swain, S., J. Alexander, and J. Weinberg. (2008). The Instability of Philosophical Intuitions: Running Hot and Cold on Truetemp. *Philosophy and Phenomenological Research*, 76(1), pp. 138–155.

Symons, J. (2008). Intuition and Philosophical Methodology. *Axiomathes*, 18(1), pp. 67–89.

Tobia, K., W. Buckwalter, and S. Stich. (2012). Moral Intuitions: Are Philosophers Experts? *Philosophical Psychology*, 5, pp. 1–10.

Turri, J. (2012). Is Knowledge Justified True Belief? *Synthese*, 184(3), pp. 247–259.

Turri, J. and O. Friedman. (2014). Winners and Losers in the Folk Epistemology of Lotteries. In J.R. Beebe, ed., *Advances in Experimental Epistemology*. London: Continuum, pp. 45–69.

Vaesen, K., M. Peterson, and B. Van Bezooijen. (2011). The Reliability of Armchair Intuitions. *Metaphilosophy*, 44(5), pp. 559–578.

van der Kuijp, L.W.J. (2003). A Treatise on Buddhist Epistemology and Logic Attributed to Klong chen Rab 'byams pa (1308–1364) and Its Place in Indo-Tibetan Intellectual History. *Journal of Indian Philosophy*, 31, pp. 381–437.

Waters, A., ed., (2003). *American Indian Thought: Philosophical Essays*. Oxford: Wiley-Blackwell.

Weatherson, B. (2003). What Good Are Counter Examples? *Philosophical Studies*, 115(1), pp. 1–31.

Weinberg, J.M. (2007). How to Challenge Intuitions Empirically without Risking Skepticism. *Midwest Studies in Philosophy*, 31(1), pp. 318–343.

Weinberg, J.M., C. Gonnerman, C. Buckner, and J. Alexander. (2010). Are Philosophers Expert Intuiters? *Philosophical Psychology*, 23(3), pp. 331–355.

Weinberg, J.M., S. Nichols, and S. Stich. (2001). Normativity and Epistemic Intuitions *Philosophical Topics*, 29, pp. 429–460.

Williamson, T. (2004). Philosophical 'Intuitions' and Scepticism about Judgment. *Dialectica*, 58(1), pp. 109–153.

Williamson, T. (2007). *The Philosophy of Philosophy*. Oxford: Wiley-Blackwell.

Wittgenstein, L. (1953) *Philosophical Investigations* (trans. G. E. M. Anscombe), Oxford: Blackwell.

Zagzebski, L. (1996). *Virtues of the Mind: An Inquiry into the Nature of Virtue and the Ethical Foundations of Knowledge*. Cambridge: Cambridge University Press.

Further Reading

Beebe, J.R. (forthcoming) *Advances in Experimental Epistemology*. London: Continuum.

Gupta, B. and J.N. Mohanty, eds. (2000). *Philosophical Questions East and West*. Lanham: Rowman and Littlefield.

Janz, B.B. (2009). *Philosophy in an African Place*. New York: Rowman & Littlefield.

Waters, A. (2003). *American Indian Thought*. Oxford: Blackwell.

PART IV

Science and Social Epistemology

21

OVERVIEW: ON SCIENCE AND SOCIAL EPISTEMOLOGY

David Henderson

If asked to point to successful classes of epistemic practice, many would respond by pointing to work in the sciences—and much of this work is both carried out in groups and benefits from results and commentary within the broader scientific community. Thus, scientific practice includes much that is taken to be paradigmatically epistemically fitting, and as a result, scientific communities constitute a reasonable central focus for social epistemology. In the four contributions that follow in this part, we find discussions of literatures that should have significant interest for social epistemologists. First, the sociology of science has raised important issues for epistemologists and philosophers of science—discussed in Chapter 22, "The Sociology of Science and Social Constructionism." Second, to what extent should consensus within an epistemic community—and a scientific community—be taken as epistemically weighty or probative? This concern is reflected in Chapter 23, "The Social Epistemology of Consensus and Dissent." Third, an emerging line of investigation pursues the question of what features of research communities are conducive to epistemic successes—for example, by distributing work across lines of research so as to pursue various "live alternatives" in a productive manner. Work on this question is the focus in Chapter 24, "Modeling Epistemic Communities." Fourth, feminist philosophy of science is a rich epistemological literature that has commonly been concerned with the various ways in which epistemic successes can be best fostered within scientific communities that reflect the full range of situated concerns and perspectives within the wider community. This literature is discussed in Chapter 25, "Feminist Philosophy of Science as Social Epistemology."

Michael E. Lynch's entry, "The Sociology of Science and Social Constructionism" (Chapter 22), picks up where Stephen Turner's piece, "The Philosophical Origins of Classical Sociology of Knowledge" (Chapter 4), leaves off. Turner's discussion traced the philosophical roots of the sociology of science. From these issued the sociology of science of Karl Mannheim ([1929] 1954). Mannheim had sought to develop a "non-evaluative general, total conception of ideology," in which "no judgments are pronounced as to the correctness of the ideas to be treated" (Mannheim, 1929 [1954], p. 80). Lynch's contribution picks up the story with Robert K. Merton's (1973) sociology of science. Merton's purported to characterize a set of "norms" that distinguished science as an institution from other modern social institutions: communism (later termed communalism), universalism, disinterestedness, and organized skepticism. These norms were understood as ideal-types in the tradition of Weber. They were to serve as approximations of the normative ideas held among members of the relevant community—and were thought to distinguish science as a general institutional form from other institutions. As Lynch notes, these putative norms were never elaborated at a level of precision that could be used to account for much of the practice of concrete situated communities of scientists.

Merton's account of the hallmark scientific norms also would not readily allow the norms, described in such idealized and general ways, to double as much of a normative epistemology; of themselves, they would not have taken one far towards regulating actual practice within a group of inquirers. But, their limitations in connection with normative epistemology do not turn just on their generality. Rather, as Lynch notes, Merton's sociology of knowledge would seem ill-suited to doubling as a normative epistemology due to its diffidence with respect to central epistemological success measures, such as attaining true beliefs and avoiding error, or attaining understanding versus misunderstanding, or attaining knowledge versus mere belief. Merton approached settled scientific theories in terms of a decidedly sociological conception of communally "certified knowledge," and thereby bracketed the question of whether they involved successfully discovering facts and laws. At the same time, in the context of the general structural–functionalist sociology with which Merton is associated, there is the unmistakable suggestion that the norms themselves were functional in the institutional pursuit of something—presumably something in the vicinity of an epistemological good.

Developments in the history of science, notably the work of Thomas Kuhn, forced important questions on sociologists of science as well as philosophers. Central here was the question of whether or not there was more to be said beyond noting that certain norms facilitated the development of episodic consensuses (paradigms) within communities. When consensus emerged, was it related to something like objective facts, recognizable as such, which might be used to leverage the discovery of further general truths about the world? What, if any, role did rationality play in the process? (Notice that such issues are central to each of the contributions to follow in this part of the handbook.) Lynch recounts several currents of thinking that led sociologists from Kuhn's talk of successive and competing paradigms to the idea that all "knowledge" is "constructed," perhaps along with the things themselves. Do we, to use the language of Pickering (1984), "construct quarks" as we construct our theories—and what would this mean?

There are multiple lines of thought among sociologists that need to be sorted out (as the sociologists were not marching in neat formation). A number of these lines of thought are reflected in David Bloor's *Knowledge and Social Imagery* (1976). Here is Lynch's summary of a central doctrine, that of symmetry:

> In an often-cited argument, [Bloor] proposed that the sociology of knowledge "would be impartial with respect to truth or falsity, rationality or irrationality, success or failure. Both sides of these dichotomies will require explanation" (1976, p. 7). And, "[i]t would be symmetrical in its style of explanation, the same types of cause would explain, say, true and false beliefs." Bloor emphasized that the strong program would provide *causal* explanations of such knowledge; explanations that also would be *reflexive*—applicable to the sociology of knowledge itself. In the years that followed, the numerous citations of Bloor's scheme often used *symmetry* as the summary term.
>
> *(Lynch, Chapter 22, this handbook, p. 220)*

Thus, the envisioned sociology of science would be symmetrical in that it would provide a unified causal account of epistemic successes and failures, our own and others—the sociologist was then looking for causal relationship, causal processes, that were exhibited alike in both cases of epistemic success and cases of epistemic failure. The same causal mechanisms are in play throughout.

From our perspective, in light of the recent decades in which there have been striking developments within cognitive psychology, it might be natural to think that such a causal account would appeal to an ensemble of psychological processes such as reflected in the heuristics and biases tradition (think for example of Kahneman & Frederick, 2005). After all, the processes there studied allow one to account for ways in which an ensemble of cognitive processes, together with informational and aspirational contexts, make for both successes and failures in the production of true belief. So, such an approach would seem to satisfy the advertised symmetry requirement. But, commonly, sociologists of science have been resistant to turning over some of their explanatory authority to the psychologists.

From an epistemological point of view, the sociological approach of the strong programme (and to some extent, of Merton) is frustrating. Insofar as it seeks a totalizing descriptive/causal account of all belief formation—and specifically one that has no place for, or connection with, parameters measuring epistemic success—it seems resistant to being informative for addressing normative epistemic concerns. It suggests that any distinction between normatively fitting and nonfitting ways of forming beliefs will need to draw normative lines where there are no significant differences in causal processes really in play—that whatever causal processes are in play, they are neither fitting nor nonfitting. It has been taken to suggest that all such normative line drawing is a matter of "social construction," where this has an antirealist and relativist suggestion. Such suspicions (many warranted) were the bases for the "science wars" of the 1990s. As Lynch notes in his entry, these intellectual skirmishes seem to have "faded away" and "without a decisive victory for either side," while fewer writers seem to be really content with constructionism.

One reason for discontent is that such a position leaves one unable to give a principled basis for drawing on the extant scientific consensus on several matters that seem practically of great moment or consequence, but which are important only if they turn on matters of fact. One such matter is that of the causal dynamics of climate change. One might note the significant consensus here, but that seems of little significance if this consensus is itself simply the result of causal processes that are found everywhere—in both truth-yielding and falsity-yielding instances. One would have no (non-special pleading) basis for thinking that a consensus so formed would be likely true. (See also "The Social Epistemology of Consensus and Dissent," Chapter 23, this handbook.)

There was always a deep tension in both the constructivist program and the (imperfectly parallel) "strong programme in the sociology of science", as represented by Bloor. The tension had to do with aspirations for a causal account of belief formation. Was this merely an aspiration for accounts couched in certain socially fashionable terms—causal terms—or was this an aspiration for accounts that allowed one to understand or describe the actual causal dynamic in the relevant epistemic communities? The latter should be of little concern to those who are content to think that all interpretive accounts are themselves a kind of fiction—something made, as Geertz (1975, pp. 15–16) would put it. Talk of the social construction of facts, and of facts as "artifacts," was at the contentious core of the so called "science wars" discussed by Lynch. But, it is noteworthy that such talk, together with the reflexivity and symmetry championed by those adhering to the strong programme, suggested that their causal accounts were similarly fictions. To give a realistic causal account, in contrast, would be to note what it was about events that made a difference, such that, were things to have been different, so would what came after. Were we to discover real dependencies in the causal dynamics within real communities, or were we only to manage more or less satisfying stories featuring "causal idiom."

Before turning our attention to the next entry in the handbook, I want to advance one observation of my own. From the epistemological point of view, the sociology of science, as reflected in its constructivist representatives, is indeed unsatisfactory. But it is not at all clear that the limits it would impose on us need be traced to the insistence that accounts should satisfy the symmetry principle—that "the same types of cause would explain, say, true and false beliefs." Rather, the epistemological limitations of such accounts seem to harken to their hesitancy to find a place for notions such as veridical belief and false beliefs or facts that are more than consensual "fictions."

To see this, we need only contrast the constructivist approaches with work in cognitive science that seems to satisfy symmetry just as well as constructivist accounts. Again, consider work on heuristics and biases (for a useful presentation of this approach, see Kahneman & Frederick, 2005). This work posits a set of heuristics—fast and frugal—processes. These heuristics commonly work by, first, intuitively gauging some simple, easily estimated matter, then using one's intuitive verdicts on this matter as verdicts concerning the more difficult matter. Such processes may fair moderately well and be serviceably reliable on certain questions, and in certain contexts and conditions, and also be systematically biased or unreliable in others. There are thought to be other processes—slower and more cognitively costly—that can, in congenial conditions, modulate our acceptance of answers afforded by the fast and frugal processes. Now, here we have a model of an ensemble of processes, their input, and their various reliabilities in settings in which they are triggered. This affords an account of a causal system—an ensemble of causal processes and their common triggers—one that can account for both epistemically denominated successes and failures. Here, the same ensemble of causal processes—"the same types of cause"—operating in various contexts and conditions, "would explain, say, true and false beliefs." Symmetry! But, one can readily find ways of putting such cognitive psychology to epistemic work. One might prescribe the use of the slower and more cognitively costly processes in modulating the use of heuristics—proscribing the simple reliance on heuristics in certain classes of cases in which they are notably biased or notably pivotal. Here, the ease of putting such cognitive psychology to epistemic work—prescribing or proscribing—has a lot to do with the ways in which this research readily finds a place for notions of objective reliability, truth, error, and the like.

In "The Social Epistemology of Consensus and Dissent" (this handbook, Chapter 23), Boaz Miller discusses a range of social epistemological work that is highly continuous with the issues raised in the sociology of science. However, one can note this striking general difference in the agenda across these two bodies of work: much of the work in the sociology of knowledge has little place for sorting the produced beliefs into such epistemically normative categories as "true" and "false," or "factual" rather than "fictional." There is some tendency to treat all beliefs as "fictional" in Geertz's sense—as something made, something produced via the relevant causal social processes. At the top of the sociological agenda is thus a concern for a unified, non-evaluative, explanatory account of the formation of beliefs within groups. In contrast, and not surprisingly, normative concerns are more prominent in the work of the social epistemologists. When is a consensus the result of group processes that are adequately truth-conducive (and thus to be normatively prescribed)? What features of group processes make for such reliability in a case of consensus? When can the fact that a given claim is a matter of consensus among investigators give one warrant or justificatory license to draw on that result? Obviously, one should epistemologically prescribe such processes, and one can warrantly forebear drawing on consensus results when these are produced in a group not having the truth-conducive or truth-indicative features.

Miller distinguishes *cognitive* from *social* accounts of knowledge-based or epistemically justified consensus.

Cognitive accounts seek to specify pivotal features of groups in virtue of which the groups manage various cognitive functions that, when issuing in consensus, makes truth likely. Plausible candidate cognitive functions include matters of the group stockpiling of reliable observation, of group openness to weighing alternative explanations or approaches, of group sensitivity to anomalies, and of group sensitivity to theoretical trade-offs in cognitive context. As an illustration, Miller mentions Naomi Oreskes, who "identifies five general hallmarks of a good scientific theory: inductive support, predictive success, resistance to falsification attempts, consilience of evidence (convergence of evidence of different types), and explanatory success" (Miller, this handbook, p. 230). This counts as a cognitive approach insofar as epistemologically approved consensus is associated with group processes that are sensitive to matters characterized in terms of relations between the contents or information possessed within the group.

Social accounts, in contrast, specify societal properties of the group yielding such a consensus. Here Miller discusses Longino's critical contextual empiricism (Longino, 2002). The pivotal societal features turn on group norms—norms and conforming institutional practices of critical deliberation that jointly serve to expose and eliminate various biases. These make for public venues of criticism and for the uptake of criticism which is then evaluated in keeping with recognized standards of evaluation of theories. Longino also requires that there be a tempered equality of intellectual authority and expertise—that the tempering of credibility within the group be sensitive to the marginal differences across agents in the extent to which their contributions match the community standards for observation and criticism. (See also Chapter 42, "Epistemic Norms as Social Norms.")

Suppose, as is at least compatible with such social accounts, that the prescribed social properties of groups might be understood in terms of norms—and the relevant norms have to do (a) with responsiveness to content relationships of sorts reflected in cognitive accounts (as illustrated above); and (b) with a responsiveness to others that functions to readily pool and facilitate the response to such content. Now, to the extent that this is the case, there should be more continuity across the cognitive and social approaches than some of their proponents might suppose. While the articulation of some epistemically desirable features might be saliently associated with one rather than the other approach, there yet would remain a kind of commensurability in the two approaches.

As might then be expected, there are also hybrid accounts, both cognitive and social. Miller has pursued one such hybrid (Miller, 2013). His seeks to identify features of groups and evidence that would make a given group's attaining knowledge (attaining warranted truths) the best explanation of that group's settling into a consensus on the relevant matters. This is to require a social epistemological account of knowledge production with this feature: suppose that we are dealing with a case in which a group has attained a consensus. Now characterize the group processes and contents in terms of the pivotal matters featured in the social epistemological account—its parameters. Suppose that we find that the processes found there conform to the social epistemology so parameterized. Ask the question, what explains the consensus obtaining here? Miller insists that a social epistemology should be such that an explanation (indeed the best explanation) of the consensus in the group comes via supposing not simply that the group conformed to the group's normative model of group processes and contents, but, additionally, via the supposition that the propositions on which there is consensus are true. Miller suggests that this makes consensus "indicative" of knowledge, but does not make consensus itself conducive to knowledge. Apparently, in certain settings involving the epistemic norms extant within the group, knowledge in a group yields and explains consensus in the group, which then serves as an indicator that it is knowledge that is productive of that consensus there. Compare: white-nose disease in a bat colony may cause and explain a significant die-off of the colony over a winter; a die-off in a colony then serves as an indicator of there having been white-nose disease in that colony. Die-off of bat colony over winter, think white-nose disease. Consensus in a group (with certain epistemic norms), think truth and knowledge.

In "Feminist Philosophy of Science as Social Epistemology" (Chapter 25), Sharon Crasnow surveys central social epistemological issues addressed in prominent feminist philosophy of science. As she makes evident, this engagement with social epistemological issues is not incidental, as feminist philosophy of science commonly focuses on respects in which scientists are socially embedded and interdependent epistemic agents. Crasnow highlights three respects of prominent concern. The first is termed the *internal* aspect of social epistemology: scientific knowing is said to be contextual in that scientific knowing and evidence are subject to community standards; scientists are able to know only by virtue of satisfying the norms of that community. Relations between knowers are understood to be central here. The second is the idea that scientific knowledge is *evidentially* social: that aspects of scientific norms having to do with evidence, worthy questions, and acceptable theoretical answers are conditioned by features of the political, social, and cultural environment in which knowledge is produced. The third reflects an *organizational* aspect of social epistemology: that understanding the ways in which research proceeds requires attention to the organization of the research community, its institutions, and the broader political, social, and cultural context in which the research takes place. Thus, relations between knowers (the internal aspect) is of concern, as are the conditioning of community norms by the wider cultural environment (the evidential aspect), and the social organization of the narrower and wider communities (the organizational aspect). Obviously, these ideas have many connections with issues pursued by Lynch and by Miller in the previous two chapters.

Crasnow first focuses on feminist empiricists including Helen Longino and two "feminist empiricist holists"—Lynn Hankinson Nelson and Elizabeth Anderson—and then considers feminist standpoint theorists.

Longino offers a naturalized epistemology on which science is conditioned both by values that are constitutive of science—which can evolve or develop over time—and by values from the wider community. The values constitutive of science include "empirical adequacy (a.k.a. accuracy) ... novelty, ontological heterogeneity, complexity of interaction, applicability to human needs, [and] diffusion or decentralization of power" (Longino, 1995, p. 385). But, scientific practice is itself conditioned by values and associated assumptions within the wider community. Longino expects and demands that ultimately theory-laden empirical information afforded by inquiry will serve to occasion ongoing refinement of substantive understandings, and changes in understanding can occasion refinements in values. She requires scientific communities to have features that are conducive to such ongoing refinement of value—which may yet come haltingly. Some degree of tempered equality will be important here (compare Fricker, 2007).

Elizabeth Anderson (2004) is also concerned to understand the place for values in science. She argues that many scientific concepts are "thick concepts" that reflect values variously drawn from communities. Alternative concepts might yield richer lines of research—ones that fittingly cast wider evidential nets, for example—and which thus afford more richly informed evidential perspectives on phenomena. Values do not just condition working with evidence—but also condition the evidence that is pursued in light of value-laden concepts in play. Values, concepts, and evidence are then deeply interrelated. Such a holistic feminist empiricism brings out ways in which values can condition evidence, and can thereby enrich or impoverish the evidential currency of theory choice.

Crasnow notes that we also need to attend to "internal relations within the community of knowers and the questions about the proper organization of the community." This was the concern of *feminist standpoint theorists*. These writers hold that, within communities, agents occupy many standpoints—locales from which knowledge may be produced. Locales are constituted by diverse characteristics of agents within communities—gender, race, economic resources, and related networks of relationships. The knowledge so produced is said to be always situated in consequence of the opportunities and concerns, the power and needs, of the agents. Standpoint theorists hold that these locations give differently situated agents "epistemic privilege" with respect to certain matters. Marginalized agents may have access to experience and knowledge that is, at best, less available (or more indirectly available) to those differently situated within the broader community. Researchers from marginalized groups might be situated so as to take advantage of a kind of "double-vision" (Collins, 1986) productive of a composite understanding—and this is notably true in connection with social understanding.

These ideas raise numerous, complex, and cross-cutting issues revolving around notions of objectivity, the usefulness of knowledge to various groups or communities, and how these might make for an interplay of evolving community norms and empirical results. Crasnow highlights some of these issues for us.

In "Modeling Epistemic Communities" (Chapter 24), Reijula and Kuorikoski discuss recent work focusing on the kind of more or less episodic epistemic communities in which agents coordinate to answer some open question or class of such questions. Scientific collaborations, research and development laboratories or groups, and related expert groups are instances of the kind of epistemic community in question. Some such epistemic communities are institutionalized and endure to pursue a series of questions in a field. In the epistemic communities of concern, one finds a division of labor: the community is composed of subgroups and agents which are understood to have responsibility for tractable epistemic chores—components of the larger epistemic problem to be solved.

The philosophical modeling of such communities is pretty recent. One might date it from Kitcher (1990, 1994), although one clearly can find roots in work by sociologists such as Robert Merton or Pierre Bourdieu. One should also mention Thagard (2000) and Thagard and Kroon (2006).

Modeling of epistemic communities seeks to deploy the tools of modeling, found in various scientific disciplines, to understand the epistemic consequences of various features at the level of groups. It is powerfully motivated by this general idea: epistemic features (virtues/vices, strengths/weaknesses) of a community need not be a simple composite of the same features being had by the members of the community. In a loose sense, epistemic properties of the community may be "emergent"—they may be different from the epistemic properties of the agents composing the group (even if they explicably supervene on the properties of the latter together with organizational features of the group). Two examples follow.

Kitcher notes that, were agents to all pursue the one most promising line of research on a given open question, they would be putting all scientific eggs in one basket. This is epistemically risky at the wider community level, even if it would be epistemically less risky for each of the individual investigators. Insofar as the answer to the question is really open—and alternative resolutions really might turn out supported in the ultimate course of research—the community would be a better epistemic engine were agents to distribute themselves so as to work somewhat in parallel on the various lines of research. Kitcher notes that such a distribution of research effort could be explained in terms of the priority rule for according credit to researchers and teams of researchers. Kitcher's economically inspired model suggests that the norm within the broad scientific community for attributing credit makes for a motivated distribution of research within that community that would not otherwise obtain from the motivations of individual researchers.

Zollman's models have addressed a similar issue. Suppose that researchers seek to be epistemically productive themselves. Suppose also that they must choose and use one of various alternative theoretical approaches within the community. Zollman models this on an analogy with a gambler choosing which slot machine to play on a casino floor. One may have richer or poorer information about which machines have been paying out at what relative levels. Similarly, communication within the broad scientific community regarding results from various approaches may be more or less full or rich. However, the richer the information on the rates at which machines or approaches have been paying off, the more there will be a tendency for gamblers or researchers to cluster in "pulling the same lever" or pursuing the same theoretical development and experimentation. This could result on all coalescing in playing some machine that just happened early to have a short run of paying off, or most investigators coalescing in pursuing one initially promising theory. In both cases, the agents would be neglecting an alternative that would be superior. The results within the wider community would be less good—or at least delayed. Reijula and Kuorikoski summarize Zollman's central result:

Perhaps counterintuitively, too much social information can be harmful. In densely connected epistemic networks, misleading evidence obtained in the early stages of the simulated research process can spread quickly through the network, suppress experimentation on alternative methods, and lead the whole community to converge on a suboptimal alternative.

(Chapter 24, p. 241)

One can worry about interpreting such modeling, and about how dependent the results are on specifics of the simplified model. But it should be clear that features of the community (its norms and incentives, its structured communication, its diversity, and the like) can make for epistemic dispositions of the whole that are not mere echoes of the features of the individual's therein. Further, the community-level epistemic dispositions of a community need not be at all obvious in light of the individual-level epistemic dispositions of agents.

Reijula and Kuorikoski discuss prominent philosophical approaches to modeling epistemic communities and they end by flagging several important questions about such modeling. One can certainly be concerned with how well-motivated the modelers' choices are—with how well features of their model reflect the features that they seek to model. For example, several of the models discussed seek to say something about the division of labor within research groups—but one may doubt that their proxies effectively reflect the kinds of diversity of competences and expertise that are commonly found in cooperative research groups (see Reijula and Kuorikoski's discussion).

Modeling clearly holds significant promise for social epistemology. We can hope that it develops into a significant branch of social epistemology, and that, as it does so, it comes to be more securely connected to historical, sociological, economic, and philosophical case studies of scientific practices, to parallel empirical data, and to social epistemology generally. Reijula and Kuorikoski's overview reflects this promise, and notes that we are at an early (but significant) stage in realizing it. As they note:

Rather than being high-fidelity representations of particular target systems "out there," [the extant models] function as proof-of-concept exercises about the possible mechanisms underlying collective intelligence. They are theoretical arguments, not virtual experiments.

(Chapter 24, p. 245)

In the contributions discussed above, one encounters several recurrent issues. One is that the structure of epistemic communities is epistemically important—who, for example, listens to whom, who checks on whose results, who looks for problems. Of course, community structure is commonly neglected in traditional individualist epistemology. Another is the idea (associated with both the history of science and naturalized epistemology) that the values in some community change over time in response to the extant information possessed at a time. Of course, such values interact with the structure of the community. It is also worth noting that many writers talk of norms—which are presumably normative sensibilities common in a group and coordinating practice there. (See also Chapter 42, "Epistemic Norms as Social Norms.") Of course, epistemic values and normative sensibilities are not so neglected in traditional epistemology, but their social dimension commonly is. In what ways, for example, do values and dispositions found among individual agents correspond or diverge from dispositions found at the level of the community? It would seem that any epistemic community is a developing, situated, structured set of interacting agents—where that structure is conditioned by extant putative information, epistemic and other values variously possessed, and norms common in the community. Social epistemic concerns revolve around the question of what constellations of these matters makes for a community whose results tend to be epistemically virtuous. To what extent is consensus in a community indicative of likely truth and knowledge? Are the processes in the community conducive of consensus—and, if so, of true shared beliefs? What features of communities conduce to, or hinder, epistemic successes—and how are this distinct from, but realized in, the dispositions of individual agents?

References

Anderson, E. (2004). Uses of Value Judgments in Science: A General Argument with Lessons from a Case Study of Feminist Research on Divorce. *Hypatia: A Journal of Feminist Philosophy*, 19, pp. 1–24.

Bloor, D. (1976). *Knowledge and Social Imagery*. London: Routledge & Kegan Paul.

Collins, P. H. (1986). Learning from the Outsider Within: The Sociological Significance of Black Feminist Thought. *Social Problems*, 33, pp. S14-S32.

Fricker, M. (2007). *Epistemic Injustice: Power and the Ethics of Knowing*. Oxford: Oxford University Press.

Geertz, C. (1975). *The Interpretation of Cultures: Selected Essays*. London: Hutchinson.

Kahneman, D., & Frederick, S. (2005). A Model of Heuristic Judgment. In: K. Holyoak & R. Morrison, eds., *The Cambridge Handbook of Thinking and Reasoning*, New York: Cambridge University Press, pp. 267–293.

Kitcher, P. (1990). The Division of Cognitive Labor. *Journal of Philosophy*, 87(1), pp. 5–22.

Kitcher, P. (1994). The Advancement of Science. *Journal of Philosophy*, 91(4), pp. 212–215.

Longino, H. (1995). Gender, Politics, and the Theoretical Virtues. *Synthese*, 104, pp. 383–397.

Longino, H. (2002). *The Fate of Knowledge*. Princeton, NJ: Princeton University Press.

Mannheim, K. ([1929] 1954). *Ideology and Utopia: An Introduction to the Sociology of Knowledge*, trans. L. Wirth and E. Shils. New York: Harcourt Brace & Company. https://archive.org/details/ideologyutopiain00mann (accessed 5 February 2016).

Merton, R. K. (1973). The Normative Structure of Science. In: R. K. Merton, ed., *The Sociology of Science*, Chicago, IL: University of Chicago Press, pp. 267–278.

Miller, B. (2013). When Is Consensus Knowledge Based? Distinguishing Shared Knowledge from Mere Agreement. *Synthese*, 190(7), pp. 1293–1316.

Pickering, A. (1984). *Constructing Quarks: A Sociological History of Particle Physics*. Chicago, IL: University of Chicago Press.

Thagard, P. (2000). *Coherence in Thought and Action*. Cambridge, MA: M.I.T Press.

Thagard, P., & Kroon, F. W. (2006). Emotional Consensus in Group Decision Making. *Mind and Society*, 5(1), pp. 85–104.

22

THE SOCIOLOGY OF SCIENCE AND SOCIAL CONSTRUCTIVISM

Michael E. Lynch

Constructivism (also known as constructionism) is a theoretical position that became prevalent in the sociology of science from the late 1970s through the 1990s. During that time, it was closely associated with the rise of a "new" sociology of scientific knowledge (SSK) that engaged critically with the "contents" of the natural sciences and mathematics, and was a prominent aspect of the development and expansion of the interdisciplinary field of science and technology studies (STS). The term "constructivism" has fallen out of favor in recent years, but variants of the position remain in play within STS. This essay begins with an account of the "new" sociology of scientific knowledge and the development of social constructivism as a key position associated with it. It then discusses some of the disputes about constructivism that culminated in the "science wars" of the 1990s. Finally, it briefly discusses the aftermath of the dissolution of constructivism in STS in favor of a variety of other approaches.

A "New" Sociology of Scientific Knowledge

When the sociology of science developed as a specialty, largely in the decades following World War II, it was closely connected with the structural–functionalist theory of institutions. An early essay by American sociologist Robert K. Merton (1942 [1973]) on the "ethos of science" became a touchstone for the sociology of science, and later became a target for critics, such as Michael Mulkay (1976), who proposed an alternative sociological approach to science and knowledge.

Merton's essay provided a concise and memorable list of "norms" that distinguished science as an institution from other modern social institutions: communism (later changed to communalism), universalism, disinterestedness, and organized skepticism. He argued that these ideal-typical properties distinguished science from other institutions in which personal connections, deference to authority, and unquestioned adherence to received ideas was the rule. Merton used this combination of institutionalized norms to explain the relative autonomy of science: the independence from religious, political, and metaphysical orthodoxy of its pursuit of knowledge. He was aware that his ideal type did not describe average tendencies or actual practices; instead, they were ideals expressed through maxims that emphasized the communal spirit of a cumulative research enterprise ("standing on the shoulders of giants"), institutionalized practices such as the policing of research through peer review, and sanctions against sources of self-deception and bias arising from individual vanity and the seductions of everyday life.

Merton's best-known work was theoretical and essayistic, but many of his students and followers conducted systematic research using surveys of scientists' attitudes, and sociometric analyses of "invisible colleges" – dispersed scientific communities made visible through citation networks and professional communications (Price 1963; Crane 1972). Research during the Mertonian era also included a few notable case studies, such as the investigation of a serendipitous discovery by Barber and Fox (1958), but, for the most part, sociologists of science at the time did not delve deeply into the technical details of scientific practices. They left that task for methodologists in specialized branches of science and, at a more general level, epistemologists.

Merton's conception of science did not amount to an epistemology. It was apparent that he held science to be exceptional among social institutions, and he also subscribed to the prospects of a scientific sociology, but refrained from giving an account of scientific truth, preferring instead a sociological conception of communally "certified knowledge" to describe historically settled theories, facts, and laws. Merton left it for philosophers to debate about verification and falsification, the requirements of experimental method, and the relationship between theory and evidence. And, for the most part, he left the contents of science to qualified specialists in the relevant fields. His norms were congruent with a logical empiricist philosophy, but his interest was in the institutionalized incentives for scientific research, rather than the personal qualities of scientists or the details of their technical practices.

During the post-war expansion of sociology through the 1960s, the sociology of science became a well-established, although relatively minor, subfield of the discipline. However, by the late 1960s, some new initiatives had begun to gain prominence. These initiatives were inspired, in part, by Thomas S. Kuhn's (1962) *The Structure of Scientific Revolutions*. In the social sciences at the time, Kuhn's historical conception of revolutionary change in scientific fields was embraced as a manifesto for ambitious social scientists who sought to initiate "paradigm shifts" in their chosen fields. The dominant structural–functionalist "paradigm" in American sociology began to lose its hold in the face of various critiques of established theories and methods, and alternative initiatives articulated by C. Wright Mills, Harold Garfinkel, Herbert Blumer, and Alvin Gouldner, among others. Their criticisms focused on the idealized conception of objective science and scientific method that was entrenched in sociology. Garfinkel (1967) turned attention to sociological research practices, such as coding interview responses and using bureaucratic records, and treated data production itself as a "topic" rather than a "resource" for sociological research. Later, under the rubric of constructivism, a further step was taken to treat *natural* science methods as practical and discursive actions to be investigated sociologically (Latour and Woolgar 1979).

One of the boldest efforts to initiate a novel line of work in the sociology of scientific knowledge was developed at the Edinburgh University Science Studies Unit. The Unit was founded in 1964, largely through the initiative of prominent scientists such as Conrad Waddington and key university administrators. The initial aim was to supplement science education with instruction on social, ethical, and historical aspects of science. David Edge, an astronomer by training who had hosted a BBC radio program on science, was the first director, and he later co-founded (with Roy Macleod) the flagship journal of the new social studies of science (initially titled *Science Studies* in its first few volumes, starting in 1971, and retitled *Social Studies of Science* in 1975). During its first decade, the Unit hired David Bloor, Barry Barnes, and Steven Shapin, and one of their early students, Donald Mackenzie, later joined the University of Edinburgh Sociology Department. Bloor and Barnes explicitly announced what they called the "Strong Programme" in the sociology of knowledge, and Shapin and Mackenzie produced historical and sociological studies that exemplified its key proposals. Others who studied and worked at Edinburgh, and elsewhere in the UK, such as Michael Mulkay, H.M. Collins, Andrew Pickering, John Law, and Simon Schaffer, were active participants in the early development of the sociology of scientific knowledge (SSK).

Bloor (1976) boldly proclaimed an interest in *explaining* scientific knowledge sociologically. An initial move in this direction was to reject the Mertonian norms as unrealistic ideals that failed to account for practical engagements and actions in and around the sciences, and to question the supposition that objective science operated independently from political ideologies and economic interests. Accordingly, the authority of science, as well as the subjection of science to social authority and interest, was open to sociological investigation, just as it would be for religious authority or political authority. The program Bloor proposed would be "strong," because it would make no exception for the most robust instances of scientific and mathematical knowledge. Bloor contrasted this program with the "sociology of error," which he attributed to prior work in sociology and social psychology that explained cognitive biases and perceptual illusions by reference to vested interests, tradition, mythology, superstition, group-think, and social pressure, but left adherence to "true" knowledge unexplained. "Error" was perhaps a misleading term, since sociologists and social anthropologists had long been comfortable with offering explanations of beliefs, attitudes, and opinions that become established within the boundaries of coherent communities, but are not universally shared. Bloor's explanatory program was, thus, not so different from conventional sociological or anthropological studies that treat systematic *variation* in belief as an initial condition for investigating the social, historical, and personal bases for such variation.

Karl Mannheim (1936: 80) had earlier struggled to develop a "non-evaluative general, total conception of ideology," in which "no judgments are pronounced as to the correctness of the ideas to be treated." This general conception differed from more familiar theories of ideology to denigrate particular beliefs as dogma, reflecting vested interests and other sources of bias. However, Mannheim's sociology of knowledge granted that some established facts and procedures diffuse so widely that they become independent of any particular community, and thus cannot be accounted for by reference to distinct "existential" factors.

Bloor was unwilling to exempt *any* knowledge from his explanatory program, regardless of how authoritative and well established it was. In an often-cited argument, he proposed that the sociology of knowledge "would be impartial with respect to truth or falsity, rationality or irrationality, success or failure. Both sides of these dichotomies will require explanation" (1976: 7). And, "[i]t would be symmetrical in its style of explanation, the same types of cause would explain, say, true and false beliefs" (ibid.). Bloor emphasized that the "Strong Program" would provide *causal* explanations of such knowledge; explanations that would also be *reflexive* – applicable to the sociology of knowledge itself. In the years that followed, the numerous citations of Bloor's scheme often used *symmetry* as the summary term.

Bloor, and others in SSK, approvingly cited Peter Winch's (1990 [1958]) *The Idea of a Social Science*, which argued that the effort in sociology to produce causal *explanations* using ordinary concepts, such as "motives" and "attitudes," was ill-conceived, and that an epistemological explication of the meaning and practical uses of such concepts in daily life was a more appropriate analytical task (also see Mills 1940). However, unlike Winch, Bloor advocated causal explanations. Bloor, thus, did not present his version of SSK as a social *epistemology*, at least not in a philosophical sense, but he and others in SSK, such as Collins (1986), supported their empirical programs by recruiting philosophical arguments about the limits of induction, the role of theory-laden observation in science, and the underdetermination of theories by "finite" observational evidence. Barnes and Bloor (1982) declared themselves to be "relativists," but they disavowed philosophical relativism in favor of historical and contemporary case studies, which delineated particular connections between scientific innovations and prior social interests, political and economic agendas, class milieus, and so forth. Perhaps the most convincing arguments in favor of what Collins (1983) called "empirical relativism" were supported by studies of scientific controversies in experimental science. These studies documented strongly held disagreements, among members of specialized fields, about particular experiments, and showed that replicating experiments was not only difficult and only occasionally attempted, but also laden with rival assumptions about the phenomena in question and the requirements for demonstrating them.

For the most part, early SSK studies focused on historical and contemporary conflicts between rival scientists, and their "symmetrical" treatments of these conflicts resisted the idea that such differences were temporary and that the truth of the matter had been (or would be) resolved in the long run. Social studies of such controversies, for the most part, did not give straightforward causal explanations, but, more often, described the divergent viewpoints and related them to the political and economic interests, and cultural conditions (including local attachments to research styles, laboratories, and networks of colleagues) that sustained them.

Bloor supported the "Strong Programme" by drawing arguments and examples from philosophy and history of science, but Collins' (1975) contemporaneous study of gravity wave experiments, and Shapin and Schaffer's (1985) historical study of the Boyle-Hobbes dispute about pneumatic experiments, provided original and detailed substantiation for SSK. These studies addressed broad topics of philosophical interest (replication of experiments in Collins' case, and experimental procedure in Shapin and Schaffer's case), but placed them in historical, political, and communicative contexts.

The argumentative style of these studies was symmetrical and impartial, as Shapin and Schaffer deliberately declined to invoke present-day assumptions that would vindicate Boyle's use of the air pump as an experimental apparatus, while dismissing Hobbes principled refusal to credit the mundane vicissitudes of practical reasoning and technical manipulation as a way to "prove" what he regarded as metaphysical theses. Unlike Collins, who focused on disputes within the restricted world of a "core set" of contending laboratories in a subfield of physics, Shapin and Schaffer related Boyle's and Hobbes' contentions about the vacuum and the pneumatic pump to contentious political and theological positions at the time. But, rather than treating the local dispute about experimental proof as a reflection of broader social forces, they explicated how the gentlemen of the Royal Society imagined that the experimental way of life would eventually provide a peaceful and decisive alternative to endless and bloody religious disputes. They summarized the hopes invested in experiment with the slogan: "Solutions to the problem of knowledge are solutions to the problem of social order" (1985: 332).

Social Constructivism

Peter Berger and Thomas Luckmann's (1966) *The Social Construction of Reality* was the first book to use the term "social construction" in its title (Hacking 1999: 24). Berger and Luckmann were mainly concerned with explaining how human social institutions are "real" and "objective" in the sense of being stable, obdurate, and impossible to wish away. They sought to show that social institutions become stable conditions for living in a given society, even though they originally are "constructed" from highly flexible situations of human action and interaction, before eventually becoming established as collective imperatives. Consequently, for well-socialized members of such a society, established institutions that originated through human actions, and are continually sustained through such actions, are taken for granted as external and impersonal facts of life. Viewed with hindsight, Berger & Luckmann's theory seems far from radical, as much of their book is an elementary synthesis of classic sociological theories that makes the case for the distinctive reality of the actions and institutions that sociologists study.

Although it now seems less provocative than it may have been in the 1960s, Berger and Luckmann's theory continues to hold critical implications, as a constructivist genealogy can counteract reified and naturalized treatments of social identities and institutionalized activities by encouraging the conviction that such identities and activities need not remain as they are. However, their theory does not suggest that socially constructed institutions are somehow defective or that they should be reformed or overthrown *because* they are socially constructed. Some socially constructed phenomena, such as the value of currency and the division of labor in an organization, are not illusory forms of *real* entities or forces; they are no less objective than proverbial rocks in the field, though their objectivity depends, essentially, on their continual enactment.

In the decades that followed the publication of Berger and Luckmann's landmark work, countless other academic books and articles adopted "social construction" in their titles, to the point of making up a movement that ran through a broad array of fields in the humanities and social sciences (Hacking 1999). Social constructivist arguments tend to be most provocative when they take aim at phenomena that other academics and professionals insist are immutable facts of life and nature. One arena where such provocation succeeded is in disputes about whether particular psychiatric and/or neurological disease categories were "constructed" or "real." As Hacking (1995) points out, conditions such as "multiple personality disorder," which underwent dramatic shifts in incidence and definition in the late 20th century, appear to have a more evident connection to historical and cultural contingency than neurological and psychiatric disorders that appear to be more stable and somatic in origin.

An optimal subject for a constructivist argument would thus be a disorder such as clinical depression, which has undergone dramatic change in recent years and yet is treated by the psychiatric profession as an intrinsic individual condition (Horwitz 2011). Although constructivist interpretations of particular diseases do not necessarily debunk them as unreal, popular writings about the "epidemic" of depression emphasize fraudulent manipulation orchestrated by interested medical practitioners and pharmaceutical companies. Like Thomas Szasz's (1974) classic account of the "myth" of mental disorder, such writings draw explicit or implicit contrasts with genuine diseases. Such uses of constructivist idioms as polemical, and often political, weapons in disputes about particular phenomena present a persistent source of confusion for efforts to establish such idioms as part of general analytical treatments. The confusion is akin to what greeted Karl Mannheim's effort to develop a general explanatory understanding of ideology that would transcend the more common dismissal of ideology as false ideas.

Constructivism and the Science Wars

With the publication of Latour and Woolgar's (1979) ethnographic study of the "construction of facts" in a microbiology laboratory at Salk Institute, constructivism explicitly entered the vocabulary in the sociology of science. Further publications followed and constructivist arguments about natural science theories and facts proliferated during the 1980s. The sociology of scientific knowledge became folded into a larger, interdisciplinary field (commonly called Science and Technology Studies, or STS). This rapidly expanding international field included explicitly constructivist studies of science (Knorr Cetina and Mulkay 1983) and of technology (Bijker et al. 1987), developing through the 1990s in a sometimes fraught alliance with explicitly normative and politicized cultural studies that took issue with both the demographic and epistemological legacy of the gentlemen of the Royal Society (Haraway 1997).

The idea that "facts" are constructed linked STS research to efforts in the humanities and cultural studies to deconstruct dichotomous distinctions between facts and values, nature and nurture, and knowledge and belief. Actor-network theorists, such as Latour (1987) and Michel Callon (1986), attempted to dissolve the very distinction between human agency and material causality, which was so central to the humanist tradition, and to replace it with heterogeneous networks in which "agency" circulated freely among human and non-human "actors." Feminist research increasingly called into question the distinction between (natural, biological) sex and (culturally constructed) gender that had once been a source of leverage for (and also against) feminist social movements. Efforts to restore "strong objectivity" by reference to standpoint epistemologies proved difficult to support in the context of a corrosive deconstruction of any and all forms of epistemic "privilege" ascribed to fixed, essential, and unitary states, statuses, and standpoints (Haraway 1988; Harding 1993).

Although STS became more established and attracted more widespread attention through the 1980s, it also attracted hostility and confusion, both within and beyond its expanding boundaries. A primary source of conceptual confusion and polemical hostility was the, by then widespread, claim that experimental findings and physical laws were "constructed." When couched at such a general level, this claim provoked interest but constructivism (and related terms emphasizing the artificial character of scientific knowledge) also invited confusion with partisan arguments in scientific research about deliberately or inadvertently constructed artifacts.

An idiomatic use of the word "artifact" is commonplace in empirical sciences to attribute an apparent object or observed property to the observational methods and instruments (Lynch 1985). Artifacts include noise from the instrumentation and environment that can be misconstrued as evidence for a possible astrophysical source. They also include precipitates from staining procedures that may be mistaken for cellular organelles in electron micrographs. Although scientists often acknowledge that sources of possible artifacts can never be fully identified and controlled, they deploy a distinction between features due to artifacts and those tentatively assigned to an object or natural process under investigation. Arguments among rival scientists often turn on questions of whether particular findings can be recast as artifacts. In the context of such arguments, to suggest that something is an artifact or construction is to call it into question; to express opposition to claims about its evidential value and significance. Given such negative or oppositional connotations in arguments among scientists, sociological arguments to the effect that scientific knowledge *in general* is "constructed," "artificial," or "manufactured" (Knorr Cetina 1981) struck some scientists, as well as many philosophers, social scientists, and journalists, as an expression of a general anti-science ideology (Gross and Levitt 1994; Sokal and Bricmont 1999). The accusations of being hostile to science and the efforts to defend against those accusations were dubbed by some writers as "the science wars" – a battleground within the broader "culture wars" that occasionally spilled beyond the borders of university campuses into the popular media.

Objections thrown at real and imagined social constructivists (often labeled "postmodernists") included that they ignored the strength of material evidence while speculatively playing up "social" and "cultural" factors. They also were accused of failing to engage with technical detail, of being ignorant of basic scientific facts and principles, and of focusing only on unsettled science. Although he did not explicitly sign on to constructivism, and was far from being hostile to science, Bloor was criticized for having denied the roles of truth, rationality, and empirical evidence, thereby pushing the constructivist bandwagon on to the path of its downward journey. However, a careful reading of how he presents his symmetry and impartiality postulates does not support crude arguments to the effect that he *denied* the validity of established science or the importance of material evidence. Bloor did not *deny* that some scientific propositions are true and others are false, just as he did not *deny* that some scientific innovations have proved to be successful and others have not. Instead, he argued that *social* causes should apply to scientific concepts, theories, and facts, regardless of whether the sociologist of knowledge (or anyone else) holds them to be true or false, rational or irrational, or successful or unsuccessful.

The ongoing controversy in the USA about the origin of species (particularly the human species) is a case in point. Public surveys in the USA consistently indicate that a substantial proportion of the population agree with statements such as, "God created human beings pretty much in their present form at one time within the last 10,000 years or so." Those of us who would strongly disagree with that statement are likely to insist that it is out of line with massive amounts of scientific and historical evidence, and that those who agree with it are under the sway of religious ideology. However, such a conviction does not necessary preclude an analysis of the controversy in the way Bloor recommends. His impartiality and symmetry postulates do not require us to place young-earth creationism on the same *epistemological* footing as current evolutionary theory. Instead, these postulates invite us to consider that evolutionist and creationist conceptions of human origins can both be understood as conditioned by social circumstances, such as variations in regional culture and religious background. Moreover, creationists have their own credentialed authorities, bodies of literature, educational and research institutes, and even museums. Unless one assumes that a "symmetrical" explanation that points to parallel sources of credibility must be exhaustive – resulting in a determination of compete equivalence and an inability to choose between the competing "beliefs" – it should offer no threat to established scientific truths that we hold dear. Instead, what it can help us to understand – and this can be quite valuable – is why "irrational" beliefs, that many of us would reject outright, are so robust and convincing among members of the particular communities for whom they are credible. They are credible for many of the same reasons as the "rational" beliefs we accept. Such an emphasis on social context and institutional supports also should provide a damper on the tendency to dismiss and demean the intelligence or honesty of the particular individuals who hold such "irrational" beliefs. However, a "symmetrical" explanation cannot settle the question of which of the competing beliefs is valid because it doesn't *address* that question.

The Constructivist's Dilemma

The science war of the 1990s faded away soon after the end of the decade without a decisive victory for either side. There was never a war in any serious sense, and the main protagonists simply stopped arguing with one another, perhaps because they grew tired of the repetitious claims and counterclaims. Constructivism also faded away; or rather, "construction" was less often used as an explicit term of art in STS, although the legacy of constructivism remained alive in commonplace refusals to accept epistemic and ontological *boundaries*, and in summary claims about the *contingent* and *uncertain* status of scientific facts, and the *messiness* of scientific research and technological projects. Some former proponents of constructivism not only avoided the term, they also publicly entertained second thoughts about the skeptical tenor that ran through many STS accounts of established science (Collins and Evans 2002; Latour 2004). These second thoughts arose in the context of debates about climate change, and the arguments and models that associated global warming and unstable weather patterns with carbon emissions from fossil fuel consumption.

The dispute about climate change is one of several contested "scientific controversies" that are being played out in a highly public way, and which involve contested legislation and litigation. Among the contested issues is whether these disputes actually constitute *scientific* controversies. A distinctive feature of the climate change dispute, as well as disputes about the theory of evolution, the link between second-hand smoke and cancer, and the link between thimerosal-containing vaccines and autism, is that one side invokes established science and insists that there is not (or not any longer) serious controversy among competent scientists, while the other side argues that dissenting voices have been marginalized and that the enforced consensus is a public front that suppresses genuine uncertainty. The concepts of controversy and consensus are themselves in dispute, and journalists and scholars who present the dispute impartially are liable to be accused of naively abetting the vacuous arguments of climate deniers or creationists.

For an STS scholar to weigh in on the side of the much-publicized consensus about climate change would mean to abandon symmetry and impartiality, and to avoid using constructivist arguments in reference to the established *facts*, because such arguments would appear to align with the political positions of climate-change deniers. However, the constructivist's dilemma – whether to support established science on its own terms or to join hands with conspiracy theorists – is only an apparent dilemma. It depends upon a subscription to a generalized constructivism akin to Mannheim's vision of a conception of ideology that would transcend partisan politics. If we assume that such transcendence is an illusory hope, then the indiscriminate use of concepts such as "ideology" and "construction" can only generate confusion. Moreover, an indiscriminate constructivism would also fail to be provocative, since it would beg the question *constructed* as opposed to what (Hacking 1999)? The constructivist's dilemma also depends upon the idea that the ability to discriminate between credible or incredible arguments (whether made by politicians, scientists, or colleagues down the hall) depends upon a general epistemology, rather than an array of particularistic judgments. An alternative way to think about the matter is to doubt that any general theory of knowledge – especially one as thin as constructivism – could be up to the task of guiding judgments about one singular case after another.

Various solutions are on offer for avoiding or getting out of the constructivist's dilemma. One, advocated by Collins and Evans (2002) is to refrain from judgments about the truth of contentious *factual* claims, and instead to develop sociologically informed normative judgments about the authenticity of the *expertise* claimed by the contending parties. A further step in this direction is to abandon symmetry and engage in direct advocacy of a contending position by deploying social science methods to compare the parties in a controversy (or manufactured controversy), and to demonstrate the imbalance of expertise and the asymmetric distribution of credentials, sources of sponsorship, vested interests, and histories of partisanship (Oreskes and Conway 2010). A different solution, advocated by Latour (2004), is to shift from "matters of fact" to "matters of concern" (a broader assemblage of commitments, actions, and entities that extends well beyond any given technical specialty or conventionally defined political group). This solution promises a shift away from the anthropocentric ontology that is continually reiterated in claims and counterclaims about anthropogenic climate change. However, the practical and political implications of such a shift appear to be remote from the alternatives for acting in contemporary political and legal domains.

Another response (though not a general solution) to the constructivist's dilemma is to identify constructivist idioms with specific moves in disputes among scientists. Consequently, constructivism is akin to an argumentative "repertoire" for opposing naturalistic claims that comes into play in particular disputatious circumstances (Gilbert and Mulkay 1984). One such circumstance is in court judgments about patents on gene sequences and genetically modified organisms. For example, legal challenges to gene patents assert that the objects in question are not *compositions of matter* (inventions, constructs), but instead are *products of nature*. Instead of committing to a constructivist position, an STS study of such disputes can identify how political and epistemic issues become intertwined with substantive biological issues, commercial interests, and legal precedents (Jackson 2015).

Conclusion

In the sociology of science, constructivism never quite attained the status of an epistemology. That is, it was never established as a general theory of knowledge that would enable discrimination between true and false belief, or between justified knowledge and mere opinion. Instead, constructivism arose from a principled effort to *avoid* making judgments about validity in sociological and historical studies of science. However, despite claims and methodic efforts to be impartial toward matters of truth and falsity when describing or explaining past and present-day sciences, the very idiom of "social construction" had strong associations with both philosophical skepticism and skeptical arguments used in particular disputes among practicing scientists. When presented as a general theoretical perspective, constructivism became a source of confusion and hostile exchange during the 1990s. Following, though not necessarily as a consequence of those disputes, constructivism was succeeded by a series of turns toward practice, materiality, and normativity, and many members of the STS field abandoned the stance of impartiality toward truth and falsity in favor of political and epistemic engagement in public controversies. Echoes of constructivist arguments can still be found in STS, but ambitious efforts to establish a general constructivist theory or explanatory program have gone the way of Mannheim's "non-evaluative general total conception of ideology."

References

Barber, B and Fox, R. (1958) "The Case of the Floppy-eared Rabbits: An Instance of Serendipity Gained and Serendipity Lost," *American Journal of Sociology* 64: 128–136.

Barnes, B. and Bloor, D. (1982) "Relativism, Rationalism, and the Sociology of Knowledge," in M. Hollis and S. Lukes (eds.), *Rationality and Relativism*, Cambridge: MIT Press, pp. 21–47.

Berger, P. and Luckmann, T. (1966) *The Social Construction of Reality*, New York: Doubleday.

Bijker, W., Hughes, T., and Pinch, T. (eds.) (1987) *The Social Construction of Technological Systems*, Cambridge, MA: MIT Press.

Bloor, D. (1976) *Knowledge and Social Imagery*, London: Routledge & Kegan Paul.

Callon, M. (1986) "Some Elements of a Sociology of Translation: Domestication of the Scallops and the Fishermen of St. Brieuc Bay," in J. Law (ed.), *Power, Action and Belief: A New Sociology of Knowledge?* London: Routledge and Kegan Paul, pp. 196–233.

Collins, H.M. (1975) "The Seven Sexes: A Study in the Sociology of a Phenomenon, or the Replication of Experiments in Physics," *Sociology* 9: 205–224.

Collins, H.M. (1983) "An Empirical Relativist Programme in the Sociology of Scientific Knowledge," in K. Knorr-Cetina and M. Mulkay (eds.), *Science Observed: Perspectives on the Social Study of Science*, London: Sage, pp. 83–113.

Collins, H.M. (1986) *Changing Order: Replication and Induction in Scientific Practice*, London: Sage.

Collins, H.M. and Evans, R. (2002) "The Third Wave of Science Studies: Studies of Expertise and Experience," *Social Studies of Science* 32(2): 235–296.

Crane, D. (1972) *Invisible Colleges: Diffusion of Knowledge in Scientific Communities*, Chicago, IL: University of Chicago Press.

Garfinkel, H. (1967) *Studies in Ethnomethodology*, Englewood Cliffs, NJ: Prentice Hall.

Gilbert, G.N. and Mulkay, M. (1984) *Opening Pandora's Box: An Analysis of Scientists' Discourse*, Cambridge: Cambridge University Press.

Gross, P. and Levitt, N. (1994) *Higher Superstition: The Academic Left and its Quarrels with Science*, Baltimore, MD: Johns Hopkins University Press.

Hacking, I. (1995) *Rewriting the Soul: Multiple Personality and the Sciences of Memory*, Princeton, NJ: Princeton University Press.

Hacking, I. (1999) *The Social Construction of What?* Cambridge, MA: Harvard University Press.

Haraway, D. (1988) "Situated Knowledges: The Science Question in Feminism and the Privilege of Partial Perspective," *Feminist Studies* 14(3): 573–579.

Haraway, D. (1997) *Modest_Witness@Second_Millennium.FemaleMan_Meets_OncoMouse: Feminism and Technoscience*, New York: Routledge.

Harding, S. (1993) "What is 'Strong Objectivity'?" in L. Alcoff and E. Potter (eds.), *Feminist Epistemologies*, New York: Routledge, pp. 49–82.

Horwitz, A. (2011) "Creating an Age of Depression: The Social Construction and Consequences of the Major Depression Diagnosis," *Society and Mental Health* 1(1): 41–54.

Jackson, M. (2015) *The Genealogy of a Gene: Patents, HIV/ AIDS, and Race*, Cambridge, MA: The MIT Press.

Knorr Cetina, K. (1981) *The Manufacture of Knowledge: An Essay on the Constructivist and Contextual Nature of Science*, Oxford: Pergamon Press.

Knorr Cetina, K. and Mulkay, M. (eds.) (1983) *Science Observed: Perspectives on the Sociology of Science*, London: Sage.

Kuhn, T.S. (1962) *The Structure of Scientific Revolutions*, Chicago, IL: University of Chicago Press.

Latour, B. (1987) *Science in Action: Following Scientists and Engineers through Society*, Cambridge, MA: Harvard University Press.

Latour, B. (2004) "Why Has Critique Run Out of Steam? From Matters of Fact to Matters of Concern," *Critical Inquiry* 30(2): 225–248.

Latour, B. and Woolgar, S. (1979) *Laboratory Life: The Social Construction of Scientific Facts*, London: Sage.

Lynch, M. (1985) *Art and Artifact in Laboratory Science*, London: Routledge & Kegan Paul.

Mannheim, K. (1936) *Ideology and Utopia: An Introduction to the Sociology of Knowledge*, New York: Harvest Books.

Merton, R.K. (1942[1973]) "A Note on Science and Democracy," *Journal of Legal and Political Sociology* 1: 115–126. Republished and revised, with the title, "The Normative Structure of Science," in R.K. Merton, *The Sociology of Science*, Chicago, IL: University of Chicago Press, 1973.

Mills, C.W. (1940) "Situated Actions and Vocabularies of Motive," *American Sociological Review* 5: 904–913.

Mulkay, M. (1976) "Norms and Ideology of Science," *Social Science Information* 15: 637–656.

Oreskes, N. and Conway E. (2010) *Merchants of Doubt: How a Handful of Scientists Obscured the Truth on Issues from Tobacco Smoke to Global Warming*, New York: Bloomsbury Press.

Price, D.J.d.S. (1963) *Little Science, Big Science*, New York: Columbia University Press.

Shapin, S. and Schaffer, S. (1985) *Leviathan and the Air Pump*, Princeton, NJ: Princeton University Press.

Sokal, A. and Bricmont J. (1999) *Fashionable Nonsense: Postmodern Intellectuals' Abuse of Science*, New York: Picador.

Szasz, T. (1974) *The Myth of Mental Illness: Foundations of a Theory of Personal Conduct*, New York: Harper.

Winch, P. (1990 [1958]) *The Idea of a Social Science and Its Relation to Philosophy*, 2nd ed, New York: Routledge. (1st ed., Routledge & Kegan Paul, 1958).

Further Reading

Lynch, M. (1993) *Scientific Practice and Ordinary Action: Ethnomethodology and Social Studies of Science*, Cambridge: Cambridge University Press.

Turner, S. (1994) *The Social Theory of Practices: Tradition, Tacit Knowledge and Presuppositions*, Chicago, IL: University of Chicago Press.

Zammito, J. (2004) *A Nice Derangement of Epistemes: Post-positivism in the Study of Science from Quine to Latour*, Chicago, IL: University of Chicago Press.

23

THE SOCIAL EPISTEMOLOGY OF CONSENSUS AND DISSENT

Boaz Miller

Consensus plays an increasingly growing role in public life. The National Institute of Health (NIH) and the Intergovernmental Panel on Climate Change (IPCC) formulate expert consensus statements to provide authoritative answers to disputed questions. The "Danish Citizen Consensus Model" is used for assessing societal dimensions of science and technology (Einsiedel et al. 2001; Medlock et al. 2007; Horst 2008). Wikipedia promotes consensus for achieving neutrality and verifiability (Wikipedia 2017). Scientific consensus is deferred to when arbitrating between rival experts in legal trials.

But when we think about the relations between knowledge and consensus, two conflicting intuitions arise. On the one hand, since when is truth determined by numbers? Are we back to the notorious Indiana House of Representatives "Pi Bill" of 1897, which redefined Pi by majority voting (Hallerberg 1977)? Wasn't Galileo right although his views contradicted common wisdom? On the other hand, for every Galileo, there are hundreds of misguided contrarians, forgotten by history. Is everybody wrong and only you are right?

Current social epistemology of consensus of dissent sorts out these conflicting intuitions.[1] Social epistemologists distinguish between knowledge-based consensus and mere agreement, explore the relations between consensus and the aims of inquiry, and distinguish legitimate from illegitimate dissent. The first section concerns the attribution of consensus to an epistemic community. The second section reviews accounts of knowledge-based or epistemically justified consensus. The third section addresses consensus as an aim of inquiry and the normative status of dissent. The final section reviews computational models of consensus.

When Does a Consensus Exist?

Deciding whether a consensus exists is not always trivial. To do so, we need to assess the scope of and depth of the agreement. Let's start with scope. Tucker (2003, 509–510) argues that a scientific agreement amounts to consensus only when there is no dissent whatsoever. While a universal consensus is not reasonable to expect, because "[t]here are still people who deny that the earth is round" (2003, 511), it is reasonable to expect complete agreement in a community of experts.

Miller (2013, 1297) argues, however, that in a large enough scientific community, chances are that some members will dissent. For example, while there are few scientists who deny that HIV causes AIDS, we cannot deny the existence of a general scientific consensus that HIV causes

AIDS. Miller argues that a consensus may be attributed to an epistemic community if the consensus view is well institutionalized, and the dissent view is marginalized.

Oreskes (2007, 66–79) analyzes abstracts extracted from the Web of Science using the search-keyword "global climate change." She codes them into groups, and shows that none falls into the climate skeptical camp. She concludes that a consensus on anthropogenic climate change exists. This method can easily be applied to other cases.

Qualitative methods for identifying consensus require extensive manual labor, and their outcome depends on researchers' subjective judgment in classifying papers. Shwed and Bearman (2010) present an algorithm for identifying a consensus that is not susceptible to these vulnerabilities. The algorithm identifies clusters within a network of citations in a large corpus of scientific papers. Shwed and Bearman assume that a citation of a paper is more likely to show agreement with it than disagreement. Bruggeman et al. (2012) argue, however, that when positive and negative citations are distinguished, other clusters emerge. This criticism may take the wind out of Shwed and Bearman's method, since it reintroduces human labor and susceptibility to subjective judgement (see Shwed and Bearman (2012) for a rebuttal).

Another factor that needs to be addressed is the depth of agreement. Fuller (2002, 208–210) distinguishes essential from accidental consensus. In an essential consensus, a group forms a collective decision for the same thing using shared standards of evidence and sense of relevance. In an accidental consensus, individuals form the same belief on and for their own reasons. A paradigmatic accidental consensus is found among a random group of surveyed people. The subjects may not understand the question in the same way, and by paraphrasing it the extent of consensus may be manipulated. For Fuller, only an essential consensus is a genuine consensus. Against this, Miller (2013, 1302–1303) argues that an agreement on shared formalisms, ontological schemes, and evidential standards is sufficient for attributing a consensus to the community, because it provides a sufficient basis for pursing research together, even if members differ in their metaphysical beliefs.

When Is Consensus Knowledge-Based or Epistemically Justified?

A common intuition is that a majority or consensus of epistemically-competent agents is more likely to be right than wrong. Several philosophers try to justify it. Jones (2002) argues that ceteris paribus, a scientific consensus is more likely to be knowledge-based than not because science strives at the truth. Anderson (2011) and Collins (2010), while not naive about the influence of biases and interests on the outcomes of scientific controversies, argue that science is still the most reliable way to the truth, thus laypeople have no better alternative than trusting a scientific consensus.

Another rationale for deferring to the majority or consensus comes from Condorcet's jury theorems, which state, roughly, that sufficiently large groups in which there is a sufficiently large subgroup of individuals who have a higher than 0.5 probability to form a correct belief on a given matter will reach the correct decision by majority voting (Odenbaugh 2012). It is unclear, however, in which concrete cases the conditions of statistical independence and higher than 0.5 probability should obtain, or how to judge whether they obtain (Vermeule 2009, 28–33).

Indiscriminate lay deference to a consensus of experts has its risks. "If the history of science teaches anything, it's humility. There are numerous historical examples where expert opinion turned out to be wrong" (Oreskes 2007, 66). Moreover, a community of experts may mask internal disagreements and present a façade of consensus for reasons like keeping their professional reputation intact and maintaining public trust in science (Beatty 2006). Beatty (2017) further argues that the existence of consensus on a theory does not imply that it has been rigorously tested, but that researchers trust each other about their results. The validity of the consensus depends on whether these mutual trust relations are justified (Miller 2015a).

Thus, other scholars recommend deference to a consensus of experts only when there are reasons to think it is *knowledge-based* or epistemically justified. We may distinguish *cognitive* from *social* accounts of knowledge-based or epistemically justified consensus. Cognitive accounts specify empirical and theoretical virtues of a credible or justified consensual view. Social accounts specify societal properties of such a consensus. There are also hybrid accounts, both cognitive and social.

Let's start with the cognitive approach. Oreskes identifies five general hallmarks of a good scientific theory: inductive support, predictive success, resistance to falsification attempts, consilience of evidence (convergence of evidence of different types), and explanatory success. Oreskes argues that because the theory of anthropogenic climate change bears these hallmarks, the scientific consensus over it is knowledge-based (2007, 79–92).

It is disputed, though, that this is sufficient for rendering a consensus knowledge-based. Miller (2013, 1012) argues that even if a scientific community unanimously accepts a theory that seemingly enjoys strong evidential support, we should still examine the societal properties of the agreement for deciding whether to trust it. Suppose there is a scientific consensus that passive smoking does not raise the chances of lung cancer. Suppose this conclusion is supported by seemingly robust studies of different types, e.g., epidemiological, in vivo, and in vitro studies. If all these studies were supported by tobacco companies, there is still good chance their conclusion is false. The upshot, so Miller argues, is that for inferring truth from social agreement, in addition to being evidentially supported, we would like it to socially diverse in relevant ways, in this case, shared by publicly-funded researchers, smokers and non-smokers, etc.

By contrast, Stegenga (2016) argues that a purely cognitive epistemic evaluation of a consensus is possible. Stegenga identifies three conditions the procedures leading to a knowledge-based consensus should satisfy: (1) *Inclusivity*: the consensus-forming processes should include all available evidence; (2) *Constraint*: these processes should constrain intersubjective assessments of the hypothesis of interest; and (3) *Evidential Complexity*: these processes should assess evidence on multiple relevant evidential criteria. Stegenga acknowledges that social diversity is positively correlated with meeting Inclusivity and Evidential Complexity, but insists that it is subordinate to them and not principally necessary. The dispute between Stegenga and Miller is whether social diversity is required for achieving Constraint by limiting subjects' excessive interpretive flexibility in assessing the evidence. While Miller thinks that it is necessary, Stegenga (2016, 46) holds that Constraint can be achieved by more rigorous evidence assessment methods, and that too much diversity actually militates against Constraint.

But cognitive accounts of knowledge-based consensus, such as Oreskes' and Stegenga's, have a more fundamental problem. For Oreskes, the existence of consensus does not actually constitute a reason for (or against) trusting it. For suppose that the theory of anthropogenic climate change that currently enjoys a consensus were supported by a minority of the scientific community, and a rival theory, which does *not* bear Oreskes' five hallmarks of good science, were supported by the majority. By Oreskes' reasoning, the minority theory would still be more credible, because it would still be better evidentially supported.

Social evidence such as the number of people who support a view, their credentials, and their social background *is* relevant to assessing the credibility of a consensus. But can the credibility of a consensus be assessed by looking *only* at social factor? *Social* accounts of knowledge-based consensus try to do that. Their advantage is that they do not require a layperson to evaluate expert claims, but only to examine social features of the consensus, which are more epistemically accessible to her.

Longino (2002a, Ch. 6) provides an influential social account of knowledge-based consensus, called Critical Contextual Empiricism, which specifies necessary and sufficient conditions for an agreement in an epistemic community to count as collective knowledge. When researchers theorize from empirical data, they may make biased background assumptions that may taint their resulting theories. Critical Contextual Empiricism prescribes four social norms of critical deliberation to expose and eliminate such biases: (1) there are public venues of criticism; (2) there is uptake of criticism; (3) there are publicly recognized standards of evaluation of theories; and (4) there is tempered equality of intellectual authority – intellectual capacity and relevant expertise are the only criteria by which people are given the right to participate in the collective critical discussion. Critical Contextual Empiricism echoes Habermas' (1984) "ideal speech situation," in which fully rational agents reach a consensus converging on the truth through free discourse.

Critics argue that Longino's four norms are either too permissive or too restrictive, and neither sufficient nor necessary for knowledge. Goldman (2002) argues that interpreted too permissively, a group of creationists with their own peer-reviewed journals may be said to satisfy Longino's norms. Interpreted too restrictively, evolutionary biologists who do not engage with creationists may be said to fail to meet them. Solomon and Richardson (2005) argue that we have successful knowledge achieved without following Longino's norms, while critical norms do not guarantee actual criticism, thus unwarranted views may survive long. They claim that conditions for knowledge cannot be formulated solely procedurally, they must say something substantive about the conditions the end product that the community reaches must meet. This criticism questions the viability of purely social accounts of knowledge-based consensus.

Empirical evidence about the epistemic performance of deliberative models of consensus is mixed. Habermas (2006) cites psychological studies that show that critical public discussion converges on the truth in real-world, and not just ideal conditions. Sunstein (2006) and Solomon (2015, 92–102) cites other studies according to which deliberation leads to group polarization and extremism. Sunstein and Solomon argue that knowledge from a group is best extracted by aggregating members' independently formed judgements, rather than deliberation within the group (see Tollefsen 2006 for a middle-ground position). Sunstein's and Solomons' views accord with Surowiecki's (2004) theory of the Wisdom of Crowds, according to which individuals' aggregated judgments may outperform experts' judgment (cf. Thicke 2017).

Tucker (2003) gives another social account of knowledge-based consensus. Tucker identifies three conditions under which shared knowledge is *the best explanation* of a consensus. First, the consensus is uncoerced. Second, the consensus is uniquely heterogeneous, namely no subgroup shares an extraneous property that may otherwise explain the agreement within it. Just like in a controlled experiment, if members of a test group do not share any property other than the one being tested, an observed effect may be attributed to the tested property, when there is a consensus in a group of people who do not share a property such a mutual power relationship, joint interest, shared ideology or bias, the consensus may be attributed to knowledge (2003, 506). This is why a third condition, that the group is sufficiently large, is required. While an accidental consensus in a small uniquely heterogeneous group is likely, it is unlikely in a large heterogeneous group.

Against Tucker, Solomon (2001) and Miller (2013) argue that an accidental aggregation of views toward a non-knowledge-based consensus is plausible. It therefore cannot be eliminated as the best explanation of a consensus even when Tucker's conditions hold. Solomon argues that the history of science shows that consensuses often emerge out of an accidental aggregation of interests and influences on individual members of a scientific community, when there are rival theories that do not get the attention they deserve (2001, 121–135). Miller (2013, 1306–1308) adds that accidental aggregation of influences that leads to a consensus is likely from a probabilistic perspective, because people have many influences on a variety of issues, thus they are likely to happen to agree on some of them. For example, while leaders of the world's orthodox religions disagree on the most fundamental doctrinal issue, they all reject homosexuality. This accidental agreement, however, does not give their view any epistemic credit (for a rebuttal, see Tucker 2014).

Solomon and Miller both offer hybrid accounts of the social epistemology of consensus, which attend to cognitive as well as social factors. In *Social Empiricism* (2001), Solomon addresses the question of when a distribution of research efforts in a scientific community is epistemically justified. Solomon conceptualizes cognitive diversity in terms of factors ("decision vectors") that influence individuals' and communities' theory choice. She distinguishes between empirical and non-empirical decision vectors. Empirical decision vectors are factors that make scientists prefer theories with empirical success. Non-empirical decision vectors are other reasons or causes for theory choice, such as ideology, pride, or preference for simpler theories (2001, 51–63).

Solomon argues that empirical decision vectors should be equitably distributed among theories in proportion to the theories' empirical success. For instance, if a theory has some technological success, a proportional number of scientists should be drawn to it *because of this success*. It follows that a consensus is epistemically justified only in rare cases in which one theory has all the empirical success (2001, 117–120).

Miller (2013) offers also a hybrid theory of knowledge-based consensus. Miller identifies four types of consensuses, three of which are not knowledge based and one is. The first is a non-cognitive consensus, which aims at promoting non-epistemic aims. The second is a "vertically-lucky" consensus. This is an agreement that happens to be correct, but could have easily been wrong. The third is an epistemically unfortunate consensus, in which parties to the consensus have the bad luck of being systematically or deliberately mislead or biased. When a consensus belongs to none of these three types, it is likely to be knowledge-based.

Miller thus argues that when we can eliminate non-epistemic factors, veritic epistemic luck, and epistemic misfortune as the best explanations of a consensus, knowledge remains its best explanation. He identifies three conditions for knowledge being the best explanation of a consensus: (1) *social calibration*: researchers give the same meaning to the same terms and share the same fundamental background assumptions; (2) *apparent consilience of evidence*: the consensus seems to be built on an array of evidence that is drawn from a variety of techniques and methods; and (3) *social diversity*: the consensus is shared by men and women, researchers from the private and public sectors, liberals and conservatives, etc. As mentioned, Miller argues that the third condition is not reducible to the second.

So far we distinguished cognitive, social, and hybrid accounts of knowledge-based or epistemically justified consensus. Following Gasparri (2013), we may also distinguish knowledge-*indicative* from knowledge-*conducive* accounts of consensus. Knowledge-indicative accounts identify signs that indicate that a consensus is credible or epistemically justified. Knowledge-conducive accounts specify conditions which should hold if a community of researchers is to converge on the truth (see Table 23.1).

Table 23.1 A taxonomy of accounts of knowledge-based or epistemically justified consensus

	Cognitive	*Social*	*Hybrid(Cognitive and Social)*
Indicative	Oreskes (2007)	Tucker (2003, 2014)	Solomon (2001); Miller (2013, 2016)
Conducive	Lehrer and Wagner (1981); Habermas (1984); Stegenga (2016)	Longino (2002a)	

Gasparri draws this distinction to scrutinize Tucker's and Miller's knowledge-indicative accounts of consensus. He compares their accounts to Lehrer and Wagner's (1981) knowledge-conducive account of consensus, which consists of a mathematical model of a group of fully-informed rational Bayesian agents who iteratively update their degrees of belief on a given proposition and the degree of credibility they assign to other members regarding this proposition until all agents converge on the same degree of belief, and a rational, knowledge-based consensus is formed. While Tucker and Miller regard Lehrer and Wagner's idealized model as irrelevant to real-world consensuses, Gasparri argues that Lehrer and Wagner's account addresses exactly the missing elements in Tucker's and Miller's accounts; namely, the dynamics of rational aggregation of beliefs and trust-building in an epistemic community.

Solomon's Social Empiricism is similarly criticized for overlooking the dynamics leading to consensus. Wylie (2006) argues that the same social factors that Solomon identifies as obstructing epistemically effective deliberation also obstruct a justified distribution of decision vectors. Thus, a question arises how such an obstruction is to be avoided. Longino (2008) argues that an epistemic appraisal of consensus should answer who should be trusted in scientific debates. Since Social Empiricism does not analyze how decision vectors affect social inquiry, so Wylie and Longino argue, it has no sufficient resources to address these questions.

Aiming for Consensus, Dealing with Dissent

Knowledge-conducive accounts of consensus assume that consensus is an aim of inquiry. We may question this assumption. Longino's Critical Contextual Empiricism strives at rational consensus, yet Longino (2002b) acknowledges that permanent rational dissent due to incompatible theoretical background assumptions between dissenters and the majority is possible. Kitcher (2002a, 2002b) denies this possibility, while Andler (2013) argue that it is both possible and normal.

For Solomon, because both consensus and dissent emerge due to accidental factors, dissent is not a temporary glitch to be overcome, and consensus is not the end of inquiry (2001, 117–120). Miller (2016) warns that through the interaction of scientific and non-scientific factors, a scientific consensus can emerge prematurely, and be unjustly deferred to in policy and legal contexts.

Solomon (2015, Ch. 2–5) is suspicious of consensus building initiatives. While such initiatives help the public legitimation and dissemination of information, they neither expedite the discovery of truths nor warrant their final conclusions. Focusing on the NIH Consensus Development Program, Solomon argues that when the available evidence is insufficient for reaching a conclusion, a consensus statement is premature, and when the evidence is clear, it is redundant. A consensus conference is useful only when the available evidence is sufficient but not yet clear. But the NIH usually misses this window of opportunities. Moreover, the main vehicle of scientific progress is empirical research, rather than social deliberation, hence the epistemic contribution of consensus conferences is minimal.

Against this, Kosolosky and Van Bouwel (2014) argue that the NIH Consensus Development Program and similar initiatives can make genuine epistemic contributions. They distinguish academic consensus, which is about issues internal to science, from interface consensus, which is about the interface of science and policy. Consensus initiatives may give reasoned answers to interface question that do not arise in standard scientific practice. Consensus initiatives may help explicate the reasoning behind their conclusions, which cannot be done by mere aggregation of evidence.

de Melo-Martín and Intemann (2013) identify epistemic and political difficulties with demands by the public or decision makers for a unified scientific front as a condition for action. Such demands convey a distorted image of science as a body that speaks unanimously. They may silence legitimate dissent and set too high a bar for science to meet (cf. Miller 2015b, 2016, 29–31).

These worries raise the problem of dealing with dissent. On the one hand, dissent may have epistemic benefits; "controversies are indispensable for the formation, evolution and evaluation of theories, because it is through them that the essential role of criticism in engendering, improving, and controlling the 'wellformedness' and the 'empirical content' of scientific theories is performed" (Dascal 1998, 147). Beatty and Moore (2010, 203) argue that effective critical deliberation requires researchers genuinely committed to a dissent view. But when they exist, the deliberation may not produce a consensus.

On the other hand, dissent may be epistemically detrimental, especially dissent stemming from *manufactured uncertainty* or *doubt mongering*. Affluent bodies opposed to a particular piece of knowledge may inhibit the formation of consensus or create the perception that it does not exist. They may insist on more and ever more critical scrutiny, no matter how strong the evidence is. Oreskes and Conway (2010) argue that the climate skeptical claims have not originated from within the scientific community but rather from politically motivated external actors who, consciously and cynically, have been manufacturing controversy on the subject.

Intemann and de Melo-Martín (2014) argue that Longino's Critical Contextual Empiricism faces special difficulties dealing with manufactured uncertainty, because of its prescribed norms of uptake of criticism. Who is to judge whether dissenters fail to follow this norm or whether their concerns are genuine? When may a community stop engaging with them and move on? Defending Critical Contextual Empiricism against this charge, Borgerson (2011, 445) argues that if we distinguish the level of certainty required for action from that required for knowledge, interested parties will be less motivated to manufacture uncertainty. In response, Miller (2015b, 118–119) argues that Critical Contextual Empiricism should still be able to determine when closure in an epistemic community is warranted despite incessant criticism.

Unlike Critical Contextual Empiricism, Tucker's and Miller's accounts of knowledge-based consensus arguably do not face difficulties with manufactured dissent. Tucker and Miller hold that consensus is knowledge-based when knowledge is the best explanation thereof. If knowledge remains the best explanation of a consensus excluding a dissent, and the dissent is best explained by non-epistemic factors, such as financial interests, then we may still legitimately infer that the consensus excluding the dissent is knowledge-based.

Biddle and Leuschner (2015) provide an inductive-risk account for distinguishing epistemically beneficial from epistemically detrimental dissent. Inductive risk is the risk of making a wrong epistemic judgment, such as accepting a false hypothesis and rejecting a true hypothesis (Douglas 2009, Ch. 5). Drawing on Wilholt (2009), who characterizes conventional scientific epistemic standards, e.g., using a critical p value of 5 percent, as reflecting conventional trade-offs between inductive risks, Biddle and Leuschner identify four conditions jointly sufficient for a dissent over a hypothesis H to be considered epistemically detrimental: (1) the non-epistemic consequences of wrongly rejecting H are likely to be severe; (2) the dissenting research that constitutes the objection violates established conventional standards; (3) the dissenting research involves intolerance for producer risks at the expense of public risks; and (4) producer risks and public risks fall largely upon different parties.

Beatty and Moore (2010, 209) propose that a scientific community allow dissent and aim at a meta consensus shared by the entire community that the deliberation process on the theory was adequate, and in this respect the theory can stand for the view of the group. The realistic prospects of this proposal remain to be seen.

Computer Simulations of Consensus and Dissent Formation

Some scholars develop computational models of a group of epistemic agents who exchange information, and revise their beliefs accordingly.[2] The models inter alia try to identify the salient factors that lead to knowledge-based consensus or permanent dissent.

Zollman presents two such models. One model (Zollman 2010) finds that in a sufficiently dense community, there is an epistemic trade-off between diversity of strong views and fast communication channels. When only one factor is present, the community is likely to converge on the truth, but not when both are. The rationale is that when both strong views and fast communication channels are present, scientists with weaker beliefs are more easily persuaded to abandon their beliefs and adopt the beliefs of scientists with stronger beliefs, such that if the abandoned beliefs are, in fact, true, the scientific community will not discover that. Another model (Zollman 2007) finds a similar trade-off between the speed of communication and its reliability. Holman and Bruner (2015, as well as as in Bruner and Holman Forthcoming) relax Zollman's assumptions and add factors such as intransigent biases. They demonstrate that convergence on a falsehood or permanent dissent may also occur under some circumstances.

Thagard presents two models that associate consensus with coherence. The first model (Thagard 2000, Ch. 10) is of "cold" (intellectual) cognitive factors. In it, a consensus in a scientific community emerges if the different pieces of information scattered in the community cohere, and the communication between the agents is sufficiently reliable. The second model (Thagard and Kroon 2006) studies the effect of "hot" (emotional) cognitive factors on consensus formation. In it, subjects interact and emotionally affect each other. Consensus on a judgement is reached when it coheres with the subjects' emotional stances toward it. The outcome is path dependent. If Alice and Bob may both emotionally affect Charlie's judgment, it may matter whether Charlie interacted first with Alice or Bob.

Such models do not make traditional philosophical argument redundant. Their external validity and applicability to concrete circumstances hinge on the validity of their background assumptions, which need to be justified by argument. They can thus still benefit from engaging with the work reviewed in the previous sections.

Notes

1 In philosophy of science until the early 1980s, scientific consensus was addressed mostly in the context of Kuhn's (1961/1970) *The Structure of the Scientific Revolutions* (see Wray in this volume). For a classic account of the interplay between data, theory, method, and rational consensus, see Laudan (1984).
2 See also Reijula and Kuorikoski, Chapter 24 in this handbook.

References

Anderson, E. (2011). Democracy, Public Policy, and Lay Assessments of Scientific Testimony. *Episteme* 8(2), pp. 144–164.

Andler, D. (2013). Dissensus in Science as a Fact and as a Norm. In: H. Andersen, D. Dieks, T. Uebel, and G. Wheeler, eds., *New Challenges to Philosophy of Science*. Dordrecht: Springer, pp. 493–506.

Beatty, J. (2006). Masking Disagreement among Experts. *Episteme* 3(1), pp. 52–67.

Beatty, J. (2017). Consensus: Sometimes It Doesn't Add Up. In: S. Gissis, E. Lamm, and A. Shavit, eds., *Landscapes of Collectivity in the Life Sciences*. Cambridge, MA: MIT Press, pp. 179–198.

Beatty, J. and Moore, A. (2010). Should We Aim for Consensus? *Episteme* 7(3), pp. 198–214.

Biddle, J. B. and Leuschner, A. (2015). Climate Skepticism and the Manufacture of Doubt: Can Dissent in Science Be Epistemically Detrimental? *European Journal for Philosophy of Science* 5(3), pp. 261–278.

Borgerson, K. (2011). Amending and Defending Critical Contextual Empiricism. *European Journal for Philosophy of Science* 1(3), pp. 435–449.

Bruggeman, J., Traag, V. A., and Uitermark, J. (2012). Detecting Communities through Network Data. *American Sociological Review* 77, pp. 1050–1063.

Bruner, J. and Holman, B. (Forthcoming). Complicating Consensus. In L. Garbayo, ed., *Expert Disagreement and Measurement*. Dordrecht: Springer.

Collins, H. M. (2010). *Elective Modernism*. Cardiff: Cardiff School of Social Sciences. Available at: www.cardiff.ac.uk/socsi/contactsandpeople/harrycollins/expertise-project/elective%20modernism%204.doc

Dascal, M. (1998). The Study of Controversies and the Theory and History of Science. *Science in Context* 11(2), pp. 147–154.

de Melo-Martín, I. and Intemann, K. (2013). Scientific Dissent and Public Policy: Is Targeting Dissent a Reasonable Way to Protect Sound Policy Decisions? *EMBO Reports* 14(3), pp. 231–235.

Douglas, H. (2009). *Science, Policy, and the Value-Free Ideal.* Pittsburgh, PA: University of Pittsburgh Press.

Einsiedel, E. F., Jelsøe, E., and Breck, T. (2001). Publics at the Technology Table: The Consensus Conference in Denmark, Canada, and Australia. *Public Understanding of Science* 10(1), pp. 83–98.

Fuller, S. (2002). *Social Epistemology,* 2nd ed. Bloomington: Indiana University Press.

Gasparri, L. (2013). Knowledge Indicative and Knowledge Conductive Consensus. *Journal of the Philosophy of History* 7(2), pp. 162–182.

Goldman, A. I. (2002). Knowledge and Social Norms. *Science* 296 (June 21), pp. 2148–2149.

Habermas, J. (1984). *The Theory of Communicative Action,* Vol. 1 & 2. Boston: Beacon Press.

Habermas, J. (2006). Political Communication in Media Society: Does Democracy Still Enjoy an Epistemic Dimension? The Impact of Normative Theory on Empirical Research. *Communication Theory* 16(4), pp. 411–426.

Hallerberg, A. E. 1977. Indiana's Squared Circle. *Mathematics Magazine* 50(3), pp. 136–140.

Holman, B. and Bruner, J. P. (2015). The Problem of Intransigently Biased Agents. *Philosophy of Science* 82(5), pp. 956–968.

Horst, M. (2008). In Search of Dialogue: Staging Science Communication in Consensus Conferences. In: D. Cheng, M. Claessens, T. Gascoigne, J. Metcalfe, B. Schiele, and S. Shi, eds., *Communicating Science in Social Contexts.* Dordrecht: Springer, pp. 259–274.

Intemann, K., and de Melo-Martín, I. (2014). Are There Limits to Scientists' Obligations to Seek and Engage Dissenters? *Synthese* 91(12), pp. 2751–2765.

Jones, W. E. (2002). Dissident Versus Loyalist: Which Scientists Should We Trust? *The Journal of Value Inquiry* 36(4), pp. 511–520.

Kitcher, P. (2002a). The Third Way: Reflections on Helen Longino's. *The Fate of Knowledge. Philosophy of Science* 69(4), pp. 549–559.

Kitcher, P. (2002b). Reply to Helen Longino. *Philosophy of Science* 69(4), pp. 569–572.

Kosolosky, L. and Van Bouwel, J. (2014). Explicating Ways of Consensus-Making in Science and Society: Distinguishing the Academic, the Interface and the Meta-Consensus. In: C. Martini and M. Boumans, eds., *Experts and Consensus in Social Science.* Dordrecht: Springer, pp. 71–92.

Kuhn, T. S. (1961/1970). *The Structure of Scientific Revolutions,* 2nd ed. Chicago: The University of Chicago Press.

Laudan, L. (1984). *Science and Values: The Aims of Science and Their Role in Scientific Debate.* Berkeley: University of California Press.

Lehrer, K. and Wagner, C. (1981). *Rational Consensus in Science and Society: A Philosophical and Mathematical Study.* Dordrecht: Reidel.

Longino, H. (2002a). *The Fate of Knowledge.* Princeton: Princeton University Press.

Longino, H. (2002b). Reply to Philip Kitcher. *Philosophy of Science* 69(4), pp. 573–577.

Longino, H. (2008). Norms and Naturalism: Comments on Miriam Solomon's Social Empiricism. *Perspectives on Science* 16(3), pp. 241–245.

Medlock, J., Downey, R., and Einsiedel, E. (2007). Governing Controversial Technologies: Consensus Conferences as a Communications Tool. In: D. Brossard, J. Shanahan, and T. C. Nsbitt, eds., *The Media, the Public and Agricultural Biotechnology.* Wallingford, Oxfordshire: CABI, pp. 308–326.

Miller, B. (2013). When Is Consensus Knowledge Based? Distinguishing Shared Knowledge from Mere Agreement. *Synthese* 190(7), pp. 1293–1316.

Miller, B. (2015a). Why (Some) Knowledge Is the Property of a Community and Possibly None of Its Members. *The Philosophical Quarterly* 65(260), pp. 417–441.

Miller, B. (2015b). 'Trust Me – I'm a Public Intellectual': Margaret Atwood's and David Suzuki's Social Epistemologies for Climate Science. In: M. Keren and R. Hawkins, eds., *Speaking Power to Truth: Digital Discourse and the Public Intellectual.* Athabasca, AB: Athabasca University Press, pp. 113–128.

Miller, B. (2016). Scientific Consensus and Expert Testimony in Courts: Lessons from the Bendectin Litigation. *Foundations of Science* 21(1), pp. 15–33.

Odenbaugh, J. (2012). Climate, Consensus, and Contrarians. In: W. P. Kabasenche, M. O'Rourke, and M. H. Slater, eds., *The Environment: Philosophy, Science, and Ethics.* Cambridge, MA: MIT Press, pp. 137–150.

Oreskes, N. (2007). The Scientific Consensus on Climate Change: How Do We Know We're Not Wrong? In: J. F. C. DiMento and P. Doughman, eds., *Climate Change: What It Means for Us, Our Children, and Our Grandchildren.* Cambridge, MA: MIT Press, pp. 65–99.

Oreskes, N. and Conway, E. M. (2010). *Merchants of Doubt: How a Handful of Scientists Obscured the Truth on Issues from Tobacco Smoke to Global Warming.* New York: Bloomsbury.

Shwed, U. and Bearman, P. S. (2010). The Temporal Structure of Scientific Consensus Formation. *American Sociological Review* 75(6), pp. 817–840.

Shwed, U. and Bearman, P. S. (2012). Symmetry Is Beautiful. *American Sociological Review* 77(6), pp. 1064–1069.

Solomon, M. (2001). *Social Empiricism.* Cambridge, MA: MIT Press.

Solomon, M. (2015). *Making Medical Knowledge.* Oxford: OUP.

Solomon, M. and Richardson, A. (2005). A Critical Context for Longino's Critical Contextual Empiricism. *Studies in History and Philosophy of Science* 36, pp. 211–222.

Stegenga, J. (2016). Three Criteria for Consensus Conferences. *Foundations of Science* 21(1), pp. 35–49.

Sunstein, C. R. (2006). Deliberating Groups versus Prediction Markets (or Hayek's Challenge to Habermas). *Episteme* 3(3), pp. 192–213.

Surowiecki, J. (2004). *The Wisdom of Crowds: Why the Many Are Smarter than the Few and How and Nations, Societies, Collectives Wisdom Shapes Business.* New York: Doubleday.

Thagard, P. (2000). *Coherence in Thought and Action.* Cambridge, MA: MIT Press.

Thagard, P. and Kroon, F. W. (2006). Emotional Consensus in Group Decision Making. *Mind & Society* 5(1), pp. 85–104.

Thicke, M. (2017). Market Epistemology. *Synthese,* in press. Available at:link.springer.com/epdf/10.1007/s11229-017-1464-2

Tollefsen, D. P. (2006). Group Deliberation, Social Cohesion, and Scientific Teamwork: Is There Room for Dissent? *Episteme* 3(1–2), pp. 37–51.

Tucker, A. (2003). The Epistemic Significance of Consensus. *Inquiry* 46(4), pp. 501–521.

Tucker, A. (2014). Epistemology as a Social Science: Applying the Neyman-Rubin Model to Explain Expert Beliefs. In: C. Martini and M. Boumans, eds., *Experts and Consensus in Social Science.* Dordrecht: Springer, pp. 155–170.

Vermeule, A. (2009). *Law and the Limits of Reason.* New York: OUP.

Wikipedia. (2017). Wikipedia: Consensus. Available at: en.wikipedia.org/wiki/Wikipedia:Consensus

Wilholt, T. (2009). Bias and Values in Scientific Research. *Studies in History and Philosophy of Science* 40(1), pp. 92–101.

Wylie, A. (2006). Socially Naturalized Norms of Epistemic Rationality: Aggregation and Deliberation. *The Southern Journal of Philosophy* 44, pp. 43–48.

Zollman, K. J. S. (2007). The Communication Structure of Epistemic Communities. *Philosophy of Science* 74(5), pp. 574–587.

Zollman, K. J. S. (2010). The Epistemic Benefit of Transient Diversity. *Erkenntnis* 72, pp. 17–35.

Further Reading

Simon (2010) identifies three types of communal epistemic closure in Internet platforms, and discusses their respective virtues and vices. Andler (2012) criticizes the notion of the Wisdom of Crowds as an epistemic panacea. Van Bouwel (2009) draws a comparison between political models of pluralism and social-epistemic models of consensus and dissent. Delborne (2008) and Martin (2008) offer empirically-based taxonomies of dissent and dissenting practices.

Andler, D. (2012). What Has Collective Wisdom to Do with Wisdom? In: H. Landemore and J. Elster, eds., *Collective Wisdom: Principles and Mechanisms.* Cambridge: Cambridge University Press, pp. 72–94.

Delborne, J. A. (2008). Transgenes and Transgressions: Scientific Dissent as Heterogeneous Practice. *Social Studies of Science* 38(4), pp. 509–541.

Martin, B. (2008). Varieties of Dissent. In: S. P. Banks, ed., *Dissent and the Failure of Leadership.* Cheltenham, UK: Edward Elgar, pp. 22–36.

Simon, J. (2010). A Socio-Epistemological Framework for Scientific Publishing. *Social Epistemology* 24(3), pp. 201–218.

Van Bouwel, J. (2009). The Problem With(out) Consensus: The Scientific Consensus, Deliberative Democracy and Agnostic Pluralism. In: J. V. Bouwel, ed., *The Social Sciences and Democracy.* New York: Palgrave Macmillan, pp. 121–142.

24

MODELING EPISTEMIC COMMUNITIES

Samuli Reijula and Jaakko Kuorikoski

Introduction

Finding solutions to genuinely important epistemic challenges typically exceeds the capabilities of a single knower. Science, research and development laboratories, and the work of expert committees are all instances of knowledge production, which require coordinated effort from several agents. Furthermore, these situations essentially involve interaction and a division of cognitive labor among the members of the group or community: Difficult problems are attacked by dividing them into more tractable sub-problems, which are then allocated to subgroups and ultimately to individual group members. In this chapter, we use the notion of epistemic community to refer to such a group of agents faced with a shared epistemic task.[1] We regard division of labor between the members of the group as a necessary property of an epistemic community, so as to distinguish such groups from mere statistical or aggregative epistemic collectives, where there is no communication or coordination between group members (cf. Surowiecki 2005; Sunstein 2006). However, as we will see, the division of labor and the associated conception of cognitive diversity can be understood in several different ways.

In this chapter, we provide a review of the modeling work, which has aimed at understanding the functioning of epistemic communities.[2] Modeling done by social epistemologists resides at an interesting junction of various strands of inquiry. Many of the themes touched upon by social epistemologists (e.g., scientific reputation and authority, reward schemes in science) had already been studied by sociologists of science such as Robert Merton (1973) and Pierre Bourdieu (1975). Furthermore, the disciplinary origins of the various modeling methodologies used in social epistemology can typically be traced back to economics and decision theory, organization science, AI, and ecology. However, within social epistemology, formal modeling work has often formed its own niche and the integration of modeling work with the rest of research in social epistemology has often been less than satisfying. Hence, it is often not clear how the simple models of epistemic communities contribute to (a) the more general problems studied by social epistemology as a whole, and (b) how they should be connected to relevant findings from disciplines such as social psychology and organization studies.

After providing an overview of some of the most prominent modeling approaches in social epistemology, in the final section of our review we try to go some way towards answering these questions. We sketch a general approach to interpreting models, thereby suggesting how they could be integrated with conceptual and empirical work (e.g., case studies) done in the rest of the field. Furthermore, by showing that the models in social epistemology are in many ways parallel to those developed in other fields that study collective knowing and problem solving, our contribution hopefully helps to position the philosophical work within this multi-disciplinary research area. We suggest that there is a clear epistemic benefit from seeing these parallels more clearly: It allows us to see where the strengths and blind spots of models presented in various fields are, and where promising future contributions might lie.[3]

The Invisible Hand in Science: From Individual Irrationality to Collective Rationality

In a now classic paper, Philip Kitcher (1990) set out to examine the division of cognitive labor in a community of scientists. By employing a combination of modeling tools from microeconomic theory (individual maximization of expected utility and equilibrium), Kitcher investigates how research resources should be allocated among alternative competing research programs, methods, or theories. In light of several examples drawn from the history of science, Kitcher argues that in many cases, a community of scientists should hedge its bets. All research effort should not be allocated only to the study of the currently most strongly confirmed or most promising alternative so as not to prematurely rule out potentially true but not yet well-confirmed hypotheses. Nevertheless, from the point of view of individual epistemic rationality, every scientist should pursue exactly the most promising avenue of research best supported by the currently available evidence.

There is, therefore, a discontinuity between the requirements of individual and collective rationality. Whereas an epistemic community might benefit from diversity provided by some stubbornness or biased appraisals of evidence, the rational behavior for each truth-motivated individual agent appears to be to join the best supported research program, method, or theory. This suggests that the rationality of individual agents (understood as each one optimizing their individual pursuit of the truth) is not sufficient for achieving good collective outcomes in research.

Kitcher's model aims to show that individual rationality is not necessary for collective epistemic efficiency either. Like Bourdieu (1975), Kitcher treats scientists as self-interested entrepreneurs in the search for personal prestige. The model suggests that under an appropriate reward allocation scheme, the individual incentives of a population of "sullied" self-interested agents, motivated not by truth as such but by individual glory garnered from finding the truth, drive the population towards the collectively optimal resource allocation.

Suppose that there are two alternative methods for finding out the structure of a Very Important Molecule. Truth, once discovered, is easy to recognize, and the probability of arriving at the truth with a given method is an increasing function of the number of people applying the method. Furthermore, suppose that when the truth is found by using a given method, each individual having used that method has an equal probability of being the one making the discovery and thus getting all the credit. Because of the way in which credit is allocated, choosing between the two alternative methods becomes a strategic decision involving not just the expected epistemic utility of the methods, but also the number of people already using them. Under these conditions, egoistic credit-seeking behavior may help to ensure that some resources are also allocated to the currently less well supported alternatives and thus to maintain crucial epistemic diversity in the community.

In the last chapter of his 1993 book *Advancement of Science,* Kitcher broadens his economics-inspired investigation of the epistemically pure and sullied agents by employing analytical machinery from population biology. This allows him to address questions about whether scientists should cooperate or go solo, how attribution of epistemic authority is done, and further questions related to trust, replication, and influence of scientific tradition on theory choice. We do not go into these arguments in detail here. Many of the topics introduced by Kitcher have been discussed in the models described in the sections that follow. Generally, the discrepancy between the micro and the macro has perhaps been the most lasting result of Kitcher's contribution to social epistemology, as it underscores the importance of studying the social processes of knowledge production (cf. Mayo-Wilson et al. 2011). Hence, epistemic communities can be studied as systems manifesting macro-level properties not reducible to the properties of their members, and the efficiency of such systems appears to be determined by at least the three following kinds of factors:

- The distribution of the cognitive properties of individual agents in the community (cognitive diversity)
- The organizational properties of the community (e.g., its communication structure, reward scheme)
- The nature and difficulty of the problem-solving task faced by the community

As we will see, the key concepts of cognitive diversity, division of cognitive labor, and resource allocation have subsequently been given several interpretations – often leading to confusion and difficulties in combining and comparing results from several models. We now turn to some of the extensions and examination of Kitcher's modeling approach.

Extending Kitcher's Approach

Kitcher's argument rested crucially on the priority rule for apportioning credit. A further development of the resource allocation view is Michael Strevens' (2003) model of the role of reward schemes in resource allocation.

Already Merton (1973) had pointed out that priority disputes have always been a feature of modern science. There are no second prizes in research, only the first person to a discovery gets the recognition and prestige and virtually nothing is left for the runner-ups. But why is credit allocated due to this priority rule, and not based on a scientist's contribution to a research program (MARGE rule), or simply the success of their research program (GOAL rule)? And why is the priority rule applied in a peculiarly rigid way, even when the time difference between discoveries is a matter of days or hours?

Strevens argues that what is special about science as a collective endeavor is that the runner-up's contribution adds nothing to the collective good. Once a result has been discovered, no value to the collective is produced by discovering it again. Strevens uses basic economic principles ("what happens at the margin when the reward scheme changes") to compare the priority rule, MARGE, and GOAL, and shows that the priority rule allocates the comparatively largest proportion resources to the most potential research program: When reward is based neither on work or effort, or even on achievement as such, but on achieving-first, the resulting distribution of research effort over competing alternatives most closely resembles the collectively optimal allocation.

Note, however, that there is a problematic functionalist step in Strevens' explanation: without an additional mechanism, the mere fact of congruence between the individual and the collective good fails to explain why the priority rule *in fact* prevails in actual scientific research. Furthermore, Piimies and Sappinen (mimeo) point out that the analytical approach taken by Kitcher (and Strevens) bears a striking resemblance to a branch of economics called neoclassical economics of innovation. A comparison to this literature reveals that most of Kitcher's model-based arguments are in fact highly sensitive to the selection of initial assumptions. Moreover, Kitcher exacerbates the problem by introducing seemingly ad-hoc modifications to his models "on the fly" – a move strictly forbidden by the modeling methodology in economics. For example, the central result about the connection between credit seeking and beneficial diversity rests crucially on the assumption that the agents are risk-neutral. Such fragility of results with respect to simplifying assumptions dramatically complicates the evaluation of the empirical implications of the models. This does not, by any means, invalidate Kitcher's (or his followers') achievements, but implies that such results should be considered more as theoretical suggestions, not as evidence or proof.

Theory Choice in Epistemic Networks

Another key aspect of research modeled in Kitcher's investigations in the *Advancement* was a scientist's decision of whether or not to borrow results from others given their (observable) rate of hitting on the truth. Recently, the tension between individual theoretical exploration and the need to converge on a solution has been explored by Kevin Zollman (2010, 2013). Using ideas from statistics, economics, and network theory, Zollman models theory choice in terms of so-called bandit problems (see below).[4] Zollman does not study epistemically sullied credit-seeking agents as Kitcher and Strevens do, but the same basic result holds: Individual rationality alone is not sufficient for reliable convergence to the truth on the social level.

Zollman portrays a scientist's choice between competing theories (or methods) as analogical to a learning problem faced by a gambler, who has to select between two slot machines with initially unknown winning rates. Each bandit is postulated to have some objective probability of success, and the payoff from winning from a machine is considered analogous to the payoff received from a successful application of a theory. Furthermore, pulling a machine amounts to getting more information about the truthfulness of a theory by running an experiment. However, because the agent's resources are limited, only a limited number of pulls can be conducted. Hence, they must devise a strategy for pulling the two levers so as to efficiently converge on the more lucrative machine.

The learning challenge presented by such bandit problems is non-trivial because of the trade-off between exploration and exploitation. In the short term, each agent gets the largest payoff by only running the best experiment so far discovered, whereas exploration of other alternatives is typically a precondition for long-term success. Zollman constrains his study to simple myopic agents who always sample only the best alternative and leave exploration to other members of their epistemic network. That is, in Zollman's simulations, in addition to individual experimentation, the agents also receive the experimental results obtained by their network neighbors. These sources of evidence are integrated with the agent's existing knowledge by Bayesian conditionalization.

The most well-known result from Zollman's models is that, perhaps counterintuitively, too much social information can be harmful. In densely connected epistemic networks, misleading evidence obtained in the early stages of the simulated research process can spread quickly through the network, suppress experimentation on alternative methods, and lead the whole community to converge on a suboptimal alternative. That is, it might be that correct hypotheses do not get a fair chance. For example, in the research on peptic ulcer disease, a single early study on the causes of the disease proved so influential in the field that the whole research community was wrongly convinced for a half a century that the illness could not be caused by bacteria (Zollman 2010).

However, densely connected networks perform comparatively better when agents' initial beliefs are strong. What these two findings together suggest is that what is common to epistemically successful communities is *transient diversity*, a proper balance between the diversity of beliefs and consensus. Such a balance allows, at first, sufficient exploration of alternatives, but eventually leads to convergence on truth.

Zollman and his co-authors have extended the bandit approach in subsequent papers (Mayo-Wilson et al. 2011; Zollman 2013). Many of Zollman's simplifying assumptions were also relaxed by Alexander (2013). He modifies Zollman's approach in three ways. First, instead of assuming Bayesian conditionalization in evidence uptake, he studies heuristic agents relying on reinforcement learning (cf. Russell and Norvig 2003, ch. 6). Secondly, the model does not assume a fixed structure of the epistemic network, but instead, network formation is assumed to be based on preferential attachment, where agents form connections to their peers based on the observed success of a peer's approach. Thirdly, Alexander further complicates the learning problem faced by the scientist agents by adding the possibility of theoretical innovation by attaching new arms to the bandit.

Alexander's model suggests that in this more difficult learning task, preferential attachment helps successful theories to spread in the population, and hence a population of connected agents can converge more quickly than individual learners. The spreading of a very good theory (of success probability close to 1) in the network is, however, conditional on the fact that either old theories get sometimes forgotten, or that agents discount old information about theories. Both mechanisms prevent the network from getting locked in into suboptimal belief and communication patterns.

Compared to Kitcher's pioneering work, the simulation methods used by Zollman and Alexander make it possible to study several important properties of epistemic communities not within the reach of the earlier analytical models (such as the dynamics of belief change, heterogeneity, details of the learning heuristics used by agents, and the influence of the communication structure of the community on its epistemic performance). The big advantage of such agent based simulation models (ABMs) is that they allow viewing group problem solving not only as a formal decision problem, but rather as a form of coordinated social behavior arising from the cognitive mechanisms and interpersonal processes involved. Importantly, the models suggest that no one learning heuristic or communication structure of an epistemic community is optimal for all research tasks. This suggests that the computational study of epistemic communities should adopt the more fine-grained strategy of mapping the dependencies between the individual properties of agents, properties of the social system, and the task addressed by the community.

However, computational modeling also has its disadvantages. Compared to analytical models, simulations often come with more parameters, and it is often hard to see what really drives the obtained results. In addition to this opaqueness of the models, the results obtained often hold only in limited parts of the parameter space. For example, the generalizability of Zollman's results have been challenged both on theoretical and empirical grounds. Rosenstock et al. (2017) demonstrate that the negative Zollman effect of connectivity is in fact highly sensitive to the selection of parameter values. In their experimental study of the problem-solving performance of epistemic networks, Mason and Watts (2012) found that – contrary to theoretical expectations – networks efficient in information diffusion outperformed slower ones even in tasks thought to be conducive to phenomena similar to the Zollman effect.[5]

Opinion Dynamics

Since the 1950s, social scientists have developed mathematical models addressing the question of why some social processes lead to polarization of opinions, whereas others lead to the formation of consensus. In the classical paradigm of opinion dynamics, agents have opinions represented by numerical quantities, and the model is used to investigate the way in which different initial profiles of opinions and different social processes of information exchange influence the convergence and clustering of opinions.

Hegselmann and Krause (2002, 2006, 2009) imported this modeling approach to social epistemology by adding to the model the effect of truth seeking: In addition to social information, some agents in the population also revise their opinions based on a signal coming from "the truth" (i.e., by running experiments). The two main analytical results from their model (HK) are (1) the funnel theorem and (2) the leading-the-pack theorem.

The first states that if all agents are truth seekers (even to a modest degree), the population will ultimately reach a consensus that lies arbitrarily close to the truth. The latter theorem concerns the more interesting situation in which only some of the agents aim at the truth while others rely solely on social information (Hegselmann and Krause's somewhat strained interpretation of the notion of division of cognitive labor). According to the theorem, for all initial profiles, even one agent with a truth signal suffices for the convergence of population on truth, on the condition that all non-truth seekers are connected[6] to a truth seeker through a chain of other agents. The extensive set of simulations conducted by the authors examines the parameter spaces of variants of the model in order to assess the generality of the analytical results.

Hegselmann and Krause's results suggest that under appropriate forms of social exchange, even a small minority of truth-guided agents in an epistemic community can lead the whole community to the truth. Riegler and Douven (2009) have recently extended the HK model by allowing the transmitted information to be noisy, and by representing agents' belief states as sets of propositions in a finite language. Like the original HK model, Riegler and Douven's model cannot directly answer the question of how much weight we should assign to the opinions of our colleagues. The model seems, however, to refine Hegselmann and Krause's findings by suggesting conditions for the quality of evidence: only sufficiently good evidence transmitted between agents facilitates convergence to the truth, whereas poor quality evidence can lead to the fragmentation of the population into several disagreeing groups.

Diversity and Collaboration

Although ostensibly about diversity – commonly associated with a division of cognitive labor and the accumulation of community results – most of the models above have surprisingly little to say about epistemic collaboration in research (D'Agostino 2009). Typically they depict a *competition* between individual agents which, under appropriate conditions, leads, as if by an invisible hand, to good collective outcomes. However, in science there is also more profound division of cognitive labor between agents, research groups, and even between scientific disciplines. The ability of a research community to solve problems that exceed the capacities of any individual actor or group is based on recursively dividing problems into smaller sub-problems solvable by finite cognitive actors, and subsequently piecing together the sub-solutions to answer the original complex question. Central aspects of cognitive diversity involved in such a *distributed problem solving process* are not represented in any of the models above: there is no representation of (a) variation in research heuristics or (b) specialization on a topic or question, which would differentiate an agent from the others.

Both heterogeneous heuristics and specialization are aspects of what we call *cognitive diversity*: due to different backgrounds, training, and talent, researchers might have different reasoning styles and, hence, different agents could contribute differentially to various aspects of the research topic. Here we discuss two recent contributions to the study of cognitive diversity and its consequences to collective problem-solving.

Michael Weisberg and Ryan Muldoon (2009) put forward a model that depicts research in a scientific field as a population of agents foraging on an epistemic landscape. Different patches of the landscape correspond to different research approaches, and the height of a patch represents the epistemic significance of that approach. That is, within each scientific field, different combinations of questions, available background theories, and methods have different potential to uncover the significant truths in the domain of research.

What makes this a model of cognitive diversity is that there are three different kinds of agents in the population: controls, followers and mavericks. Each kind of agent has a different way of doing research. Followers tend to adopt approaches already examined by others, mavericks avoid them, and controls are insensitive to social information and rely solely on their own information about how to improve their epistemic lot. Weisberg and Muldoon's simulations suggest (once again) the intuitively plausible result that diversity is good for a scientific community. Their most surprising finding is, however, that the maverick social learning strategy which uses information about others to *avoid* doing the same as others is the most effective way to promote the progress of research on a scientific field.

By importing a fitness-landscape based modeling approach from ecology, Weisberg and Muldoon introduced a new way of implementing cognitive diversity in a simulation model. However, the reliability and generality of their results have been called into question. The problem is, yet again, in the non-robustness of the results. Critics have shown that replacing some of the assumptions made by Weisberg and Muldoon by other, just as plausible, ones, different and even contradictory results regarding the role of cognitive diversity can easily be derived (Alexander et al. 2015; Thoma 2015; Poyhonen 2016).

An influential approach to modeling cognitive diversity, which has received attention in economics, organization science, and recently also in philosophy, was introduced by Lu Hong and Scott Page (2001; 2004). Building on Newell and Simon's (1972) view of problem-solving as heuristic search, Hong and Page portray diversity as consisting of two components: each agent having their particular (a) way of representing the problem ("perspective") and a (b) set of rules for devising new problem solutions from earlier ones ("heuristic").

In Hong and Page (2001), the problem faced by a community of problem-solvers is represented as that of constructing a bitstring – a sequence of ones and zeros – associated with the highest possible payoff. The bitstring in effect represents a structured solution to a complex problem, each bit standing for a possible solution to a subproblem. Each agent is characterized by a set of heuristics for flipping the states of the bits in the string, and an agent's individual performance level is the expected value of the value function at the local optimum at which the individual's search is drawn to a halt. Collaborative group performance, in turn, is determined by the value of the configuration reached by having the agents sequentially apply their own heuristics to manipulate the same binary string. Once an agent cannot improve on a solution, the turn is given to the next agent employing a different bit-flipping rule.

In such a setting, the diverse perspectives and heuristics used by agents can lead to globally optimal collective solutions, although no individual agent can reach the optimum on their own. Hong and Page use the model to argue that in group problem solving, adding a new problem solver to the group often does not have a diminishing marginal utility for the collective: Depending on the order in which agents' heuristics are applied to the problem, it can even be so that the addition of the last agent has the largest marginal contribution to collective performance, if the last agent happens to contribute the missing piece to the puzzle by applying a novel heuristic that helps the population to escape a local optimum.

Using a similar model, Hong and Page (2004) derived several additional results about the usefulness of cognitive diversity in problem solving. They show that under quite general conditions, a diverse group of randomly chosen agents can outperform a homogenous group consisting of individually best-performing problem solvers. The diversity-trumps-ability theorem suggests, roughly, that to maximize problem-solving efficiency, a company should rather hire 20 random problem solvers than 20 of the best performers, who, being the best and hence equally good, would have to be cognitively similar. The result also suggests a conjecture regarding science policy: Perhaps the current emphasis on individual "excellence" in science funding should be tempered with policies aimed at maintaining diversity?

Conclusion: What Can Philosophers Learn from Models?

So what, in the end, have models of collective knowing thus far achieved and what are the future prospects for the field? Whereas much, even most of, science has become fundamentally model-based, in philosophy modeling methodology is still relatively new. Consequently, work in the field is sometimes characterized by the lack of a clear understanding about the goals and the added value of modeling in general, and of common agreed-upon methodological constraints.

What makes a good model? First of all, worthwhile model results should not be immediately obvious logical consequences of the used assumptions. Models, both analytical and simulation, are externally supported arguments, and the model as such does not do any work, if seeing the assumptions already suffices to make the conclusions obvious (Kuorikoski and Pöyhönen unpublished). With hindsight, some of the early analytical models of science suffer from such theoretical sterility (see, for example, Goldman and Shaked 1991). Second, a model should be theoretically well-motivated in that it should be built on clear theoretical ideas, from which further implications are drawn with the help of the model.[7] In social epistemology, however, much of the modeling work appears to be driven by the modeling framework itself. Model templates are often borrowed from elsewhere and simply given a new (not necessarily very convincing) interpretation in terms of epistemic properties of social systems.

Thirdly, models should be reliable in the sense that the results depend only on the empirically interpretable substantial assumptions and do so in a way which makes the empirical interpretation of the results as straightforward as possible. As we have already pointed out, many of the models in social epistemology are problematic in these respects, because the central results often only hold in a very restricted part of the parameter space or under very specific technical assumptions. If the key results are not robust with respect to essentially arbitrary modeling assumptions, which are made only for the sake of making the model "work," and which lack a clear empirical interpretation, then inferring from the demonstrated results to real epistemic social systems amounts to little more than guesswork. Running models and simulations can be seen as a new exciting method for philosophers, but we have a lot to learn from scientists engaged in modeling.

Nevertheless, we firmly believe modeling to be a valuable methodology for thinking about epistemically well-designed social systems. Theorizing in natural language about "emergent" properties that arise from complex organization and interaction is extremely limiting and prone to error – especially since when faced with structurally and interactionally complex systems, our pre-theoretic intuitions often tend to become increasingly unreliable. Modeling is in many cases a prerequisite for having theoretical understanding about the dynamics of collective cognitive systems: convergence, equilibria, and the micro-mechanisms involved. Working with models is an invaluable part of theorizing and analysis, because it forces us to make ideas precise, and allows the transparent examination of their coherence. ABMs in particular make it possible to examine complex scenarios where our intuitions and reasoning falter. The combination of a large group of heterogeneous agents following simple rules often leads to results that are impossible to anticipate by using only analytical or "conceptual" methods.

One possible strategy for improving the abstract models in social epistemology would be to calibrate them with empirical data. However, relevant data about properties of research fields, problems, and research strategies employed by scientists is not readily available – and often it is not even clear how such evidence should be obtained. So while empirical calibration is a laudable aim, we are not there yet. However, we see the models reviewed here as serving a different purpose. Rather than being high-fidelity representations of particular target systems "out there," they function as proof-of-concept exercises about the possible mechanisms underlying collective intelligence. They are theoretical arguments, not virtual experiments.

The most promising way forward in the modeling work in social epistemology is to aim at a better integration with the existing modeling traditions in neighboring fields. As things stand, the existing philosophical models are often isolated from empirical literature as well as from each other, and do not form a methodologically coherent progressive research program. However, the research literature on human problem solving, both in individual and social contexts, is extensive, and various research fields such as cognitive science, sociology of science, social psychology, and economics have contributed to explaining both the failures as well as the surprising strengths of problem-solving groups. Furthermore, there is a long-standing modeling tradition on collective heuristic problem solving in management studies and organization science. If we take Kitcher's original definition of social epistemology seriously, there should not be any reason for social epistemologists to ignore such work, nor should there be any discontinuity between philosophical social epistemology and the empirical social science of group problem solving.

Notes

1 Following a usage common in the modeling literature, we understand an epistemic community as a social system consisting of producers of knowledge. In a broader sense of the notion (cf. Longino 1990), epistemic communities can be seen to encompass also the consumer side, i.e. those consulting the results.
2 For alternative ways of organizing the material, see Weisberg (2010) and Muldoon (2013).
3 In this chapter, most of the attention is on epistemic communities in science. One might object to this by pointing out that the scope of social epistemology is broader than science. We focus on scientific problem solving for the following reasons: First, science has been the main target of much of the work that we review. Secondly, scientific problem solving is a particularly challenging example: it is often not routine-like, nor is the social process of research hierarchically organized. Instead, the questions addressed by scientists are often open-ended, and the process is largely self-organized.
4 Zollman's model generalizes a framework proposed in economics by Bala and Goyal (1998).
5 For experimental results providing some support for the Zollman effect, see Mason et al. 2008. Open questions regarding the effect do not compromise the more general exploration-exploitation trade-off observed already by March (1991) and Lazer and Friedman (2007): A well-functioning epistemic community must strike a balance between exploration and exploitation. Whereas efficient dissemination and uptake of information between the nodes of a network improves the behavior of the epistemic community in the short term, allocating sufficient resources to exploratory activities is necessary for long term success.
6 Connectedness here means that the opinions are not too far from each other and, consequently, communication between the two agents remains possible.
7 An elegant example of such model building can be found in Hegselmann and Will (2013).

Acknowledgements

Thanks to David Henderson for his helpful comments and suggestions on the manuscript. The research for this chapter has been funded by The Academy of Finland and the University of Helsinki.

References

Alexander, J. (2013). Preferential attachment and the search for successful theories. *Philosophy of Science*, 80(5), pp. 769–782.
Alexander, J., Himmelreich, J. and Thompson, C. (2015). Epistemic landscapes, optimal search, and the division of cognitive labor. *Philosophy of Science*, 82(3), pp. 424–453.
Bala, V. and Goyal, S. (1998). Learning from neighbours. *Review of Economic Studies*, 65, pp. 565–621.
Bourdieu, P. 1975. The specificity of the scientific field and the social conditions of the progress of reason. *Social Science Information*, 14, pp. 19–47.
D'Agostino, F. (2009). From the organization to the division of cognitive labor. *Politics, Philosophy & Economics*, 8(1), pp. 101–129.
Goldman, A. and Shaked, M. (1991). An economic model of scientific activity and truth acquisition. *Philosophical Studies*, 63, pp. 31–55.
Hegselmann, R. and Krause, U. (2002). Opinion dynamics and bounded confidence models, analysis and simulation. *Journal of Artificial Societies and Social Simulation*, 5(3).
Hegselmann, R. and Krause, U. (2006). Truth and cognitive division of labour. First steps towards a computer aided social epistemology. *Journal of Artificial Societies and Social Simulation*, 9(3).
Hegselmann, R. and Krause, U. (2009). Deliberative exchange, truth, and cognitive division of labour: A low-resolution modeling approach. *Episteme*, 6(2), pp. 130–144.

Hegselmann R. and Will, O. (2013). From small groups to large societies: How to construct a simulator? *Biological Theory*, 8(2), pp. 185–194.

Hong, L. and Page, S. (2001). Problem solving by heterogeneous agents. *Journal of Economic Theory*, 97, pp. 123–163.

Hong, L. and Page, S. (2004). Groups of diverse problem solvers can outperform groups of high-ability problem solvers. *PNAS*, 101(46), pp. 16385–16389.

Kitcher, P. (1990). The division of cognitive labor. *The Journal of Philosophy*, 87(1), pp 5–22.

Kuorikoski, J. and Pöyhönen, S. (unpublished). Simulations as virtual experiments: An inferentialist approach. In review.

Lazer, D. and Friedman, A. (2007). The network structure of exploration and exploitation. *Administrative Science Quarterly*, 52, pp. 667–694.

Longino, H. (1990). *Science as Social Knowledge*. Princeton: Princeton University Press.

March, J. (1991). Exploration and exploitation in organizational learning. *Organization Science*, 2(1), pp. 71–87.

Mason, W. A., Jones, A., and Goldstone, R. L. (2008). Propagation of innovations in networked groups. *Journal of Experimental Psychology: General*, 137(3), 422com.

Mason, W. and Watts, D. (2012). Collaborative learning in networks. *PNAS*, 109(3), pp. 764–769.

Mayo-Wilson, C., Zollman, K. and Danks, D. (2011). The independence thesis: When individual and social epistemology diverge. *Philosophy of Science*, 78(4), pp. 653–677.

Merton, R. (1973). *The Sociology of Science. Theoretical and Empirical Investigations*. Chicago: The University of Chicago Press.

Muldoon, R. (2013). Diversity and the division of cognitive labor. *Philosophy Compass*, 8, pp. 117–125.

Newell, A. and Simon, H. (1972). *Human Problem Solving*. Englewood Cliffs, NJ: Prentice Hall.

Piimies, J-P and Sappinen, J. (mimeo). The advancement of science by means of economics. Unpublished manuscript.

Riegler, A. and Douven, I. (2009). Extending the Hegselmann–Krause model III: From single beliefs to complex belief states. *Episteme*, 6(2), pp. 145–163.

Rosenstock, S., Bruner, J. and O'Connor, C. (2017). In epistemic communities, is less really more? *Philosophy of Science*, 84(2), 234–252.

Russell, S. J. and Norvig, P. (2003). *Artificial Intelligence: A Modern Approach* (2nd ed.). London: Prentice Hall/Pearson Education.

Strevens, M. (2003). The role of the priority rule in science. *The Journal of Philosophy*, 100(2), pp. 55–79.

Sunstein, C. (2006). Deliberating groups versus prediction markets (or Hayek's challenge to Habermas). *Episteme*, 3(3), pp. 192–213.

Surowiecki, J. (2005). *The Wisdom of the Crowds*. London: Abacus.

Thoma, J. (2015). The epistemic division of labor revisited. *Philosophy of Science*, 82(3), pp. 454–472.

Weisberg, M. (2010). New Approaches to the Division of Cognitive Labor. In: P. Magnus and J. Busch, eds., *New Waves in Philosophy of Science*. London: Palgrave Macmillan, pp. 250–269.

Weisberg, M. and Muldoon, R. (2009). Epistemic landscapes and the division of cognitive labor. *Philosophy of science*, 76(2), pp. 225–252.

Zollman, K. (2010). The epistemic benefit of transient diversity. *Erkenntnis*, 72(1), pp. 17–35.

Zollman, K. (2013). Network epistemology: Communication in epistemic communities. *Philosophy Compass*, 8, pp. 15–27.

25

FEMINIST PHILOSOPHY OF SCIENCE AS SOCIAL EPISTEMOLOGY

Sharon Crasnow

Introduction

Feminist philosophy of science is social epistemology in that it insists on the relevance of gender to scientific knowledge and considers the effects of social values on the production of knowledge. There are at least three ways in which this concern with the social nature of scientific knowledge shows up in feminist philosophy of science. First, feminist philosophies of science do not conceive of the knower as an abstracted, decontextualized individual, but rather as embedded within a community and able to know only insofar as they are members of that community. As Lynn Hankinson Nelson puts it,

> What I know depends inextricably on what *we* know, for some we. My claims to know are subject to community criteria, public notions of what constitutes evidence, so that, in an important sense, I *can* know only what *we* know, for some we.
>
> *(Nelson 1990: 255)*

As a consequence, questions of the interrelations among knowers and their effect on knowledge production are salient to understanding scientific knowledge. I refer to this as the *internal* aspect of social epistemology. Second, the examination of episodes from the history of science shows that what theories are accepted, what is considered to be relevant evidence, and what questions are thought worth asking are dependent on features of the political, social, and cultural environment in which knowledge is produced. This is a lesson feminists take from the naturalistic turn in philosophy of science in the second half of the twentieth century. Scientific knowledge can be described as *evidentially* social in this sense. A third way in which philosophy of science can be seen as social epistemology has to do with the organization of the research community, its institutions, and the broader political, social, and cultural context in which the research takes place. This last is the *organizational* aspect of social epistemology. Feminist philosophies of science have considered the social nature of knowledge in each of these aspects.

Sandra Harding's (1986) classification of feminist epistemologies into feminist empiricism, feminist standpoint theory, and feminist postmodernism has come to be a standard starting point for discussing feminist philosophy of science.[1] As Kristen Intemann points out, it is probably no longer fully adequate to the way feminist epistemology has developed subsequently (Intemann 2010: 793–4), nonetheless, I will use it as a way of framing the discussion. I examine two feminist empiricist approaches: Helen Longino's contextual empiricism and several approaches that I call feminist empiricist holism. The third account I consider is standpoint theory. The characterizations of these accounts are brief and none is complete. I focus primarily on features that highlight aspects of feminist philosophy of science that mark it as a social epistemology – the extent to which they display the internal evidential, and organizational aspects of social epistemology. I conclude by arguing that feminist philosophy of science has been focused primarily on the social nature of knowledge and given less attention to the social nature of the knower and knowledge communities. I offer some recommendations for addressing this weakness.

Longino's Contextual Empiricism

In her 1990, *Science as Social Knowledge: Values and Objectivity in Science*, Helen Longino argues that what counts as evidence is at least partially determined by the background assumptions of the scientific community in the context of research. This argument depends on the rejection of the possibility of an independent observation language that serves as evidence – an idea that anchored the rational reconstructionist project of the early twentieth century. Her argument is based on conclusions drawn by Thomas Kuhn from the examination of historical cases. Kuhn describes the empirical evidence that researchers use to support their theories as interpreted through the background assumptions and beliefs that these researchers come to the project with. These beliefs are in turn a result of their training as scientists, but also depend on the elements of the social context in which their research takes place (which would affect that training). This analysis leads Kuhn to conclude that observation is theory-laden. Longino follows Kuhn in understanding observation as theory-laden and gives an account of evidence in which what observations count as evidence is dependent on the background assumptions shaped by the historical, political, social, and cultural context of the research. This is so in two ways. First, the context mediates the relation between evidence and hypothesis and so background assumptions contribute to theory acceptance. Second, the social context of the research needs to ensure that the assumptions that play a role in identifying evidence are not idiosyncratic. She calls this view contextual empiricism: "It is empiricist in treating experience as the basis of knowledge claims in the sciences. It is contextual in its insistence on the relevance of context ... to the construction of knowledge" (Longino 1990: 219).

Among the background assumptions that are relevant to the determination of evidence are values. Longino distinguishes two types of values. Constitutive values that are generated by the goals of science and that specify what counts as good scientific practice. Contextual values stem from the political, social, and cultural environment in which the research takes place. Longino's distinction between constitutive and contextual values differs from a distinction that is often made between epistemic and non-epistemic values. Epistemic values guide science as a search for truth. Non-epistemic values are social, political, and cultural values. While they may affect the choice of research questions, for example, they are not to play a role in the justification of hypotheses. This is the ideal of science as value free, where "value" refers to non-epistemic values.

Longino is a pluralist about the goals of science (see particularly Longino 2013); truth may not be the only goal. The constitutive/contextual distinction leaves open the possibility that shared community standards might evolve relative to alternate goals. While she identifies one broad aim of science – to give good explanations – she points out that there are a variety of ways in which that goal could be achieved depending on how "good explanation" is understood.

This is perhaps clearer if we contrast her discussion of constitutive values with Kuhn's discussion of epistemic virtues – virtues that exemplify epistemic values. Kuhn settled on five such epistemic virtues, "not because they are exhaustive, but because they are individually important and collectively sufficiently varied to indicate what is at stake" (Kuhn 1977: 321). His five are accuracy, internal and external consistency, broad scope, simplicity, and fruitfulness. Kuhn notes that such virtues often cannot all be maximized at the same time and so scientists make trade-offs among them. In doing so, they make pragmatic decisions guided by non-epistemic values.

Longino agrees with Kuhn about such trade-offs, since the virtues of theories reflect constitutive values – the shared standards – of the scientific community, her assessment of the role context plays differs from Kuhn's.

> The particular weighting and interpretation assigned these standards will vary in different social and historical contexts as a function of cognitive and social needs.... [I]t is the existence of standards that makes the individual member of a scientific community responsible to something besides themselves.
>
> *(Longino 1990: 77)*

For Longino the standards can change, not just the different weightings that such standards receive. She considers, for example, some alternate constitutive values that she takes from work done by feminist scholars: "empirical adequacy (a.k.a. accuracy),... novelty, ontological heterogeneity, complexity of interaction, applicability to human needs, diffusion or decentralization of power" (Longino 1995: 385). Although there is some overlap with the previous list of virtues (for example, empirical adequacy or accuracy, reflecting her empiricist commitment to experience as "the least defeasible legitimator of knowledge claims") her consideration of alternative constitutive values is a departure from the spirit of Kuhn's approach (Longino 1995: 384).

Thus, for Longino, scientific knowledge is social knowledge both in the role that the community's background assumptions play (evidentially social) and in the ways in which those background assumptions are mediated by the community in order to mitigate the subjectivity that such background assumptions might produce (organizationally social).

> What controls the role of background assumptions is interaction among scientists, interaction consisting in criticism of assumptions involved in observation, of assumptions involved in reasoning, of assumptions involved in thinking a given hypothesis plausible, of assumptions involved in the application of particular methods to the solution of particular problems.
>
> *(Longino 1995: 384)*

It is through the controls on background assumptions that Longino addresses the question of the objectivity of science as social knowledge. She proposes that the communities in which such critical interactions take place must be organized along particular lines in order to be more objective – something that she argues is only achieved by degrees. She offers four criteria that the scientific community should meet:

1　*Venues.* There must be publicly recognized forums for the criticism of evidence, of methods, and of assumptions and reasoning;
2　*Uptake.* There must be uptake of criticism;
3　*Public Standards.* There must be publicly recognized standards by reference to which theories, hypotheses, and observational practices are evaluated and by appeal to which criticism is made relevant to the goals of the inquiring community;
4　*Tempered Equality.* Communities must be characterized by equality of intellectual authority.[2]

While the first and third seem primarily focused on the organization of the community, arguably the second and fourth of these requirements say something about the internal structure of the knowledge community. For example, factors that affect uptake of criticism may have to do with the internal social relations and the distribution of power within the community. The testimony of some members of the community may not get uptake as a result of a credibility deficit due to their position within the social structure (Fricker 2007: 17). The final requirement, tempered equality of intellectual authority, also speaks at least obliquely to the internal social relations within a group, attempting to address the question of differential power among the individuals within that group.

Feminist Empiricist Holism

While Longino's contextual empiricism is a holist approach in that observations are theory-laden, evidence depends on background assumptions, and she does not make a sharp fact/value distinction, it differs from the empiricist holistic approaches primarily in the way values are treated. The four requirements that Longino offers for the organization of scientific communities are intended to mitigate any idiosyncratic values that could distort science. Other feminist empiricist holisms treat values as part of an interconnected system of beliefs that is subject to empirical constraint. Values are thus empirical as part of a system that answers to empirical evidence. Miriam Solomon makes this point in a discussion of varieties of feminist empiricism. "Lynn Hankinson Nelson (1990) was the first feminist empiricist to suggest that values be considered along with scientific theories for the empirical success of the aggregate" (Solomon 2012: 441).

Nelson's account is a naturalized philosophy of science explicitly derived from her reading of Quine.[3] By "naturalized" she means it is a philosophy of science that pays attention to the history and contemporary practice of science, it is grounded in sciences relevant to knowing, e.g., psychology, cognitive science, biology, and sociology, and it treats science as an extension of everyday reasoning. A naturalized philosophy of science recognizes that the actual practice of science incorporates political, social, and cultural values and they function as part of the interconnected system of beliefs that is subject to empirical constraint. Nelson's empiricism differs from traditional empiricism in that evidence includes observations that are theory-laden, but also "a body of accepted standards and theory" informed by social beliefs and values (Nelson 1997: 100). The account is empiricist in that experience serves as evidence and it is also holist in that experience is mediated by current theories and theories, including those informed by social values and beliefs, consequently serve as evidence as well.

Nelson's account works as social epistemology in several ways. Individuals, both scientists and non-scientists are always understood as part of a knowing community.

> What I know depends inextricably on what *we* know, for some we. My claims to know are subject to community criteria, public notions of what constitutes evidence, so that, in an important sense, I *can* know only what *we* know, for some we.
>
> *(Nelson 1990: 255)*

This addresses the internal aspect of social epistemology, but only minimally since it says nothing about the nature of the relationship of the individual to the community. While Nelson identifies the community as the knower, she does so primarily to focus on the knowledge the community shares and in what way that works as evidence along with experience, she is primarily focused on the evidential aspect of social knowledge production.

Nelson also does not address the structure of scientific communities. Consequently, of the three ways in which knowledge is social, her account only deals with the second.[4] The "social" nature of Nelson's epistemology rests primarily on the idea that what we know is known by a community and that the values, beliefs, currently accepted theories, and methodological commitments of that community are all part of both the evidence and what is adjudicated by experience.

Elizabeth Anderson offers another example of a holist approach. She also treats values as subject to empirical constraint although she only claims that this is so for at least *some* values. The example she offers is the way emotions are evidence for what matters to us – what we value. For example we value California redwoods because we experience awe when we see them. When values are of this sort, they can serve as evidence in her view. She illustrates this through a case study of research – Abigail Stewart et al.'s research on divorce (Anderson 2004).

Anderson begins by noting that many of the concepts that are used in research on divorce are "thick" concepts in the sense that they include evaluative aspects. "Divorce" and "family" are examples. For example, "divorce" might be understood as the breaking apart of a family, "family" understood as a unit living under one roof made up of a heterosexual couple and children. These are indeed readings that are implicit in previous research on divorce. Stewart's research team replaces these values with explicitly feminist values understanding divorce as a transition rather than a one time traumatic event. Family is treated as continuing to exist but in a new form.

Anderson argues that Stewart's assumptions allow for greater empirical scrutiny because they allow researchers to cast the net more broadly for empirical evidence. Previous research on divorce targeted negative experience as evidence because of the way divorce was understood. By conceiving of divorce as a transition Stewart's team broadened their understanding of what counted as evidence and consequently they were able to see both reports of positive and negative experiences as relevant.

Holistic accounts answer to a question not addressed by contextual empiricism. Longino addresses the question of the appropriate social organization of knowledge communities through a commitment to democratic, egalitarian principles. However, her inclusiveness suggests the possibility that even values that are clearly problematic should be included – that all voices should be listened to given that it is through the participation of those with differing perspectives and experiences that background assumptions that include value judgments that shape evidence can be unearthed and evaluated. But as Intemann points out, "This is worrisome, as it suggests that the ideal scientific community is one where all values and interests are represented, including those that are potentially problematic" (Intemann 2010: 791). Feminist empiricist holists address this problem by arguing that values can be adjudicated *empirically*. If values inform an empirically inadequate belief system they should be rejected. Clough and Loges argue, for example, that racist and sexist beliefs are shown to be inadequate in this way (Clough and Loges 2008). In doing so they appeal to Clough's holism based in a Davidsonian philosophy of language (Clough 2003).

It is not clear how well a holistic feminist empiricism can eliminate problematic values however. Miriam Solomon (2012) has argued that while the holist web of belief metaphor offers a way of conceiving of empirical constraint on the entire network of beliefs, it is not clear how it provides a means of picking out particular beliefs (values) as being problematic if the network fails to be empirically successful. Holism stresses the evidential role of the social. That emphasis leaves questions about both the effect of the internal relations within the community of knowers and the questions about the proper organization of the community answered inadequately.

Standpoint Theory

On Harding's original characterization, feminist standpoint approaches to philosophy of science provide an alternative to feminist empiricism. Recent accounts of standpoint theory address some of the concerns that were originally raised to the approach – for example, that it failed to acknowledge diversity among women by treating all women as have one "standpoint" (an issue that I will return to in the final section). (Crasnow 2013, 2014; Intemann 2010; Wylie 2003). Many of these newer accounts highlight shared features of standpoint theory and feminist empiricism. Intemann suggests that this merging of approaches might yield a hybrid – "feminist standpoint empiricism" (Intemann 2010: 794).

Although there are shared features, I focus on elements that are common among standpoint approaches. All endorse some version of the following three theses: the situated knowledge thesis, the thesis of epistemic privilege, and what I refer to as "the achievement thesis" (Crasnow 2013, 2014). The thesis of situated knowledge is that knowledge is *for* and *by* socially situated knowers and so is always *local*. The claim is that needs (including what people need to know) and interests depend at least to some degree on the distribution of power within a society and so where one is socially situated is epistemically relevant both in terms of what one wants to know, what one is able to know, and what knowledge would count as addressing those needs and interests. The thesis of epistemic privilege is that there are some social locations that offer epistemic advantage – that is, it is possible to know things as a result of one's social location that may not be accessible to those at another social location for a variety of reasons. Specifically, those who are marginalized or oppressed – those who do not hold power – have access to experiences and insights that are not accessible to those in power. The understanding of this thesis should be tempered through the third thesis: the achievement thesis. Social location does not confer epistemic advantage automatically but epistemic advantage is achieved. This is done through "studying up" and requires mapping "the practices of power, the ways the dominant institutions and their conceptual frameworks create and maintain oppressive social relations" (Harding 2004: 31). All three theses are social, all depend on the social location of the knowers and the last also depends on an understanding of the power dynamic that produces and sustains social location.

Standpoint theory differs from other approaches in that it deals directly with an aspect of knowledge that they do not directly address – power. It is the distribution of power in society that creates the circumstances under which standpoint becomes a tool for knowledge – social location is shaped by socially salient characteristics such as gender and race. These are characteristics that also track the distribution of power within society. The differential distribution of power affects interests (what is valued) and thus results in differences in knowledge. As Dorothy Smith puts it, "From the point of view of 'women's place' the values assigned to different aspects of the world are changed" (1974: 7).

Patricia Hill Collins (1986) describes the researcher who is marginalized as having "double-vision" – she is both an insider and outsider and as such may recognize that many of the concepts and procedures adopted by the discipline are not able to capture the lived experience of those who are being studied. The knowledge produced cannot be knowledge "for them" – it is not appropriate to their interests. Starting from the lives of women – starting research from that social location – alters the knowledge produced.

Some examples of how standpoint works to change science can be seen in feminist social science. Smith presents research that starts with interviewing women about their daily routine – paying attention to their lived reality. The work that they do is both shaped by, and sustains, the economic structure and institutions in which they live (Smith 1987). When their children come home from school is not their choice, for instance. This reality contrasts with the way labor is conceived of within those structures however. The tension between sociologists' accounts of labor and the actual working lives of women creates a kind of "fault line" that calls for reconceiving labor so that it takes into account domestic labor. The political scientist Pamela Paxton challenges standard accounts of the spread of democracy since the eighteenth century, noting that they depend on understanding universal suffrage as universal male suffrage (either explicitly or implicitly) (Paxton 2000). She sees this, in part, because she is an insider/outsider. Lin Farley comes up with the term "sexual harassment" to describe experience reported by women in consciousness raising (Farley 1978). This concept was grounded in the lived experience of women as identified and described in consciousness-raising groups. These are the sorts of changes in the concepts through which inquiry is conducted that the critical stance of feminist standpoint theory uncovers.

Harding argues that standpoint theory carries with it an ideal of "strong objectivity". Strong objectivity requires that the processes through which knowledge is produced be subject to the same scrutiny as the knowledge itself. This means that the underlying assumptions made in the dominant scientific community need to be identified and examined. Those who are members of the dominant community are less likely to be able to do so, since their positions are secured in part through adopting these very assumptions. Diversity alone will not uncover these assumptions according to Harding. Diversity may bring different perspectives to the table, but it does not bring insights of the oppressed specifically and so will not address their needs. The strong objectivity associated with standpoint theory "demands interrogation of just which cultural commitments can advance growth of the kinds of knowledge a particular community desires" (Harding 2015: 36).

Intemann sees this as one of the main remaining differences between feminist empiricism and feminist standpoint theory (Intemann 2010: 793). If we consider the two approaches from the perspective of the evidential and organization aspect of social epistemology, this difference is also apparent. For contextual empiricism, objectivity is a matter of form – the organization of the community. For Harding, decisions about the organization of science communities have value content and consequently they affect evidential choices as well. My characterization of feminist empiricism holism has it faring somewhat better on this dimension since values are adjudicated empirically, but whether this adjudication is robust enough to distinguish desirable from undesirable values is questionable.

From the discussion of standpoint theory thus far, it is clear that it is sensitive to socio-political factors as they affect knowledge. The organization (distribution of power) within a society affects knowledge production. Normatively standpoint recommends "studying up" – both in the sense of starting from the lives of women and in the sense of working to achieve standpoint. What evidence is relevant to knowledge production depends on who the knowledge is for, the interests served, and the achievement of standpoint – all social factors. The internal dimension of social epistemology is also relevant in that differential distribution of power is a factor in knowledge production. But another internal feature – social identity – is not fully addressed. Social identities are complex intersections of race, gender, sexuality, ethnicity, ability, and class – all of which interact in a variety of ways depending on context. It is unclear how this complexity fits with the idea of knowledge communities, how an account of communities should incorporate it, or how stable such communities are given that complexity.

Neither version of feminist empiricism nor current versions of standpoint theory address either how knowledge communities are formed or the potential fragmentation of the community of knowers through their multiple identities. To address this question requires a more adequate account of the relations among the individuals who make up those communities.

Extending Feminist Epistemology: Individuals and Communities of Knowers

Some clues to addressing the problem of knowing communities and the individuals that comprise them appear in the literature on feminist standpoint theory. Gaile Pohlhaus (2002) suggests that there are distinctive features of feminist standpoint theory that need to be more fully developed. To do so, she first critiques standpoint's metaphor of social location, arguing that it individualizes the knower, since only one individual can occupy a place at one time. She argues that standpoint theory needs a more social conception of knowers – one that more clearly identifies the knower as a community and acknowledges the political nature of such communities. Where this comes into play can be seen particularly in relation to standpoint's achievement thesis.

Standpoint is described most frequently as achieved by struggling *against* a dominant understanding but political struggle includes both struggling against and struggling *with*. "To struggle-with would involve building relations with others by which we may come to know the world and understand one another, that is the project of building knowing communities" (Pohlhaus 2002: 292). Pohlhaus is calling for a better account of the political aspect of standing, an element that appears in the original Marxist sources of standpoint theory but drops out of versions that appear in feminist philosophies of science. The idea of struggling with aligns with the achievement thesis and would make the idea of achievement clearer. The building of communities involves identifying, forging, and/or negotiating shared interests – fundamentally political activities. The role of social values in knowledge, both their evidential role and their organizational role, requires these community building activities.

There is another way in which the social location metaphor is misleading. A spatial location is a fixed point, but social locations are not. They may change since individuals have different social identities in different contexts. This speaks to an early criticism of feminist standpoint theory – that feminist standpoint or women's standpoint seemed to suggest a universal or essential notion of "woman" – attributing characteristics to all women in the same way that early feminist critique of science identified bias that came from attributing the characteristics of some males (those in the dominant group) to all humans. Standpoint theory seemed to threaten to ignore or "disappear" race, ethnicity, sexual orientation, gender identity, class, and ability differences among women and the complex interactions between various forms of oppression associated with membership in these groups. On the other hand, to acknowledge these many identities as all possible locations for standpoints seems to impossibly fragment knowing communities.

Pohlhaus calls attention to struggling with as a way of thinking about standpoint that addresses both of these issues. Political communities are built on shared interests. Building such a community requires acknowledging diversity and working to find those shared interests. This is coalition building. A feminist standpoint is not a perspective derived from a social location – this mistaken view is what the achievement thesis is intended to correct. The struggling with others to find the sources of oppression brings about standpoint. This struggling with requires identifying with at least some interests of others and forming a knowing community. It does not result from some essential feature of womanhood, or some other category recognized in others. The shared interests are forged or even negotiated in order to form the community, the political group, the coalition.

While I have used standpoint theory as the path to make the point, the more general claim is that the least explored aspects of feminist philosophy of science as a social epistemology are the internal relations among individuals that make up knowledge communities. This is true in all three approaches examined here. How the individual is social – self-identified and other-identified both with and through social categories – and how individuals make up communities – specifically knowledge communities – are the key elements that are in need of exploration. The feminist philosophies of science that I have examined all acknowledge the knower as a community, but communities are composed of individuals who are, in turn, identified through social categories that affect the degree to which they have power in the community. Their identities are myriad and complex, which allows various different alliances – different communities within the broader social context in which they find themselves.

Feminist philosophies of science have focused primarily on what I have called the evidential and organization social aspects of knowledge. These features have more to do with *what* is known and in some ways it is not surprising that this is where the focus has been. Feminist philosophy of science first came of age during the science wars of the 1990s and the fear that claims that the socio-political nature of knowledge implied the demise of ideal of science as objective knowledge drove much of the work discussed here. The value-free ideal is no longer widely accepted and with its demise the discussion has turned from questions of whether social values play a role in science to how they play a role. Most of this discussion focuses on the effect of values on knowledge and less on the sources of those values within scientific communities. Addressing this issue requires addressing the question of the community of knowers more fully.

Notes

1 Feminist epistemology and feminist philosophy of science are often treated as synonymous.
2 Versions of these appear in (Longino 1993, 1995, 1997, 2002). The list here is adapted from (Longino 2002: 129–32).
3 Other accounts use Davidson (Clough 2003) and Sellars (Sobstyl 2004) to develop versions of feminist empiricist holism.
4 She does discuss a dissenting community in examining a feminist critique of androcentric assumptions in one of her case studies (Nelson 1997: 107–14) but in doing so makes no normative claims about the need for dissenting voices or other features that might have to do with the structure of a scientific community.

References

Anderson, E. (2004) Uses of Values Judgments in Science: A General Argument, with Lessons from a Case Study of Feminist Research on Divorce, *Hypatia: A Journal of Feminist Philosophy*, 19, pp. 1–24.
Clough, S. (2003) *Beyond Epistemology: A Pragmatist Approach to Feminist Science Studies*. Lanham: Rowman and Littlefield.
Clough, S. and W. E. Loges (2008) Racist Value Judgments as Objectively False Beliefs: A Philosophical and Social-Psychological Analysis, *Journal of Social Philosophy*, 39(1), pp. 77–95.
Collins, P. H. (1986) Learning from the Outsider Within: The Sociological Significance of Black Feminist Thought, *Social Problems*, 33, pp. S14–S32.
Crasnow, S. (2013) Feminist Philosophy of Science: Values and Objectivity, *Philosophy Compass*, 8(44), pp. 13–23.
Crasnow, S. (2014) Feminist Standpoint Theory. In: N. Cartwright and E. Montuschi, eds., *Philosophy of Social Science: A New Introduction*, Oxford: Oxford University Press, pp. 145–161.
Farley, L. (1978) *Sexual Shakedown: The Sexual Harassment of Women on the Job*. New York: McGraw-Hill.
Fricker, M. (2007) *Epistemic Injustice: Power and the Ethics of Knowing*. Oxford: Oxford University Press.
Harding, S. (1986) *The Science Question in Feminism*. Ithaca: Cornell University Press.
Harding, S. (2004) A Socially Relevant Philosophy of Science? Resources from Standpoint Theory's Controversality, *Hypatia: A Journal of Feminist Philosophy*, 19(1), pp. 25–47.
Harding, S. (2015) *Objectivity and Diversity: Another Logic of Scientific Research*. Chicago: University of Chicago Press.
Intemann, K. (2010) Twenty-Five Years of Feminist Empiricism and Standpoint Theory: Where Are We Now? *Hypatia: A Journal of Feminist Philosophy*, 25(4), pp. 778–796.
Kuhn, T. S. (1977) Objectivity, Value Judgment, and Theory Choice. In: *The Essential Tension: Selected Studies in Scientific Tradition and Change*, Chicago: University of Chicago Press, pp. 320–339.
Longino, H. (1990) *Science as Social Knowledge: Values and Objectivity in Social Inquiry*. Princeton: Princeton University Press.
Longino, H. (1993) Subjects, Power and Knowledge: Description and Prescription in Feminist Philosophies of Science. In: L. Alcoff and E. Potter, eds., *Feminist Epistemologies*, London: Routledge, pp. 101–120.
Longino, H. (1995) Gender, Politics, and the Theoretical Virtues, *Synthese*, 104, pp. 383–397.
Longino, H. (1997) Cognitive and Non-Cognitive Values in Science: Rethinking the Dichotomy. In: L. H. Nelson and J. Nelson, eds., *Feminism, Science, and the Philosophy of Science*, Dordrecht, The Netherlands: Kluwer Academic Publishers, pp. 39–58.
Longino, H. (2002). *The Fate of Knowledge*. Princeton: Princeton University Press.
Longino, H. (2013). *Studying Human Behavior: How Scientist Investigate Aggression and Sexuality*. Chicago: University of Chicago Press.
Nelson, L. H. (1990) *Who Knows: From Quine to a Feminist Empiricism*. Philadelphia: Temple University Press.

Nelson, L. H. (1997) Empiricism without Dogmas. In: L. H. Nelson and J. Nelson, eds., *Feminism, Science, and the Philosophy of Science*, Dordrecht: Kluwer Academic Publishers, pp. 95–120.

Paxton, P. (2000) Women's Suffrage and the Measurement of Democracy: Problems of Operationalization, *Studies in Comparative International Development*, 43, pp. 92–111.

Pohlhaus, G. (2002) Knowing Communities: An Investigation of Harding's Standpoint Epistemology, *Social Epistemology*, 16(3), pp. 283–293.

Smith, D. (1974) Women's Perspective as a Radical Critique of Sociology, *Sociological Inquiry*, 44(1), pp. 7–13.

Smith, D. (1987) *The Everyday World As Problematic*. Boston, MA: Northeastern University Press.

Sobstyl, E. (2004) Re-radicalizing Nelson's Feminist Empiricism, *Hypatia*, 19(1), pp. 119–141.

Solomon, M. (2012) The Web of Valief: An Assessment of Feminist Radical Empiricism. In: S. Crasnow and A. Superson, eds., *Out from the Shadows*, New York: Oxford University Press, pp. 435–450.

Wylie, A. (2003) Why Standpoint Matters. In R. Figueroa and S. Harding (eds.) *Science and Other Cultures: Issues in Philosophies of Science and Technology*, New York: Routledge, pp. 26–48.

Suggestions for Further Reading:

Grasswick, H. E. (ed.) (2011) *Feminist Epistemology and Philosophy of Science: Power in Knowledge*. New York: Springer. This relatively recent collection includes work from contemporary feminist epistemologists and philosophers of science dealing with issues of the relationship between feminist philosophy of science and feminist epistemology, the relationship between traditional and feminist epistemologies, political issues of oppression and liberation in relation to epistemology, and case studies that show the role of social values.

Kourany, J. A. (2010) *Philosophy of Science after Feminism*. New York: Oxford. Kourany examines varieties of feminist philosophy of science, critiquing each, and argues for another approach, which she calls "socially responsible science".

Solomon, M. (2001) *Social Empiricism*. Cambridge, MA: MIT Press. Solomon offers an alternative to discussions about epistemic vs. non-epistemic values by describing decisions about theory acceptance as based on epistemic and non-epistemic decision vectors. She argues that such epistemic and non-epistemic decision vectors both play a role in theory acceptance but that they should be equitably distributed.

Rolin, K. (2015). Values in Science: The Case of Scientific Collaboration, *Philosophy of Science*, 82, pp. 157–177. Rolin looks at the way values function in research communities. She argues that it is more productive for understanding how values function than either looking at the role of values in the decisions of individuals or considering the proper functioning of larger scientific communities.

Garry, A. (2012) Who Is Included? Intersectionality, Metaphors, and the Multiplicity of Gender. In: S. Crasnow and A. Superson, eds., *Out from the Shadows: Analytical Feminist Contributions to Traditional Philosophy*, Oxford: Oxford University Press. Garry explores various concerns that the complexity of identities creates for feminism and proposes an intersectional account as a solution to these difficulties.

PART V

The Epistemology of Groups

26

THE EPISTEMOLOGY
OF GROUPS

Deborah Perron Tollefsen

Introduction

The epistemology of groups (also called *collective epistemology*) is a subfield of social epistemology that explores the possibility of epistemic properties and processes at the group level.[1] Over the past decade the field has grown rapidly, evidence by three dedicated anthologies (Schmid et al. 2011; Lackey 2014a; Brady & Fricker 2016), several special issues of journals, (e.g. *Protosociology* 2002, vol. 16; *Episteme* 2004, vol. 2(1); *Social Epistemology* 2007, vol. 21(3)), and a number of national and international conferences.

Traditional epistemology has been criticized for exhibiting two forms of individualism. First, it takes the individual in isolation from its social setting. The S that knows in "S knows that p" is often stripped of her location in a social setting and viewed as an independent and solitary knower. Social epistemology developed, in part, as response to this form of individualism and studies the ways in which the social influences, for good or bad, influence the acquisition of knowledge and the justification of beliefs had by individual agents.

Second, traditional epistemology presumes the individual to be the locus of epistemic properties such as belief, knowledge, cognition, rationality, epistemic virtue, and objectivity. Call this form of individualism, *epistemic agent individualism* (Tollefsen 2007). The epistemology of groups has developed, in part, as a response to this form of epistemic individualism. In what follows, I survey some of the basic issues, concepts, and debates in this developing field.

Groups

Before we discuss the epistemology of groups, it will be useful to distinguish between different types of groups. Much of the literature has been focused on what we might call small task groups (e.g. scientific research teams, committees, and juries). The members of these groups know that they are members of the group and they interact with other members to do various things—solve problems, complete experiments, develop policies, decide on a verdict. These groups are sometimes temporary and do not necessarily maintain identity when group membership changes. A small task group could be formed to complete one task and then dissolve when the task is complete.

Some of the literature in collective epistemology[2] has focused on more stable and structured groups—those with a decision making mechanism and defined roles that allow for members to leave the group without the group thereby dissolving. These would include larger groups such as institutions and corporations. Both of these types of groups, the small task oriented group and the institution, can be contrasted with aggregate groups, such as the collection of people waiting at the bus stop or the class of red-haired women.

Though the literature has tended to focus on either small task groups or institutions, there are interesting phenomena involving aggregate groups that are of epistemological interest.[3] *Collective intelligence* is a growing field of study informing artificial intelligence. Modeled on the idea of swarm intelligence—the ability of animals and insects to navigate their environment and solve problems collectively—collective intelligence often results in better predictions than anything an individual epistemic agent could produce.[4] How crowds are sourced in order to extract information, in what way "big data" is collected and processed, whether collective intelligence is *intelligence*, are important questions for social epistemology.[5] One interesting exploration of these ideas can be found in a volume of *Episteme* dedicated to the Philosophy of Mass Collaboration (2009, 6(1)).[6]

Group Belief

The traditional analysis of knowledge has it that knowledge is justified true belief. Although the traditional analysis has been challenged, the role of belief in knowledge has played a relatively stable role. To say that S knows that p is, to many, to say that S has a certain sort of belief.[7] It is not surprising, then, that group belief should play a prominent role in discussions of the epistemology of groups. Recent discussions of group belief have their origin in the field of collective intentionality.[8] Collective intentionality is a relatively new area of philosophy that studies various types of social phenomena including, group belief, shared intention, collective responsibility, and the construction of social reality.[9]

Prima facie, the idea that groups could have beliefs is a bit puzzling. Groups don't have a collective mind or brain, so how could they have mental states like belief? Yet, we have a robust practice of attribution belief to groups. As group members we attribute beliefs to "us" such as "We believe that our institution should pay adjuncts a fair wage." In addition, we often take the intentional stance toward groups and attribute beliefs to groups from the third person perspective (e.g. "The committee believes candidate A is the best candidate," "Corporation X believes that they are not polluting the environment").

One might argue that our attributions to groups are simply shorthand ways of referring to the sum of the beliefs of group members or to the commonly held beliefs within a group.[10] Margaret Gilbert (1987, 1989, 2000, 2002) was the first to argue against this "summative" approach. The summative account clearly isn't sufficient for group belief. Every member of the CIA probably believes that 2 + 2 = 4 but it is not likely to be a belief that we attribute to the CIA. We can also imagine cases where there are two groups with the same members and yet attribution of a belief to one is appropriate whereas attribution to another is completely inappropriate. Consider the case of two committees, the dress code committee and the budget committee whose members are co-extensive (i.e. they are the same individuals). The dress code committee might believe that tank tops are inappropriate for work whereas the budget committee has no view on the matter.

Whether a group believes something seems to depend on more than what the individual members believe. Somehow the proposition attributed to the group must play a role in the life of the group—in its deliberations, policy making, guiding its joint actions. Gilbert has also argued that the summative account doesn't provide necessary conditions for group belief. According to Gilbert, we can imagine cases where no member of a group personally believes that p but p is appropriately attributed to the group. This "divergence argument" (Mathiesen 2011) is a staple in the literature on group belief.

According to Gilbert (1987, 1989, 2000, 2002), group beliefs are formed when members express their willingness to be jointly committed to believing p as a group. This does not entail that members of the group personally believe p. Thus, her view allows for the divergence between group belief and individual belief. The existence of joint commitments explains why members feel compelled to act, qua group members, in accordance with the group belief and why other members are entitled to expect such behavior. If, for instance, a member of the group boldly states "not p" when the group believes that p then other things equal the member is rightly subject to some degree of rebuke for reneging on his part in the joint commitment to p. The normativity of group belief—that group members are entitled to expect a certain sort of behavior from each other—is something, according to Gilbert, any account of group belief must explain. Raimo Tuomela's account of group belief appeals to the distinction between belief and acceptance. Although the details of Tuomela's account are complex, the basic idea is that a group, G, believes that p if and only if the operative members of G accept that p is the view of the group (Tuomela 1992). Tuomela's account of group belief is more easily extended to larger groups such as institutions because he distinguishes between operative members (who are in positions of authority to form group beliefs) and non-operative members who play no decision-making role within an institution.

Gilbert's and Tuomela's account of group belief raise the following question: Are group beliefs really beliefs? On a joint commitment account members of a group are simply accepting that a certain proposition is the view of the group and acting as if they were a single body that believed it. On an acceptance account the members jointly accept a proposition, they don't actually believe the proposition. No one, not even the group itself, seems to believe that p. This has led some philosophers to argue that group belief is not really belief at all but is a species of acceptance (Wray 2001; Meijers 2002). The debate between *Rejectionists* (those who reject the idea of group belief) and the *Believers* (those who think groups have beliefs) rests on the distinction between belief and acceptance. Belief is directed at the truth, whereas acceptance is something pragmatically guided (we accept p if we take p as a sound basis for action); belief is involuntary, whereas acceptance is voluntary. *Rejectionists* have argued that many of Gilbert's examples of group belief are practical in nature and so are better thought of as acceptances (Wray 2001; Hakli 2006); and that among the examples of propositions supported by reasons there are no cases in which the reasons a group has to accept p are not also shared by its individual members (Meijers 2002; McMahon 2003). In response to this, *Believers* have argued that belief is in any case a form of acceptance (Tollefsen 2003), group beliefs are often directed at the truth (Tollefsen 2003), and groups have epistemic goals (Mathiesen 2006, 2011; Fallis 2007) so there is no obstacle to regarding groups as having genuine beliefs. Gilbert and Pilchman (2014) have recently argued that we ought to stop trying to fit group belief in to the individual belief mold because doing so risks ignoring the unique features of group belief.

List and Pettit offer an account of group belief that rests on the divergence between the aggregation of individual beliefs about a matter and what the group believes about a matter (2013). This process of "collectivizing reason" is a result of the fact that groups must maintain coherence and consistency over time. The "discursive dilemma" is often appealed to in making the divergence argument (2013). I discuss the discursive dilemma in more detail below.

Finally, Tollefsen has argued that, on a certain conception of what beliefs are, certain groups can, themselves, be the appropriate subject of belief ascription (2015). Beliefs, according to Tollefsen, are best thought of as dispositional states characterized in terms of counterfactuals that are true of the agent. To say that a group believes that p is to say that the group would behave in certain ways under certain circumstances.

The Justification of Group Belief

If group belief is possible, the question of how and to what extent a group's beliefs are justified is a natural question. Schmitt (1994b) argues that process reliabilism can be extended to make sense of the justification of group belief. Tollefsen (2002) develops a similar proposal arguing that it will require, however, giving up on the idea that the processes that are relevant to justification are within the head of individuals alone.

Recently, Alvin Goldman has broadened his conception of a reliable process to include social processes (2014). Goldman remains agnostic regarding the nature of group belief but adopts List and Pettit's account in order to develop a theory of the justification of group belief. For List and Pettit group beliefs are the result of decision-making processes that take individual votes or attitudes as an input and issues the group belief as an output. Goldman calls the function that takes individual attitudes as inputs and yields collective beliefs as output a *belief aggregation function* (BAF). He then proposes a way of aggregating the justification of group belief. He calls this a *justification aggregation function* (JAF). According to Goldman, the greater proportion of members who are justified in believing that p and the smaller the proportion of members who are justified in rejecting that p, the greater the justification of the group belief that p. Goldman now accepts that, at least in collective contexts, belief-forming processes extend across "agential gaps" along the lines suggested by Sanford Goldberg (2010) for the case of testimony. Goldberg (2010) argues that in cases where we rely on the testimony of another the justificatory base extends beyond the individual hearer. When I form the belief that it is 2 p.m. on the basis of your testimony, the justification I have for this belief rests on more than the reliability of my cognitive processes. It also rests on whether your cognitive processes are working reliably. Acknowledging this, however, does not commit one to active externalism (Clark & Chalmers 1998). The belief itself remains in the head of the individual.[11]

Raul Hakli (2011) provides an account of justification of group belief, understood as voluntary acceptance of a proposition on the part of individuals within the group, on the basis of dialectical justification. The basic idea of dialectical justification is that an agent is justified in so far as he or she can defend the proposition against reasonable challenges. Hakli extends this to the group case. The group belief is justified insofar as the group can defend the proposition it accepts against challenges within and outside the group.

An interesting discussion of the justification of group belief that predates some of these more recent accounts can be found in Solomon (2006). Solomon argues that there is an assumption that joint deliberation within a group will result in beliefs (both individual and group) that are more rational and hence justified. But social psychological research suggests that group contexts can result in poorer decision-making. She argues that this form of internalism (that reasons need to be accessed by members of the group in order for the group judgment to be justified) ought to be replaced with an externalism in which, as long as the process of forming group judgments is reliable, there isn't a need for explicit accessibility of reasons. She points to the phenomenon of crowdsourcing and appeals to a number of examples from Suroweicki's *Wisdom of the Crowds* (2004).[12]

Group Knowledge

The literature on group knowledge can be divided into two main approaches (Bird 2014).The approaches are not mutually exclusive but they have tended to be pursued in isolation. On one hand, there are accounts that build on theories developed in the collective intentionality literature (Gilbert 1989, 2004; Tuomela 1992, 2011; Hakli 2007; Mathiesen 2011; Tollefsen 2002, 2015). On the other hand, the second approach (Palermos & Pritchard 2013; Carter et al. forthcoming) combines virtue reliabilism (Greco 2010) from mainstream epistemology with the hypothesis of distributed cognition (Hutchins 1995; Tollefsen 2006; Sutton 2008; Sutton et al. 2010; Theiner et al. 2010) from philosophy of mind in order to account for group knowledge as the product of distributed cognitive abilities. Group deliberation, for instance, involves a process by which reasoning is distributed across members of a group.

The most developed account of group knowledge that appeals to shared intentional states is that of Raimo Tuomela (2004). Tuomela begins with his acceptance account of group belief in which a group belief is formed when members jointly accept p as the view of the group. He develops an account of group knowledge on this basis and with a traditional analysis of knowledge in mind. Group knowledge occurs when members are justified in accepting that p and justification in this case is a matter of having reasons for accepting p as the view of the group. Tuomela specifies that the reasons are group reasons. A group's reasons might differ from an individual's reasons for accepting a proposition. A group, for instance, might have reasons for accepting a proposition because it will result in a group view that is more consistent with the other views they hold. Tuomela's account has an internalist theory of justification built into it. In order for the group to have knowledge its members must have access to the relevant reasons (either of the personal or group kind). As we saw above an externalist approach might provide an alternative to this.

Raul Hakli (2007) defends Tuomela's account from critics and argues that despite the fact that Tuomela's account begins with the notion of acceptance rather than belief it can ground a theory of group knowledge. Mathiesen (2011) makes an important contribution to this debate by shifting the focus from knowledge to epistemic agency. Contrary to arguments made by Meijers (2002) and McMahon (2003), groups are, according to Matheisen, independent epistemic agents in the sense that what they jointly accept may differ from what their members individually believe. Mathiesen argues that there are forms of acceptance that are truth directed and therefore epistemically evaluable. In some cases a group's acceptance is not reducible to each individual accepting that p because individuals can be working with different evidence sets. If the divergence argument can still be made for group acceptance then it forms the basis for a form of collective epistemic agency and sidesteps the issue of group belief.

The extended knowledge approach (Palermos & Pritchard 2013; Palermos 2016; Carter et al. forthcoming) promises to offer a way of extending credit (and hence knowledge on the credit account of knowledge) without having to attribute beliefs to groups. This alternative approach to group knowledge couples distributed cognition with virtue reliabilism. Virtue reliabilism upgrades traditional process reliabilism by focusing on the notion of a cognitive ability. According to virtue reliabilism, knowledge is not simply the result of a reliable process but the result of belief that is true in virtue of cognitive ability (e.g. Sosa 1988, 1991, 2007, 2009; Greco 2007, 2009, 2010; Pritchard 2009, 2010). Specifically, virtue reliabilists hold that a belief-forming process is knowledge-conducive only if it is a reliable process that is integrated into an agent's cognitive character. According to Pritchard and Palermos (2013), if we couple virtue reliabilism with active externalism, the view that cognitive processing might extend beyond the skull, we can account for epistemic group agents. The cognitive character of a group is constituted by its members' mutual interactions. In the case of a scientific research team, for instance, the knowledge-conducive belief forming processes will be distributed across several experts and their experimental artifacts. These individual experts will be mutually interacting and the collective cognitive success of believing the truth of some (scientific) proposition will be creditable to the group's cognitive agency—the set of organismic cognitive faculties of its individual members (2013, 115). Individual scientists will "have" the belief. The credit and, hence, knowledge will be properly attributed to the group.

There have been a number of critics who have argued that groups cannot be knowers or epistemic agents. Ronald Giere (2007), for instance, argues that just because cognition is distributed across a group (e.g. a scientific research group) doesn't mean that the group constitutes an agent that knows; Heimir Geirsson (2004) argues groups cannot be epistemic agents because they lack consciousness; and Szigeti (2015) argues, contra List and Pettit (2013), that group rationality does not entail that groups are epistemic agents.

If groups can know there remains the question of *which* groups can know.[13] On the shared intentionality approach group members need to form certain attitudes vis-a-vis a proposition in order for the group to know that p. This would, it seems, restrict knowledge to groups that are relatively cohesive and whose membership is stable—something like small task groups. What about larger groups? We often attribute knowledge to institutions and even communities. Alexander Bird has recently argued that in some cases it is the scientific community that knows (2014).[14] This idea can also be found in the work of Lynn Hankinson Nelson (1990, 1993).[15,16]

Group Epistemic Virtue

In book IV of the *Republic*, Plato discusses the virtues of a city. His focus is on the moral virtue of justice. More recently there have been a number of attempts to unpack the idea that groups could have epistemic virtues.

Virtue epistemology can be divided roughly into two groups: virtue reliabilism and virtue responsibilism. The virtue reliabilist identifies virtues with faculties or processes that are responsible for producing true belief. On this account a well-functioning perceptual system is virtuous or exhibits virtue. The virtue responsibilist (e.g. Zagzebski), on the other hand, uses virtue in the rich sense of motive-based character traits, traits such as open-mindedness, courage, and integrity. As we have seen there have been attempts to extend virtue reliabilism to groups and establish a theory of group knowledge by coupling it with distributed cognition. A variety of other discussions of group epistemic virtue have arisen.

Reza Lahroodi (2007) argues that an account of group virtue in terms of the sum of individual virtue in a group will fail just as a summative account of group belief fails. He adapts Gilbert's account of group belief (2002) in terms of joint commitment to provide an account of group virtues, in particular group open-mindedness. A group is open-minded when its members jointly commit "with others under conditions of common knowledge to accord contrary ideas initial plausibility" (2007, 291). Miranda Fricker (2010) offers an account of institutional virtues that also builds on the work of Margaret Gilbert. Anita Konzelman Ziv (2011) extends a virtue responsibilist account of epistemic agency to groups. Attributions of collective virtue, according to Ziv, will require that individual intentions, beliefs, and emotions align with the collective character of a group.

Sarah Wright (2014) has extended a stoic conception of epistemic virtues to groups. According to such an account, the *skopoi* [goal] of a group on a stoic virtue epistemic model would be true group beliefs. Since for the stoic one's beliefs and actions are both equally the result of choice and equally reflect one's character, one strand of the worry that group beliefs are not really beliefs is avoided.

Group Rationality and Objectivity

There are a variety of other epistemic properties that one might think are attributable to groups. Consider, for instance, the property of rationality. We certainly seem to judge whether groups are rational or irrational. Are such judgments simply a way of judging the individuals within the group? List and Pettit (2013), as mentioned above, have argued that in some cases rationality is *collectivized*. They appeal to the discursive dilemma in order to make their case. Consider the following case (Pettit 2010). A panel of judges must find the defendant liable if and only if it finds: (1) that the defendant was negligent and that their negligence was responsible for the injury to the plaintiff, and (2) that the defendant had a duty to care for the plaintiff. Imagine that the judges A, B, and C vote on those issues and on the related matter of whether the defendant is liable.

There are two ways that the court might make its decision. They might vote simply on the issue of liability and let the majority view on that issue determine the court's decision. Pettit calls this the *conclusion-driven approach*. Given the above matrix, the defendant would not be found liable since there are two votes against liability. The court could also aggregate the votes with

	Cause of Harm?	*Duty of Care?*	*Liable?*
A	Yes	No	No
B	No	Yes	No
C	Yes	Yes	Yes

respect to the individual issues of cause and duty of care and let the conclusion be accepted—that the defendant is guilty—if and only if both premises are endorsed by a majority of the court. Pettit calls this approach the *premise-driven approach*. Given the matrix, the defendant would be found liable, since there are two votes to one for both cause and duty of care. If they adopt the conclusion-driven approach, the court will be endorsing a conclusion that is inconsistent with how the majority voted regarding the related issues. And if the court adopts the premise-driven approach, then they will collectively endorse a conclusion that a majority of them individually reject. The premise-driven approach, thus, clearly reveals the ways in which a group's belief or judgment can *diverge* from the belief or judgment of its members.

So why would any group choose the premise-driven approach? The justification for this approach becomes apparent only when we acknowledge that the norms of rationality apply to groups as well as individuals. The constraints we recognize as applying to our own judgment govern collective judgments. If the court has already established that the relevant issues will determine the verdict they cannot simply disregard the fact that a majority believes that the relevant factors obtain. The premise-driven approach avoids the possibility that the court collectively endorses an inconsistent or incoherent set of propositions. Thus, the premise-driven approach preserves the rationality of the group. The irrationality of the conclusion-driven approach can be seen more clearly in diachronic rather than synchronic cases. In these cases the verdict is determined on the basis of precedence of previous court judgments some of which may not be the judgments of the current court. There is pressure for consistency across time.

While List and Pettit focus on the rationality of groups (and the related notions of coherence and consistency in group judgements), feminist philosophers of science such as Helen Longino (1990) have argued that objectivity is something achieved by groups, rather than individuals, because individual epistemic agents are naturally biased. The only way to overcome that bias is to engage in joint deliberative processes that engage many different perspectives. Deliberative practices within a group produce more objectivity.

Conclusion

The epistemology of groups is a rapidly growing subfield of social epistemology. This brief overview highlights the variety of issues and approaches that philosophers are exploring. There is, however, a single methodology that unites the majority of these approaches. The study of the epistemology of groups begins with an interest in the possibility that the theories and concepts we have developed in relation to the individual can be extended (or not) to the group. The method is rehearsed over and over again: raise the possibility of group X (group belief, group knowledge, group testimony, group rationality), pick your favorite theory of individual X, and show how your favorite theory of individual X can or, in the case of skeptics, cannot be extend to groups.

Interestingly Margaret Gilbert (2002) warns that this approach risks missing the ways in which group epistemic phenomena can be used to challenge and shape epistemic theories and theories of cognitive states. It also risks overlooking the ways in which groups might be different from individuals and therefore require a unique analysis. Gilbert and Pilchman (2014) suggest that rather than try to fit collective epistemology into the individual epistemology mold we should be developing a general epistemological theory which can handle both the individual and group case. They don't offer such a general epistemology but their idea is intriguing. Perhaps the epistemology of groups may ultimately serve a dual role, not only as a way of making groups visible as epistemic agents, but also as a heuristic for seeing the limitations of the epistemology of the individual.

Notes

1 Goldman (2010) labels this type of social epistemic inquiry as "expansionist" social epistemology. Expansionism appears to violate one of Goldman's "central features" of epistemology (as we know it, in the analytic fashion) namely that "the epistemic agents of traditional epistemology are exclusively individuals" (2010, 2). This is an explicit statement of the epistemic agent individualism discussed above. Since expansionism doesn't respect this feature it would appear that it isn't "real" epistemology, though Goldman glosses over this. It is unclear, given Goldman's recent work (2014), whether he still thinks that collective epistemology is not "real" epistemology.

2 See, for instance, Tuomela (1992, 2004, 2011) whose accounts of proper group belief, positional belief, operative membership, and group knowledge extend most easily to the institutional case.

3 Consider, for instance, some of the examples we find in James Surowiecki's book *The Wisdom of the Crowd* (2004). In 1906, Dalton asked fairgoers to guess the weight of an ox. He then averaged their answers and the average answer was extremely close to the true weight. The group of fairgoers was somehow able to guess the weight of the ox though no individual fair goer was able to do so. The fair goers were not a task group or an institution. They did not even know that their answers would contribute to a final answer on the matter. They acted independently rather than jointly.

4 An AI collective intelligence algorithm was recently used to predict, with accuracy, the 2016 Kentucky Derby winners. "AI startup taps human 'swarm' intelligence to predict winners." www.cnet.com/news/swarm-ai-unu-boasts-it-can-predict-winners-using-humans/#ftag=CADf28c2b9

5 See Mulgan (2014) for an interesting discussion of this emerging new field.

6 See also Fallis (2010).

7 The exception here are those who think knowledge is a distinct mental state and not reducible to a type of belief. See, for instance, Williamson (2000).

8 Historically, the discussion of group belief can be traced to late 19th and early 20th century social scientists. Emile Durkheim, for instance, argued that there were collective representations that played a role in guiding human behavior (Durkheim 1953).

9 For an introduction to issues in this field see Tollefsen (2004), Roth (2011), and Schweikard and Schmid (2012).

10 This view is attributed to Anthony Quinton (1976).

11 Joseph Shieber (2013) has argued that this extended justification can also be found in processes that extend across groups. He, too, rejects the idea that this constitutes a case of extended cognition. The epistemology may extend but the metaphysics does not.

12 Solomon's view highlights the following issue: if one adopts a process reliabilist approach to the justification of group belief then we need to be able to identify which processes are reliable. Just as traditional process reliabilism deferred to the cognitive sciences to tell us which cognitive processes reliably produced true belief, social process reliabilism will have to defer to the empirical sciences (the social sciences in this case) to tell us which group processes reliably produce true group belief. We should also keep in mind here that all of the problems that plague process reliabilism—the generality problem (that the "process" identified might be anything as general as "vision" or as specific as "Jane's eyesight with her reading glasses on"); the Gettier problem (that there can be cases of justified true belief that are not knowledge); and so on—will have to be dealt with at the level of group knowledge.

13 The issue of group knowledge is related to the topic of group testimony. We seem to gain knowledge from the testimony of groups, such as scientific research teams. If knowledge is transmitted in cases of testimonial knowledge then one might argue that groups can know. Unfortunately word limits precluded the discussion of this important topic.

14 For an argument against this view see Lackey (2014b).

15 For arguments against the idea that the scientific community could be the bearer of knowledge see Wray (2007).

16 A related issue is the question of group knowledge ascriptions. Jennifer Lackey (2012) argues that William Craig's hypothesis that the function of knowledge attributions is to flag reliable informants is undermined by the fact that we attribute knowledge to groups. She argues that the attribution of knowledge to groups often fails to identify reliable informants. Rather than tracking *reliable informants*, knowledge attributions to individuals or groups, according Lackey, serves the purpose of flagging reliable *sources of information*.

References

Bird, A. (2014). When is there a group that knows? Distributed Cognition, Scientific Knowledge, and the Social Epistemic Subject. In: J. Lackey, ed., *Essays in Collective Epistemology*, Oxford: Oxford University Press, pp. 42–63.

Brady, M. & Fricker, M. (eds.) (2016). *The Epistemic Life of Groups*. Oxford: Oxford University Press.

Carter, J. A., Clark, A., Kallestrup, J., Palermos, O., & Pritchard, D. (eds.) (forthcoming). *Socially Extended Knowledge*. Oxford: Oxford University Press.

Clark, A. & Chalmers, D. (1998). The Extended Mind. *Analysis*, 58(1), pp. 7–19.

Durkheim, E. (1953). *Sociology and Philosophy*. London: Cohen & West.

Fallis, D. (2007). Collective Epistemic Goals. *Social Epistemology*, 21(3), pp. 267–280.

Fallis, D. (2009). Introduction: The Epistemology of Mass Collaboration. *Episteme*, 6(1), pp. 1–7.

Fallis, D. (2010). Wikipistemology. In: A. I. Goldman & D. Whitcomb, eds., *Social Epistemology: Essential Readings*. New York: Oxford University Press, pp. 297–313.

Fricker, M. (2010). Can There Be Institutional Virtues? In: T. S. Gendler & J. Hawthorne, eds., *Oxford Studies in Epistemology* (Special Theme: Social Epistemology) Vol. 3, Oxford: Oxford University Press, pp. 235–252.

Geirsson, H. (2004). Contra Collective Epistemic Agency. *Southwest Philosophy Review*, 20(2), pp. 163–166.

Giere, R. N. (2007). Distributed Cognition without Distributed Knowing. *Social Epistemology*, 21(3), pp. 313–320.

Gilbert, M. (1987). Modelling Collective Belief. *Synthese*, 73(1), pp. 185–204.

Gilbert, M. (1989). *On Social Facts*. London: Routledge.

Gilbert, M. (2000). *Sociality and Responsibility: New Essays in Plural Subject Theory*. Lanham, MD: Rowman & Littlefield Publishers.

Gilbert, M. (2002). Belief and Acceptance as Features of Groups. *Protosociology*, 16, pp. 35–69.

Gilbert, M. (2004). Collective Epistemology. *Episteme*, 1(2), pp. 95–107.

Gilbert, M. & Pilchman, D. (2014). Belief, Acceptance, and What Happens in Groups. In: J. Lackey, ed., *Essays in Collective Epistemology*. Oxford: Oxford University Press, pp. 189–214.

Goldberg, S. (2010). *Relying on Others: An Essay in Epistemology*. Oxford: Oxford University Press.

Goldberg, S. C. (2015). *Assertion: On the Philosophical Significance of Assertoric Speech*. Oxford: Oxford University Press.

Goldman, A. (2010). Why Social Epistemology is Real Epistemology. In: A. Haddock, A. Millar & D. Pritchard, eds., *Social Epistemology*, Oxford: Oxford University Press, pp. 1–28.

Goldman, A. (2014). Social Process Reliabilism: Solving Justification Problems in Collective Epistemology. In: J. Lackey, ed., *Essays in Collective Epistemology*, Oxford: Oxford University Press, pp. 11–41.

Greco, J. (2007). The Nature of Ability and the Purpose of Knowledge. *Philosophical Issues*, 17(1), pp. 57–69.

Greco, J. (2009). Knowledge and Success from Ability. *Philosophical Studies*, 142(1), pp. 17–26.

Greco, J. (2010). *Achieving Knowledge: A Virtue-Theoretic Account of Epistemic Normativity*. Cambridge: Cambridge University Press.

Hakli, R. (2006). Group Beliefs and the Distinction between Belief and Acceptance. *Cognitive Systems Research*, 7, pp. 286–297.

Hakli, R. (2007). On the Possibility of Group Knowledge without Belief. *Social Epistemology*, 21(3), pp. 249–266.

Hakli, R. (2011). On Dialectical Justification of Group Beliefs. In: H. B. Schmid, D. Sirtes & M. Weber, eds., *Collective Epistemology*, Hessen, Germany: Ontos Verlag, pp. 119–153.

Hutchins, E. (1995). *Cognition in the Wild*. Cambridge, MA: MIT Press.

Lackey, J. (2012). Group Knowledge Attributions. In: J. Brown & M. Gerken, eds., *Knowledge Ascriptions*, Oxford: Oxford University Press, pp. 243–269.

Lackey, J. (ed.) (2014a). *Essays in Collective Epistemology*. Oxford: Oxford University Press.

Lackey, J. (2014b). Socially Extended Knowledge. *Philosophical Issues*, 24(1), pp. 282–298.

Lahroodi, R. (2007). Collective Epistemic Virtues. *Social Epistemology*, 21(3), pp. 281–297.

List, C. & Pettit, P. (2013). *Group Agency: The Possibility, Design and Status of Corporate Agents*. New York: Oxford University Press.

Longino, H. (1990). *Science as Social Knowledge: Values and Objectivity in Scientific Inquiry*. Princeton, NJ: Princeton University Press.

Mathiesen, K. (2006). The Epistemic Features of Group Belief. *Episteme*, 2(3), pp. 161–175.

Mathiesen, K. (2011). Can Groups Be Epistemic Agents? In: H. B. Schmid, D. Sirtes & M. Weber, eds., *Collective Epistemology*, Hessen, Germany: Ontos Verlag, pp. 20–23.

McMahon, J. (2003). Two Modes of Collective Belief. *Protosociology*, 18/19, pp. 347–362.

Meijers, A. (2002). Collective Agents and Cognitive Attitudes. *Protosociology*, 16, pp. 70–85.

Mulgan, G. (2014). True Collective Intelligence? A Sketch of a Possible New Field. *Philosophy and Technology*, 27(1), pp. 133–142.

Nelson, L. H. (1990). *Who Knows: From Quine to a Feminist Empiricism*. Philadelphia, PA: Temple University Press.

Nelson, L. H. (1993). Epistemological Communities. In: L. Alcoff & E. Potter, eds., *Feminist Epistemologies*. New York: Routledge, pp. 121–160.

Palermos, O. (2016). Spreading the Credit: Virtue Reliabilism and Weak Epistemic Anti-Individualism. *Erkenntnis*, 81(2), pp. 305–334.

Palermos, O. & Pritchard, D. (2013). Extended Knowledge and Social Epistemology. *Social Epistemology Review and Reply Collective*, 2(8), pp. 105–120.

Pettit, P. (2010). Groups with Minds of Their Own. In: A. I. Goldman & D. Whitcomb, eds., *Social Epistemology: Essential Readings*. New York: Oxford University Press, pp. 242–270.

Pritchard, D. (2009). Knowledge, Understanding and Epistemic Value. *Royal Institute of Philosophy Supplement*, 64, pp. 19–43.

Pritchard, D. (2010). *The Nature and Value of Knowledge: Three Investigations*. Oxford: Oxford University Press.

Quinton, A. (1976). Social Objects. *Proceedings of the Aristotelian Society*, 76, pp. 1–27.

Roth, A. S. (2011). Shared Agency. *Stanford Encyclopedia of Philosophy*.

Schmid, H. B., Sirtes, D., & Weber, M. (2011). *Collective Epistemology*. Hessen, Germany: Ontos Verlag.

Schmitt, F. (ed.) (1994a). *Socializing Epistemology: The Social Dimensions of Knowledge*. Lanham, MD: Rowman and Littlefield.

Schmitt, F. (1994b). The Justification of Group Beliefs. In: F. Schmitt, ed., *Socializing Epistemology: The Social Dimensions of Knowledge*, Lanham, MD: Rowman and Littlefield, pp. 257–287.

Schweikard, D. P. & Schmid, H. B. (2012). Collective Intentionality. *Stanford Encyclopedia of Philosophy*.

Shieber, J. (2013). Toward a Truly Social Epistemology: Babbage, the Division of Mental Labor, and the Possibility of Socially Distributed Warrant. *Philosophy and Phenomenological Research*, 86(2), pp. 266–294.

Solomon, M. (2006). Groupthink versus The Wisdom of Crowds. *Southern Journal of Philosophy*, 44 (Supplement), pp. 28–42.

Sosa, E. (1988). Knowledge in Context, skepticism in Doubt: The Virtue of our Faculties. *Philosophical Perspectives*, 2, pp. 139–155.

Sosa, E. (1991). *Knowledge in Perspective*. Cambridge: Cambridge University Press.

Sosa, E. (2007). *A Virtue Epistemology*. Oxford: Oxford University Press.

Sosa, E. (2009). *A Virtue Epistemology: Apt Belief and Reflective Knowledge, Volume I*. Oxford: Oxford University Press.

Surowiecki, J. (2004). *The Wisdom of the Crowds: Why the Many Are Smarter than the Few and How Collective Wisdom Shapes Business, Economies, Societies and Nations*. New York: Doubleday.

Sutton, J. (2008). Between Individual and Collective Memory: Interaction, Coordination, Distribution. *Social Research*, 75(1), pp. 23–48.

Sutton, J., Harris, C. B., Keil, P. G., & Barnier, A. J. (2010). The Psychology of Memory, Extended Cognition, and Socially Distributed Remembering. *Phenomenology and the Cognitive Sciences*, 9(4), pp. 521–560.

Szigeti, A. (2015). Why Change the Subject? On Collective Epistemic Agency. *Review of Philosophy and Psychology*, 6(4), pp. 843–864.

Theiner, G., Allen, C., & Goldstone, R. L. (2010). Recognizing Group Cognition. *Cognitive Systems Research*, 11(4), pp. 378–395.

Tollefsen, D. (2002). Challenging Epistemic Individualism. *Protosociology*, 16, pp. 86–120.

Tollefsen, D. (2003). Rejecting Rejectionism. *Protosociology*, 18, pp. 389–405.

Tollefsen, D. (2004). Collective Intentionality. *Internet Encyclopedia of Philosophy*.

Tollefsen, D. (2006). From Extended Mind to Collective Mind. *Cognitive Systems Research*, 7(2), pp. 140–150.

Tollefsen, D. (2007). Collective Epistemic Agency and the Need for Collective Epistemology. In: N. Psarros & K. Schulte-Ostermann, eds., *Facets of Sociality*, Hessen, Germany: Ontos Verlag, pp. 309–329.

Tollefsen, D. (2015). *Groups as Agents*. Cambridge: Polity.

Tuomela, R. (1992). Group Beliefs. *Synthese*, 91(3), pp. 285–318.

Tuomela, R. (2004). Group Knowledge Analyzed. *Episteme*, 1(2), pp. 109–127.

Tuomela, R. (2011). An Account of Group Knowledge. In: H. B. Schmid, D. Sirtes & M. Weber, eds., *Collective Epistemology*, Hessen, Germany: Ontos Verlag, pp. 75–118.

Williamson, T. (2000). *Knowledge and Its Limits*. Oxford: Oxford University Press.

Wray, K. B. (2001). Collective Belief and Acceptance. *Synthese*, 129(3), pp. 319–333.

Wray, K. B. (2007). Who Has Scientific Knowledge? *Social Epistemology*, 21(3), pp. 337–347.

Wright, S. (2014). The Stoic Epistemic Virtues of Groups. In: J. Lackey, ed., *Essays in Collective Epistemology*, Oxford: Oxford University Press, pp. 122–141.

Ziv, A. K. (2011). Collective Epistemic Agency: Virtue and the Spice of Vice. In: H. B. Schmid, D. Sirtes & M. Weber, eds., *Collective Epistemology*, Hessen, Germany: Ontos Verlag, pp. 45–72.

Further Reading

Brady, M. & Fricker, M. (eds.) (2016). *The Epistemic Life of Groups*. Oxford: Oxford University Press.

Lackey, J. (ed.) (2014). *Essays in Collective Epistemology*. Oxford: Oxford University Press.

Schmid, H. B., Sirtes, D., & Weber, M. (2011). *Collective Epistemology*. Hessen, Germany: Ontos Verlag.

27

GROUP BELIEF AND KNOWLEDGE

Alexander Bird

Introduction

We ascribe, so it appears, beliefs and knowledge, as well as other states normally regarded as mental states, to groups and social collectivities as well as to individual persons:

> "Our poetry reading group believes that Browning is more challenging than Tennyson."
> "The court believes that the defendant is guilty."
> "GlaxoSmithKline believes that it has discovered a cure for dementia."
> "The stock market believes that Brexit will be bad for British business."
> "Neuroscientists know that the brain is plastic."
> "North Korea knows how to build an atomic bomb."

This article looks at different ways of understanding statements such as these. (At the outset, we should note that there may be no uniform phenomenon of group belief—it might be that different kinds of group belief statement have different correct readings.)

While the foreground topic falls within social epistemology, in the background are questions of social ontology. The nature of the individual believer and their existence are not especially pertinent questions for those trying to understand the nature of individual belief. By contrast, the nature of the group or of the collectivity and whether it really exists, and if so what makes it exist, are important background questions for those trying to understand group belief and knowledge.

Consider the following statement. "With their team three–nil down, the crowd of Rangers fans knew that its team could not win, and began leaving the stadium before the final whistle." In this statement, the Rangers fans are treated as some kind of collectivity—as a group they began leaving the stadium early, which is to say, roughly, that some sizeable proportion left early, not that they all or most made a move to leave early. The statement also attributes *knowledge* to the body of fans. How should we understand that? It looks clear that the simplest analysis is correct: all or most of the fans knew that Rangers could not win.

This is an instance of an analysis of attributions of a state to a group that is known as the *summative* account, as articulated by Anthony Quinton (1976: 19):

> To ascribe mental predicates to a group is always an indirect way of ascribing such predicates to its members. With such mental states as beliefs and attitudes the ascriptions are of what I have called the summative kind. To say that the industrial working class is determined to resist anti-trade-union laws is to say that all or most industrial workers are so minded.

More formally:

>   (S) The group G has property Φ iff all/most of the members of G have property Φ.

While the summative account looks right for some cases, we shall see that there are reasons for doubting that it can cover all cases in which belief and other states are attributed to groups. A slightly more complex view may reject (S) for some cases while nonetheless still holding that G's relationship to a property Φ depends in some less simple way on the relationship of members of G to the property Φ. Above, I said that "the crowd began leaving the stadium before the final whistle" did not mean that most members of the crowd started leaving early. Nonetheless, it does mean that some sizeable proportion of the crowd actually left the stadium early. Consider the belief expressed in "The stock market believes that Brexit will be bad for British business". This doesn't mean that the majority of investors in the stock market have that belief. The relevant criterion is how the stock market responded to the news of the Brexit vote—falling indicates that the market took a negative view of its implications for business. How the stock market behaves depends not just on the number of investors taking an action such as selling shares, but on the size of the holdings that they sold and at what price they sold them. So the relationship of the collective belief of the stock market is rather more like a weighted average of the beliefs of the investors constituting the market.

Rejecting the Summative View

It is useful to define *mutual knowledge/belief* (Vanderschraaf and Sillari 2005) thus:

> Members of a group have mutual knowledge/belief that *p* iff each individually knows/ believes that *p*.

This is distinct from *common knowledge/belief* (Lewis 1969):

> Members of a group have common knowledge/belief that *p* iff each individually knows/ believes that *p* and each individually knows/believes that each individually knows/believes that *p* and each individually knows/believes that each individually knows/believes that each individually knows/believes that *p* and … etc.

The summative view, (S), says that group belief is mutual belief or is an approximation to mutual belief (in the case of a group belief where most but not all individuals have the relevant belief). Likewise, (S) says that group knowledge is mutual knowledge or an approximation to mutual knowledge. The summative view will fail in cases where mutual belief/knowledge is not sufficient for group belief/knowledge. And it will fail when there is group belief/knowledge without mutual belief/knowledge or any approximation to it.

Mutual Belief Not Sufficient for Group Belief

(S) is refuted as a general account of group belief by cases where although all members of a group share belief *p*, the group itself does not believe *p*. Several kinds of example of such cases have been given:

- Some groups are *established* groups—for example a court, a union, or rugby club. Established groups will often have a formal set of rules or a constitution governing their existence and means of decision making. An established group can also exist with an informal but widely understood set of procedures and norms. The members of an established group may all have a belief without that belief being a *belief* of the group if that belief has not been adopted by that group *as a group*. Margaret Gilbert (1987: 189) gives the example of the Food Committee and the Library Committee of a college. The two committees happen to be coextensive. All the individuals believe that there is too much starch in the college diet. But it is only the Food Committee that believes this whereas the Library Committee has no opinion on the matter. (We may imagine that the Food Committee has discussed the matter and agreed on the point, whereas the Library Committee has not.) Members of a jury or of a panel of judges may, at some point in a trial, all believe that the defendant is guilty. But until the jury or court have at least discussed the question, it would not be correct to say that they have a belief as a jury or court about the defendant's guilt.

- All members of a group believe *p* but for some reason deny and behave as if they do not believe *p*, each member thinking that they are the only one with this strange belief. In such a case it would be a mistake to say that the group believes *p* (Gilbert 1989: 257–8; Bird 2010: 29–30).
- All members of a group believe *p* but this is such a mundane piece of information ("the sky is blue") that it is not distinctive of the group nor has it been discussed by the group nor do those individual beliefs stem from membership of the group (Schmitt 1994: 261; Corlett 1996: 88).

The first two reasons are compelling. The third, in my opinion, is not. That a belief is not distinctive of a group is not a reason to deny that the group has that belief—after all, it is not a reason for denying such a belief to an individual. Even if mundane propositions are not *adopted* as group beliefs, they may still play a role in group deliberations. It would be difficult to explain a group's reasoning without attributing to it belief in mundane propositions as well as distinctive ones. (The Library Committee believes that it will have a storage problem because the library has space for 100,000 books but recent acquisitions will lead to a collection of 107,000. How do we explain that if we deny that the Library Committee has the mundane belief that 107,000 is greater than 100,000?)

Mutual Belief Not (Approximately) Necessary for Group Belief

In other cases, a group may have a belief without all members having that belief. The football crowd may believe that their team will not win even if a few extreme optimists believe there will be an unprecedented turnaround. The committee may take a view as a result of a vote, even if the vote is not unanimous or some members are absent. For such reasons statements of the summative view, such as (S), do not require full mutual belief but only a weak approximation to it—group belief requires only that *most* members of the group should have the belief in question.

Other kinds of case suggest that even the weaker version of (S) is false:

- All the members of a group may want the group to endorse *p* but few or none of the individuals believe *p*. They may have a variety of reasons for wanting the group to have a belief that they do not themselves share. It might be politically expedient that group adopts the belief *p* even if the members individually believe otherwise (it may even be common knowledge within the group that they believe otherwise) (Gilbert 1987: 187).
- The group has decision-making rules that are not simple majorities (as in the stock market case). Certain members might have additional weight. It may even decide what it believes by deferring to a leader or policy committee. A group (such as a political party) that comes

to its views in such a manner may have a belief that is the belief of only a small proportion of the individual members of the group.

- A group may come to its opinion not by aggregating the opinions of its members but by a division of labour among them. Different individuals are given different cognitive roles and feed the different bits of information to those in the group whose role it is to collate that information and take a decision based on it. (This is *distributed cognition*—see below.)

The Commitment Model

The committee is a paradigm of group decision making. The members of the committee meet, discuss, deliberate, and decide. They know that they are meeting as a committee and that the decision that they take is a decision of the committee. They will understand how the committee reaches its decision and will be aware of the fact that they have made that decision as a committee. The members of the committee will thereby be committed to its decision in a certain way: they will acknowledge the decision as a decision of the committee they constitute and they may even be under some obligation not to disavow that decision as an individual beyond the committee. Furthermore, such commitments are not simply commitments that each takes on individually, but are commitments that they jointly undertake. When the decision is one to endorse some proposition, then we have a case of the committee believing a proposition as a group.

This picture of group belief finds its articulation in the commitment model, developed by Margaret Gilbert (1987, 1989, 1994, 2004). A group believes *p* when it is jointly committed to accepting or believing *p* as a body (Gilbert 2004: 100). What does this joint commitment amount to? Joint commitment requires that the individuals in question openly express their individual commitment conditional on a like commitment by others and that this open expression by each is common knowledge within the group (Gilbert 1994: 245–6; Gilbert 2004: 100). A joint commitment to accepting/believing *p* as a body is a joint commitment to letting *p* stand as the view of the group. In summary, then:

(G) A group G believes *p* just in case the members of G jointly accept *p*, where the latter happens just in case each member is openly committed to letting *p* stand as the view of G, conditional on a like open expression of commitment by other members of G, and this open expression is common knowledge in G.

(See Gilbert 1987: 195; Gilbert 1989: 306)

Raimo Tuomela (1984, 1992, 2004) develops a similar account, differing in certain details. For example, Tuomela prefers the idea of an unconditional commitment that *presupposes* the commitments of others, rather than a conditional commitment. He thinks that open expression is unnecessary—tacit acceptance may be sufficient. In an important departure from Gilbert's view, Tuomela distinguishes between operative and non-operative agents within a group. The group's structure of authority may permit a certain subset of members, the operative members, to make decisions on behalf of the whole group. The group believes *p* when the operative members jointly accept *p* and as a result the non-operative members tend, as members of the group, tacitly to accept *p*.

The Distributed Model

Above, I mentioned that a group may decide to form its beliefs not by aggregating the opinions of its members on each proposition but instead by dividing the labour among its members. The aggregative approach to group decision making may be the one to adopt when it is easy to furnish all members with the same evidence but it is difficult to know how exactly that evidence bears on the proposition in question. In Francis Galton's (1907) famous anecdote about the crowd at a country fair, the average of the individual guesses of the weight of an ox was very accurate (and more accurate than the large majority of individual estimates). In this case the evidence is available to all the crowd was for the most part the same—they could all see and inspect the ox. What is tricky is to infer the weight from that information. In other cases the problem is not one of making the inference from the evidence, but is a matter of gathering the evidence accurately and deploying it is a timely fashion. Edwin Hutchins (1995a) gives the example of the problem of navigating a large warship, the USS *Palau*, into harbour. This is an information-driven exercise: the ship's crew needs to gather information about the ship's location relative to landmarks, about the ship's current course and speed, about tide and wind, and so forth. With this information the problem of plotting the ship's course, while a technically skilled task, is not one that requires debate and discussion but is, relatively speaking, mechanical. What is important is that the information employed is accurate and delivered in good time. Clearly a bad way of solving this problem would be for many crew members to take a view on each of the relevant input propositions concerning location, speed, and such like, then to come to a conclusion about the proper course, and finally to aggregate those individual conclusions into a group view. The individuals' views on the input propositions would be too inaccurate and so would their conclusions, and they would not be able to do the required work rapidly enough to navigate a moving ship.

Clearly the best way of solving the problem of plotting a ship's course is to divide the task into parts. Different sailors and officers have distinct roles in collecting the various pieces of information required, while others have roles in collating the information and using it to plot the course. In this case specialization increases accuracy as well as speed. This model of group belief formation, with its division of cognitive labour, is known as *distributed cognition* (or the *distributed model*). This model is not inconsistent with the commitment model. For the group could satisfy the commitment model by committing themselves individually to whatever conclusion the distributed system produces. The two models are easiest to reconcile on Tuomela's conception of the commitment model. For Tuomela holds that a group's commitment to the group belief may be tacit rather than explicit; in a distributed system the individuals may well have no knowledge of the conclusion reached by the system. And Tuomela's model implies the possibility of the division of cognitive labour to the extent that it allows for operative members of a group to determine the group's belief; in the distributed model the operative members (in Tuomela's sense) would be those who draw the relevant conclusions from the evidence gathered by other members.

Nonetheless, many actual examples of distributed cognition do not satisfy the commitment model because commitment is not required in the distributed model. It is simply not relevant to understanding how the USS *Palau* knows its correct course to consider whether the crew members are committed to the conclusion reached by those plotting the course. All that matters is that they perform their allotted tasks in collecting the required information and passing it on in the appropriate manner.

Another important difference between the two models concerns the role of inanimate objects in the cognitive system. Hutchins emphasizes the importance of various tools for representing information in distributed systems. In another of his examples, "How a cockpit remembers its speed", Hutchins (1995b) explains that the cognitive task of landing a passenger aeroplane involves not only a division of cognitive labour between the two pilots but also the use of various mechanisms for the representation of data. For example, the correct airspeeds for the different stages of the descent are determined by one of the pilots (the "pilot not flying") who represents these speeds with moveable "speedbugs" around the rim of the airspeed indicator. The other pilot (the "pilot flying") is able to use these in real time to adjust the aeroplane's speed as it descends as well as the configuration of flaps and slats on its wings. The airspeed indicator and its speedbugs are a key part of the cognitive system.

Cognition is distributed not only among the human parts of the system but also its inanimate components. Hutchins regards the result as a cognitive state of the system—it is the *cockpit* that remembers its correct speeds.

Some Key Issues in Understanding Group Belief and Knowledge

The Discursive Dilemma

Let us return to the committee as the paradigm of the commitment model. It forms its opinions by simple majority vote on the proposition in question. As Pettit and others point out, this can lead to the group forming inconsistent beliefs. Imagine a committee made of three individuals, A, B, and C, who consider three propositions, p, q, and $p \wedge q$. A holds p to be true but q to be false, and so holds $p \wedge q$ to be false. B holds p to be false but q to be true, and so also holds $p \wedge q$ to be false. C holds both p and q to be true and so holds $p \wedge q$ to be true. A, B, and C now vote on the propositions in order to decide the committee's views on each. Accordingly they regard p as true (A and C vote in favour), and q as true (B and C vote in favour), and they also regard $p \wedge q$ as false (since A and B both vote for the falsity of $p \wedge q$). Consequently, the group beliefs are inconsistent. This is the discursive dilemma.

According to Pettit (2003) a group becomes a "social integrate", which is to say an institutional person capable of intentional action and intentional states such as belief, only if it adopts a belief aggregation procedure that can avoid the dilemma. If the latter is correct, the discursive dilemma constitutes a refutation of (S), insofar as (S) allows the group view to be determined by the majority of individual beliefs. It does not refute (G) in its general form, since (G) says nothing about how the group belief is formed. But it does constrain how (G) is implemented. Group belief cannot be formed in all cases by simple majoritarian voting. (G) is, however, consistent with there being a single guru who fixes the group belief—so long as the other members of the group are jointly committed to accepting whatever the guru opines. The distributed model in effect bypasses the discursive dilemma—it simply does not face the question of aggregating multiple opinions on the same proposition, because different individuals are given different propositions on which to focus.

Supervenience

Because the summative account analyses group states in terms of the corresponding states of individuals, it satisfies this supervenience claim (assuming knowledge is itself a mental state):

> (SUP) The beliefs/knowledge of a group supervene on the mental states of the individual members of the group.

The commitment model the analyses belief and knowledge in terms of a wider range of mental states, including the intentions and commitments of individuals, and so conforms to (SUP) or something close to it. The requirement for the open expression of individual commitment, which Gilbert promotes but Tuomela rejects, goes beyond the mental states of individuals, but not beyond their actions. So a slightly weaker version of (SUP) remains true for the Gilbert's version of the commitment model:

> (SUP*) The beliefs of a group supervene on the mental states and actions of the individual members of the group.

While Tuomela (2004: 112) explicitly commits himself to a supervenience claim about group states and Schmitt (2003: 2) regards it as "nearly uncontroversial", I (Bird 2010, 2014) argue that it is false. The distributed model, as Hutchins presents it, also very clearly rejects both (SUP) and (SUP★). For that model is happy to regard inanimate objects as parts of systems that have cognitive properties such as belief, knowledge, and memory. The airspeed indicator and the speedbugs showing the correct speeds are a part of the cognitive system required to fly and land an aeroplane. In this respect the distributed model can be seen as moving even further away from the summative account than the commitment model.

Social Ontology

According to Quinton (1976: 19), the use of "belief" is metaphorical when applied to groups. Insofar as the summative account applies, there is no such thing as the group to which doxastic and epistemic attitudes can appropriately be ascribed in a non-metaphorical way. Those rejecting the summative account may be thought of as advancing two claims (i) there really is some non-trivial entity that is the group, and (ii) genuine doxastic and epistemic states may be possessed by that entity. In this section I address (i) and in the next section I look at (ii).

Trivial conceptions of group existence would be conceptions that apply to almost any collection of objects: for example, the group as the set of its members or the group as the mereological sum of its members. In going beyond trivial conceptions of a group we are looking for a principle of composition for groups that does justice to their being social entities, and, furthermore, that permits them to be possessors of doxastic and epistemic states. The commitment model and the distributed model may both be seen as supplying putative principles of composition for groups. The commitment model regards the group's existence as consisting in the joint commitment of its members, whereas the distributed model regards the group being constituted by those members being connected in a network of cognitive dependencies.

One might see this as a disagreement about what the correct principle of composition of a group is. Alternatively, one might also think that both are genuine ways in which individuals may be bound together into a social entity. In which case, one might think that there are, importantly, two different kinds of group—the bound-by-joint-commitment kind and the linked-by-a-cognitive-network kind. And maybe there are further types, too, corresponding to other modes of social composition, if there are other modes. (One perhaps should think that there are, insofar as we have been considering modes of composition that are explicitly doxastic/cognitive. And, presumably, there should be modes of composition that are not doxastic/cognitive. For example, a group can be united by shared grief or joy.)

One might then also wonder whether the term "group" is properly applied to both (or all) such kinds. For while it seems appropriate to think of a poetry reading group, a rugby club, a court, or the British cabinet, as a "group", it is less clear that the USS *Palau* or the cockpit of a commercial airliner are appropriately termed a "group". And so, if we are talking about *group* belief specifically (and that is the title of this article), then is not the commitment model the correct account (while the distributed model is an account of something else other than groups)? While that may be a correct observation about the term "group" and what it applies to, our broader interest ought to be with social entities more generally or at least that subset of social entities to which doxastic and epistemic states can be attributed. Some such entities may be called "groups" and others may be better termed "institutions" or something else.

Analogy with Individual Belief

A further question is whether it is appropriate to attribute *beliefs* to social groups or institutions. The summative account does not regard the groups as (non-trivial) entities and a fortiori does not ascribe *beliefs* to them. The use of the term "belief" is just a transference from the states of the individuals in the group. The commitment model and distributed model claim to describe states of genuine social entities. But why regard them as beliefs?

The best reason to regard the states in question as beliefs is that they bear a sufficiently close analogy to the beliefs of individuals.

An individual believer has a certain kind of commitment to a proposition: they will be disposed to assert that proposition and to deny its negation. The commitment model of group belief mirrors this feature of individual belief; the group's members are jointly committed to letting the proposition stand as the belief of the group. Furthermore, this is reinforced by requiring some degree of commitment by the individual members to the proposition. Gilbert emphasizes that members of a group that believe *p* should not disavow *p* and may be rebuked by the group if they do.

Asserting what one believes is a special case of a more general relationship between belief and action. While the commitment model does not directly mention action (other than openly expressing commitment, according to Gilbert), the model is typically accompanied by a corresponding account of social action (Tuomela 1984, 1995; Gilbert 2013). Just as a group may be committed as a group to a belief it may similarly be committed to an action, and presumably, if the individual members are rational and the group's decision making is appropriately organised, the group's beliefs and actions will be related just as individual belief and action (assuming also that the decision making process ensures avoidance of the discursive dilemma) (see List and Pettit 2013).

Contrasting with the commitment model, the distributed model makes the relationship to the action of a social entity more central to its conception of belief but does not place any special emphasis on the "commitment to a proposition" aspect of belief. The best way to see the analogy implicit in the distributed model is in terms of the analogy between social institutions and organisms originating with Émile Durkheim (1893) and developed as "structural functionalism" by Talcott Parsons (1961) and others. At the grand scale this view sees the whole of society as an organism, with the various institutions (the law, parliament, business, the security services, etc.) performing different functions in order to contribute to social cohesion. The analogy may also be applied to social entities below the level of society, such as the institutions themselves. The institution will have a set of roles or goals it pursues. It will do so by giving distinct functions to subgroups or to individuals. This parallels the different functions of the systems and organs of a biological organism that contribute to its organic unity and stability and to the pursuit of its overall goals. Furthermore, those functions in the social entity may have direct analogues with specific functions in the individual organism. In particular the pursuit of institutional goals (itself involving the analogue of action) will require social analogues of belief and desire or intention. An institution cannot pursue its goals without institutional beliefs.

One may think that this relationship to assertion and other kinds of action do not exhaust what is essential to belief. (After all, one would get the same pattern of behaviour in someone who is just pretending that *p* is the case.) Also important is a connection to the *truth*. Belief involves thinking that a proposition is true. Furthermore, normally beliefs are somewhat sensitive to evidence. If you see clouds and heavy rain, you do not believe that it is currently sunny and dry. While it is possible for an individual to hold on to a belief in the face of counter-evidence, such a belief may be thought to fail in some important way. Such a belief is not sensitive to the truth. Some philosophers try to capture this by saying that it is in the nature of belief to *aim* at the truth. One feature of the commitment model is that there is no clear connection of group belief to the truth. Since that account does not tell us how or why a group belief is formed, it is no part of the account that the group belief formation process is even normally sensitive to the truth. Tuomela (1992: 291) notes that this is a point of disanalogy between group and individual belief. The distributed model, on the other hand, starts from the idea of a cognitive system—a system whose function it is to gather and process information in order to guide action. So that model has the connection to truth as well as to action built into its account of group belief.

There is a clear parallel between the distributed account of group belief and the account of individual belief given by the functionalist theory of mind. Indeed one might suppose that this parallel could support the claim that both individual and social beliefs are states of one and the same more general type *belief*. In my view, this functionalist approach to group belief—and quite probably to other properties of groups also—promises to be a fruitful avenue for future inquiry.

Group Knowledge

In concert with the bulk of the literature on group epistemology, I have hitherto largely focussed on belief. Many of the same points apply, *mutatis mutandis*, to group knowledge. For example, the summative account (S) applies equally to knowledge and to belief. Similarly the supervenience thesis (SUP) applies to both, so long as knowing is held to be a mental state. Does group *knowledge* raise any particular further questions beyond those arising for group belief?

Given the emphasis on belief, a natural approach starts from the traditional view that individual knowledge is true belief plus some additional component—warrant, justification, causal connection, or reliability, *etc.* Then group knowledge is group belief that is true and accompanied by the group analogue of the additional component (Corlett 1996). For example, one might take knowledge to be justified (true) belief, in which case one needs to supplement one's account of group belief with an account of group justification. This may lead to asking, for example, when it is that a reason is a reason for a group (rather than simply for individual members of the group) (Tuomela 2004).

According to the knowledge-first programme (Williamson 2000), knowledge should not be analysed as belief plus some additional component. Instead, knowledge is the principal kind of state in epistemology, and other kinds of state (such as belief and justification, etc.) should be understood in terms of their relationship to it. This makes trouble for an account of group knowledge under the commitment model. Because the commitment model is a model of group belief, those who start from the commitment model tend to take the approach to group knowledge just outlined: group knowledge is group belief plus some additional (social) component. The distributed model, on the other hand, is not focussed on belief. Since its concern is with social cognitive systems, it is better suited to a knowledge-first account of group knowledge. For some, this may prove a decisive difference.

References

Bird, A. (2010). Social knowing. *Philosophical Perspectives*, 24, pp. 23–56.

Bird, A. (2014). When is there a group that knows? Scientific knowledge as social knowledge. In J. Lackey, ed., *Essays in Collective Epistemology*. Oxford: Oxford University Press., pp. 42–63.

Corlett, J. A. (1996). *Analyzing Social Knowledge*. Lanham, MD: Rowman and Littlefield.

Durkheim, E. (1893). *De la division du travail social*. Paris: Alcan. Translated as *The Division of Labor in Society*, by W. D. Halls, New York, NY: The Free Press, 1984.

Galton, F. (1907). Vox populi. *Nature*, 75, pp. 450–451.

Gilbert, M. (1987). Modelling collective belief. *Synthese*, 73, pp. 185–204.

Gilbert, M. (1989). *On Social Facts*. London: Routledge.

Gilbert, M. (1994). Remarks on collective belief. In F. F. Schmitt, ed., *Socializing Epistemology: The Social Dimensions of Knowledge*. Lanham, MD: Rowman and Littlefield., pp. 235–256.

Gilbert, M. (2004). Collective epistemology. *Episteme*, 1, pp. 95–107.

Gilbert, M. (2013). *Joint Commitment: How We Make the Social World*. Oxford: Oxford University Press.

Hutchins, E. (1995a). *Cognition in the Wild*. Cambridge, MA: MIT Press.

Hutchins, E. (1995b). How a cockpit remembers its speeds. *Cognitive Science*, 19, pp. 265–288.

Lewis, D. K. (1969). *Convention: A Philosophical Study*. Cambridge, MA: Harvard University Press.

List, C. and Pettit, P. (2013). *Group Agency*. Oxford: Oxford University Press.

Parsons, T. (1961). *Theories of Society: Foundations of Modern Sociological Theory*. New York NY: Free Press.

Pettit, P. (2003). Groups with minds of their own. In F. F. Schmitt, ed., *Socializing Metaphysics*. Lanham, MD: Rowman and Littlefield., pp. 167–193.

Quinton, A. (1976). Social objects. *Proceedings of the Aristotelian Society*, 76, pp. 1–27.

Schmitt, F. (1994). The justification of group beliefs. In F. F. Schmitt, ed., *Socializing Epistemology: The Social Dimensions of Knowledge*. Lanham, MD: Rowman and Littlefield., pp. 257–287.

Schmitt, F. (2003). Socializing metaphysics: An introduction. In F. F. Schmitt, ed., *Scoializing Metaphysics*. Lanham, MD: Rowman and Littlefield., pp. 1–37.

Tuomela, R. (1984). *A Theory of Social Action*. Dordrecht: D. Reidel.

Tuomela, R. (1992). Group beliefs. *Synthese*, 91, pp. 285–318.

Tuomela, R. (1995). *The Importance of Us*. Stanford, CA: Stanford University Press.

Tuomela, R. (2004). Group knowledge analyzed. *Episteme*, 1, pp. 109–127.

Vanderschraaf, P. and G. Sillari (2005). Common knowledge. In E. N. Zalta, ed., *The Stanford Encyclopedia of Philosophy*. Available at: http://plato.stanford.edu/archives/win2005/entries/common-knowledge/[Accessed Winter 2005].

Williamson T. (2000). *Knowledge and its Limits*. Oxford: Oxford University Press.

Further reading

Bird, A. J. (2014). When is there a group that knows? Scientific knowledge as social knowledge. In J. Lackey, ed., *Essays in Collective Epistemology*. Oxford: Oxford University Press. (Rejecting the supervenience thesis, this article emphasizes the importance of the distributed model for understanding group belief.)

Gilbert, M. (1987). Modelling collective belief. *Synthese*, 73, pp. 185–204. (A classic of the group belief literature, articulating the commitment model. The starting point for many subsequent discussions.)

Hutchins, E. (1995b). How a cockpit remembers its speeds. *Cognitive Science*, 19, pp.265–288. (The source of the idea of distributed cognition.)

Pettit, P. (2003). Groups with minds of their own. In F. F. Schmitt, ed., *Socializing Metaphysics*. Lanham, MD: Rowman and Littlefield. (Pettit starts from the discursive dilemma and discusses its implications for thinking of groups as having intentions and beliefs.)

Tuomela, R. (1992). Group beliefs. *Synthese*, 91, pp.285–318. (Another classic of the group belief literature promoting a version of the commitment model that, among other things, allows for "operative members" of a group to determine a group's belief.)

28

THE REFLEXIVE SOCIAL EPISTEMOLOGY OF HUMAN RIGHTS

Allen Buchanan

Perhaps the most persistent complaint about the modern human rights enterprise is that although it aims to ensure that all societies meet certain standards, it is founded on parochial moral values, not universal ones. Often the charge is that so-called universal human rights are rights that are valid, if at all, only from a Western or liberal-individualist point of view. In this chapter, I will focus on one especially important version of the parochialism objection, what I call The Different Goods Argument. It asserts that there are significant differences in the basic interests of men and women as such—natural differences whose proper appreciation allows or even requires different treatment of women in violation of antidiscrimination rights in international human rights law. The complaint is that the human rights movement's goal of ensuring that all individuals have access to the conditions for a minimally good life has been compromised by a failure to recognize that there are morally relevant differences between the good of men and the good of women because it has not appreciated the natural differences between these two distinct types of human beings.

This version of the parochialism objection does not assume that men and women share no basic interests and it is compatible with acknowledging that universal rights against certain forms of gender discrimination are warranted. Instead, the claim is that the human rights enterprise, at least in its understanding of which rights ought to be part of international human rights law, fails to appreciate the extent to which the natures and hence the interests of men and women differ and that this failure reveals a parochial point of view.

I suspect that many readers of this chapter—because they are highly educated members of Western societies and most likely trained in moral and political philosophy as well—will find it hard to take the Different Good Argument seriously. They may be tempted to regard it as simply a matter of false beliefs rooted in antiquated religious dogma or flawed folk theories of human nature. They might dismiss such benighted views as unworthy of critique in the pages of a volume on social epistemology. After all, it is not a view that enjoys any prominence, if it occurs at all, in the philosophical or legal literature on human rights. A second response, instead of dismissing the objection as unworthy of philosophical attention, is to assume that the power of the Different Goods Argument can be undercut by citing evidence about the capacities of women.

The first dismissive response (no one in "the literature" advances the Different Good Argument) betrays a problematic assumption about the proper subject matter of investigations in moral and political philosophy, namely, they should be confined to engagement with the views of moral and political philosophers—or, more accurately, those moral and political philosophers whose works are part of the standard Western literatures. That assumption is unfortunate, because if taken seriously it would preclude moral and political philosophers engaging critically with some views that are widely held and exert a significant influence on individual behavior and social practices. In brief, being important in "the literature" (*our* literature) is not the same as being important. Moreover, the Different Good Argument does actually find expression in other literatures, including some strains of Islamic jurisprudence, in the justification of inferior rights of due process for women in some Sharia-influenced legal systems. For example, the official justification for the Iranian legal system's provision that the testimony of two women counts only as much as the testimony of one man in certain cases (including rape), is that women's testimony is less reliable, due to their greater emotionality and lesser rationality.[1]

The second response—combatting the parochialism objection by trying to convince those who hold it that they have mistaken beliefs about the facts, is, as I shall show, epistemically and psychologically naïve. It assumes that providing information (or sound arguments) is sufficient, thereby overlooking the fact that an individual's social experience can predispose her toward sustaining false beliefs in the face of information that contradicts them and sound arguments to refute them. The second response ignores the fact that individuals function as knowers within a particular social-epistemic environment, a set of social practices and institutions through which they come to know—or mistakenly believe they know—together, as part of an epistemic community. The knowledge that the members of an epistemic community are capable of achieving depends upon the character of its social experience, as that experience is categorized and interpreted through the medium of shared epistemic norms and cultural values.

In order to provide an effective response to the Different Goods version of the parochialism objection, a deeper explanation of the appeal of the objection is needed: one that explains the existence and persistence of false beliefs about natural differences and also their uneven distribution among human populations. One needs to know why in some societies many people hold these false beliefs and continue to cleave to them in the face of contradictory information about the capacities of women. One also needs to know why the Different Goods Argument and the beliefs about natural differences it relies on have so little traction with many people in other societies. This chapter will provide the needed explanations and in so doing shed light on how progress in understanding and realizing human rights can best be achieved. The practical message of the inquiry will be that changing false beliefs about natural differences is not likely to be achieved simply by providing information or engaging in argument; changing social practices and thereby transforming the social experience to which they give rise will likely be required. For individuals to come to realize that various human rights are valid for all human beings, women as well as men, it may be necessary to achieve a transformation of their social experience and with it the character of the epistemic collective in which they function as knowers. What "we" all know about differences between men and women may be altered only if social experience changes.

An Epistemic Argument against the Different Good Objection

My criticism of the Different Good Argument emphasizes the *epistemic value* of avoiding the social practices prohibited by various legal human rights, including, preeminently rights against discrimination on grounds of gender and race. It begins by pressing a question that proponents of the Different Goods Argument fail to ask: under what conditions are judgments about individuals' innate capacities and hence about their basic interests and good likely to be reliable? My answer is that the circumstances in which such judgments are likely to be reliable include, *inter alia*, the substantial realization of various human rights, in particular rights against gender discrimination, but also rights to freedom of association, expression, and political participation.

The epistemic argument, in simplest form, can be outlined as follows:

1 Whether social orders that include pervasive discrimination against the members of some group are compatible with securing those individuals' basic interests (or more strongly, are compatible with the optimal well-being of all members of a society) cannot be determined *a priori*; it must be determined empirically.

2 For most people, empirical evidence for what is conducive to well-being and, more specifically, for determining which interests are basic interests, comes from experience, including social experience that reveals the capacities of human beings, because what is conducive to an individual's well-being or helps secure her basic interests depends to some extent upon her capacities.

3 Only under social conditions in which individuals can freely develop and exercise their capacities does social experience provide reliable evidence about innate human capacities and about natural differences among groups of humans and hence about what the basic interests common to all human beings are.[2]

4 Social conditions in which there is pervasive discrimination on grounds of gender (or race or ethnicity or caste, etc.), severely limit the exercise and in some cases the development of the capacities of the victims of discrimination and thereby create a social experience that encourages false beliefs about natural differences between men and women (and between members of different races, ethnicities, etc.).

5 Therefore, in social conditions in which there is pervasive discrimination, social experience does not provide reliable evidence about innate human capacities and hence about what the basic interests common to all human beings are.

6 The only conditions under which (the majority of) women can freely develop and exercise their capacities are those in which rights against discrimination are substantially realized.

7 Therefore, the only conditions in which social experience provides reliable evidence about natural differences and innate capacities, and hence about what is conducive to the realization of basic interests shared by all individuals, include the substantial realization of rights against discrimination on grounds of gender (and similarly for race, ethnicity, sexual preference, etc.).

8 Therefore, the only conditions under which one can reliably ascertain, on the basis of social experience, whether efforts to realize rights against discrimination are facilitating or impeding the realization of basic interests are those under which rights against discrimination are substantially realized.

9 Whether human rights law should include rights against discrimination depends in part upon whether the implementation of such rights is compatible with such law effectively fulfilling the basic interest function, that is, ensuring that all individuals have access to the conditions generally necessary for realizing their basic interests.

10 Therefore, (from (7), (8), (9)) whether human rights law should include rights against discrimination can be reliably ascertained, on the basis of social experience, only where rights against discrimination have been substantially realized.

The key idea is that the only conditions under which one can reliably know on the basis of social experience what basic interests individuals share and what is conducive to their realization— and therefore can know whether the realization of rights against discrimination helps ensure the conditions under which individuals can realize their basic interests—are those in which rights against gender discrimination are already substantially realized. It follows that the social moral epistemology of human rights can properly be described as reflexive: success in the realization of certain key human rights may be required if we are to know whether our understandings of human rights are parochial or not. And where such success has been achieved, there is reason to believe that one important version of the charge of parochialism—the allegation that the human rights project ignores important differences in the basic interests of men and women—is unjustified.

The qualifier "on the basis of social experience" (from the beginning of the previous paragraph) is important. One could form an undistorted understanding of the capacities on the basis of testimony that is ultimately grounded in social experience that is available in societies in which rights against discrimination are substantially realized, even if one lived in a society that featured pervasive discrimination. For various reasons, however, it appears that many individuals who live in societies where discrimination is pervasive rely heavily on their own social experience or on the testimony of supposed authorities in their own society in forming and sustaining their beliefs about natural differences between men and women. Such individuals either lack access to reliable testimony about the capacities of women (due to illiteracy or lack of education or government restrictions on information) or discredit such testimony because they distrust its sources, in some cases because of dogmatically held religious or ideological views. The extent to which individuals are open to testimony based on the social experience of societies other than their own may vary greatly, depending upon the character of the epistemic collective of which they are a part. If an individual's epistemic collective features norms that accord virtually unconditional epistemic deference to religious leaders and these leaders deny that other societies, structured by different religious practices, are credible sources of beliefs, then he or she and other members of that epistemic community will not heed testimony about social experiences that contradict shared beliefs. There will be some facts that the group cannot know and that individual members of it are very unlikely to be able to know. My epistemic argument focuses on cases where the charge that international anti-discriminatory legal human rights reflect a parochial point of view is supported, at least implicitly, by appeal to social experience in the objector's own society or societies like it, rather than to testimony about the social experience of other, different societies.

The upshot of this epistemic argument against the parochialism objection to the Different Goods argument can be put, if somewhat provocatively, as follows: The Different Goods Argument version of the parochialism objection against human rights is itself an example of parochial moral thinking. Those who live in societies in which human rights against discrimination are not substantially realized are in a worse epistemic position for determining whether those rights are tainted by parochialism than those who live in societies in which they are. A society in which discrimination prevents women from developing and exercising their capacities is a poor epistemic environment for determining what women are capable of and hence for ascertaining what is most conducive to their well-being. That epistemic environment includes formidable obstacles to forming accurate, evidence-based judgments about the natural capacities of women.

The same is true, I shall argue shortly, for societies in which there is significant discrimination on grounds of race or sexual orientation: they are poor epistemic environments in which to make judgments about the facts relevant to determining whether these other forms of differential treatment are permissible or instead are discriminatory in the pejorative sense. Discriminatory environments do not provide good epistemic standpoints from which to determine whether rights against discrimination are tainted by parochial bias.

If we assume that an important function of human rights is to protect basic human interests, then certain rights that are now commonly regarded as human rights ought to be implemented because their realization is necessary for creating an epistemic environment in which human rights generally, including those rights themselves, can be reliably identified. Because pervasive discrimination produces a distorted social experience that encourages and sustains false beliefs about human interests, efforts to overcome such discrimination are justified, in part, because they are needed if we are to be in a good position to make accurate judgments about human interests and hence about the sorts of rights that are needed to ensure their protection. Call this the epistemic boot-strapping argument.

Why Understandings of Human Rights are Subject to Revision

Suppose one assumes, as many philosophical theorists of human rights do, that an important function of human rights law and the human rights practices that are anchored on it is to ensure that each individual has access to what is needed to realize her basic interests.[3] On this assumption, the justification for including various rights in international human rights law requires certain empirical assumptions about what human beings' shared basic interests are, about what the standard threats to the interests are in our world (for the foreseeable future), and about which legal rights help to protect those interests against the standard threats. There is reason to believe that those empirical assumptions are corrigible, not only because of the possibility of errors in judgments about current interests and threats, but also because changing circumstances can produce new interests and threats. For the purposes of this inquiry, the chief point is that various biases, including parochial moral perspectives, are potential sources of errors in how human interests and hence human rights are conceived.

The question, then, is whether we can identify and achieve the most epistemically reliable conditions for making the needed empirical assumptions and for revising them over time. My contention is that although we do not know what the full set of optimal feasible epistemic conditions is, we do know that some social arrangements are detrimental to the formation of justified beliefs about human interests and that they include forms of discrimination that create a social experience that appears to confirm false beliefs about natural differences and innate capacities.[4] When discrimination is pervasive, judgments about the basic interests of various subgroups of humanity are likely to be distorted. Ironically, such judgments are likely to be tainted by parochialism: they will tend to be partial, biased views because they will be shaped by arbitrarily limited experience, and those who hold them will be oblivious to this limitation. That is what it means to say they are likely to be parochial. If that is so, then it is the proponents of the parochialism objection who are guilty of the very error they accuse proponents of the human rights project of perpetrating.

Having outlined the argument, I shall now flesh it out through the use of examples. The examples have two features in common: (i) discriminatory practices produce a kind of experience that appears to confirm the false beliefs that are invoked to justify the practices and (ii) the distorted experience would not occur were human rights against discrimination successfully implemented. In each case, discriminatory social practices prevent the victims of discrimination from exhibiting behavior that would disconfirm false beliefs about their natures and innate capacities, and this in turn renders judgments about their basic interests and more generally about their good unreliable. And in each case, realization of rights against discrimination would allow those victims to act in ways that provide sound evidence as to what their basic interests are. I will consider in turn epistemic distortions produced by gender discrimination, racial discrimination, and discrimination against gays and lesbians. The three cases also have this in common: (i) discriminatory social practices are epistemically debilitating in ways that create the illusion that the beliefs invoked to justify them are true, (ii) the effects of discrimination are mistaken for valid grounds for discrimination, and (iii) the epistemic disabilities are epistemic injustices insofar as they are epistemic disadvantages grounded in injustice.

Gender Discrimination

Consider two examples from different ends of a spectrum of discrimination that runs from more to less extreme. The first is the case of the severe forms of gender discrimination practices in some societies in which Islam is the dominant religion. Most women are excluded from education altogether or from anything but basic education, prevented from engaging in economic activity outside the home of sufficient scale to enable them to live independently, excluded from holding public office and in some cases from any meaningful form of political participation, have significantly restricted property rights, and their mobility outside the home is curtailed by the requirement that they be accompanied by a male relative. The pervasive ideology of gender differences invoked to justify these discriminatory practices portrays the actual condition of women in such a society as their natural condition—that is, as the condition that is most consonant with their natures as women.

In such societies, most women will have little opportunity to develop some of the capacities that men freely exercise and those women who somehow manage to develop these capacities will have few opportunities for exercising them—or at least for exercising them in public view. Under these conditions, the dominant experience of what women are like will appear to confirm the ideology's claims about the natural differences between men and women. Mistaken inferences about the supposedly inferior innate capacities of women will be drawn from experience of the severely truncated exercises of capacities of women suffering severe discrimination. These epistemic errors will afflict both individuals and society as a whole, or the dominant group within it. That is, if beliefs can be attributed not just to individual members of the society but to the society as a collective, or to a dominant group within society, then distorted social experience, categorized and interpreted according to social epistemic norms, will produce beliefs that preclude collective knowledge of what women are really like. Collective knowing typically occurs through an array of social-epistemic practices that feature a division of epistemic labor characterized by hierarchies of epistemic deference.[5] What "we" know, as members of an epistemic collective, depends upon a shared social experience categorized and interpreted according to shared norms that confer epistemic deference upon some sources of testimony and dismiss others as unreliable. If the social experience is distorted by patterns of discrimination and shared epistemic norms serve to reinforce the distortions rather than remedy them, then "we" will not know what "we" think "we" know.

People who live in such societies are generally in a poor epistemic position when it comes to judging what the basic interests of women are. They are also generally in a poor epistemic position to claim that proponents of rights against gender discrimination have a parochial understanding of the basic interests shared by all people, whether male or female.

A less extreme example of gender discrimination exhibits the same pattern. Until quite recently, it was quite common for schoolteachers in the United States to assume that girls were innately or naturally inferior in mathematical ability compared to boys. Social scientists have shown that this belief encourages teachers to act in ways that produce an experience that seems to confirm it.[6],[7] When they believe that girls are inferior in mathematical ability, teachers spend less time helping them to develop their ability than they do with boys. The result is that girls less frequently excel at mathematics. The poorer performance of girls is then taken to confirm the assumption that they have lesser ability.

Racial Discrimination

Racial discrimination produces its own distorted experience. In the Jim Crow American South and in South Africa under Apartheid, a dense and pervasive web of discriminatory practices severely limited the educational and occupational opportunities of Blacks. Predictably, under these conditions one rarely encountered an educated Black person or one who engaged in anything other than menial labor. Discrimination thus prevented most Blacks from exhibiting higher mental capacities and in some cases inhibited their development.[8] Experience of what Blacks are like seemed to confirm the belief that they were inferior by nature, so far as mental capacities were concerned—the very belief that was invoked to justify the discriminatory practices that produced that social experience. Only when a significant reduction of discrimination occurred was it possible for the true capacities of Black people to be known. People ensnared in the self-perpetuating delusion of this distorted experience were in a poor epistemic position to assert that their social practices conformed to natural differences between Whites and Blacks. Nor were they on solid epistemic ground when they claimed, as they typically did, that those who condemned their discriminatory practices did not understand what Blacks are like.

Discrimination against Gays and Lesbians

The case of discrimination on grounds of sexual orientation is similar to those of gender and racial discrimination, but with some differences. When "homosexual acts" were subject to criminal liability, gays and lesbians had to live in the shadows and in some cases developed a kind of underground culture that differed significantly from mainstream heterosexual culture. Because the underground culture included anonymous, episodic sexual encounters, often conducted in bathhouses, public restrooms, or other dubious venues, heterosexuals developed distorted views of "the gay life-style", often assuming that gays were interested only in sex, not intimacy and stable relationships.

Once the legal restrictions were lifted, the costs of living openly as a gay or lesbian person dropped dramatically. When gays and lesbians could afford to stop disguising their sexual preferences, and could integrate more fully into the larger society, increasing numbers of heterosexual people came to realize that they had gay or lesbian friends, relatives, co-workers, and co-religionists. On the basis of the new experience that the increasing realization of rights against discrimination on grounds of sexual preference produced, they came to understand that gays and lesbians were people just like themselves, only with different sexual preferences. In contrast, in societies in which gay and lesbians are subject to serious and pervasive discrimination, especially in the form of the criminal law, it is very difficult for heterosexuals to have an accurate picture of what gay and lesbian people are like. Discrimination creates a social experience that prevents people from recognizing that they hold distorted stereotypes of the victims of discrimination. Both individual and collective knowing can be impaired by reliance on the distorted social experience that discrimination produces.

The Self-Reinforcing Testimonial Injustice of Discriminatory Practices

Where racial, gender, or ethnic discrimination is pervasive, the victims of discrimination are likely to suffer serious "testimonial injustice" in Miranda Fricker's sense of that term. For Fricker, testimonial injustice occurs when some people, by virtue of their being identified as members of a particular group, are wrongly excluded from or disadvantaged in the social processes by which knowledge is created—they are wrongly viewed as unreliable or comparatively inferior sources of true beliefs.[9] Discriminatory practices that relegate them to an inferior status will tend to discredit them as sources of knowledge generally, including and perhaps especially knowledge about their own interests. In some cases, the discriminatory practices will exclude these individuals from important spaces in which public perception is formed, as when women are confined to the household or people of color or lower caste are excluded from certain public venues. When this occurs, they will not have the opportunity to shape public perceptions of their basic interests, nor to correct for the distortions that social experience grounded in discriminatory practices produces.

A Deeper Epistemic Injustice: Unjust Deprivation of Opportunities for Developing an Accurate Understanding of One's Own Interests and the Threats to Them

If discrimination extends to restrictions on educational opportunities, the victims of discrimination will be less able to articulate their understanding of what is conducive to their interests. And if discrimination restricts their freedom of association, they may be unable to draw on each other's experiences in order to gain a more accurate knowledge of their common interests and of how existing social practices thwart their realization.[10] Discrimination in education and discrimination that bars individuals from freely associating with other victims of discrimination can also produce what Fricker calls hermeneutical injustice: individuals may, as a consequence of injustices of discrimination that they suffer, be deprived of the concepts needed for effectively articulating their interests and identifying the injustices that thwart their realization. Further, the victims of discrimination will, as I have argued, be deprived, as a result of the injustice they suffer, of the sort of experience that would provide reliable evidence of the nature of their own capacities and hence of their own interests.[11] In all of these ways, the victims of discrimination will be epistemically disadvantaged as a result of unjust social practices and will therefore suffer epistemic injustices. They will be excluded from the epistemic collective and yet be expected to acknowledge and conform their behavior to the "truths" the epistemic collective claims to know. And the epistemic injustices they suffer will contribute to sustaining the unjust social practices that cause them.

The Reflexive Flawed Social Moral Epistemology of Discrimination

My epistemic argument against the Different Good version of the parochialism objection emphasizes the reflexive nature of the social epistemology of human rights—that the conditions under which certain human rights are substantially realized provide the best epistemic environment for having an accurate understanding of the basic interests that human rights are supposed to protect and hence for forming sound understandings of human rights so far as they are supposed to help realize basic interests.

I now want to emphasize that the flawed social epistemology of discrimination is also reflexive, but in a deeply pernicious way. The key point is that the injustice of discrimination fosters a distorted social experience that is then invoked as evidence for the truth of the beliefs about natural differences that serve to justify the discrimination, while at the same time discrimination produces testimonial and hermeneutical injustices that make it difficult for individuals to understand or to reveal to others the distorted character of social experience.[12]

Conclusion

One of the most prominent forms of the objection that the modern human rights enterprise is infected with parochial moral bias is that the attempt to impose universal standards intended to realize basic human interests overlooks relevant differences between the basic interests of men and women. In this essay, I have argued that the social moral epistemology of human rights is reflexive in this sense: the best epistemic environment for determining what basic interests all human beings share is one in which rights against discrimination are substantially realized. I have also argued that the social moral epistemology of environments in which these human rights are systematically violated is also reflexive in a negative sense: the violation of these rights creates an epistemic environment in which testimonial and hermeneutical injustices, as well as distorted social experience, reinforce the injustice of discrimination.

Notes

1   This inequality of testimony (and often of compensation for death) is most thoroughly applied in Saudi Arabia and Iran, but also exists in some form in most of the countries in the Middle-East/North Africa region. Notable *de jure* exceptions are Oman and Tunisia. See Freedom House's report: *Women's Rights in the Middle East and North Africa: Progress Amid Resistance*. Sanja Kelly and Julia Breslin (eds). (New York: Rowman & Littlefield, 2010). That the justification for the rule is due to the inferior nature of women's intellect is most clearly seen in Sahih al-Bukhari, hadith 3:48:826: "Isn't the witness of a women equal to half that of a man?" The women said "yes". He said "This is because of the deficiency of the women's mind." transl. M. Muhsin Khan (Omar Ibn Al Khattab Foundation, & USC Center for Religion and Civic Culture: [website] http://www.usc.edu/org/cmje/religious-texts/hadith/bukhari/048-sbt.php#003.048.826).

2   John Stuart Mill makes this point in *The Subjection of Women*. (Online Library of Liberty, 1869).

3   I have argued at length that this is only one of the two important functions of the realization of international legal human rights, the other being the public affirmation and protection of equal basic status. Allen Buchanan, *The Heart of Human Rights* (Oxford: Oxford University Press, 2011).

4 Charles Mills, "White Ignorance." In *Race and Epistemologies of Ignorance*. Ed.Shannon Sullivan and Nancy Tuana. (Albany: SUNY Press, 2007).

5 James Bohman, "Democracy as inquiry, inquiry as pragmatic: pragmatism, social science, and the cognitive division of labor." *American Journal of Political Science* vol. 43, no.2 (1999), pp. 590–607.

6 Qing Li, "Teacher's beliefs and gender differences in mathematics: a review." *Educational Research* vol. 41, no.1 (1999), pp. 63–76.

7 Elizabeth A. Gunderson, et al. "The role of parents and teachers in the development of gender-related math attitudes." *Sex Roles* vol. 63, no.3–4 (2012), pp. 153–166.

8 Claude Steele and Joshua Aronson, "Stereotype threat and the intellectual performance of African Americans." *Journal of Personality and Social Psychology* vol. 69, no. 5 (1995), p. 797.

9 Miranda Fricker, *Epistemic Injustice*. (Oxford: Oxford University Press, 2001).

10 Mills (2007) ibid., Martín Alcoff (2007) ibid.

11 If hermeneutical injustice consists in being unjustly deprived of concepts needed to articulate one's predicament, then this last sort of epistemic justice is not the same as hermeneutical injustice, because one might have all the concepts needed to understand that one is being treated unjustly, but fail to apply them properly because one had false beliefs resulting from the distorted experience that injustice produces. Take the concept of sexual harassment as an example: many women are aware in the abstract of what constitutes sexual harassment, but paradoxically, victims often doubt that their own experience falls under this category. Martín Alcoff (2007) argues that victims often have good reasons to "maintain their own ignorance about the social order … reasons that have to do with overall mental health and functional social relations" (p. 44). Linda Martín Alcoff, "Epistemologies of Ignorance: Three Types." In *Race and Epistemologies of Ignorance*. Ed.Shannon Sullivan and Nancy Tuana. (Albany: SUNY Press, 2007).

12 My claim is that ending or reducing discriminatory practices may be necessary for spreading better understandings of human rights, not that it is sufficient. False beliefs about the capacities of members of various groups may persist unless the notion of equal basic status that is central to the modern human rights movement becomes part of the culture.

References

Alcoff, L. (2007). Epistemologies of Ignorance: Three Types. In: S. Sullivan and N. Tuana, eds., *Race and Epistemologies of Ignorance*, 39–58. Albany: SUNY Press.

Bohman, J. (1999). Democracy as inquiry, inquiry as pragmatic: pragmatism, social science, and the cognitive division of labor. *American Journal of Political Science*, 43(2), pp. 590–607.

Buchanan, A. (2011). *The Heart of Human Rights*. Oxford: Oxford University Press.

Fricker, M. (2001). *Epistemic Injustice*. Oxford: Oxford University Press.

Gunderson, E., et al. (2012). The role of parents and teachers in the development of gender-related math attitudes. *Sex Roles*, 66(3–4), pp. 153–166.

Kelly, S. and Breslin, J. (eds.). (2010). *Women's Rights in the Middle East and North Africa: Progress Amid Resistance*. New York: Rowman & Littlefield Publishers.

Li, Q. (1999). Teacher's beliefs and gender differences in mathematics: a review. *Educational Research*, 41(1), pp. 63–76.

Mills, C. (2007) White Ignorance. In: S. Sullivan and N. Tuana, eds., *Race and Epistemologies of Ignorance*, 13–38. Albany: SUNY Press.

Steele, C. and Aronson, J. (1995). Stereotype threat and the intellectual performance of African Americans. *Journal of Personality and Social Psychology*, 69(5), pp. 797–811.

Further Reading

Anderson, E. (2012). Epistemic justice as a virtue of institutions. *Social Epistemology* 26(2): pp. 163–173.

Buchanan, A. (2004). Political liberalism and social epistemology. *Philosophy and Public Affairs*, 32(2), pp. 95–130.

Buchanan, A. (2009). Social Moral Epistemology and the Tasks of Ethics. In: A. Davis, R. Keshen and J. McMahan, eds., *Ethics and Humanity: Themes From the Philosophy of Jonathan Glover*. Oxford: Oxford University Press.

Fricker, M. (2016). Epistemic Injustice and the Preservation of Ignorance. In: R. Peels and M. Blaauw, eds., *The Epistemic Dimension of Ignorance*, eds. Rik Peels and Martjn Blaauw, 160–177. Cambridge: Cambridge University Press.

PART VI

Feminist Epistemology

29

FEMINIST EPISTEMOLOGY

Heidi Grasswick

Introduction

At its core, feminist epistemology seeks to expose and understand the epistemic salience of gendered social relations. Its interests lie in both descriptive questions concerning how gendered relations affect knowing, and in normative questions concerning how knowers can know well within social contexts shaped by gender, and how we can design robust and successful knowledge practices within such contexts. Its inclusion of normative issues ensures that it is a social *epistemology* as opposed to simply a *sociology* of knowledge (Grasswick, 2013, 2014a), and its central concern with the relationship between gender and knowing places it squarely within the purview of *social* epistemology (Anderson, 1995; Grasswick, 2013) as opposed to what many refer to as mainstream *individualistic* epistemology.

But it would be a mistake to frame feminist epistemology as an enterprise exclusively focused on gender. Rather, as feminists have become increasingly attuned to the intersectional nature of social identities, recognizing that experiences of gender cannot be understood in isolation from numerous other aspects of one's social identity, their work has attended to the epistemic relevance of other social categories such as those drawn along the lines of race, ethnicity, sexuality, able-bodiedness, and class (to name a few) (Alcoff and Potter, 1993). Ultimately, feminist epistemologists are concerned with how social relations and their associated power dynamics structure our epistemic practices and make a difference to who knows, how we know, and what knowing amounts to. Gendered relations, even when understood on an intersectional model, offer only one example of socially structured power relations that carry epistemic ramifications and are therefore of interest to feminist epistemologists.

Social epistemology itself is a broad-ranging field and has been described as a "loosely related family of disputes" that vary in focus with respect to different kinds of knowledge, and the different ways in which knowledge can be social (Schmitt, 1994, p. 1). The relationship of feminist epistemology to social epistemology can be characterized in at least two different ways. On the one hand, feminist epistemology can be viewed as a *sub-field* of social epistemology, in that it contributes to a certain collection of topics and debates that fall within social epistemology's "loosely related family of disputes" and draws attention to the social dimensions of certain kinds of knowledge. For example, feminists are particularly interested in knowledge of social relations and the phenomenon of oppression, both how it works and how it can be transformed. They have found individualistic epistemologies that assume a singular appropriate epistemic perspective across social positions to be inadequate for developing this kind of knowledge of structured social relations. Instead, they have developed sophisticated accounts of how particular social positions can offer potential insights into the workings of oppression that would be missed if one's analysis did not take seriously the differences in perspectives and insights that can accompany social position. Though knowledge of oppression might be considered a very specific topic, feminists have also made substantial contributions to broader epistemological issues, such as the epistemic role of testimony. Analyses of testimony have formed one of the largest and most active areas of discussion in contemporary social epistemology. Feminists' attention to the role of social power relations in the economies of credibility has provided a distinct angle from which to develop insightful descriptive and normative assessments of testimony across differently situated agents. The burgeoning literature on epistemic injustice including testimonial injustice (see Daukas, this volume) is evidence of the widespread interest in such feminist contributions.

On the other hand, feminist epistemology can be understood not so much as a sub-field but rather as an overall approach to doing social epistemology—an approach that begins with the idea that knowing is *socially situated* and critically investigates epistemic practices and revisits key epistemological questions with this in mind. In spite of substantial differences between particular versions of feminist epistemology, this tenet of situated knowing remains a key feature of a feminist approach (Grasswick, 2014a). First articulated by Donna Haraway, the tenet of situated knowing holds that the social situation of a knower both shapes and limits their knowing (Haraway, 1988). Feminists investigate both the ways in which differences in the social location of various (individual) knowers can shape and limit their respective knowing, and also the ways in which shared features of social life and practices inevitably shape and limit the knowledge that is produced within particular communities and cultures.

The basic idea of socially situated knowing amounts to a denial of the traditional framing of the epistemic point of view as a "view from nowhere," embracing instead the idea that knowing is inherently perspectival, with perspectives being tied to our materially and socially grounded position in the world. This sets it apart from some approaches in social epistemology that remain committed to a conception of knowledge as aperspectival while working within such a framework to engage in certain social epistemic questions such as (to give just one example) how to optimize the cognitive division of labor in order to maximize the generation of true (aperspectival) claims (Kitcher, 1990).

An "approach" to social epistemology, as I am using the phrase, marks the starting assumptions, or the starting orientation of one's epistemological investigations. But it does not specify the end point of those investigations. Accordingly, to say that feminists operate with a starting assumption of socially situated knowing does not imply that they insist that every form of knowledge is socially situated in the same way or to the same extent. There may well be exceptions, and investigations into how a particular form of knowing is socially situated may or may not bear fruit. Epistemic contexts differ, and the ways in which social situation affects knowing differ accordingly (Wylie, 2003). The point of a socially situated approach, however, is to provide a tool that will help reveal the workings of social situation in knowing where such workings are present. Epistemological approaches that are impervious to the epistemic specificities of social location, whether those be differences between knowers or shared cultural frameworks, will be incapable of revealing any marks of social situation that may in fact be present. For example, feminists have found the adoption of a socially situated approach to be a crucial tool in revealing many of the ways in which gender bias has affected various areas of knowledge production, and have argued that traditional individualistic and aperspectival approaches necessarily miss such important dimensions of knowledge production.

A situated approach also leads feminists to develop new normative visions for what is involved in knowing the world well. For example, rather than retreating into a straightforward relativism that might be thought to follow from the claim that knowing is both shaped and limited by social situation, many feminist epistemologists have understood the implications of socially situated knowing to demand engagement across social situations and perspectives (Longino, 1990), and a critical awareness of the role of one's own social location (Harding, 1991) in order to achieve a robust form of objectivity in our knowing.

Understood as an "approach" to social epistemology, it should be no surprise that feminists have used the general idea of situated knowing to investigate many different topics of interest to social epistemologists. In what follows, I describe its historical development as an approach, and highlight several different areas of social epistemology to which feminists have contributed.

The Historical Development of Feminist Epistemology and Its Situated Approach

Feminist epistemology first emerged in the early 1980s on the heels of early developments in feminist social and political philosophy as feminists began to widen their interests across multiple areas of philosophy, seeking to understand the philosophical implications of their initial analyses of gender oppression. At the same time, feminist researchers in other disciplines, and especially the social sciences, were struggling to explain why androcentricism and other forms of gender bias in their fields were only becoming visible as self-identified feminists entered their fields. For them, it was becoming increasingly clear that traditional epistemological frameworks that isolated standards of objectivity and measures of high quality research from the social contexts of knowing and the corresponding identities of the knowers were inadequate for what they took to be an important epistemic phenomenon in need of explanation (Harding, 1983; Longino, 1999). The situated approach I described above was not just randomly selected as a starting point for feminist explorations into epistemology. Rather, it developed out of feminist attempts to address just such epistemological puzzles as the persistence of gender bias in knowledge production, and the ways in which shifts in the demographics of research communities historically made a difference to their abilities to perceive such bias in the research and develop new research directions in the process.

Early pieces in feminist epistemology such as Lorraine Code's "Is the Sex of the Knower Epistemically Significant?" (Code, 1981) and Sandra Harding's "Why has the Sex/Gender System Become Visible Only Now?" (Harding, 1983) began to explore the idea that gender might make a difference to what and how one knows. As feminist epistemology progressed throughout the 1980s, theorists became increasingly aware that a distinction needed to be made between what one might consider a "feminine" epistemology that took there to be essential differences in knowing and reasoning between the sexes (a "women's ways of knowing" approach), and a "feminist" epistemology that understood gender to be a culturally defined social position embedded in structured power relations that could impact knowledge-seeking enterprises.[1] While feminist epistemology grew, the likes of "feminine epistemology" came to be increasingly left behind as the field of feminist theory itself became more conscious of the problems of essentializing any aspect of womanhood, given the vast evidence of differences in women's experiences and the intersectional nature of identities (Lugones and Spelman, 1983).

At the time of these early 1980s developments in feminist epistemology, there was no well-developed vibrant field of social epistemology like the one we recognize today. In fact, Frederick Schmitt acknowledges the work of feminist philosophers of science as one of the two major inspirations (alongside naturalized epistemology) for the developments of social epistemology through the 1980s (Schmitt, 1994), and many of the significant appearances of special journal issues and major full-length works in feminist epistemology predate similar markers in social epistemology (Grasswick, 2013). During this time, epistemology as a whole remained very much in the grip of an analytic approach that worked with abstract conceptions of rational individual knowers and idealized accounts of necessary and sufficient conditions for knowledge. Feminists found this paradigm extremely limiting and incapable of addressing their most pressing epistemological concerns, such as figuring out how to identify and correct for bias in knowledge production practices, and how to appropriately value epistemic contributions from those who might have less social and epistemic influence than others. Furthermore, many of their early critiques suggested not just that such abstract models of knowledge were limiting, but that they actually contributed to some of the problems in knowledge production, by masking male bias behind a facade of having achieved the "view from nowhere" (Code, 1991; Scheman, 1993). It was not just a question of feminists adopting existing epistemological tools and applying them to newly revealed topics of feminist interest. Rather as Lorraine Code argued, feminists needed to "remap the epistemic terrain" (Code, 1991).

One of feminists' major critiques of the dominant epistemological framework concerned its conception of knowers as atomistic: not only did the paradigm operate on the assumption that knowers were primarily individuals, but it also conceptualized these individuals as self-sufficient and generic (or interchangeable) from the epistemic point of view (Code, 1991; Grasswick, 2004; Nelson, 1993; Potter, 1993). Accordingly, there was nothing special about knowers' particularities or social locations that needed accounting for in standard epistemological analyses, and thus no reason to pay any attention to the social identities of knowers or their relationship to other knowers. But feminist epistemologists challenged these opening assumptions, finding that attention to questions such as *who is it that knows?* and *who is claiming knowledge?* could in fact provoke important investigations and reveal features of our epistemic practices that had previously passed unnoticed. As feminists began to trace the epistemic effects of power relations between knowers, they were able to see how some epistemic agents had more control over the epistemic agenda than others, and more power to determine the assumptions that would govern research processes and shape the very standards of knowledge itself. Feminists noted differences in the credibility attributed to differently situated knowers, differences that allowed some more than others to have their understandings of the world circulated and taken up by others as authoritative accounts. Such realizations also led feminists to grapple with making sense of the normative demands of a theory of knowledge: how were different epistemic perspectives represented by differently located knowers to be negotiated, such that a robust conception of knowing and knowledge could emerge? Their original criticisms of the individualism of traditional epistemology turned out to have rather far-reaching effects for a theory of knowledge.

Though much attention has been paid to feminists' critiques of the standard rendition of knowers within traditional epistemology, it is worth noting that feminists found other aspects of the dominant framework troubling as well. The standard framework promoted rarified and idealized epistemological analyses that worked best for extremely simple forms of knowing such as basic perceptual claims and claims about medium-sized material objects (Code, 1991). However, feminists were especially interested in more complex kinds of knowledge, such as coming to understand social phenomena, social experience, and what it might mean to "know" other people (Code, 1991). Additionally, as epistemologists focused on idealized accounts of knowledge and attempts to defeat the skeptic, their abstractions seemed to many feminists to be far removed from the practical issues of how knowers could "know well" within an imperfect and embodied world where the epistemic challenges facing agents are deeply embedded in social interactions and material situations. Some feminists also made a plea for the need to reorient epistemology in a way that would offer guidance on how to generate the kinds of knowledge that we most need in order to promote human flourishing. For them, the ethical is thoroughly embedded in the epistemic.

Given its concern with practical issues of knowledge production, then, feminist epistemology can also be characterized as a call for a more contextualized and pragmatic approach to theorizing knowledge and knowing (Grasswick, 2014a). Much feminist work marks a shift in focus toward the *activities* of knowing and away from a fixation on the product of knowledge itself. As feminists quickly discovered, detailed attention to our actual activities of knowing revealed epistemic dependencies between knowers, and multiple social dimensions of knowing activities, making for a deeply social epistemology on this front as well.

Although feminists found the dominant analytic epistemological paradigm difficult to work with, in the development of their own work they were able to find and build upon other philosophical movements that they found to be more conducive to their projects, including some of the contemporary directions in philosophy of science. For example, although Quine's initial formulation of a naturalized epistemology was highly individualistic and not at all social, many feminists drew inspiration from his and other naturalists' rejection of idealized accounts alongside their insistence on the epistemological import of careful descriptions of our activities and practices of knowing (Nelson, 1990). Additionally, the post-Kuhnian development of a historicized approach to philosophy of science opened many pathways for investigating the communal dimensions of scientific knowledge and theory choice, offering models of the kinds of epistemological conclusions that could be drawn from the study of actual epistemic practices. Such resources have assisted feminist epistemologists and philosophers of science as they attempt to connect the critiques of specific cases of scientific research that feminist science studies scholars have provided with their normative interests in trying to see a way forward, outlining what good science looks like if the knower's perspective cannot be removed (Harding, 1991; Longino, 1990; Nelson, 1990).

Over the years, feminist epistemology has grown tremendously in both depth and scope. The situated approach itself has been developed by different theorists in distinct directions, and it has resulted in a wealth of feminist contributions to a wide variety of topics in social epistemology. I highlight a few examples of some of the prominent research directions below.

Epistemic Dependencies Between Knowers

Feminists have theorized a multitude of ways in which we are epistemically dependent on each other. First, they have argued that we are epistemically dependent on others in a developmental sense (Grasswick, 2004). Lorraine Code, for example, adapts Annette Baier's work on "second personhood" (Baier, 1985) to the epistemic realm, arguing that many of our most coveted cognitive skills are socially acquired "arts of personhood" (Baier's term), cultivated through histories of interaction with each other and mutual acknowledgement. As Code notes "even the ability to change one's mind is learned in a community that trains its members in conventions of criticism, affirmation, and second thinking" (Code, 1991, p. 83). Without long histories of dialogue and exchange, we would not have the cognitive skills of developed reasoning that traditional epistemologists cite as being key to an individual's epistemic agency. One of the repercussions of this line of reasoning is that our very epistemic agency is dependent upon how we have been and are treated by others. Another is that the very forms of reasoning and argumentation in which we engage with each other in pursuit of knowledge may be culturally shaped, and open to change (Moulton, 1983; Rooney, 1995, 2012)

Second, we are epistemically dependent on each other as sources of knowledge. We rely on others' testimony for claims that we do not, and often cannot, have evidence for ourselves. The limitations of our embodied locations, our epistemic capacities, and our time mean that the scope of our knowledge would be miniscule if we did not have access to others' testimony and be in a position to confidently use it. While feminists are in good company with other social epistemologists in stressing the importance of testimony, the feminist emphasis on differences between various social locations and the epistemic perspectives that accompany these positions makes the need for a philosophical analysis of testimony all the more compelling. Feminists have been at the forefront of discussions concerning the differential credibility assigned to variously situated knowers and the testimonial injustices that occur with many such assignments (Alcoff, 2001;

Collins, 1991; Fricker, 2007; Jones, 2002; Medina, 2013). Most clearly Fricker claims that the social exchange of knowledge is so important to our ways of knowing that to deny someone the credibility they are due because of prejudicial stereotypes constitutes an injustice in virtue of compromising their very epistemic agency (Fricker, 2007).

Feminists have not only recognized the credibility deficits that accrue to those in socially marginalized positions (and credibility excesses that accrue to the privileged), but they have also sought to understand what the workings of the credibility economy means for knowers who wish to know responsibly within such power-infused contexts of knowing. Implicit biases and their impact on our beliefs, actions, and reception of the ideas of others have become a serious area of investigation not just for psychologists, but also for feminist epistemologists who seek to make sense of their role in epistemic responsibility: they ask how epistemic agents who are by definition unaware of their *implicit* biases can know responsibly, either by finding ways to prevent the influence of implicit biases or working to improve our social epistemic practices overall (see Holroyd and Puddifoot, this volume). Concern with testimonial injustices and their effect on the development and sharing of knowledge has also sparked feminist analyses of the role of trust and trustworthiness in healthy epistemic relationships between individuals, communities, and institutions (Anderson, 2012; Daukas, 2006; Grasswick, 2010, 2014b; Scheman, 2001). Relatedly, feminist epistemologists have also sought to understand the ethical dimensions of epistemic relationships between knowers (Addelson, 1993; Code, 2006).

Cultural Dependencies within Knowledge Production

To generate knowledge, conceptual frameworks and assumptions are required, and many of these are culturally and socially influenced. Feminists have pointed out myriad ways in which the conceptual schemas required for knowledge often bear the markers of their makers. For example, taking a Quinean approach yet emphasizing the communal nature of knowing, Lynn Hankinson Nelson argues that one of the key elements of an epistemic community is its shared standards of evidence. Such standards are dynamic, and sometimes their changes trace social change. Accordingly, science that relied on androcentric assumptions and may have been acceptable at one time will no longer be acceptable once androcentrism comes to be questioned (Nelson, 1990, 1993).

In another example of the epistemic impact of culturally embedded conceptual frameworks, when white men have a substantial amount of power to control the institutions of knowledge-making, we can expect that these institutions, their practices, and the knowledge generated will bear the marks of this group's experiences, employing conceptual frameworks and assumptions that they have found to be most helpful in the generation of their understandings of the world. While their experiences may be well represented and understood within the pool of knowledge, those who do not occupy such socially privileged positions may find it challenging to understand and articulate their own (differing) experiences given that the culturally available conceptual resources have not been generated from those experiences, and may be inadequate to the task. Fricker has identified these situations as *hermeneutical injustices*, offering examples such as the difficulty women had in understanding their experiences of sexual harassment before the idea was articulated and culturally accepted as representing a recurrent phenomenon (Fricker, 2007). The idea of hermeneutical injustice has generated a rich body of literature (see Daukas, this volume). While many have focused on the injustice of being unable to access the resources needed to adequately understand one's social experience, others have argued that conceptual resources are actually more dispersed within society; socially underprivileged groups may be able to generate and share common understandings of their experiences, but without uptake from dominant groups, these understandings are not given the cultural credence they deserve, nor are they able to be widely circulated and acted upon (Dotson, 2011; Mason, 2011; Medina, 2013; Pohlhaus,

2012). This line of reasoning has also emphasized the importance of the close interactive relationship between testimonial and hermeneutical injustices (see also Fricker, 2016).

Feminists' attention to hermeneutical injustices represents just one of the ways in which they have broadened their analyses to consider the social influences of not just knowledge, but also ignorance. Feminists have drawn attention to many of the ways in which ignorances can be "culturally and politically induced" and can serve the interests of social domination (Code, 2007). Opening up social epistemology to include analyses of both knowledge and ignorance allows the opportunity to investigate the important interactions between the two (including some of the tradeoffs that occur) (Townley, 2006, 2011), and to understand how particularly situated knowers may be invested in maintaining particular ignorances in ways that then challenge their abilities to know responsibly from their social positions (Code, 2007; Mills, 2007).

Social Analyses of Objectivity

The socially situated approach of feminists has also led to substantial reworkings of the idea of objectivity. Again, it is the differences between socially situated knowers and their perspectives that generates the challenge. In the absence of an appeal to a neutral perspective, feminists have sought to negotiate the relationship between variously positioned perspectives in an attempt to best characterize an epistemic goal of objectivity. One obvious trend across feminist epistemologies has been the characterization of objectivity in terms of certain forms of social interaction. For example, in philosophy of science, Helen Longino has set out criteria of social conditions of epistemic communities that foster transformative criticism, and has characterized objectivity as a matter of how well epistemic communities live up to these conditions (Longino, 1990, 1993). Building on a recognition of the importance of inquirers' interactions and the assumptions that they bring to the communal table, many feminists have also argued that objectivity requires a diversity of perspectives to be represented within epistemic communities (Intemann, 2011; Longino, 1993). These arguments suggest that certain social relations need to be in place before knowledge generation can be said to be objective, and draw connections between epistemic objectivity and democratic practices (Anderson, 2012).

Perhaps one of the most controversial, yet also the most fruitful lines of theorizing within feminist epistemology has been the developments of feminist standpoint theory (see Tanesini, this volume). The situated approach to knowing that I described thus far only captured the fact that knowing is perspectival, with perspectives being connected to social and material location. In various forms of standpoint theory, the social situatedness of knowing combines with arguments for the epistemic privilege of some perspectives over others, based on certain features of the social structure itself. Though arguments vary regarding what epistemic privilege amounts to, Sandra Harding has focused on standpoint theory's demand that attention be paid to the positions of the marginalized. For her, we need "strong objectivity" that expresses a commitment to "starting research" from the lives of the marginalized (Harding, 1993, 1991). Differences in socially situated perspectives means that, in order to be robustly objective, researchers need to be critically reflexive, aware of the relationship between their own perspective and the perspectives of those situated differently. Interaction with those situated differently from oneself becomes an important feature of strong objectivity, as researchers strive to come to know and appreciate the socially situated perspectives of others that can inform their research.

Feminist epistemology is a vibrant and wide-ranging field, and it continues to develop its situated approach in multiple directions. It remains to be seen just where its future developments go, but no doubt they will include concepts and analyses that probe many different social dimensions of knowing, offering significant contributions to the broader field of social epistemology.

Note

1 For example, in Lorraine's Code's revised essay "Is the Sex of the Knower Epistemologically Significant?" that appears in her 1991 book *What Can She Know?* she notes that she no longer endorses the "essentialism with respect to masculinity and femininity" that could be found in her original 1981 version of the essay (Code, 1991, p. 1).

References

Addelson, K. (1993) Knowers/Doers and Their Moral Problems, In: L. Alcoff and E. Potter, eds., *Feminist Epistemologies*, New York: Routledge, pp. 265–294.

Alcoff, L. and Potter E. (1993) Introduction: When Feminisms Intersect Epistemology, In: L. Alcoff and E. Potter, eds., *Feminist Epistemologies*, New York: Routledge, pp. 1–14.

Alcoff, L. (2001) On Judging Epistemic Credibility: Is Social Identity Relevant? In: N. Tuana and S. Morgen, eds., *Engendering Rationalities*, Albany: SUNY, pp. 53–80.

Anderson, E. (1995) Feminist Epistemology: An Interpretation and a Defense, *Hypatia*, 10, pp. 50–84.

Anderson, E. (2012) Epistemic Justice as a Virtue of Social Institutions, *Social Epistemology*, 26, pp. 163–173.

Baier, A. (1985) *Postures of the Mind: Essays on Mind and Morals*, Minneapolis: University of Minnesota Press.

Code, L. (1981) Is the Sex of the Knower Epistemologically Significant? *Metaphilosophy*, 12, pp. 267–276.

Code, L. (1991) *What Can She Know?: Feminist Theory and the Construction of Knowledge*, Ithaca: Cornell University Press.

Code, L. (2006) *Ecological Thinking: The Politics of Epistemic Location*, Oxford: Oxford University Press.

Code, L. (2007) The Power of Ignorance, In: S. Sullivan and N. Tuana, eds., *Race and Epistemologies of Ignorance*, Albany: State University of New York Press, pp. 213–229.

Collins, P.H. (1991) *Black Feminist Thought: Knowledge, Consciousness, and the Politics of Empowerment*, New York: Routledge.

Daukas, N. (2006) Epistemic Trust and Social Location, *Episteme*, 3, pp. 109–124.

Dotson, K. (2011) Tracking Epistemic Violence, Tracking Practices of Silencing, *Hypatia*, 26, pp. 236–257.

Fricker, M. (2007) *Epistemic Injustice: Power and the Ethics of Knowing*, Oxford: Oxford University Press.

Fricker, M. (2016) Epistemic Injustice and the Preservation of Ignorance, In: M. Blaauw and R. Peels, eds., *The Epistemic Dimensions of Ignorance*, Cambridge: Cambridge University Press, pp. 160–177.

Grasswick, H. (2004) Individuals-in-Communities: The Search for a Feminist Model of Epistemic Subjects, *Hypatia*, 19, pp. 85–120.

Grasswick, H. (2010) Scientific and Lay Communities: Earning Epistemic Trust Through Knowledge Sharing, *Synthese*, 177, pp. 387–409.

Grasswick, H. (2013) Feminist Social Epistemology, In: E. Zalta, ed., *The Stanford Encyclopedia of Philosophy (Spring 2013 Edition)*, URL=http://plato.stanford.edu/archives/spr2013/entries/feminist-social-epistemology/

Grasswick, H. (2014a) Understanding Epistemic Normativity in Feminist Epistemology, In: J. Matheson and R. Vitz, eds., Ethics of Belief: Individual and Social, New York: Oxford University Press, pp. 216–243.

Grasswick, H. (2014b) Climate Change Science and Responsible Trust: A Situated Approach, *Hypatia*, 29, pp. 541–557.

Haraway, D. (1988) Situated Knowledges: The Science Question in Feminism and the Privilege of Partial Perspective, *Feminist Studies*, 14, pp. 575–599.

Harding, S. (1983) Why Has the Sex/Gender System Become Visible Only Now? In: S. Harding and M. Hintikka, eds., *Discovering Reality: Feminist Perspectives on Epistemology, Metaphysics, Methodology, and the Philosophy of Science*, Dordrecht: D. Reidel, pp. 311–324.

Harding, S. (1993) Rethinking Standpoint Epistemology: What Is 'Strong Objectivity'? In: L. Alcoff and E. Potter, eds., *Feminist Epistemologies*, New York: Routledge, pp. 49–82.

Harding, S. (1991) *Whose Science? Whose Knowledge?: Thinking from Women's Lives*, Ithaca, NY: Cornell University Press.

Intemann, K. (2011) Diversity and Dissent in Science, In: H. Grasswick, ed., *Feminist Epistemology and Philosophy of Science: Power in Knowledge*, Dordrecht: Springer, pp. 111–132.

Jones, K. (2002) The Politics of Credibility, In: L. Antony and C. Witt, eds., *A Mind of One's Own: Feminist Essays on Reason and Objectivity*, Boulder: Westview Press, pp. 154–176.

Kitcher, P. (1990) The Division of Cognitive Labor, *The Journal of Philosophy*, 87, pp. 5–22.

Longino, H. (1990) *Science as Social Knowledge: Values and Objectivity in Scientific Inquiry*, Princeton NJ: Princeton University Press.

Longino, H.E. (1993) Subjects, Power, and Knowledge: Description and Prescription in Feminist Philosophies of Science, In: L. Alcoff and E. Potter, eds., *Feminist Epistemologies*, New York: Routledge, pp. 101–120.

Longino, H.E. (1999) Feminist Epistemology, In: J. Greco and E. Sosa, eds., *Blackwell Guide to Epistemology*, Malden: Blackwell, pp. 327–353.

Lugones, M.C. and Spelman, E.V. (1983) Have We Got a Theory for You! Feminist Theory, Cultural Imperialism and the Demand for 'The Woman's Voice', *Women's Studies International Forum*, 6, pp. 573–581.

Mason, R. (2011) Two Kinds of Unknowing, *Hypatia*, 26, pp. 294–307.

Medina, J. (2013) *The Epistemology of Resistance: Gender and Racial Oppression, Epistemic Injustice, and Resistant Imaginations*, Oxford: Oxford University Press.

Mills, C. (2007) White Ignorance, In: S. Sullivan and N. Tuana, eds., *Race and the Epistemologies of Ignorance*, Albany: State University of New York Press, pp. 13–38.

Moulton, J. (1983) A Paradigm of Philosophy: The Adversarial Method, In: S. Harding and M. Hintikka, eds., *Discovering Reality: Feminist Perspectives on Epistemology, Metaphysics, Methodology and Philosophy of Science*, Dordrecht: Reidel, pp. 149-164.

Nelson, L. (1990) *Who Knows: From Quine to a Feminist Empiricism*, Philadelphia: Temple University Press.

Nelson, L. (1993) Epistemological Communities, In: L. Alcoff and E. Potter, eds., *Feminist Epistemologies*, New York: Routledge, pp. 121-159.

Pohlhaus, G. (2012) Relational Knowing and Epistemic Injustice: Toward a Theory of, *Willful Hermeneutical Ignorance, Hypatia*, 27, pp. 715–735.

Potter, E. (1993) Gender and Epistemic Negotiation, In: L. Alcoff and E. Potter, eds., *Feminist Epistemologies*, New York: Routledge, pp. 161–186.

Rooney, P. (1995) Rationality and the Politics of Gender Difference, *Metaphilosophy*, 26, pp. 22–45.

Rooney, P. (2012) When Philosophical Argumentation Impedes Social and Political Progress, *Journal of Social Philosophy*, 43, pp. 317–333.

Scheman, N. (1993) *Engenderings: Constructions of Knowledge, Authority, and Privilege*, New York: Routledge.

Scheman, N. (2001) Epistemology Resuscitated: Objectivity as Trustworthiness, In: N. Tuana and S. Morgen, eds., *Engendering Rationalities*, Albany: State University of New York Press, pp. 23–52.

Schmitt, F. (1994) Socializing Epistemology: An Introduction through Two Sample Issues, In: F. Schmitt, ed., *Socializing Epistemology: The Social Dimensions of Knowledge*, Lanham, MD: Rowman & Littlefield, pp. 1–27.

Townley, C. (2006) Toward a Revaluation of Ignorance, *Hypatia*, 21, pp. 37–55.

Townley, C. (2011) *A Defense of Ignorance: Its Value for Knowers and Roles in Feminist and Social Epistemologies*, Lanham MD: Lexington Books.

Wylie, A. (2003), Why Standpoint Matters, In: R. Figueroa and S. Harding, eds., *Science and Other Cultures: Issues in Philosophies of Science and Technology*, New York: Routledge, pp. 26–48.

Further Readings

Anderson, E. (2015) Feminist Epistemology and Philosophy of Science, In: E.N. Zalta, ed., *The Stanford Encyclopedia of Philosophy (Fall 2015 Edition)*, https://plato.stanford.edu/archives/fall2015/entries/feminism-epistemology/.

Crasnow, S. (2014) Feminist Standpoint Theory, In: *Philosophy of Social Science: A New Introduction*, Oxford: Oxford University Press, pp. 145–161.

Intemann, K. (2010) 25 Years of Feminist Empiricism and Standpoint Theory: Where Are We Now? *Hypatia*, 25, pp. 778–796.

Nelson, L. H. and J. Nelson (eds.) (1997) *Feminism, Science and the Philosophy of Science*, Dordrecht: Kluwer.

30

RACE AND GENDER AND EPISTEMOLOGIES OF IGNORANCE

Linda Martín Alcoff

Social epistemology is by definition concerned with the ways in which knowledge inquiries are pursued within a social context. Arguably, all knowledge involves the sphere of the social in the sense that the available concepts, practices, and norms delimit any given knower's domain of intelligibility. This significantly influences their epistemic activity, even that which is conducted in solitude, as we imagine Descartes' meditations to have taken place. Thus, in the quiet of our isolated thoughts, we are still operating in a social field of meanings.

These fields of meaning vary, however, and there may be several operating within a society, community, or institution. Often, as this essay will discuss, there are aspects of the fields of meaning we have at our disposal that are related in some respects to our identities. For this reason, it makes an epistemic difference in some, perhaps most, projects of inquiry as to whether the identities of the individuals involved are fairly uniform across the group or are diversified (Keller 1985; Harding 1986; Longino 1990).

Think of some typical social contexts in which knowledge is produced: large laboratories, research institutes, newspaper offices, national security agencies. Philosophers sometimes imagine that *our* context of knowing is more individualized than these sorts of institutions: all one needs to do philosophy is a library, or even just a capacity to think. Yet philosophy is just as much a collective enterprise as any other, with classrooms, journals and books, conferences, workshops, and other means by which we develop arguments in a process of engaging with others. Often, our projects of inquiry concern highly general questions that might well be relevant to the lives of human beings across the planet, and yet we have a very restricted set of identity types with whom we directly interact, or whose work we read, or whose books are included in our library, while we are developing our philosophical ideas and arguments.

A concern with the social context of knowledge directs epistemology toward these decidedly non-ideal realities. Actual social contexts in which knowledge is pursued today usually exhibit patterns of exclusion, often involving race and gender among other forms of identity. Further, as this entry will argue, these contexts operate with inadequate epistemic norms to reflect upon and address these exclusions or the impact that these exclusions have on their projects of inquiry. This is the sort of problem that constitutes, as we will see, an epistemology of ignorance: structurally supported and normalized sets of epistemic practices that are adopted and followed by both individuals and organizations, and which keep ignorance in place.

One of the most astounding examples of group-related ignorance occurred during the Jim Crow era in the southern United States. Historian Jason Sokol's fascinating portrait of white southern attitudes toward civil rights, appropriately titled *There Goes My Everything* (2006), documents these through newspaper editorials, personal narratives, and interviews from the time. "Most of us have a deep and abiding affection for the Negro," one typical Mississippi native recounts (2006, 57). Violence was only necessary, such men believed, when the rules of nature were abrogated. As long as segregation was upheld, everyday interactions could be enacted on the model of a kind paternalism, or so whites thought. A more perceptive analysis given by a white South Carolinian, from the hindsight of the late 1960s, noted the utility of these contradictions: "In our inmost [ears], we knew we were wrong. And so ... we didn't talk about justice, we talked about love" (Sokol 2006, 58).

Maybe affection was quite truly felt, but what was it they were feeling the affection for? Consider this. The resounding majority of white southerners expressed surprise at the movement for civil rights: middle-class whites were convinced their servants were content. The "trouble," as they called the movement, was caused by outsiders, such as Yankees, communists, and Jews. Sokol finds in community after community white perplexity, surprise, and resistance to the idea that African Americans wanted social equality. And they compounded this error with a claim of epistemic privilege *as white southerners* to "know" black people. The owner of a lumber mill in Albany Georgia expressed this idea without a blush, assuring "his fellow white southerners that federal judges 'simply don't know the American Negro as you and I do'" (Sokol 2006, 69). Whites thought they knew black people, and they liked what they thought they knew. In truth, the affection such fellows might have felt was for a mask held up by black people to soothe their egos and relax their trigger fingers.[1]

As most societies are currently configured, in matters of large social consequence—from nuclear weapons production to natural energy transport—many of the people with the relevant knowledge and/or direct and immediate interest are likely to be absent from "the room where it happens," to quote the lyrics of the hit musical, *Hamilton*. This is just to say that every major institution in every western society engaged in the pursuit of knowledge remains exclusionary in its membership, and that these exclusions are often relevant to the matter under discussion. *De facto* exclusions linger long after *de jure* segregation has been reformed, but this just indicates the power and longevity of our historically formed social contexts. Even in matters of more personal or local consequence, it is a rare person whose familial and communal networks extend to a significant diversity of people or of global knowledge sources. And it is a rare institution that enables truly honest communication on matters of political significance across group-related differences of identity and power.

Hence, most of our real world practices of knowing continue to occur in segregated social contexts with distorted patterns of communication (Fricker 2007; Dotson 2011, 2014). In some cases, there may be no epistemic loss incurred in this, but in many cases, the pattern of exclusion limits the participation of whole groups of people in a variety of critical topics of wide public concern to which their input could make a significant difference. A variety of scientific and political institutions responded to the HIV-AIDS epidemic that emerged in the 1980s, but collectively failed to provide the public with clear and accurate information or to develop medical responses in an efficient manner. The resistance movement that soon emerged found that they had to contest the epistemic arrangements in which victims were left out of the deliberative process, uninvolved in developing or debating treatment options (France 2016). Gay activists began to school themselves on the science of clinical trials and the policies and market considerations affecting the production of new drugs, and the movement made their inclusion in decision-making a key demand. Their subsequent ability to become involved in the developments of treatment was pivotal in transforming HIV-AIDS from a fatal diagnosis to a manageable disease.

Ignorance, as will be argued here, is usually an effect of histories of social exclusions based on various kinds of social ranking, as well as the protection of epistemic norms that deflect attention from the deleterious effects of exclusion. But before turning to the question of how ignorance comes about, let us first be clear on what we mean by the concept itself. Webster's Unabridged Dictionary identifies synonyms of the word "ignorant" as "unenlightened," "illiterate," "uneducated," "uninstructed," and "uninformed." The implication here is that there exists available knowledge of which the ignorant are not making use. In this usage ignorance is understood to be a remediable epistemic state. Indeed, we generally do not use the term to refer to a state of lacking knowledge about something no human being currently knows. I can be ignorant about the history of U.S. slavery, but not about whether the Andromeda Galaxy actually contains life.

We might yet want to distinguish between ignorance that is a vice and ignorance that is not. One can lack education through no fault of one's own, without ever having taken an action or made a choice. Conversely, one may be actively resistant to certain kinds of readily available information or know-how, such as when someone claims to be incapable of changing diapers only because they would rather not. Some such resistance we might classify as the purview of individual choice and not morally blameworthy, but if a parent resists learning the basics of infant care, we might judge their resistance as a moral failing. The concept of epistemology of ignorance is concerned with ignorance of this problematic kind, in which individuals or groups exhibit active resistance to readily available knowledge.

So let us define ignorance as a remediable lack of knowledge that involves, at least some of the time, substantive practices (such as avoidance of sources or of reflection) and norms (such as those that justify or excuse avoidance). Some such willful ignorance may be ethically innocuous, such as not wanting to know the details of medical procedures, but our concern is with a willful resistance against the kinds of knowledge that threatens one's unfair privileges. This turns out to be a very large set, and to include almost everyone in regard to some aspect of our lives.

In light of how widespread such resistance is, we need norms of knowing, including norms of everyday justification as well as scientific methods, that are capable of addressing the phenomenon. Ignorance is a growing topic of study in the behavioral and psychological sciences, but what philosophy offers is to go beyond the description of the problem to prescribing antidotes in the form of realistic but effective reforms, such as heuristic guides of behavior as well as justificatory norms that will raise the bar for adequacy and redress the specific support systems that maintain ignorance in our own contexts. Part of this work requires that philosophers take a critical look at our house. Before we assume that the norms of justification put forward in western theories of knowledge can operate as antidotes to ignorance, we need to see whether they actually have, or can today. European traditions of thought may in fact harbor an epistemology of ignorance within epistemology itself.

But many people may still believe that, despite the fact that ignorance is an epistemic state, it mainly has non-epistemic causes. For example, ignorance may appear to be the product of an emotionally motivated, willful commitment to irrationality, of the sort Jean-Paul Sartre analyzed in his study of anti-Semitism. What is most interesting about the anti-Semite, Sartre suggests, is his (or her) passionate refusal to entertain counter-arguments or counter-evidence, whether these are logical, historical, or empirical. This refusal indicates that anti-Semitism is "first of all a passion," as Sartre puts it (1944, 6). By this Sartre means that attachment to anti-Semitism is dogmatic; the facts must be made to conform to one's prior belief, or they will be rejected as false reports, "fake news," or otherwise invalid.

What Sartre describes is not a pursuit of knowledge done badly but a refusal to pursue knowledge, and so this may look to be more properly studied by some other field of behavioral analysis. But the fact remains that the anti-Semite has beliefs and makes factual claims. He may assert, as in Sartre's example, that he was robbed and cheated by Jews, which may well be true, but he then goes on to claim that it was the *Jewish* identity that *explains* the behavior. So here, the anti-Semite is not simply stating a personal preference, but offering an explanation with a causal account. Despite his refusal to countenance countervailing evidence, he is operating in the domain of reasoned belief.

Sartre's interest in writing a book on this topic in 1942 was to show why the anti-Semite's view should not be classified under the rubric of "opinion" that might then become protected as free speech. Anti-Semitism is a claim about the shared social world, and thus it requires a response that a mere description of one's subjective preference for vanilla over strawberry ice cream would not. And, as he points out, it is a claim that is action-guiding in that it implicates those who hear it if they fail to reject the legitimacy, even the necessity, of certain social exclusions and directed forms of violence.

Most importantly for our purposes, Sartre's analysis helps to show why we should not take this sort of ignorance to be a passive state in which one simply lacks information. Counter-evidence to anti-Semitism may not be part of one's required school curriculum, and yet it is not on the far side of the moon. The passive acquiescence to noxious but widely accepted ideas is a form of laziness, and laziness is itself a choice. Neglecting to respond to the sort of claim that implicates me in a shared orientation to the world works as a confirmation that supports the claim's continuation.

Following in this line of thought, José Medina provides an account of ignorance that views it as necessarily active. It can involve actively resisting certain kinds of knowledge that would contradict one's favored view, or actively resisting criticism. Medina refers to this as "active ignorance," to indicate that ignorance is not merely passive but involves the performance of some conscious practices such as avoidance and refusal. He explains that:

> active ignorance has deep psychological and sociopolitical roots: it is supported by psychological structures and social arrangements that prevent subjects from correcting misconceptions and acquiring knowledge because they would have to change so much of themselves and their communities before they can start seeing them differently.
>
> *(2013, 57)*

Medina thus characterizes active ignorance as an individual practice that has personal and psychological motivation but is also enabled by social conditions of certain sorts, such as segregated social arrangements. This bears further exploration.

Inside of segregated institutions or communities, whether these have been created *de jure* or are simply *de facto*, we can imagine a given individual who is operating with good norms of epistemic behavior and yet ends up with faulty beliefs. He may be diligently consulting sources, carefully observing and analyzing, but all within a restricted set that may ultimately distort his results. Even the anti-Semite can appeal to standard epistemic conventions to justify his epistemic practices: he might discount the sources and arguments that seek to refute anti-Semitism as biased, characterizing these as lacking objectivity. His reliance on highly respected, mainstream media sources, such as were common in France when Sartre wrote, might well be considered entirely reasonable choices within his restricted milieu. In the 1940s, one did not have to be a committed Nazi to be an anti-Semite; such ideas were the normal backdrop of the public culture in many countries, even, or especially, among the educated classes. One could read the standard, accepted sources of news, receive a good quality public education, and have one's predilection toward anti-Semitism challenged little if not fully supported. Refutations of anti-Semitism primarily existed outside of the mainstream, and so could have been characterized as harboring a political agenda or vested interests.

So in this scenario, although counter-evidence to anti-Semitism existed, it could be ignored without necessarily flouting the standard and accepted epistemic conventions among French Gentiles of the educated classes. In this context, demobilizing or diverting anti-Semitism would require an active intervention. Thus one might argue that the ignorance in this case is the result of passivity rather than the outcome of a concerted effort, or conversely, that the effort required was small.

While Sartre gives us examples of individual anti-Semites who actively pursue contrived justifications for their passionate commitments, Medina's account suggests that we need to consider both individual and structural causes in order to explain the sorts of "normalized" or accepted ignorance as I described above. Certain kinds of social arrangements and conventional norms of belief formation can play an important supportive role in enabling ignorance, in conjunction with personal, individual motivations or acts. Consider again the effects of exclusionary, segregated institutions: in these contexts an individual might be enacting responsible epistemic practices and yet retain ignorance.

Here is where the project of an epistemology of ignorance must begin its work. We need to consider whether any norms of justification under consideration will be capable of redressing common patterns of ignorance. We also need to consider whether conventional ideas and practices advocated in contemporary philosophical methodology might create obstacles for redressing ignorance; if the answer to this is yes, then these may qualify as part of the "structural arrangements" that Medina describes that work to excuse and thus enable ignorance.

Generally in societies it is obvious that those in dominant social groups that materially benefit from the current ranking system have motivations that incline them against rocking the epistemic boat, or challenging conventional belief-forming practices of certain sorts (Mills 1997, 2007). For example, the general conventions of epistemic practice, as well as highly influential theories of justification, have too often taken the exclusionary character of many sorts of social institutions and contexts as epistemically benign, or as nothing that requires immediate melioration on *epistemic* grounds. The recent challenges to these conventions that have emerged from feminist epistemologists have been rebuffed with insufficient and sometimes biased arguments (Lloyd 1995). Traditional-leaning philosophers have often wanted to maintain a rigid boundary between sociological considerations and philosophical ones, and any critique that looks to be grounded in sociological concerns, or moral ones for that matter, are set aside. Concerns about diversity are tagged as value concerns, and the pursuit of knowledge, some argue, should aspire to be as value-free as possible (Harding 2015). As a result, although some will acknowledge that *de facto* segregated institutions (such as the academic discipline of philosophy itself) have moral, and political, deficiencies, they deny that this poses an epistemic deficiency.

Exclusion is a practice, not an absence, even if part of that practice involves avoidance or passivity. But it takes a certain amount of work to characterize exclusivist or segregated contexts as legitimate and epistemically benign. This work typically includes the development, defense, and application of criteria to determine and maintain borders and boundaries. Some of this work involves keeping a bright and sharp line between the sphere of knowledge and the sphere of political values, and then policing this border on the hunt for transgressions. Hence it is no accident that norms of justification rarely list diversity in the research team or learning community as an epistemically relevant issue of concern, and may explicitly deflect such considerations as illegitimate.

In these ways epistemologies of ignorance may be quietly operating in modern epistemology, and in the normative conventions of epistemic practice occurring across many sectors of societies, to legitimate the typical exclusionary ways of knowing. In some recent political discourse, the requirement to expand the coterie of sources from which we draw is taken to be nothing more than a demand for "political correctness," which is a way of characterizing it as a defective value that would undermine our knowledge, and which thus should not be encouraged under any circumstances. The critique of "political correctness" can then operate to maintain borders and legitimate ignorance.

Medina describes three bad personal qualities that generate the bad epistemic practices that make up active ignorance: arrogance, laziness, and close-mindedness. Arrogance is manifest when knowers are impervious to criticism in a peremptory way; laziness causes knowers to omit pursuing relevant sources and failure to act upon new information; and closed-mindedness is manifest in the sort of dogmatic circular reasoning that Sartre describes. We might want to impose a "reasonableness" consideration in their formulation and in the prescriptions they imply for our epistemic activity, and there may be disagreements about where the boundary of reasonable effort lies (see e.g. Dotson 2012; Medina 2013; Fricker 2016). And yet the three components of active ignorance that Medina outlines remain useful desiderata.

What we now need to understand is how the social arrangements that Medina refers to can provide support for these bad practices by mischaracterizing them as benign, excusable, or even legitimate. What we also need to understand is how epistemic practices that appear defensible can yet result in the maintenance and protection of ignorance. This will be the burden of the remainder of this essay, and it will require connecting the discussion of epistemic real world conditions with the real world of social identities. As we will see, all identities are not positioned in exactly the same ways in regard to the seductions of ignorance or the structural arrangements that are conducive to ignorance.

Part of the way in which social contexts influence projects of inquiry concerns the frameworks of interpretation, starting belief sets, and learned methods of analysis such as ways of categorizing and conceptualizing. Our background frames of meaning are built up in part out of historical stock images that confer apparent inductive legitimacy on the expectation that a woman will be comparatively worse at physics or chess than a man, that a Latino will be comparatively more macho than an Anglo, that a working class person will know little about Shakespeare, and that knowledge of Shakespeare is a reasonable criterion to use in determining cultural sophistication, and so on. The patterns that exist in our accessible digital, literate, and visual fields silently but significantly inform our current practices of perception, comparison, and judgment, affecting what we find "naturally" attractive, or credible, how we slot objects and persons into categories, and the way we assess merit (P. C. Taylor 2016).

Unless we become critically self-reflective about the historically produced social ingredients that inform our judgment, those judgments can contain and perpetuate falsehoods. This demonstrates that we have a reason to be epistemically interested in the social and political conditions of the production of knowledge. Such conditions affect the fact that individuals with group-related differences sometimes have notably different background frames that inform their interpretations of new events. There might also be group-related differences in economic or personal interests that affect motivations in knowing, as well as in our starting belief sets that exert coherence constraints on new claims (Harding 2015). Political conditions can also affect the quality of communicative interactions that occur across differences of identity, having an impact on who speaks and how sincerely and comprehensively they relate their views.

Building from a tradition of analysis in African American art theory and philosophy, Paul Taylor develops a concept of "Black invisibility" to name the phenomena in which a presence— a person or an object, such as an art object—is rendered beneath notice. In this scenario it is not that black people are completely absent from shared social spaces but that perception of them is attenuated to their role as waiter, doorman, servant. Their artifacts may also be observable yet taken as beneath aesthetic analysis. Notably, such attenuated modes of perception are not universal or common to all who enter a shared space. He says,

> ... certain ways of seeing are more likely to recommend themselves to people who occupy different racial positions in a racialized society. This follows from the recognition ... that one of the fields of political contestation is the field of public meaning. White supremacy is constituted in part by the colonization of public meaning by whitely assumptions and prejudices ...
>
> *(P. C. Taylor 2016, 59)*

Let us unpack this claim. Perception involves forms of attentiveness that operate to foreground some aspects of a tableau, rendering the rest into a backdrop. Clearly, no one can pay equal attention to every visible or audible intrusion on our senses. The manner in which sensory inputs are organized into categories of relative importance is affected by what Taylor calls "hegemonic ways of seeing." In the passage above, this is referred to as a domain of public meanings that establishes both content and significance from a white dominant point of view. To say that white supremacy has colonized public meaning is to say that the dominant texts—visual, literary, and so on—that are available to all, and that we are required to learn in many sorts of venues, such as school curriculum, have an implicit frame that indicates a specific rather than general or universal point of view.

Toni Morrison has called this "playing in the dark," in which black presence is systematically erased from or marginalized in the accepted canons of the national literature marked as "American." She argues that the whiteness of the canon has been protected by a method of literary criticism and analysis that "argues *against noticing* …" (1992, 10). She explains that, "A criticism that needs to insist that literature is not only 'universal' but also 'race-free' risks lobotomizing that literature, and diminishes both the art and the artist" (1990, 12). This argument shows why the aspiration for an entirely value-free judgment and analysis may be curtailing the very reflective critique we need in order to discern epistemic deficiencies.

The Black Lives Matter movement in the United States has focused on the ongoing problem of police killings of unarmed black men and women who pose them no threat (K. Y. Taylor 2016). Part of what has made the movement so successful in garnering wider public attention beyond black communities is the use of cameras, usually on cell phones, to record many of these kinds of killings. Thus it is now possible for larger numbers of people to see for themselves that the victims are not posing a threat, nor could they reasonably be interpreted as posing a threat.

Thus, wider segments of the public now have more knowledge about the kinds of events that occur in U.S. society. But, of course, this is not actually news to everyone. Black communities have largely known about such violence perpetrated by the police, through their direct personal experience or the communication of experiences among friends and family. The attempt to communicate this information outside black communities was too often rebuffed, considered implausible because it contradicted other groups' starting belief sets based on their own typical interactions with the police. The fact that it has taken camera footage to establish these problems is unfortunate, and suggests that, despite this new visibility of the problem, the epistemic practices of non-black communities may not change as much as they should with respect to giving credibility to verbal reports of police misconduct.

One of the principal challenges to changing dominant norms of knowing is the very categories of social identity this essay has been using. To imagine knowers as disembodied and unlocated in any specific place allows for the maintenance of ideas about the goals of neutrality and color-blindness. Before concluding, then, we need to gain some philosophical clarity on what we mean by social identities, and how these affect knowledge. Let us start with race. Today, in general, race concepts are not taken to mean biological kinds, or natural kind distinctions between human types, but to refer to historically created groups (P. C. Taylor 2013). When "black," "Asian American," "Native American," or "white" categories are used, it is a way to refer to a grouping demarcated by race rather than ethnicity, nationality, or class. (I will set aside the category of Latinos here since it requires special argumentation to link it to race.) There are many ethnic differences within each of these groupings, as well as differences of national origin and class. By referring to racial categories, we are intending to identify that specific feature of persons that was used historically for the purpose of organizing and demarcating labor markets, whether slave, free, indentured, or otherwise constrained to certain kinds of jobs. Race has also been relevant to: legal treatment; immigration and citizenship possibilities; whether one could testify in court, and against whom; and where one could purchase real estate or attend school. These rules were often correlated primarily to race and not to ethnicity, nationality, or class, even though these additional features of one's identity could mitigate one's treatment.

When we define race as a historically created form of group demarcation, we can begin to see how identity categories can affect knowledge. The historical experiences of exclusion, enslavement, legal curtailment of rights, and so on, produce some specific group-related knowledge about how one's society works—how, in effect, the sausage gets made. If we define race, then, not as a natural or a biological kind, but as a historically created human group with an associated set of group-specific experiences, we can see why racial exclusions may have important epistemic effects on the fields of meaning knowers have available to them.

Racial identities have had a long history of boundary control, with legal proscriptions as well as negative social costs for boundary crossers. Boundaries between racial groups are in transition, and yet the cross-generational experiences of the difference race makes continue to inform us. Race does not represent some sort of electromagnetic border that is impossible to penetrate; it is possible, and desirable, for racial groups to gain knowledge about the experience of other groups. But, as Supreme Court Justice Sonia Sotomayor argued, race can make a difference in our starting position, or the basic background information that we already have at our fingertips to interpret a new event (Alcoff 2010). Race can also affect the motivations we have to pursue knowledge in areas that we lack: I might have no idea why it is relevant to a particular domain of inquiry, or I might be disinclined to pursue some sorts of knowledge out of fear it will adversely affect my comfort or self-perception. Racial difference, then, does not impose a border beyond which it is impossible to gain knowledge, but, much like other variations in human experience, it does pose some special obstacles that are not distributed equally to all.

Although all of us, with effort, would seem to have the ability to learn the knowledge others have more readily, some knowledge has a first person perspective that is not entirely transmissible. I can read up on reservation life in the United States, for example, but that cannot confer the richness, complexity, or the depth of knowledge gained from direct experience from the inside of reservations for indigenous peoples. The same is true for many other sorts of knowledge, such as the knowledge about what it is like to cross borders illegally, or to play football or competitive chess, and yet racial, ethnic, gender, and other sorts of identities can have a multi-local reach across many of the contexts in which we operate. In other words, my identity as a Latina has a manifest impact on my first person experience of crossing borders, playing football, or competing in chess tournaments.

Some experiences are simply not open to all. I can join a chess club but I cannot "join" a racial group different from my own. Race is often considered to have associated bodily features, even though the variations and gradations within groups can make these almost indistinguishable from other groups for some individuals. Hence the experience of specific embodiments are among the range of race-related first person knowledge, such as the experience of having group-related bodily features that are viewed by the mainstream as exotic or strange or ugly.

Gender similarly involves specific bodily experiences that are not shared or sharable, such as menstruation, pregnancy, childbirth, and lactation, all of which are profound human experiences. Not all of those people designated as female experience these but most do, and this gives some epistemic content to the different bodily potentialities that have been grouped in gender categories. Gender identity also has a purely social specificity in relation to the history of male supremacy, enforced gender binaries, the persistent segmentation of labor markets, and the specific ways in which many societies have disauthorized women as credible knowers, reliable rememberers, capable of learning science and math, and so on.

Such historical forms of discrimination have also operated in regard to racial forms of identity as well as other forms, producing a kind of epistemic ranking of human types in regard to their knowledge and their capacity to be knowers. It is alarming to find a recurrent isomorphism between the traditional rankings of group identities that many people today consider to be arbitrary and illegitimate, and ideas about epistemic capacities that continue to affect the inclusion of actual personnel who make up large laboratories, research institutes, newspaper offices, colleges, and universities.

We can operate responsibly with broad identity categories such as race and gender if we understand these to be socially created, and in some cases enforced and policed, rather than natural kinds. Even though these categories are not produced with criteria that "carves nature at its joints," they function to distinguish some significant aspects of bodily experiences that affect first-person knowledge, whether that bodily experience is the product of social histories or biological capacities. Rooting out the epistemic norms that obscure these group-related epistemic differences is critical in rendering our ignorance more visible and subject to reform.

Note

1   This example is taken from Alcoff (2015).

References

Alcoff, L. M. (2010). Sotomayor's Reasoning. *Southern Journal of Philosophy*, 48(1), pp. 122–138.
Alcoff, L. M. (2015). *The Future of Whiteness*. Malden, MA: Polity Press.
Dotson, K. (2011). Tracking Epistemic Violence, Tracking Practices of Silencing. *Hypatia*, 26(2), pp. 236–257.
Dotson, K. (2012). A Cautionary Tale: On Limiting Epistemic Oppression. *Frontiers: A Journal of Women's Studies*, 33(1), pp. 24–47.
Dotson, K. (2014). Conceptualizing Epistemic Oppression. *Social Epistemology*, 28(2), pp. 115–138.
France, D. (2016). *How to Survive a Plague: The Inside Story of How Citizens and Science Tamed AIDS*. New York: Knopf.
Fricker, M. (2007). *Epistemic Injustice: Power and the Ethics of Knowing*. Oxford: Oxford University Press.
Fricker, M. (2016). Fault and No-Fault Responsibility for Implicit Prejudice: A Space for Epistemic "Agent-Regret". In *The Epistemic Life of Groups: Essays in the Epistemology of Collectives*, M. S. Brady and M. Fricker eds. Oxford: Oxford University Press, 33–50.
Harding, S. (1986). *The Science Question in Feminism*. Ithaca, NY: Cornell University Press.
Harding, S. (2015). *Objectivity and Diversity: Another Logic of Scientific Research*. Chicago, IL: University of Chicago Press.
Keller, E. F. (1985). *Reflections on Gender and Science*. New Haven, CT: Yale University Press.
Lloyd, E. A. (1995). Objectivity and the Double Standard for Feminist Epistemologies. *Synthese*, 104, pp. 351–381.
Longino, H. E. (1990). *Science as Social Knowledge: Values and Objectivity in Scientific Inquiry*. Princeton, NJ: Princeton University Press.
Medina, J. (2013). *Epistemologies of Resistance: Gender and Racial Oppression, Epistemic Injustice, and Resistant Imaginations*. New York: Oxford University Press.
Mills, C. (1997). *The Racial Contract*. Ithaca, NY: Cornell University Press.
Mills, C. (2007). White Ignorance. In *Race and Epistemologies of Ignorance*, S. Sullivan and N. Tuana eds. Albany, NY: State University of New York Press, 11–38.
Morrison, T. (1992). *Playing in the Dark: Whiteness and the Literary Imagination*. New York: Vintage Books.
Sartre, J. P. (1944). *Anti-Semite and Jew*. Translated by George J. Becker. New York: Schocken Books.
Sokol, J. (2006). *There Goes My Everything: White Southerners in the Age of Civil Rights, 1945–1975*. New York: Vintage Books.
Taylor, K. Y. (2016). *From #BlackLinesMatter to Black Liberation*. Chicago, IL: Haymarket Books.
Taylor, P. C. (2013). *Race: A Philosophical Introduction*. 2nd ed. New York: Polity Press.
Taylor, P. C. (2016). *Black Is Beautiful: A Philosophy of Black Aesthetics*. Malden, MA: Wiley Blackwell.

Further Readings

De Sousa Santos, B. (2007). *Another Knowledge is Possible: Beyond Northern Epistemologies*. New York: Verso.
Harding, S. (1993). *The Racial Economy of Science: Toward a Democratic Future*. Bloomington, IN: Indiana University Press.
Moya, P. M. (2002). *Learning from Experience: Minority Identities, Multicultural Struggles*. Berkeley, CA: University of California Press.
Sullivan, S. and Tuana, N. (2007). *Race and Epistemologies of Ignorance*. Albany, NY: State University of New York Press.

31

IMPLICIT BIAS AND PREJUDICE

Jules Holroyd and Katherine Puddifoot

Recent empirical research has substantiated the finding that very many of us harbour implicit biases: fast, automatic, and difficult to control processes that encode stereotypes and evaluative content, and influence how we think and behave. Since it is difficult to be aware of these processes – they have sometimes been referred to as operating 'unconsciously' – we may not know that we harbour them, nor be alert to their influence on our cognition and action. And since they are difficult to control, considerable work is required to prevent their influence. We here focus on the implications of these findings for epistemology. We first look at ways in which implicit biases thwart our knowledge-seeking practices (see 'Good Epistemic Practice' and 'Epistemic Benefits of Implicit Bias?' below). Then we set out putative epistemic benefits of implicit bias, before considering ways in which epistemic practices might be improved (see 'Improving Epistemic Practice below). Finally, we consider the distinctive challenges that the findings about implicit bias pose to us as philosophers, in the context of feminist philosophy in particular (see 'Challenges for Philosophers' below).

Good Epistemic Practice

Let us start by noting various hallmarks of good epistemic practice, as we find them in the epistemology literature, and the ways that implicit biases have been argued to thwart good epistemic practice.

Implicit Bias and Distortion

Central to the idea of good epistemic practice is the notion of standing in the right sort of relation to the world by tracking the truth in our belief formation and judgement:

> TRUTH-TRACKING: S's belief forming processes are in good epistemic standing if S's belief formation tracks the truth.

For example, suppose at a philosophy conference you form the belief that Jessica is an epistemologist. In order to meet the norm TRUTH-TRACKING you would only believe that Jessica is an epistemologist if it is true that she is; you track the way the world is.

Suppose that we have reason to believe that our belief forming processes lead to systematic distortion of our beliefs and judgements. This would indicate that our belief forming processes do not meet norms such as TRUTH-TRACKING. Jennifer Saul argues that this is precisely what we should conclude from the findings about implicit bias. She claims that 'the research on implicit bias shows us that we are actually being affected by biases about social groups *when we think we are evaluating evidence or methodology*' (Saul 2013, 248). Her concern is that we systematically have our judgements and beliefs distorted by considerations of gender and race and other social identities since, in the normal course of things, when evaluating evidence or methodology these considerations are not relevant to our enquiries. Irrelevant considerations distort our judgements. Let us consider an example of the sort of thing Saul has in mind.

Imagine you are taking part in a psychological study, and your task is to evaluate the importance of traits that you find on the CV in front of you to the role for which individuals are applying (the role of police chief, say). If you are tracking the truth then you will form judgements based on the assessment of the relevance of the traits to the role at issue. Those judgements should be consistent across the CVs you look at: if you think that certain qualifications are very important when possessed by candidate A, but irrelevant when possessed by candidate B, then your assessment of the importance of those qualifications appears not to track the truth about which traits are really relevant to the role.

Yet, this is just the pattern of judgements that Uhlmann and Cohen (2007) found when they asked participants to make such evaluations. When considering the importance of being 'streetwise' to being a police chief, participants tended to judge this as important when a male applicant possessed it, but not when a female applicant did.[1] This led them to make more positive hiring recommendations for the male candidates, irrespective of their differing qualifications for the post. Ulhmann and Cohen conclude that implicit associations between men and police chief roles distorted individuals' clear-eyed evaluation of the importance of qualifying characteristics.

To fully appreciate how people's judgements violate the truth-tracking norm in their responses in this study, consider how they fail to meet some norms which have been taken by various epistemologists to capture what it is for an epistemic agent to track the truth:

SENSITIVITY: *S*'s belief that *p* is sensitive if and only if, if *p* were false, *S* would not believe that *p*.

(cf. Nozick 1981)

SAFETY: S's belief that *p* is safe if and only if *p* could not easily have been false.

(Williamson 2000, Pritchard 2005)

Suppose that when evaluating the streetwise woman's CV you form the belief: *being streetwise is not important to the role of police chief*. For the sake of argument, suppose it is true that it is not so important to the role. Does this belief track the truth? On one view, we ask: is this belief sensitive, or would you still believe it if it were false? In these scenarios, where the only difference is the gender of the applicant but different responses are made, you seem not to be sensitive to the truth or falsity of the belief – you'd falsely believe it important if a man had that trait. What about SAFETY? Is your belief unsafe; could your true belief easily have been false? It would seem so. Even where your belief is true, it could easily have been false: if you had formed your belief in a situation where the only difference was the gender of the applicant for the job, you may have reached a different belief about the weighting of the trait. If this is right, then it looks like these implicit associations lead people to occupy a poor epistemic situation, forming beliefs that are insensitive or unsafe, even when their beliefs are true.

314

Implicit Bias and Perceptual Evidence

Consider another marker of good epistemic practice that epistemologists have identified:

> EVIDENCE: S's beliefs have positive epistemic status if (a) the believer has good supporting evidence for those beliefs and (b) the belief is based on that evidence.

We might think that a paradigm case of having good supporting evidence for our beliefs is when we appeal to perceptual evidence under normal circumstances. Suppose you perceive that Jessica is at the conference and form the belief that she is in attendance. Unless you have reason to suppose your perceptual systems to be unreliable under the circumstances in which you perceived Jessica, your belief appears to be evidentially supported. However, some philosophers have worried that implicit biases sometimes pose problems even for our reliance on perception. Jennifer Saul (2013) and Susanna Siegel (2012) have each pointed to studies that indicate that implicit associations lead to distortion of our perceptual judgements. (One way of putting this worry might be that our biases 'cognitively penetrate' our perceptions (Siegel 2012)).

To see the worry, imagine that you are participating in an experiment in which you are asked to identify a picture of an object that is flashed before your eyes – a weapon, such as a gun, or a non-harmful object, such as a tool. You might expect the perceptual judgements that you form to be solely determined by the evidence before you (shape of object, features manifest, etc.). However, Keith Payne's (2006) study showed that whether or not a picture of a Black or White male's face was flashed before the picture of the object made a significant difference to individuals' perceptual judgements. If you are primed to think about Black persons, you are more likely to perceive that the object is a weapon. This means that the presence of a prime can determine the way the object is perceived. These findings suggest that implicit bias 'affects our very perceptions of the world' (Saul 2013, 246), preventing our perceptions from being fully determined by the relevant evidence available in our environments.

Implicit Bias and Internalist Justification

A further norm of good epistemic practice that some epistemologists advocate is the following:

> ACCESSIBILITY: S's belief that *p* is justified if and only if S has access to good, undefeated and consciously accessible reasons for believing *p*.

Those who endorse this norm argue that factors that are under the radar of consciousness are irrelevant to the justificatory status of a belief: they can neither justify nor defeat the justification of a belief.

But now imagine again that you are taking part in the CV study, or Payne's object perception study. Notwithstanding the impact of biases that we have outlined above, it may nonetheless seem, from your own perspective, that you have access to good reasons for your belief – your perceptions of the object, for example. Moreover, the influence of implicit bias on perception may operate under the radar of consciousness: therefore it is irrelevant to the justification of your beliefs according to ACCESSIBILITY. According to this norm, you have justified beliefs, although your beliefs are affected by implicit biases (Puddifoot 2015).

These observations pose difficulties for those who endorse ACCESSIBILITY. There is a strong case for saying that where you form a belief based on bias-inflected perceptions your belief does not conform to the norms of good epistemic practice. But this cannot be captured by the norm ACCESSIBILITY (ibid.). Although firmly committed accessibilists might bite this bullet, this commits them to accepting that their account cannot capture the various ways that implicit biases lead people to deviate from good epistemic practice.

Implicit Biases, Responsibility and Virtues

Some epistemologists have emphasised that good epistemic practice involves forming beliefs responsibly, giving priority to the following norm:

> RESPONSIBILITY: good epistemic practice requires forming beliefs responsibly, in a way that fits with the evidence, coheres with one's previous beliefs, and is based on good reasons.
>
> *(Kornblith 1983, Bonjour 1985)*

From what we've already seen – the CV example and the weapons bias case – implicit biases pose difficulties for forming beliefs responsibly: biases prevent us from responding to the evidence that is available to us and from being aware of the real reasons for our beliefs. A subset of epistemologists who place responsibility at the heart of their account of good epistemic practice are virtue responsibilists, who give priority to norms such as the following:

> VIRTUE: good epistemic agents exercise a suite of epistemic virtues, including intellectual carefulness, perseverance, flexibility, open-mindedness, fair-mindedness and insightfulness.
>
> *(Zagzebski 1996, 155)*

> VICE AVOIDANCE: good epistemic agents avoid the exercise of a suite of epistemic vices, including intellectual pride, negligence, conformity, rigidity, prejudice, closed-mindedness and lack of thoroughness.
>
> *(Zagzebski 1996, 152)*

Psychologists have emphasised that implicit biases function in the service of efficiency (see Moskowitz & Li 2011): these sorts of automatic processes are useful to us when we're under time pressure, or preoccupied with other tasks. But whilst this arguably might sometimes be useful (see'Improving Epistemic Practice' above), it is in tension with intellectual virtues such as carefulness, flexibility, and perseverance. The person whose beliefs and judgements are influenced by implicit bias displays epistemic vices like negligence and lack of thoroughness. And since implicit biases often encode stereotypes, they are a hindrance to the achievement of virtues such as open-mindedness, leading to prejudice and closed-minded responses. Note that in some circumstances – e.g. limited evidence of social equality or in which little is known about implicit bias – agents might demonstrate these vices even whilst doing all they can to live up to their epistemic responsibilities. This may be a case of what Fricker (2016) calls 'no fault' epistemic responsibility: non-culpable epistemic responsibility for a biased response even whilst it is unreasonable to expect her to have avoided it. Implicit biases therefore make both VIRTUE and VICE AVOIDANCE difficult to achieve, even for those who make substantial efforts to meet these norms.

Implicit Bias and Appropriate Trust

Finally, consider the dispositions involved in responding appropriately to testimonial evidence. Elizabeth Fricker (1995) endorses:

TRUST: good epistemic agents should adopt an appropriately critical stance towards the testimony of others.

(Fricker 1995)

For example, imagine you tell me that Jessica was at the conference in May. According to TRUST, I should adopt the appropriately critical stance, using markers of credibility to evaluate whether your testimony has evidential value, before trusting (or not) your testimony about Jessica's whereabouts.

As Patricia Hill Collins argued, decisions about 'whom to trust and what to believe' are key to what version of the truth will prevail. And such decisions have often been guided by sexist and racist assumptions (2010, 252). Stereotypes that reduce Black women's credibility have been used to disregard Black women's testimony and exclude them from the domain of knowers (2010, 254, see also 69–97). More recently, Miranda Fricker (2007) has elucidated the way prejudice can inflect trust in her development of the idea of 'testimonial injustice'. Fricker describes how judgements about whether a source of testimony is credible can rely on negative prejudices that track social identity, such as gender or race. Fricker illustrates this with the example from *The Talented Mr Ripley*: Dickie Greenleaf's girlfriend Marge has valuable testimonial evidence about the circumstances of his disappearance, but she is written off as proffering merely 'women's intuition', and as being unreliable due to her distress. Knowledge is lost as she is excluded from the domain of knowers. More generally, TRUST is unlikely to be met in interactions with members of stigmatised groups stereotyped as epistemically inferior in this way: a default position of suspicion which fails to track true markers of credibility may be manifest and an inappropriately critical stance adopted in assessing the testimony of members of such groups.

We might think that so long as we are free from the sorts of prejudices that beset the agents in *Mr Ripley* – outright, or paternalistic, sexism – we are not hindered in our development of appropriate dispositions of trust. But implicit biases might be implicated in our dispositions to trust in complex ways. Some autonomic responses may subtly inflect our interactions in a way that undermines TRUST. For example, Dovidio et al. (1997) found differences in the automatic aspects of behaviour of White participants towards Black and White interaction partners. In interactions with Black partners, White participants' rates of eye-blink, which reflects tension, were higher; and rates of eye-contact, reflecting intimacy and respect, were lower. Interestingly, since the White individuals were not readily aware of these aspects of their behaviour, this also led to divergent impressions of how pleasant the interactions were: the Black participants noted the signals of discomfort, whilst the White participants were not aware they were displaying such behaviour (Dovidio et al. 2002). The tension that besets, and discrepant impressions of these interactions, Dovidio et al claim, means that these automatic behaviours operate 'in a way that interfere[s] with a foundation of communication and trust that is critical to developing long-term positive intergroup relations' (2002, 89). Kristie Dotson (2011) characterises such micro-behaviours as ways in which hearers demonstrate 'testimonial incompetence' and fail to provide the appropriate uptake for the testimony. Having these biases hinders interlocutors in meeting norms of TRUST and important testimonial evidence may be lost (cf. Fricker 2007).

Implicit Bias, Exclusion and Epistemic Practice

It is worth noting that in various endeavours to address under-representation it has been argued that implicit biases are part of the (complex) explanations for continued marginalisation and exclusion of individuals – in particular women and Black and minority ethnicity individuals – from communities of enquirers (Saul 2013). If this is so, then on views according to which diverse communities of enquirers are better positioned to identify errors and biases, implicit biases will be doubly implicated in undermining good epistemic practice: first in distorting the judgement of individuals; secondly in sustaining a homogeneous community of enquirers in which those distortions cannot well be detected and corrected (cf. Longino's model of enquiry, 1990).

Implicit Bias and Scepticism

We might wonder how widespread the difficulties we have outlined are. Saul (2013) argues that these findings mean that we have strong reasons not to trust our own 'cognitive instruments' (to use Hookway's (2010) terminology). Very many of our judgements may be distorted by implicit biases and the chances of detecting and correcting all of these are slim. We may never be sure, Saul argues, that we are forming good judgements – especially if perception itself is subject to distortion, and especially if we can't even detect the occasions on which we are getting things wrong. This sort of 'bias-induced doubt', Saul claims, is more pressing than that induced by more traditional sceptical challenges: we have strong reason to suppose that the challenge is realised (rather than just a theoretical possibility, such as that we are brains in vats); and, the scope of the challenge is broad – it would undermine very many of our judgements and beliefs (rather than some subset of them, as may be the case if we learn we have reason to doubt our probabilistic reasoning). Moreover, it is not clear that this kind of doubt can be overcome by individual exercises of reasoning; social resources may be required to mitigate bias-related doubt (see 'Improving Epistemic Practices' below). As such, the phenomenon of implicit bias should lead us to a radical form of scepticism.

One of the premises that provides the basis for the move to pervasive bias-related doubt is that we cannot be sure whether we are affected by biases. Recently, though, contention has emerged regarding whether we can be aware of implicit biases: in part this might depend on the sense of awareness at issue (see Nagel 2014, Holroyd 2015). Recent empirical studies suggest that, at least under certain conditions, individuals can become aware that their behaviours manifest bias (Hahn et al 2013). If we are able to deploy strategies to reliably track this, the scope of the sceptical challenge could be somewhat limited, by helping us to be aware of those cases in which our judgements are indeed beset by biases. However, the efficacy of those strategies needs further investigation.

Note that this line of scepticism supposes that implicit biases are always epistemically defective – leading us away from epistemic norms such as TRUTH-TRACKING, and hindering our cultivation of good dispositions such as VIRTUE, or TRUST. This stands in stark contrast to another line of reasoning, which has proposed that, whilst morally problematic, implicit biases might nonetheless yield some epistemic benefits.

Epistemic Benefits of Implicit Bias?

Here we consider whether (a) there is a case for accepting that implicit biases can sometimes be epistemically beneficial; and (b) there are costs to strategies intended to reduce the influence of implicit bias. Given the claims made under the previous heading 'Good Epistemic Practice', it may seem obvious that implicit biases are damaging and that it is epistemically beneficial rather than costly to reduce the influence of implicit bias. However, these assumptions have been challenged by, in turn, Jennifer Nagel (2012, 2014) and Tamar Szabo Gendler (2011).

Benefits of Implicit Biases?

Nagel (2014) disputes what she describes as a misinterpretation of empirical evidence that 'intuitive' forms of thought – 'type 1', fast, automatic, implicit cognitions – are irrational and likely to lead to errors, in contrast to 'reflective' – 'type 2', slow and deliberative – forms of thought, which are taken to be rational.[2]

Nagel defends intuitive reasoning in general – and indeed, there is no reason to suppose that all cognition that is non-reflective is therefore defective – but pertinent to our concerns is her defence of implicit biases in particular. The latter rests on empirical findings suggesting that implicit attitudes can be updated to reflect stimuli presented to the thinker. In an experimental setting, participants were exposed to pairings of Black individuals with positive words and images and White individuals with negative words and images. Following exposure to these pairings some implicit associations altered, even in the absence of any change of their explicit attitudes (Olson & Fazio 2006, cited in Nagel 2012). These findings suggest that implicit biases may be as evidence sensitive as explicit attitudes. If this is correct, there is reason to think that implicit biases can be epistemically beneficial: that under some circumstances we are more likely to make accurate judgements that reflect the available evidence if we are influenced by implicit biases than if we are not so influenced.

However, in evaluating Nagel's claims, we should bear in mind the distinction between (i) individuals who hold implicit associations being responsive to evidence and (ii) implicit associations being responsive to evidence. The Olson and Fazio study suggests that implicit biases can be responsive to evidence, and that our associations can change due to exposure to stimuli. But in a way, this is unsurprising, since the associations are held by many psychologists to be the result of associations in our environment to which we are exposed. Moreover, that the associations may be responsive to stimuli does not show that people who hold, and are influenced by, such implicit associations are more responsive to evidence than they would be if they were not subject to biases. It is consistent with Olson and Fazio's claim that being influenced by implicit bias brings epistemic costs, leading to distorted judgements, and prevention of forming beliefs based on the evidence. This is so even if the association itself can be altered through strategies such as counter-stereotyping used in the Olson and Fazio study.

Epistemic Costs of Reducing Bias?

A distinct challenge is presented by Tamar Szabo Gendler (2011) who agrees that there are serious epistemic costs to being influenced by implicit bias, but argues that there are also epistemic costs to choosing not to be influenced by implicit bias. To so choose, Gendler argues, is to choose not to be influenced by social category information. For example, to avoid weapons bias of the sort described above, you could ignore social category information about high rates of crime among the Black population of the United States. The result of this choice would be that you would no longer more strongly associate the members of the social category group (e.g. Black people in the US) with the undesirable features (e.g. weapons, or crime) and you could avoid relying on implicit associations that you explicitly repudiate. However, Gendler argues, this choice involves the explicit irrationality of choosing base-rate neglect; the neglect of important and relevant background information (Tversky & Kahneman 1974). Gendler's argument presents a dilemma between two epistemic aims: between avoiding the epistemic costs of base-rate neglect, or avoiding the epistemic costs of the influence of implicit associations (though see Mugg 2013 for a rejection of the claim that there are epistemic costs of being biased to the bearer of the bias).

Another potential dilemma we may face is between ignoring base-rate information – an alleged epistemic cost – and utilising it – an alleged ethical cost, insofar as implicit biases lead to discriminatory differential treatment of members of groups targeted by the biases (see Kelly & Roedder 2008, Brownstein 2015, for articulation of the ethical/epistemic dilemma).

Either way of setting up the dilemma supposes that there are some epistemic costs to not utilising implicit biases, since doing so involves a form of base-rate neglect. Focusing on implicit bias:

319

relating Black people with violence or crime, Puddifoot (2017) challenges this claim, arguing that our ordinary ways of using social category information about race and crime that occur in the absence of strategies to prevent implicit bias are substantially different from ideal base-rate use. Whilst ideal base-rate information use involves using accurate and relevant background information, our ordinary social category judgements involve inaccurate stereotypes, deploying them where they are irrelevant, and allowing them to distort our perception of, for example, case-specific information about individual crimes, suspects or victims. Accordingly, preventing our judgements being influenced by social category information in order to change or remove implicit biases is not equivalent to ignoring useful information, and so does not involve the same epistemic cost as base-rate neglect.

Another response accepts that there is a dilemma, but argues that we can minimise the costs we face. Madva (2016) argues that if we can limit the influence of implicit associations on judgement and behaviour, we could use information about social reality only where appropriate. For example, associations between Black men and crime might influence our thought if we are aiming to understand the social forces that culminate to bring Black males into contact with the criminal justice system, without implicit associations (e.g. between Black males and crime) then distorting judgement on other occasions. It is an open empirical question, however, whether and under what conditions it is possible to prevent our awareness of background information about social categories from inflecting our cognition with implicit biases. Further, the claim that it is possible to control implicit biases in this way will turn, ultimately, on debates concerning the nature of implicit bias (see Levy 2014, Mandelbaum 2015, Holroyd 2016) and the methods available to mitigate its influence.

Improving Epistemic Practice

Insofar as at least sometimes implicit biases hinder our epistemic practice then we should consider ways in which our epistemic practices might be adapted or transformed in order to avoid the distortions of implicit bias. The discussion above highlights that strategies for combating bias may be not only morally required, but also required if we are to avoid poor epistemic practice. However, there may be competing epistemic considerations that must be weighed in deciding what to do.

Insulating from Implicit Bias

One way in which we might avoid the epistemic distortions of implicit bias is by insulating our epistemic practices from the possibility of bias: deploying procedures to remove bias-triggering demographic information. For example, anonymised CVs can avoid gender or race biases inflecting the evaluation of the quality of the applicants, and could bring practice into line with norms of TRUTH-TRACKING, or EVIDENCE, and help agents with AVOIDING VICES. However, such anonymisation processes may also involve unwanted epistemic limitations. Suppose we know that women and Black or minority ethnicity individuals receive significantly less mentoring in a particular profession. Knowledge of an applicant's race or gender, therefore, could help to contextualise some of the information provided on the CV, and to understand qualifications as achieved despite less mentoring.

De-Biasing

Other strategies aim to remove the bias from our cognitions. This includes measures either to 'retrain' associative thinking or affective responses to remove problematic biases, or to train other aspects of cognition to effectively manage and block the manifestation of bias. Studies have suggested a range of surprising measures may be effective in retraining association, such as: imagining counter-stereotypical exemplars (Dasgupta & Asgari 2004); imagining interactions with individuals from stigmatised racial groups (Crisp & Turner 2012); retraining approach/avoidance dispositions (Kawakami et al. 2007. Other successful stragegies to block the influence of bias measures include imagining cases in which one has failed to act fairly, thereby activating 'egalitarian goals' (Moskowitz & Li 2011), or deploying 'implementation intentions' – cued cognitive or behavioural responses to environmental stimuli – (Webb et al. 2012).

Nagel (2014) has raised concerns about the specific epistemic costs of some of these strategies: implementation intentions, she argues, generate a general loss of accuracy in object identification studies (the weapon/tool studies outlined above). The main general concern for such strategies, however (setting aside for now the issue of whether debiasing involves epistemic loss), are the epistemic difficulties in knowing how effective these debiasing strategies are. On the one hand, some studies have failed to replicate success in mitigating biases, on the other, even if the studies robustly demonstrate bias reduction, it can be difficult to generalise outside of the lab, or to other kinds of bias. Since biases are varied in content and, it seems, in operation, measures which are successful in combating one kind of bias may not be so for others (see Holroyd & Sweetman 2016, Madva & Brownstein 2018). For example, bias reduction strategies may aim to reduce certain stereotypical associations, such as those between Black people and physical (rather than intellectual) constructs (cf. Amodio & Devine 2006). Yet it is unlikely that this same bias is implicated in e.g. perceptions of greater hostility in Black facial expressions (Hugenberg & Bodenhausen 2003), or in weapons biases (Payne 2006) – for which different interventions may be required.

Individualistic and Interpersonal Correctives

Some have argued that individual virtues are an important corrective to combating the distortions of prejudice and implicit biases (see Fricker 2007, Webber 2016). For example, Miranda Fricker has proposed the virtue of 'testimonial justice' as required to avoid unjustly underestimating the credibility of interlocutors. One way in which this sensibility may manifest, Fricker suggests (2010), is in alertness to cognitive dissonance between judgements of credibility (which may be infected by implicit biases) and the anti-discrimination norms to which one subscribes. Dissonance can provide 'cues for control' and prompt critical assessments of the evidence.

Note that this strategy supposes that individuals can at least sometimes become cognisant of their susceptibility to bias – arresting prejudicial tendencies when it is noticed that they are in operation. Is such awareness possible? There are at least three senses of awareness at issue in the literatures of philosophy and psychology: introspective awareness of the associations; observational awareness of our behaviour being inflected by bias; inferential awareness of our propensity to bias given the empirical findings (Holroyd 2015). Notwithstanding obstacles to awareness such as self-deception or misleading introspective evidence, some recent studies suggest that whilst we are individually poor judges of the extent to which we have or manifest implicit biases, we are nonetheless better at noticing the effects of bias when prompted in interpersonal interactions to reflect on this (Hahn et al. 2013).

Even if individuals are able to ascertain that their behaviours manifest bias, it is difficult to detect *to what extent* this is so. It is not the case that whenever we find implicit bias influencing belief, the counterfactual 'She would not believe that but for the bias' will be true: in some cases biases might shore up a belief, make it peculiarly insensitive to revision, but ultimately provide bad epistemic grounds for a belief that has independent epistemic support. So assessing the ways in which biases have affected our beliefs requires careful weighing of evidence with the likely contribution of bias: yet we are not often in an epistemic position to do this (for an example of the difficulties that beset attempts to 'correct' judgements which might be inflected by implicit bias, see Kelly and Roedder's (2008) discussion of grading student papers).

Structural Correctives

Haslanger (2015) has suggested that if the correct analysis of injustice is primarily structural, then individual corrective responses are unlikely to effectively target injustice. Moreover, correcting individual implicit biases may be ineffective in the absence of broader social change; few de-biasing strategies have lasting effects, as problematic associations remain in our social environment. Similarly, Elizabeth Anderson has worried that if problems of improper credibility assignment are systemic and structural, then individual virtue as a corrective is unlikely to be sufficient to address the problem: not only because it can be hard to identify when such correctives are needed, and hard for individuals to be constantly vigilant to going wrong; but also because broader structural solutions are needed (2012, 167).

Anderson describes three ways structural change can be beneficial: first, enabling individual corrective measures to work – for example by having institutional procedures that clearly specify explicit grounds for decision-making, sufficient time for making decisions carefully in accordance with those criteria, and accountability for discriminatory outcomes (Anderson 2012, 168). Second, structural changes can instantiate individual virtues at a collective level – an institution may endorse institutional policies that accord with the norm of TRUST or VIRTUE (2012, 168–169). Finally, Anderson proposes a more radical kind of structural change: we might hope to foster social and structural arrangements that promulgate 'epistemic democracy: universal participation on terms of equality of all inquirers' (Anderson 2012, 172). This involves ending patterns of informal segregation that structure educational provision, and communities of inquiry.

Avoiding Scepticism?

Given that epistemic difficulties beset the remedial strategies themselves – how effective they are, when they are needed, whether they can be successful in the absence of broader structural change – the threat of scepticism may remain until our social and epistemic environment is refigured along the lines of Anderson's 'epistemic democracy' (cf. Saul 2013). An alternative response to bias-related scepticism has been proposed by Louise Antony (2016): confronted by the pervasiveness of bias, Antony suggests, we should not retreat to scepticism, but rather adopt a naturalised epistemology of inquiry based evaluation into which biases are a hindrance to good epistemic practice, and which are not. We may be unable to function bias free, but we can weed out the bad ones, and use methods of scientific enquiry to do so.

Challenges for Philosophers

Finally, philosophical engagement with empirical research on implicit bias raises distinctive epistemic challenges.

Repligate

The discipline of social psychology is itself presently facing a crisis of replication – so called 'repligate'. In a wide-ranging attempt to replicate important findings, only 39 of 100 studies reproduced the original results,[3] prompting critical reflection on the methods of empirical psychology: whether null results should be published, data widely and openly available, methods and analyses pre-registered to avoid selective analysis, and so on. We are not suggesting that this provides decisive reason to doubt all of the findings of empirical psychology – especially since some findings have been replicated via robust methods. However, there is reason to adjust our confidence in the outcomes of empirical studies until they have been robustly replicated. And whilst a large number of studies have demonstrated the existence and effects of implicit bias (see Jost et al. 2009), attempts to mitigate bias have been less successfully replicated (Lai et al. 2014).

Under-Developed Conceptual Frameworks

A second difficulty is that the psychological research deploys notions that are constructed with experimental purpose, rather than philosophical rigour, in mind. Most simply, psychologists may use terminology ('belief', 'judgement', 'stereotype', 'desire', 'affect') in different ways from philosophers. More problematically, philosophers may inherit modes of discourse – 'implicit bias' itself being a case in point – that is not robustly worked out. Few psychologists agree on what is meant by 'implicit', and some understandings of it – e.g. accessible (though not exclusively) by implicit measure (De Houwer et al. 2009) – certainly depart from what is commonly meant in philosophical discourse (where this is often conflated with 'unconscious'). These differences are not benign – normative conclusions to do with accountability and remedial obligation may turn on the sense in which biases are 'implicit', and whether this is incompatible with 'awareness' (see Holroyd 2015).

This means that there is scope for what philosophers may sometimes do best – bringing conceptual clarity to a discourse! But whilst the empirical evidence is fast changing, it may be difficult to reach firm conclusions. We take this to speak in favour of more, rather than less, interaction between philosophers and psychologists – to enable fruitful and conceptually clear discourse across disciplinary differences.

Positioning the Literature in Relation to Extant Claims

The findings of empirical psychology are often presented as showing to us surprising and troubling aspects of our cognitions, and their implication in perpetuating injustices. But we should ask why these findings are surprising, and what this tells us about our epistemic disposition towards sources of evidence. One putative and unsatisfactory answer would be that empirical psychology reveals a domain of discriminatory behaviour which it was simply impossible to know about prior to the advent of this research. This answer is unsatisfactory in that in supposing knowledge of such discrimination was inaccessible to us, we fail to engage with other sources of evidence of these patterns of discrimination and ignore testimonial evidence from individuals stigmatised by such biases. Gloria Yamato provides such testimonial evidence, in her writing from 1988, which pre-dates the recent upsurge of interest in implicit bias within psychology and philosophy:

> Unaware/unintentional racism drives usually tranquil white liberals wild when they get called on it, and confirms the suspicions of many people of color who feel that white folks are just plain crazy. [...] With the best of intentions, the best of educations, and the greatest generosity of heart, whites, operating on the misinformation fed to them from day one, will behave in ways that are racist, will perpetuate racism by being 'nice' the way we're taught to be nice.
>
> *(Yamato 2004, 100)*[4]

The point is not that empirical psychology adds nothing to our understanding of patterns of discrimination – of course it has helped us to develop nuanced models of how aspects of our cognition may be implicated in, and perpetuate, various injustices. But we should not suppose that it reveals patterns of discrimination that were invisible prior to this; to do so privileges certain sources of evidence – from communities of academic scientists – over others, namely, the testimony of individuals targeted by those patterns of discrimination and injustice. Indeed, the value of lived experience as a source of knowledge has been emphasised by Patricia Hill Collins. She suggests that within Black-feminist thought lived experience reveals itself as a more reliable source of understanding than those produced by exclusionary institutions, quoting Hannah Nelson's remark that for her, 'distant statistics are certainly not as important as the actual experience of a sober person' (Nelson, quoted at 257). Yet, this source of knowledge – testimony on the basis of lived experience – has not been valued accordingly in academic communities. The proposal is that we should think carefully about the epistemic status of the empirical literature: for example, we might regard it as providing evidential support for, and thereby vindicating, the lived experiences of individuals who have long reported on this discrimination, whilst also reflecting on which norms dictate that such testimony requires 'vindicating', rather than as evidence about newly discovered patterns of discrimination. Such a stance highlights the importance of attending to historically marginalised testimonies, and may help to avoid what Kristie Dotson (2012) has named 'contributory injustice'. In a context where various conceptual resources – some marginalised – co-exist, contributory injustice is the maintenance and deployment of structurally prejudiced and exclusionary hermeneutical resources. Whilst being able to articulate experiences via non-mainstream hermeneutical resources, some speakers may fail to receive uptake for their testimony due to the impoverished resources of the hearer.

Feminist epistemology also offers us resources to account for why testimony has been ignored or marginalised. One might see the literature on implicit bias as filling a 'hermeneutical gap' (a notion developed in Fricker 2007), and offering us conceptual resources that better enable discourse on discrimination and injustice to proceed. Whilst the findings on implicit bias help us to correct that lack of interpretative resources, they also prompt reflection on how those findings are positioned in relation to other sources of evidence, and on the appropriate epistemic dispositions towards both empirical findings and heretofore marginalised narratives of social reality.

Notes

1 Ulhmann and Cohen used certain experiences, by which the candidates were ranked, to indicate the extent to which a candidate was 'streetwise': e.g. 'worked in tough neighbourhoods', 'got along with other officers'. This was contrasted with qualifications pertaining to being well educated: 'well schooled', 'with administrative experience'.

2 Ultimately, Nagel endorses a way of distinguishing intuitive and reflective thinking that identifies the ways each draws on working memory. Each depends on the other (228–231). See also Carruthers (2013).

3 See Open Science Collaboration (2015), DOI: 10.1126/science.aac4716; however, it is worth considering http://alexanderetz.com/2015/08/30/the-bayesian-reproducibility-project/ [accessed 13.01.2016] for useful critical discussion of how to interpret these failures of replication.

4 It is worth noting that this paper was not available in any of our university libraries, despite being reproduced in many volumes on gender and race – testament itself to what sources of knowledge are deemed important, perhaps.

References

Amodio, D. M., & Devine, P. G. (2006). Stereotyping and evaluation in implicit race bias: Evidence for independent constructs and unique effects on behaviour. *Journal of Personality and Social Psychology*, 91(4), p. 652.

Anderson, E. (2012). Epistemic justice as a virtue of social institutions. *Social Epistemology*, 26(2), pp. 163–173.

Antony, L. (2016). Bias: Friend or Foe? Reflections on Saulish Skepticism. In M. Brownstein & J. Saul, eds., *Implicit Bias and Philosophy*. Oxford: Oxford University Press, pp. 157–190.

Bonjour, L. (1985). *The Structure of Empirical Knowledge*. Cambridge, MA: Harvard University Press.

Brownstein, M. (2015). Attributionism and moral responsibility for implicit bias. *Review of Philosophy and Psychology*, 4, pp. 1–22.

Carruthers, P. (2013). Evolution of working memory. *Proceedings of the National Academy of Sciences*, 110 (Supplement 2), pp. 10371–10378.

Crisp, R. J., & Turner, R. N. (2012). The imagined contact hypothesis. *Advances in Experimental Social Psychology*, 46, pp. 125–182.

Dasgupta, N., & Asgari, S. (2004). Seeing is believing: Exposure to counterstereotypic women leaders and its effect on the malleability of automatic gender stereotyping. *Journal of Experimental Social Psychology*, 40(5), pp. 642–658.

De Houwer, J., Teige-Mocigemba, S., Spruyt, A., & Moors, A. (2009). Implicit measures: A normative analysis and review. *Psychological Bulletin*, 135(3), p. 347.

Dotson, K. (2011). Tracking epistemic violence, tracking practices of silencing. *Hypatia*, 26(2), pp. 236–257.

Dotson, K. (2012). A cautionary tale: On limiting epistemic oppression, *Frontiers. A Journal of Women Studies*, 33(1), pp. 24–47.

Dovidio, J. F., Gaertner, S. E., Kawakami, K., & Hodson, G. (2002). Why can't we just get along? Interpersonal biases and interracial distrust. *Cultural Diversity and Ethnic Minority Psychology*, 8(2), p. 88.

Dovidio, J. F., Kawakami, K., Johnson, C., Johnson, B., & Howard, A. (1997). On the nature of prejudice: Automatic and controlled processes. *Journal of Experimental Social Psychology*, 33(5), pp. 510–540.

Fricker, E. (1995). Critical notice: Telling and trusting: Reductionism and anti- reductionism in the epistemology of testimony. *Mind*, 104, pp. 393–411.

Fricker, M. (2007). *Epistemic Injustice: Power and the Ethics of Knowing*. Oxford: Oxford University Press, p. 7.

Fricker, M. (2010). Replies to Alcoff, Goldberg, and Hookway, book symposium on *epistemic injustice: Power and the ethics of knowing*, in *Episteme. A Journal of Social Epistemology*, 7(2).

Fricker, M. (2016). Fault and No-fault Responsibility for Implicit Prejudice—A Space for Epistemic Agent-regret. In M. S. Brady & M. Fricker, eds., *The Epistemic Life of Groups: Essays in the Epistemology of Colectives*. Oxford: OUP.

Gendler, T. S. (2011). On the epistemic costs of implicit bias. *Philosophical Studies*, 156(1), pp. 33–63.

Hahn, A., Judd, C. M., Hirsh, H. K., & Blair, I. V. (2013). Awareness of implicit attitudes. *Journal of Experimental Psychology: General*, 143(3), p. 1369.

Haslanger, S. (2015). Distinguished lecture: Social structure, narrative and explanation. *Canadian Journal of Philosophy*, 45(1), pp. 1–15.

Hill Collins, P. (2010). *Black Feminist Thought: Knowledge, Consciousness and the Politics of Empowerment*, 2nd Edition. New York: Routledge.

Holroyd, J. (2015). Implicit bias, awareness and imperfect cognitions. *Consciousness and Cognition*, 33, pp. 511–523.

Holroyd, J. (2016). What do we want from a model of implicit cognition? *Proceedings of the Aristotelian Society*, 116(2), pp. 153–179.

Holroyd, J., & Sweetman, J. (2016). The Heterogeneity of Implicit Bias. In M. Brownstein & J. Saul, eds., *Implicit Bias and Philosophy*. Oxford: Oxford University Press.

Hookway, C. (2010). Some varieties of epistemic injustice: Reflections on Fricker. *Episteme*, 7(2), pp. 151–163.

Hugenberg, K., & Bodenhausen, G.V. (2003). Facing prejudice: Implicit prejudice and the perception of facial threat. *Psychological Science*, 14(6), pp. 640–643.

Jost, J. T., Rudman, L. A., Blair, I. V., Carney, D. R., Dasgupta, N., Glaser, J., & Hardin, C. D. (2009). The existence of implicit bias is beyond reasonable doubt: A refutation of ideological and methodological objections and executive summary of ten studies that no manager should ignore. *Research in Organizational Behavior*, 29, pp. 39–69.

Kawakami, K., Dovidio, J. F., & Van Kamp, S. (2007). The impact of counterstereotypic training and related correction processes on the application of stereotypes. *Group Processes & Intergroup Relations*, 10(2), pp. 139–156.

Kelly, D., & Roedder, E. (2008). Racial cognition and the ethics of implicit bias. *Philosophy Compass*, 3(3), pp. 522–540.

Kornblith, H. (1983). Justified belief and epistemically responsible action. *Philosophical Review*, 92(1), pp. 33–48.

Lai, C. K., Marini, M., Lehr, S. A., Cerruti, C., Shin, J. L., Joy-Gaba, J. A., Ho, A. K., Teachman, B. A., Wojcik, S. P., Koleva, S. P., Frazier, R. S., Heiphetz, L., Chen, E., Turner, R. N., Haidt, J., Kesebir, S., Hawkins, C. B., Schaefer, H. S., Rubichi, S., Sartori, G., Dial, C. M., Sriram, N., Banaji, M. R., & Nosek, B. A. (2014). Reducing implicit racial preferences: I. A comparative investigation of 17 interventions. *Journal of Experimental Psychology: General*, 143, pp. 1765–1785.

Levy, N. (2014). Neither fish nor fowl: Implicit attitudes as patchy endorsements. *Noûs*, 49(4) (2015), pp. 800–823.

Longino, H. (1990). *Science as Knowledge: Values and Objectivity in Scientific Inquiry*. Princeton, NJ: Princeton University Press.

Madva, A. (2016). Virtue, Social Knowledge, and Implicit Bias. In M. Brownstein & J. Saul, eds., *Implicit Bias and Philosophy*. Oxford: Oxford University Press.

Madva, A., & Brownstein, M. (2018). Stereotypes, prejudice, and the taxonomy of the implicit social mind. *Noûs*, 52(3), pp. 611–644.

Mandelbaum, E. (2015). Attitude, inference, association: On the propositional structure of implicit bias. *Noûs*, 50(3) (2016), pp. 629–658.

Moskowitz, G. B., & Li, P. (2011). Egalitarian goals trigger stereotype inhibition: A proactive form of stereotype control. *Journal of Experimental Social Psychology*, 47(1), pp. 103–116.

Mugg, J. (2013). What are the cognitive costs of racism? A reply to gendler. *Philosophical Studies*, 166(2), pp. 217–229.

Nagel, J., (2012). Gendler on alief. *Analysis*, 72(4), pp. 774–788.

Nagel, J. (2014, June). II—Intuition, reflection, and the command of knowledge. *Aristotelian Society Supplementary Volume*, 88(1), pp. 219–241.

Nozick, R. (1981). *Philosophical Explanations*. Cambridge, MA: Harvard University Press.

Olson, M. A., & Fazio, R. H. (2006). Reducing automatically activated racial prejudice through implicit evaluative conditioning. *Personality and Social Psychology Bulletin*, 32(4), pp. 421–433.

Payne, B. K. (2006). Weapon bias split-second decisions and unintended stereotyping. *Current Directions in Psychological Science*, 15(6), pp. 287–291.

Pritchard, D. (2005). *Epistemic Luck*. Oxford: Oxford University Press.

Puddifoot, K. (2015). Accessibilism and the challenge from implicit bias. *Pacific Philosophical Quarterly* 97(3), pp. 421–434.

Puddifoot, K. (2017). Stereotyping: the multifactorial view. *Philosophical Topics*, 45(1), pp. 137–156.

Saul, J. (2013). Scepticism and implicit bias. *Disputatio*, 5(37), p. 248.

Siegel, S. (2012). Cognitive penetrability and perceptual justification. *Noûs*, 46(2), pp. 201–222.

Tversky, A., & Kahneman, D. (1974). Judgment under uncertainty: Heuristics and biases. *Science*, 185(4157), pp. 1124–1131.

Uhlmann, E. L., & Cohen, G. L. (2007). I think it, therefore it's true: Effects of self-perceived objectivity on hiring discrimination. *Organizational Behavior and Human Decision Processes*, 104(2), pp. 207–223.

Webb, T. L., Sheeran, P., & Pepper, J. (2012). Gaining control over responses to implicit attitude tests: Implementation intentions engender fast responses on attitude-incongruent trials. *British Journal of Social Psychology*, 51(1), pp. 13–32.

Webber, J. (2016). Instilling Virtue. In A. Masala & J. Webber, eds., *From Personality to Virtue*. Oxford: Oxford University Press.

Williamson, T. (2000). *Knowledge and Its Limits*. Oxford: Oxford University Press.

Yamato, G. (2004). Something About the Subject Makes It Hard to Name. In M. Anderson & P. Hill Collins eds., *Race, Class and Gender*, 5th Edition. New York: Thomson/ Wadsworth, pp. 99–103.

Zagzebski (1996). *Virtues of the Mind*. Cambridge: Cambridge University Press.

32

EPISTEMIC JUSTICE
AND INJUSTICE

Nancy Daukas

Analytic philosophy conventionally represents epistemological concerns as distinct from ethical and political concerns. Since the 1980s, a critical movement in epistemology (which I will call *liberatory social epistemology*) has challenged that convention by showing that social power affects practices through which communities produce, share, acknowledge, understand, and reward knowledge and knowledge claims, in ways that benefit the more powerful and harm the less powerful (Code 1991, 1995, Collins 1990, Fricker 1998, 1999, Mills 1997, Alcoff 1999). Miranda Fricker identifies the distinctively epistemic harms inflicted by the politics of knowing as *epistemic injustices*, and defines an epistemic injustice as "a wrong done to someone specifically in their capacity as a knower" (2007: 2). With the publication of Fricker's influential book, *Epistemic Injustice: Power & the Ethics of Knowing* (2007), the political character of epistemic concepts and practices is becoming more broadly recognized in social epistemology.

In that book, Fricker distinguishes two types of epistemic injustice: *testimonial* and *hermeneutical*. David Coady proposes that there are also *distributive* epistemic injustices: members of socio-economically disadvantaged groups are harmed as knowers when they are denied full access to epistemic goods such as educational opportunities, information and communication technologies, libraries, and so on (Coady 2010). The work in liberatory social epistemology discussed below focuses primarily on the ideas of testimonial and hermeneutical injustices. This chapter explains those ideas and their connections to related work in liberatory social epistemology (although space limitations make it impossible to provide a comprehensive review), and briefly discusses several proposals for how to change epistemic practices to avoid or counteract epistemic injustices.

Testimonial Injustice and the Epistemology of Testimony

In epistemology, "testimony" refers to communicative acts, such as spoken, signed, and written utterances, through which a speaker asserts something to an audience with the intention of encouraging the audience to believe that what they[1] say is true. Whenever a speaker tells someone something, they are giving testimony. Conventionally, the epistemology of testimony represents testimony as involving a generic speaker, S, who utters a generic proposition, P, to a generic audience or hearer, H, in circumstance C. The standard questions are: Is testimony a reliable source of beliefs, on a par epistemologically with an individual's own perceptual experiences and reasoning? Or does the justification of the belief that P that H acquires when S asserts that P depend on H's independent evidence that S is a reliable informant?

From the perspective of liberatory social epistemology, the abstract generality of this picture conceals the fact that audiences often respond differently to speakers who occupy different social positions, and that such responsive differences can profoundly affect a speaker's ability to participate fully in public epistemic life. When an audience respectfully attends and appropriately responds to a speaker's utterance, the audience acknowledges the speaker as a knower, provides the social recognition necessary for their attempt at communication to succeed (Hornsby and Langton 1998), and enables them (and what they say) to participate in the conversations and inquiries through which the community's public knowledge is produced and disseminated. When an audience withholds that recognition, they undermine the speaker as a knower. On Fricker's view, when an audience's prejudice concerning the speaker's social identity causes that withholding of recognition, the audience inflicts a *testimonial injustice* upon the speaker. Testimonial injustices often fuel other sorts of injustices: they may affect legal proceedings; the distribution and quality of health care; how educators respond to particular students; how employers evaluate resumes or job performance; how voters view political candidates; who is and is not granted institutionalized social power; and so on.

Feminist epistemologist Lorraine Code argues that a realistic framework for understanding testimony would acknowledge that testimonial exchanges occur in "rhetorical spaces" shaped by "hierarchies of power and privilege," so that whether or not a given knowledge claim "goes through" depends on "who is speaking where and why" (1995: ix–x). Fricker provides precisely such a framework for her epistemology of testimony. She argues that audiences spontaneously use stereotypes (or assumed empirical generalizations) "about the trustworthiness of different social types in different social contexts" to form "credibility judgments" that attribute a higher or lower degree of credibility to particular speakers regarding a given topic under the given circumstances. (2007: 72).

Often, stereotypes steer an audience in the right direction. For example, it makes good sense to assume that a physician employed by a reputable medical practice is a credible authority regarding issues of routine health care. However, it is wrong, epistemically and ethically, to doubt a physician's diagnosis because she is a black woman, for example. When an audience's credibility judgment relies on a *prejudicial* stereotype (or a stereotype that misaligns with and resists correction by evidence) that attributes a "credibility deficit" to the speaker, the audience inflicts a testimonial injustice on that speaker. For Fricker, then, the "central case" of testimonial injustice occurs when a speaker receives a credibility deficit due to "identity prejudice in the hearer" (2007:28). Where social conditions are shaped by a history of unjust power relations among social groups, individuals routinely form credibility judgments on the basis of culturally inherited prejudicial stereotypes that distort the ways that they perceive one another as knowers and speakers. They are likely to perceive speakers who belong to socially privileged groups as more credible than the available evidence suggests, and speakers who belong to socially marginalized groups as less credible than the evidence suggests.

Toward a Broader Understanding of Testimonial Injustice

Elizabeth Anderson argues that individuals' prejudices are not the only causes of credibility deficits—structural forces cause credibility deficits regardless of whether or not individual participants are prejudiced. For example, socio-economic segregation may deny members of disadvantaged groups access to the educational resources through which to develop the styles and patterns of communicative behavior that members of privileged groups recognize as "markers of credibility". The absence of those markers confers a credibility deficit on the speaker. And ethnocentrism (or "bias in favor of groups to which one belongs") may cause members of privileged groups to see one another as more credible than members of other groups, again resulting in a credibility deficit being attributed to a given member of a less privileged group, and inflicting a testimonial injustice (2012: 169).

Along with the "standard case" of testimonial injustice that Fricker delineates, there are other patterns that we might also identify as testimonial injustices. These include patterns in whose testimony is (and is not) solicited, who tends to be interrupted, whose claims are remembered, who takes or receives credit for whose ideas, whose intellectual labor is acknowledged, whose questions and comments receive engaged follow-up, who is permitted to steer a conversation, and so on. Further, when the powerful *speak for* the oppressed (even with good intentions), they may create the appearance that the oppressed are not adequately articulate or informed to speak for themselves, or that the more powerful understand the lives, needs, and experiences of the marginalized better than the marginalized understand themselves (Alcoff 1991, Okin 2003).

When audiences inflict testimonial injustices, they inflict harm by denying speakers acknowledgment as knowers. Being, and being seen as, a knower is a core aspect of personhood. Therefore Fricker considers testimonial injustice to provide "a direct route to undermining [speakers] in their very humanity" (44). Further, when audiences systematically deny speakers acknowledgment as knowers due to social group membership, they reinforce the grip of prejudicial stereotypes over social perceptions and so contribute to reinforcing existing power relations that disadvantage some groups while benefiting others. All of this ultimately impoverishes the broader community's shared knowledge by blocking the (potentially transformative) benefits that diversity in beliefs, understandings, and interpretive resources generally offers. This brings us to Fricker's second category of epistemic injustice.

Hermeneutical Injustice

Fricker defines hermeneutical injustice as

> the injustice of having some significant area of one's social experience obscured from collective understanding owing to a structural identity prejudice in the collective hermeneutical resource.
>
> *(2007: 155, italics in original)*

By "the collective hermeneutical resource," Fricker refers to the stock of meanings, concepts, and understandings broadly available to all for making one's experiences intelligible to oneself and/or to others in a given community. Where there is social inequality, the more powerful will tend to enjoy disproportionate control over those resources and the less powerful are likely to be "*hermeneutically marginalized*" vis-a-vis some area(s) of their social experience (153). The resources that are publically validated and widely disseminated therefore serve the communicative needs and interests of the powerful more effectively than they serve the communicative needs and interests of the marginalized. As a result, according to Fricker, the community's collective hermeneutical resources may "have a lacuna where the name of a distinctive social experience should be," causing "an acute cognitive disadvantage" for members of marginalized groups (2007: 150–151). That disadvantage is a hermeneutical injustice, a kind of epistemic injustice that may cut so deeply as to "cramp the very development of the self":

> When you find yourself in a situation in which you seem to be the only one to feel the dissonance between received understanding and your own intimated sense of a given experience, it tends to knock your faith in your own ability to make sense of the world.
>
> *(Fricker 2007: 163)*

It is easiest to recognize hermeneutical injustices retrospectively, after the responsible hermeneutical gaps have been filled. For example, what we now recognize as sexual harassment was long represented as harmless flirting—an understanding that expresses the experience of the harasser and conceals or invalidates the experiences of the harassed. The introduction and dissemination of the expression "sexual harassment" enhanced the ability of the harassed to understand their experiences, and shifted public understandings in ways that helped to promote gender justice (2007: 149–151). Other concepts that, once validated, have enhanced shared interpretive resources and supported social activism include *ableism, homophobia, transphobia*, and *white privilege*, to name only a few. Fricker's *epistemic injustice* belongs on this list as well.

Perhaps the most powerful reverberations of hermeneutical injustice emerge from their role in the *social construction* of social identity categories, such as gender, race, class, and so on. Control over hermeneutical resources allows meanings that express the perspective of the powerful to be normatively enforced, so that the social world becomes as those meanings represent it to be. That is, hermeneutical power exerts control over how things are, including how people are socialized to be. Therefore, continues Fricker,

> hermeneutical injustice can mean that someone is socially constituted as, and perhaps even caused to be something they are not, and which it is against their interests to be seen to be.
>
> (168)

Toward a Broader Understanding of Hermeneutical Injustice

We might consider Fricker's definition of hermeneutical injustice to have a broader scope than her account of it suggests. Fricker clarifies her view of hermeneutical injustice by explaining that, in contrast to testimonial injustice, "no agent perpetrates hermeneutical injustice—it is a purely structural notion" (2007: 159). In response, Jose Medina argues that hermeneutical injustices can be both agential and structural: "hermeneutical gaps are performatively invoked and recirculated— *reenacted*, we could say—in the speech acts of daily life" (2013: 110). An example might be when a co-worker responds to the complaints of a victim of sexual harassment by advising them to lighten up and enjoy the compliment. In that sort of case, background conditions "erupt into [hermeneutical] injustice" through the agency of an individual to undermine an "actual attempt at intelligibility" (Fricker 2007: 159).

Fricker characterizes both hermeneutical and testimonial injustices as *episodic*, that is, as occurring in particular times and places, during particular communicative exchanges (or attempted communicative exchanges). But although it seems clear that testimonial injustices and *some* hermeneutical injustices are episodic (such as the co-worker's failure to comprehend the speaker in the above example), other hermeneutical injustices do not seem episodic. One of Fricker's central cases is an example: consider a woman suffering from post-partum depression before the expression was widely available (2007: 149). If she keeps her suffering to herself, she may never endure a localized episode of agent-enacted hermeneutical injustice. Yet there is a hermeneutical gap in shared resources (due to the traditional hermeneutical marginalization of women) that denies the subject self-understanding and prevents her experiences from being understood in public space, thus harming her as a knower. Here, a gap in shared resources creates sustained, persistent epistemic harm to members of a subordinated social group.

On Fricker's account of hermeneutical injustice, gaps in available resources leave both the marginalized and the powerful without resources for adequately understanding the experiences of the marginalized. But hermeneutical gaps in the resources preferred by the powerful often prevent only the powerful from understanding the experiences of the marginalized. The marginalized use resources of their own to understand and successfully communicate with one another about their experiences, but the powerful are either oblivious to, or illiterate in, those alternative resources. Gaile Pohlhaus identifies the refusal "to acknowledge already developed epistemic resources for knowing the world from situations other than their own" as a form of *willful hermeneutical ignorance* (Pohlhaus 2011:19). Kristie Dotson links such ignorance to a further kind testimonial injustice: it creates an environment in which the oppressed are likely to censor or withhold their own testimony to avoid the predictable and potentially harmful misinterpretations of the privileged. Dotson calls such self-censoring *testimonial smothering* (2011).

Dotson identifies the root source of hermeneutical injustices as *contributory epistemic injustice*, which occurs when the hermeneutical ignorance of the powerful "thwarts a knower's ability to contribute to shared epistemic resources within a given epistemic community" (2012: 32). We might extend the category of contributory epistemic injustice to include cases in which the powerful *knowingly* exclude the epistemic resources of the marginalized from the stock of favored or preferred resources, as when a colonial power deliberately suppresses the traditional resources of the colonized. Even more broadly, we can think of systemic contributory epistemic injustice, together with the resulting problems of systematic hermeneutical and testimonial injustice, as forms of *participatory* epistemic injustices, where participatory epistemic injustice is understood to include injustices of recognition (Cf McConkey 2004).

Epistemic Injustices and Social Epistemic Harm

We have seen that epistemic injustices harm individuals and entire social groups. Over time, systemic patterns of epistemic injustice also harm a community's knowledge system itself. Most obviously, they prevent it from being as extensive as it could be, by excluding contributions and withholding opportunities for epistemic development. This sort of harm may seem to be straightforwardly quantitative: because of epistemic injustice, the stock of broadly shared public beliefs is smaller than it could be. But epistemic injustices impoverish a community's belief system in a further way: they sustain cultural biases and perspectival narrowness, and so make the belief system less objective than it could and should be. This sort of harm is particularly evident in the sciences.

When we identify *objectivity* as an epistemic standard, we (minimally) express the conviction that what a community accepts as knowledge ought not to be biased by prejudice or parochial narrowness. The practices through which the sciences produce knowledge are conventionally understood to promote objectivity by rooting out biases. But historically, the sciences (and philosophy) have been dominated by members of powerful groups. Members of powerful groups are likely to share sorts of background experiences and culturally inherited presuppositions, and unlikely to notice how those shared presuppositions bias their epistemic practices and products. A large body of work in feminist science studies argues that social diversity, together with an equitable distribution of epistemic authority amongst diverse participants, promotes objectivity, because participants with diverse backgrounds are able to notice how one another's presuppositions bias their inquiry (Longino 1990). In a field with a history of social exclusion, centering inquiry on experiences and understandings of members of excluded or underrepresented groups therefore is likely to enhance objectivity (Harding 1993). Since epistemic injustices sustain such exclusions and authorial inequities, they obstruct objectivity in the sciences, and undermine the epistemic integrity and potential of the epistemic community.

Overcoming Epistemic Injustices: Virtue-Theoretical Responses

Fricker and others propose virtue-theoretical responses to problems of epistemic injustices. *Virtue epistemology* analyzes epistemic practices and concepts by reference to the enduring character states of epistemic agents and the sorts of dispositions and habits those character states support. Virtue-theoretical responses to problems of epistemic injustice offer normative guidance for cultivating character states and sensitivities that would dispose us to avoid inflicting, disrupt, or rectify epistemic injustices. My own work is an example: it emphasizes the importance of cultivating a critical self-awareness through which to recognize and alter the ways that epistemic politics affect our assumptions regarding our own, and others', epistemic trustworthiness. (Daukas 2006, 2011).

Fricker's virtue theoretical response to testimonial injustice urges individuals to specifically cultivate the virtue of *testimonial justice,* that is, a sensitivity to "*the impact of prejudice in [their] credibility judgments*", to develop strategies for neutralizing that impact (2007: 92, italics in original).[2] To overcome tendencies to contribute to hermeneutical injustice, Fricker urges agents to cultivate the virtue of *hermeneutical justice,* that is,

> an alertness or sensitivity to the possibility that the difficulty one's interlocutor is having as she tries to render something communicatively intelligible is due not to its being nonsense or her being a fool, but rather to some sort of gap in collective hermeneutical resources.
>
> *(169)*

Medina's virtue-theoretical proposal engages with the willful ignorance that often fuels epistemic injustice. Medina diagnoses willful hermeneutical ignorance as a symptom of the epistemic shortcoming (or vice) of "meta-insensitivity", that is, insensitivity to one's insensitivity toward others. As a remedy, he urges epistemic agents to cultivate "*meta-lucidity*", or awareness of their cognitive "blind spots," and a "communicative openness and responsiveness to indefinitely plural interpretive perspectives" (2013: 112–113).

In response to Fricker and Medina, Jack Kwong argues that there is no need to multiply our stock of recognized epistemic virtues to respond to problems of epistemic injustice, since already recognized virtues such as open-mindedness and humility provide the needed resources (2015). Kwong is right to point out that tendencies to inflict epistemic injustices reveal failures of open-mindedness and epistemic humility. But in the past, virtue epistemologists have attended to and promoted those virtues, while remaining oblivious to the routine patterns of epistemic injustice that widespread failings of those very virtues express. Introducing new resources into virtue epistemology (such as the idea of the virtue of testimonial justice) stimulates new patterns of attention and facilitates productive change (Cf Daukas 2018).

However, as Linda Alcoff argues, virtue-theoretical responses to problems of epistemic injustice may be too demanding: we may not be able to achieve the degree of critical self-awareness necessary to discern our prejudices and patterns of ignorance (2010) Further, it is not clear how engaging in projects of self-transformation can enable scattered individuals to effectively transform the deeply entrenched social structures responsible for long-standing, systematic participatory and distributive epistemic injustices. For this, we need to consider other possibilities.

Institutional Reform and Structural Change

Karen Jones recounts a case in which a US judge denied a Ghanaian woman's legitimate petition for political asylum as a result of inflicting a testimonial (and perhaps also a hermeneutical) injustice. The judge saw her as confused and irrational, and for that reason, disbelieved her testimony. Jones proposes a methodological principle or heuristic for avoiding such epistemic injustices: an audience ought to assess the plausibility of what is said separately from, and prior to, forming credibility judgments about the speaker (2002). Introducing such a methodological reforms in high-stakes institutionalized settings would clearly provide an effective means by which to avoid many testimonial injustices in those particular settings. However, it would not effectively disrupt the web of meanings, assumptions, and ignorance that sustain patterns responsible for much distributive and participatory epistemic injustices.

Code argues that to rid our epistemic practices of harmful power inequities, we must institute a "new social imaginary" or set of meanings, expectations, and imagined possibilities through which to understand ourselves as mutually independent, socially positioned knowers. She seeks to institute such a change in epistemology (2006). How might we bring about such a change in the broadly prevailing social consciousness? Medina looks to successful activist movements of the past for an answer to that question. He recommends creating "communities of resistance" coordinating multiple consciousness-raising efforts into highly visible "chained actions" (2013). But given the extent of the willful ignorance that needs to be overcome, it is not clear how broadly effective even organized consciousness-raising activism can be. Anderson argues that structural problems call for structurally instituted change, and surely she is right. Since she sees ongoing socio-economic segregation as the root cause of epistemic (and other) injustices, she urges reforms that would effectively end segregation. (2012)

Clearly multiple avenues of structural and individual response are needed. I think that effective structural changes must include educational reform, including reforms that counteract the long history of socioeconomic segregation at all levels of education. But genuinely successful integration must effect equitable redistributions of epistemic authority. That sort of change calls for educational reform specifically aimed at cultivating epistemic virtues and reversing a widespread public ignorance regarding the character of knowledge itself. That is, we need to habituate young minds to skills and attitudes that promote critical epistemic self-awareness and open-mindedness. And we need to teach basic principles of liberatory social epistemology at all levels, to inform that critical awareness and inspire that open-mindedness. That is, we need to teach that knowing subjects are always socially positioned; that epistemic communities and their beliefs are shaped by their cultural histories (including histories of conquest and prejudice); that the practices and products of western science bear the marks of their cultural histories; that scientific knowledge continually evolves through critique and social change; and that diversity is epistemically valuable.

Conclusion

Recent decades have carved out a rich and evolving area of work in social epistemology that bridges the conventional divide separating epistemology and justice theory. Work on epistemic injustice lies at its center. Epistemic injustices permeate epistemic practices in communities shaped by unjust power relations. They inflict harm on individuals and on historically oppressed social groups by sustaining unjust institutional practices and social structures, they undermine objectivity in the sciences, and avoidably impoverish public knowledge. Analyses of epistemic injustices clearly demonstrate the need for significant reform in accepted epistemic practices. Such reform requires continued theoretical work on multiple fronts, paired with sustained, coordinated, focused activism. Such reform promises to make us better knowers, better community members, and better epistemologists.

Notes

1 Throughout, I use conventionally plural pronouns (they, them, their) as gender-neutral singular (and plural) pronouns.
2 This virtue informs the normative component of Fricker's epistemology of testimony: when an audience comes to believe testimony through exercising the virtue of testimonial justice, they are justified in their testimonial beliefs (2007:77).

References

Alcoff, L. (1991). The Problem of Speaking for Others, *Cultural Critique*, (20), pp. 5-32.

Alcoff, L. (1999). On Judging Epistemic Credibility: Is Social Identity Relevant? *Philosophic Exchange Annual Proceedings*, 29, pp. 73–93.

Alcoff, L. (2010). Epistemic Identities, *Episteme* 7(2), pp. 128–137.

Anderson, E. (2012). Epistemic Justice as a Virtue of Social Institutions, *Social Epistemology* 26(2), pp. 163–173.

Coady, D. (2010). Two Concepts of Epistemic Injustice, *Episteme* 7(2), pp. 101–113.

Code, L. (1991). *What Can She Know? Feminist Theory and the Construction of Knowledge*, Ithaca: Cornell University Press

Code, L. (1995). *Rhetorical Spaces: Essays on Gendered Locations*, London and New York: Routledge.

Collins, P. (1990). *Black Feminist Thought: Knowledge, Consciousness and the Politics of Empowerment*, London: Routledge.

Daukas, N. (2006). Epistemic Trust and Social Location, *Episteme: A Journal of Social Epistemology* 3(1–2), pp. 109–124.

Daukas, N. (2011). Altogether Now: A Virtue-Theoretic Approach to Pluralism in Feminist Epistemology, In: H. Grasswick, ed., *Feminist Epistemology and Philosophy of Science: Power in Knowledge*, Dortrecht: Springer, pp. 45–67.

Daukas, N. (2018). Feminist Virtue Epistemology, in H. Battaly, ed., *Routledge Handbook of Virtue Epistemology*, Routledge, pp. 379-391.

Dotson, K. (2011). Tracking Epistemic Violence, Tracking Practices of Silencing, *Hypatia* 26(2), pp. 236–257.

Dotson, K. (2012). A Cautionary Tale: On Limiting Epistemic Oppression, *Frontiers: A Journal of Women Studies* 33(1), pp. 24–47.

Fricker, M. (1998). Rational Authority and Social Power, *Proceedings of the Aristotelian Society*, pp. 159–177.

Fricker, M. (1999). Epistemic Oppression and Epistemic Privilege, *Canadian Journal of Philosophy* 25, pp. 191–210.

Fricker, M. (2007). *Epistemic Injustice: Power and the Ethics of Knowing*, Oxford: Oxford University Press.

Harding, S. (1993). Rethinking Standpoint Epistemology: What is Strong Objectivity? In: L. Alcoff and E. Potter, eds., *Feminist Epistemologies*, New York and London: Routledge, pp. 49–82.

Hornsby, J., and Langton, R. (1998). Free Speech and Illocution, *Legal Theory* 4, pp. 21–37.

Jones, K. (2002). The Politics of Credibility, In: L.M. Antony and C.E. Witt, eds., *A Mind of One's Own: Feminist Essays on Reason and Objectivity*, Boulder, CO: Westview Press, pp. 154–176.

Kwong, J. (2015). Epistemic Injustice and Open-Mindedness, *Hypatia* 30(2), pp. 337–351.

Longino, H. (1990). *Science as Social Knowledge*, Princeton: Princeton University Press.

McConkey, J. (2004). Knowledge and Acknowledgement: 'Epistemic Injustice' as a Problem of Recognition 1. *Politics*, *24*(3), pp. 198-205.

Medina, J. (2013). *The Epistemology of Resistance: Gender and Racial Oppression, Epistemic Injustice, and Resistant Imaginations*, Oxford: Oxford University Press.

Mills, C. (1997). *The Racial Contract*, Ithaca and London: Cornell University Press.

Okin, S. (2003). Poverty, Well-Being, and Gender: What Counts, Who's Heard? *Philosophy and Public Affairs* 31(3), pp. 280–316.

Pohlhaus, G. (2011). Relational Knowing and Epistemic Injustice: Toward a Theory of Willful Hermeneutical Ignorance, *Hypatia* 27(4), pp. 715–735.

Further Reading

Code, L. (2006). *Ecological Thinking: The Politics of Epistemic Location*, New York: Oxford University Press. (Presents a model of knowing called "ecological thinking" to counteract the harmful affects of social power on epistemic practices and epistemological understandings, and reshape practices and understandings to promote social and environmental well-being.)

Fricker, M. (2013). Epistemic Justice as a Condition of Political Freedom? *Synthese* 190, pp. 1317–1332. (Argues that epistemic justice is a necessary condition for political freedom).

33

STANDPOINT THEN AND NOW

Alessandra Tanesini

Some things are best understood from the standpoints of those who are less powerful, less economically privileged, less entitled. This, initially counterintuitive, claim is the distinctive feature of standpoint epistemology, which is one of the most controversial and most discussed feminist approaches to the study of knowledge.[1] In the social sciences where, arguably, standpoint has had its widest appeal, this approach has often been interpreted as offering some broad methodological recommendations in favour of listening to the views of the subjects one studies even when those subjects may appear unreflective or uneducated.[2] In philosophy, standpoint has generally been interpreted as a theory about the epistemic practices involved in attributing, claiming, discovering, justifying or communicating (putative) knowledge and understanding.[3]

The theory centers on three tenets: the *situated knowledge thesis,* which states that (many) claims put forward as knowledge are socially situated because they are based on putative evidence that is more accessible from some social locations or perspectives than others (Wylie, 2003: 31; Intemann, 2010: 784–787); *the standpoint thesis*, which asserts that some socially situated perspectives (standpoints) are epistemically privileged in that they offer a less partial, less distorted understanding or because they contain a higher number of (significant) truths than those provided by other perspectives (Intemann, 2010: 787–789); and *the inversion thesis*, which claims that the perspective(s) of the socially subordinated are epistemically privileged compared with those of dominant groups (Wylie, 2003: 26). Standpoint shares the first two tenets with other feminist epistemologies; it is, arguably, differentiated from them by its endorsement of the third.[4]

In this overview I explain the nature of standpoint epistemology; detail its evolution through the responses offered by its supporters to their critics; and briefly point to the continued fruitfulness of the approach.

Social Situatedness, Epistemic Privilege and Inversion

It is commonplace in feminist philosophy to think of standpoint as one of three distinctively feminist approaches in the philosophy of science (Harding, 1986). These are in addition to standpoint, feminist empiricism and feminist postmodernism. Standpoint theory shares with postmodernism a commitment to the situated knowledge thesis.[5] In what follows I first offer an overview of each of the three theses characteristic of standpoint before discussing its evolution since its earliest versions in the mid-1980s.

The thesis that knowledge is socially situated has been formulated in a number of different ways (Hartsock, 1983; Harding, 1986, 1993; Haraway, 1991). However, the guiding thought often is that individuals who occupy the same or similar social roles, and/or belong to the same social group, and/or subjectively identify with one such group are likely, because of these facts, to develop the same cognitive and practical skills and a similar point of view on numerous issues, questions and topics.[6] Once the claim is fleshed out in this manner, it is an empirical question as to whether there is a unique point of view that is the product of any given social location.[7] If the notion of standpoint is to have any plausibility, it cannot imply that without exception all those who share a social location must share a perspective. But, although this fact is less often appreciated, even weaker interpretations that make hedged generalizations are for many social locations equally problematic. The claim that there are any significant theories, beliefs, understanding or experiences that a preponderance of women are likely to share in virtue of occupying the same or similar social locations is an empirical one. It also appears to be false (Spelman, 1990).

These considerations have led some recent supporters of the socially situated knowledge thesis to a reformulation of it in more individualistic terms. Given this understanding, an agent's social location is said to affect that person's access to the evidence, the cognitive and practical skills that one is able to develop, and which experiences one is likely to have (Wylie, 2003: 29 and 31; Anderson, 2015: 1–14). This claim, however, may or may not support generalizations about different areas of inquiry and across individuals who occupy the same or similar social location. So interpreted, the situatedness thesis would belong to a form of social epistemology that takes individuals rather than groups or collectives as the primary object of study.

There is, however, another very different understanding of the thesis that knowledge is socially situated. In this reading social location is explained in terms of shared objective interests rather than subjective identification with, or membership in, a social group.[8] Putative knowledge is thus said to be socially situated in the sense that, given their shared interests, some knowledge claims are more useful than others for collectives and their members.[9] For instance, they may help members of groups to understand better their situation, and to improve it, and in general may reveal aspects of the social world that are important to them. On this understanding a standpoint is defined by its pragmatic features. It is a set of theories, beliefs, explanations or skills that work for some people because they are of assistance in achieving their social and political goals. This interpretation of the thesis is much more faithful than those presented above to the earliest incarnations of standpoint epistemology as a version of critical theory deeply inspired by Marxist thought (Hartsock, 1983). It explains why standpoint is not automatic but is an achievement, since it requires the acquisition of a point of view that is in fact helpful to understand and improve the position of those who share some interests.[10] It also explains why the scope of standpoint is likely to be limited to knowledge of the social world; this is the field of study that is more likely to be affected by the interests of different social groups. In this account the thesis that knowledge is socially situated is unashamedly normative. It states that acceptance of some claims as knowledge serves the interests of some groups whilst acceptance of different claims is of benefit to other collectives. It takes skill and effort to figure out which claims are actually in the interest of one's own group.

The second tenet of standpoint theory defines the view's opposition to relativism since it states that not all standpoints are epistemically on a par. There are several dimensions to epistemic privilege. A collection of theories, explanations, beliefs and the range of evidence in their support (including experiences) may be superior to another because it includes more truths, or more significant truths, because it affords a better understanding of the situation as a whole. But it could also be superior because it is more readily applicable to solving pressing problems or because it opens up useful avenues of thought about different topics. It would seem that the kind of epistemic privilege afforded by given perspectives might vary from case to case and be also relative to a number of pragmatic considerations.[11]

Finally, the inversion thesis is the most distinctive feature of standpoint. It claims that the perspective of the downtrodden is epistemically privileged. I began this overview by highlighting the initial implausibility of the thesis. Since those who are systematically disadvantaged are less likely to have received a formal education, lack the leisure to read and reflect, and are likely to be psychologically damaged because of oppression and discrimination, it is at least plausible that they are less likely than those who are educated to have a good theoretical understanding of the social world in which they find themselves (Narayan, 1988: 36). Whilst there is truth to this claim, it is not an objection to standpoint once both the notions of a standpoint (as a socially situated body of putative knowledge) and of epistemic privilege are adequately clarified.

If, as I suggested above, the thesis that knowledge claims are socially situated is interpreted as the claim that some bodies of putative knowledge are more useful than others to groups of individuals that share the same interests, then the inversion thesis is best understood as the view that knowledge claims that are most useful to the downtrodden to understand and improve their situation are also epistemically superior to those that are employed by the privileged because they offer a more truthful, or less distorted, account of the social world or a deeper understanding of some of its features. Following Sandra Harding's stronger objectivity thesis one may argue that any theory of the social world that gives central stage to the facts about the lives of the oppressed and aims first and foremost to explain and understand them is likely to be epistemically superior (more truthful and insightful) to any account that ignores them (Harding, 1991, 1993). Whilst it remains an open question as to whether theories or approaches that aim to serve the interests of the oppressed are more empirically adequate or more insightful than theories suited to serve a different range of interests, much of the intuitive implausibility of the inversion thesis is thus dissipated.

Two further points emerge from these considerations. First, the inversion thesis—if true at least in some localized cases—would show that empirically adequate or true theories may be formulated more effectively by epistemic agents who are socially and politically engaged. That is to say, more objective theories may be developed if the agents who formulate them are not dispassionate or politically neutral (Wylie, 2003: 33). Second, they may explain why, although standpoints are not automatically acquired and lack of access to education damages those who are oppressed, those who are downtrodden have a better chance of accessing a viewpoint that serves their interests than members of privileged groups. They have an incentive, which members of dominant groups lack, to acquire this putative knowledge. Arguably, powerful individuals actually have strong self-interested reasons *not* to know.[12] Hence, even if it is true that the majority of the oppressed have not acquired a standpoint on oppression, nevertheless the barriers in their path to this achievement are, despite being extremely powerful, less insurmountable than those to be found on the road that members of dominant groups must travel to acquire that same standpoint.

From Marxist Beginnings to a Pluralist Present

In its earliest formulation feminist standpoint theory is based on an analogy with Marxian accounts of the standpoint of the proletariat (working class). According to the latter the working class occupies a unique social position within the capitalist system. Capitalism is defined in part as a system of production predicated on a division of labor by class. The manual labor of members of the proletariat is essential to the perpetuation of the system. Yet, the system primarily serves the interests of the capitalists or bourgeoisies. Marxists propose that a deeper understanding of the economic laws governing the capitalist system is gained if one studies it with the aim of developing a theory that serves the interests of the working class and helps them to address their oppression. Marxist justifications in favor of this point of view are complex and need not detain us here but they are centered on the thought that theories that serve the interests of the working class would be instrumentally more effective in bringing about social change in the interest of the whole of humanity (and not only of the proletariat).

Marxists also think that individual members of the working class have fewer obstacles than capitalists in gaining this understanding. Firstly, they have first-hand experience of the working of the system since their labor is essential to it. Second, they have an incentive to acquire the viewpoint that is in the service of their interests. Nevertheless, achieving the standpoint of the proletariat remains a difficult task. However, even individuals who, like Marx himself, are not members of the working class are not precluded from this accomplishment.

This account provides the basis for Nancy Hartsock's hugely influential formulation of a feminist standpoint (1983, 1997). In Hartsock's view women occupy a unique social position in patriarchy, defined as a system that organizes the division of reproductive labor by gender. Women's reproductive labor in creating and sustaining the next generation—by giving birth to, feeding and nuturing it—is essential to the perpetuation of this situation. The system, however, does not serve their interests. Hartsock proposes that we gain a better understanding of the social relations between the genders if we aim to develop theories that would serve the interests of women by revealing the shortcomings of the current system. The arguments for the epistemic privilege of this viewpoint are partly pragmatic. Developing it is more likely to lead to accounts that are of help to change society so that the needs of all of its members are served more fairly. But they are also partly epistemic. Standpoints that aim to serve the interests of those who do not benefit from the current system are less likely to be distorted by self-serving interests. Hence, empirically adequate theories about gender relations are more likely to be formulated if one carries out inquiries whilst bearing in mind the interests of those who are in a subordinate position.[13]

Once the view is explicated in these terms it becomes clear why in response to her critics Hartsock often pointed out that hers was an account of a feminist standpoint rather than a womanly one (Hartsock, 1983, 1997). In this regard her views have been largely misunderstood by her earliest feminist critics who argue that standpoint is guilty of essentialism and that it assumes that the views of members of oppressed groups should be automatically granted epistemic privileges.[14] It is, however, a misunderstanding that has been facilitated (and partly warranted) by the second half of Hartsock's original paper where she invokes object relation psychoanalytic theory apparently to argue for the existence of a distinctive cognitive style that pertains to women under patriarchy. This aspect of the account largely disappears in Hartsock's later writings but it is responsible for giving the impression that a standpoint is a point of view that all actual women share because they are women.[15]

Among these critics are Spelman (1990) and Hooks (1982), who have argued convincingly that there are no experiences that are shared by all women since one cannot neatly separate out in one's experience those aspects which follow from one's gender from those that pertains to one's race, ethnicity or sexual orientation. In response feminist standpoint epistemologists have, accepting the criticism, endorsed pluralism about standpoints. They have acknowledged that there is no single feminist standpoint but a plurality of standpoints each related to a different social location.[16] This approach is generally associated with the work of Patricia Hill Collins (1991) who, while developing the notion of a black feminist standpoint, has also provided a novel rationale for the epistemic privilege of the view from the margins.

Collins convincingly argues that at least some individuals who belong to marginalized groups are capable of acquiring a dual focus or bifurcated consciousness. They are able to observe social reality both from the point of view of the privileged and from that of the underprivileged. This is an ability that is born out of necessity. The subordinated need to know how the privileged think in order to outwit them so as to deflect the worst consequences of oppression and discrimination. They also know how things look from the perspective of the marginalized because they have first-hand experience of occupying this position. The dual point of view of outsider-within confers an epistemic advantage on those who are capable of adopting it, because by aggregating the insights offered by two perspectives, it is less partial than each of them individually (Collins, 1991: 11–13).[17]

More recently, Alison Wylie (2003) has, building on the work of Collins and earlier standpoint theorists, developed arguments for the inversion thesis that bring standpoint closer to feminist empiricism. In her view we should not be surprised to learn that members of subordinated groups have developed, because of their social and economic positions, cognitive skills and heuristics that are at variance with those deployed by more privileged members of society. Further, she points out, it is possible that for some kind of inquiries and in some local contexts the skills developed by the underprivileged produce true beliefs and genuine understanding more reliably than those nurtured in privileged individuals. The issue, as Wylie also notes, is empirical and can only be addressed on a problem by problem basis as a 'second-order application of our best available research tools to the business of knowledge production itself' (2003: 40).[18]

I have claimed above that standpoint theory has been often misunderstood by its feminist critics. Some of the objections that have been levelled against it by less sympathetic opponents have been even cruder. Perhaps the most common among these, which has been levelled against feminist epistemology as a whole, is the claim that it endorses feminist propaganda, disregards the objectivity of science and simply wishes to silence those whose values feminists oppose (Haack, 1997; Pinnick et al., 2003). These criticisms have been ably rebutted on behalf of feminist empiricism by Anderson (2002, 2004, 2015). In her view one must distinguish the impartiality of a theory from its value-neutrality.

The latter pertains to theories that have no value-laden consequences or assumptions. If it is granted, as seems sensible, that the goal of inquiry is to find out truths that are significant rather than trivial and that are not misleading, then good scientific theories cannot be value neutral since values are essential in deciding which truths are significant rather than trivial. What can save value-laden theories from the objection that they must lack objectivity, however, is impartiality.

A theory is accepted on impartial grounds if the only considerations taken into account when deciding on its adoption are whether it exemplifies cognitive values such as simplicity or explanatory power and whether there is sufficient evidence in its support (2002, 2004). Thus Anderson recommends that we keep issues of truth and of significance distinct. The truth of a theory must be assessed on impartial grounds but its significance is dependent on the values that guide one's inquiry. Similar defenses have been adopted by those who, like Wylie (2003), think that standpoint has essentially merged with empiricism. In response to the critics Wylie can point out that it is perfectly possible that those who subscribe to some political values rather than to others may as a result of their political commitments be more reliable in their attempts to figure out the truth about some features of social reality. For example, primatologists committed to feminist values have paid attention to the behavior of female apes and by doing so have been able to acquire more reliable information about primate social organizations (Cf. Anderson, 1995).

Arguably, however, these defenses may concede too much to standpoint's opponents. If it is granted, as it is plausible, that standpoint epistemology is limited to assessing theories about the social world, then its focus is on beliefs and assumptions that involve the use of concepts purporting to refer to social kinds. In this context standpoint epistemology can be seen as engaged in an ameliorative project of the sort described by Sally Haslanger (2012). Such a project begins with the awareness that social reality can be categorized in different ways, each of which is based on existing shared properties. However, only some of these taxonomies are helpful when one is trying to formulate theories that facilitate the pursuit of political projects. Ameliorative analyses are attempts to formulate new concepts and modify old ones so that they become serviceable for the purpose of formulating theories that are effective in illuminating those aspects of the social world that the underprivileged need to understand and to do so in a manner that makes them readily usable for political action. The notion of an ameliorative analysis thus offers a way of developing further the interpretation of the notion of standpoint that I have favored in this overview. Knowledge claims that constitute a standpoint are socially situated in the sense of relying on a conceptual framework that is adopted because of its predictive and explanatory power but also because of its emancipatory potential. It is a consequence of this view that, contrary to Anderson's proposal, evidential considerations cannot be sufficiently disentangled from pragmatic ones to allow any assessment of the empirical adequacy of theories to proceed on completely impartial grounds.

An example discussed by Anderson herself may help to clarify the issue. Some social scientists committed to feminist values have conceptualized divorce not as the breaking up of a family but as the separation of the adults' parental roles from their role as spouses. Conceiving of divorce in these terms has made it possible to think that on some occasions divorce is not the dissipation of a family but the creation of a new two-household family structure. Research, employing this novel conceptualization of what counts as a family, can help to see when family restructuring is beneficial to vulnerable parties (Cf. Anderson, 2004). In cases such as this one, it is not possible to distinguish neatly issues of truth from issues of significance since the very concepts in which the theory is formulated are chosen in light of their emancipatory potential.

It may be granted that this response, even when more fully developed, is less likely to convince standpoint non feminist opponents than Anderson's reply. Nevertheless, it has the advantage of highlighting the fact that standpoint theorists do not share the presupposition, implicitly made by their opponents, that all values are equally just propaganda. Instead, supporters of standpoint are committed to the belief that some values are better than others and that these can be rationally defended.[19]

The Continued Fruitfulness of Standpoint

I have argued so far that there are different versions of standpoint theory in the contemporary literature. In some accounts standpoint is of a piece with naturalized epistemology and claims that individuals who occupy underprivileged social locations are likely to have developed more reliable views than dominant individuals about some specific aspects of the social world. In other accounts standpoint is a form of critical theory that asserts that perspectives selected for their emancipatory potential also offer a deeper understanding of the nature of power relations in deeply unequal societies (Cf. Rolin, 2009). Either way standpoint has motivated feminist philosophers and critical race theorists to ask novel questions and these have generated burgeoning research programmes.

Two stand out among many: work on epistemic injustice and on the epistemology of ignorance. The first studies how members of subordinated groups can be harmed and wronged in their epistemic capacities. This area of research is based on Miranda Fricker's account of testimonial and hermeneutical injustices (2007). It has emerged because of a switch of focus when studying epistemic practices to exploring what happens to those who are less powerful when they come into contact with members of dominant groups. The second explores epistemic practices that produce and sustain ignorance of many aspects of social reality (Tuana, 2004, 2006; Mills, 2007; Medina, 2013). According to this programme the privileged are often ignorant of the facts about their privilege because they have an incentive not to know the truth about themselves. This programme too can be traced back to some of the themes that standpoint theorists have explored since the inception of this approach.

In summary, standpoint epistemology has all the trademarks of a productive research programme in the social epistemology of the social sciences. It has been refined and modified in response to pertinent criticisms and it continues to generate new hypotheses and research questions that lead to fruitful discoveries.[20]

Notes

1 See Anderson (2015) for an excellent overview.

2 For this approach see Smith (1987) and, arguably, Rolin (2009). For a critic, see Walby (2001).

3 Hence, standpoint theorists are usually interested in what people claim to know, how they go about discovering things, how they justify their beliefs. They often use the term 'knowledge' non-factively to include both knowledge and other items which are put forward as knowledge (even though they may be false).

4 But as Anderson (2015: 69) notes in recent years the three views have largely converged into hybrid versions.

5 Contemporary feminist empiricists also subscribe to this thesis. In Harding's (1983) original characterization empiricists would limit the thesis application to the context of discovery claiming that social location may make a difference to the range of claims one puts forward as true, but does not affect their actual justification.

6 Hence, the expression 'social location' is used capaciously to include social role, subjective identification with a social group or objectively characterised membership of such a group.

7 Walby's main objection to standpoint in her (2001) is that these questions when they have been scientifically investigated have generally received a negative answer.

8 There might be robust correlations between having the same interests and occupying the same social role or being assigned membership to the same social group. The correlations between subjective identification and interests may be weaker.

9 Here and in what follows I use the expression 'knowledge claim' as a shorthand for knowledge attributions in general.

10 Recently, and following Harding (1991) the claim that standpoint is an achievement has been understood to entail self-reflective awareness of one's own point of view and of the effects that social locations have on it. See also Wylie (2003). In my view this transforms standpoint into an exclusively intellectual kind of achievement and forgets that in its original formulation it was intended to be also an example of political emancipatory success.

11 This is a complex issue. Once it is granted that the goal of inquiry is not simply to maximise true beliefs and minimise false ones, but that what matters is the maximisation of true beliefs that are significant (rather than trivial), it becomes hard to disentangle purely epistemic from partly pragmatic considerations. Anderson (2002, 2004) has offered one of the best attempts to keep them distinct.

12 The idea that dominant individuals are committed to remaining ignorant about the reality of unearned privilege is one the central insights of theepistemologies of ignorance (Cf. Tuana, 2004, 2006; Mills, 2007).

13 I have formulated this claim in terms of the factors that affect the formulation of theories (context of discovery) rather than factors that affect their justification (context of justification). I have done so because the claim is most obviously true in this interpretation. But it can also be defended in the case of justification. One way of doing so is to argue that theories whose conceptual framework is value-laden may be more empirically adequate or have more explanatory power of rival theories which are laden with a different set of values. See Anderson (2002) for a similar claim.

14 Some of these charges, however, are not groundless. Although Hartsock does not presuppose that all women share the same experiences of womanhood she assumes that there is a significant number of interests which they all share. This is, as critics have pointed out, at least debatable.

15 For reasons of space I cannot explore this facet of standpoint but it figures prominently in the work of several feminist philosophers of science and epistemologists. See for example Keller (1985).

16 In this manner standpoint has become closer to postmodernism since the latter has always been associated with the view that there are plural situated knowledges (Haraway, 1991).

17 In addition, one may say that the point of view of the insider-outsider is epistemically advantaged because these individuals have no vested interest in the continuation of the system of social relations that marginalise them whilst having an incentive to understand it fully so as to minimise its negative impact on their lives.

18 An assessment of whether despite recent rapprochements disagreements between standpoint and feminist empiricism persist is beyond the scope of this overview. See Intemann (2010) for an excellent evaluation of these issues.

19 There is also another common objection to standpoint according to which it is a theory that promotes women's ways of knowing. Although early cases of reliance on psychoanalytic theory may be plausibly read as developing this theme, as I have shown in this text these tendencies are not present in contemporary accounts of standpoint theory.

20 I would like to thank Miranda Fricker for her helpful comments on an earlier draft.

References

Anderson, E. (1995). Feminist Epistemology: An Interpretation and a Defense, *Hypatia*, 10(3), pp. 50–84.

Anderson, E. (2002). Situated Knowledge and the Interplay of Value Judgements and Evidence in Scientific Inquiry. In: P. Gärdenfors, J. Wolenski and K. Kijania-Placek, eds., *In the Scope of Logic, Methodology, and Philosophy of Science: Volume One of the 11th International Congress of Logic, Methodology and Philosophy of Science, Cracow, August 1999*, Dordrecht and Boston: Kluwer Academic Publishers, 497–517.

Anderson, E. (2004). Uses of Value Judgments in Science: A General Argument, with Lessons from a Case Study of Feminist Research on Divorce, *Hypatia*, 19(1), pp. 1–24.

Anderson, E. (2015). Feminist Epistemology and Philosophy of Science. In: E. N. Zalta, ed., *The Stanford Encyclopedia of Philosophy (Fall 2015 Edition)*, http://plato.stanford.edu/archives/fall2015/entries/feminism-epistemology/

Collins, P. H. (1991). *Black Feminist Thought: Knowledge, Consciousness, and the Politics of Empowerment.* New York: Routledge.

Fricker, M. (2007). *Epistemic Injustice.* Oxford: Clarendon.

Haack, S. (1997). Science as Social? – Yes and No. In: L. H. Nelson and J. Nelson, eds., *Feminism, Science and the Philosophy of Science*, Dordrecht: Kluwer Academic Publishers, 79–93.

Haraway, D. (1991). Situated Knowledges: The Science Question in Feminism and the Privilege of Partial Perspective. In: D. Haraway, ed., *Simians, Cyborgs and Women: The Reinvention of Nature.* London: Free Association Books, 183–201.

Harding, S. (1986). *The Science Question in Feminism.* Ithaca: Cornell University Press.

Harding, S. (1991). *Whose Science? Whose Knowledge?: Thinking from Women's Lives.* Ithaca: Cornell University Press.

Harding, S. (1993). Rethinking Standpoint Epistemology: 'What Is Strong Objectivity'? In: L. Alcoff and E. Potter, eds., *Feminist Epistemologies*, New York and London: Routledge, 49–82.

Hartsock, N. (1983). The Feminist Standpoint: Developing the Ground for a Specifically Feminist Historical Materialism. In S. Harding and M. B. Hintikka, eds., *Discovering Reality*, Dordrecht: Reidel, 283–310.

Hartsock, N. (1997). Standpoint Theories for the Next Century, *Women and Politics*, 18(3), pp. 93–102.

Haslanger, S. (2012). *Resisting Reality: Social Construction and Social Critique.* New York: Oxford University Press.

Hooks, B. (1982). *Ain't I a Woman: Black Women and Feminism.* London: Pluto Press.

Intemann, K. (2010) 25 Years of Feminist Empiricism and Standpoint Theory: Where Are We Now? *Hypatia*, 25(4), pp. 778–796.

Keller, E. F. (1985). *Reflections on Gender and Science.* New Haven: Yale University Press.

Medina, J. (2013). *The Epistemology of Resistance: Gender and Racial Oppression, Epistemic Injustice, and Resistant Imaginations.* Oxford: Oxford University Press.

Mills, C. W. (2007). White Ignorance. In: S. Sullivan and N. Tuana, eds., *Race and Epistemologies of Ignorance*, Albany: State University of New York Press, 13–38.

Narayan, U. (1988). Working Together across Difference: Some Considerations on Emotions and Political Practice, *Hypatia*, 3(2), pp. 31–48.

Pinnick, C., Noretta K. and Robert A. (eds.) (2003). *Scrutinizing Feminist Epistemology: An Examination of Gender in Science.* New Brunswick: Rutgers.

Rolin, K. (2009). Standpoint Theory as a Methodology for the Study of Power Relations, *Hypatia*, 24(4), pp. 218–226.

Smith, D. E. (1987). *The Everyday World as Problematic: A Feminist Sociology*, Boston: Northeastern University Press.

Spelman, E. V. (1990). *Inessential Woman: Problems of Exclusion in Feminist Thought.* London: Women's Press.

Tuana, N. (2004). Coming to Understand: Orgasm and the Epistemology of Ignorance, *Hypatia* 19(1), pp. 194–232.

Tuana, N. (2006). The Speculum of Ignorance: The Women's Health Movement and Epistemologies of Ignorance, *Hypatia*, 21(3), pp. 1–19.

Walby, S. (2001). Against Epistemological Chasms: The Science Question in Feminism Revisited, *Signs*, 26(2), pp. 485–509.

Wylie, A. (2003). Why Standpoint Matters. In: R. Figueroa and S. G. Harding, eds., *Science and Other Cultures: Issues in Philosophies of Science and Technology*, New York and London: Routledge, 26–48.

Further Reading

In addition to the works cited above the reader may wish to consult the following:

Crasnow, S. (ed.) (2009). Symposium on Standpoint Theory, *Hypatia*, 24(4).(Includes several articles revisiting standpoint theory and its usefulness for feminist epistemology.)

Narayan, U. (1989). The Project of Feminist Epistemology: Perspectives from a Nonwestern Feminist. In: A. M. Jaggar and S. Bordo, eds., *Gender/Body/Knowledge: Feminist Reconstructions of Being and Knowing*, New Brunswick and London: Rutgers University Press.(A lucid account of some of the disadvantages of having to occupy the position of the outsider/within and thus adopt a so-called double vision.)

Potter, E. (2006). *Feminism and Philosophy of Science*. London and New York: Routledge.(A comprehensive discussion of both empiricism and standpoint epistemology.)

Tanesini, A. (1999). *An Introduction to Feminist Epistemologies*. Oxford: Blackwell.(A comprehensive introduction.)

Alessandra Tanesini is Professor of Philosophy at Cardiff University. She is the author of *An Introduction to Feminist Epistemologies* (Blackwell, 1999), of *Wittgenstein: A Feminist Interpretation* (Polity, 2004), and of several articles in feminist philosophy, the philosophy of mind and language, epistemology and on Nietzsche. Her current work lies at the intersection of ethics and epistemology and focuses on epistemic vice, prejudice and ignorance.

34

SYMPATHETIC KNOWLEDGE AND THE SCIENTIFIC ATTITUDE

Classic Pragmatist Resources for Feminist Social Epistemology[1]

Shannon Dea and Matthew Silk

Introduction

The affinities between contemporary feminist pragmatism and feminist social epistemology are well known. However, the connections between feminist social epistemology and classic pragmatism[2] deserve more attention than they have typically received. In this chapter, we sketch some of the main similarities between the two approaches in support of our view that classic pragmatists' conception of science as an attitude is an important precursor to some of the central insights of contemporary feminist social epistemologists.

We adopt Robert Talisse and Scott Aikin's distinction between *meaning* and *inquiry* pragmatism, and argue that it is classic inquiry pragmatism that is of especial relevance for contemporary feminist social epistemologists. We survey a range of relevant figures and identify three themes that are central to both feminist social epistemology and classic inquiry pragmatism: the conception of inquiry as social, the entanglement of knowledge with practices and interests, and emphasis on the perspective of the knower. Jane Addams is a particularly clear exemplar of all three views. As we show, Addams is fundamentally committed to the importance of perspective for knowledge, and to the possibility of understanding perspectives that are different from our own. We argue that Addams's approach is paradigmatic of early pragmatists' conception of science as an attitude. We flesh out what this attitude requires, and then conclude by drawing connections between the scientific attitude, as conceived by historical pragmatists, and feminist standpoint theorists' conception of strong objectivity.

Varieties of Pragmatism

It can be challenging to define pragmatism as a philosophical movement in a way that is neither too general nor too exclusive.

Among broader conceptions of pragmatism are those that emphasize pragmatists' concern with applicability and practical consequences. However, to define pragmatism in this way arguably trivializes it. First, pragmatists' practical "cash value" thinking has been notoriously exaggerated and misrepresented. Second, lots of philosophers from a range of different philosophical traditions have been and continue to be interested in practical consequences. This is not the exclusive province of pragmatism. Nor is it sufficiently specific to be useful as a heuristic for identifying pragmatists.

One narrower conception takes the central feature of the movement to be the application of some version of the so-called pragmatic maxim. The earliest, and for some the canonical, version of this maxim is Peirce's: "Consider what effects, that might conceivably have practical bearings, we conceive the object of our conception to have. Then, our conception of these effects is the whole of our conception of the object" (W3:266).[3] Both Peirce and James go on to offer accounts of truth derived from their respective versions of the pragmatic maxim.[4] There is considerable debate even among pragmatists about whether pragmatism constitutes a theory of truth, but most scholars agree that pragmatism offers a theory of meaning. However, to insist that to be a pragmatist one must invoke a pragmatic theory of meaning is to exclude figures generally accepted as part of the pragmatist canon. Jane Addams, for instance, does not seem to employ any version of the pragmatic maxim.

Talisse and Aikin (2005) divide pragmatists into two broad camps – *meaning pragmatists* and *inquiry pragmatists*. Meaning pragmatists place greater emphasis on pragmatic methods of elucidating meaning, such as that expressed in the Peirce quote, above. By contrast, inquiry pragmatists are more concerned with adopting pragmatic approaches to inquiry, broadly conceived. Such approaches are characterized by pluralism about types of evidence and methodologies, grounding in experience, fallibilism, and an emphasis on inquiry as evolution and growth.[5] Talisse and Aikin do not take meaning and inquiry pragmatism to be mutually exclusive categories. However, they hold that most pragmatists tend to emphasize either meaning or inquiry.

Extending the conception of pragmatism to include not only *meaning pragmatism* but *inquiry pragmatism* makes the movement much more inclusive, and in particular inclusive of feminist pragmatists.[6] As we note above, Addams[7] does not seem to be motivated by, or particularly interested in, pragmatic theories of meaning. However, she is an exemplary inquiry pragmatist. Her approach to inquiry is pragmatic in all four senses we identify above: it is pluralistic about evidence and methods, it is grounded in experience, it is fallibilist, and it is evolutionist. Further, Talisse and Aikin's conception of inquiry pragmatism is more specific, and hence less trivial, than the characterization of pragmatists as concerned with practical consequences. While Addams is often characterized as a pragmatist because of her concern with practical actions, we can better capture what is distinctively pragmatist, as opposed to merely practical, about her thought by emphasizing her approach to inquiry.

Thus, if we define a pragmatist as anyone who is either a meaning pragmatist or an inquiry pragmatist or both, we arrive at a conception that is inclusive without being so broad as to include just any philosopher who is concerned with practical matters. Further, most contemporary feminist pragmatists in one way or another adopt all four of the features of inquiry pragmatism that we have identified. While we focus in this chapter on elements of social epistemology that emerge in the work of early pragmatists (that is, in the work of pragmatists who predate feminist pragmatism), it is striking to observe that contemporary feminist pragmatists, such as Sullivan, McKenna, Rooney and McHugh, in general align much more closely with inquiry pragmatism than with meaning pragmatism. Unsurprisingly, it is primarily inquiry pragmatism that offers resources to contemporary social epistemologists. In the next section, we discuss in greater detail some of the commonalities between inquiry pragmatism and feminist social epistemology.

Pragmatism and Feminist Social Epistemology: Three Themes

The affinities between pragmatism and feminism are well known. Scholars have pointed out that pragmatists share with feminists a scepticism about *a priori* thinking and fixed thinking (Rooney

1993), criticism of foundationalism (Duran 1993), and objections to the dichotomies between theory and practice, subject and object, nature and culture, and emotion and reason (Gatens-Robinson 1991). Further, three themes that are central to feminist social epistemology are likewise at the heart of inquiry pragmatism: the conception of inquiry as social, the entanglement of knowledge with practices and interests, and emphasis on the perspective of the knower. We elaborate on each of these in this section.

Pragmatist epistemology considers social factors central to what it means to call something true. Peirce describes truth as that which any community of inquirers would believe if inquiry were pushed far enough (Peirce, W3:273). Dewey notes that inquirers depend upon the experiences of the community for confirmation, and that until there is agreement, "the conclusions that are announced by an individual inquirer have the status of an hypothesis" (1938a, 490). James explains that, "there can be no final truth [...] until the last man has had his experience and said his say" (1891, 330).

Moreover, like many feminist epistemologists, pragmatists conceive of knowledge as growing out of practices and activities. For the pragmatist, inquiry is the attempt to understand and control our experiences as we navigate the world and become more intelligent in our behavior.[8] Phyllis Rooney points out this insight is important to both feminist and pragmatist epistemological processes (1993, 21). Thus, pragmatism understands knowledge as socially and historically embedded as inquiry grows out of and responds to social factors around us.[9] Inquiry is a result of the particular interests and uncertainties in the situations we face. This fits well with the feminist position that what allows for satisfactory interaction with the world has to do with our social and cultural standing in it (Rooney 1993, 31). Values and conduct are intertwined. The pragmatist understands values to play a direct role in the conduct of inquiry. Dewey and C. I. Lewis see the task of evaluating courses of action as necessary for inquiry, and thus regard value judgments as indispensable. Both describe pragmatism as the view that all judgments are judgments of value (Dewey 1998b, 240; Lewis 1970, 108). Such value judgments drive what conceptions and ontologies we adopt. Like many feminist ontologies, pragmatist ontologies stress objects in their relations to persons rather than in themselves (Duran 1993, 166).[10] In other words, the ontologies we adopt are a response to human social conditions and problems rather than being a reflection of a metaphysically fixed world structure.

Seigfried notes that the pragmatist position that human knowledge is an expression of particular perspectives, including values, makes it "particularly attractive to feminist reconstruction" (1996, 31). James for instance, regards some of our intellectual needs as passional; for him, sentiments and satisfactions are a legitimate and irreducible part of our intellectual lives (Rooney 1993, 23). For Dewey, "All inquiry proceeds within a cultural matrix which is [...] determined by the nature of social relations" (Dewey 1938a, 487). This matrix includes social factors, habits, and traditions that can lead us to emphasize certain kinds of problems, many of which may only exist against a given historical background.

For Dewey, "knowledge is a function of association and communication; it depends upon tradition, upon tools and methods socially transmitted, developed and sanctioned" (1980b, 335). In other words, how we think and what we know is a function of social habits and traditions that have been passed down from previous generations and can be modified.[11] That our thinking is conditioned by such habits and traditions can be problematic. He maintains that "Failure to examine the conceptual structures and frames of reference which are unconsciously implicated [...] is the greatest single defect that can be found in any field of inquiry" (Dewey 1938a, 507). Dewey's warning aligns with recent feminist work on implicit bias. For instance, feminist science scholars argue that certain methodologies and assumptions of scientists can be a product of androcentric and sexist biases. There are further echoes of Dewey in feminist criticisms of the received view of objectivity, to wit, that the male perspective is taken as objective. Feminists and pragmatists agree that values play a role in science, and so both are concerned with reconstructing the concept of objectivity, a project we explore in Section 5.

There are further resources for feminist social epistemologists in the pragmatist conception of experience. Many pragmatists adopt a notion of the "double barreled" nature of experience. According to this notion, experience is an intersection of various physical and mental processes and is thus both subjective and objective, although these characterizations may be functionally distinguished from each other (James 1912, 12).

This conception of experience was important to early women pragmatists.[12] Helen Thompson Bradford (1903) and Elsie Ripley Clapp (1909) both criticized the notion of experience as merely subjective. Seigfried notes that for many of the first generation of female students of pragmatism,

> The thesis that theory arises directly from and is accountable to experience allowed them to trust their own experiences even when those experiences ran counter to accepted dogma. They were thus able to claim as sources of genuine knowledge those of their insights that had been dismissed throughout their education as merely deviant opinions or untrustworthy female sentiments.
>
> *(1996, 57)*

Unsurprisingly, pragmatists were from early days attuned to contemporary standpoint theorists' insight that inquiry is affected by the particularity of the inquirer's experience. When examining what women can bring to philosophy, Dewey notes, "we cannot conceive that it will be the same in viewpoint or tenor as that composed from the standpoint of the different masculine experience of things" (1998a, 73). Social habits, customs, and authorities condition how we experience things, and thus what we believe. However, those personal elements of experience can emancipate us from social habit so long as they are used as part of a controlled inquiry towards checking custom and tradition rather than being considered to be merely personal and "subjective" (1929, 14). Seigfried explains that experience, even when personal, is also social. She observes that

> pragmatists [...] show that each person's perspective is unique and irreplaceable. Until each person's perspective on a situation that includes her or him is heard and acknowledged, the complexity of the situation cannot be grasped, and the possibly relevant insights may be lost.
>
> *(1996, 79)*

One early pragmatist who is particularly distinctive for her embrace of the epistemic importance of standpoint is Jane Addams. We explore her social epistemology in the next section.

Jane Addams's Social Epistemology

At the heart of Jane Addams's social epistemology are two notions – that perspective makes a difference to knowledge, and that it is possible to acquire understanding of perspectives different from our own.

Addams's perspectivalism is arguably most salient in her social democracy. For Addams (as for Dewey), true democracy is not the merely arithmetic question of who gets to vote and who doesn't. Put differently, suffrage is not a sufficient condition for democracy. The question of whether or not one's vote is counted cannot indicate what is more essential to democracy – to wit, the opportunity to participate fully in dialogue and deliberation about the character of one's society. For Addams, a society in which some groups are prevented from such participation is not a truly democratic society, regardless of what happens at the ballot box.

If we support democracy, then we have a duty to seek out the company of those who do not share our political and religious convictions. She writes, "We are under a moral obligation in choosing our experiences, since the result of those experiences must ultimately determine our understanding of life" (1907, 9–10). For Addams, engaging in dialogue with those who occupy a different standpoint than we do is both a moral-political duty and an epistemic one. Indeed, for Addams, moral and epistemic duties are importantly entangled:

> We know at last, that we can only discover truth by a rational and democratic interest in life, and to give truth complete social expression is the endeavor upon which we are entering. Thus the identification with the common lot that is the essential idea of Democracy becomes the source and expression of social ethics.
>
> *(1907, 11)*

In her discussion of the role of "charity visitors" in *Democracy and Social Ethics*, Addams elaborates a series of examples to draw out the perspectival gap between the charity visitor and the down-at-heel people she seeks to aid. One of the most striking of these examples illustrates two very different perspectives on the saloon.

> [The charity worker] refers quite naturally to the "horrors of the saloon," and discovers that the head of her visited family does not connect them with "horrors" at all. He remembers all the kindnesses he has received there, the free lunch and treating which goes on, even when a man is out of work and not able to pay up; the loan of five dollars he got there when the charity visitor was miles away and he was threatened with eviction. He may listen politely to her reference to "horrors," but considers it only "temperance talk."
>
> *(1907, 32)*

Addams often gave public addresses about her work with Chicago's poor at Hull House, the settlement house she co-founded with Ellen Gates Starr in 1889. Her conviction of the importance of the perspectives of Hull House's users led her to adopt the policy always of bringing Hull House users with her when she gave public addresses. She writes,

> I never addressed a Chicago audience on the subject of the Settlement and its vicinity without inviting a neighbor to go with me, that I might curb my hasty generalization by the consciousness that I had an auditor who knew the conditions more intimately than I could hope to do.
>
> *(1923, 96)*

While Addams was deeply committed to the idea that people with different experiences and from different communities have a range of different, equally legitimate perspectives, she did not think that these differences in perspectives were insuperable. For Addams, there is no Kuhnian incommensurability between the perspectives of members of different groups. On Addams's account, we can indeed learn from each other. However, she rejected the idea that this can occur by means of rendering the other an object of research. When the University of Chicago Department of Sociology sought to take over the operation of Hull House in order to study the users, she fought the bid – both because she was ethically committed to treating Hull House users as neighbours, not research subjects, but also for methodological reasons.[13] For Addams, we learn about others' perspectives not by as it were putting them under the microscope, but through what she termed "sympathetic knowledge" or "sympathetic understanding."

On Addams's account, sympathetic knowledge is "the only way of approach to any human problem" (1913, 11). To engage in sympathetic knowledge requires putting oneself – really or imaginatively – in the perspective of the other. By living and working near people different from oneself, and by spending time with them, we can enter into community with them and come to empathize with them. However, we can also imaginatively take on their perspective through literature, theatre or various kinds of play. Addams founded initiatives that permitted both kinds (literal and imaginative) of proximity.

To understand another sympathetically is to start not from our own ethical or epistemic precepts, but from the other's own account of the world. Thus, much of Addams's writing about the poor of Chicago with whom she worked proceeds by way of anecdote. One of the most famous of these is her story of the devil baby of Hull House.

In 1913, a rumour broke out that a devil baby had been born in Chicago and was living at Hull House. People began lining up at Hull House, hoping to see the child. Of course, there was no devil baby, so its would-be visitors were never admitted to its presence. However, Addams spent hours listening to the conversations about the putative devil baby by people in the queue, and by other Hull House users.

Among these overheard conversations, Addams reported being most interested in those of the old immigrant women. Listening to their discussions of the devil baby helped Addams to understand some of the character of their lives and struggles. For many of these women, the devil baby reminded them of their own hardships – and in particular the violence and losses they had endured. One old woman attributed a scar on her face to her having seen her father kill her mother. On her view, the appearance of the devil baby similarly reflected the underlying violence and injustice of the world. Another old woman saw analogies between the origins of the devil baby and her own son's violent treatment of her:

> You might say it's a disgrace to have your son beat you up for the sake of a bit of money you've earned by scrubbing – your own man is different – but I haven't the heart to blame the boy for doing what he's seen all his life, his father forever went wild when the drink was in him and struck me to the very day of his death. The ugliness was born in the boy as the marks of the Devil was born in the poor child up-stairs.
>
> *(1916, 12)*

The common thread that Addams discerned among the old women's accounts was an effort to seek patterns in and thereby make sense of a world in which cruelty and suffering were endemic. In these shared experiences of loss and fragility the women were able to muster solidarity with each other and indeed with other sufferers.

For Addams, those who quickly dismissed the devil baby myth as non-veridical were thereby unable to acquire the sympathetic knowledge made possible by bracketing the myth's veridicality. While the claim that there was a devil baby at Hull House was not true, taking seriously the old women's belief in the devil baby gave Addams access to other pragmatically consequential truths about the lives of some of Chicago's most vulnerable people.

At bottom, sympathetic knowledge was for Addams a scientific method, one that, as Thomas Burke argues, was crucial in the experimental approach to settlement work that she championed. Burke argues that Addams was committed to taking a scientific approach towards charity efforts. For her, this meant eschewing dogmatism, and adopting instead open-mindedness, a "scientific conscience" and "scientific patience" (Burke 2013, 120–1). For Addams, both settlement work and inquiry require fallibilism, a commitment to listening carefully to different perspectives, and the conviction that proposed solutions to problems must ultimately be judged by the standards of those affected (Seigfried 1996, 200). It is easy to see Addams's approach as an expression of the broader inquiry pragmatist approach to science. In the next section, we will take up the scientific attitude at the heart of inquiry pragmatism.

The Scientific Attitude

Sympathetic understanding exemplifies the broader pragmatist understanding of science. For the pragmatist, science is not just a method or a collection of laws, but an *attitude*.

Even for Peirce, probably the most realist of the pragmatists, the method of science requires not only the hypothesis of a real world – "something upon which our thinking has no effect" (W3:253) – but also fallibilism and the will to learn. For Peirce, fallibilism, the practice of "holding for true" our beliefs, and the corresponding willingness to revise those beliefs in the face of new evidence, permits scientists to consider a wide range of evidence and methods that would be inadmissible if Cartesian certainty were the standard of belief.[14] Further, for Peirce, the scientific thinker has a will to learn. In order to learn, Peirce tells us, one must desire to learn. The pragmatic test of this willingness is whether or not the inquirer sets up obstacles to inquiry in the form of dogmatism or skepticism. (Peirce, EP2:48–50. See also Agler and Durmus 2013, 308; Dea 2015).

Dewey characterizes the scientific attitude as the tendency towards intelligent action, rather than acting from routine, prejudice, dogma, unexamined tradition, or sheer self-interest (Dewey 1938b, 30). It requires that we accept ideas as hypotheses that need to be tested according to evidence, that we address problems that bear on how both our and others' lives are lived, and that we inquire into such problems in concert with those affected by them.

While pragmatists take science as the model for the scientific attitude, they commend the scientific attitude to both scientists and to non-scientists. For the pragmatist, striving to live well is a process of inquiry. Further, Dewey argues that the spread of the scientific attitude is necessary for a mature democracy to respond to social problems. The scientific attitude allows a society to address problems in a spirit of inquiry rather than relying on dogma, habit, and propaganda (Dewey 1988, 167).

For Dewey, the scientific attitude is at once experimental and "intrinsically communicative" (1980c, 115). Echoing Addams's conception of sympathetic understanding, Dewey notes, "To formulate the significance of an experience a man must take into conscious account the experiences of others. He must try to find a standpoint which includes the experience of others as well as his own" (1980a, 236). George Mead notes that personal development and participation in any social activities requires that people put themselves "to some degree in the experiential places of, or to take the attitudes of, the other individuals belonging to that society" (1934, 300). Thus participation in inquiry – whether scientific, social or ethical – requires sympathetic understanding.

For the pragmatist, science as a social process is bound together with social progress. Sympathetic knowledge is a component of the practices required of us by the scientific attitude. The practice of sympathetic understanding makes us less dogmatic and more inclusive, and requires us to consider the effects of our ideas from standpoints other than our own. As Dewey notes, scientific inquiries are only fully tested through a "widening circle of consequences" into the non-scientific field:

> [Public] agreement is an integral part of a *complete* test of physical conclusions wherever their public bearings are relevant. The point involved comes out clearly when the social consequences of scientific conclusions invoke intensification of social conflicts. For these conflicts provide presumptive evidence of the insufficiency, or partiality, and incompleteness of the conclusions as they stand.
>
> *(1938a, 490)*

Elizabeth Anderson praises the epistemic merits of Dewey's experimentalist approach to democracy, and agrees with Dewey that when we exclude diverse perspectives in our deliberations we risk arriving at conclusions that are not in the public interest. She continues that exclusion "undermines the ability of collective decision-making to take advantage of ... the fact that citizens from different walks of life have different experiences of problems and policies of public interest, experiences that have evidential import for devising and evaluating solutions" (2006, 14). Using the example of Community forestry groups in India and Nepal as a case study, she notes that excluding women's views there was problematic as they were traditionally tasked with gathering firewood and thus faced hardships because of the adopted policies. Yet, they were also in the unique position to provide useful feedback regarding reforms (2006, 18). To reason in a way that excludes their perspectives, is both unjust and epistemically unsound.

Perhaps unsurprisingly, several early feminists drew on pragmatism and its characterization of the scientific attitude to champion feminist causes. In her doctoral dissertation, *Psychological Norms in Men and Women,* Helen Bradford Thompson adopted an experimentalist and pragmatist approach to challenge the widely held view that women's intelligence is different than men's (Morse 2002, 126). Charlotte Perkins Gilman shared numerous views with the pragmatists (Seigfried 2001; Upin 1993), and in particular argued that freedom from dogma lies in science. On Gilman's account, the "scientific mind has developed a new attitude – that ideas are hypotheses" that need to be tested (quoted in Upin 1993, 46). Finally, Peirce's former student, Christine Ladd-Franklin, when faced with exclusion from a psychological group known as the Experimentalists because she was a woman, argued against the ban on the basis that it hindered inquiry: "So unconscientious, so immoral, – worse than that – so unscientific!" (Scarborough and Furumoto 1987, 126).

In sum, both for the canonical early pragmatists and for the proto-feminists working within pragmatist circles, a properly scientific attitude – that is, an attitude characterized by fallibilism, the desire to learn, and in particular a desire to consider a range of perspectives – makes us better inquirers because it prevents us from valorizing views merely because they are produced by the dominant group. Pragmatists' scientific attitude is thus an historical precursor to standpoint theorists' notion of strong objectivity. In the next (and final) section, we conclude by sketching the similarities.

Conclusion

In recent decades, feminist epistemologists of science have increasingly taken up the view that socially-situated knowledge requires a new conception of objectivity – what Sandra Harding terms "strong objectivity" (Harding 1993). On Harding's account, the old value-free ideal for science encodes particular biases – the biases of the dominant group – into science. By balancing dominant beliefs against the range of often-ignored perspectives, Harding argues that we can produce a stronger objectivity, less subject to historico-political vagaries.

Harding's demand for stronger objectivity was anticipated by the early pragmatists. As exemplified by Addams's sympathetic understanding, the scientific attitude of the pragmatists leads inquirers to seek out diverse perspectives, and in particular the perspectives of those most affected by the object of the inquiry, in order to escape the bond of dogmatism. Dewey endorses "scientific experimental inquiry marked not the elimination of social aims and interests, but their emancipation from bondage and routine." He continues that "to be intellectually objective is to be impartial; to have no ax to grind; no preconceived purpose to maintain at any cost; no particular consequence to insist upon at any hazard" (1998b, 123–5).

From Addams's sympathetic knowledge to Dewey's injunction that we widen the circle of consequences in our pragmatic reasoning, to applications of the scientific attitude by such figures as Bradford Thompson and Ladd-Franklin, pragmatism has from its earliest days been committed to the idea that knowledge is social. For early pragmatists as for contemporary feminist social epistemologists, not only the demands of justice, but in particular the epistemic demands of inquiry oblige us to seek out a wide range of perspectives and values and to test the consequences of our beliefs for the full range of people most affected by them.

Notes

1 Many thanks to Miranda Fricker for her kind suggestions on an earlier draft of this chapter.
2 Roughly, 1860s to 1930s.
3 Peirce himself was never completely satisfied with this formulation. He reformulated the maxim at least six times in subsequent years.
4 See, for instance, Peirce W3:273, and James (1907, 76).
5 This is not Talisse and Aikin's characterization. Indeed, as their (2005) title makes explicit, they argue that pragmatists cannot be pluralists.
6 As we suggest in what follows, this understanding of pragmatism also captures the spirit of pragmatism as a scientific attitude.
7 While Addams did not describe herself as a feminist, her work is infused with feminism in ways that will become clear in Part 4.
8 We here use "intelligent" in Dewey's sense. For Dewey, "intelligence" describes a way of behaving, not a measurable cognitive capacity. For Dewey, to become more intelligent is for one's inquiry about the world to make one more discriminating and observant, and to bring one's knowledge and behavior into better alignment.
9 As numerous scholars have pointed out (Moen 1991; Rooney 1993; Seigfried 1996), Peirce's work fits less easily into the feminist framework than that of other pragmatists. However, Marcia Moen notes that some elements of Peirce's account of experience may be a resource for feminism.
10 Peirce's ontology takes seriously objects' relations not only to persons but also to each other.
11 James makes a similar argument in Pragmatism (1907).
12 In general, when we discuss early women pragmatists, we do not describe them as feminist pragmatists since they did not typically identify as feminists. See also, n. 6.
13 Addams also rejected the predominantly male University of Chicago sociologists' characterization of Hull House as a "sociological laboratory." See Feagin et al. (2015, 62–64).
14 Lewis echoes Peirce's fallibilism in his own characterization of science as "attitude of regarding all accepted findings as in some degree provisional, and as attesting themselves by their value as working hypotheses and their usefulness in application" (Lewis 1970, 100).

Works Cited

Addams, J. (1907). *Democracy and Social Ethics*. New York: MacMillan.
Addams, J. (1913). *A New Conscience and an Ancient Evil*. New York: MacMillan.
Addams, J. (1916). *The Long Road of Woman's Memory*. New York: MacMillan.
Addams, J. (1923). *Twenty Years at Hull House with Autobiographical Notes*. New York: MacMillan.
Agler, D. W. and Durmus, D. (2013). Christine Ladd-Franklin: Pragmatist Feminist. *Transactions of the Charles S. Peirce Society*, 49(3), pp. 299–321.
Anderson, E. (2006). The Epistemology of Democracy. *Episteme*, 1(2), pp. 8–22.
Burke, F. T. (2013). *What Pragmatism Was*. Bloomington: Indiana University Press.
Clapp, E. R. (1909). Dependence of Imagination of the Subject-Object Distinction. *The Journal of Philosophy, Psychology and Scientific Methods*, 6(17), pp. 455–460.
Dea, S. (2015). Meaning, Inquiry, and the Rule of Reason: A Hookwayesque Colligation. *Transactions of the Charles S. Peirce Society*, 51(4), pp. 401–418.
Dewey, J. (1929). *Experience and Nature*. London: George Allen & Unwin, Ltd.
Dewey, J. (1938a). *Logic: The Theory of Inquiry*. New York: Henry Holt and Company.
Dewey, J. (1938b). Unity of Science as a Social Problem. In O. Neurath, R. Carnap, and C. Morris, eds., *Foundations of the Unity of Science, Vol. 1*. Chicago: The University of Chicago Press, 29–38.
Dewey, J. (1980a). Democracy and Education. In J. Boydson, ed., *The Middle Works of John Dewey, Volume 9, 1899–1924*. Carbondale, IL: Southern Illinois University Press.
Dewey, J. (1980b). The Public and its Problems. In J. Boydson ed., *The Later Works of John Dewey, Volume 2, 1925–1953*. Carbondale, IL: Southern Illinois University Press, pp. 235–372.

Dewey, J. (1980c). Individualism, Old and New. In J. Boydson, ed., *The Later Works of John Dewey, 1925–1953, Volume 5: 1929–1930*. Carbondale, IL: Southern Illinois University Press, pp. 41–144.

Dewey, J. (1988). Freedom and Culture. In J. Boydson, ed., *The Later Works of John Dewey, Volume 13, 1925–1953*. Carbondale, IL: Southern Illinois University Press, pp. 63–188.

Dewey, J. (1998a). Philosophy and Democracy. In L. Hickson and T. Alexander, eds., *The Essential Dewey, Vol. 1*. Bloomington: Indiana University Press, pp. 136–171.

Dewey, J. (1998b). The Logic of Judgments in Practice. In L. Hickson and T. Alexander, eds., *The Essential Dewey, Vol. 2*. Bloomington: Indiana University Press., pp. 136–171.

Duran, J. (1993). The Intersection of Pragmatism and Feminism. *Hypatia*, 8(2), pp. 159–171.

Feagin, J., Vera, H., and Ducey, K. (2015). *Liberation Sociology*. 3rd Edition. New York: Routledge.

Gatens-Robinson, E. (1991). Dewey and the Feminist Successor Science Project. *Transactions of the Charles S. Peirce Society*, 27(4), pp. 417–433.

Harding, S. (1993). Rethinking Standpoint Epistemology: What is 'Strong Objectivity'. In L. Alcoff and E. Potter, eds., *Feminist Epistemologies*. New York: Routledge, pp. 49–82.

James, W. (1891). The Moral Philosopher and the Moral Life. *International Journal of Ethics*, 1(3), pp. 330–354.

James, W. (1907). *Pragmatism*. New York: Longmans, Green, and Co.

James, W. (1912). *Essays in Radical Empiricism*. New York: Longmans, Green, and Co.

Lewis, C. I. (1970). Logical Positivism and Pragmatism. In J. D. Goheen and J. L. Mothershead, Jr., eds., *Collected Papers of Clarence Irving Lewis*. Stanford: Stanford University Press, pp. 92–112.

Mead, G. H. (1934). *Mind, Self, and Society*. C. W. Morris, ed. Chicago: The University of Chicago Press.

Moen, M. K. (1991). Peirce's Pragmatism as a Resource for Feminism. *Transactions of the Charles S. Peirce Society*, 27(4), pp. 435–450.

Morse, J. F. (2002). Ignored But Not Forgotten: The Work of Helen Bradford Thompson Woolley. *NWSA Journal*, 14(2), pp. 121–147.

Peirce, C. S. (1986). *Writings of Charles S. Peirce: A Chronological Edition. Vol. 3*. Peirce Edition Project, ed., Indianapolis: Indiana University Press.

Peirce, C. S. (1998). *The Essential Peirce. Vol. 2*. Peirce Edition Project, ed., Bloomington: Indiana University Press.

Rooney, P. (1993). Feminist-Pragmatist Revisionings of Reason, Knowledge, and Philosophy. *Hypatia*, 8(2), pp. 15–37.

Scarborough, E. and Furumoto, L. (1987). *Untold Lives: The First Generation of American Women Psychologists*. New York: Columbia University Press.

Seigfried, C. H. (1996). *Feminism and Pragmatism: Reweaving the Social Fabric*. Chicago: University of Chicago Press.

Seigfried, C. H. (2001). Can a "Man-Hating" Feminist Also be a Pragmatist?: On Charlotte Perkins Gilman. *The Journal of Speculative Philosophy*, 15(2): 74–85.

Talisse, R. and Aikin, S. (2005). Why Pragmatists Cannot Be Pluralists. *Transactions of the Charles S. Peirce Society*, 41(1), pp. 101–118.

Thompson, H. B. (1903). A Critical Study of Bosanquet's Theory of Judgment. In J. Dewey ed., *Studies in Logical Theory*, Chicago: The University of Chicago Press, pp. 86–126.

Upin, J. S. (1993). Charlotte Perkins Gilman: Instrumentalism Beyond Dewey. *Hypatia*, 8(2), pp. 38–63.

Further Reading

Addams, J. (2002). *The Jane Addams Reader*. In E. Jean ed., New York: Basic Books. (A handy single volume selection of Addams' works.)

Dewey, J. (1998). *The Essential Dewey Volume 1: Pragmatism, Education, Democracy*. In L. Hickson and T. Alexander, eds., Bloomington: Indiana University Press. (Dewey published prolifically. No single volume survey can do justice to his corpus. However, this volume anthologizes several works in which Dewey elaborates the scientific attitude and other matters relevant to social epistemology; so, it's a good place to start.)

Seigfried, C. H. (1996). *Feminism and Pragmatism: Reweaving the Social Fabric*. Chicago: University of Chicago Press. (An elaboration of the pragmatism's relevance for feminist philosophy from a distinguished scholar of early women pragmatists.)

Talisse, R. and Aikin, S. (2011). *The Pragmatism Reader: From Peirce through the Present*. Princeton: Princeton University Press. (An excellent, if male-dominated, survey of the pragmatist canon from two important historians of the movement.)

PART VII

The Epistemology of Democracy

35

THE EPISTEMOLOGY
OF DEMOCRACY

An Overview

Robert B. Talisse

Preliminaries

The relationship between democracy and epistemology is tense. In theory, democracy embraces commendable epistemic ideals that in practice it seems doomed to violate. To explain, familiar democratic norms—equality, open discussion, a free Press, fair majoritarian elections—embody the aspiration for informed, well-considered, and reason-based political decision-making. Democracy embraces the idea that a group makes better decisions when its members discuss, debate, and challenge each other's ideas; democratic norms appear to be designed to foster precisely these activities. Furthermore, democracy upholds an ideal of political accountability that presupposes an engaged citizenry that can contest standing policies. In a democracy, citizens may demand *reasons* from their government; and where these are lacking, citizens may rightly object, and perhaps resist or even revolt. In general, one might say that democracy is the political manifestation of the individual aspiration to practical rationality. As Cass Sunstein puts it, a democracy aims to be a "republic of reasons" (1993: 20).

As appealing as the democrat's image of collectively rational self-government may be, it prompts an obvious query: Does democracy in fact enhance the epistemic quality of political decisions? Here trouble looms. Not only is it unclear that democratic norms epistemically improve decision-making, it may be that they tend to *diminish* the epistemic worth of public opinion. After all, democratic norms of free expression and open discussion enable propagandists, demagogues, and strategic actors of other kinds to manipulate and mislead democratic citizens.[1] As will be discussed below, when these norms are coupled with rights to free association, they can contribute to distinctive group-epistemic pathologies. We also know that the communications environment that is enabled by modern technology has exacerbated our epistemic vulnerabilities (Sunstein 2007). What's more, there is good reason to think that these dysfunctions are especially active in contemporary democracies: Democratic citizens not only tend to be strikingly ignorant with regard to their political order, they also seem increasingly unable to countenance reasonable political disagreement.[2] One recent study suggests that politically divided citizens in the United States inhabit "separate realities" (Kull 2004). Despite its laudable epistemic ideals, real democracy is at best an epistemically mixed bag.

Given this, it is not surprising that a good deal of contemporary democratic theory attempts to understand democracy in non-epistemic ways. The leading proposals cast democracy in *moral* terms. On these views, democratic norms do not reflect a grand epistemological aspiration, but instead respond to the moral requirement that governments and societies treat persons as equals

(Dworkin 2000; Christiano 2008). Other views of this kind contend that democracy is that political order that performs the moral function of constraining power and avoiding domination (Pettit 2012; Shapiro 2016), or achieving a properly inclusive (Young 2002) or free (Gould 1988) society. Still others propose that democracy's driving aim is something that is neither moral nor epistemic, but prudential, such as political stability (Riker 1982; Posner 2003). Nevertheless, many of the moral conceptions, and (as we will see below) even some of the stability views in currency invoke epistemic considerations. In any case very few theorists think that the epistemic performance of democracies is entirely *beside the point*; that is, it would be difficult to find any theorist who contends that entrenched, widespread, and irreparable incompetence among a citizenry and government does not compromise the legitimacy of a democracy.

Hence much of the democratic theory now in currency aims to show how democracy might yet be a "republic of reasons." Some theories focus particularly on the task of enhancing the epistemic value of democratic *outputs* (decisions, policies), whereas others seek to enhance the capacity of democracy to epistemically improve democratic *inputs* (popular political opinion, votes). To be sure, the better-developed views devote attention to the epistemic improvement of *both* the inputs and the outputs. As these currents can be fruitfully viewed as continuations of long-standing trends, it will be useful to begin this overview with a brisk (thus highly selective) survey of the relevant background in democratic theory.

A Longstanding Tension

The tension between democracy's epistemic ideals and its practical reality has been evident since the dawn of political theory. In his famous funeral oration, Pericles celebrated democracy largely on epistemic grounds. He lauded democracy's capacity to foster civic participation and debate among its citizens, affirming that these activities serve to "instruct" citizens about political matters, who thereby in turn can hold their governors (and each other) accountable (2011: 797). Yet many of the same epistemic considerations are central to the formidable anti-democratic arguments launched by Plato. Plato condemned democracy as that form of government which apportions political power equally to the wise and the unwise (1997: 558c). He reasoned that as the unwise vastly outnumber the wise in any populace, democracy is simply the rule of the foolish; this arrangement, Plato thought, is not only imprudent, but also manifestly unjust and morally preferable only to tyranny (1997: 562a). His infamous conclusion is that those who seek a political order based in reason should embrace a kingship of the wise (1997: 473d).[3] Aristotle adopted a slightly moderated view in his *Politics*. He acknowledged that under certain conditions a group of unwise people might be epistemically superior to a few wise ones (1984: 1281a42).[4] Still, he regarded democracy as "deviant" (1984: 1289a27), as it gives individuals access to the highest offices regardless of their intellectual excellence.

In the Modern period, several philosophers fashioned epistemic arguments for democracy. Jean-Jacques Rousseau is one example; he argued that democracy is uniquely legitimate because it alone could reveal and enact the General Will. He went so far as to claim that in a well-functioning democracy, those who find themselves on the losing side of an election must conclude that they had been mistaken to vote as they did; again, when a proper democracy votes, the result discloses the General Will, which is inerrant. According to Rousseau, democratic majorities are, in this sense, infallible (1988: 100). Thus their authority: By submitting one's judgment to the General Will, one is guaranteed to arrive at the truth. Hence in a democracy the individual "[unites] himself with all" and yet "[obeys] himself alone," and "[remains] as free as before" (1988: 92).

Rousseau's conception of the General Will is notoriously obscure, and consequently its relevance to democratic theory remains unclear.[5] Yet Rousseau's contemporary Marquis de Condorcet

(1785) seems to have supplied a precise version of what Rousseau may have had in mind.[6] Condorcet's renowned "jury theorem" shows that, assuming relatively weak conditions regarding individuals' competence and cognitive independence, the majority vote in even a modestly-sized population is nearly infallible when presented with a binary decision. Although the formal elements of the theorem are straightforward, the institutional details are complicated and cannot be explored here.[7] But note that even if it is supposed that the details can be sorted out, the jury theorem is not univocal in its support for democracy. The theorem entails that the majority in a modestly sized group that fails to satisfy the weak competence condition is nearly surely mistaken, and it offers no way to discern whether this condition has been satisfied in a given group. Additionally, it is implausible to think that the actual political questions are adequately framed as binary choices; it is similarly implausible to think that voters typically are cognitively independent in the respect that is called for. Thus the applicability of the jury theorem is questionable.[8]

The nineteenth century saw other attempts to reconcile real-world democracy with its epistemic ideals. John Stuart Mill argued that since democracy aims to promote the common good, and those with higher levels of education and "mental superiority" are thereby better at discerning the common good, those who "work with their heads," or have graduated from universities should be given "two or more" votes at the polls (1861: 336). Perhaps sensing trouble, Mill was sure to add that this arrangement reflects the "true ideal" of democracy (1861: 337).[9] Still, those who accept Mill's claim that plural voting is consistent with (or even required by) the kind of political equality that democracy upholds must address the question of whether such a scheme would indeed enhance the epistemic value of collective decision. That being a "graduate of a university" enhances one's ability to discern the general good is not evident. Neither is it obvious that higher levels of education are positively correlated with a tendency to serve the general good.

New difficulty for democracy's epistemic self-image emerged in the twentieth century, which saw important advances in the social sciences as well as pioneering achievements in communications technologies. Writing in the earlier half of the century, Walter Lippmann (1922, 1925) observed that the new technology placed in the hands of an elite strikingly reliable techniques for manufacturing mass public opinion; he argued that, in this new communications environment, democratic politics is dominated by opinions crafted by political insiders, while the democratic citizenry is rendered a mass of ineffectual bystanders (1925: 110) by the overwhelming onslaught of messages, symbols, and images provided by elites.

Lippmann's arguments explicitly called into question the very idea of a democratic public whose will could be represented in an election result or enacted in policy. On his view, the epistemic situation of modern politics is so complex that the very idea of a citizen exercising political "judgment" or forming a political "opinion" is misplaced. Following on this skepticism, there emerged a conception of democracy that sought to fully jettison democracy's epistemic ambitions. The so-called "realist" conception of democracy, championed by Joseph Schumpeter (1942), holds that democracy is "that institutional arrangement for arriving at political decisions in which individuals acquire the power to decide by means of a competitive struggle for the people's vote" (1942: 269). Here there is no appeal to the common good, and no claim about the ability of democratic processes to disclose the people's will; according to the realist, democracy rather is a mechanism that produces stable government by holding popular elections to select "bosses" (1942: 269) who hold office for a limited period of time. On this view, the role of the citizenry is not to discuss, deliberate, or debate, but simply to vote on Election Day, and thereafter to attend to other matters (1942: 295).

By the middle of the twentieth Century, the Lippmann and Schumpeter line was bolstered significantly by social choice theory. Results associated with Kenneth Arrow (1951) brought into prominence the view that epistemic goods that democracy seeks to realize are not hard to measure or merely difficult to achieve in practice, but conceptually incoherent. In particular, Arrow's impossibility theorem showed that there could be no collective decision procedure that reliably avoids certain forms of irrationality.[10] Consequently, the very idea of a popular will fell under greater suspicion; social choice theory suggests that the very thing that democracy was supposed to reveal—the General Will, the common good, the public interest, the majority opinion, and so on—was a fiction, "empty" (Riker 1982: 239).

According to such views, democracy cannot deliver a more rational citizenry or better-justified decisions, because democracy is inescapably vulnerable to collective irrationality. Hence these views maintain that democracy's choice-worthiness derives from non-epistemic consider-ations, such as stability. The social choice theorists claimed that democracy's central virtue con-sists in its ability to "restrain officials" (Riker 1982: 9) by empowering citizens to "get rid of rulers" (1982: 244) who "offend" (1982: 242) by not performing to the citizens' satisfaction. As Riker puts it, then, democracy is "not popular rule, but rather an intermittent, sometimes random, even perverse, popular veto" (1982: 244).

Yet this view is fragile. If the idea of a "popular will" is "empty," how could a vote count as a "veto"? How could democratic electoral mechanisms impose discipline on elected rulers (Cohen 1986; Coleman and Ferejohn 1986; Miller 1992)? In order for elections to impose discipline, results must *express* the prevailing opinion of an official's performance; that is, votes must be treated as *judgments* if elections are to impose political restraint. But if votes express *judgments*, they manifest epistemic properties; they can be well-informed, highly-justified, ignorant, erroneous, and so on. Thus the tension between democracy's epistemic ideals and its practical reality simply re-emerges.

John Dewey set the stage for the contemporary modes of democratic theory that concern us here. Largely reacting to Lippmann, Dewey introduced two reorientations that have since become central to theorizing the epistemic dimensions of democracy.[11] First, Dewey expanded the *site* of democracy. Second, Dewey proposed an expanded, socialized epistemology. Each bears comment.

First, Dewey contends that democracy is *not* primarily a form of government, but a type of society, a "way of life" (1939: 155).[12] This extension of democracy's site calls theorists to look beyond the institutional mechanisms of democracy (votes, electoral systems, campaigns, represen-tative bodies) that previously had been their nearly exclusive focus, and towards a larger social environment, where citizens daily interact, cooperate, communicate, compete, discuss, and work together. The fundamental question for an enlarged democratic theorist regards the *character* of these encounters; thus the democratic theorist's concern expands to encompass the system of public education, the economy, the workplace, the media, civic associations, and more.

Second, Dewey promotes an epistemology that takes inquiry as the primary epistemological activity. Inquiry, Dewey holds, is fundamentally the social process of experimentally addressing emergent problems (1938: 108). Hence he sees problem-solving, not the acquisition of justified true belief, as the primary epistemic goal.[13] Epistemology hence becomes the study of a distinctive kind of conduct. Accordingly, the scope of epistemology expands to include matters that are today regarded as distinctively *social epistemic*, including the social distribution of informa-tion, the channels by which new problems are recognized and taken up by communities, the division of social-epistemic labor, and the social role of experts.

These reorientations enable one to locate the epistemic ideals of democracy within the oper-ations of the *society*, and not exclusively in electoral processes and outcomes. Democracy then can be understood as a society devoted to the ongoing collective epistemic enterprise of addressing shared problems. Hence the epistemic power of democracy lies not in its ability to render correct electoral outcomes, but rather in its capacity to pool information, harness socially distributed cogni-tive resources, incorporate new perspectives and considerations, and revise its practices and policies in light of new findings (Anderson 2006). Democracy becomes a "republic of reasons" in virtue of being a society of citizens committed to sharing epistemic resources in their continuing effort to resolve common problems. The familiar mechanisms of democracy hence derive their legitimacy from the democratic quality of the broader society in which they function.[14] Thus well-established data concerning the extent of public ignorance, the vulnerability of democratic populations to epistemic pathologies, and the general tendency of democracy to make epistemically sub-optimal decisions do not pose a refutation of democracy's epistemic ideals, but rather identifies *problems* that democratic societies must address.[15] Hence for Dewey, as for many contemporary epistemic democrats, the most urgent issue for modern democracy is "the improvement of the methods and conditions of debate, discussion, and persuasion" that prevail in society (1927: 365).

Some Current Trends

We turn to the contemporary scene. *Deliberative democracy* has been the predominant framework in democratic theory for several decades. Deliberativists disagree over a range of issues, but all hold that the legitimacy of democratic government, and the bindingness of its decisions, require more than fair elections among political equals; democratic decisions must be *preceded* by opportunities for citizens to *deliberate publicly* about the social and political issues they face. Thus deliberativists embrace the enlarged vision of democracy's site: Democratic political mechanisms must function within a society characterized by norms of open and inclusive discussion, debate, critique, and civic participation. Importantly, as deliberation is understood explicitly as *reason exchanging*,[16] deliberativists also embrace a *social epistemological* stance: The epistemic goods of democracy are not to be sought exclusively in its outputs, but also in the quality of the social processes of reasoning that democracy enables.

The deliberativist framework opens several distinctive avenues of research concerning the epistemology of democracy. In the remainder of this overview, I discuss briefly only three major and interlocking trends: (1) the epistemic capabilities of groups; (2) vulnerabilities to group-epistemic pathologies; (3) the epistemic character of public discourse.

The first trend picks up on themes found in both Aristotle and Rousseau. Much of this literature has roots in Scott Page's "diversity trumps ability" theorem, which holds that, given the satisfaction of a few relatively undemanding conditions, "a randomly selected collection of problem solvers outperforms a collection of the best individual problem solvers" (2007: 162). Although some—notably Elizabeth Anderson (2006)—have questioned the value of Page's theorem, Helene Landemore (2013) recently has developed a series of arguments showing that majority rule under democratic norms of inclusive deliberation within a large and cognitively diverse population tends to produce decisions of greater epistemic value than decision-making processes that involve only experts. On her view, democracy uniquely realizes a powerful form of collective intelligence, which she calls "democratic reason" (2013: 233).

Others working on the epistemic abilities of groups have attended to the ways in which individuals' preferences and judgements change within the context of well-ordered group deliberation. Here James Fishkin's experiments with "deliberative polls" have been especially influential. A deliberative poll "models what an electorate *would* think if, hypothetically, it could be immersed in intensive deliberative processes" (1991: 81). The idea is to take a sample of citizens, record their antecedent views regarding some political question, and then have them participate in an orchestrated deliberation event focused on that question. These events involve, among other things, presentations by experts who hold opposing viewpoints, question-and-answer sessions with the experts, and open dialogue within the deliberating group. The point is to chart *opinion change* among the group's members and to get a sense of what an "informed and engaged public opinion" on the question at hand would be (Ackerman and Fishkin 2003: 12).

Large-scale deliberative polling events have been staged, and Ackerman and Fishkin (2003) have even proposed a "new national holiday" devoted to public deliberation. However, some have questioned the *relevance* of the results of deliberative polls (Richardson 2010), and others have found that deliberative events can actually encourage extremism, entrenchment, and division (Schkade, Sunstein and Hastie 2007). Relatedly, Diana Mutz (2006) has found that discussion in heterogeneous groups positively correlates with political nonparticipation, whereas those who discuss politics only with like-minded others are more likely to vote. The conclusion of this research is that, in order for it to be democratically enriching, deliberation must be conducted under highly specific conditions.

The question, then, is what the appropriate conditions are. Hence a second trend of research explores distinctive types of epistemic dysfunction that can affect deliberating groups. The touchstone is Cass Sunstein's work on group polarization. Group polarization means that, in the course of a discussion, "members of a deliberating group predictably move toward a more extreme point in the direction indicated by the members' predeliberative tendencies" (Sunstein 2003: 81); in other words, deliberation with like-minded others can cause individuals to shift to more extreme versions of their original positions. The phenomenon has been studied across an impressively broad range of deliberative contexts; it affects groups irrespective of political orientation, level of education, economic class, ethnicity, and gender. It has been documented around the world, in groups ranging from political parties, corporate boards, judicial panels, consumer groups, and local citizen assemblies (Sunstein 2009: 1ff.). The result is remarkably robust.

That deliberation can *encourage* extremism is troubling. Note that polarization apparently is not driven by reason or argument, but by group dynamics. Individuals shift to more extreme versions of their prior views mainly in order to affirm their group identity and solidarity. And as individuals polarize, they become less able to see their opponents as rational (Hardin 2002); hence polarizing groups tend towards epistemic insularity, which generates further polarization. Consequently, deliberation within doxastically homogeneous groups not only breeds extreme versions of individuals' prior beliefs, it also engenders *extremism*. The problem, of course, is that social movements and activist projects *require* a good deal of in-group discussion and solidarity.

What can be done? Sunstein has found that polarization is counteracted when groups adopt norms that go beyond free participation and open discussion. In order to guard against polarization, groups must also develop mechanisms to protect—and perhaps even incentivize—contestation, challenge, and dissent (2003: 211–212) within their membership, as well as norms that expose the group to criticisms and objections from without (2003: 165). However, the mere *exposure* to dissenting voices and countervailing considerations is not yet sufficient; what is needed is for dissenters not only to have a voice, but to get a *hearing*. This means that citizens must bring to the deliberative activity a set of competencies that enable them to engage in civil disputation.

Thus a third research trend concerns the epistemic nature and quality of public discourse. If, indeed, public deliberation is the key to a legitimate, accountable, and inclusive democracy, then citizens and institutions must be able not only to reason well together; they must also be equipped to manage disagreement. After all, public deliberation is necessary largely because citizens hold different beliefs concerning political matters. Often these differences run deep, engaging citizens' fundamental value commitments (Talisse 2009: 11, ff.). Accordingly, public deliberation is likely to incite heated disagreement, perhaps even hostility, among citizens. So, if deliberation is to serve democracy's epistemic ideals, citizens must bring to the enterprise the capacities that enable them to argue well, even under heated conditions.

Hence some work in this area has been focused on the nature of civility in public discourse (Carter 1998; Kingwell 2012), though others have challenged the thought that proper public discourse always calls for this (Estlund 2001; Young 2001). Still others have pursued a distinctively Rawlsian (2005: 217) conception of civility by restricting the *kind of reason* that is admissible into public deliberation. Here the thought is that political disagreement can be domesticated by introducing a norm of *reciprocity* whereby citizens may offer only those reasons that other citizens can be expected to recognize the force of (Gutmann and Thompson 2004: 133). Of course, the issue here concerns the contours of the restraints; many have argued that the very idea is objectionable (Eberle 2002; Vallier 2014).

Another strand within this general trend focuses on the dynamics of political argumentation, including argumentation mediated by contemporary media and technology (Walton 2007; Lynch 2016). One concern has to do with the ways in which political argumentation conducted for the sake of an onlooking audience can satisfy the usual requirements for acceptable and even civil debate among the interlocutors, while nonetheless activating within the onlookers the epistemic pathologies mentioned above. Aikin and Talisse (2006, 2008, 2014) have developed the concept of a *dialectical* fallacy to capture these phenomena.[17] One particularly vivid case is the "weak man" fallacy. In the "weak man," one soundly refutes an especially feeble critic of one's view, but then proceeds as if the feeble critic is the best the opposing side has to offer, thereby signaling to one's audience a distorted view of the argumentative state of play. The effect of dialectical fallacies is to project to an audience the view that there is no serious opposition to one's favored position; when successful, one's audience is disinclined to seek out cogent opposition, and thus primed for polarization and insularity. Again, the lesson is that the epistemic power of democracy depends largely on the *epistemic character* of its citizens and their interactions. In this way, research in the epistemology of democracy is increasingly integrated with social epistemology as such. Hence it may be time for there to be recognized within the field of social epistemology a sub-field of "political epistemology."

Notes

1 See Stanley (2015) for a recent discussion of how democratic norms secure the conditions that enable their own undermining. Kelly (2013) examines how framing effects can be employed for the purpose of manipulating citizens. See also Lakoff (2016).

2 Ackerman and Fishkin write, "If six decades of moral public opinion research establish anything, it is that the general public's political ignorance is appalling by any standard" (2003: 8). The literature on public ignorance in democratic societies cannot be surveyed here but see Delli Carpini and Keeter (1997); Somin (2016); and the essays collected in Elkin and Soltan, eds. (1999).

3 Ahlstrom-Vij (2013) and Brennan (2016) both argue for epistemic elitism.

4 See Surowiecki (2004) and Page (2007) for contemporary versions of this.

5 Cohen (2010) provides a current interpretation.

6 See Grofman and Feld (1989), and responses by Estlund (1989) and Waldron (1989).

7 Goodin (2008: 80ff). provides a nice discussion of both the simplicity of the math and the complexity of the institutional details, as does Sunstein (2006: 25ff).

8 For reasons similar to the ones stated, Estlund (2008: Ch. XII) declares the jury theorem "irrelevant." Anderson (2006) also doubts that the jury theorem is of use to democracy. Others have sought to salvage the theorem; see List and Goodin (2001), and Dietrich and Spiekermann (2013). See also Peter (2016).

9 Lopez-Guerra (2014) argues for a significant deviation from democracy's standard conception of franchise. Estlund (2000) develops an epistemic argument for plural voting.

10 See Maskin and Sen (2014) for helpful discussions of Arrow's theorem.

11 Dewey's 1927 *The Public and its Problems* is self-consciously a direct response to Lippmann's *The Phantom Public* (1922). See Bohman (2010) for an assessment; see also Rogers (2009).

12 Elsewhere I have criticized Dewey's conception of "democracy as a way of life" for being an untenable form of political perfectionism. That matter is not in play here. One can follow Dewey in holding that democracy is fundamentally a mode of social association without accepting Dewey's conception of the *content* of that mode of society. See my (2007) and (2011) for discussion.

13 See Peter (2009: 117ff). For helpful discussion.

14 Hence Dewey, "Majority rule, just as majority rule, is as foolish as its critics charge it with being. But it never is *merely* majority rule ... the way a majority comes to be a majority is the more important thing: antecedent debates, modification of views to meet the opinions of minorities, the relative satisfaction given the latter by the fact that it has had a chance and that next time it may be successful in becoming a majority." (1927: 365)

15 See my (2005) for discussion.

16 Some early critics, notably Iris Young (1997) and Lynn Sanders (1997), objected that the focus on reasoning revealed exclusionary tendencies within deliberativism. The force of these arguments is challenged effectively by Dryzek (2000: 64ff.). In any case, most deliberativists subsequently have been keen to espouse a broad conception of reasoning that preempts such concerns.
17 See also Aikin and Casey (2011), and Aikin and Casey (forthcoming).

References

Ackerman, B. and Fishkin, J. (2003) *Deliberation Day*, New Haven: Yale University Press.

Ahlstrom-Vij, K. (2013) *Epistemic Paternalism: A Defence*, New York: Palgrave Macmillan.

Aikin, S. and Talisse, R. (2006) Two Forms of the Straw Man, *Argumentation* 20, pp. 345–352.

Aikin, S. and Talisse, R. (2008) Modus Tollens, *Argumentation* 22, pp. 521–529.

Aikin, S. and Talisse, R. (2014) *Why We Argue (And How We Should)*, New York: Routledge.

Aikin, S. and Casey, J. (2011) Straw Men, Weak Men, and Hollow Men, *Argumentation* 25, pp. 87–105.

Aikin, S. and Casey, J. (forthcoming) Straw Men, Iron Men, and Argumentative Virtue, *Topoi*.

Anderson, E. (2006) The Epistemology of Democracy, *Episteme* 3, pp. 9–23.

Aristotle. (1984) *Politics*, C. Lord (tr.), Chicago: University of Chicago Press.

Arrow, K. (1951) A Difficulty in Social Welfare, *Journal of Political Economy* 68, pp. 328–346.

Bohman, J. (2010) Participation Through Publics: Did Dewey Answer Lippmann? *Contemporary Pragmatism* 7, pp. 49–68.

Brennan, J. (2016) *Against Democracy*, Princeton: Princeton University Press.

Carter, S. (1998) *Civility*, New York: Harper.

Christiano, T. (2008) *The Constitution of Equality*, New York: Oxford University Press.

Cohen, J. (1986) An Epistemic Conception of Democracy, *Ethics* 97, pp. 26–38.

Cohen, J. (2010) *Rousseau*, Cambridge: Cambridge University Press.

Coleman, J and Ferejohn, J. (1986) Democracy and Social Choice, *Ethics* 97, pp. 6–25.

Condorcet, M. (1785) *Essay on the Application of Analysis to the Probability of Majority Decisions*, New York: Chelsea Press.

Delli Carpini, M. and Keeter, S. (1997) *What Americans Know About Politics And Why It Matters*, New Have: Yale University Press.

Dewey, J. (1927) The Public and its Problems, In: J. Boydston, ed., *The Later Works of John Dewey, Vol. 2*, Carbondale: Southern Illinois University Press, pp. 235–372.

Dewey, J. (1938) Logic: The Theory of Inquiry, In: J. Boydston, ed., *The Later Works of John Dewey, Vol. 12*, Carbondale: Southern Illinois University Press.

Dewey, J. (1939) Freedom and Culture, In: J. Boydston, ed., *The Later Works of John Dewey, Vol. 13*, Carbondale: Southern Illinois University Press, pp. 63–188.

Dietrich, F. and Spiekermann, K. (2013) Epistemic Democracy with Defensible Premises, *Economics and Philosophy* 29, pp. 87–120.

Dryzek, J. (2000) *Deliberative Democracy and Beyond*, New York: Oxford University Press.

Dworkin, R. (2000) *Sovereign Virtue*, Cambridge: Harvard University Press.

Eberle, C. (2002) *Religious Conviction in Liberal Politics*, Cambridge: Cambridge University Press.

Elkin, S. and Soltan, K. (1999) *Citizen Competence and Democratic Institutions*, University Park: Pennsylvania State University Press.

Estlund, D. (1989) Democratic Theory and the Public Interest: Condorcet and Rousseau Revisited, *American Political Science Review* 83, pp. 1317–1322.

Estlund, D. (2000) Political Quality, *Social Philosophy and Policy* 17, pp. 127–160.

Estlund, D. (2001) Deliberation, Down and Dirty: Must Political Expression be Civil?, In: T. Hensley, ed., *The Boundaries of Freedom of Expression and Order in American Democracy*, Kent: Ohio State University Press, pp. 49–67.

Estlund, D. (2008) *Democratic Authority*, Princeton: Princeton University Press.

Fishkin, J. (1991) *Democracy and Deliberation*, New Haven: Yale University Press.

Goodin, R. (2008) *Innovating Democracy*, New York: Oxford University Press.

Gould, C. (1988) *Rethinking Democracy*, Cambridge: Cambridge University Press.

Grofman, B. and Feld, S. (1989) Rousseau's General Will: A Condorcetian Perspective, *American Political Science Review* 82, pp. 567–576.

Gutmann, A. and Thompson, D. (2004) *Why Deliberative Democracy?* Princeton: Princeton University Press.

Hardin, R. (2002) The Crippled Epistemology of Extremism, In: B. Albert, ed., *Political Extremism and Rationality*, Cambridge: Cambridge University Press, pp. 3–22.

Kelly, J. (2013) *Framing Democracy*, Princeton: Princeton University Press.

Kingwell, M. (2012) *Unruly Voices: Essays on Democracy, Civility, and the Human Imagination*, Toronto: Biblioasis.

Kull, S. (2004) The Separate Realities of Bush and Kerry Supporters, *PIPA/Knowledge Networks Poll*, www.pipa.org/OnlineReports/Iraq/IraqRealities_Oct04/IraqRealitiesOct04rpt.pdf

Lakoff, G. (2016) *Moral Politics: How Liberals and Conservatives Think*, 3rd edition, Chicago: University of Chicago Press.

Landemore, H. (2013) *Democratic Reason*, Princeton: Princeton University Press.

Lippmann, W. (1922) *Public Opinion*, New York: Free Press.

Lippmann, W. (1925) *The Phantom Public*, New Brunswick: Transaction Publishers.

List, C. and Goodin, R. (2001) Epistemic Democracy: Generalizing the Condorcet Jury Theorem, *Journal of Political Philosophy* 9, pp. 277–306.

Lopez-Guerra, C. (2014) *Democracy and Disenfranchisement*, Cambridge: Cambridge University Press.

Lynch, M. P. (2016) *The Internet of Us*, New York: Norton.

Maskin, E. and Sen, A. (2014) *The Arrow Impossibility Theorem*, New York: Columbia University Press.

Mill, J. (1861) Considerations on Representative Government, In: J. Gray, ed., *On Liberty and Other Essays*, New York: Oxford University Press, pp. 203–470.

Miller, D. (1992) Deliberative Democracy and Social Choice, *Political Studies* 40, pp. 54–67.

Mutz, D. (2006) *Hearing the Other Side*, Cambridge: Cambridge University Press.

Page, S. (2007) *The Difference*, Princeton: Princeton University Press.

Pericles (2011) Funeral Oration, In: S. Cahn, ed., *Political Philosophy: The Essential Texts*, New York: Oxford University Press.

Peter, F. (2009) *Democratic Legitimacy*, New York: Routledge.

Peter, F. (2016) The Epistemic Circumstances of Democracy, In: M. Brady and M. Fricker, eds., *The Epistemic Life of Groups*, New York: Oxford University Press, pp. 133–149.

Pettit, P. (2012) *On the People's Terms*, New York: Oxford University Press.

Plato. (1997) Republic, In: J. Cooper, ed., *Plato: Complete Works*, Indianapolis: Hackett Publishing, pp. 971–1223.

Posner, R. (2003) *Law, Pragmatism, and Democracy*, Cambridge: Harvard University Press.

Rawls, J. (2005) *Political Liberalism*, New York: Columbia University Press.

Schkade, D., Sunstein, C. and Hastie, R. (2007) What Happened On Deliberation Day, *California Law Review* 95 (3), http://scholarship.law.berkeley.edu/californialawreview/vol95/iss3/6

Shapiro, I. (2016) *Politics Against Domination*, Cambridge: Harvard University Press.

Richardson, H. (2010) Public Opinion and Popular Will, In: D. Kahane, D. Weinstock, D. Leydet and M. Williams, eds., *Deliberative Democracy in Practice*, Vancouver: UBC Press, pp. 172–193.

Riker, W. (1982) *Liberalism against Populism*, Long Grove, IL: Waveland Press.

Rogers, M. (2009) *The Undiscovered Dewey*, New York: Columbia University Press.

Rousseau, J. (1988) *The Social Contract, in Rousseau's Political Writings*, New York: Norton.

Sanders, L. (1997) Against Deliberation, *Political Theory* 25, pp. 347–376.

Schumpeter, J. (1942) *Capitalism, Socialism, and Democracy*, New York: Harper.

Somin, I. (2016). *Democracy and Public Ignorance*, 2nd edition, Stanford: Stanford University Press.

Stanley, J. (2015) *How Propaganda Works*, Princeton: Princeton University Press.

Sunstein, C. (1993) *The Partial Constitution*, New York: Oxford University Press.

Sunstein, C. (2003) *Why Societies Need Dissent*, Cambridge: Harvard University Press.

Sunstein, C. (2006) *Infotopia*, New York: Oxford University Press.

Sunstein, C. (2007) *Republic.Com 2.0*, Princeton: Princeton University Press.

Sunstein, C. (2009) *Going to Extremes*, New York: Oxford University Press.

Surowiecki, J. (2004) *The Wisdom of Crowds*, New York: Doubleday.

Talisse, R. (2005) Does Public Ignorance Defeat Deliberative Democracy? *Critical Review* 16, pp. 455–463.

Talisse, R. (2007) *A Pragmatist Philosophy of Democracy*, New York: Routledge.

Talisse, R. (2009) *Democracy and Moral Conflict*, Cambridge: Cambridge University Press.

Talisse, R. (2011) A Farewell to Deweyan Democracy, *Political Studies* 59, pp. 509–526.

Vallier, K. (2014) *Liberal Politics and Public Faith*, New York: Routledge.

Waldron, J. (1989) Democratic Theory and the Public Interest: Condorcet and Rousseau Revisited, *American Political Science Review* 83, pp. 1322–1328.

Walton, D. (2007) *Media Argumentation*, Cambridge: Cambridge University Press.

Young, I. (1997) Communication and the Other: Beyond Deliberative Democracy, In: J. Bohman and W. Rehg, eds., *Deliberative Democracy*, Cambridge: MIT Press, pp. 120–136.

Young, I. (2001) Activist Challenges to Deliberative Democracy, *Political Theory* 29, pp. 670–690.

Young, I. (2002) *Inclusion and Democracy*, New York: Oxford University Press.

Further Reading

Brennan, J. (2016) *Against Democracy*, Princeton: Princeton University Press.

Estlund, D. (2008) *Democratic Authority*, Princeton: Princeton University Press.

Landemore, H. (2013) *Democratic Reason*, Princeton: Princeton University Press.

Landemore, H. and Elster, J. (eds.) (2012) *Collective Wisdom: Principles and Mechanisms*, Cambridge: Cambridge University Press.

Peter, F. (2016) The Epistemic Circumstances of Democracy, In: M. Brady and M. Fricker, eds., *The Epistemic Life of Groups*, New York: Oxford University Press.

Sanders, L. (1997) Against Deliberation, *Political Theory* 25, pp. 347–376.

Somin, I. 2016. *Democracy and Public Ignorance*, 2nd edition, Stanford: Stanford University Press.

Sunstein, C. (2003) *Why Societies Need Dissent*, Cambridge: Harvard University Press.

36

PRAGMATISM AND EPISTEMIC DEMOCRACY

Eva Erman and Niklas Möller

Pragmatism could be described as a philosophical view that gives primacy to human practices, encouraging a way of philosophising more apt to dealing with problems of everyday life. While it has had a major impact on issues in epistemology, metaphysics, meta-ethics and the philosophy of language, relatively little attention has been devoted to political philosophy. This started to change with John Dewey, who placed politics at the heart of pragmatist philosophy. And in the last decades, we have witnessed an increased interest in pragmatism in several debates in political philosophy, not least in democratic theory, where the Deweyan view has had a major impact. Pragmatism in democratic theory today displays a rich variety of doctrines and approaches that are impossible to even try to do justice to here. Instead, this chapter is devoted to reviewing and evaluating the influence of pragmatism in current democratic theory with regard to epistemic aspects of democracy. More narrowly still, we focus on what we see as the three most interesting pragmatist approaches to epistemic democracy in the current literature and discuss possible challenges they face: we have labelled them "democracy as collective problem-solving" inspired by Dewey, "democracy as truth-seeking" inspired by Pierce, and "democracy as stance-taking" inspired by current political realism and non-ideal theory.

Democracy as Collective Problem-Solving

Pragmatist democratic theorists usually describe democracy as a shared political enterprise and a device for collective problem-solving and inquiry. Through a democratic organization, Dewey argued, information can easily spread across the public and help citizens make informed decisions by acting as organized intelligence (Dewey 1935: 56). Dewey depicted this shared political enterprise as a way of life, both on the communal level as "community life" and on the individual level as a personal way of associated living. Acting co-jointly, individuals and their society are seen as an organic whole. In contrast to the view of democracy as a decision procedure applicable only to society's basic institutions, democracy for Dewey is a social organization that impregnates all modes of human association (Dewey 1916, 1927). The good life and human flourishing can only be achieved within a democracy and citizens can only be properly represented insofar as they are "organically related to one another, or are possessed of unity of purpose and interest" (Dewey 1888: 231). Moreover, there is no meaningful *a priori* distinction to be made between ethics and politics for Dewey, since values are constructed to resolve practical problems. In contrast to traditional consequentialist and deontological approaches, criteria of correctness are thus not external but internal to the practice in which the problem occurs (Dewey 1922: 199).

Various criticisms have been levelled at Deweyan democracy. One of the more forceful criticisms is directed at the demanding form of perfectionism it presupposes. Perfectionism usually refers to accounts of the good human life and human well-being. In democratic theory, perfectionists commonly argue that the main task of the political community (the state) is to cultivate among citizens the dispositions and habits required for human flourishing (Kymlicka 1990: 199–203; Talisse 2014: 124). The standard criticism of a perfectionist defense of democracy is that it has difficulty accommodating what John Rawls famously calls "the fact of reasonable pluralism", according to which citizens in modern, pluralist and complex societies reasonably disagree over the nature of human flourishing and the aims of social institutions (Rawls 2005: 36–38). This becomes all the more challenging for Deweyan democracy, which is remarkably demanding by being applied not only to the basic institutions but also to a wide range of social relationships (Talisse 2014: 124).

To respond to these concerns, most Deweyan pragmatists in contemporary democratic theory have weakened or abandoned the arduous communal and perfectionist elements of Dewey's view and instead focused more on democracy as collective inquiry and problem-solving (Putnam 1990; Westbrook 2005; Anderson 2006; Festenstein 2007). Indeed, the idea that democracy is best understood as a community of inquirers has in recent years injected liberal theory and generated a cluster of accounts under the label "pragmatist political liberalism," which draws together strands from pragmatism, Rawls' political liberalism, and epistemic democracy (Festenstein 1997, 2007; Bacon 2010; MacGilvray 2010, 2014).

Anderson's Experimentalist Model

One of the more interesting Deweyan accounts is the experimentalist model of democracy developed by Elizabeth Anderson. In her view, this model has advantages over competing epistemic models of democracy, of which the most influential one rests on the Condorcet Jury Theorem (see, e.g. Cohen 1986).[1] This theorem roughly states that if voters face two options, vote independently of one another and in light of their judgment of what is the right solution, as well as have a greater than 50% probability of being right, then as the number of voters increases the majority vote will increasingly yield the right answer (Condorcet 1995[1785]; Anderson 2006: 11).

There are several problems with the Condorcet model from an epistemic viewpoint of democracy, according to Anderson. First, it works even if voters are epistemically homogeneous, yet an important epistemic case for democracy is precisely that it is able benefit from the diversity of citizens (Anderson 2006: 11). Second, as the Condorcet model presupposes that citizens vote independently, it runs the risk of working against the deliberative qualities of democracy, such as public discussions on matters of common concern before voting. Without such discussions voters are left with their own private preferences as input when deciding on how to cast their vote (Anderson 2006: 11). Moreover, the openness between public space and majoritarian decision-making procedures is essential for citizens to even determine what should count as a problem of public concern in the first place (Habermas 1996: 183; Erman 2016: 277–278). Third, the Condorcet model fails to capture the dynamism of the epistemic functions of democracy, according to Anderson. Whether a law succeeds in solving what it was designed for depends on its consequences, and majorities often decide on an inefficient solution simply because they do not anticipate its consequences. Since the model "suggests that majorities are nearly infallible from the start", it is presumed that they do not need to correct their original policy (Anderson 2006: 12). But democratic decision-making needs feedback and accountability mechanisms, Anderson stresses, to develop better solutions in light of new information about the consequences of policies. However, in focusing only on the moment of voting, the Condorcet model "disables investigation into how to improve the epistemic functioning of democratic institutions beyond the voting booth" (Anderson 2006: 12).

In contrast to the Condorcet model, Anderson argues, the Deweyan experimentalist model is able to accommodate all the constitutive features of democracy above: diversity, discussion and dynamism. Whatever epistemic democrats presume about what Anderson calls "internal" criteria of success for democratic institutions – i.e. procedural criteria of what makes an outcome democratically legitimate or fair – they largely agree that pure internalism neglects the important instrumental functions of democracy and "external" criteria of success – i.e. criteria external to the decision-making process. From an external standpoint, whether a law is successful depends on its external consequences, not on the fairness of the procedure through which it was adopted (Anderson 2006: 10). A strength of the experimentalist model, according to Anderson, is that the universal inclusion of diverse individuals satisfies both the internal and external criteria of success for democratic decision-making. Whereas exclusion both raises suspicion about whether identified problems are truly of general interest to the public and fails to take advantage of citizens' situated knowledge, universal inclusion in the decision process makes maximal use of such knowledge (2006: 14). However, to ensure that voting and deliberation reinforce one another as much as possible, Anderson argues, institutions such as a free press, public opinion pooling, protests, and so on are important feedback and accountability mechanisms necessary to institutionalize fallibilism and an experimental attitude towards policies (2006: 14).

Even if Anderson is correct that the experimentalist model accommodates diversity, discussion and dynamism, it does not give us much support for its superiority. First, it is far from clear to what extent a theorem can be regarded as a full-fledged account or model of democracy. Presumably, it would have to be complemented with several additional features to be represented as a model or account of democracy comparable with Deweyan democracy. Moreover, it seems that a proponent of the Condorcet Theorem may well endorse all the feedback and accountability mechanisms proposed by Anderson as well as endorse fallibilism in the design of democratic institutions. For these reasons, claiming that the Condorcet model "disables investigation into how to improve the epistemic functioning of democratic institutions" seems way too strong. Second, since largely all accounts of deliberative democracy in the contemporary debate (as well as all alternative pragmatist accounts of democracy) seem equally or at least sufficiently fit to accommodate diversity, discussion and dynamism, it is still an open question which approach to epistemic democracy is most favourable.

In our view, this cannot be settled by looking at external criteria of democracy alone. As Anderson acknowledges, internal criteria of success are necessary for any plausible epistemic model. However, Anderson is silent about what internal criteria she defends and how they are justified alongside the external ones. Although universal inclusion is supposed to secure both, very little is said about inclusion as an internal criterion. Since focus is almost exclusively directed at instrumental benefits, Anderson does not explain why citizens, independent of whether the law is correct, have a duty to comply with it. At the same time, to properly assess the superiority of the Deweyan experimentalist model – not only over theorems but also over other pragmatist models as well as models of deliberative democracy – it seems to us that we need a defense of both internal (moral)[2] and external (epistemic) criteria as well as an account of how they hang together.

Democracy as Truth-Seeking

As mentioned above, pragmatism has recently generated a number of accounts in political theory sometimes referred to as "pragmatist political liberalism", which draw together ideas from pragmatism, Rawls' political liberalism and epistemic democracy. However, pragmatist criticism has also been levelled at approaches influenced by Rawls. The motivating force behind the critique is foremost a failure of Rawslian liberal theory to deal with what Robert Talisse calls "the paradox of democratic justification," which emerges from the fact that democracy requires consent among a citizenry combined with the fact that citizens in pluralistic societies inevitably and reasonably disagree on fundamental moral matters. When citizens are deeply divided at the most fundamental moral level, Talisse argues, it would be impossible to offer a moral justification of democracy that is justifiable to all citizens, which is what democracy requires (Talisse 2009: ch. 1 and 2). A similar worry is expressed by Cheryl Misak: "Rawls does not provide us with an independent or neutral justification of the liberal or democratic virtues; he just assumes those virtues" and thereby fails to offer normative resources to those who do not already accept them, such as the Schmittian (Misak 2000: 25, 5).

It is in response to this challenge that pragmatists have set out to justify democracy on purely epistemic grounds, that is, without recourse to any moral values or principles. It is thus a freestanding justification of democracy in the sense that it rests only on epistemic premises (Misak 2000; Talisse 2005; 2007, 2009, 2014; Misak and Talisse 2014). This route is allegedly superior to the Rawlsian alternative because epistemic principles are universally shared despite moral disagreement.

Misak's and Talisse's Pragmatist Epistemic Argument

This freestanding argument – let us call it the "pragmatist epistemic argument" – is an argument of what it is rational to believe given a set of premises that are constitutive of being a thinking person, a believer. In a nutshell, it goes like this:

1 As believers, we are committed to a number of fundamental principles.
2 These fundamental principles entail a number of interpersonal epistemic commitments.
3 From these epistemic commitments, a commitment to democracy follows.
4 Ergo: As believers, we are committed to democracy.

The fundamental principles of step one revolve around truth-seeking and reason-responsiveness. A belief is by definition something that aims to be true, and by being committed to a belief we take on the commitment of giving reasons for it as well as being prepared to abandon it if it turns out not to be justified (Misak 2004: 12–14; Talisse 2009: 87–88).

The second step of the argument is that these fundamental principles entail a set of epistemic commitments or virtues. Misak, for example, argues that a believer is committed to *epistemic honesty* ("following reasons and evidence, rather than self-interest"), *modesty* ("taking your views to be fallible"), *charity* ("willingness to listen to the views of others") and *integrity* ("willingness to uphold the deliberative process, no matter the difficulties encountered") (Misak 2008: 103). Talisse similarly argues that we are committed to "engaging with those whose experiences differ from our own", that "we must seek out new and unfamiliar challenges" and that "the norms of belief entail interpersonal norms of equality, participation, recognition, and inclusion" (Talisse 2014: 127).

The third step, finally, concludes that a commitment to democracy follows from these epistemic commitments. Engaging in reason-giving and inquiry is only possible in an enabling social structure, and so we need to be participants in a community of inquirers in order to fulfill our epistemic commitments. Such participation, Misak and Talisse argue, entails a commitment to a full-blown deliberative democracy (Misak 2000: 94, 106; Talisse 2009: 15, 123).

Two features of this argument are of central importance. First, it is a *coherence* argument. If the believer does not accept democracy, she is incoherent, since she fails to be committed to something which follows from core commitments she cannot abandon (since they are constitutive of being a believer/thinker). Second, the argument is *internal*: not endorsing democracy makes the believer irrational *in her own light,* not from some outside perspective (Talisse 2009: 122–123; Misak and Talisse 2014: 372).

While these features make up a convincing case if successful, it also makes the argument sensitive to criticism. We will here grant the first premise (step one) for the sake of argument. Still, the inference to the second and the third step both face grave difficulties.[3]

Do the fundamental principles justify the epistemic deliberative commitments? Since the epistemic commitments of listening to others, upholding the deliberative process, etc., are clearly conducive to truth-finding, the inference from the first to the second step of the argument might seem correct. The challenge, however, comes from the strong form of this commitment.

There are two main ways of interpreting a commitment to a certain principle or norm: as absolute, allowing for no exceptions, or as defeasible, as a *pro tanto* norm holding for the most part but not always. Talisse and Misak have chosen the former, stronger interpretation. According to Talisse, for example, our truth-aim entails that we "must seek out new and unfamiliar challenges" (2014: 127). And Misak adds that integrity entails upholding the deliberative process "no matter the difficulties encountered" (Misak 2009: 36). While a weaker *pro tanto* interpretation of the epistemic commitments would be easier to defend, Misak and Talisse's absolutist interpretation is in fact necessary for the pragmatist epistemic argument to be successful. A mere *pro tanto* interpretation would fail to provide the sought conclusion that anti-democrats are irrational in their own light, since it could then always be objected that other commitments may trump without threatening irrationality or incoherence.

Necessary as the absolutist interpretation of the epistemic commitments is for the freestanding argument, there are at least two reasons to believe that our commitment to truth is more limited than the argument allows. First, while we aim for our beliefs to be true, this is not our *only* rational concern. For example, our objection to torture and ethically problematic experiments with human subjects are an expression of the idea that gaining knowledge, while important, is not an absolute commitment.

A second limitation has both a metaphysical and psychological dimension. Whereas there are endless propositions (true and false) out there, we are all both cognitively and temporally limited. So while we may grant that we should revise a belief when faced with convincing arguments against it, it would be a self-defeating commitment were we forced to listen to all arguments for and against every belief we hold, not to mention having to search for new perspectives and challenges at all costs.

In sum, while we may always *aim* for truth rather than falsehoods, the epistemic commitments Misak and Talisse argue for do not follow from this aim. Talisse argues that "[w]ere it not the case that we took our moral and political beliefs to be subject to [the epistemic premises], there would be no need to react in any way to our opponents, much less to discredit them" (Talisse 2010: 46). We agree, but a proper reaction may take many forms. We may be reluctant to uphold (not to mention *at any cost*) the deliberative process with people we think are unlikely to contribute anything of worth, and we may think there are times when the search for the truth in a certain topic has to give way to other concerns. Still, we may still perfectly well endorse the aim for truth in the relevant, pragmatist sense.

Do the epistemic commitments justify deliberative democracy? So far we have shown that several challenges face the claim that the epistemic commitments of step two follow from the fundamental epistemic principles of step 1. However, even if we *endorse* the epistemic commitments of step two, democracy (step three) does not seem to follow.

In their argument, Misak and Talisse point out that a commitment to *equality, participation* and *inclusion* constitute central tenets of democracy. The content of the epistemic commitments is that we are equally entitled to state our beliefs and support them with reasons, and that we therefore should be included and have a right to participate in the epistemic enterprise, since the ultimate goal is truth (Misak 2008: 94; Talisse 2009: 124–125). However, the *democratic* counter-parts of equality, participation and inclusion are different. Being equally entitled to state our beliefs and engage in reason-exchange, for example, is different from the democratic idea that we are equally entitled to influence the *decision-making*. Indeed, even having *no say* in the decision-making seems compatible with the former. Many alternatives to democracy may respect the epistemic commitment to equality, such as different forms of expert rule or meritocracy securing the relevant conditions for citizens as epistemic peers and equal participants in the epistemic enterprise – e.g. freedom of speech and expression, freedom of information etc. – but still distribute political power according to merit.

The same is true for participation and inclusion, which in their democratic form differ substantially from the epistemic version. Democratic participation should of course include reason-exchange, but ultimately its aim is to secure that a sufficient number of individuals in a democracy takes part in the decision-making. And democratic inclusion is ultimately about whom should be included in this decision-making. This so-called "boundary problem" in democratic theory clearly raises questions other than the purely epistemic question of truth-finding. Here, theorists have mainly argued either for an "all affected interests principle" as a criterion of inclusion – that anyone whose interests are significantly affected by a decision should have a say in the decision-making – or an "all subjected principle" – that all subjected to the policies and laws should have a say in their making (see e.g. Habermas 1996; Goodin 2007; Abizadeh 2012; Erman 2014). However, no one in this debate would suggest that the *epistemic* criterion to include anyone with a good argument in the epistemic endeavor applies directly to *democratic* inclusion. The justifications given for the all-affected or all-subjected principles are *moral* (or at least extra-epistemic), such as the egalitarian idea that people's fundamental interests should count equally (all affected) or that people should be the authors of their own laws in order for the laws to be binding upon them (all subjected). For Misak and Talisse's freestanding argument, however, the justification must be purely epistemic. But no such argument is offered.

This justificatory lack is especially pressing since such an epistemic criterion seems to have counter-intuitive consequences from the standpoint of democracy: while there may be good reasons for including any reasonable *argument* for, say, the best policy of parental allowance, it seems far-fetched to take this as entailing a Swede a right to vote on Brazilian policies on the matter. It seems to us that a purely epistemic justification of democracy is a chimera. Democracy needs to be grounded in values, and such values must go beyond the purely epistemic.

Democracy as Stance-Taking

Interestingly, another pragmatist approach to epistemic democracy has recently emerged in political philosophy that also wishes to eschew moral principles in theorizing political legitimacy. Far from a unified position, it is best described as a recent current in pragmatist democratic theory that draws inspiration from non-ideal theory and political realism.

In brief, non-ideal theory has emerged as a criticism of mainstream liberal theory ("ideal theory") – represented by egalitarians such as Rawls and Dworkin – for not taking seriously the non-ideal circumstances under which principles of justice are supposed to be justified and applied. Above all, non-ideal theorists have highlighted problems pertaining to action-guidance, practical import and feasibility (e.g. Mills 2005: 165–184; Farrelly 2007: 844–864; Sen 2009). A similar criticism against ideal theory has emerged in democratic theory, where political realism throws doubt on ideal theory's commitment to political moralism. According to political realists, political moralism wrongly regards the political domain mainly as an arena for the application of moral principles. By giving priority to morality over politics, realists argue, political moralism overlooks that the political is an autonomous domain with its own distinctive conditions, normative sources and standards. Hence realists reject political moralism and its attempt to justify principles of political legitimacy through some pre-political principle and instead emphasize that principles of political legitimacy must be justified *within* the political (e.g. Williams 2005; Geuss 2008; Bellamy 2010; Galston 2010; Sleat 2010; cf Erman and Möller 2013: 215–216).

It is perhaps not strange that pragmatists find these ideas attractive. As Matthew Festenstein points out, there are several shared commitments between pragmatism and political realism, such as to the primacy of practice, to the focus on agency, and to the doubts about "antecedent a priori criteria" for success external to practice, experience and social learning (Festenstein 2016: 42). Some argue that classical pragmatism in fact anticipates contemporary non-ideal theory and political realism (Koopman 2016: 28).

Fossen's Socio-Pragmatic Project

The most systematic attempt to develop a pragmatist account in democratic theory in this realist and non-ideal spirit has recently been made by Thomas Fossen, who utilizes Robert Brandom's socio-pragmatic account of language and meaning to theorize political legitimacy. According to some pragmatists, Fossen's approach is the most promising to date to escape the predominant political moralism in mainstream political philosophy (Festenstein 2016).[4]

In Fossen's reading of political moralism (which he labels "normativism"), morality is seen as prior to politics in the sense that the question about what political legitimacy is, is answered by "applying a particular form of moral knowledge," which comes in the shape of moral principles and criteria that are supposed to tell us under what conditions a political authority has a right to rule (Fossen 2013: 429–430). Furthermore, moralists seek a "privileged standpoint" from where to offer a general and definitive theoretical solution concerning legitimacy (2013: 432, 442, 446). From a Brandomian perspective, by contrast, we start "by asking what one does in taking authority to be legitimate, rather than what it means for authority to be legitimate" (2013: 432). On this socio-pragmatic view, politics is understood as a practice of *stance-taking*, such that calling a political authority legitimate is to make explicit a political stance towards it (Fossen 2013: 428). The theoretical concept of political legitimacy labels the political predicament to speak and act "to alter the patterns of commitments and entitlements subjects and authorities attribute to one another, convincing others to shift their stances and rethink their responsibilities" (Fossen 2013: 439). Further, Fossen emphasizes the contestatory and agonistic character of politics (Fossen 2014).[5]

What makes this approach a genuine alternative to mainstream moralist approaches, in Fossen's view, is that what is distinctly political about political legitimacy is explained in terms of a practical situation revolving around attempts to rule (2013: 434, 428). By under-standing the concept of legitimacy in terms of the pragmatic role it plays in political situations, Fossen argues that distinguishing what is actually legitimate cannot be done from a disengaged and "privileged standpoint" as supposed by political moralism (2013: 446), but is something that must be settled provisionally through lived experience (2013: 445–446). While Fossen does not (yet) offer an alternative first-order normative theory of legitimacy, he claims to provide an alternative by supplying a pragmatist framework for answering the question of what makes an authority legitimate, which leads to a number of constraints on what a positive normative account of legitimacy should look like, pointing to a new way of going forward when theorizing legitimacy. He also points to some recent approaches, notably those of James Tully and Aletta Norval, that "take us a bit further" on this alternative path (Tully 1989; Norval 2006).

Fossen thus puts forward a number of meta-normative constraints on how the theorist should view political legitimacy, which allegedly would generate alternative normative theories. For example, the theorist is supposed to recast the predicament in a pragmatic way to enable her to "frame political judgment as an ongoing task that calls for practical engagement, rather than a philosophical problem calling for a general solution" (Fossen 2013: 442). A fundamental challenge for Fossen's account, however, is that his considerations are for the most part direct applications of Brandom's *fully general* theory of meaning. So when Fossen says that we may elucidate explicitly claiming legitimacy in terms of stance-taking, this is true only in a sense that does not distinguish legitimacy from any other concept: we may replace "legitimacy" not only with any political term but with *any term at all* (Erman and Möller 2014: 492).

Another example of this challenge concerns Fossen's meta-constraint that we should "explicate what is political about political legitimacy in terms of the kind of social practice in which 'legitimacy' is used in a political sense, that is, in terms of where and how the concept occurs" (Fossen 2013: 434). This application of Brandom's view is completely generic as well; so we may say that we explicate what is mathematical about mathematical subtraction in terms of the kind of social practice in which "subtraction" is used in a mathematical sense, that is, in terms of where and how the concept occurs. On Brandom's account, meaning is conferred by the practice in which our performances are to be found, and that goes for the natural kind concepts that figure in our explanation of scientific phenomena (mass, mammal) as well as mathematical concepts (addition, imaginary numbers) and even semantic ones (truth, meaning) (Brandom 1994).

Fossen thus takes a grounding feature of Brandom's systematic account, how practice grounds meaning, and concludes that political *engagement* rather than theory is the solution when we focus on the political domain. But since he has utilized fully general features of Brandom's account, Fossen's conclusions about *political* judgment goes for *any* judgment, and so when Fossen says that we should "frame political judgment as an ongoing task that calls for practical engagement, rather than a philosophical problem calling for a general solution" (2013: 442) he must conclude that *no* problem calls for a general solution. This turns Brandom's account into an extremely radical, anti-theoretical theory. Such a theory would come at a great cost, since the prospect for the generality of mathematics, logics, and natural science would be undermined. Fortunately, Brandom is in no way making such claims. On his account, there is nothing troubling with making explicit theoretical commitments that are general in scope. On the contrary, *he* puts forward a systematic theoretical account of meaning and content – a solution, if you will – which definitely has general pretensions (Erman and Möller 2014: 492).

However, the problem with Fossen's pragmatist account is not only that the inference from Brandom's theory to meta-normative constraints on theories of legitimacy does not go through. He has also not shown that his socio-pragmatist perspective of legitimacy suggests other first-order normative theories than those put forward by moralists. On the contrary, we have good reasons to believe that nothing in normative democratic theory is in fact changed by the socio-pragmatist viewpoint. The reason is twofold: first, there seems to be no reason for moralists to deny the aspects of linguistic practice extracted from Brandom's account; second, Fossen's own characterization of political legitimacy is conventional and therefore congenial to any normative account, moralist or other.

With regard to the former, Brandom's account offers a way of understanding what we do (i.e., how meaning is conferred through practice), but it is not telling us to do anything differently from what we already do. With regard to the latter, moralists may well agree that the role of legitimacy in political speech and action revolves around the "attempt to rule" (Fossen 2013: 436) and involves stance-taking between subjects and authorities, in particular since the term "political legitimacy" in this literature is described as the right to rule.[6]

Notes

1 Apart from the Condorcet Theorem, Anderson also discusses the Diversity Trumps Ability Theorem.
2 As we will see in the third section, though, political realists prefer to label such considerations normative rather than moral in theorizing political legitimacy.
3 For a comprehensive analysis of Misak and Talisse, see Erman and Möller (2016).
4 In the debate on political legitimacy, typical moralists ("normativists") according to Fossen, are Nagel (1991); Simmons (1999); Buchanan (2002); and Christiano (2004).
5 For an in-depth analysis of Fossen's Brandomian project, see Erman and Möller (2014).
6 See, e.g. the alleged moralist Allen Buchanan (2002: 703).

References

Abizadeh, A. (2012) On the Demos and Its Kin: Nationalism, Democracy, and the Boundary Problem. *American Political Science Review*, 104, pp. 867–882.
Anderson, E. (2006) The Epistemology of Democracy. *Episteme*, 3(1–2), pp. 8–22.
Bacon, M. (2010) The Politics of Truth: A Critique of Peircean Deliberative Democracy. *Philosophy & Social Criticism*, 36, pp. 1075–1091.
Bellamy, R. (2010) Dirty Hands and Clean Gloves: Liberal Ideals and Real Politics. *European Journal of Political Theory*, 9, pp. 412–430.
Brandom, R. (1994) *Making It Explicit*. Cambridge, MA: Harvard University Press.
Buchanan, A. (2002) Political Legitimacy and Democracy. *Ethics*, 112, pp. 689–719.
Christiano, T. (2004) The Authority of Democracy. *The Journal of Political Philosophy*, 12, pp. 266–290.
Cohen, J. (1986) An Epistemic Conception of Democracy. *Ethics*, 97(1), pp. 26–38.
Condorcet, M. de (1995[1785]) An Essay on the Application of Analysis to the Probability of Decisions Rendered by a Plurality of Votes. In I. McLean and A. Urken, eds., *Classics of Social Choice*. Ann Arbor: University of Michigan Press, pp. 91–112.
Dewey, J. (1888) The Ethics of Democracy. In J. Boydston, ed., *John Dewey, the Early Works 1882–88, Vol. 1.* Carbondale: Southern Illinois University Press, pp. 227–252.
Dewey, J. (1916) Democracy and Education. In J. Boydston, ed., *John Dewey, the Middle Works, Vol. 9.* Carbondale: Southern Illinois University Press.
Dewey, J. (1922) Human Nature and Conduct. In J. Boydston, ed., *John Dewey, the Middle Works, Vol. 14.* Carbondale: Southern Illinois University Press.
Dewey, J. (1927) The Public and Its Problems. In J. Boydston, ed., *John Dewey, the Later Works, Vol. 2.* Carbondale: Southern Illinois University Press, pp. 235–372.
Dewey, J. (1935) Liberalism and Social Action. In J. Boydston, ed., *John Dewey, the Later Works, Vol. 11.* Carbondale: Southern Illinois University Press, pp. 1–65.
Erman, E. (2014) The Boundary Problem and the Ideal of Democracy. *Constellations*, 21, pp. 535–546.
Erman, E. (2016) Representation, Equality, and Inclusion in Deliberative Systems: Desiderata for a Good Account. *Critical Review of International Social and Political Philosophy*, 19(3), pp. 263–282.
Erman, E. and Möller, N. (2013) Political Legitimacy in the Real Normative World: The Priority of Morality and the Autonomy of the Political. *British Journal of Political Science*, 45, pp. 215–233.
Erman, E. and Möller, N. (2014) Brandom and Political Philosophy. *The Journal of Political Philosophy*, 22(4), pp. 486–498.
Erman, E. and Möller, N. (2016) Why Democracy Cannot be Grounded in Epistemic Principles. *Social Theory & Practice*, 42(3), pp. 449–473.
Farrelly, C. (2007) Justice in Ideal Theory: A Refutation. *Political Studies*, 55, pp. 844–864.
Festenstein, M. (2007) Inquiry and Democracy. In P. Baert and B. Turner, eds., *Pragmatism and European Social Theory*. Cambridge: Bardwell Press, pp. 115–136.
Festenstein, M. (2016) Pragmatism, Realism and Moralism. *Political Studies Review*, 14(1), pp. 39–49.
Fossen, T. (2013) Taking Stances, Contesting Commitments: Political Legitimacy and the Pragmatic Turn. *Journal of Political Philosophy*, 21, pp. 426–450.
Fossen, T. (2014) Politicizing Brandom's Pragmatism: Normativity and the Agonal Character of Social Practice. *European Journal of Philosophy*, 22(3), pp. 371–395.
Galston, W. (2010) Realism in Political Theory. *European Journal of Political Theory*, 9, pp. 385–411.
Geuss, R. (2008) *Philosophy and Real Politics*. Princeton, NJ: Princeton University Press.
Goodin, R. (2007) Enfranchising All Affected Interests and Its Alternatives. *Philosophy & Public Affairs*, 35, pp. 40–68.

Habermas, J. (1996) *Between Facts and Norms*. Trans., W. Rehg, Cambridge, MA: MIT Press.

Koopman, C. (2016) Unruly Pluralism and Inclusive Tolerance: The Normative Contribution of Jamesian Pragmatism to Non-ideal Theory. *Political Studies Review*, 14(1), pp. 27–38.

Kymlicka, W. (1990) *Contemporary Political Philosophy*. Oxford: Oxford University Press.

MacGilvray, E. (2010) Reply to Festenstein. *Contemporary Political Theory*, 9, pp. 50–55.

MacGilvray, E. (2014) Democratic Doubts: Pragmatism and the Epistemic Defense of Democracy. *Journal of Political Philosophy*, 22, pp. 105–123.

Mills, C. (2005) 'Ideal Theory' as Ideology. *Hypathia*, 20, pp. 165–184.

Misak, C. (2000) *Truth, Morality, Politics: Pragmatism and Deliberation*. New York: Routledge.

Misak, C. (2004) *Truth and the End of Inquiry: A Peircean Account of Truth*, 2nd ed. Oxford: Clarendon Press.

Misak, C. (2008) A Culture of Justification: The Pragmatist's Epistemic Argument for Democracy. *Episteme*, 5, pp. 94–105.

Misak, C. (2009). Truth and Democracy: Pragmatism and the Deliberative Virtues. In R. Geenens et al., eds., *Does Truth Matter? Democracy and Public Space*, Berlin: Springer, pp. 29–39.

Misak, C. and Talisse, R. (2014) Pragmatist Epistemology and Democratic Theory: A Reply to Eric MacGilvray. *Journal of Political Philosophy*, 22(3), pp. 366–376.

Nagel, T. (1991) *Equality and Partiality*. Oxford: Oxford University Press.

Norval, A. (2006) Democratic Identification: A Wittgensteinian Approach. *Political Theory*, 34, pp. 229–255.

Putnam, H. (1990) A Reconsideration of Deweyan Democracy. *Southern California Law Review*, 63, pp. 1671–1697.

Rawls, J. (2005) *Political Liberalism*. New York: Columbia University Press.

Sen, A. (2009) *The Idea of Justice*. Cambridge, MA: Harvard University Press.

Simmons, J. (1999) Justification and Legitimacy. *Ethics*, 109, pp. 739–771.

Sleat, M. (2010) Bernard Williams and the Possibility of a Realist Political Theory. *European Journal of Political Theory*, 9, pp. 485–503.

Talisse, R. (2005) *Democracy After Liberalism*. New York: Routledge.

Talisse, R. (2007) *A Pragmatist Philosophy of Democracy*. New York: Routledge.

Talisse, R. (2009) *Democracy and Moral Conflict*. New York: Cambridge University Press.

Talisse, R. (2010) Reply to Festenstein. *Contemporary Political Theory*, 9, pp. 45–49.

Talisse, R. (2014) Pragmatist Political Philosophy. *Philosophy Compass*, 9, pp. 123–130.

Tully, J. (1989) Wittgenstein and Political Philosophy: Understanding Practices of Critical Reflection. *Political Theory*, 17, pp. 172–204.

Westbrook, R. (2005) *Democratic Hope: Pragmatism and the Politics of Truth*. Ithaca, NY: Cornell University Press.

Williams, B. (2005) *In the Beginning Was the Deed: Realism and Moralism in Political Argument*, G. Hawthorn (ed.). Oxford: Princeton University Press.

Further Reading

Erman, E. and Möller, N. (2018) *The Practical Turn in Political Theory*. Edinburgh: Edinburgh University Press.

Festenstein, M. (1997) *Pragmatism and Political Theory*. Chicago: University of Chicago Press.

Gutman, A. and Thompson, D. (2009) *Why Deliberative Democracy?* Princeton: Princeton University Press.

Misak, C. (2016) *Cambridge Pragmatism: From Peirce and James to Ramsey and Wittgenstein*. Oxford: Oxford University Press.

37

EPISTEMIC PROCEDURALISM

Michael Fuerstein

Introduction

Pure epistemic arguments for democracy defend democratic institutions and procedures by reference to their tendency to produce good decision outcomes.[1] Pure epistemic arguments thus point to the tendency of democracies to make decisions that protect human rights and civil liberties, promote justice, protect against ecological disasters, avoid war, etc. (Arneson 2004; Ober 2008; Landemore 2013). Pure procedural arguments for democracy focus instead on the respects in which democracy constitutes a morally good procedure for making those decisions, independently of their outcomes. Pure procedural arguments thus point to the fact that democratic procedures are fair, egalitarian, and/or respectful in the right ways, without regard for whether the decisions thereby produced tend to be justice-promoting, rights-protecting, etc. (Waldron 1999; Christiano 2008).[2]

In general terms, epistemic proceduralism (EP) offers a defense of democracy that combines elements of both epistemic and procedural arguments. In David Estlund's canonical formulation, it holds that "democratic laws are legitimate and authoritative because they are produced by a procedure with a tendency to make correct decisions" (Estlund 2008: 8). Crucially, though, this condition is not sufficient. The legitimacy and authoritativeness of democratic procedures also depends on the fact that they are "acceptable from all qualified points of view" (Estlund 2008: 41). Thus, EP is epistemic insofar as it makes reference to the tendency of democracy to produce "correct" decisions. And EP is procedural insofar as it focuses on outcome-independent virtues of democratic procedures, i.e., their acceptability from all "qualified" perspectives. EP is also procedural in a second respect insofar as it defends democracy by reference to the epistemic qualities of its characteristic procedures rather than epistemic qualities of decisions themselves. Thus, for example, one might hold that democratic decisions are legitimate strictly insofar as they conform to the relevant correctness standard. EP rejects this stronger epistemic requirement, however. It accepts the legitimacy and authoritativeness of individual decisions that are "incorrect" by epistemic standards just so long as the procedures which produce them have a sufficient tendency to get things right and are acceptable from all qualified points of view.

In a broader context, EP has been perhaps the most prominent view amidst a wider resurgence of epistemic arguments for democracy, and a wider interest in democracy's epistemic features. A long tradition of democratic naysayers, going back to Plato (2000) and continuing up to the present, has argued that the uninformed masses could never be qualified to make good political decisions. Lacking time, virtue, and expertise, the citizenry at large would tend to rule as a reckless mob. One traditional defense against this sort of argument is to suggest that democracy's virtues as a fair procedure trump any such concerns. But that response seems unsatisfactory if democratic decisions are really as bad as the critics claim. Thus, in recent years, democratic theorists have drawn on some new (or rekindled) resources to challenge the presumption of democracy's epistemic deficiencies. The Condorcet Jury Theorem and the Diversity Trumps Ability theorem, in particular, both offer formal results that support a "wisdom of crowds" argument, according to which large groups of non-expert decision makers tend under certain conditions to beat out smaller and/or more elite groups (Grofman and Feld 1988; List and Goodin 2001; Hong and Page 2004). Likewise, the empirical work of James Fishkin and others suggests that properly structured forms of group deliberation can substantially enhance the tendency of political decision-making to reflect important background information (Fishkin 2009). But it is at best unclear how well the background conditions underlying these results hold up when applied at scale in real world politics (Carpini et al. 2004; Steiner 2012).

Thus, both procedural and epistemic arguments seem to have a natural role to play in justifying democracy. And yet both arguments also seem to confront important objections when taken on their own. In general terms, then, the success of EP depends on how well it is able to exploit the resources of both these types of argument while, at the same time, avoiding the crucial limitations they reveal when considered independently. Below, we will consider the apparent virtues of the view, the primary objections to it, and the crucial interpretive issues on which it depends. Since David Estlund's version of EP has been dominant in the scholarly literature, it will be our primary focus. However, Fabienne Peter's important alternative will also be discussed.

The Primary Argument for EP

Given the enormous complexity and difficulty of political decision-making, the argument for democracy seems, at first blush, to be absurd. On Plato's famous analogy, democracy seems to be the equivalent of turning over the responsibility for steering a ship to warring factions of drunken, untrained sailors. That kind of argument is echoed by more recent critics, such as Bryan Caplan, who points to survey data suggesting that democratic citizens are, in general, hopelessly misinformed on basic matters of relevant social science (economics in particular) (Caplan 2007). Such worries are easily reinforced by casual observations of the state of public opinion on such matters as climate change.

Given these concerns, it is tempting to focus on the fact that democracies make decisions in a free and fair way, even if those decisions often fail to reflect important forms of evidence and expertise. The procedural fairness of democracy is reflected, at the most fundamental level, in the basic principle of "one citizen, one vote," along with the standard package of protections for civil liberties that goes along with the voting franchise. In recent decades democratic theory has been overtaken by the idea of "deliberative democracy," which characterizes the ideal of democracy in terms of an inclusive, respectful exchange of arguments about matters of public concern (Cohen 1989; Bohman and Rehg 1997). From this point of view, the basic notion of fairness and equality embodied in voting procedures can be supplemented by a richer notion of reciprocity and respect embodied in this kind of broad, deliberative process (Gutmann and Thompson 1996).

There are a few important problems, however, with procedural arguments when they are taken on their own.

(i) *Can procedural merits alone differentiate democracy from alternatives?*

The first problem, as Estlund emphasizes, is that the procedural norms to which democrats tend to appeal do not clearly favor democracy over a range of decision-making alternatives.

Estlund thus asks us to consider a couple of alternatives to conventional democratic decision-making (Estlund 2008: 65–84). On one alternative, we make political decisions by soliciting policy preferences from all citizens and then choosing among them using a "coin flip" or some other random selection mechanism. On another alternative, we govern via "queen for a day": every day a different citizen is randomly appointed to serve as an all-powerful decision-making dictator. Both of these options give all citizens an equal chance to have their policy views realized. And both of these options appear to employ a fair means of selecting from among the various views distributed amongst the citizenry. It thus seems that a full justification of democracy must appeal to something else besides these procedural considerations. Under these conditions, the tendency of democracy to get things right – if it has such a tendency – appears to be the obvious "something else" that would set it apart from fair but non-democratic alternatives.

Relatedly, one might point out that there is a wide range of specific forms that conventional democracy takes, including various forms of majoritarianism, plurality rule, run-off mechanisms, parliamentary rules for agenda-setting, and devices for assigning representation. Democracies also incorporate a range of non-democratic mechanisms into their standard operation, including super majoritarian rules (e.g., constitutional provisions) and the bureaucratic delegation of various policy objectives. Thus, even if one takes for granted that democracy defeats alternatives like queen-for-a-day on procedural grounds, it remains difficult to see how procedural considerations alone could support a rational choice among the infinite array of specific forms that democratic decision-making might take. Here, once again, epistemic considerations appear to be a compelling, if only partial, way of supporting these kinds of specific institutional decisions.

As an ideal, deliberative democracy seems similarly vulnerable to these kinds of objections. Deliberative engagement very plausibly reflects – at its best – a certain kind of egalitarian respect among citizens. Taking the arguments of others seriously and responding to them in a reciprocal spirit seems to manifest a deep regard for their autonomy and equal status as citizens. But deliberation is also an activity which seems to have intrinsically epistemic elements: it is hard to make sense of the endeavor to present and receive good arguments, to be faithful to the evidence, and to present information, unless these activities are in some way oriented towards the truth (Fuerstein 2014).

(ii) *Are procedural merits sufficient when weighed against epistemic flaws?*

If we imagine a democratic population freely and fairly deciding (by majority vote, for example) to enslave some minority, it seems doubtful that procedural merits alone could justify the decision. Likewise, if a citizenry consistently decides to implement policies with catastrophic effects – consider our present climate policy, for example – the fact that those policies are freely and fairly chosen shouldn't suffice to vindicate the democratic system. Thus, even if democracy is not the best system, or even a very good system from an epistemic point of view, some minimal threshold of epistemic adequacy seems at least to be a necessary condition for the system's validity.

If purely procedural approaches confront crucial challenges, purely epistemic approaches seem equally vulnerable to important objections.

(i) *The "expert/boss fallacy"*

In seeking to justify democracy, it is not enough to show that it is, in general terms, a system with great merit. As a political system, democracy involves the right to rule, i.e., to use coercive power and, in that respect, it seems to require a very specific kind of justification. As Estlund observes, the mere fact that someone is an expert in some domain does not in itself entail that he/she has the right to rule over others. The belief that expertise does entail the right to rule is thus what Estlund labels the "expert/boss fallacy" (2008: 22–39). Certainly, it is plausible that expertise in some domain gives other individuals a reason to endorse their right to rule. But that still remains distinct from the claim that expertise in itself entails such a right. Relatedly, as Estlund notes, the mere fact that some individual is an expert political ruler does not mean that everyone knows or believes that the individual is an expert. In general, within the liberal tradition, legitimacy is tied in crucial ways to consent, because consensual rule is a basic condition of being ruled without sacrificing fundamental freedoms.

If expertise alone is not enough, then, it looks as if it must be supplemented by some kind of procedural requirement grounded in consent: the validity of the democratic system depends in part on the fact that it would under appropriate conditions be accepted by all appropriate or qualified parties. Estlund refers to this as the "Qualified Acceptability" requirement (Estlund 2008: 40–64). The precise contents of the requirement depend on how one spells out the idea of "qualified" parties and, likewise, how one interprets the counterfactual notion of "acceptability." Exploring these issues in full detail exceeds the scope of this entry, but it is worth noting that, by coupling epistemic arguments to this kind of acceptability requirement, EP brings itself very much in line with post-Rawlsian "public reason" liberalism which likewise treats idealized acceptability as the definitive condition of legitimacy. Like public reason views more generally, EP must grapple with a range of concerns about the acceptability ideal: Whose acceptance matters? What happens to the "non-qualified"? And how do we make the counterfactual calculation of acceptability in relation to an agent's actual beliefs? One could of course try to abandon the acceptability requirement altogether, but one would then need an alternative response to the challenge presented by the expert/boss fallacy.

(ii) *Is the truth safe for democracy?*

A second problem with purely epistemic approaches to justifying democracy is the one that Plato originally introduced: What if democracy just isn't very good from an epistemic point of view? Or, more optimistically, what if it is pretty good relative to alternatives, but not the best? One might wonder, as Estlund puts it, whether the truth is "safe" for democracy (24). As I noted earlier, there has been some promising, empirically informed work of late suggesting that, at least under the right conditions, democracy might be quite good from an epistemic point of view, and this has prompted some to pursue a purely (or at least very strongly) epistemic approach. Historically, John Dewey and John Stuart Mill also attributed substantial epistemic merits to democracy (Dewey 1954; Mill 1991). But there remains substantial evidence against those merits (Brennan 2016), at least if one takes democracy as it is rather than as it could be under the best conditions. From this point of view, introducing procedural elements to the defense of democracy can be seen as a kind of bet-hedging approach. Even if democracy is not epistemically the best available system, one could try to argue that it is the best among those that surpass a necessary condition of procedural legitimacy. This is Estlund's strategy, and it has the effect of lowering, while still preserving, the epistemic bar.

Defining the Standard of Epistemic Reliability

There are a few different issues that arise in thinking about the epistemic reliability of democracy. One concerns the rate of epistemic success that we attribute to democracy. Estlund holds that democracy can be vindicated as the "best" system among those that satisfy the procedural requirement of qualified acceptability. The fact that it is the best among those procedurally legitimate is not enough however; as noted above, it seems necessary that a political system surpass some minimal threshold of epistemic reliability. For Estlund, the threshold is randomness. That is, it is a condition of democracy's authoritativeness and legitimacy that it achieves correct answers to political questions at a better than random rate (Estlund 2008: 98–116). This kind of standard, however, introduces a variety of vexing questions about probability. What is the baseline rate of success against which we are to define "better than random"? And how should we define the set of possible policies that could be implemented? Is any conceivable policy a member of the set? Or only those existing on the agenda (Gaus 2011)? The answers to such questions could make a difference to our assessment of democracy relative to alternatives, whether or not one goes with Estlund's "better than random" threshold. In addition, one of the primary virtues of democracy is arguably that it constructs, in a fair way, the very set of policy options to be considered by a political community (Anderson 2008). This creates a further complication in defining the set of policy options against which epistemic success is to be measured.

A second issue in this context concerns the demandingness of the reliability standard itself. Why is "better than random" good enough, particularly if there are alternatives to democracy that would do much better? If an aristocratic regime would protect human rights at a 95% rate, but democracy does it at a 51% rate, then it isn't obvious that democracy's "better-than-randomness" should be satisfactory. The problem here is that, once one concedes that epistemic considerations should play some role in justifying democracy, it is not clear exactly why epistemic considerations don't push us toward some fairly demanding standard. Are procedural considerations strong enough to justify that 44% difference in human rights-reliability? Maybe, but it's not clear exactly why that is the case. But if a more demanding epistemic standard is in fact the right one, we will be stuck once again with the worry that the truth is not safe for democracy.

A third issue concerns the particular moral standard of values that provides content to the correctness standard (Gaus 2011). A classical liberal, for example, will argue that the priority for government is avoiding coercion. A Marxist, however, will argue that the priority for a government is mitigating or eliminating structural injustices in the economic system. Pacifists will argue that correctness involves avoiding war at all costs. Humanitarians will argue that correctness requires intervening to prevent genocide, even if that requires engaging in the killing of some innocents. Etcetera. The problem is that there does not seem to be any way of applying a correctness standard without privileging moral commitments which themselves are legitimately contested. One possible line of response is to limit the applicable correctness standard to a circumscribed list of more-or-less universally accepted commitments. Estlund's particular strategy is to focus on a list of "primary bads" – such as war and famine – and argue that we can assess epistemic reliability by focusing on the rate at which political regimes avoid these things (Estlund 2008: 160). But even if there is some such list, there is likely to be significant disagreement about the relative priority of the items on that list as weighed against others not on the list. That may undermine the significance of this particular, circumscribed metric of epistemic reliability.

Meeting the Procedural Standard

(i) *Can consent-based procedural requirements pass their own test?*

Is the principle that a procedure is only legitimate if it is acceptable to all qualified points of view (Estlund's "qualified acceptability" principle) itself acceptable to all qualified points of view? Critics of Estlund have noted that there are plenty of philosophers out there who disagree with his particular conception of legitimacy (Copp 2011). It is possible, of course, that all of these philosophers are unqualified in Estlund's sense merely in virtue of having false beliefs about (some aspects of) the theory of legitimacy (Estlund 2011: 362–365). At least on its face, however, that seems to make Estlund's standard of who is qualified implausibly demanding. One thus worries that the qualified acceptability requirement itself fails the test of qualified acceptability. Any consent-based standard is likely to confront concerns of this kind.

(ii) *Can democracy meet the qualified acceptability standard?*

Is universal suffrage subject to no qualified rejection, even possible qualified rejection? Interestingly, there are some contemporary political theorists working within the mainstream Western liberal framework defending "lottocratic" alternatives to democracy, which employ a random selection of representatives rather than the standard voting model (Guerrero 2014). There are others arguing for more substantial elements of technocracy within the political system (Brennan 2016). And there are yet others defending more strongly aristocratic Confucian alternatives to the democratic model (Bell 2015). Whether or not any of these possibilities can actually be vindicated over democracy is very much an open question. Nonetheless, they suggest that conventional democracy is at least vulnerable to qualified objections. One thus worries that there is no system at all which survives all possible qualified objections. Perhaps the qualified acceptability requirement is simply too demanding.

In response, Estlund argues that democracy has default advantages over many alternatives insofar as it is premised on the fundamentally equal status of all. Systems that presuppose "invidious comparisons," by contrast, have a higher bar to justification because they are less likely to be acceptable to all qualified points of view (Estlund 2008: 35–37). Still, even if the bar to justifying aristocracy is higher than it is for democracy, that doesn't quite show that there are no reasonable aristocratic objections to democracy. One way of handling this problem is to attribute some kind of default status to democracy, such that it counts as justified unless there is any alternative which lacks qualified rejections. But that seems to beg the question against non-democratic possibilities. Perhaps a more attractive response would be for the epistemic proceduralist to relax the acceptability requirement. Perhaps it is enough that democracy is widely acceptable to qualified parties, even if there remain possible qualified objections. Or perhaps the actual wide acceptance of democracy is sufficient (Copp 2011).

Fabienne Peter's Alternative: "Pure Epistemic Proceduralism"

Earlier, we observed that the content of the epistemic standards by which democracy is to be judged are themselves likely to be reasonably contested in a democratic society. We also observed that this presents a certain problem for epistemic approaches: How are we to determine which epistemic standards we may appeal to, and what are we supposed to do about inevitable disagreements in this domain? Fabienne Peter has developed a version of this worry that she dubs the "authority dilemma": "If practical authority is justified on epistemic grounds, then legitimate practical authority is non-democratic. If, on the other hand, the practical authority of democracy is to be legitimate, it must be justified on non-epistemic grounds" (Peter 2016: 138). The problem is that an epistemic justification of democracy requires us to identify the appropriate epistemic standard of judgment among the various possibilities on offer. If there are in fact individuals who know what the correct standard is, Peter argues, then from an epistemic point of view there is no need for democracy; we should simply appoint those positioned to identify the correctness standard. But if we don't think that anyone is qualified to pronounce what the correct epistemic standard is, then democracy can't be justified on epistemic grounds. A broader, related question here concerns the manner in which epistemic approaches respond to the characteristic pluralism of democratic societies, which are characterized by a variety of competing conceptions of the good life. How are we to make sense of such pluralism if we conceptualize political questions as having a uniquely correct answer?

Peter's solution to the authority dilemma is to focus on the procedural epistemic value of democracy, and specifically of democratic deliberation. "Procedural epistemic value" refers to the epistemic goods realized through procedures for doing inquiry, as opposed to "instrumental" epistemic goods realized through improved accuracy of belief. Peter proposes what she dubs "pure epistemic proceduralism": democratic decisions are legitimate if they are produced via procedures that realize particular virtues: political fairness *and* epistemic virtues of fairness (Peter 2008) and mutual accountability (Peter 2012). For the instrumentalist epistemic democrat, good outcomes are defined independently of procedure, and democracy is justified at least in part by reference to its tendency to produce decisions which track that standard. For the pure epistemic proceduralist, good outcomes are to be defined in terms of procedures that realize epistemic virtues, and cannot be defined independently of those procedures.

In the specific case of democracy, Peter argues that democratic disputes may have features of epistemic peer disagreement writ large. That is, there are cases where citizens sincerely disagree with one another and yet, in general, have no basis for ascribing to themselves superior evidence or competence relative to many of their peers. Just as in local peer disagreement we ought to lower confidence in our beliefs in light of what our peers believe, Peter argues that democratic political disagreements entail a similar procedural requirement to temper our beliefs (Peter 2012). Democratic disputes are also cases in which a plurality of competing values and interests are at stake, and in which good answers to political questions are at least partly constructed through a process of reciprocal engagement (as Elizabeth Anderson also notes; see discussion above). Justified answers to political questions are thus those that emerge from a fair procedure of deliberative engagement. The epistemic value of democracy is thus to be defined in terms of a procedurally appropriate response to pluralism and disagreement – the manifestation of mutual "epistemic accountability" and "epistemic fairness" (Peter 2007) – rather than in terms of some truth-tracking tendency. In this respect, her view of democracy parallels Longino's influential social account of scientific epistemology, where the epistemic rationality of science is defined in terms of procedural tendencies that allow for the superior representation of diverse perspectives (Longino 1990).

Peter characterizes her position in contrast to instrumental views such as Estlund's, which understand epistemic value in terms of outcomes. Still, one might reasonably understand procedural value in instrumental terms. Thus, tempering belief confidence in the face of disagreement may not lead to more accurate belief in any individual case; but the epistemic value of this behavior is plausibly a function of the fact that, in general, it tends to produce beliefs that better track the truth. Likewise, there are compelling instrumentalist arguments for diversity and inclusiveness in democratic deliberation, particularly given the need for correct answers to respect a broad range of perspectives. Drawing on such considerations, Estlund might argue that democracy is epistemically the best among those political systems that satisfy moral procedural requirements of acceptability, at least in part because democracy's norms of fairness and inclusion produce truth-tracking tendencies under conditions of disagreement.

Like Estlund's view, Peter's view also remains vulnerable to worries about the epistemic properties of democracy. On complex policy matters, it is hardly clear that the model of peer disagreement is most apt, particularly if we are considering the democratic community as a whole. Even if no individual is in a position to identify the correct epistemic standard, one might see the community of experts as far better positioned to arrive at a good outcome through their own internal deliberations. Indeed, the primary point of traditional criticisms of democracy is that democratic citizens are incompetent and thus should not be included among the deliberative community devoted to making political decisions. Peter's view entails that if there are recognizable experts, then we should turn to them over the democratic citizenry. Appealing to epistemic fairness would not get us past this point, though one might observe that there are typically reasonable disputes among experts, and among the general population about which experts are right. As such, the conditions of peer disagreement would push us back towards the epistemic procedural values of inclusiveness and fairness. Still, the epistemic priority of those values ultimately seems to ride on the premise that a system realizing them is, overall, more epistemically successful than systems that do not realize them. It is not clear how to justify claims of epistemic success, however, except via some appeal to a tendency to track the truth. But that seems to bring us back to the very instrumentalist approach that Peter wanted to avoid.

Notes

1 I am grateful to David Estlund and Fabienne Peter for reading and commenting on earlier drafts of this entry.
2 It is not clear whether anyone holds a view that is strictly indifferent to outcome quality. Waldron's and Christiano's views, however, place a characteristically strong emphasis on procedural qualities.

References

Anderson, E. (2008). An Epistemic Defense of Democracy: David Estlund's Democratic Authority. *Episteme*, 5, pp. 129–139.

Arneson, R. (2004). Democracy Is Not Intrinsically Just. In: K. Dowding, R. E. Goodin & C. Pateman, eds., *Justice and Democracy* (pp. 40-58). Cambridge: Cambridge University Press.

Bell, D. A. (2015). *The China Model: Political Meritocracy and the Limits of Democracy*. Princeton, NJ: Princeton University Press.

Bohman, J. & Rehg, W. (eds.) (1997). *Deliberative Democracy: Essays on Reason and Politics*. Cambridge, MA: MIT Press.

Brennan, J. (2016). *Against Democracy*. Princeton, NJ: Princeton University Press.

Caplan, B. (2007). *The Myth of the Rational Voter: Why Democracies Choose Bad Policies*. Princeton, NJ: Princeton University Press.

Carpini, M. X. D., Cook, F. L. & Jacobs, L. R. (2004). Public Deliberation, Discursive Participation, and Citizen Engagement: A Review of the Empirical Literature. *Annual Review of Political Science*, 7, pp. 315–344.

Christiano, T. (2008). *The Constitution of Equality*. New York: Oxford University Press.

Cohen, J. (1989). Deliberation and Democratic Legitimacy. In: J. Bohman & W. Rehg, eds., *Deliberative Democracy: Essays on Reason and Politics* (pp. 67-91). Cambridge, MA: MIT Press.

Copp, D. (2011). Reasonable Acceptability and Democratic Legitimacy: Estlund's Qualified Acceptability Requirement. *Ethics*, 121, pp. 239–269.

Dewey, J. (1954). *The Public and Its Problems*. Chicago: Swallow Press.

Estlund, D. (2011). Reply to Copp, Gaus, Richardson, and Edmundson. *Ethics*, 121, pp. 354–389.

Estlund, D. M. (2008). *Democratic Authority: A Philosophical Framework*. Princeton, NJ: Princeton University Press.

Fishkin, J. S. (2009). *When the People Speak: Deliberative Democracy and Public Consultation*. Oxford: Oxford University Press.

Fuerstein, M. (2014). Democratic Consensus as an Essential Byproduct. *The Journal of Political Philosophy*, 22, pp. 282–301.

Gaus, G. F. (2011). On Seeking the Truth (Whatever That Is) through Democracy: Estlund's Case for the Qualified Epistemic Claim. *Ethics*, 121, pp. 270–300.

Grofman, B. & Feld, S. L. (1988). Rousseau's General Will: A Condorcetian Perspective. *The American Political Science Review*, 82, pp. 567–576.

Guerrero, A. A. (2014). Against Elections: The Lottocratic Alternative. *Philosophy and Public Affairs*, 42, pp. 135–178.

Gutmann, A. & Thompson, D. F. (1996). *Democracy and Disagreement: Why Moral Conflict Cannot Be Avoided in Politics and What Should Be Done about It*. Cambridge, MA: Belknap Press.

Hong, L. & Page, S. (2004). Groups of Diverse Problem Solvers Can Outperform Groups of High-Ability Problem Solvers. *Proceedings of the National Academy of Sciences*, 101, pp. 16385–16389.

Landemore, H. (2013). *Democratic Reason: Politics, Collective Intelligence, and the Rule of the Many*. Princeton, NJ: Princeton University Press.

List, C. & Goodin, R. E. (2001). Epistemic Democracy: Generalizing the Condorcet Jury Theorem. *Journal of Political Philosophy*, 9, pp. 277–306.

Longino, H. E. (1990). *Science as Social Knowledge: Values and Objectivity in Scientific Inquiry*. Princeton, NJ: Princeton University Press.

Mill, J. S. (1991). Considerations on Representative Government. In: J. Gray, ed., *On Liberty and Other Essays* (pp. 203-470). Oxford: Oxford University Press.

Ober, J. (2008). *Democracy and Knowledge: Innovation and Learning in Classical Athens*. Princeton, NJ: Princeton University Press.

Peter, F. (2007). Democratic Legitimacy and Proceduralist Social Epistemology. *Politics, Philosophy, and Economics*, 6, pp. 329–353.

Peter, F. (2008). Pure Epistemic Proceduralism. *Episteme*, 5, pp. 33–55.

Peter, F. (2012). The Procedural Epistemic Value of Deliberation. *Synthese*, 190, pp. 1253–1266.

Peter, F. (2016). The Epistemic Circumstances of Democracy. In: M. S. Brady & M. Fricker, eds., *The Epistemic Life of Groups: Essays in the Epistemology of Collectives* (pp. 133-149). New York: Oxford University Press.

Plato. (2000). *The Republic*. Cambridge: Cambridge University Press.

Steiner, J. (2012). *The Foundations of Deliberative Democracy: Empirical Research and Normative Implications*. Cambridge: Cambridge University Press.

Waldron, J. (1999). *Law and Disagreement*. Oxford: Clarendon Press.

Further Reading

Goodin, R. E. (2003). *Reflective Democracy*. Oxford: Oxford University Press. (Thorough discussion of democracy's epistemic and non-epistemic properties, including some relevant formal models.)

Quong, J. (2011). *Liberalism without Perfection*. New York: Oxford University Press. (Illuminating critical discussion of idealized acceptability as it figures in contemporary liberalism.)

Rawls, J. (1993). *Political Liberalism*. New York: Columbia University Press. (The definitive contemporary account of how political legitimacy depends on acceptance among qualified – "reasonable" – points of view.)

Somin, I. (2016). *Democracy and Political Ignorance: Why Smaller Government Is Smarter*. 2nd ed., Stanford, CA: Stanford University Press. (Thorough, empirically driven challenge to democracy's epistemic virtues.)

Viehoff, D. (2011). Procedure and Outcome in the Justification of Authority. *Journal of Political Philosophy*, 19, pp. 248–259. (Useful discussion of procedural vs epistemic values in democratic theory that attempts to integrate the two.)

38

JURY THEOREMS

Franz Dietrich and Kai Spiekermann

Introduction

Jury theorems form the technical core of arguments for the 'wisdom of crowds', the idea that large democratic decision-making bodies outperform small undemocratic ones when it comes to identifying factually correct alternatives. The popularity of jury theorems has spread across various disciplines such as economics, political science, philosophy, and computer science. A 'jury theorem' is a mathematical theorem about the probability of correctness of majority decisions between two alternatives. The existence of an objectively correct (right, better) alternative is the main metaphysical assumption underlying jury theorems. This involves an epistemic, outcome-based, rather than purely procedural, conception of democracy: the goal of democratic decision-making is to 'track the truth', not to fairly represent people's views or preferences (Cohen 1986). Typical jury theorems conclude that 'crowds are wise' in one or both of two senses:

> *The growing-reliability thesis*: Larger groups are better truth-trackers. That is, they are more likely to select the correct alternative (by majority) than smaller groups or single individuals.

> *The infallibility thesis*: Huge groups are infallible truth-trackers. That is, the likelihood of a correct (majority) decision tends to full certainty as the group becomes larger and larger.

Jury theorems differ considerably in their premises (axioms) about voters. They often rest on two premises, an 'independence' axiom and a 'competence' axiom, each of which may take various forms. For instance, the first of all jury theorems, attributable to the French enlightenment philosopher and mathematician Nicolas Marquis de Condorcet (1785), concludes that both of the aforementioned theses hold, based on particularly simple premises:

> *Condorcet's independence premise*: The voters have independent probabilities of voting for the correct alternative.

> *Condorcet's competence premise*: These probabilities exceed 1/2, and are the same for all voters.

Following our analysis with revised premises, the infallibility thesis emerges as incorrect in almost all real applications. Worse, this thesis does not even seem helpful as an approximation, idealization or paradigm of how large-scale democracy performs. It is fair to say that those classical jury theorems which conclude that huge groups are infallible – however beautiful they might be – have played a misleading role as a model of democratic decision making. Their overly optimistic conclusion has led the debate astray, suggesting to some that the infallibility thesis might be true after all, while suggesting to others that 'something' must be wrong with jury-theorem-based arguments in general. Neither reaction is justified. We shall (i) pinpoint what goes wrong in (the premises of) some naive jury theorems, and (ii) show how other jury theorems avoid flawed premises. Non-naive jury theorems reach the growing-reliability conclusion, but not the infallibility conclusion. This suggests that the growing-reliability thesis is the more appropriate formal rendition of the wisdom of crowds. That thesis, by itself, gives strong epistemic support for (majoritarian) democracy. The infalli-bility thesis would have given additional support – but it is not tenable, and should be taken off the agenda after having haunted the literature for decades.

We shall give a selective review of jury theorems and our own critical assessment of their suitability for formal arguments for the 'wisdom of crowds'. We begin with a naive Condorcetian jury theorem, which we then gradually refine into jury theorems with more plausible premises. We then discuss further jury theorems, key objections, and strategic voting, before offering a concluding assessment.

A Naive Jury Theorem

We consider a group of individuals deciding by majority vote between two alternatives, such as to convict or acquit a defendant, or to keep or abolish a law. To be able to vary the group size, we consider an infinite reservoir of individuals labelled $i = 1,2, \ldots$ and take the group of size n to consist of the first n individuals $1, \ldots, n$. Each individual votes for exactly one alternative. The alternative receiving more votes wins. To avoid ties, the group size n is throughout an *odd* number: $n \in \{1,3,5, \ldots\}$.[1] Exactly one of the alternatives is 'correct' or 'better' in an objective, voter-independent sense; it is called the unknown *state (of the world)*.

We first state the jury theorem in a simple and common (yet as we shall see problematic) version. The only model ingredients are events $R_1, R_2, \ldots$ representing correct voting by indi-viduals $1,2, \ldots$, respectively. Alternatively, the model ingredients could be random variables $\mathbf{v}_1, \mathbf{v}_2, \ldots$ representing the votes of individuals $1,2, \ldots$ and another random variable represent-ing the true state, all ranging over the same binary set of alternatives, e.g., the set {'convict', 'acquit'}, or {'abolish', 'keep'}, or $\{0,1\}$; each correctness event R_i is then defined as the event that $\mathbf{v}_i$ coincides with the state.[2]

We are ready to state the simple Condorcetian jury theorem, beginning with its two axioms (e.g., Grofman et al. 1983).

> *Unconditional independence (UI)*: The correctness events $R_1, R_2, \ldots$ are (unconditionally) independent.
> *Unconditional competence (UC)*: The (unconditional) correctness probability $p = P(R_i)$, the *(unconditional) competence*, (i) exceeds $1/2$ and (ii) is the same for each voter i.

Theorem 1. *Assume UI and UC. As the group size increases, the probability of a correct majority*[3] *(i) increases*[4] *(growing reliability), and (ii) tends to one (infallibility).*

Mathematically, the infallibility conclusion is an easy consequence of the law of large num-bers, which implies that, under UI and UC, as the group size tends to infinity, the correctness proportion converges to the correctness probability $p = P(R_i)$ (with probability one), so that the probability of a correct majority tends to one. The growing-reliability conclusion is harder to prove.[5]

A State-Sensitive Jury Theorem

The independence assumption UI is highly problematic, even if voters do not communicate with each other. Why? This section explains *one* of the problems, and presents a jury theorem that fixes it (other problems are addressed below). Binary decision problems often display an asymmetry between the alternatives: one alternative is simpler to identify as correct than the other one. Guilt of a defendant might be easier to detect than innocence, or vice versa; global warming might be easier to detect than its absence, or vice versa; and so on. This sort of truth-tracking asymmetry is the rule, not the exception. It renders the event R_i that individual i identifies the state positively correlated with the event of the simpler-to-identify state, because correct voting is more likely given the simpler-to-identify state than given the harder-to-identify state. For example, if guilt is simpler to identify than innocence, a juror is more likely to get it right given guilt than given innocence. As all correctness events $R_1, R_2, \ldots$ correlate positively with the same event (of the simpler-to-identify state), they normally correlate positively *with one another*.[6] So UI is violated.

This problem of correlation 'via' the state can be avoided by holding the state fixed, that means, conditionalizing on the state. We first enrich Section 2's model by another ingredient: a random variable $\mathbf{x}$, interpreted in this section as the state, i.e., the correct alternative.[7] Formally speaking, nothing hinges on this interpretation of $\mathbf{x}$ which could be almost any random variable.[8]

We can now revise the axioms and theorem as follows.

Conditional Independence (CI): The correctness events $R_1, R_2, \ldots$ (or equivalently the votes $\mathbf{v}_1, \mathbf{v}_2, \ldots$[9]) are independent conditional on any value of $\mathbf{x}$.

Conditional Competence (CC): For any value x of $\mathbf{x}$, the conditional correctness probability $p^x = P(R_i|x)$, the *competence (conditional on x)*, (i) exceeds $1/2$ and (ii) is the same for all voters i (but may vary with x).

Theorem 2. *Assume CI and CC. As the group size increases, the probability of a correct majority (i) increases (growing reliability), and (ii) tends to one (infallibility).*

This jury theorem reaches the same conclusions as Theorem 1, but on the basis of 'state-conditional' axioms. The state x with higher competence p^x (if it exists) is the easier-to-identify state discussed at the start of the section.

The Fundamental Tension between Independence and Competence

Different votes can be correlated via the objective state they track – a problem solved above by working with the independence axiom CI rather than UI, thereby fixing the state and blocking the correlation via the state. Unfortunately, votes can also be correlated via several other circumstances. So fixing just the state – the most common form of conditionalization in the literature – does not yet secure independence (Dietrich and List 2004, Dietrich 2008, Dietrich and Spiekermann 2013a; see also Ladha 1992, 1995). *Any common cause* of votes is a potential source of dependence. Consider common evidence, such as, in a court case, witness reports and the defendant's facial expression, or, among scientists, experimental data. Evidence may or may not support the truth: it may be truth-conducive or misleading. For instance, the defendant's friendly facial expression presumably supports innocence and is misleading in case of guilt. Plausibly, the correctness events $R_1, R_2, \ldots$ correlate positively with the event of truth-conducive (i.e., non-misleading) common evidence, and thereby correlate positively *with one another*. Voters can also be influenced by common causes that are *non-evidential* such as distracting heat: such causes lack an objective bearing on the true state, and yet they influence people's epistemic performance and thereby threaten independence. Jurors are more likely to vote well in agreeable room temperature; votes are thus correlated via room temperature.[10]

The strategy to restore independence should by now be familiar: one should conditionalize on the common causes of votes. So we now reinterpret the variable x on which we conditionalize in axioms as representing not just the state, but in addition all common causes of votes, the 'circumstances'. In the terminology of Dietrich (2008) and Dietrich and Spiekermann (2013a), x represents the specific *decision problem* faced by the group. For such x, axiom CI becomes plausible. Have we thus rehabilitated Theorem 2 as a formal argument for the 'wisdom of crowds'? Unfortunately not, because our rich interpretation of x renders the competence axiom CC implausible. Why?

Generally, whether a voter is competent – i.e., more often right than wrong – depends on the reference class considered. Plausibly, a voter is more often right than wrong among all conceivable yes/no questions, or all guilty/innocent questions. While competent within such an all-encompassing reference class, a voter is presumably not competent within a reference class in which certain misleading evidence is always present, such as all guilty/innocent questions where the defendant is guilty even though he has an alibi. Once we conditionalize on the full decision problem, we fine-grain the reference classes and effectively randomize only over parameters other than the state, common evidence, and other common causes.[11] Just imagine a decision problem (a value of x) characterized by severely misleading evidence, say a decision problem in which an innocent defendant unluckily looks exactly like the true murderer captured on CCTV. In this reference class a juror will be incompetent: within it he will get it right only rarely, e.g., when inattentive to (misleading) evidence. Most court cases (or decision problems) are not of this unfortunate kind: most have mainly truth-conducive evidence. So the voter is more often right than wrong across a wider cross-problem reference class. This observation is, however, irrelevant for the problem-conditional competence axiom CC, which conditionalizes on a specific decision problem rather than 'averaging out' the unlucky cases of misleading evidence. Ironically, the *problem-conditional* notion of probability renders independence (CI) defensible but competence (CC) unjustified, whereas a cross-problem-randomizing notion of probability – whether Section 2's *unconditional* or Section 3's *state-conditional* notion – renders competence (UC or CC) more justified but independence (UI or CI) implausible. So, Theorems 1's and 2's premises are not jointly justifiable, regardless of how much we conditionalize on, i.e., 'pack' into x. The table below summarizes this dilemma.[12]

A Problem-Sensitive Jury Theorem

Following the previous section, we interpret the variable x as capturing the group's specific decision problem, including the common causes of voters. So the independence axiom CI is plausible, but the competence axiom CC is untenable. It is tempting to replace CC by the unconditional competence axiom UC, but unfortunately the combination of CI and UC – two potentially justified premises – does not lend itself to a jury theorem: it does not imply the growing-reliability thesis. We therefore weaken CC to a more plausible axiom: *tendency to competence*. Stating this axiom requires a short preparation. A voter i's problem-specific competence $p^x = P(R_i | x)$ depends on the (randomly drawn) problem x, and is thus itself a random variable.

	Unconditional	State-conditional	Problem-conditional
Independence axiom	UI implausible	CI for $x = state$ implausible	CI for $x = problem$ plausible
Competence axiom	UC plausible in homog. groups	CC for $x = state$ plausible in homog. groups	CC for $x = problem$ implausible

Its value is above 1/2 for 'easy' problems (values of **x**), and below 1/2 for 'difficult' problems with misleading evidence or other epistemically harmful circumstances. A discrete real-valued random variable, in our case the competence variable, *tends to exceed* 1/2 if the value $1/2 + \varepsilon$ is at least as probable as the symmetrically opposed value $1/2 - \varepsilon$, and this for all $\varepsilon > 0$. An illustration is given in Figure 38.1.[13] Here the competence level is for, instance, more likely to be $0.7 = 0.5 + 0.2$ than to be $0.3 = 0.5 - 0.2$. This and all other symmetrical comparisons are indicated by dashed lines.

> *Tendency to Competence (TC)*: A voter i's competence $p^{\mathbf{x}} = P(R_i | \mathbf{x})$ (as a function of **x**)
> (i) tends to exceed 1/2, and (ii) is the same for all voters i.

Axiom TC weakens CC: it retains CC's homogeneity part, but weakens CC's first part by allowing voters to sometimes be incompetent. By using TC rather than the implausible axiom of CC, we no longer reach the implausible infallibility conclusion, while retaining the growing-reliability conclusion (Dietrich and Spiekermann 2013a):

> **Theorem 3**. *Assume CI and TC. As the group size increases, the probability of a correct majority (i) increases (growing reliability), and (ii) tends to a value which is below 1 (no infallibility) unless CC holds.*[14]

This theorem gives group deliberation and communication a new role. Classical jury theorems suggest that deliberation might be harmful by threatening independence (e.g. Rawls 1971, pp. 314–5, Anderson 2006). But deliberation does not undermine the new problem-conditional independence axiom CI: insofar as deliberation leads to information exchange and hence to additional common-evidence, this common evidence is incorporated into the decision problem, so that common-evidence-caused correlations are automatically 'conditionalized away'. Instead, deliberation is beneficial: it ideally renders voters more competent[15] and thereby the group's majority judgment more reliable.

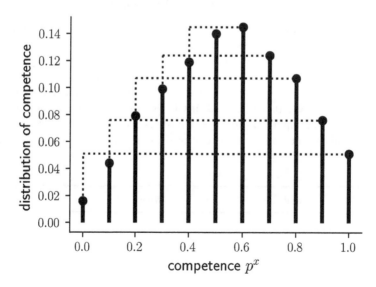

Figure 38.1 Example of Tendency to Competence.

Further Jury Theorems

In this section we provide a short, non-exhaustive overview of other jury theorems (setting aside the sort of concerns raised above, although they still apply). The most frequent starting point is the classic Theorem 1, in which either axiom could be weakened.

Weakening axiom UC by simply dropping its homogeneity condition, hence allowing voter-specific competence $p_i = P(R_i)$, has dramatic consequences: neither the growing-reliability nor the infallibility thesis still follows. Instead the probability of a correct majority can *decrease* in group size and converge to 1/2, so that huge groups are as bad as a fair coin. This happens if the sequence of competence levels p_1, p_2, ... strictly decreases towards 1/2, so rapidly that newly added voters are much less competent than existing voters and thereby pull the majority's reliability down (Paroush 1998). Some restriction on *how* competence varies across voters is thus needed for any 'wisdom of crowds' conclusion. One could weaken UC either to the condition that all p_i exceed $1/2 + \varepsilon$ for a voter-independent $\varepsilon > 0$ (Paroush 1998), or to the condition that average competence $\frac{1}{n}\sum_{i=1}^{n} p_i$ converges to a value above 1/2 (Dietrich 2008; for related or more general results, see Berend and Paroush 1998 and Owen et al. 1989). This preserves the infallibility conclusion, but not the growing-reliability conclusion – the 'wrong' conclusion is preserved, one might complain. Alternatively, one no longer assumes fixed identity of voters but draws the group of any given size n randomly from a given huge (finite) pool of potential voters i with competence levels $p_i > 1/2$. The probability of a correct majority vote is then doubly random: the identity of the voters and their votes are random. The growing-reliability conclusion is then restored (Berend and Sapir 2005).

The other candidate for modification is the independence axiom. Boland (1989) and Boland et al. (1989), for example, discuss the influence of an opinion leader. Before the opinion leader is consulted, voters' judgments obey UI and UC. Afterwards, each voter (other than the opinion leader) has the same independent probability of following the opinion leader in his vote; votes thus violate UI. The infallibility conclusion is still reached if (and only if) the probability of following is not too high, specifically below $1 - \frac{1}{2p}$ (see also Goodin and Spiekermann 2012). There are many other ways to adapt or weaken independence. For instance, some jury theorems assume votes to be interchangeable rather than independent, giving up the infallibility conclusion (Ladha 1993, Dietrich and Spiekermann 2013a); others are based on causal networks, again giving up infallibility (Dietrich and List 2004, Dietrich and Spiekermann 2013b); Kaniovski (2010) analyses the group's reliability as a function of the dependence structure among voters; and Pivato (2016) shows that the infallibility conclusion is still reachable under surprisingly strong forms of dependence, using suitable voting rules.

List and Goodin (2001) importantly generalize Theorem 2's infallibility conclusion to the case of $k \geq 2$ options, still assuming one option is correct. They generalize CC: given the correct option x, a voter is more likely to vote for x than for y, and this for every incorrect option y. Interestingly, the probability of correct voting no longer needs to exceed 1/2 for $k > 2$ options. It can be conjectured that the growing-reliability conclusion also generalizes to $k \geq 2$ options. The upshot is that jury theorems and 'wisdom of crowds' arguments need not be restricted to binary decision problems.

Going beyond majority voting, some work asks which voting rule is epistemically optimal, where 'optimality' could be cashed out differently, e.g., by maximizing the probability of a correct outcome (e.g., Nitzan and Paroush 1982, Shapley and Grofman 1984, Ben-Yashar and Nitzan 1997, Dietrich 2006, Pivato 2013). The generic finding is that, under an independence axiom of type UI or CI, the optimal rule is a weighted super-, sub- or simple majority rule in which a voter's weight is well-calibrated as a function of his competence (and becomes negative in case of incompetence). Simple majority rule is optimal in case of equal competence and symmetric options.

Objections and Replies

One objection is David Estlund's 'disjunction problem' (Estlund 2008, pp. 228–30). We give a new reconstruction of the problem, showing its appeal but also its limits. In a choice, say between building a roadbridge or a footbridge, each option is a disjunction of several finer sub-options. For instance, a roadbridge might have one, two or more lanes, and might or might not have street lights and plants. Alternatively, the voters could decide between a *specific* roadbridge (say one with 2 lanes, no street lights, but plants) or any other road- or footbridge. The first option has become finer, the second coarser.[16] The change in options may considerably alter a voter's pair of state-conditional competence levels (the correct-voting probabilities given correctness of the first or second option). This by itself is not a problem, but just a feature, we maintain. What *is* a problem is the following. If one option is much more specific than the other, then a voter's conditional competence may easily be below 1/2 given the specific state of the world (and close to 1 given the unspecific state). For correctness of a highly specific option is often subjectively unlikely, hence not recognized – just as it seems unlikely that you ate exactly 139 corn flakes this morning, even if you did. This argument threatens the plausibility of the competence axiom CC, but only for decision problems whose options are highly unequal in specificity. Also, the competence axioms UC and TC remain plausible.[17] Since Estlund neither distinguishes between conditional and unconditional competence nor explicitly restricts the scope of the problem, his objection is overstated.

The disjunction problem is not the only objection raised against competence axioms. Some scholars question competence on empirical grounds. There is, however, one theoretical argument against systematic incompetence: systematically worse-than-random judgments are *unstable*, since once a voter becomes aware of his incompetence he can normally achieve competence by simply reversing all of his judgments (Dietrich 2008, Goodin and Spiekermann 2012).

Another frequent objection is that jury theorems invoke variables whose exact nature is unknown in practice. One usually knows neither exact competence levels nor the precise nature and distribution of the decision problem **x** in Theorem 3, as the precise common causes are unknown. However, accepting a competence axiom (UC, CC or TC) only requires ascertaining some inequalities, without having to know the exact behaviour of the variables involved.

Finally, on the most fundamental level, some critics suggest that there often is no truth to be tracked (e.g. Black 1958, p. 163, Miller 1992, p. 56). For instance, it is sometimes claimed that there is no objective truth in political choices, which are supposedly not about facts but about values or preferences. Whether this is so arguably depends on how the question is asked (Landemore 2013, ch. 8). Asking British voters whether they 'prefer' the United Kingdom (UK) to remain in the European Union (EU) suggests a non-epistemic preference elicitation. Asking whether EU membership is 'better' or 'better for the UK' seems to ask two (different) epistemically framed questions. In fact, the question in the EU referendum on 23 June 2016 was whether the UK 'should' remain in or leave the EU. Whether this is an epistemic issue, i.e., whether there is a fact about what the UK 'should' do, depends on how one interprets 'should' and on meta-ethical commitments.

An interesting hybrid view is that, while there *is* an objective fact, it is a group-specific fact about which option is *preferred* by the majority, i.e., the 'will of the majority'. The question then is: does a voter vote according to his own preference, or according to his belief about the majority preference? In the latter case, the standard jury-theorem setup directly applies. In the former case, majority outcomes may seem to be correct by definition. But, on a more sophisticated version of the view, a voter can be mistaken about his own true preference, so that his vote tracks a *voter-specific truth* about his preference. Under plausible conditions, large groups are likely to track the majority preference (Miller 1986, Goldman 1999, p. 323ff, Goodin and Spiekermann 2015, List and Spiekermann 2016).

Strategic Voting

It is well-known that conflicts of interests between voters may lead to strategic incentives. Surprisingly, strategic voting may also occur in purely epistemic contexts where voters share the common goal of objectively correct group decisions; this insight has sparked a large and active literature, particularly among economists (Austen-Smith and Banks 1996, Feddersen and Pesendorfer 1999, Peleg and Zamir 2012, Bozbay et al. 2014, among many others). We only sketch the basic idea. Suppose you are one of 11 jurors voting on whether to convict the defendant. Your private information suggests guilt. Should you vote 'convict'? Strategically, your vote should be chosen on the assumption that it makes a difference (is 'pivotal'); so that 5 other jurors vote 'convict' and 5 vote 'acquit'. In any other situation your vote would be irrelevant for the outcome and can therefore be ignored. Hence, after adding the hypothetical information about other voters to your own information, 'convict' is supported 6 times, and 'acquit' 5 times. This is almost an informational tie, which (let's assume) does not justify conviction. You should vote 'acquit', although your private information alone suggests conviction. Paradoxically, if every voter reasons like this, all jurors vote to acquit even when they all hold private information suggesting guilt. In game-theoretic terms, truthful voting may be irrational, and the situation that everyone votes truthfully may fail to be a (Bayes-Nash) equilibrium of the voting game.[18] A key goal of this literature is to determine the (often non-majoritarian) voting rules which render truthful voting rational and generate efficient decisions in light of all information spread across voters.

But will voters really engage in such strategic reasoning? The reasoning depends on an extreme motivational assumption: voters care exclusively about the correctness of group outcomes. The rationality of non-truthful voting breaks down quickly as the voter's motivation is enriched by an intrinsic concern for the truthfulness of his own vote, in addition to the concern for the group outcome. For the expressive part of a voter's motivation quickly crowds out the outcome-driven part as the probability of pivotality is usually very small. Besides, even voters with purely outcome-oriented preferences might lack the strategic sophistication for engaging in strategic voting.

Concluding Assessment

Whether jury theorems are useful for social epistemology and democratic theory is highly controversial. To see clearly through the large variety of proposed theorems, approaches, and objections, we have classified and evaluated theorems based on their premises and their conclusions. Theorems usually make *independence* and *competence* assumptions about voters' correct-voting probabilities; the core question is how these probabilities are understood. Probabilities could be unconditional (Theorem 1), conditional on the state (Theorem 2), or conditional on the full decision problem which includes not just the state but also the common causes of votes (Theorem 3).

Our analysis shows that there is a fundamental tension between independence and competence premises: independence is plausible only for a rich conditionalization, whereas competence is only plausible for a thin conditionalization. Indeed, independence is untenable when construed unconditionally or state-conditionally; but competence is untenable when construed problem-conditionally. As a result, classical jury theorems fail to have jointly justified premises, which is responsible for their (implausible) conclusion that huge groups are infallible. Our suggested response is to use a rich (problem-conditional) conditionalization, while weakening the competence axiom to *tendency to competence*: voters are more often competent than incompetent rather than always competent. The resulting jury theorem no longer concludes that huge groups are infallible; but it still concludes that larger groups perform better, thereby giving support for majoritarian democracy.

Notes

1 One could work without excluding even n, by assuming that ties are broken using a fair coin.

2 Events and random variables are of course defined relative to a background probability space, i.e., a set of possible worlds Ω, a notion of 'events' (one could count all subsets of Ω as events, or, more generally, all subsets in a given σ-algebra of subsets), and a probability function P defined on the set of events. We shall never mention the probability space explicitly as a model ingredient.

3 This is the probability that the number of individuals i $\in \{1, ..., n\}$ such that R_i obtains exceeds $n/2$.

4 Throughout, 'increases' is used in its weak sense. In fact, the increase in Theorem 1 is strict, provided the correctness events R_i do not have probability one. In the other theorems stated the increase is also strict, except for extreme cases.

5 The proof relies on a recursive formula for the probability of a correct majority as a function of n. This formula is stated in Grofman et al. (1983), but its proof is hard to find (see however Dietrich and Spiekermann 2013a, Step 2 in Appendix C).

6 We say 'normally' rather than 'necessarily' since there are some far-fetched mathematical counterexamples.

7 Recall that Section 2's initial model has as ingredients the correctness events $R_1, R_2, ...,$ or alternatively the votes $\mathbf{v}_1, \mathbf{v}_2, ...$ and a state variable (with R_i then defined as the event that $\mathbf{v}_i$ matches the state). If we adopt the alternative ingredients and if the new ingredient $\mathbf{x}$ is itself the state (following our current interpretation), then the initial model already contains $\mathbf{x}$ and need not be extended.

8 $\mathbf{x}$ could take any sort of values, with the only constraining assumption that each value has positive probability in order to render conditionalization meaningful. This implies that $\mathbf{x}$ is a discrete random variable, i.e., takes only finitely or countably infinitely many values. (Everything could be generalized to possibly continuous $\mathbf{x}$.)

9 The equivalent formulation in terms of votes assumes that $\mathbf{x}$ is or more generally subsumes (determines) the state, an assumption in line with our current and later interpretations of $\mathbf{x}$. Under this assumption, the equivalence holds since R_i and $\mathbf{v}_i$ are then interdefinable given $\mathbf{x}$: R_i holds if and only if $\mathbf{v}_i$ matches the state determined by $\mathbf{x}$.

10 Common causes, whether evidential or non-evidential, threaten not just unconditional independence UI but also state-conditional independence since the correlations do not disappear by conditionalizing on the state.

11 What can still vary is, say, the voter's level of awakeness, attention, hunger, or back pain, all of which may indeed influence the voter's truth-tracking ability and hence his correctness probability.

12 An altogether different approach avoids the need of conditionalizing on the decision problem and defends the independence axiom in its unconditional form UI by interpreting probabilities differently in the first place: the probabilities captured by the function P are now taken to already incorporate (be 'posterior on') the decision problem. The state and the common causes are thus fixed rather than drawn randomly. This interpretation of probability turns Theorem 1 into Dietrich's (2008) fixed-problem jury theorem. Theorem 1's independence axiom UI is now justified, but its competence axiom UC is no longer justified. The problem is not that UC *must* fail, but that it is *unknown* whether it holds: since the fixed state is unknown, so is the question of whether the fixed problem has truth-conducive or misleading circumstances. So the alternative interpretation of probability also fails to render Theorem 1's premises jointly justified. We shall not adopt this interpretation.

13 We thank the developers of the open source matplotlib library.

14 To disambiguate, 'unless' means 'if and only if it is *not* the case that'. See Dietrich and Spiekermann (2013a) for the generalization to possibly non-discrete $\mathbf{x}$, and for a version of the result which concludes that the group's performance increases *strictly* (something achieved by strengthening TC through using a strict notion of 'tendency to exceed $1/2$').

15 A voter's problem-specific competence $p^{\mathbf{x}}$ presumably tends to exceed $1/2$ *more strongly* for a 'post-deliberation decision problem' $\mathbf{x}$ enriched by new common evidence than for a 'no-deliberation decision problem' $\mathbf{x}$ with less or no common evidence.

16 Presumably the new first option, the specific roadbridge, can be the correct option only if the old first option, the unspecific roadbridge, was the correct option.

17 Regarding UC, a voter is unconditionally likely to vote correctly since he is likely to believe the unspecific option is correct and since that option is itself likely to be correct. It is only conditional on correctness of the specific option that the voter is likely to get it wrong.

18 In voting, voters effectively play a strategic game with asymmetric information and common preferences (for objectively correct outcomes).

References

Anderson, E. (2006). The Epistemology of Democracy. *Episteme* 3(1-2), pp. 8–22.

Austen-Smith, D., and Banks, J. S. (1996). Information Aggregation, Rationality, and the Condorcet Jury Theorem. *American Political Science Review* 90(1), pp. 34–45.

Ben-Yashar, R. C., and Nitzan, S. I. (1997). The Optimal Decision Rule for Fixed-Size Committees in Dichotomous Choice Situations: The General Result. *International Economic Review* 38(1), p. 175.

Berend, D., and Paroush, J. (1998). When is Condorcet's Jury Theorem Valid? *Social Choice and Welfare* 15, pp. 481–488.

Berend, D., and Sapir, L. (2005). Monotonicity in Condorcet Jury Theorem. *Social Choice and Welfare* 24(1), pp. 83–92.

Black, D. (1958). *The Theory of Committees and Elections*. Cambridge: Cambridge University Press.

Boland, P. J., Proschan, F., and Tong, Y. L. (1989). Modelling Dependence in Simple and Indirect Majority Systems. *Journal of Applied Probability* 26(1), pp. 81–88.

Boland, P. J. (1989). Majority Systems and the Condorcet Jury Theorem. *Journal of the Royal Statistical Society. Series D (The Statistician)* 38(3), pp. 181–189.

Bozbay, I., Dietrich, F., and Peters, H. (2014). Judgment Aggregation in Search for the Truth. *Games and Economic Behaviour* 87, pp. 571–590.

Cohen, J. (1986). An Epistemic Conception of Democracy. *Ethics* 97(1), pp. 26–38.

Condorcet, Marquis de. 1785. *Essai sur l'application de l'analyse á la probabilité des décisions rendues á la pluralité des voix*.

Dietrich, F. (2008). The Premises of Condorcet's Jury Theorem Are Not Simultaneously Justified. *Episteme* 5(1), pp. 56–73.

Dietrich, F. (2006). General Representation of Epistemically Optimal Procedures. *Social Choice and Welfare* 26(2), pp. 263–283.

Dietrich, F., and List, C. (2004). A Model of Jury Decisions Where All Jurors Have the Same Evidence. *Synthese* 142, pp. 175–202.

Dietrich, F., and Spiekermann, K. (2013a) Epistemic Democracy with Defensible Premises. *Economics and Philosophy* 29(1), pp. 87–120.

Dietrich, F., and Spiekermann, K. (2013b). Independent Opinions? *Mind* 122(487), pp. 655–685.

Estlund, D. M. (2008). *Democratic Authority: A Philosophical Framework*. Princeton: Princeton University Press.

Feddersen, T., and Pesendorfer, W. (1999). Elections, Information Aggregation, and Strategic Voting. *Proceedings of the National Academy of Sciences* 96(19), pp. 10572–10574.

Goldman, A. I. (1999). *Knowledge in a Social World*. Oxford: Clarendon.

Goodin, R. E., and Spiekermann, K. (2012). Epistemic Aspects of Representative Government. *European Political Science Review* 4(3), pp. 303–325.

Goodin, R. E., and Spiekermann, K. (2015). Epistemic Solidarity as a Political Strategy. *Episteme* 12(4), pp. 439–457.

Grofman, B., Owen, G., and Feld, S. (1983). Thirteen Theorems in Search of the Truth. *Theory and Decision* 15, pp. 261–278.

Kaniovski, S. (2010). Aggregation of Correlated Votes and Condorcet's Jury Theorem. *Theory and Decision* 69 (3), pp. 453–468.

Ladha, K. K. (1992). The Condorcet Jury Theorem, Free Speech, and Correlated Votes. *American Journal of Political Science* 36(3), pp. 617–634.

Ladha, K. K. (1993). Condorcet's Jury Theorem in Light of de Finetti's Theorem. *Social Choice and Welfare* 10 (1), pp. 69–85.

Ladha, K. K. (1995). Information Pooling through Majority-Rule Voting: Condorcet's Jury Theorem with Correlated Votes. *Journal of Economic Behavior & Organization* 26(3), pp. 353–372.

Landemore, H. (2013). *Democratic Reason: Politics, Collective Intelligence, and the Rule of the Many*. Princeton, N. J.: Princeton University Press.

List, C., and Goodin, R. E. (2001). Epistemic Democracy: Generalizing the Condorcet Jury Theorem. *Journal of Political Philosophy* 9(3), pp. 277–306.

List, Christian, and Spiekermann, K. (2016). The Condorcet Jury Theorem and Voter-Specific Truth. In: H. Kornblith and B. McLaughlin, eds., *Alvin Goldman and His Critics*. Chichester, UK: Wiley., pp. 216–233.

Miller, D. (1992). Deliberative Democracy and Social Choice. *Political Studies* 40(1 Suppl), pp. 54–67.

Miller, N. R. (1986). Information, Electorates, and Democracy: Some Extentions and Interpretations of the Condorcet Jury Theorem. In: B. Grofman and G. Owen, eds., *Information Pooling and Group Decision Making*. Greenwich, Conn.: JAI Press, pp. 173–192.

Nitzan, S., and Paroush, J. (1982). Optimal Decision Rules in Uncertain Dichotomous Choice Situations. *International Economic Review* 23(2), pp. 289–297.

Owen, G., Grofman, Bernard., and Feld, S. L. (1989). Proving a Distribution-Free Generalization of the Condorcet Jury Theorem. *Mathematical Social Sciences* 17, pp. 1–16.

Paroush, J. (1998). Stay Away from Fair Coins : A Condorcet Jury Theorem. *Social Choice and Welfare* 15, pp. 15–20.

Peleg, B., and Zamir, S. (2012). Extending the Condorcet Jury Theorem to a General Dependent Jury. *Social Choice and Welfare*, 39(1), pp. 91–125.

Pivato, M. (2013). Voting Rules as Statistical Estimators. *Social Choice and Welfare* 40(2), pp. 581–630.

Pivato, M. (2016). Epistemic Democracy with Correlated Voters. Available at: https://mpra.ub.uni-muenchen.de/69546/ (July 18, 2016).

Rawls, John. (1971 [rev. ed. 1999]). *A Theory of Justice*. Revised edition. Oxford: Oxford University Press.

Shapley, L., and Grofman, B. (1984). Optimizing Group Judgmental Accuracy in the Presence of Interdependencies. *Public Choice* 43(3), pp. 329–343.

Further reading

Goodin, R. E., and Spiekermann, K. (2018). *An Epistemic Theory of Democracy*. Oxford: Oxford University Press.

Landemore, H., and Elster, J. (eds.). (2012). *Collective Wisdom: Principles and Mechanisms*. Cambridge: Cambridge University Press.

39

THE EPISTEMIC ROLE OF SCIENCE AND EXPERTISE IN LIBERAL DEMOCRACY

Klemens Kappel and Julie Zahle

The Classical View

What is the proper role of science and scientific experts in decision-making in liberal democracy? What we might call *the Classical View* endorses a distinctive division of epistemic and deliberative labor: science should deliver the facts, and just the facts, needed for political decision-making, whereas liberal democracy should make decisions on the basis of these. This view, or similar enough views, is associated with Weber and Merton, but have had many other proponents (Merton 1938, 1942; Weber 2011). Views of this sort are widely adopted among scientists and policy makers, though they are surely not always adhered to in practice (see e.g. Pielke (2007), Resnik (2009), Maasen and Weingart (2005)). In more recent debates, however, many philosophers and sociologists of science have questioned or rejected the Classical View as utopian, misconceived or even harmful. In the following, our focus will be on this criticism of the Classical View, as well as on what can be said on its behalf.

We start by outlining a slightly more detailed, if still sketchy, version of the Classical View. First, it is important to note that the view only specifies the role of science in democratic decision-making. Science may, of course, have many other roles and purposes. Next, strictly speaking, science cannot deliver facts, as facts are not the sort of entities that can be handed over from one person to another. But science can, of course, make assertions about facts. It might then be suggested that science should deliver knowledge, i.e. assert known facts. Again, this is not plausible. Science often makes assertions that are very likely to be true, but yet not strictly known to be true, and some even hold that science never knows its assertions to be true. A better view, then, is that science should make factual assertions where these are well supported by evidence generated by scientific methods. Note here that many philosophers think that there are normative facts. The Classical View could concede this, and with this qualification, the view holds that science should make assertions about non-normative facts, and only non-normative facts, that are well supported by evidence generated by scientific methods.

A common argument for the Classical View trades on the distinction between facts and values. Science should only make assertions in matters where it has a special epistemic authority. No method exists that could discover values or answer basic normative questions in a scientifically respectable way. So, science has no special epistemic authority regarding substantive normative questions, such as those involved in ethics and politics. Hence, science should not make assertions about substantive normative questions.

This argument only shows that science should make assertions about non-normative facts, but not about matters of value. It does not demonstrate that or why liberal democracy should care about science or the findings of science. So, one might ask, why should democratic decision-making take special notice of the views of science, maybe at the expense of other types of institutions? This question is less elaborated in the literature. However, there is a fairly obvious argument indicating that democracy should accord science a special role (Compare (Root 1993), Chapter 1): Rational decision-making needs both a factual and an evaluative component, in that rational choices between options require factual information about the options as well as an evaluation of the options. Decision-making in liberal democracy covers various forms of public deliberation, voting and political decision-making. In decision-making in liberal democracy, the evaluative component derives from the core values of liberal democracy, deliberation and from various democratic procedures. The factual component needed for decision-making in liberal democracy, generally has to come from elsewhere, as the core values and decision-making processes in liberal democracy mostly cannot generate all the factual input needed. In general, liberal democracy would want this factual component to be supplied by the institutions best suited for doing so. In a wide range of domains, science or scientific institutions are the best to provide the factual component needed for decision-making in liberal democracy. Hence liberal democracy would want the factual input needed for decision-making to be supplied by science.

The above provides a rationale both for according science a distinctive role in democratic decision-making, and for imposing certain constraints on how science should fulfill this role. On the one hand liberal democracy should *respect the epistemic authority of science*: when relevant and otherwise feasible, policy makers as well as wider democratic deliberation should seek out scientific opinion regarding the relevant factual input needed, and policy makers and public opinion should not question, reject, undermine, or distort findings of science, unless they have specific epistemic reasons to doubt the veracity of the messages. On the other hand, science should supply the factual input needed in a way that is most conducive to democratic decision-making, where this covers various forms of public deliberation, voting and political decision-making. This obviously requires that the messages from the scientific community be *relevant* to the deliberation and political choices on the agenda, and *reliable*. Moreover, science, and the communication from science, should be *normatively neutral* in that it should not rig the scientific process or distort its communication of findings in order to promote certain political ends over others, or in other ways distort or undermine democratic decision-making. So, as motivated by the needs of liberal democracy, the Classical View holds that liberal democracy should respect the epistemic authority of science, while science should make assertions about non-normative facts only, while being relevant, reliable and normatively neutral. These two norms specify a division of epistemic and deliberative labor that complement each other. One norm makes practical sense only when the other is in place. Willingness to comply with one norm may generally depend on the perceived compliance with the other. Science will accept a role of the neutral arbiter of facts, but not if its epistemic authority is constantly attacked for political reasons. Politics will tend to accept the epistemic authority of science, but not if science is perceived as being non-neutral or irrelevant.

As we said, views like the Classical View or parts of it has been subject to much controversy. One issue has concerned value freedom in science. According to critics, science cannot be, or should not be, free from values in the way that is allegedly required by the Classical View. We review some of these objections below. Another source of concern is that the Classical View accords science or scientific experts a role in decision-making that conflicts with democratic ideals, or is otherwise unwarranted. We also review some of these objections and offer a brief reflection on these criticisms.

Value Freedom in Science

Traditionally, it has been assumed that in order for science to deliver the facts, as it were, research must live up to what is sometimes known as the *ideal of value free science*. There are different formulations of the ideal. Here is one version: *Nonepistemic values*, like moral, political and social values, should not affect the *internal phases of research*, that is, the researcher's collection and interpretation of data and her establishment of research findings on the basis of the data. Among other things, this ideal implies that a researcher should not abstain from collecting certain data because they are likely to support a research result that does not go well together with her political commitments; she should not decide on a certain interpretation of her data because it fits best with her moral views; and she should not reject a hypothesis because it does not line up with her social values.

While the ideal of value free science states that nonepistemic values should not affect the internal phases of research, it does not make any such claim in relation to the *external phases of research*. These include the choice of research question and method, and the use of the research findings. Typically, proponents of the ideal of value free science agree that nonepistemic values may influence both the choice of research question and the application of research findings, and that nonepistemic values in the form of an ethical concern for the research participants should affect the choice of methods and their manner of application.

Within the recent – and very lively – debate on values in science, the ideal of value free science has been heavily criticized. Perhaps the most prominent objection is *the argument from inductive risk* which classic formulation may be found in a paper by Richard Rudner (Rudner 1953). Rudner maintains that a researcher accepts or rejects hypotheses. However, since there is never complete evidence for a hypothesis, the researcher must decide whether the evidence is sufficiently strong to accept it. When making this decision, he continues, the researcher should assess and take into account the moral graveness of the consequences in case she wrongly accepts the hypothesis. Heather Douglas has further extended the scope of the argument by pointing out that, as part of the research process, the researcher makes other decisions, such as how to characterize the data and interpret the evidence, that may also involve uncertainty and hence risk of error. When this is the case, the researcher should likewise assess and take into account the nonepistemic consequences of making a wrong choice (Douglas 2000). The upshot of these considerations is that the ideal of value free science should be dismissed since it fails to acknowledge various ways in which nonepistemic values should affect the internal phases of research.

Another widely discussed objection to the ideal of value free science is *the argument from underdetermination*. Helen Longino is a well-known proponent of this line of reasoning (Longino 1990). Longino maintains that data only serve as evidence for hypotheses relative to background beliefs and assumptions: In the absence of these, data underdetermine hypotheses. Further, she continues, nonepistemic values may, and often do, motivate the choice of background beliefs and assumptions. When there is little or no available evidence in support of a background belief or assumption, values may legitimately inform their choice. Since the ideal of value free science fails to make room for this, it should be discarded.

In response to the criticisms of the ideal of value free science, a number of alternative ideals for the role of values in science have been offered (see, e.g. Longino 1990; Solomon 2001; Douglas 2009; Kourany 2010; Steel 2015). While taking into account objections to the value free ideal, the alternative ideals purport to offer more adequate accounts of the constraints that should be placed on values in research. Here, we briefly sketch two such alternative ideals. Both ideals are meant to capture what the role of values in research should be given that science aims to deliver the facts – facts that may also serve as a basis for decision-making in liberal democracy.

Longino has proposed an alternative ideal as part of her social account of objectivity (Longino 1990). According to this account, scientific communities are objective to the extent that they satisfy certain criteria: Within a community, there must be recognized venues where researchers can criticize each other's work and there must be shared standards to which they can appeal when offering their criticism. Further, the scientific community as a whole must be responsive to the ongoing critical discussion just as all qualified parties to the discussion must be regarded as being on an equal footing in terms of intellectual authority (Longino 1990: 76ff). Under these conditions, consider a researcher who proposes a theory based on several background assumptions which adoption is motivated by her nonepistemic values. In Longino's view, insofar as these assumptions have not been disputed in the ongoing critical discussion, their underlying nonepistemic values play a legitimate role in the research.

Douglas's alternative to the ideal of value free science holds that throughout the research process, values should play an indirect role only in decision-making about which empirical claims to make (Douglas 2009). A researcher makes these sort of decisions when she decides how to characterize the evidence, how to interpret it, and whether to accept a hypothesis. Douglas' ideal trades on a distinction between values being able to play direct and indirect roles. Values play a direct role when they directly motivate the making of a claim, as exemplified by a researcher who accepts a hypothesis simply because it goes well along with her nonepistemic values. By contrast, values play an indirect role when they are used to assess whether the evidence offered in support of a claim is sufficient to accept it. The indirect role is illustrated by the researcher who thinks that the evidence in support of a hypothesis is insufficient on the ground that if the hypothesis were wrongly accepted (it is actually false) this would have terrible social consequences. Thus, on this account, values, including nonepistemic values, are legitimate in the research process as long as they play the proper indirect roles.

Neutral Science?

Whereas the above concerns value freedom in the internal phases of research, much discussion has also concerned various forms of neutrality in other phases of research. According to the Classical View science should deliver the facts and only the facts, as it were. It has been thought that this would require that values are entirely eliminated from scientific communication. It has often been pointed out that this is hardly possible, at least in the social sciences, but arguably similar problems arise in biology. The problem is that scientific communication may need to make essential use of expressions with an ineliminable value content, e.g. expressions such as "terrorist", "illness", "rape", or "poverty". These expressions have a non-evaluative meaning, which if needed can be stipulated in more precise definitions. Yet, in ordinary use these expressions typically retain an evaluative meaning. Even if a statement such as "The incidence of Islamic terrorism in Europe reached a peak in 2016" expresses a purely factual assertion, the term "terrorism" is normatively laden, and its use in a context like the above normally conveys a distinct moral evaluation of a particular kind of behavior. This has been taken to count against the Classical View – the idea that science should deal only with facts. There is no way that science can entirely avoid values when communicating its results, so at best the value freedom required by Classical view is an illusion. (see for example Root 1993; Dupre 2007)

A further concern relates to the idea that science should live up the *ideal of liberal neutrality*. This ideal requires that *states* should be neutral in the sense that they should not promote certain conceptions of the good over others (see e.g. Dworkin 1978; Larmore 1987; Rawls 1993). However, given the above justification of the Classical View, it seems natural to require that science should abide by the ideal of liberal neutrality.

Many have argued that at least social science does not, and cannot, live up to this ideal of liberal neutrality. An instance of the problem is the following (cf. Root 1993, Chapter 7, following Foucault, Hacking, and many others). Social science often makes use of kinds, that is, concepts used for categorizing data and for theorizing. Typically, these are *social kinds,* i.e. kinds that in various ways depend upon legislation, institutional designs, administrative practices, and wider moral and political views. Think for example of kinds such as "marriage", "mental illness", or "terrorist" all of which only make sense on the background of particular institutional settings and political and moral views, giving heterosexual married people certain legal privileges, and deeming certain kinds of behavior abnormal, unwanted, in need of treatment, politically illegitimate, or dangerous. However, the argument goes, even if the kinds themselves do not have a normative content, by merely employing such normatively dependent kinds, scientists risk promoting or legitimizing the underlying institutional, legal, political or moral views upon which they depend, whether this is intended or not. Social science may even have a significant role in shaping social reality in virtue of the choice of social kinds to be used in research.

So, while research practices may seem entirely free from values, they may nonetheless effectively promote certain views of the good through the conceptual choices that need to be made. Of course, researchers may explicitly want to avoid normatively infested social kinds, or they may through their conceptual choices seek to contribute to developing new categories that they find more appropriate (e.g. a redefinition of the concept of marriage to cover same-sex partnerships). But again, such conceptual decisions are not neutral among conceptions of the good. When conceptualizing items to be researched in a morally or politically charged domain, deciding to employ certain concepts rather than others will often effectively favor one side of the struggle over the other, and it may be impossible to stay neutral. Depending on details of definition, this problem may arise in external or internal phases of research. But the issue is not that researchers ignore relevant evidence or prefer one interpretation or hypothesis over another for moral or political reasons or that they fail to refrain from using expressions like "terrorist" with an ineliminable value content.

Expertise and Democratic Legitimacy

The Classical View, as we have stated it, specifies a distinctive division of epistemic and deliberative labor between science and democracy. Many have worried that according science and scientific experts this distinct epistemic authority lacks democratic legitimacy. One problem concerns the difference in power or influence that may accompany the distinctive role accorded to experts. As Stephen Turner phrases it, "Expertise is a kind of violation of the condition of the rough equality presupposed by democratic accountability." (Turner 2003: 19). But a second separate problem, according to Turner, concerns how liberal democracy can legitimately privilege the scientific perspective:

> If the liberal state is supposed to be neutral with respect to opinions, that is to say it neither promotes nor gives special regard to any particular belief, world view, sectarian positions, and so on, what about expert opinion? Do they enjoy a special status that these things lack?
>
> *(ibid: 19)*

The charge here is that there is something democratically illegitimate about according science the role of epistemic authority. After all, isn't science just one among several outlooks that liberal democracy should allegedly be neutral between? This objection may be viewed as a matter of extending the idea of liberal neutrality to cover the factual domain: it is not just that science should not promote one conception of the good over others, but that science itself is just one perspective among many between which liberal democracy should be neutral.

A related but distinct concern is that the epistemic authority of science is unwarranted for epistemic reasons. In a widely discussed paper sociologists of science Collins and Evans write that:

> One of the most important contributions of sociology of scientific knowledge (SSK) has been to make it much harder to make the claim: "Trust scientists because they have special access to truth". Our question is "If it no longer is clear that the scientists and the technologists have special access to the truth, why should their advice be specially valued?" This, we think, is the pressing intellectual problem of the age.
>
> (Collins and Evans 2002: 236)

The worry is that there is no compelling reason to believe that science or experts have a privileged access to truth and therefore genuinely have earned a special epistemic authority. So, if one wants to uphold the division of epistemic and deliberative labor distinctive to the Classical View, one needs to defend it in other ways.

What Sort of Science Should Liberal Democracy Want?

Let us now briefly reflect on these criticisms and consider what can be said on behalf of the Classical View as motivated by the requirements of liberal democracy.

1   The ideal of value free science holds that the internal phases of science should be unaffected by non-epistemic values, but leaves it fairly open how non-epistemic values may influence external phases, where this includes the choice of research question, choice of method, and communication of findings. The Classical View as we see it is more demanding in some respects, but perhaps less in others. Scientists could legitimately decide to focus on a particular issue because they believe that gaining more knowledge about it would change the political agenda, or would change the outcome of political decision-making in a better direction. But scientists cannot legitimately decide to *neglect* a question because they think that *ignorance* in the general population or among policy-makers will better promote their favored political view. Opting for ignorance is not a way of supporting democratic deliberation, but a way of distorting it. Likewise, the choice of research method is not free. There are, of course, moral constraints in the choice of methods having to do with moral obligations not to harm and to obtain informed consent. But there are additional constraints motivated by the role that science should have in democratic decision-making. Scientists cannot, for example, pick a less reliable method because they think that uncertainty or conflicting evidence in a particular domain will promote favored political ends. This would be a way of distorting democratic decision-making (cf. (Kitcher 2001) for related discussion of constraints on free inquiry and allocation of resources in science).

2   Whereas the ideal of value free science imposes no constraints on how non-epistemic values may affect the external stages, the Classical View would support some constraints. It could agree that scientists could be motivated by non-epistemic values to invest an effort in communicating results in one area rather than another, because they think it more important that rational political decisions are expedited in some areas rather than others. However, in the general case it would appear illegitimate if scientists were to withhold reporting some issue because they think that ignorance about that issue would lead to what they considered a better political outcome. Again, this particular way of influencing the outcome of the political process – by deciding not to support it – would run counter to the values of liberal

democracy. Liberal democracy would also permit that communication to the public may involve values. First, the communication may make use of expressions featuring ineliminable value content, i.e. expressions such as "terrorist", "illness", "rape", "poverty", as long as it is clear to the intended audience what factual content is being asserted, and that the epistemic authority regards the factual content only. Second, it may be fully appropriate for scientists to assert or make their personal value judgments known in public, as long as it is clear that science or experts assert no special epistemic authority regarding these value judgments.

3   Liberal democracy would agree that non-epistemic values should not distort the internal stages of research. However, the ultimate concern for liberal democracy is not values as such, but relevance, reliability and neutrality of the outcome of scientific processes. In so far as the non-epistemic values affect the reliability of research negatively, it should be banned or minimized. On the other hand, researchers are of course permitted to be motivated by moral and political concerns or personal interests to do highly reliable research. Hence, the internal phases may well be affected by non-epistemic values in that sense. For these reasons, the Classical View could welcome Longino's view. Science is a social process aiming at generating epistemically highly qualified claims. This process involves critical discussion, the outcome of which may improve significantly from certain forms of value diversity. Thus, individuals participating in critical discussion may well be motivated by non-epistemic values, affecting their initial judgments about acceptance and interpretation of evidence, background theories and so on, and this would make the internal stages replete with values. However, as long as the process produces a relevant and reliable output, this is fully acceptable.

4   According to Douglas, there are cases where scientists are morally obliged to make their own judgments about possible risks that their research involves. These judgments are in part based on non-epistemic values, and at least in some cases they cannot be fully delegated to democratic decision-making. If this is right, the question is how liberal democracy should accommodate it. First, even if there are exceptions, in the general cases it is surely possible to communicate transparently about the various types of uncertainty that surround particular findings. It can typically be communicated, for example, whether methods employed a high or a low margin of error, whether they are likely to overestimate or underreport a given phenomenon, and it can be communicated whether the interpretation of results depend on controversial background assumptions or not, and whether these are independently testable or not, and so on. It would then be up to liberal democracy to decide whether the findings should be considered solid enough to warrant certain political decisions. Scientists would, of course, play an indispensable role in offering their views about the levels of uncertainty surrounding various findings. And scientists having this role would not exempt them from making morally sensible choices in the internal parts of the research process, and these choices would have to be in part based on values.

5   Second, scientists could be criticized from the point of view of liberal democracy if their judgments of risk pertaining to the internal stages of research are based on illegitimate values, say highly idiosyncratic values or values inconsistent with the basic tenets of liberal democracy, say the view that certain possible negative outcomes were not worth bothering with because they mainly affect women or underrepresented ethnic groups.

6   An important charge is that social science and perhaps other parts of science is bound to be partisan because there are too many cases where no neutral conceptual choices are possible (among other reasons). Clearly, a partisan science would be highly problematic as it would impede or bias democratic decision-making. A natural response on behalf of liberal democracy would be that such intentional or unwitting partisanship of science should be challenged and laid bare in the deliberative process itself. Liberal democracy should respect the epistemic authority of science, but this is compatible with scientific claims being legitimately contested for

reasons not having to do with their truth, or the scientific evidence adduced in their favor, but because they employ concepts or kinds that come with links to institutions, legislations, or moral or political views that are perceived to be objectionable. So, democratic deliberation and scrutiny could seek to identify ways that conceptual choices in science may illicitly promote certain conceptions of the good over others, or in other ways distort public deliberation, and democratic deliberation could urge science to rethink its categories if necessary. Of course, this is a very blunt answer on behalf of liberal democracy to a large and complex problem – and some hold that that this strategy is not even possible as various sorts of science or scientific expertise already have the upper hand. (cf. the discussions in Turner 2003)

7   Consider finally the charge that it is not democratically legitimate to accord science or scientific experts the epistemic authority implied in the Classical View. One worry is that science or scientific experts enjoy an unduly large share of political influence, thus violating an ideal of political equality. However, in so far as the division of decision-making between the factual part and the value part is in fact observed, there seems to be no violation of the ideal of political equality. Scientists do not get to have a greater say than others regarding which policies we should adopt. A somewhat different objection goes that liberal democracy should be neutral between different worldviews, where the scientific outlook is just one view among several worldviews. If we accept this premise, it might well be indefensible to accord science any special role in democratic decision-making. This problem merits a longer discussion, but suffice it here to say that normally proponents of liberal neutrality do not endorse such a wide interpretation of liberal neutrality.

Collins and Evans pressed the different charge that science studies reveals that there is no justification for thinking that science or scientific experts has any special access to truth. For liberal democracy such skepticism about the epistemic merits of science would imply that there is no justification for involving scientific expertise in democratic decision-making. The skeptical claim about the capacity of scientific institutions is strong and very controversial, and we cannot discuss it here. For general discussions of these and related sweeping claims, see for example (Goldman 1999; Boghossian 2006).[1]

Note

1   Klemens Kappel has written "The Classical View", "Neutral Science?", "Expertise and Democratic Legitimacy", and "What Sort of Science Should Liberal Democracy Want?"; Julie Zahle has written "Value Freedom in Science". They have of course discussed, and commented on, each other's sections.

References

Boghossian, P.A. (2006). *Fear of Knowledge : Against Relativism and Constructivism*. Oxford: Clarendon Press.
Collins, H.M. and R. Evans. (2002). The Third Wave of Science Studies: Studies of Expertise and Experience. *Social Studies of Science*, 32(2), pp. 235–296.
Douglas, H. (2000). Inductive Risk and Values in Science. *Philosophy of Science*, 67, pp. 559–579.
Douglas, H. (2009). *Science, Policy, and the Value-Free Ideal*. Pittsburgh: University of Pittsburgh Press.
Dupre, J. (2007). Fact and Value. In H. Kincaid, J. Dupre, and A. Wylie, eds., *Value-Free Science: Ideals and Illusions*. Oxford: Oxford University Press, pp. 27–41.
Dworkin, R. (1978). Liberalism. In S. Hampshire, ed., *Public and Private Morality*. Hampshire, Cambridge: Cambridge University Press, pp. 113–145.
Goldman, A.I., (1999). *Knowledge in a Social World*. Oxford, New York: Oxford University Press.
Kitcher, P. (2001). *Science, Truth, and Democracy*. Oxford, New York: Oxford University Press.
Kourany, J.A. (2010). *Philosophy of Science after Feminism*. Oxford: Oxford University Press.
Larmore, C.E. (1987). *Patterns of Moral Complexity*. Cambridge: Cambridge University Press.

Longino, H. (1990). *Science as Social Knowledge. Values and Objectivity in Scientific Inquiry*. Princeton, NJ: Princeton University Press.

Maasen, S. and P. Weingart. (2005). *Democratization of Expertise? Exploring Novel Forms of Scientific Advice in Political Decision-Making*. Dordrecht: Springer.

Merton, R.K. (1938). Science and the Social Order. *Philosophy of Science*, 5, pp. 321–337.

Merton, R.K. (1942). A Note on Science and Democracy. *Journal of Legal and Political Sociology*, 1, pp. 115–126.

Pielke, R.A. (2007). *The Honest Broker: Making Sense of Science in Policy and Politics*. Cambridge: Cambridge University Press.

Rawls, J. (1993). *Political Liberalism*. New York: Columbia University Press.

Resnik, D.B. (2009). *Playing Politics with Science: Balancing Scientific Independence and Government Oversight*. Oxford, New York: Oxford University Press.

Root, M., (1993). *Philosophy of Social Science: The Methods, Ideals, and Politics of Social Inquiry*. Oxford: Blackwell.

Rudner, R. (1953). The Scientist Qua Scientist Makes Value Judgments. *Philosophy of Science*, 20, pp. 1–6.

Solomon, M. (2001). *Social Empiricism*. Cambridge, MA: MIT Press.

Steel, D. (2015). *Philosophy and the Precautionary Principle. Science, Evidence, and Environmental Policy*. Cambridge: Cambridge University Press.

Turner, S.P. (2003). *Liberal Democracy 3.0: Civil Society in an Age of Experts*. London; Thousand Oaks, CA: SAGE Publications.

Weber, M. (2011). *Methodology of Social Sciences*. Somerset, N.J., Transaction; London: Eurospan [distributor].

Further Reading

Carrier, M., D., Howard, and J. Kourany eds. (2008). *The Challenge of the Social and the Pressure of the Practice: Science and Values Revisited*. Pittsburgh: University of Pittsburgh Press.

Elliott, K.C. (2017). *A Tapestry of Values. An Introduction to Values in Science*. Oxford: Oxford University Press.

Elliott, K.C. and D. Steel eds. (2017). *Current Controversies in Values and Science*. New York: Routledge.

Kincaid, H., J. Dupré, and A. Wylie eds. (2007). *Value-Free Science?: Ideals and Illusions*. Oxford: Oxford University Press.

40

THE EPISTEMIC BENEFITS OF DEMOCRACY

A Critical Assessment

Kristoffer Ahlstrom-Vij

Introduction

Democracy is rule by the people, and people sometimes make bad choices on account of ignorance. In particular, when people vote, they influence what policies are implemented in society, which is why we rightly worry about ignorance among the electorate. So, are we ignorant? In an overview of survey data about the American voter from 1940 to 1994, Michael Delli Carpini and Scott Keeter (1996) found that "[o]nly 13 percent of the more than 2,000 political questions examined could be answered correctly by 75 percent or more of those asked, and only 41 percent could be answered correctly by more than half the public," and moreover that "[m]any of the facts known by relatively small percentages of the public seem critical to understanding—let alone acting in—the political world" (101–102). In what Jeffrey Friedman (2005) describes as an "ocean of findings about political ignorance" (x), results such as these are the norm. Indeed, according to Larry Bartels (1996), "[t]he political ignorance of the American voter is one of the best-documented features of contemporary politics" (194). I will assume that Americans are not unique in this respect.

That said, we cannot *infer* from widespread public ignorance that we have reason to worry about bad policy. There might be epistemically relevant features of democracies that alleviate ignorance. Indeed, this is exactly the possibility we will be concerned with below, although our conclusion will be largely negative: even if we consider the most promising candidates for such features, we have good reason to worry about public ignorance. More specifically, the chapter starts by showing that the worry remains despite the Condorcet Jury Theorem and the so-called "miracle of aggregation." It then moves on to widen the scope of the challenge to encompass liberal and deliberative conceptions of democracy. Finally, the chapter surveys the non-democratic alternative of expert rule found in Plato and Mill, and considers a recent case for that alternative provided by Jason Brennan in response to David Estlund's claim that expert rule can never be politically legitimate.

Public Ignorance and Voting

A natural place to start when considering the challenge posed by public ignorance for democracy is with voting. There are two prominent views on the nature of voting. We have reason to worry about public ignorance on either view.

On one theory, voting involves making a *statement*, and specifically a statement about policies conforming with the general will (Rousseau 1978/1762) or being in the common interest (Estlund 1990). On this theory, there is such a thing as voting *incorrectly*. According to Rousseau (1978/1762), "[w]hen [...] a view which is at odds with my own wins the day, it proves only that I was deceived, and that what I took to be the general will was no such thing" (273). This is because

> [i]f the People, engaged in deliberation, were adequately informed, and if no means existed by which the citizens could communicate with one another, from the great number of small differences the general will would result and the decision reached would always be good.
>
> *(194)*

Several commentators have noted the similarity between Rousseau's conditions and those of *the Condorcet Jury Theorem* (e.g., Grofman and Feld 1988; Wolff 2006). Condorcet (1976/1785) famously suggested that, provided each voter is *competent*, by being more likely than not to answer the question voted on right, and votes *independently*,[1] in not just voting in the way that other people vote, the probability that the majority vote answers the question voted on correctly increases with the size of the voting group. Are voters *in fact* competent (and independent, although I will set aside that aspect here)? Condorcet himself doubted it:

> A very numerous assembly cannot be composed of very enlightened men. It is even probable that those comprising this assembly will on many matters combine great ignorance with many prejudices. Thus there will be a great number of questions on which the probability of the truth of each voter will be below ½.
>
> *(Condorcet 1976: 49)*

Condorcet's conjecture is consistent with the empirical data considered above. For now, however, the main thing to note is that, rather than highlighting a means to *removing* voter ignorance, Condorcet's theorem *presupposes* that the voters are, as Rousseau put it, "adequately informed." Consequently, if votes are statements about what conforms with the general will, public ignorance means that it is unlikely that the popular will, as revealed through voting, will track the general will.

It might be argued that this worry is unfounded on account of the "miracle of aggregation" (Converse 1990), i.e., the idea that, "[u]nder the right conditions, individual measurement errors will be independently random and will tend to cancel each other out" (Page and Shapiro 1993: 41).[2] The problem is that, if mistaken voter beliefs tend to point in one direction rather than randomly in different directions, individual errors will *not* cancel each other out. Bryan Caplan (2007) argues that public ignorance about economics is systematic in this sense. While this does not entail that we systematically err in *other* politically relevant domains, it does put the burden of proof onto the defender of the miracle of aggregation to give us reason to believe otherwise.[3]

But maybe votes are not so much statements (about the general will or otherwise) as expressions of *preferences* (e.g., Arrow 1977; Caplan 2007). And if so, it might be suggested that the question of voter ignorance does not enter the picture, since preferences are not the sort of things that are true or false. However, preferences can be more or less informed, and as a result more or less likely to be frustrated. For example, if we prefer a society where no one lives in economic destitution to one where some do, but have wildly inaccurate views about what political candidates or policies will realize the kind of society we thereby prefer, then our preference might end up frustrated.[4] This gives us reason to worry about public ignorance, even if votes express preferences.

Epistemic Benefits of Liberal Democracy

If what was argued in the previous section is on point, we have reason to worry about public ignorance, irrespective of whether we understand votes as statements or as expressing preferences.[5] It might be objected, however, that in so far as we are attracted to democracy, we are typically not attracted to it merely as a way to aggregate votes, but also as a political system protecting certain basic *rights*. In other words, what we are attracted to is a specifically *liberal* democracy. Chief among those rights is that of free speech. Beyond being a right we want to protect on moral grounds, it might also carry with it certain epistemic benefits, assuaging worries about public ignorance.

The most famous epistemic defense of free speech is that of John Stuart Mill. According to Mill,

> [i]f all mankind minus one, were of one opinion, and only one person were of the contrary opinion, mankind would be no more justified in silencing that one person, than he, if he had the power, would be justified in silencing mankind.
>
> *(2008/1859: 21)*

At the heart of Mill's argument is the assumption that "[w]rong opinions and practices gradually yield to fact and argument" (24). This is a questionable assumption. Convincing-sounding falsities often win out in discussion, while unpopular truths often are rejected. This is not to say that Mill's assumption is uncommon. Alvin Goldman (1999) argues that Mill's argument has been revived recently among those maintaining that the truth stands the best chance of winning out in a "marketplace of ideas." The problem, Goldman argues, is that, if we understand the relevant idea to be appealing to a *literal* market, it neither follows from economic theory, nor receives any support from the practice of the markets; and if we understand it in *metaphorical* terms, it comes down to the overly optimistic idea that restrictions on speech are epistemically objectionable because more speech is always epistemically better.

In light of this, it makes sense for defenders of the epistemic benefits of liberal democracy to rest their case on a wider set of considerations than Mill does. For example, Allen Buchanan (2004) suggests that "key liberal institutions [...] contribute significantly to the reduction of the moral and prudential risks to which we are all vulnerable by virtue of our ineliminable social dependence" (99). Moral risks consist in risks of doing the morally wrong thing, while prudential risks involve the risk of harming oneself, e.g., in the way that false beliefs might lead one to make bad choices. In order to avoid these risks in a context where we're inescapably dependent on others for information, we need to defer to reliable sources. According to Buchanan, the key liberal institutions that help us do so are (A) freedom of thought, conscience, expression and association, and opportunities for equal participation; (B) a large role for merit in the social identification of reliable sources of beliefs (i.e., of experts); and (C) epistemic egalitarianism, which involves a willingness to challenge others as well as to listen.

As for (A), Buchanan acknowledges that Mill is too optimistic, and suggests that "more specific institutional mechanisms and psychological dispositions are needed for reliable selection of true beliefs and correction of false ones" (110). The most important mechanisms and dispositions here are "effective processes for identifying epistemic authorities on grounds of merit, understood as the possession of objective qualifications, and a widespread, though not necessarily universal, limited epistemic egalitarianism" (110). That's to say that, while there is certainly something distinctly liberal about (A), the weight of Buchanan's argument rests, not on (A), but on (B) and (C) above. Let us consider the latter two in reverse order.

Buchanan spells out (C) with reference to a "widespread [...] attitude of basic moral egalitarianism" that has people "view themselves as competent to form and revise their beliefs and to give reasons capable of prompting others to form and revise their beliefs" (117). As in the case of (A), there is certainly something distinctly liberal about (C). But for a practice of epistemic egalitarianism to make for a reliable check on experts—which is required if it's to provide "a significant constraint on epistemic deference and hence on the moral and prudential risk that results from excessive or misplaced epistemic deference" (117–18)—people need to *be* competent in forming and revising their beliefs about the competency of others, and not just *view* themselves as competent in that regard. But if so, people being reliable judges of the competency of others is a *precondition* on a practice of epistemic egalitarianism reducing moral and prudential risk, rather than a *consequence* thereof.

The upshot is that Buchanan's entire case for the role of liberal democracy in reducing moral and prudential risk rests on (B), the "merit-based competition for expert status" (106). But there is nothing distinctly liberal about (B). Science, when done correctly, assigns expertise solely on merit, as does the market. But it's not clear that science and the market thereby are liberal. In other words, to the extent that liberal democratic institutions generate epistemic benefits of the kind Buchanan is interested in, it's due to a practice that ultimately has nothing to do with liberalism.

Epistemic Benefits of Deliberative Democracy

So far, we have seen that there is widespread public ignorance, and that the Condorcet Jury Theorem, the miracle of aggregation, and liberal institutions such as free speech and epistemic egalitarianism do not serve to assuage the worries associated with such ignorance. But perhaps we need to understand the relevant liberal institutions in a broader way, as involving a deliberative process of reason-exchange among the public. This line of reasoning has been defended by deliberative democrats, and perhaps most prominently by Amy Gutmann and Dennis Thompson (2004).[6]

According to Gutmann and Thompson, deliberative democracy involves an inclusive and dynamic exchange of reason, wherein any output of the process is open to revision, and the process as such is self-correcting. What's good about such a process? Gutmann and Thompson point to two kinds of value: an *instrumental* and an *expressive*. The instrumental value arises out of the fact that, "when [people] deliberate, they can expand their knowledge" (12), and that, "[b]y deliberating with their fellow citizens, decision-makers can arrive at better, more adequately justified decisions" (23). The expressive value, by contrast, comes about because, "[b]y deliberating with one another, decision-makers manifest mutual respect toward their fellow citizens" (22). Let us consider the instrumental value first.

According to Gutmann and Thompson, deliberation *can* expand people's knowledge and *can* increase their justification. Given the fact of widespread public ignorance as well as the fact of bias and power asymmetries, why think that deliberation will tend to do what it arguably can do? Here, Gutmann and Thompson appeal to "one of the most effective antidotes to both the misuse of deliberation and the neglect of undesirable forms of power politics—the use of deliberation itself to publicly expose the unjustified exercise of power" (46). So, if there's a problem with deliberation, the solution is *more* deliberation. To see why this is implausible, consider what we want social deliberation to do in political contexts. Since politics is complicated, we can at most expect a minority of citizens to be informed—an expectation borne out in the empirical studies on public ignorance considered above. Consequently, what we want social deliberation to do is (at the very least) help the informed minority educate the uninformed majority. Is that something we can expect social deliberation to do?

In situations in which there is a minority opinion, there are two possibilities. One possibility is that the minority doesn't share their information, in which case that opinion cannot possibly have any influence on the majority opinion. This possibility is far from unlikely, given both the informational pressure of the majority position—leading the minority to infer that they're probably mistaken—or social pressure associated with the risk of social sanctions against dissenters (Sunstein 2006). These pressures can be resisted, which brings us to the second possibility: the minority shares their information. Still, the impact on the group judgment is likely to be small due to the so-called *common knowledge effect*. Daniel Gigone and Reid Hastie (1993) explain: "The influence of a particular item of information [on the judgment of a group] is directly and positively related to the number of group members who have knowledge of that item before the group discussion and judgment" (960).

In light of these social psychological facts, we should expect it to be unlikely that social deliberation will enable the minority to educate the majority. On account of informational pressures, social pressures, and the common knowledge effect, what makes a difference is not *quality* of information but *quantity* of people bringing a particular piece of information to the table. Consequently, it's not clear that any problem owing to deliberation will tend to be corrected by further deliberation; if anything, deliberation will tend to simply *reinforce*, not educate or otherwise challenge, the majority position.[7]

This calls into question the instrumental value of social deliberation. By extension, it also undermines the expressive value of social deliberation, since Gutmann and Thompson (2004) suggest that, "[i]f deliberation tended to produce worse decision than other processes in the long run, then it would not serve the expressive purpose" (22). As it turns out, there are other, non-deliberative processes that harnesses the insight of minorities more successfully than socially deliberating groups, in exactly the kind of contexts we can expect to find ourselves in on political matters, namely ones wherein the majority is likely to be uninformed (Ahlstrom-Vij 2012). The relevant non-deliberative processes, including ones involving so-called information markets—markets aggregating bets on future or otherwise unknown events—thereby enable us to reach better decision than we would through social deliberation.[8]

The points made here about Gutmann and Thompson are likely to apply to other deliberative democrats who emphasize the epistemic benefits of social deliberation, such as Seyla Benhabib (1996), Iris Marion Young (2000) and Robert Talisse (2005).[9] They might also extend to deliberative democrats, such as Joshua Cohen (1997), who follow John Rawls (1997) in restricting the role of social deliberation to constitutional essentials and matters of basic justice. After all, while it is controversial whether the propositions thereby deliberated over have truth-values, the fact that we lack reason to believe that the empirical results showing that social deliberation consistently favors the majority view do not generalize to *moral* deliberation suggests that those results should worry Rawlsians, particularly given Rawls's stated interest in respecting pluralism.

It might be objected that the arguments above ignore the fact that Gutmann and Thompson (2004) take deliberative democracy to be "an aspirational ideal" (37). That is, while social psychology might present those defending deliberative practices with a genuine challenge, it does not go so far as to suggest that deliberative democracy isn't *possible*—perhaps people just need some help. Indeed, Bruce Ackerman and James Fishkin (2004) have provided evidence suggesting that good information can be properly harnessed, spread, and utilized in highly controlled and monitored settings. Still, they are the first to acknowledge that mirroring the relevant conditions in actual, everyday deliberations would require "a rethinking of the deliberative process from the ground up" (5). This raises a question: If what was initially attractive about deliberation was its (presumed) epistemic benefits, and it turns out that large-scale reform is required to at all reap those benefits, why keep bothering with social deliberation? In particular, why not just let those who are informed rule?

Expert Rule

Plato famously defends a form of expert rule in the *Republic*, on which (1) the competent should rule, and (2) the competent are philosophers. The former claim is supported primarily by his ship analogy: like a ship, the state requires a competent captain (488b-e). In defense of (2), Plato offers a two-pronged argument. First, the alternative to rule by philosophers would be rule by sophists. The problem with the sophist is that he simply teaches whatever "convictions that the majority express when they are gathered together", but "knows nothing about which of these convictions is fine or shameful, good or bad, just or unjust, [and simply] applies all these names in accordance with how the beast reacts—calling what it enjoys good and what angers it bad" (493a-c).[10] Second, only philosophers, who are in touch with the eternal forms in accordance with which society is to be shaped, do have knowledge about what is fine, good, and just, and are on that account the appropriate rulers (501b-c).

If we reject Plato's metaphysics and epistemology, (2) starts to look questionable. However, we might still accept (1). This is the position taken by Mill (2008/1861), who defends a version of expert rule in the context of universal suffrage. His argument is straightforwardly utilitarian. While maintaining that "it is a personal injustice to withhold from any one, unless for the prevention of greater evils, the ordinary privilege of having his voice reckoned in the disposal of affairs in which he has the same interest as other people" (329), he also takes it that "the benefits of completely universal suffrage cannot be obtained without bringing with them [...] a chance of more than equivalent evil" (339). Preventing said evil requires two things: First, people are to be excluded from the political franchise unless they can read, write, and do basic arithmetic, and know some history and politics (330–331). Second, some people should be allowed plural votes on the basis of "mental superiority" (366).

Critics of utilitarianism might find Mill's argument problematic. However, more recently, Jason Brennan (2011a) has defended a version of (1) on non-utilitarian grounds.[11] He maintains that "universal suffrage is unjust, because it violates a citizen's right not to be subject to high stakes decisions made by incompetent and morally unreasonable people" (702). He makes his point partly by way of an analogy to a jury trial: just like an ignorant or morally unreasonable jury would lack authority and legitimate power over a defendant, an ignorant or morally unreasonable voter lacks authority and legitimate power over others. This motivates a *competence principle*, on which political decisions are to be restricted to competent and morally reasonable people. That principle, Brennan argues, is violated in the case of universal suffrage. Hence, universal suffrage is unjust.

According to Estlund (2008), the problem with Plato and Mill is that they commit what he calls "the expert/boss fallacy," which consists in inferring from someone knowing what should be done that they have political authority over those who don't. Brennan (2011a) isn't committing that fallacy; on his competence principle, competency (or expertise) is necessary but not sufficient for authority (710). Still, his account violates the requirement that, according to Estlund, accounts for the fallacy being a fallacy: the qualified acceptability requirement, on which "[n]o one has authority and legitimate coercive power over another without a justification that could be accepted by all qualified points of view" (33). Estlund doesn't specify exactly what makes points of views qualified, but makes clear that it has something to do with being reasonable (63–64). And since reasonable people can disagree about where to draw the line between the competent and the incompetent, any form of epistemically restricted suffrage violates the acceptability criterion. Brennan (2011a) grants that the restricted suffrage he has in mind violates the acceptability criterion, but suggests that "the way in which democracy violates the competence principle is intrinsically worse than the way in which epistocracy [i.e., expert rule] violates the qualified acceptability requirement" (717). Factoring in that restricted suffrage is likely to make for better outcomes on account of the voters being competent, Brennan contends that we have reason to prefer restricted to universal suffrage nonetheless.

Conclusion

Public ignorance presents a genuine challenge to democracy. Moreover, that challenge remains in the face of the Condorcet Jury Theorem and the miracle of aggregation), and fails to be countered by liberal or deliberative theories of democracy. In fact, the challenge might just be driving us towards some form of expert rule of the kind defended by Plato, Mill and more recently by Brennan. Of course, while Brennan's rights-based and as such explicitly moral case against the universal franchise should certainly give us pause, there being few (if any) epistemic benefits to democracy is compatible with there being ample non-epistemic benefits thereof, including *moral* benefits. As such, the negative but hopefully still constructive conclusion of our investigation is this: in so far as we want to defend democracy, we should probably not look to epistemology.

Notes

1 Ladha (1992) argues that the theorem holds even in the absence of complete independence, provided the average interdependence between votes is sufficiently low.
2 See also Landemore (2013: 156–160) and Surowiecki (2004: 10) who invoke a similar explanation to account for "the wisdom of crowds."
3 See Huemer (2015), who argues that the best explanation for widespread political disagreement is that people are systematically biased when it comes to politics generally, not just economics.
4 Note that the relevant preferences need not be strictly *self-interested* attitudes. In fact, empirical research suggests that people tend to vote, not on the basis of narrow self-interest, but for what they perceive to be in the *national* interest (see, e.g., Funk and Garcia-Monet 1997).
5 This conclusion is compatible with the view, popular among economists, that "it is irrational to be politically well-informed because the low returns from data simply do not justify their cost in time and other resources" (Downs 1957: 259). After all, it might be *individually* rational for someone not to do something, even if we have reason to worry about the *social* costs of everyone not doing it, as illustrated by the cases of recycling and other polluting behaviors.
6 See Bohman and Rehg (1997) and Elster (1998) for a sample of the wide variety of views included under the heading of "deliberative democracy."
7 This conclusion remains despite Lu Hong and Scott Page's (2004) so-called *diversity trumps ability* theorem, according to which "a random collection of agents drawn from a large set of limited-ability agents typically outperforms a collection of the very best agents from that same set" (16386). First, Hong and Page's model does not take into account *communication* (16389) and as such has nothing to do with social deliberation. Second, as Landemore (2013) points out, since the theorem is decreasingly likely to hold as the number of agents increases, it "could seem slightly sobering from a democratic point of view favoring maximal inclusiveness" (164). Third, for the theorem to hold, the agents involved need to be, as Page (2007) puts it, "pretty smart" (137), an assumption that's unlikely to hold in the contexts we're concerned with, in light of the public ignorance data.
8 For more on the epistemology of information markets, see Ahlstrom-Vij (2016).
9 For an argument to this effect, see Ahlstrom-Vij (2012).
10 All translations from Plato are from Cooper (1997).
11 By contrast, Brennan (2011b) defends, not the view that incompetent people should not be allowed to vote, but simply that they have a moral obligation not to.

References

Ackerman, B., and Fishkin, J. (2004). *Deliberation Day*. New Haven, CT: Yale University Press.
Ahlstrom-Vij, K. (2012). Why Deliberative Democracy is (Still) Untenable. *Public Affairs Quarterly*, 26(3), pp. 199–220.
Ahlstrom-Vij, K. (2016). Information Markets. In D. Coady, K. Lippert-Rasmussen, and K. Brownlee, eds., *The Blackwell Companion to Applied Philosophy*. Oxford: Wiley-Blackwell, pp. 89–122.
Arrow, K. (1977). Current Developments in the Theory of Social Choice. *Social Research*, 44, pp. 607–622.
Bartels, L. (1996). Uninformed Voters: Information Effects in Presidential Elections. *American Journal of Political Science*, 40(1), pp. 194–230.
Benhabib, S. (1996). Toward a Deliberative Model of Democratic Legitimacy. In S. Benhabib, ed., *Democracy and Difference*. Princeton, NJ: Princeton University Press., pp. 67–94.

Bohman, J., and Rehg, W. (1997). *Deliberative Democracy: Essays on Reason and Politics*. Cambridge, MA: MIT Press.

Brennan, J. (2011a). The Right to a Competent Electorate. *The Philosophical Quarterly*, 61(245), pp. 700–724.

Brennan, J. (2011b). *The Ethics of Voting*. Princeton and Oxford: Princeton University Press.

Buchanan, A. (2004). Political Liberalism and Social Epistemology. *Philosophy and Public Affairs*, 31(2), pp. 95–130.

Caplan, B. (2007). *The Myth of the Rational Voter: Why Democracies Choose Bad Policies*. Princeton: Princeton University Press.

Cohen, J. (1997). Deliberation and Democratic Legitimacy. In B. James, and R. William, eds., *Deliberative Democracy: Essays on Reason and Politics*. Cambridge, MA: MIT Press., pp. 67–91.

Condorcet, M. J. A. N. C. (1976). Essay on the Application of Mathematics to the Theory of Decision-making. In K. M. Baker, ed., *Condorcet: Selected Writings*. Originally published in 1785. Indiana: Bobbs-Merrill.

Converse, P. (1990). Popular Representation and the Distribution of Information. In J. Ferejohn, and J. Kuklinski, eds., *Information and Democratic Process*. Urbana: University of Illinois Press., pp. 369–388.

Cooper, J. M. (1997). *Plato: Complete Works*. Indianapolis: Hackett.

Delli Carpini, M., and Keeter, S. (1996). *What Americans Know about Politics and Why It Matters*. New Haven, CT: Yale University Press.

Downs, A. (1957). *An Economic Theory of Democracy*. New York: Harper and Row.

Elster, J. (1998). *Deliberative Democracy*. Cambridge, MA: Cambridge University Press.

Estlund, D. (1990). Democracy Without Preference. *The Philosophical Review*, 99(3), pp. 397–423.

Estlund, D. (2008). *Democratic Authority: A Philosophical Framework*. Princeton, NJ: Princeton University Press.

Friedman, J. (2005). Popper, Weber, and Hayek: The Epistemology and Politics of Ignorance. *Critical Review*, 17(1–2), pp. i–lviii.

Funk, C., and Garcia-Monet, P. (1997). The Relationship between Personal and National Concerns in Public Perceptions about the Economy. *Political Research Quarterly*, 50(2), pp. 317–342.

Gigone, D., and Hastie, R. (1993). The Common Knowledge Effect: Information Sharing and Group Judgment. *Journal of Personality and Social Psychology*, 65(5), pp. 959–974.

Goldman, A. (1999). *Knowledge in a Social World*. Oxford: Oxford University Press.

Grofman, B., and Feld, S. L. (1988). Rousseau's General Will: A Condorcetian Perspective. *The American Political Science Review*, 82(2), pp. 567–576.

Gutmann, A., and Thompson, D. (2004). *Why Deliberative Democracy?* Princeton, NJ: Princeton University Press.

Hong, L., and Page, S. (2004). Groups of Diverse Problem Solvers Can Outperform Groups of High-Ability Problem Solvers. *Proceedings of the National Academy of Sciences of the United States of America*, 101(46), pp. 16385–16389.

Huemer, M. (2015). Why People Are Irrational About Politics. In A. Jonathan, B. Geoffrey, M. Michael, and S. Geoffrey, eds., *Philosophy, Politics, and Economics*. New York: Oxford University Press, pp. 456–467.

Ladha, K. (1992). The Condorcet Jury Theorem, Free Speech, and Correlated Votes. *American Journal of Political Science*, 36(3), pp. 617–634.

Landemore, H. (2013). *Democratic Reason: Politics, Collective Intelligence, and the Rule of the Many*. Princeton and Oxford: Princeton University Press.

Mill, J. S. (2008/1859). On Liberty. In J. Gray, ed., *On Liberty and Other Essays*. Originally published in 1859. Oxford: Oxford University Press., pp. 5–130.

Mill, J. S. (2008/1861). Considerations on Representative Government. In J. Gray, ed., *On Liberty and Other Essays*. Originally published in 1859. Oxford: Oxford University Press., pp. 205–470.

Page, B. and Shapiro, R. (1993). The Rational Public and Democracy. In G. Marcus, and R. Hanson, eds., *Reconsidering the Democratic Public*. University Park: Pennsylvania State University Press., pp. 33–64.

Page, S. E. (2007). *The Difference*. Princeton and Oxford: Princeton University Press.

Rawls, J. (1997). The Idea of Public Reason. In B. James, and R. William, eds., *Deliberative Democracy: Essays on Reason and Politics*. Cambridge, MA: MIT Press., pp. 93–141.

Rousseau, J. (1978/1762). Of the Social Contract. In E. Barker, ed., *Social Contract: Essays by Locke, Hume and Rousseau*. Originally published in 1762. Oxford: Oxford University Press.

Sunstein, C. (2006). *Infotopia: How Many Minds Produce Knowledge*. New York: Oxford University Press.

Surowiecki, J. (2004). *The Wisdom of Crowds: Why the Many are Smarter than the Few*. London: Abacus.

Talisse, R. (2005). *Democracy after Liberalism: Pragmatism and Deliberative Politics*. New York: Routledge.

Wolff, J. (2006). *An Introduction to Political Philosophy*, revised edition. Oxford: Oxford University Press.

Young, I. M. (2000). *Inclusion and Democracy*. New York: Oxford University Press.

Further Reading

As far as comprehensive overviews of the empirical data on public ignorance are concerned, it's hard to beat Michael Delli Carpini and Scott Keeter's *What Americans Know about Politics and Why It Matters* (New Haven, CT: Yale University Press, 1996). Also relevant is Scott Althaus's work [in his *Collective Preferences in Democratic Politics* (Cambridge: Cambridge University Press, 2003) on how to model what an informed citizenry might look like. Similar modeling has been done by Bryan Caplan in his *The Myth of the Rational Voter* (Princeton, NJ: Princeton University Press, 2007). Whether ultimately successful, one of the most sophisticated attempts to rebut the challenges posed for democracy by public ignorance can be found in Hélène Landemore's *Democratic Reason: Politics, Collective Intelligence, and the Rule of the Many* (Princeton and Oxford: Princeton University Press, 2013). Jason Brennan's most recent case against democracy can be found in his *Against Democracy* (Princeton, NJ: Princeton University Press, 2017).

PART VIII

Further Horizons for Social Epistemology

41

SOCIAL EPISTEMOLOGY: DESCRIPTIVE AND NORMATIVE

Sanford C. Goldberg[1]

Recent work in social epistemology has exploded in the last three decades. There can be little doubt but that this reflects an increasingly popular commitment to two claims. The first claim is that there are important social dimensions to the acquisition, processing, retention, distribution, and assessment of knowledge; the second is that these dimensions ought to be represented in epistemological theorizing itself. But precisely how should epistemology represent the social dimensions of knowledge? On this matter there is no consensus even among those who call themselves social epistemologists. In fact, two distinct methodological paradigms would seem to have emerged.

One paradigm, typified by research in science and technology studies as well as in the sociology of knowledge, focuses on describing the actual practices by which we acquire, process, retain, distribute, and assess knowledge, as well as the institutions that are implicated in these practices, which I will call our *socio-epistemic practices*.[2] A premium is placed on having accurate descriptions of the practices and institutions themselves. The goal of accurate descriptions includes describing the evaluative standards that participants bring to these practices, as well as the (perhaps implicit) norms employed as participants resolve disputes and occasionally re-assess the very standards themselves.

Another paradigm, typified by the veritistic research programme initiated by Alvin Goldman in his influential (1999, 2002), focuses on *evaluating* our knowledge practices by assessing the extent to which following these practices leads to reliable belief-formation among those who participate in the practices. A premium here is placed on the identification of all of the downstream epistemic effects of a socio-epistemic practice, as well as on the accuracy of our evaluative assessment of the practices themselves (in terms of those effects). Social epistemologists working in this tradition often compare and contrast different epistemic regimes, comparing them as to which, if any, yields better outcomes along the reliability dimension.

To be sure, neither one of the methodological paradigms themselves, which I will call the descriptive and the normative paradigms, ignores the other. After all, the descriptive paradigm includes descriptions of participants' evaluations (and meta-evaluations) of the knowledge practices themselves, thereby aiming to incorporate a "normative" dimension to its models. And the normative paradigm purports to be a normative assessment of *the very knowledge practices* that characterize the epistemic community itself, and so it cannot succeed in its aim unless it is based on an accurate characterization – often in the form of a description – of those practices.

Even so, the paradigms tend to emphasize the one over the other, in ways that can only distort our understanding of the social dimensions of knowledge.

In focusing too much on the descriptive, for example, we might lose sight of the evaluative aims of traditional epistemology. After all, it is one thing to describe the norms and standards that actually inform a practice (and that participants rely on in their dealings with one another); it is another to evaluate those norms and standards. Even if we are careful to describe how participants themselves criticize the norms and standards of their own practices, and how they resolve any resulting disputes, even so we might want to be able to assess their resolutions as well.

In focusing too much on the normative, on the other hand, we might abstract away from the messy details of our actual practices, and in this way lose sight of what it was we were supposed to be evaluating in the first place. Admittedly, there is nothing special about the abstractions in normative social epistemology; *any* research that engages in abstraction – which is to say, *all* research – runs this risk. Still, I think it is fair to worry that, if what we want out of our social epistemology is an assessment of the reliability effects of our socio-epistemic practices, we will ignore all aspects of that practice that we do not regard as having any such effects, and it is reasonable to fear that the result will be an impoverished understanding of our socio-epistemic practices themselves.

I recognize that these criticisms will likely not move those already committed to one or the other methodological paradigm. I will not try to convince these folks here.[3] Instead, what I want to offer is a conception of social epistemology for those who are not already committed. In doing so, my aim is twofold. First, I aim to present a conception of social epistemology that properly acknowledges both the normative and the descriptive dimensions of our knowledge communities. Second, I aim to motivate this conception by appeal to considerations that make clear both how and why we ought to pay particular attention to the social dimension itself as we seek to understand the nature of knowledge. I will begin there, with a brief discussion of the point of and motivation behind a distinctly "social" epistemology.

Distinctively Social Epistemology

In the last thirty years or so, philosophers, social scientists, and others have begun to speak of and pursue inquiry within a distinctly "social" epistemological framework. In one sense, the fact that there should be a "social" epistemology is easy to explain. As standardly conceived, epistemology is the theory of knowledge. As standardly practiced, the theory of knowledge is interested in the various *sources* of knowledge. We might think to explain the existence of a distinctly "social" epistemology, then, in terms of the existence of distinctly social sources of knowledge. While there is much to this explanation, I believe that at best it is incomplete: our community is implicated in our body of knowledge in ways that go far beyond that of being a source of information. Once we appreciate this, we will be in a position to appreciate the variety of different ways in which knowledge acquisition is (often, and perhaps even typically) a social activity.[4]

Traditional epistemology is individualistic in its orientation: it focuses on the states, skills, capacities, and background information of individual epistemic subjects. As such it recognizes only two general ways for an individual to acquire knowledge of her environment: through perception (broadly construed), or through inference (relying on her own background information). On this framework, others' antics and appearances – their doings and sayings, their dress and manner of presentation etc. – are no different in principle from the antics and appearances of *any* of the objects in one's environment. In particular, all of these things have the status of *evidence* from which one can come to know things through inference. On this picture, when I come to know, for example, that the Dean is in London through your telling me that she is, my route to knowledge here is no different in kind than the route by which I come to know that we have a mouse problem by observing the mouse droppings under the sink. In both cases perception makes available to me a piece of evidence – an utterance of yours; mouse droppings – from which I go on to make inferences. In making these inferences, I am relying on my background information, both for interpreting the evidence in the first place (you have *asserted that the Dean is in London*; those things are *mouse droppings*), and for knowing which inferences to draw from my evidence (e.g. *your asserting something is highly correlated with the truth of what you've asserted; the presence of mouse droppings is highly correlated with the nearby presence of mice*).[5]

I believe that this approach to the role others play in one's pursuit of knowledge fundamentally mischaracterizes that role. While we often do draw inferences from others' antics, speech, and appearances (and so treat these things as evidence), there are also cases in which we rely on others *as epistemic subjects in their own right*. Perhaps the clearest and most straightforward example of this is the case of testimony. When we accept another's word for something, we regard them not merely as providing potential evidence, but also, and more centrally, as manifesting *the very results of their own epistemic sensibility*. Nor is this the only way in which we rely on others as epistemic subjects in their own right. We so rely whenever we participate in our community's socio-epistemic practices – that is, in social practices whose point is (or includes) the acquisition, processing, storage, dissemination, or assessment of knowledge.

This last point is worth illustrating in some detail. To give just one (admittedly overly simplified) example, consider my reliance on a thermometer for reaching a belief about the ambient temperature. When I use a thermometer I have not previously employed, I do so against a host of expectations regarding the manufacture of such objects.[6] These include expectations regarding the construction, testing, and sale of the instrument: I rely on the manufacturer to have made their thermometers so that they give reliable information regarding the temperature; I also expect the thermometer to be easy to read, so that the information it provides is easily apprehended; I expect the manufacturer not to bring their instruments to market if they fail to meet these conditions; and so forth. What is more, if a particular thermometer is saliently placed in a public park overseen by the local community, I expect the vigilance of those tasked with the upkeep of the park: I assume that they would have replaced that particular thermometer if it were not working properly. Each of these expectations is fallible: any one of them can fail to be satisfied. And while none of the expectations individually, nor the set of them as a whole, entitle(s) me to accept the thermometer's readout *come what may*, they do lessen the epistemic burdens on me as I seek to come to know the temperature. For insofar as the temperature I take to be indicated on the thermometer is plausible (relative to my background beliefs about the temperature ranges around here during this time of year), I can properly accept what it "tells" me. In particular, I do not need to know anything else about the track record of this particular thermometer (i.e. to have independent knowledge that it is reliable), nor do I need to have conducted any experiments on thermometers in general (i.e. to have independent knowledge that they are generally reliable); and I do not need any further knowledge of how thermometers work. I am relying on the various people in my community to have played their roles, and this lightens the epistemic burdens on me as I come to form beliefs through my reliance on the instrument(s) they have made available to me.

When one comes to acquire knowledge in these and many other ways, it is plausible to think that the epistemic task has been socially distributed. What is more, we might speculate that subjects who are implicated in the relevant socio-epistemic practices constitute (part of) an epistemic community. That is to say, they are members of a group whose knowledge environment is structured by various social practices regarding the acquisition, processing, storage, transmission, and assessment of knowledge.

Epistemic Subjects, Agents, and Communities

The foregoing picture is clearly controversial, especially among those who grew up in the more traditional, individualistic orientation that characterizes orthodox epistemology. For my purposes here, however, I want to suggest how social epistemology looks from the vantage point of those who take this picture seriously. For such theorists, we stand in a fundamentally different relation to other epistemic subjects than we do to the rest of the items in our environment. Since the point at issue reflects the roles epistemic subjects play as epistemic agents in a common epistemic community, and since a proper characterization of these roles will require characterizing the descriptive and normative dimensions in play in the epistemic community itself, it will be helpful to begin by saying a few words about epistemic subjects, epistemic agents, and epistemic communities.

Here and in what follows I will use "epistemic subject" to refer to the sort of entity of whom we can intelligibly ascribe knowledge and other epistemic states (such as justified or rational belief). I will sometimes want to highlight the various roles that epistemic subjects play in acquiring, processing, storing, transmitting, or assessing information. When I want to highlight these roles, I will speak of them (not as epistemic subjects, which they remain, but rather) as "epistemic agents." This difference in nomenclature marks a *notional* difference: to speak of an epistemic agent is to speak of an epistemic subject, albeit in a way that highlights the role(s) played by the subject in the process(es) by which knowledge is acquired, processed, stored, transmitted, or assessed. Finally, I will also be speaking of the socio-epistemic practices, institutions, and norms that structure the relations between epistemic agents as they go about their information-seeking business (both individually and socially); to do so I will speak of their shared "epistemic community."

Consider now how our relations to other epistemic subjects differ from our relations to the rest of the items in our environment. Here I highlight three dimensions of difference, each of which ought to be captured in our social epistemological theories.

The first way in which our relations to other epistemic subjects differ from our relations to the rest of the items in our environment is this: epistemic subjects stand in various *epistemic dependency relations* to other epistemic subjects in their shared epistemic community. The basic idea of an epistemic dependency relation can be brought out in terms of the nature of epistemic assessment itself, in which we assess a subject's belief (or her degree of belief) in a proposition. Such assessment aims to characterize how well-supported her belief is (alternatively: whether that degree of belief is warranted by her evidence). This sort of assessment is a fully normative affair, since it appeals to standards (e.g. of rationality, epistemic responsibility, and/or reliability, among other standards) whose satisfaction is required if the subject's (degree of) belief is to count as amounting to justified belief or knowledge. I describe one subject (S_2) as *epistemically dependent* on another subject (S_1), then, when an epistemic assessment of S_2's belief – an assessment along one or more of the dimensions just described – requires an epistemic assessment of the role S_1 played in the process through which S_2 acquired (or sustained) the belief. It is of course a substantial assumption that we do exhibit epistemic dependence on others; traditional epistemology would deny this. But social epistemology as I understand it embraces this assumption, and with it recognizes that our epistemic tasks are often socially distributed among the members of our epistemic community. Relying on another person's say-so is *one* kind of epistemic dependence (for which see Goldberg (2010)); but it is not the only kind, and it is a task of social epistemology to enumerate and describe the variety of kinds of epistemic dependence exhibited in our interactions with others.[7]

A second way in which our relations to other epistemic subjects differ from our relations to the rest of the items in our environment lies in the variety of norms that enable us to calibrate our expectations of one another as epistemic agents, as we pursue our inquiries (whether individually or jointly).[8] Consider, for example, the expectations you have when you rely on your doctor, or your lawyer, or your accountant. You expect them to be knowledgeable in certain ways, to be apprised of the best practices, to be responsive to any relevant developments in their specialties, and so forth. Alternatively, consider the expectations you have of the other members of your research team, or of your business partners. You expect them to do their jobs properly, to notify the rest of the team (the other partners) if there are any developments that bear on the research of the whole team (the success of the business), and so forth. Or consider the expectations you have of your neighbors, friends, and family members. When you have long and mutually acknowledged traditions of informing one another of the news in certain domains, you come to expect this of one another. Or, to take a final example, consider the mutual expectations that a speaker and audience have of one another when the former tells the latter something. The audience expects the speaker to be relevantly authoritative regarding the truth of what she said,[9] and the speaker expects the audience to recognize her (the speaker) as performing a speech act that purports to be epistemically authoritative, and so which demands to be treated in the manner appropriate to acts of that kind.[10] In many and perhaps even all of these cases, the expectations themselves reflect various norms that regulate our interactions with other epistemic agents. In some cases, these norms are provided by professional or institutional organizations, and rationalize our reliance on members of those professions or institutions; in other cases, the norms in question are established explicitly, as a matter of agreement e.g. among team members or - business partners; in still other cases, the norms themselves are part of the practices (e.g. of information-sharing) that emerge over the course of repeated interaction between the parties, after the parties mutually (if perhaps only implicitly) acknowledge their mutual reliance on certain aspects of the practice; and in still other cases, the norms are part of sophisticated social practices (such as those regarding the practice of assertion) whose features are, if only implicitly, mutually acknowledged by all participants. (This is not intended to exhaust the possibilities.)

Norm-sanctioned expectations, I submit, are not so much *predictions* of the behavior of our fellows – although they may give rise to such predictions – as they are *normative expectations* of our fellows. For example, your expectation that your doctor knows best practices for the treatment of your condition is not (or not merely) based on the evidence that doctors *are* generally reliable in these ways; rather, it constitutes something you normatively expect of her. It is akin to parents' expectation that their teenager will be home by midnight (an expectation to which they are entitled even if their teenager has a long history of staying out too late). These expectations enable us to solve complicated coordination problems we face as we seek to acquire knowledge in communities that exhibit a highly differentiated division of intellectual labor.[11] I regard it as a central task for social epistemology to enumerate and describe the norms that underwrite these expectations, to articulate their epistemic bearing on the *predictive* expectations they underwrite, and ultimately to evaluate the norms themselves in terms of their role in securing true belief and knowledge.[12]

It is important to be clear about the relationship between normative and predictive expectations. To a first approximation, one epistemic agent, S_2, *normatively* expects something from another epistemic agent, S_1, when S_2 holds S_1 *responsible* in the relevant way. Such normative expectations are warranted by the norms of prevailing practice, when that practice is a legitimate one (for a defense of which see Goldberg (2017a, 2017b)). In such cases we can speak of agents' *entitlement* to have the normative expectation in question. There are three fundamental theoretical questions regarding normative expectations. The first is a question primarily for ethics and political philosophy: when is a practice legitimate, so that the expectations it sanctions are ones to which its participants are entitled? But the next two are core questions for social epistemology. One asks whether the expectations sanctioned by the norms of a given practice actually conduce to epistemically good outcomes. In asking this, we are taking a critical perspective on the norms and practices of a given community, with the aim of assessing how well these norms and practices serve epistemological ends. (This is one place where the traditional normative vocabulary of epistemology will come in handy.) The other asks how the normative expectations to which an agent is entitled relate to corresponding *predictive* expectations she has. The latter expectations are a species of belief (about the future), and hence are straightforwardly assessable from an epistemic point of view. But it remains to be seen how being entitled to hold someone responsible for an outcome relates to the justification one has for *believing* that one will get that outcome. And this point brings me to the third way in which our relations to other epistemic subjects differ from our relations to the rest of the items in our environment.

Given the normative expectations one has on those on whom one epistemically relies, as well as the epistemic dependence that results thereby, the epistemic assessment of beliefs formed through one of the "social routes" to knowledge (Goldman 2002; see also, 1999, 2009) is decidedly different from the epistemic assessment of beliefs not so formed. Insofar as epistemic tasks really are socially distributed, our assessment itself must be a social one. It must take into account not only the other individual(s) on whom the belief epistemically depends, but also the social practices and the norms that regulate these practices. This will include the various practices and norms that constitute what we might call the "epistemic environment" in which agents go about their knowledge-seeking business – and (as noted in the preceding paragraph) their relationship to the justification of belief. To the extent that one's epistemic environment bears on the proper assessment of one's beliefs, we will need to rethink the nature of epistemic assessment itself, in a way that reflects the various epistemic dependencies and social norms that are implicated in the production and sustainment of belief. I regard it as a task for social epistemology to reconceive the nature of epistemic assessment, and, where needed, to reconceive the categories employed in the assessment.

Three Lessons

We can summarize the previous section's three points by portraying them as capturing what I have elsewhere called the *epistemic significance of other minds*. This significance can be seen in (i) the various forms taken by our epistemic dependence on others, (ii) the variety of norms that underwrite our expectations of one another as we make our way in the common epistemic environment, and (iii) the distinctive epistemic assessment(s) implicated whenever a doxastic state is the result of a "social route" to knowledge. In characterizing (i) to (iii) we aim to capture the ways in which our relations to other epistemic agents differ from our relations to the rest of the items in our environment. And it is this, I propose, that provides the rationale for a distinctly social epistemology: social epistemology ought to be the systematic investigation into the epistemic significance of other minds, where this is understood to involve the epistemic tasks I have described in connection with each of (i) to (iii).

There are three lessons I want to draw from the foregoing rationale.

First, if it is to be adequate, social epistemology must include a detailed description of our socio-epistemic practices – those social practices through which we acquire, process, store, disseminate, and evaluate knowledge. These will include the following (and no doubt much more): the practices whereby (1) we establish and certify expertise, as well as those by which experts are identified; (2) we institute and enforce the standards of assertoric speech and writing; (3) we implement peer review; (4) our professions govern themselves and regulate their members' professional (including intellectual) behavior; (5) we devise technologies aimed at enabling us to discern more of nature's secrets, and to train others in how to use that technology; and (6) we educate our young to become thoughtful, critical, productive members of society. In all of these (and no doubt many other) ways, we depend on each other epistemically. It is the task of social epistemology to enumerate and describe these ways, and to characterize the norms that underwrite our expectations of one another in these efforts.

Second, if it is to be adequate, social epistemology must include an evaluation of these practices. It is not enough to describe, even when these descriptions include a characterization of the norms by which we hold one another responsible as participants in the practice. Rather, we need to evaluate these norms in terms of their role in securing true belief and knowledge. As we do so we will need to distinguish the true from the false, and to do so we will appeal to our own best lights, of course. Still, we must recognize that our own epistemological accounts are fallible, and can stand corrected by subsequent evidence.

Third and finally, it is an open question as to whether the solitary epistemic subject is the only proper unit of analysis at which to conduct epistemic assessment. So far I have been speaking as if the unit of analysis *is* the individual subject. But many social epistemologists will take issue with this assumption. The development and evaluation of the case for and against this assumption ought to be on the agenda of social epistemology.[13]

In short, I submit that the pursuit of social epistemology is the attempt to come to terms with the epistemic significance of other minds. There is a straightforward rationale for making such an attempt: other people are (not mere sources of knowledge, but) epistemic subjects in their own right who, through their epistemic agency, bring their own epistemic sensibility to bear in all sorts of ways as we shape and operate within a common epistemic environment. In recognizing this we will appreciate the overriding importance of the social dimension in the theory of knowledge. What is more, we must recognize that to capture this dimension we cannot but incorporate a descriptive and a normative component to the study of our epistemic communities.

Notes

1 This paper borrows heavily from parts of Goldberg (2015b).
2 For an overview see Fuller (2012).
3 I have tried to do this in Goldberg (2017).
4 "often" or "typically": I want to remain neutral on the issue whether ordinary perceptual knowledge is social in any interesting sense. (Those who think it is often appeal to the social dimension brought in by one's public language in shaping one's perceptual capacities.)
5 For an defense of something in the neighborhood in the epistemology of testimony, see E. Fricker (1987, 1994, 1995).
6 Below I will characterize these expectations as *normative* in nature.
7 I make some initial taxonomic distinctions in Goldberg (2011).
8 For an extensive discussion of epistemic norms as social norms, see Graham (2015) and Graham and Henderson (2017). For my part, in Goldberg (2017a) I attempt to ground epistemic normativity itself in our social expectations of one another as epistemic subjects.
9 This idea is prevalent in the literature on the so-called "norm of assertion." See e.g. Williamson (2000), Lackey (2007), and the various papers in Brown and Cappelen (2011). Arguably, this idea can be traced back to a "deontic scorekeeping" view of assertion developed by Robert Brandom in his (1983, 1994). However, Brandom's approach to assertion is explicitly distinguished from the approach favored by the "norm of assertion" crowd in MacFarlane (2011). See also Goldberg (2015a) for my attempt to take this idea and develop it into a full theory of the speech act of assertion.
10 The speaker's expectations of her audience were forcefully brought to the attention of epistemologists by M. Fricker (2007).
11 See Bicchieri (2006, 2017) for a discussion of how normative expectations can be fruitfully employed in characterizations of information-sharing games.
12 I offer a framework in terms of which to theorize about these norms in Goldberg (2017a, 2017b).
13 See e.g. Tollefsen (2006, 2011), Pettit and List (2011), Lackey (2012), M. Fricker (2012).

Bibliography

Bicchieri, C. (2006). *The Grammar of Society: The Nature and Dynamics of Social Norms*. Cambridge: Cambridge University Press.

Bicchieri, C. (2017). *Norms in the Wild: How to Diagnose, Measure, and Change Social Norms*. Oxford: Oxford University Press.

Brandom, R. (1983). Asserting. *Noûs*, 17(4), pp. 637–650.

Brandom, R. (1994). *Making It Explicit*. Cambridge: Harvard University Press.

Brown, J., and Cappelen, H. (2011). *Assertion: New Philosophical Essays*. Oxford: Oxford University Press.

Fricker, E. (1987). The Epistemology of Testimony. *Proceedings of the Aristotelian Society*, Supplemental 61, pp. 57–83.

Fricker, E. (1994). Against Gullibility. In B. Matilal and A. Chakrabarti, eds., *Knowing from Words*. Amsterdam: Kluwer Academic Publishers, pp. 125–161.

Fricker, E. (1995). Telling and Trusting: Reductionism and Anti-Reductionism in the Epistemology of Testimony. *Mind*, 104, pp. 393–411.

Fricker, M. (2007). *Epistemic Injustice: Power and the Ethics of Knowing*. Oxford: Oxford University Press.

Fricker, M. (2012). Group Testimony? The Making of a Collective Good Informant? *Philosophy and Phenomenological Research*, 84(2), pp. 249–276.

Fuller, S. (2012). Social Epistemology: A Quarter-Century Itinerary. *Social Epistemology*, 26, pp. 267–283.

Goldberg, S. (2010). *Relying on Others: An Essay in Epistemology*. Oxford: Oxford University Press.

Goldberg, S. (2011). The Division of Epistemic Labour. *Episteme*, 8, pp. 112–125.

Goldberg, S. (2015a). *Assertion: On the Philosophical Significance of Assertoric Speech*. Oxford: Oxford University Press.

Goldberg, S. (2015b). A Proposed Research Program for Social Epistemology. In P. Reider, ed., *Social Epistemology and Epistemic Agency*. Maryland: Rowman and Littlefield, pp. 3–20.

Goldberg, S. (2017a). *To the Best of Our Knowledge: Social Expectations and Epistemic Normativity*. Oxford: Oxford University Press.

Goldberg, S. (2017b). Should Have Known. *Synthese*, 194, pp. 2863–2894.

Goldman, A. (1999). *Knowledge in a Social World*. Oxford: Oxford University Press.

Goldman, A. (2002). *Pathways to Knowledge: Public and Private*. Oxford: Oxford University Press.

Goldman, A. (2009). Social Epistemology: Theory and Applications. *Royal Institute of Philosophy Supplement*, 64, pp. 2–18.

Graham, P. (2015). Epistemic Normativity and Social Norms. In D. Henderson and J. Greco, eds., *Epistemic Evaluation: Purposeful Epistemology*. Oxford: Oxford University Press, pp. 247–273.

Henderson, D., and Graham, P. (2017). Epistemic Norms and the "Epistemic Game" they Regulate: The Basic Structured Epistemic Costs and Benefits. *American Philosophical Quarterly*, 367–382.

Lackey, J. (2006). It Takes Two to Tango: Beyond reductionism and Non-Reductionism in the Epistemology of Testimony. In J. Lackey and E. Sosa, eds., *The Epistemology of Testimony*. Oxford: Oxford University Press, pp. 160–192.

Lackey, J. (2007). Norms of Assertion. *Noûs*, 41, pp. 594–626.

Lackey, J. (2008). *Learning From Words*. Oxford: Oxford University Press.

Lackey, J. (2012). Group Knowledge Attributions. In J. Brown and M. Gerken, eds., *Knowledge Ascriptions*. Oxford: Oxford University Press, pp. 243–269.

MacFarlane, J. (2011). What is an Assertion? In J. Brown and J. Cappelen, eds., *Assertion: New Philosophical Essays*. Oxford: Oxford University Press, pp. 79–96.

Pettit, P., and List, C. (2011). *Group Agency: The Possibility, Design, and Status of Corporate Agents*. Oxford: Oxford University Press.

Tollefsen, D. (2006). From Extended Mind to Collective Mind. *Cognitive Systems Research*, 7, pp. 140–150.

Tollefsen, D. (2011). Groups as Rational Sources. In H.B. Schmid, D. Sirtes, and M. Weber, eds., *Collective Epistemology: Epistemic Studies 20*. Piscataway, NJ: Transaction Books, pp. 11–22.

Williamson, T. (2000). *Knowledge and Its Limits*. Oxford: Oxford University Press.

42

EPISTEMIC NORMS AS SOCIAL NORMS

David Henderson and Peter J. Graham

Among other topics, epistemology studies how the folk—individual agents and communities of agents—ought to form beliefs. In social epistemology, for example, a familiar set of issues focuses on how agents in communities ought to share beliefs that they form, and how agents ought to look for suitable informants. Relatedly, there are normative issues concerning the production of beliefs in communities: how agents (individually or in groups) ought to form beliefs, especially beliefs that are suitable for sharing. Both sets of issues call attention to the possibility that many of our epistemic norms are social norms. We believe we stand to gain understanding of our lives as epistemic agents by investigating whether and to what extent our epistemic norms are social norms.

What are Epistemic Norms?

How are we using the phrase "epistemic norm" in this chapter? By way of background, we find it useful to distinguish, following Kvanvig, two dimensions: the *evaluative* and the *normative* (Kvanvig 2014: 118):

> *The evaluative dimension* concerns value—a scale for better and worse results. It has to do with whether what we have managed is good—and how good—with respect to some set of epistemic values. Commonly, our epistemic evaluation revolves around forming true beliefs, or, relatedly, understanding ourselves and our world. Let us take the veritistic perspective for illustration. One then evaluates the results of one's belief formation in terms of whether the resulting belief is true—or whether the resulting set of beliefs is comprised of many truths and relatively few falsehoods.

> *The normative dimension*: has to do with the ways in which we go about inquiry, belief-formation, review and revision, and belief-distribution. Were these processes fitting—the ones one *ought* to have used? By what processes *ought* we form and revise our beliefs? Did we inquire as we ought? Did we revise as we ought? Did we share as we ought?

As we are using the term, epistemic norms fall within the normative dimension, as opposed to the evaluative, dimension.

Of course, the two dimensions are related. What processes are normatively fitting for critters like us is a matter of what processes are, on the best extant information, "well calculated" to produce evaluatively good results: knowledge, warrant, and true belief, among other goods. As information accumulates over time, one gets a better understanding of what these evaluatively good or better processes are—and one seemingly can do no better that use those informedly calculated to have the best results. Arguably our processes of scientific belief formation are evaluatively better now than they were, say ... four hundred years ago. As a community, and as trained epistemic agents within our community, we have gotten better. This turns on our refining our understanding of fitting or acceptable processes, and on *our holding ourselves in community to such standards* (Kvanvig 2014: 121). Thus, we are already in the neighborhood of social norms, the norms we share.

As we understand norms here, norms are then rules, or normative sensibilities, that influence what we do and think. Roughly speaking, norms are psychologically real. And we write of sensibilities here, because there should be no presumption that the relevant normative sensibilities can be fully articulated. Epistemic norms are the normative sensibilities by which folk regulate their epistemic practices. Like the rules of grammar, epistemic rules guide epistemic activity without necessarily being fully articulated in the minds of those who are guided by them.

Note that one might have formed one's belief in utterly normatively fitting ways—deploying the best attainable norms at the time—and yet have failed in that instance to have attained the relevant epistemic evaluative good. One might have failed to have gotten the truth on that matter, or one might be Gettiered and not know as a result. The evaluative and normative dimensions can yield differing results.

Epistemic norms as our normative sensibilities are then not necessarily the same as objectively valid principles of epistemic inquiry, belief-fixation and belief sharing. In some cases they may be the same. In many cases they are not.

Aware of the ideal, both evaluative and normative, it follows that any given time, our best-informed processes (and our epistemic norms) are to some extent (yet) to be refined. So, from the point of view of what maximizes evaluative good, extant processes (and associated evaluative perspectives) are always wanting to some degree—they are always objectively criticizable (were we to know more than we now know).

We improve our processes over time, and do evaluatively better, by using extant processes (with their extant warts). At the same time, extant processes (warts and all) might yet be maximally normatively fitting in being responsive to the best information presently possessed, and one cannot get better information without using those processes.

Given this use of "norm", those that write of knowledge (or truth, or understanding) as "the *norm* of belief" are making a mistake—conflating the evaluative dimension with the normative dimension. There are more or less "fancy" ways of making this mistake. One can conflate norms with what one's normative sensibilities would be were one to have all information relevant to their refinement. If one insists that such idealized refinements-in-the-limit were one's norms even now, then one understands the change in normative sensibilities across time as "the historical unfolding" of "*the* one norm"—the some Hegelian limit—as is suggested in (Brandom, 1994).

It seems helpful to think of the production and dissemination of epistemic results as parallel to other contexts in which some valued good is produced and shared within a community. Just as food may be produced or acquired well or poorly, and just as the results of that acquisition may then be shared, so epistemic results may be produced well or poorly, and may be shared within a community. To a first approximation, the production of belief is a matter of inquiry or belief fixation (or re-fixation—revision). This has been the principle focus of traditional epistemology and much philosophy of science. The sharing is a matter of assertion or testimony, and the reception of testimony. This had been somewhat neglected in much of traditional epistemology. But it has come to be a subject of much concern over the last two decades (see the relevant sections of this handbook).

Epistemic norms (as we are conceiving of them here) are thus the extant epistemic normative sensibilities possessed by agents that influence the production and dissemination of an important epistemic good. Such norms reflect (more or less well) the information available at the time—information bearing on what has apparently been reliable, in what combinations, with what weaknesses, and how such weaknesses may be patched.

At root, these sensibilities are individually held. They guide our intellectual lives as individuals. But they also clearly come to be more or less shared or similar across individuals within epistemic communities. We train children and initiates into the norms of our epistemic communities—as is reflected in home, elementary school, university, and various professional contexts. We teach some of these norms in critical thinking and research methods courses. We hold ourselves and others to such norms—and coordinate as a community thereby. Could our epistemic norms be social norms?

What are Social Norms?

We believe there is good reason to think that many of our epistemic norms—many of our psychologically real epistemic sensibilities, our epistemic normative attitudes—are social norms, in a broad sense of the term.

What then are social norms? Simple examples involving driving on the right in the United States, not belching at dinner in the United Kingdom, passing the port to the left among Oxford dons, not littering in public parks (in many but not all countries), and not interrupting the speaker to raise an obvious objection during presentations at philosophy conferences. In philosophy we are also expected to respond to objections to our preferred theories when writing a paper. Whether we should read all the footnotes when reading journal articles, or whether we should cite all the relevant research, may or may not be extant norms within philosophy. Some norms are universal across cultures: keep promises and tell the truth, for example.

There are many accounts of social norms in the literature. We find an account from Geoffrey Brennan, Lina Eriksson, Robert Goodin, and Nicholas Southwood (2013) useful.[1] Their account is in terms of normative *principles* and normative principle involving *normative attitudes*.

A normative *principle* is an abstract rule such as *one ought to X in conditions C*. The principles involved in a social norm need not be objectively valid. Indeed, many are not.

Normative *attitudes* are then normative beliefs or judgements, normative expectations, reactive attitudes, and dispositions to have reactive attitudes that involve a normative principle. I have a normative principle corresponding normative attitude when:

- I judge that one must X in C;
- I disapprove of those who do not X in C;
- I judge that it is appropriate to disapprove of those who do not X in C
- I demand that others X in C;
- I acknowledge the legitimacy of criticisms and demands from others that I do X in C;
- I see myself (and others) as entitled to sanction those who do not X in C.

A normative principle is then a *norm* within a group when enough people have normative attitudes corresponding to the principle, and enough people know that others in the group have those attitudes. Here is Brenna et al.'s definition of a norm:

A normative principle P is a norm within a group G if and only if:

i   A significant proportion of the members of G have P-corresponding normative attitudes; and
ii A significant proportion of the members of G know that a significant proportion of the members of G have P-corresponding normative attitudes.

Norms are then norms of groups, a "social" norm. We will then call these (group) norms "social norms in the broad sense." A norm of a group—a social norm in the broad sense—is then a widely embraced (and widely known to be embraced) normative principle, embraced via a collection of principle involving normative attitudes.

Individuals in the group are frequently motivated to act in accord with the norm, to act in accord with the principle. They may be motivated by their agreement with the principle, or by the existence of the norm (with the known prevalence in the group of the principle corresponding normative attitudes), or by the threat of sanctions (of various kinds, including disapproval) for failure to act in accord, or a number of other reasons.

Even so, not all norms are followed. In many parts of the world it's a norm not to pee in the swimming pool. Because it is so hard to verify violations, people often help themselves, even though they themselves think one ought not pee in the pool.

When individuals are motivated by agreement with the principle, Brennan et al call the (group) norm a *moral* norm (though it need not correspond to an objectively valid principle of morality—moral norms are the elements of the moral code of a group). When individuals are motivated by the existence of the (group) norm and the presumption that members of the group follow the norm ("this is what we do around here"), Brennan et al call the (group) norm a *social* norm (we will call this their narrow sense of "social norm.") When enough members of the group act in accord with the (group) norm, whether "moral" or "social", then the norm is also a *social practice*. Not peeing in the pool is not a social practice. Passing the port to the left, on the other hand, is.

Why Think Epistemic Norms are Social Norms?

We all have our own epistemic normative sensibilities, our personal normative attitudes. We then have our own normative attitudes corresponding to epistemic normative principles about how to inquire, how to form, revise and sustain beliefs, and how and when to share. With Brennan et al.'s broad sense of social norms on the table, we now ask whether own personal epistemic norms could also be social norms? Could our personal normative attitudes be widely shared in a group, and known to be shared?

Within a community that relies on each other epistemically, individuals are often alike in their personal epistemic normative sensibilities. This is no accident. One not only acquires information from others—beliefs—one learns from others how to inquire.[2] One learns how to evaluate one's own and others' learning. One regulates both one's own belief formation and one's reception of other's beliefs accordingly. Further, one regulates others as one makes clear to them when one thinks that they have not formed beliefs acceptably. One thereby suggests that they have let the epistemic team down. Of course, one also sometimes expresses one's epistemic sensibilities in systematic instruction. Finally, one preferentially associates with those one understands to conform to epistemic sensitivities that are (as best one can tell) at least as good as one's own. Minimally, such agents then do for one what one would do for oneself were one able to be more places at once. Commonly, if those agents' sensibilities are better than one's own, they do for one something epistemically better than what one would have done. In such cases, we expect the community of relevant experts to police their epistemic house—to insure fitting quality control themselves.

Epistemic norms as social norms serve goods that individuals in a group have reason to pursue. Shared epistemic norms allow for a coordinated community pursuit of epistemic goods. To the extent that epistemic practice in a community is regulated by shared norms, people can readily rely on results gotten elsewhere in the community. In effect, the results gotten through the conforming community practices constitute an epistemic stock of reliably produced belief. One's conforming compatriots will have formed beliefs in a way one would have sought to produce beliefs for oneself (and others) were one able to be more places at once.

It will be important to inculcate the norms in initiates, to be attentive to which folk fail to conform, to marginalize those who do not conform, to mark those who are particularly adept in their conforming practice. In so doing, agents are not merely insisting that others are "like us"—following the same fashions—rather, they are insisting that others coordinate and cooperate in the production of an individual and public epistemic good. Sanctions serve compliance with the norm.

There are at least three strands in the dynamic by which agent's epistemic sensibilities come to be more or less shared, thereby making our personal epistemic norms not only personal but social.

The first is a matter of how normative sensibilities can be transmitted. Folk learn from others how to learn. This can be done by explicit instruction—we initiate new community members (we school children, instruct university courses, and oversee labs). We articulate general practices, and caution folk concerning common pitfalls. But, significant transmission of epistemic sensibilities also may be managed by example rather than by general instruction. We evaluate our own and others' practices—and often enough do so in a public fashion. In countless episodes, we critique our own practices, the practices of others, and that of our initiates (think, for example, of conference presentations, commentaries, and class discussions). In these episodes we present—and are presented with—a rich diet of object lessons and feedback.[3] In all this we hope to impart practices that have benefited from ongoing refinement—practices that are informed by past successes and failures within the community. Both in early epistemic training and in advanced contexts, people take the lessons and the more or less gentle nudges to heart. The training that is associated with becoming a member of a scientific community or sub-community that Kitcher (1993) discusses is itself just an advanced stage of the training that is a part of becoming a member of more general kinds of everyday epistemic community.

The second component of the dynamic by which epistemic norms come to be shared turns on feedback from the world: some practices may produce more or less successes (or frustrations) than others. This can condition the normative sensibilities of individuals. Information about these matters may be communicated within the community (as was already noted). Thus, there will be a tendency for epistemic practices to be informed by epistemic successes, and for direct and communicated sensitivity to successes and failures to make for an imperfect tendency for sharing of the relatively successful norms. We do not merely get "on the same page" with others in our epistemic community, we tend to get on the same informed page. The result is a kind of "cultural ratchet" given a general characterization by Tomasello:

> Human artifacts and behavioral practices commonly become more complex over time (they have a "history"). An individual invents an artifact or way of doing things, and others quickly learn it. [The artifacts and the associated practices spread through the group.] But if another individual makes some improvement [in such artifacts and the associated productive practices], everyone tends to learn the new improved practices. [A different class of artifacts come to be common.] This produces a kind of cultural ratchet, as each version [each class of artifacts and practices] stays solidly in the group's repertoire until someone comes up with something even newer and more improved.
>
> (Tomasello 2009: x-xi)

The third component of the dynamic by which epistemic norms come to be shared turns on selective association. Again, think of an epistemic community as a collection of folk who interact with each other epistemically. Beliefs are transmitted, and considerations thought to be pertinent are communicated. If one has reason to believe that some agents within one's community do not form beliefs as one thinks fitting—in a way at least as fitting as one would seek for oneself—one would presumably hesitate to draw on the epistemic results gotten by those agents. This would amount to a graded cutting of epistemic ties with those agents. One would decline their attempts to transmit beliefs. One might still raise considerations that one thinks fitting—nudging them towards one's own sensibilities. If this has no effect, one might ultimately selectively disassociate from those agents. The reverse is also true of course. To the extent that others thought that your own alternative epistemic practice was less than fitting, they would likely minimize their dependency on you. Neither party would want to be dependent on flows of beliefs from the other. As a result of selective association, folk in a given epistemic community would come to have personal epistemic sensibilities that are similar.[4]

Of course, selective association is commonly a graded and targeted phenomena. For example, one often notes that the shortcomings (violations of one's epistemic sensibilities) found in some group or subgroup are associated with some specific domain or topic. The partisans who follow particular teams may be particularly apt to violate one's sensibilities regarding how to gauge probabilities when forming beliefs about who will win an impending matchup. In this case, one's epistemic disassociation will be selective. Or, one's neighborhood conspiracy theorist may yet be accounted a good source of information regarding matters where conspiracy is not an issue. With respect to these unaffected topics—perhaps auto repair, or Italian cooking—the person may be fully integrated into one's epistemic community.[5]

Similar processes may lead to various kinds of epistemic divisions of labor within a heterogeneous, structured, epistemic community. Suppose that one judges that the relevant community does not form beliefs in a given domain in ways at least as good as those one would seek for oneself, and suppose that those in the relevant community agree that their general practice is not as good as one's own. One then will likely be recruited as a source concerning the relevant topic. The transmission of beliefs concerning that domain will come to have a decided directionality.

We conclude that there are many reasons for thinking that our epistemic norms—our epistemic principle involving normative attitudes—are not just our own, but widely shared and known to be so shared. We conclude there are reasons for thinking our epistemic norms are social norms.

Preferences and Expectations: Tools for Rational Reconstruction

The argument for our thesis so far has been pitched at the level of descriptive sociology, or what we might call "social phenomenology." In the remainder of the paper we want to broach another avenue for discovering whether and to what extent our epistemic norms are social norms (in the broad sense): rational reconstruction. A rational reconstruction uses game-theoretic techniques within the framework of rational choice theory to see why a certain equilibrium might emerge or persist. Social norms (in both the broad and the narrow sense) are often a part of such rational reconstructions. So is there a case that we might uncover through modeling possible combinations of preferences and expectations that would show why epistemic norms as social norms would emerge and persist?

Before we address this question head on, we will review some of Christina Bicchieri's taxonomy of social kinds. She distinguishes different kinds of social facts in terms of different clusters of preferences and expectations. Understanding those different kinds of clusters will then help us understand how social norms work in rational reconstructions. So in the rest of this section we will lay out her taxonomy. In the next section we'll make an initial stab at modeling our preferences and expectations in the epistemic domain.

Bicchieri (2006, 2017) works within the framework of rational choice theory. The idea is to explain the behavior of individuals in terms of their preferences and expectations. Bicchieri distinguishes the following social kinds in terms of different kinds of preferences and expectations: habits, customs, fashions and fads, and coordinating conventions, social norms and moral norms. When Brennan et al define "norm", they are thinking of clusters of normative principle involving normative attitudes, whether people are motivated by those normative attitudes or not (though in most cases they are). When Bicchieri defines her categories, she is thinking of cluster of preferences and expectations that motivate and explain behavior.

What are the kinds of *preferences* and *expectations* that forms the basis of Bicchieri's taxonomy of regularities in behavior? A preference is a disposition to act a certain way in a specific situation. If I regularly choose chocolate instead of vanilla ice cream, then I prefer chocolate over vanilla. This is still true even if I like the taste of vanilla better, but do not choose it, for I have a mild allergy to vanilla.

Expectations are beliefs. The relevant expectations are beliefs about other people. She distinguishes between *empirical* and *normative* expectations. Empirical expectations are beliefs about what other people do in certain situations. They are first-order beliefs about behavior. Normative expectations are beliefs about what other people believe ought to be done in certain situations, including their tendency to sanction violations. They are second-order beliefs about the normative attitudes of other people, about whether other people approve or disapprove of the behavior. Here's the contact with Brennan et al.'s account of norms.

Preferences can be socially conditional or unconditional. A preference is socially unconditional when one's choice is not influenced by knowing how others act (empirical expectations) or what they approve or disapprove of (normative expectations). A preference is socially conditional when one's choice is influenced by knowing how others act in similar situations (empirical expectations) and/or what other people approve or disapprove of (normative expectations). People with conditional social preferences care about what others (who matter to them) do and/ or approve/disapprove of.

Bicchieri then distinguishes between habits, customs, fashions and fads, coordinating conventions, social and moral norms, based on the relevant clusters of preferences and expectations.

- *Habits.* When an individual finds a solution to a need and repeatedly uses that solution, the solution is a habit. Whenever it rains, I take an umbrella. My preference is not conditional on what others do. Social expectations are irrelevant here. If you didn't take an umbrella, I'd still take one to stay dry.
- *Customs.* When everyone in a group has the same need, and finds the same solution, the solution is a custom. When it rains, we all take umbrellas. And though we all take umbrellas, our preferences are still not conditional on what others do. Social expectations are still irrelevant here.
- *Fashion/Fads.* Humans tend to imitate the successful as well as to imitate the majority. Imitating the successful or the majority are often effective (though not foolproof) learning strategies. We also like to fit in, to belong, and to do as others do. Here we act on a conditional preference to do as others do. If a famous person uses a red umbrella, of if most people do, then we are apt to use not just any umbrella, but a red one, when it rains. Social expectations now play a leading role.
- *Coordinating Conventions.* We often have a mutual need to coordinate. You and I want to communicate, so we need to coordinate on one of many different ways to use words for meanings. You and I need to drive to work safely, so we need to coordinate on whether to drive on the right or to drive on the left. I prefer to drive on the right if I believe others drive on the right (a socially conditional preference, based on an empirical expectation). A coordinating convention is a behavioral rule—drive on the right—that is followed because it solves our mutual problem. Coordinating conventions solve coordination games. Once in place, conventions are self-reinforcing. In other words, once they are in place, there is no temptation to defect. For if I defect, I lose out on the benefit of coordination. If I quit using a shared language to communicate, no one will understand me. If I drive on the left instead of the right, I might just get killed. Our preference to coordinate and our social empirical expectation about what others do drives our behavior.

• *Social Norms.* Not only do we have empirical expectation (beliefs about what other people do). We often have beliefs about how other people think we ought to behave. These are beliefs about norms in Brennan et al.'s sense: beliefs about the rules or principles that people in the group believe we ought to follow. We then have normative expectations—beliefs about the normative attitudes of other people in our reference networks. Importantly for Bicchieri, these beliefs go along with beliefs about the possibility of sanctions. We know if we violate these expectations, we may lose esteem, status, access to resources, and so on. We then at least have a conditional preference to conform to the rule. Women in many countries and cultures wear a *hijab* because they believe that's the norm, and they at least have the conditional preference to conform. Oxford dons pass the port to the left because of their conditional preference to do what others expect them to do. Left to their own devices, they might prefer to do otherwise.

Social Norms Solve Cooperation Games

Many social theorists are interested in social norms (and especially the motivating role of conditional preferences and normative expectations) because of their potential to solve cooperation games. A cooperation game is a mixed-motive game.[6] Here there is a good to be attained by cooperating—a good in which all members of the groups can partake to the extent that it is produced—and an individual cost to be paid in coordinating. In these games, the marginal benefit gotten by the individual from the individual's own contribution (cooperating) is less than the cost to the individual of the individual's cooperation.

The Prisoner's Dilemma is the classic example of a mixed-motive game. In the Prisoner's Dilemma, the dominant strategy for each player is defection. If the other player cooperates, you are better off by defecting. If the other player defects, you are better off defecting. Thus, no matter what the other person does, you should defect. But since this reasoning applies to both players, both should defect. But—and this is why it is a cooperation game—it would be better if both players cooperated instead of both defecting. There is then a motive to cooperate as well as defect.

Other examples of mixed-motive games include public goods games. In a public goods game, each player is issued a stake and can choose to contribute all or part of it to a public pool. For each unit contributed to the public good pool, the individual (and all other players) get back something less than a unit. Hence there is a temptation not to contribute, for if everyone else contributes but you don't, you get a bigger payoff. As a result of the temptation payoff, individuals are tempted to "free-ride"—to partake of the public good that the others provide, while not contributing themselves. At the same time, this return on each contribution insures that if all players contribute, they all come out better off than they would were they not to have contributed.

To "solve" a mixed-motive game would then require adding another motive to the game—another payoff—that would make cooperation instead of defection the best choice for the players. In the Prisoner's Dilemma, if there were a social norm against defection ("don't be a rat!") then the players of the game would have different preferences; they would have the conditional preference to conform to the norm, either perhaps because they endorse the legitimacy of the principle ("friends don't rat on friends") or because they fear sanctions. Once the norm is in place—once players have the "right" social conditional preferences and empirical and normative expectations about others in their reference network—we've changed the incentive structure, and thereby "solved" the game by changing the game (changing the payoff structure) so that cooperation (not defection) is the best strategy for all players. The temptation payoff no longer looks so rational after all. Social conditional preferences and social normative expectations can then transform a mixed-motive game into a coordination game—and they serve to specify which equilibrium (within that coordination game) folk are to choose (Bicchieri 2006: 33–4).

Could we then model epistemic norms as social norms that solve cooperation games, or even as solutions to coordination games? Is that one thing that epistemic norms do for the folk?

Modeling Epistemic Games: Initial Thoughts

Returning to epistemic norms in our sense, we find that Bicchieri's approach encourages us to think about what is gotten by coordination and cooperation within epistemic communities—and what is then afforded by the regulation of self and others by the shared epistemic sensibilities. How do epistemic standards or epistemic normative sensibilities come to be shared in epistemic communities—how and why do communities of interdependent agents develop shared normative epistemic sensibilities, facilitating epistemic cooperation, issuing in behavior furthering individual and community goods? What do the folk get from having various normative sensibilities—what goods do they serve and what problems do they solve—and what shapes their normative sensibilities? Her framework invites a rational reconstruction of the emergence and persistence of our epistemic norms as social norms that would help us understand what they do for the folk.

In other words, it is not a straightforward matter of showing that our epistemic norms solve a coordination or a cooperation problem, or if they do, what exactly those problems are. It takes effort to run through a number of models and see what the results might be.

Here's why it is not a straightforward matter to see our epistemic norms as solutions to a cooperation game. In its fundamentals, and thus to a first approximation at least, the epistemic choice situation—the epistemic game—does not seem to have the payoff structure of a mixed-motive game such as the public goods game, provided we think of the simplest epistemic gain as where everyone is after true belief, and only true belief, and so everyone's individual epistemic norms are solely tailored towards true belief. In a public-goods game, one contributes at an initial loss from one's original endowment, and one's marginal return on one's own contribution is less than what one has contributed. One can come out ahead, provided enough others contribute similarly, but for any set of contributions from others, one does best by not contributing oneself. In contrast, when one contributes by conforming to epistemic norms (thus producing a belief that is likely true, let us say) and by sharing that belief, it is not as though one does so at an *epistemic loss* to oneself. One has the epistemic gains of one's production, gotten via conformity to epistemic norms. Further, unlike sharing food or money, an instance of epistemic sharing does not leave one with fewer truths for oneself. If the norm is indeed significantly truth conducive, conformity to is on balance a personal gain in terms of narrowly epistemic (that is strictly veritistic) value.[7] Further, it is not as though, one gives something away (the true belief), only to get back part of it back from some community stock (from the set of true beliefs jointly produced). One need not loose part of produced belief by sharing it with others. One still has the belief. Sharing a true belief is more like sharing fire than sharing your lunch. From the epistemic point of view—thinking here solely in terms of veritistic value—one has no incentive to defect from norms for the production or sharing of beliefs.[8]

There also is reason to doubt our epistemic norms solve a coordination problem. The kinds of coordination that epistemic norms provide do not seem best understood in terms of coordination games. One faces a coordination game when the payoff for one's own choice turns on one's somehow coordinating on *one of several alternative* Nash equilibria—none of which dominates the others for the individual players.[9] In the epistemic case, the choice problem seems instead to have to do largely with agents coordinating on a practice that of itself is near enough dominant for each of the agents. That the practice would be for each individual satisfactorily close to being better than alternative practices *independent of what others do*. However, this involves several simplifying assumptions. Notably, it denominates payoffs in terms of veritistic epistemic gains and losses. Our epistemic life and choices are conditions by wider payoffs, and there are reasons to think that these make for temptations for cutting corners, for example.

Focusing only on veritistic payoffs—epistemic norms do not seem to involve highly conditional preferences. This suggests that at least some significant aspects of the choice dynamic associated with epistemic norms is not to be modeled in terms of Bicchieri's social norms or coordinating conventions.

These results should come as no surprise. For focusing on the pursuit of truth alone, we individually have reasons for relying on our own belief forming process (etc.) independent of what others will do, or think we ought to do. Thus to some extent, our epistemic coordination or cooperation need not rest on conditional preferences to coordinate or conform to normative expectations.

Of course we all know our epistemic activities are influenced by a host of other considerations—not just the pursuit of truth. To fully understand out epistemic norms—and to what extent they emerge and persist as solutions to coordination or cooperation games—will require considerable reflection—armchair and empirical—on the various incentives epistemic agents bring to inquiry, belief and interaction. When we think through the costs and benefits of our epistemic activity in wider terms, there is reason to think that our epistemic norms regulate ("transform") mixed-motive games. If you want that sandwich for yourself, you'll keep your true belief about where it is locked away well hidden. If you want to know how something works, but can't be bothered to inquire on your own, you'll slack until someone else fills you in. If believing your tribe is in the right is more valuable to you than facing the facts, you'll rationalize away the counterevidence as best you can. There are plenty of temptations to defect from norms legislating the impartial pursuit of the truth. Adding in the various temptations and payoffs, one at a time, will lead to a number of interesting models that promise to deepen our understanding of the emergence and persistence of epistemic norms as social norms, both in the broad and narrower senses.[10]

Even so, focusing on the pursuit of truth alone, shared epistemic norms can be at least partially understood as what Bicchieri terms customs: A custom is a pattern of behavior such that individuals (unconditionally) prefer to conform to it because it meets their needs. The custom then arises and conformity to it is motivated by the individuals' payoffs of their own individual behaviors. So focusing on truth alone, our epistemic norms are at least customs, and for similar reasons, given our desire to imitate the successful as well as the majority, they may also fall into the (somewhat strangely labeled category) of fashions and fads. Perhaps "traditions" or "practices" might be a better label (for persistent, long-standing "fashions" within a group).

It is relatedly noteworthy that Bicchieri recognizes that norms such as norms of hygiene may have characteristics of social norms or coordinating conventions, as well as characteristics of customs. We might take a cue from this remark:

> There are many collective behaviors that *may look like customs* but are instead influenced by social expectations. These collective behaviors depend on expectations about what others do or expect one to do in a similar situation. Such behaviors display various degrees of interdependence, depending on whether expectations are normative or empirical, unilateral or multilateral.
>
> *(Bicchieri 2017, emphasis added)*

Even customs generate normative expectations. Shared solutions sometimes generate social norms.

Conclusion

Bicchieri's approach serves as a springboard by focusing one's attention on the gains and losses faced by agents in the epistemic game—gains to be gotten by one's individual practice, and gains to be gotten by a more or less coordinated practice within one's community. It helps us understand how shaped and shared normative sensibilities help individuals in groups to attain such goods.

As far as "social phenomenology" goes, we believe we have made a case for supposing that our epistemic norms (as sensibilities about how we ought to inquire, form and sustain belief, and share information with others) are social (in the broad sense). We believe modeling what epistemic norms might do for us should prove illuminating. But as we've just noted, it is not straightforward given a simple view of the payoffs. But with more elbow grease, we should find reconstructions that make sense of our normative sensibilities, for there is reason to think that epistemic norms have features that are characteristic of social norms. They allow for the coordination within a community of interdependent agents, a coordination that allows us to cooperate so as to get more of a pivotal good than we could have gotten alone. Further, we do transmit these norms to new members of our community, and in various ways, we marginalize folk who fail to conform. Our social expectations make a difference.

Notes

1 See also Pettit 1990, Miller 2001, Henderson 2012, and Green 2016. We discuss Bichhieri's work later in the text.

2 The rudiments of an understanding of the motivated shaping of others in such a community are discussed in (Dogramaci, 2012), who argues that instilling one's rules in others allows one to depend on them for information. (See also Graham, 2015). Tebben and Waterman (2015) argue that more is needed than Dogramaci provides. In particular, they seek an account for why agents in such a community would pay the costs of policing others. This is, in effect, to raise the problem of second order free riding. In norms regulating cooperation games (see below) there will be a need for such policing, because there is a temptation to defect from the rule that is the community norm. Their concern seems fitting, but only insofar as epistemic norms regulate a situation aptly understood as a mixed-motive game. The important question of whether this obtains is pursued here.

3 Here the anthropological literature on conformist transmission and success-biased transmission is worth our attention (J. Henrich & Boyd, 2001; N. Henrich & Henrich, 2007). A closely related literature has to do with the evolution of direct social learning and related capacities such as those for skill rankings deference displays.

  Deference to individuals judged to have high domain-specific skills affords individuals the advantage of opportunities for receiving information from others possessing it, and means that those individuals need not "re-invent" the wheel, acquire information anew.

4 It should also be acknowledged that wider cultural phenomena can condition these processes of transmission and selective association in morally objectionable and epistemically very undesirable ways—witness epistemic injustice, a matter of groups being accorded disadvantages in an epistemic community for reasons having no objective connection with the epistemic capacities of their members (Fricker, 2007).

5 The components of the dynamic here discussed are also associated with the literature on "cultural evolution." For an overview of this literature, and its conceptual and empirical challenges, see (Lewens, 2015).

6 For a useful discussion of various types of games, and of a representative set of cooperation games, see Camerer and Fehr (2004).

7 Note that we are here thinking of the coin of the epistemic realm—the goods to be gotten epistemically, and the costs to be incurred—as veritistic: true beliefs are a gain, false beliefs are a loss. One might seek to factor in a richer understanding of epistemic value, but we use simple veritistic value for purposes of our unabashedly exploratory development here.

  One should take care not to over-read the above observations. When epistemic choices are understood in terms of a broader set of values, one's choice situation may come to look more like a mixed-motive game on the order of a public goods game, as we note when concluding. Compare (Henderson & Graham, 2017b).

8 For a development of these considerations, consult (Henderson & Graham, 2017a, 2017b).

9 A Nash equilibrium is set of strategies (one for each player) such that each is the best response (has highest expected utility) to the other player's strategies. No player has any incentive to unilaterally change his strategy. A dominant strategy is a strategy that is better than any alternative, no matter what strategy the other players use.

10 We begin such reflections in Henderson & Graham (2017b). For related discussions of epistemic norms as social norms, see Faulkner (2010), Reynolds (2017) and Graham (forthcoming).

References

Bicchieri, C. (2006). *The Grammar of Society: The Nature and Dynamics of Social Norms.* New York: Cambridge University Press.

Bicchieri, C. (2017). *Norms in the Wild: How to Diagnose, Measure, and Change Social Norms.* New York: Oxford University Press.

Brandom, R. (1994). *Making It Explicit: Reasoning, Representing, and Discursive Commitment.* Cambridge, MA: Harvard University Press.

Brennan, G., Eriksson, L., Goodin, R., & Southwood, N. (2013). *Explaining Norms* (1st ed.). Oxford: Oxford University Press.

Camerer, C., & Fehr, E. (2004). Measuring Social Norms and Social Preferences Using Experimental Games: A guide for Social Scientists. In J. Henrich, R. Boyd, S. Bowles, C. Camerer, E. Fehr, & H. Gintis (Eds.), *Foundations of Human Sociality: Economic Experiments and Ethnographic Evidence from Fifteen Small-Sclae Societies.* Oxford; New York: Oxford, pp. 55–95.

Dogramaci, S. (2012). Reverse Engineering Epistemic Evaluations. *Philosophy and Phenomenological Research, 84* (3), 513–530.

Faulkner, P. (2010). Norms of Trust. In Haddock, A., Millar, A., & Pritchard, D. (Eds.), *Social Epistemology* Oxford: Oxford University Press, pp. 129–147.

Fricker, M. (2007). *Epistemic Injustice: Power and the Ethics of Knowing.* Oxford: Oxford University Press.

Graham, P. (2015). Epistemic Normativity and Social Norms. In D. Henderson & J. Greco (Eds.), *Epistemic Evaluation.* Oxford: Oxford University Press, pp. 247–273.

Graham, P. (forthcoming). The Function of Assertion and Social Norms. In S. Goldberg (Ed.), *The Oxford Handbook of Assertion* Oxford: Oxford University Press.

Green, A. (2016). *The Social Contexts of Intellectual Virtue: Knowledge as a Team Achievement.* New York: Routledge.

Henderson, D. (2012). Norms. In H. Kincaid (Ed.), *The Oxford Handbook of Philosophy of Social Science.* Oxford; New York: Oxford University Press, pp. 409–435.

Henderson, D., & Graham, P.J. (2017a). Epistemic Norms and the "Epistemic Game" that they Regulate: The Basic Structured Epistemic Costs and Benefits. *American Philosophical Quarterly, 54,* 367–382.

Henderson, D., & Graham, P.J. (2017b) A Refined Account of the "Epistemic Game": Epistemic Norms, Temptations and Epistemic Cooperation". *American Philosophical Quarterly, 54,* 383–395.

Henrich, J., & Boyd, R. (2001). Why People Punish Defectors: Weak Conformist Transmission can Stabilize Costly Enforcement of Norms in Cooperative Dilemmas. *Journal of Theoretical Biology, 208,* 79–89.

Henrich, N., & Henrich, J. (2007). *Why Humans Cooperate: A Cultural and Evolutionary Explanation.* Oxford; New York: Oxford University Press.

Kitcher, P. (1993). *The Advancement of Science: Science without Legend, Objectivity without Illusions.* New York: Oxford Univ Press.

Kvanvig, J. (2014). Epistemic Normativity. In C. Littlejohn & J. Turri (Eds.), *Epistemic Norms* (pp. 115–134). Oxford: Oxford University Press.

Lewens, T. (2015). *Cultural Evolution: Conceptual Challenges.* Cambridge: Cambridge University Press.

Miller, S. (2001). *Social Action: A Teleological Account* (Vol. {Miller, 2001 #4262}). Cambridge; New York: Cambridge University Press.

Pettit, P. (1990). Virtus Normatia: Rational Choice Perspectives. *Ethics,* 100, 725–755.

Reynolds, S. (2017). *Knowledge as Acceptable Testimony.* New York: Cambridge University Press.

Tebben, N., & Waterman, J. (2015). Epistemic Free Riders and Reasons to Trust Testimony. *Social Epistemology: A Journal of Knowledge, Culture, and Policy,* 29(3), 270–279. doi:10.1080/02691728.2014.907835

Tomasello, M. (2009). *Why We Cooperate.* Cambridge, MA: MIT Press.

43

EDUCATING FOR GOOD QUESTIONING AS A DEMOCRATIC SKILL

Lani Watson

Questioning is a vital skill for gathering information, helping us to learn, to communicate, and to understand our world. As an essentially collaborative, information-seeking enterprise it is of central social epistemological significance. This can be seen in education where questioning has the power to shape individual learning and promote critical, collaborative, and informed student engagement. Despite this, schooling today places substantial emphasis on the ability to answer questions and little or no emphasis on the skill of raising and refining questions themselves. I argue that we should rethink this dominant answer-oriented education model and educate for good questioning. In this chapter, I present a central line of argument in support of educating for good questioning, namely, that doing so advances the aims of democracy and so benefits democratic society. Good questioning helps us to identify and inform ourselves and others about issues of societal and political import, and to engage in constructive deliberation and debate. In this sense, good questioning is not merely an essential information-gathering skill, but a democratic one: good questioning is an essential skill to educate for in a democracy. I present three arguments in support of this central claim. First, I argue that good questioning aids *understanding* of democratic processes and institutions. Second, I argue that good questioning facilitates *participation* in democratic processes and institutions. Third, I argue that good questioning enables *informed decision-making,* to the advantage of democratic citizenship and society.

Preliminaries

In order to present the case in support of educating for good questioning as a democratic skill, I draw on two distinct but complementary movements in the philosophy of education: democratic education and skills-based education. A brief sketch of each of these movements will be useful.

Democratic Education

Democratic education was brought to the forefront of educational theory in the early 20th century, primarily due to the work of John Dewey (1916, 1933). It has subsequently been advanced by prominent philosophers and educational theorists over the past century (Gutmann 1987; Galston 1989; Ostrom 1998; Boyte 2004). Democratic education aims to educate students for democratic citizenship, placing democratic ideals, such as equality, freedom of speech, and the common good, at the heart of formal education. As a form of civic character education, democratic education promotes active participation in democratic society, furnishing students with the tools to collaboratively shape the social and political institutions of their present and future. As Dewey contends, in *Democracy and Education* (1916), '[Democratic] society must have a type of education which gives individuals a personal interest in social relationships and control, and the habits of mind which secure social changes without introducing disorder' (p.49). Thus, from its inception, the democratic education movement has sought to advance the case in support of educating for behaviours, attitudes and dispositions conducive to political progress in democratic societies.

This explicitly political objective is a distinctive, and accordingly contentious, feature of the democratic education movement. Critics of such a politicized educational objective contend that it limits, rather than broadens the educational enterprise, in an objectionably prescriptive manner. Such a view can be traced back at least as far as Plato, within the Western philosophical tradition, who famously opposed the democracy of his day, and proposed an education system based on educating the few to rule over the many (see esp. *Republic,* Books II, III, V and VII). According to this Platonic system, not all students should receive the same education, nor should all students be expected to actively participate in or influence political processes and institutions. These privileges, or duties, should be preserved for those students who exhibit a natural capacity for reason, which their education should cultivate and refine. Dewey engaged with this line of thought in Plato's work. In *Democracy and Education* (1916), for example, he praises Plato's educational insight regarding the significance of the individual capacities of the student, contending, '[I]t would be impossible to find a deeper sense of the function of education in discovering and developing personal capacities, and training them so that they would connect with the activities of others' (p.85). Yet, Dewey argues, Plato was inhibited by the society in which he lived, from appreciating the sense in which this notion should extend to all students, regardless of which capacities they exhibit, or what social class or status they are deemed to have. For Dewey, a fair and democratic education was paramount to a fair and democratic society. The democratic education movement, following from Dewey, thus maintains that the aim of education is to educate all students, according to their natural capacities and interests, so as to produce productive, informed, and engaged members of democratic society.

Skills-Based Education

Skills-based education also traces its origins, at least in part, to the work of Dewey, and indeed, to Plato, given the attention paid by both to the individual capacities of the student. More recently, the argument for skills-based education has been advocated by leading educational theorists over the past fifty years (Freire 1970; Scheffler 1973; Siegel 1988; Paul 1990; Lipman 1991). Skills-based education identifies the student's intellectual skills as the primary focus of education, juxtaposing this with the more traditional educational objective of transferring information, knowledge, and understanding between student and teacher. Paulo Freire (1970) an early, influential advocate of skills-based education, argues that, '[L]iberating education consists in acts of cognition, not transferrals of information' (p.61). Skills-based education aims to train the student's intellectual skills, providing them with the tools to acquire information, knowledge, and understanding for themselves, and engage in a critical and informed way with society at all levels, both inside and outside the classroom. This educational objective has been prominently advocated through the critical-thinking movement, first emerging in the 1970s and now well-established in the philosophy of education (Ennis 1962; McPeck 1984; Siegel 1988; Paul 1990). The critical thinking movement is unified by an emphasis on the student's reasoning skills, as well as their intellectual autonomy. Israel Scheffler (1973), for example, identifies 'the ideal of rationality [as] a unifying perspective' (p.1) and endorses 'autonomous ideals of inquiry' (p.134) in schools. Skills-based education, fueled largely by the critical thinking movement in contemporary philosophy of education, aims to advance the case in support of educating for autonomous rationality.

More recently, this approach has been adopted and adapted by virtue epistemologists who argue that education should aim to cultivate intellectual character, comprising both intellectual skills and intellectually virtuous motivations (Baehr 2011; Pritchard 2013; Watson 2016a). This notion of intellectual character is found, either implicitly or explicitly, in much of the work produced by the critical thinking movement, notably, in Harvey Siegel's (1988) advocacy of the 'critical spirit' and the centrality of dispositions to his argument in support of educating for reason. This aligns skills-based education closely with intellectual character education. By introducing the vocabulary of intellectual virtues, virtue epistemologists working in the epistemology of education, aim to advance the case for the cultivation of intellectual virtues such as open-mindedness, inquisitiveness, and intellectual humility. This represents a further contemporary development of the skills-based education movement, whilst maintaining the central aim of educating students in their capacity to become competent and independent thinkers and learners, moving beyond the mere transferal of information, knowledge, and understanding. This reorientation of educational objectives, towards the development of intellectual skills and character, can be seen in recent US-based educational reforms, advanced by groups such as the Partnership for 21st Century Education (P21) and the Common Core State Standards Initiative (CCSSI).

The democratic education movement and the skills-based education movement together provide a rich theoretical framework for advancing the case in support of educating for good questioning as a democratic skill. Drawing on both of these movements, I make the case, in the remainder of the paper, with a *democratic, skills-based education model* in mind. This model emphasizes the value of educating, not only for democratic citizenship, or for intellectual skills, but for the skills that contribute to democratic character: I call these democratic skills. What, then, is good questioning, how can it be understood as a democratic skill, and why should we educate for this skill in a democracy. The following sections will address these questions.

What Is Good Questioning

Questioning is a familiar practice. Good questioning, correspondingly, is an intuitively recognisable skill. Particularly, we can often tell when someone is struggling to engage in good questioning, when they have asked the wrong person, at the wrong time, or when they have failed to communicate what it is that they want to know. Despite its intuitive familiarity, however, good questioning is a complex and dynamic skill. A full treatment of this skill demands more attention than I can afford here. In this section, I will attempt to offer a sufficiently substantive account of good questioning in order to illuminate the subsequent argument in support of educating for this skill in a democracy. As a starting point, I take the act of questioning to be a form of information-elicitation. When one engages in questioning (good or bad), one is typically in the business of 'finding things out'. When one engages in good questioning one is engaged in this activity in a skilful manner. This elevates the skill of good questioning above the act of information-elicitation in two ways. In cases of good questioning we do not simply want to elicit information, rather we want to 1) *competently* elicit information that is 2) *worth having*. We will examine each of these conditions in turn.

First, good questioning requires competent information-elicitation. Competent information-elicitation does not permit information that is acquired by accident or luck, in contrast to successful information-elicitation which permits any manner of acquisition as long as the information is acquired. Moreover, whilst successful information-elicitation requires that the information is acquired, competent information-elicitation does not. Rather, in certain circumstances one may competently engage in information-elicitation without actually acquiring the information sought. One may competently attempt to elicit information from a young child by asking her name, for example. If the child is immediately distracted and fails to answer we would not say that one's attempt was not thereby competent, even though unsuccessful. Good questioning requires competent information-elicitation.

Second, good questioning requires that the information elicited is worthwhile. This draws attention to the normative dimension of the skill. When engaging in *good* questioning we do not merely want to elicit any information, however competently. The aim is to elicit information that is worthwhile, relevant or significant in some sense; information that is *worth having*. There are two senses in which information can be considered worthwhile in the context of good questioning. In the first sense, good questioning excludes cases of trivial or disvaluable information-elicitation. Examples of trivial or disvaluable information occur throughout contemporary epistemology. Counting blades of grass (Kvanvig 2014) or motes of dust (Sosa 2003), or memorising all the entries in the Kansas phonebook (Grimm 2008) are three examples from the literature. Similarly, instances of questioning that aim at trivial or disvaluable information can be easily constructed; 'how many blades of grass are there in the courtyard', 'how many motes of dust on the desk', and, plausibly, 'how many cupcakes did Kim Kardashian eat at her birthday party'. Determining why these are cases of trivial or disvaluable information and information-elicitation is a complex and contentious issue, faced by epistemologists across the board (e.g. Lynch 2004; Grimm 2008; Treanor 2013). There is not yet a clear consensus on this. There is however, a broad consensus that some information is indeed trivial, at least in the sense that we do not generally consider it epistemically worthwhile to possess it. As such, it is also broadly uncontentious to maintain that one can attempt to elicit trivial information by means of questioning and, furthermore, that doing so is not something we generally consider to be epistemically worthwhile. Good questioning requires the questioner to avoid eliciting trivial or disvaluable information.

Worthwhile information-elicitation, in the second sense, requires the good questioner to exercise judgement with respect to the most relevant or significant information given her aims and context. The good questioner will aim to elicit only the information that she needs or desires in a given context and, in doing so, avoid the large amount of irrelevant or insignificant information that is also available to her. If one wants to find out when the next train is due, for example, it is no good asking a fellow traveller what they are planning to vote in an upcoming referendum. Whilst this information is not in itself trivial or disvaluable, it is certainly not the most relevant or significant information to elicit when one wants to know the time of the next train. As with trivial or disvaluable information-elicitation, determining what renders information relevant or significant in a given context is a complex and contentious issue. Nonetheless, it is not hard to see that some instances of questioning falter precisely in virtue of the questioner's failure to elicit the most relevant or significant information. In this second sense one can fail to elicit information that is *worth having*. As well as avoiding trivial or disvaluable information-elicitation, good questioning requires the questioner to elicit the most relevant or significant information according to her aims and context. Thus, the skill of good questioning requires worthwhile information-elicitation, both in the avoidance of trivial or disvaluable information and in the acquisition of information that is relevant or significant given one's aims and context.[1]

Questioning is good in virtue of competent and worthwhile information-elicitation. A good questioner *competently elicits worthwhile information*. We can now return to the central question; why is good questioning a skill that we should educate for in democratic society.

Why Should We Educate for Good Questioning as a Democratic Skill

I identify three distinct contributions that the skill of good questioning makes to democratic society, drawing on examples both inside and outside the classroom. My aim is to highlight the ubiquity and import of questioning in contemporary democracy at both the individual and societal levels. Ultimately, it is the significant and pervasive role that good questioning plays in democracy itself that provides the principal case in support of educating for this skill.

Good Questioning Aids Understanding

Firstly, good questioning aids understanding. The case in support of this is not hard to make. It is not difficult to see that asking questions, especially good questions, typically helps a person enhance their understanding of a subject matter. Indeed, it would be difficult to deny this. A child who asks why the sky is blue is *more likely* to gain some understanding of why the sky is blue than a child who does not. The same is true at any age. A Wall Street trader who asks what the assets comprising a set of collateral debt obligations are actually worth is *more likely* to understand their true value than a trader who does not.[2] Asking good questions is an effective way to gain and enhance understanding. This is all that the present claim amounts to and it is, I think, uncontentious. It is worth, however, highlighting the significance of this in education and drawing attention to the ways in which it might be underestimated or overlooked. The following example will illustrate this.

Imagine a student attending his first history lesson at a new school. His class has been learning about British politics for several weeks but the student is joining late in the school term and is unfamiliar with the term 'democracy'. Consequently, he struggles to understand key ideas that the teacher introduces at the start of the lesson, struggles to follow the discussion and cannot complete the set exercise asking him to list reasons why voting is important in a democracy. From the student's perspective this experience may be one of confusion, bewilderment or frustration. It may also involve feelings of embarrassment, anxiety, even anger or simply induce a lack of interest in the topic, the discussion, and the task. For the most part this will not be conducive to his learning. Imagine, then, that instead of sitting through a lesson in which he doesn't understand the central concept, the student asks the teacher at the outset, 'what is democracy'. The teacher is then able to provide an explanation and offer assistance throughout the lesson to ensure that the student isn't left behind in the discussion and can complete the task. Of course, a good teacher in a favourable environment may pick up on the problem and offer an explanation without the need for the student to ask outright. Given the many competing demands on a teacher's time and attention in any standard classroom, however, and the difficulty of identifying and responding to the diverse needs of multiple individuals, we cannot assume that this will always be the case. At any rate, it is difficult to deny that the student increases his prospects for understanding in the case in which he asks the question, compared to the case in which he does not. The consequences of failing to ask, as noted, are significant: confusion, frustration, anxiety, disengagement. Not being able to identify the source of these experiences, moreover, is likely to exacerbate them further.

In order to overcome these pitfalls, the student must formulate and pose a question that targets the information that he needs. This requires a degree of proficiency that we cannot assume he already has. It requires the skill of good questioning. Without this, the student's understanding of the subject matter is *more likely* to be inhibited. Good questioning empowers the student to access the precise information that he needs and so to direct his own learning in a small but significant manner. Understanding what the term 'democracy' means will enable him to engage with the class discussion and share in the ideas that it generates. This will expose him to further information and alternative viewpoints which will, over time, facilitate a deeper understanding of democracy. The same can be said for many similar examples. Good questioning provides students with a tool that they can employ in any educational environment, empowering them to determine the information that they acquire and ensuring that it is relevant to their aims and context.

This example illustrates two related points relevant to the central claim; that we should educate for good questioning in a democracy. First, it demonstrates the straightforward but significant sense in which good questioning aids understanding, of any subject matter. Second, it illustrates this in the case of key ideas and concepts required in order to understand democracy, in particular. The first is perhaps the more substantial point. The fact that good questioning aids understanding, for any subject matter, demonstrates the sense in which this skill plays a key role in education; at least in so far as facilitating, deepening or refining a student's understanding plays a key role in their being educated. If an educated population is vital to a functioning democratic society, then educating for good questioning serves the aims of democracy itself. The fact that good questioning aids understanding of key democratic ideas and concepts, moreover, illustrates the significance of good questioning for understanding democratic processes and institutions, in particular. In so far as facilitating, deepening or refining a student's understanding of democracy is desirable within democratic society, good questioning also serves this aim.

Good Questioning Facilitates Participation

Second, good questioning facilitates participation in a democratic society. This can be illustrated by observing the valuable role that questioning plays in discussion and debate. Return to the class discussion from the example above. In this case the class is being asked to discuss whether voting is important in a democracy. From the outset, the discussion is both initiated and framed by a question. The question indicates the topic of the discussion and acts as its catalyst. Indeed, posing questions is a common and effective way to incorporate class discussion into a lesson, on any topic, and the posing of educative and stimulating questions by teachers has been the subject of extensive theoretical and empirical work in educational research (Bloom 1956; Dillon 1984; Wilen 1984; Elder & Paul 2005; Sattes and Walsh 2005). Good teacher-questioning is viewed as an important pedagogical device in this literature. Even on occasions where no explicit question is posed at the start of a discussion, moreover, it is unlikely that discussion will get very far in the absence of questioning. In order to engage in any kind of discussion a group must exchange comments and ideas. These will most often lead to questions posed to participants as the discussion unfolds which, in turn, spur the discussion on: 'what do you mean by freedom', 'what do you mean by civic duty', 'why do you think your vote doesn't count', 'what *really is* democracy'. One need only attempt to have a genuinely collaborative discussion *without* questions to see the essential role that they play. Indeed, try having any kind of discussion without asking or answering questions. Questions are the hidden oil that fuel our discussions, and our collaborative information-seeking practices, in general.

In addition, not only do questions serve as the fuel for collaborative discussion, they *shape* discussion. Questions direct a discussion and its participants with a force that is surprisingly hard to resist. A well-articulated and emphatically posed question is hard to ignore or divert in the course of discussion. Doing so may leave one open to criticism by the standards of ordinary discourse; a truth often manifested (and exploited) in the context of political journalism. Questions, by their nature, suggest the need for a response and, at the same time, limit the form that that response can take. A class discussion framed by the question 'how many cupcakes did Kim Kardashian eat at her birthday party', is unlikely to provoke commentary on democratic voting rights and responsibilities. Questions determine the content of a discussion.

This is perhaps no more explicitly apparent in a democracy, than in the context of formal political debate. The series of US presidential debates in 2016 offers a salient example. Notable emphasis was placed in the media run-up to the third debate, on the questions that the debate chair, Fox News anchor Chris Wallace, would ask the presidential candidates. The emphasis here is warranted; the questions determined the content of the debate itself. In this case, they are the basis on which a large proportion of those casting votes in the US election (alongside a massive international audience) gained access to the ideas, beliefs, policies, and values of the key rival candidates for the job. Or, at least, an insight into what they were willing to say about these things. Think also of the questions posed by members of the public in the 'town-hall' presidential debate, or, indeed, in any political debate, from the real town hall to a national election. Not only do questions shape the debate but they allow the individuals asking them, and those whom they, knowingly or unknowingly, represent, to take part in the discussion. Questions enable and empower us to actively participate in, and impact upon, democracy. What is asked, in the classroom, or in the wider world, determines to a significant degree, what is discussed, considered, noticed, and understood. By asking questions, an individual can participate in discussion. The good questioner targets worthwhile information with their questions, ensuring that the opportunity for discussion is not wasted on trivial or irrelevant topics and that it speaks to their concerns.

A second point relevant to the central claim has thus been highlighted: good questioning plays a valuable (and often unnoticed) role in discussion and debate. Questions both enable (and frequently initiate) discussion, and they often determine its content. Productive, collaborative, and critical discussion and debate, in societal and political settings and institutions at all levels, from the classroom, to the pub, to the highest levels of government – these are the hallmarks of a functioning democracy. If active participation in discussion, deliberation and debate is an important feature of a functioning democratic society, then educating for good questioning once again serves the aims of democracy.

Good Questioning Enables Informed Decision-Making

Third, good questioning facilitates informed decision-making. This can be illustrated by returning to the analysis of good questioning offered above: the good questioner competently elicits worthwhile information. This translates directly into the context of decision-making. Specifically, the ability to identify and seek out worthwhile information – both non-trivial and relevant to one's aims and context – is required in many everyday decision-making scenarios. Consider the array of information one encounters when deciding, for example, which newspaper to read, which supermarket to shop at, which eggs to buy, which mode of transport to use. Not all of the information one encounters in these types of decision-making scenarios will be non-trivial, relevant, or significant. In fact, much of it is likely to be information that one should not consider at all, and some will be information that actively works against the ability to make a decision. Yet decisions such as these comprise the everyday workings of democratic society. The freedom to make *informed* decisions about these things, and many others, is a freedom which fundamentally underwrites democracy itself. No more so than when deciding which box to tick on one's ballot paper. We must, at least, aspire to a democracy in which this decision, for all those making it, is based on an informed evaluation of the options available.

Importantly, the notion in operation here is a normative one; the informed decision is one based on information that is *worth having*. The ability to identify information that is worth having is key to an individual's ability to make informed choices. This ability is also key to the skill of good questioning. Thus, good questioning enables informed decision-making. Furthermore, in a society in which the most worthwhile information is not always readily available to its citizens, as voters or consumers, protected and distorted, as is often the case, by corporate needs and greeds, the need to educate individuals so that they can identify and seek information out for themselves, as well as critically assess the information that is presented to them, is all the more significant. If having an informed populace is a cornerstone of a functioning democracy, then educating for good questioning is a means of achieving this. A populace that can identify the information that it needs, seek this out, and/or critically assess it, can 'inform itself', so to speak. The significance of good questioning for decision-making can be seen at all levels of democratic society; from the egg-buying decisions of everyday life to the decisions of war and governance. If one lacks the ability to identify and elicit the most worthwhile information in a given situation, then one lacks the ability to make an informed decision, when required. Good questioning provides a valuable tool to counter this. Just as students in the classroom are empowered by good questioning to incrementally direct their learning in line with their informational needs and desires, a populace comprised of such individuals can do the same.

This highlights a final point relevant to the central claim. The skill of good questioning requires an individual to identify, and elicit worthwhile information. Doing so is key to informed decision-making. Good questioning thereby enables informed decision-making in democratic society. This enhances an individual's ability to dismiss or challenge the information that they encounter, and identify worthwhile information that is not provided, or is obscured in some way, by drawing attention to the informational features of their environment and enabling them to act within it. Democracy flourishes when those living under it are free to make informed decisions about their lives and their government. At its best, a society in which individuals are educated for good questioning is one in which this goal can be realised. Educating for good questioning as a democratic skill thereby serves a third important aim; to prepare students for democratic citizenship.

Conclusion

Educating for the skill of good questioning serves three key aims of democracy. First, it aids understanding, in general, and understanding of democratic processes and institutions, in particular. Second, it facilitates participation in democratic society, providing the opportunity and tools to share in and shape democratic discussion and debate. Third, it enables informed-decision making, preparing students for democratic citizenship. By cultivating and refining questioning skills, students are equipped with the tools to raise and pursue their own inquiries, as well as actively engage with and challenge those of others. Without such cultivation, learning is in danger of becoming passive and compliant. Active learning and critical engagement is central to the cultivation of democratic character, extending beyond the schools and classrooms in which formal education takes place to the attitude that a learner carries with them throughout their life and to the constitution of democratic society as a whole. At its best, good questioning leads to active, collaborative, and critical democratic citizenship. In this sense, good questioning is an essential democratic skill to educate for.

Acknowledgements

This publication was made possible through the support of a grant from the John Templeton Foundation to the *Institute for the Study of Human Flourishing* at *The University of Oklahoma*. The opinions expressed in this publication are those of the author(s) and do not necessarily reflect the views of the John Templeton Foundation or the *Institute for the Study of Human Flourishing*.

Notes

1 I have distinguished these two senses of 'worthwhile' for the purposes of exposition. However, it is plausible that they are not, in fact, distinct in real-world information gathering contexts. One's questioning will not, for example, be deemed good merely in virtue of satisfying one's aims, if one's aim is to elicit information about the number of blades of grass in the courtyard, for no good reason. Conversely, one's questioning will not be deemed bad merely on the basis that one's aim is to elicit information about the number of blades of grass in the courtyard, if, for example, one is responding to the fact that someone is holding a gun to one's head and demanding to know. The worthiness of any epistemic good is plausibly closely tied to the practical interests of the epistemic agent. I leave this open for the present discussion.

2 Not to mention, make an enormous fortune as a result, as per the 2008 financial crisis.

Bibliography

Baehr, J. (2011). *The Inquiring Mind*. Oxford: Oxford University Press.

Berelson, B. and Steiner, G. (1964). *Human Behavior: An Inventory of Scientific Findings*. New York: Harcourt, Brace.

Bloom, B. ed., (1956). *Taxonomy of Educational Objectives: The Classification of Educational Goals*. New York: Longman Green.

Boyte, H. C. (2004). *Everyday Politics*. Philadelphia: University of Pennsylvania Press.

Dewey, J. (1916). *Democracy and Education*. New York: Macmillan.

Dewey, J. (1933). *How We Think*. Chicago: Henry Regnery.

Dillon, J. T. (1984). Research on Questioning and Discussion. *Educational Leadership*, 42(3), pp. 50–56.

Elder, L. and Paul, R. (2005). The Art of Asking Essential Questions. [online]. www.criticalthinking.org. Available at: www.criticalthinking.org/store/products/the-art-of-asking-essential-questions-5th-edition/168 [Accessed 01 Nov. 2016].

Ennis, R. (1962). A Concept of Critical Thinking. *Harvard Educational Review*, 32, pp. 81–111.

Freire, P. (1970). *Pedagogy of the Oppressed*. Translated by M. Bergman Ramos. New York: The Seabury Press.

Galston, W. (1989). Civic Education in the Liberal State. In N. Rosenblum, ed., *Liberalism and the Moral Life*, 1st ed. Cambridge: Harvard University Press. pp. 89–102.

Grimm, S. (2008). Epistemic Goals and Epistemic Values. *Philosophy and Phenomenological Research*, 77(3), pp. 725–744.

Gutmann, A. (1987). *Democratic Education*. Princeton: Princeton University Press.

Kotzee, B. (2011). Education and "Thick" Epistemology. *Educational Theory*, 61(5), pp. 549–564.

Kvanvig, J. (2014). *Rationality and Reflection*. Oxford: Oxford University Press.

Lijphart, A. (1997). Unequal Participation: Democracy's Unresolved Dilemma. *The American Political Science Review*, 91(1), pp. 1–14.

Lipman, M. (1991). *Thinking in Education*. New York: Cambridge University Press.

Lynch, M. (2004). Minimalism and the Value of Truth. *The Philosophical Quarterly*, 217, pp. 497–517.

McPeck, J. (1984). *Critical Thinking and Education*. London: Palgrave Macmillan.

Ostrom, E. (1998). A Behavioral Approach to the Rational Choice Theory of Collective Action: Presidential Address, American Political Science Association, 1997. *The American Political Science Review*, 92(1), pp. 1–22.

Paul, R. (1990). *Critical Thinking: What Every Person Needs to Survive in a Rapidly Changing World*. Rohnert Park: Center for Critical Thinking and Moral Critique.

Plato. (1997). Republic. Translated by G.M.A Grube and Rev. C.D.C. Reeve. In J. M. Cooper, ed., *Plato, Complete Works*. Indiana: Hackett Publishing Company.

Pritchard, D. (2013). Epistemic Virtue and the Epistemology of Education. *Journal of Philosophy of Education*, 47 (2), pp. 236–247.

Sattes, B. D. and Walsh, J. (2005). *Quality Questioning: Research-Based Practice to Engage Every Learner*. Thousand Oaks: Corwen Press.

Scheffler, I. (1973). *Reason and Teaching*. London: Routledge and Kegan Paul.

Siegel, H. (1988). *Educating Reason: Rationality, Critical Thinking, and Education*. New York and London: Routledge.

Sosa, E. (2003). The Place of Truth in Epistemology. In M. DePauland and L. Zagzebski, eds., *Intellectual Virtue: Perspectives from Ethics and Epistemology*. Oxford: Oxford University Press, pp. 155–180.

Treanor, N. (2013). The Measure of Knowledge. *Nous*, 47(3), pp. 577–601.

Watson, L. (2016a). Why Should We Educate For Inquisitiveness? In J. Baehr, ed., *Intellectual Virtues and Education: Essays in Applied Virtue Epistemology*. New York: Routledge. pp. 38–53.

Wilen, W. (1984). Implications for Research On Questioning for the Teacher Educator. *Journal of Research and Development in Education*, 17, pp. 21–25.

Further Reading

Baehr, J. (2013). The Cognitive Demands of Intellectual Virtue. In T. Henning and D. Schweikard, eds., *Knowledge, Virtue and Action: Putting Epistemic Virtues to Work*. New York: Routledge, pp. 99–118.

Cremin, L. (1959). John Dewey and the Progressive-Education Movement, 1915–1952. *The School Review*, 67 (2), pp. 160–173.

Facione, P. (1990). *Critical Thinking: A Statement of Expert Consensus for Purposes of Educational Assessment and Instruction*. Report commissioned by *American Philosophical Association*.

Gosnell, H. F. (1927). *Getting Out the Vote: An Experiment in the Stimulation of Voting*. Chicago: University of Chicago Press.

Kotzee, B. (2013). Introduction: Education, Social Epistemology and Virtue Epistemology. *Journal of Philosophy of Education*, 47(2), pp. 157–167.

Oppenhuis, E. V. (1995). *Voting Behaviour in Europe: A Comparative Analysis of Electoral Participation and Party Choice*. Amsterdam: Het Spinhuis.

Robertson, E. (2009). The Epistemic Aims of Education. In H. Siegel, ed., *The Oxford Handbook of Philosophy of Education*. Oxford: Oxford University Press, pp. 11–34.

Scheffler, I. (1965). *The Conditions of Knowledge: An Introduction to Epistemology and Education*. Chicago: Scott, Foresman.

Siegel, H. (2004). Epistemology and Education: An Incomplete Guide to the Social-Epistemological Issues. *Episteme*, 1, pp. 129–137.

Siegel, H. (2008). Is 'Education' a Thick Epistemic Concept? *Philosophical Papers*, 37(3), pp. 455–469.

Sockett, H. (2012). *Knowledge and Virtue in Teaching and Learning*. New York: Routledge.

Topf, R. (1995). Electoral Participation. In H. Klingemann and D. Fuchs, eds., *Citizens and the State*. Oxford: Oxford University Press, pp. 52–92.

Watson, L. (2015). What is Inquisitiveness. *American Philosophical Quarterly*, 52(3), pp. 273–288.

Watson, L. (2016b). The Epistemology of Education. *Philosophy Compass*, 11(3), pp. 146–159.

44

INTELLECTUAL VIRTUES, CRITICAL THINKING, AND THE AIMS OF EDUCATION

Jason Baehr

The so-called "value turn" in epistemology has led to increased attention to the upper normative dimensions of the cognitive life—to states like understanding and wisdom and to the sorts of character traits or "intellectual virtues" that facilitate the acquisition of these epistemic goods.[1] This richer, more normative focus has brought with it a renewed interest in the intersection of epistemology and the philosophy of education.[2] The present chapter explores this intersection by examining the relationship between critical thinking conceived of as an educational ideal and intellectual virtues like curiosity, open-mindedness, intellectual courage, and intellectual perseverance.[3] How exactly are intellectual virtues related to critical thinking? Can a person be intellectually virtuous while failing to be a critical thinker? Or do intellectual virtues secure a certain level of competence at critical thinking? In light of these issues, which of these two ideals is a more suitable educational aim?

In responding to these questions, I take as my focus Harvey Siegel's (1988) influential account of critical thinking, according to which critical thinking has two main components: a "reason assessment" component and a "critical spirit" component. I argue, contra Siegel (2009; 2016), that intellectual virtues cut across both of these components. The argument sheds light, in particular, on how the sorts of skills or abilities proper to intellectual virtues are related to the reasoning skills involved with critical thinking. Next I consider and respond to some of Siegel's recent arguments (2009; 2016) to the effect that critical thinking is the superior educational ideal. I close with a brief argument to the contrary.

Siegel's Account of Critical Thinking: "Reason Assessment" and the "Critical Spirit"

The concept of critical thinking is at least quasi-technical. This is evident in ordinary usage of the term "critical thinking," which fails to pick out any very specific, determinate, or univocal activity or set of competencies. Nevertheless, among theorists of critical thinking, there is reasonably broad agreement about its general features and structure. One of the more prominent and sophisticated models of critical thinking is Siegel's, which he initially developed in his influential 1988 book *Educating Reason* (1988) and has continued to refine and defend in recent decades (see e.g. 1997; 2009; 2016).

According to Siegel (1988), critical thinking has two main components. The first is a "reason assessment" (RA) component, which he describes as follows:

The basic idea here is simple enough: a critical thinker must be able to assess reasons and their ability to warrant beliefs, claims and actions properly. This means that the critical thinker must have a good understanding of, and the ability to utilize, principles governing the assessment of reasons.

(34)

These principles are of two main types: "subject-specific principles which govern the assessment of particular sorts of reasons in particular contexts" and "subject-neutral, general principles which apply across a wide variety of contexts and types of reason." The former include principles applicable to, for example, the "proper assessment of works of art, or novels, or historical documents," while the latter consist of "all those principles typically regarded as 'logical,' both formal and informal," including "principles regarding inductive inference, avoiding fallacies, proper deductive inference," and so on (34–5).

While some theorists have equated critical thinking with the use or possession of such reasoning skills,[4] Siegel argues convincingly that the RA component of critical thinking is not sufficient:

> In order to be a critical thinker, a person must have, in addition to what has been said thus far, certain attitudes, dispositions, habits of mind, and character traits, which together may be labelled the "critical attitude" or "critical spirit." Most generally, a critical thinker must not only be *able* to assess reasons properly, in accordance with the reason assessment component, she must be *disposed* to do so as well; that is, a critical thinker must have a well-developed disposition to engage in reason assessment.
>
> *(39)*

Siegel elaborates on the "critical spirit" (CS) component of critical thinking as follows:

> One who has the critical attitude has a certain *character* as well as certain skills: a character which is inclined to seek, and to base judgment and action upon, reasons; which rejects partiality and arbitrariness; which is committed to the objective evaluation of relevant evidence; and which values such aspects of critical thinking as intellectual honesty, justice to evidence, sympathetic and impartial considerations of interests, objectivity, and impartiality ... A possessor of the critical attitude is inclined to seek reasons and evidence; to demand justification; to query and investigate unsubstantiated claims. Moreover, a person who possesses the critical attitude has habits of mind consonant with the just-mentioned considerations. Such a person habitually seeks evidence and reasons, and is predisposed to so seek—and to base belief and action on the results of such seeking.
>
> *(39)*

Situating Intellectual Virtues

How, then, should we understand the relationship between critical thinking and the sorts of intellectual character strengths noted above? Specifically, where in Siegel's model of critical thinking do intellectual virtues figure?

Intellectual Virtues and CS

The answer to this question may appear to be obvious. Intellectual virtues are sometimes described as the character traits of a good thinker, learner, or inquirer.[5] They include qualities like attentiveness, open-mindedness, fair-mindedness, as well as *intellectual* carefulness, thoroughness, autonomy, rigor, honesty, humility, courage, and tenacity. Such qualities appear to be at the very heart of the CS component of critical thinking. In one of the excerpts above, for instance, Siegel describes CS as involving the possession of a certain type of *character*—one which "rejects partiality and arbitrariness; which is committed to the objective evaluation of relevant evidence; and which values such aspects of critical thinking as intellectual honesty, justice to evidence, sympathetic and impartial considerations of interests, objectivity, and impartiality" (39). At first pass, this looks to be a description of precisely what virtue epistemologists think of as intellectual virtues.

Other elements of Siegel's description of CS offer additional support for this picture. Siegel describes CS as a "global disposition," the possession of which involves being "a certain sort of *person*" (8, emphasis added; cf. 10). He views CS as related to "the importance of character, values, and other moral dimensions [of critical thinking]" (10). Finally, he describes CS as involving the following: "intellectual honesty," "justice to evidence" (9), "love of reason" (39), "rational passions," a "love of truth," a "concern for accuracy in observation and inference," a "passionate drive for clarity, accuracy, and fair-mindedness ... for listening sympathetically to opposition points of view," "humility" (40), and "rational virtues" such as "impartiality of judgment, ability to view matters from a variety of non-self-interested perspectives" (43). Again, the apparent conceptual and terminological overlap with intellectual virtues is striking and substantial.

At first glance, then, intellectual virtues appear to be an integral part of the CS component of critical thinking.[6] Whether they constitute the whole of CS, that is, whether there is anything more to CS than the possession of intellectual virtues, is not something I will try to settle here. Rather, in the section that follows, I argue that the suggested account of the relationship between intellectual virtues and critical thinking is importantly incomplete.

Intellectual Virtues and RA

Siegel marks a sharp distinction between the CS and RA components of critical thinking, claiming, for instance, that a person can be very strong in CS while being very weak in the sorts of skills and abilities that comprise RA.[7] He makes a similar claim about the relationship between intellectual virtues and RA:

> [A]ll the abilities that mark the execution (and so the possession) of the virtues—taking up alternative points of view, judging open-mindedly and fair-mindedly, attending to important details, asking thoughtful questions, etc.—can be done well or badly from the epistemic point of view: One can judge open-mindedly but irrationally; attend to important details but misevaluate their evidential significance; ask thoughtful but irrelevant questions; etc. Consequently, the manifestation of [these abilities] ... while perhaps indicators of possession of the virtues, won't indicate anything about the quality of thought the virtues are supposed to secure.
>
> *(2016: 101; cf. 107)*[8]

I argue below that this is an incorrect account of the relationship between intellectual virtues and RA.[9] However, it contains a couple grains of truth that are worth noting. First, it is important to bear in mind a distinction between (mere) traits and virtues. A person who regularly but indiscriminately considers views very different from her own could be said to have the *trait* of open-mindedness (she would be, in some sense, an open-minded person); however, her open-mindedness will not be an intellectual *virtue* (intellectual virtues being traits that meet a certain standard of intellectual or epistemic *value* or *excellence*). To possess the virtue of open-mindedness, a person must be disposed to consider views different from her own at the right time, in the right way, in the right amount, and so on.[10] The same point can be made in connection with other intellectual traits and virtues. Accordingly, Siegel is right to suggest that a person can be open-minded in some sense while being deficient in the sorts of skills proper to RA. However, this leaves open whether such a person can possess the *virtue* of open-mindedness.

Second, intellectual virtues often manifest in intellectual activity that has little or nothing to do with the kind of discursive reasoning or epistemic assessment proper to RA. Creativity and open-mindedness, for example, involve conceiving of new possibilities or standpoints. Attentiveness involves looking and listening in a focused way. And curiosity involves the formulation of insightful questions. None of these activities (imagining, looking, listening, questioning) is a matter of assessing reasons or drawing inferences. As such, they are distinct from the territory covered by RA. It follows that a person can be competent in *aspects* of certain intellectual virtues without satisfying the requirements of RA. However, it does not follow that such a person can possess the virtues themselves (possessing an aspect of a virtue may be insufficient even for the minimal possession of the virtue itself). Nor does this provide any reason for thinking that intellectual virtues sometimes manifest in discursive intellectual activity that is epistemically subpar.

Indeed, as I turn now to show, virtuous intellectual activity is partly a matter of manifesting the sorts of skills and abilities proper to RA, such that being intellectually virtuous requires being a critical thinker along the lines of RA. There are, more specifically, at least two main ways in which the possession of intellectual virtues requires being a competent reasoner.

The first is related to what I have elsewhere (2015) described as the "judgment" component of an intellectual virtue. The idea, roughly, is that part of what it is to possess an intellectual virtue V is to be disposed to manifest good judgment with respect to engaging in V-relevant activity, that is, with respect to when, to whom, to what extent, and so on, to engage in said activity. So, for instance, part of what it is to be intellectually courageous, say, is to know when and how much to risk in one's pursuit of epistemic goods. Put another way, like moral virtues, intellectual virtues involve an element of *phronesis*.[11] While I cannot pause here to defend this claim, I assume that it has considerable intuitive appeal.

How, then, does satisfying the judgment requirement on intellectual virtues require the possession of the sorts of skills or abilities proper to RA? As noted above, on Siegel's view, RA centrally involves the *assessment of reasons*. This includes reasons for action (1988: 33–4). Similarly, the judgment component of an intellectual virtue involves the assessment of reasons for *intellectual action* or conduct (e.g. reasons pertaining to whether or how much to engage in a certain virtue-relevant activity). It follows that a person cannot possess an intellectual virtue without manifesting at least an element of the kind of rational competence proper to RA.

This is not the only way in which the judgment component of intellectual virtues involves RA abilities. This component also manifests in purely epistemic assessments. For instance, part of what it is to possess the virtue of open-mindedness is to be competent at judging when (or to what extent) to take up and give serious consideration to a competing standpoint. This in turn requires making judgments about the epistemic credibility of the standpoint (if the standpoint has no credibility, then open-mindedness may not be called for), that is, it requires competent assessment of the reasons for and against its truth. In this respect as well one cannot possess the kind of judgment proper to an intellectual virtue while failing to possess any of the abilities proper to RA.

A second main way in which intellectual virtues require being a competent reasoner concerns what I have elsewhere (2015) described as the "skill" component of an intellectual virtue. Here the idea is that to possess an intellectual virtue V, one must be skilled or competent with respect to the kind of intellectual activity characteristic of V. In the case of open-mindedness, this involves being skilled at taking up and giving serious consideration to an opposing point of view.

With intellectual carefulness, it involves being alert to and avoiding intellectual errors. And with intellectual humility, it involves identifying and "owning" one's intellectual limitations and mistakes.[12]

These virtue-specific skills are not identical with the sorts of reasoning skills that Siegel identifies with RA. However, the two sets of skills overlap in important ways. In particular, virtue-specific skills involve the use or deployment of RA skills, such that unless one possesses the latter, one cannot possess the former. We can begin to see this, first, by reflecting on the operation of several specific virtues. As indicated above, intellectual carefulness involves being alert to the possibility of and successfully avoiding intellectual errors, including inferential and related epistemic errors. As such, it involves making *correct* epistemic judgments. Intellectual humility involves recognizing and "owning" one's intellectual limitations and mistakes. To do this, one must be appropriately responsive to indicators of these limitations and mistakes, for example, by taking notice of them and correctly assessing their significance. Finally, consider fair-mindedness. A fair-minded person uses a common set of (apt) criteria to judge or evaluate different but relevantly similar claims and viewpoints. He does not employ a double standard, but rather is consistent in his epistemic assessments, treating "like cases alike." In this and each of the other cases just noted, an intellectual virtue manifests in precisely the kind of epistemic activity that is characteristic of RA. Thus the "reach" of intellectual virtues extends well into the territory of RA.

A similar conclusion can be arrived at on a theoretical basis. A corollary of the earlier account of the "judgment" component of intellectual virtues is that a person's intellectual activity manifests an intellectual virtue only if the person has *good reason to believe* that engaging in this activity is likely to be helpful for reaching the truth.[13] If a person engages in open-minded or intellectually courageous activity, say, without any reason to think that doing so is likely to bring her closer to the truth or to improve her epistemic standing (e.g. if she does so randomly or indiscriminately), then this activity will be less than intellectually virtuous. Typically, however, a person has good reason to think that her intellectual activity is likely to get her closer to the truth only if this activity is itself reasonable or epistemically up to par. If a person's efforts at being open-minded, say, tend to be very clumsy or irrational, then this person is unlikely to possess good reason to think that her open-minded activity is truth-conducive.[14] In this way, the satisfaction of the judgment requirement on intellectual virtues at least makes highly probable a reasonably high level of the kind of first-order rational competence that is characteristic of RA.

By way of response, Siegel might argue that while the possession of intellectual virtues requires meeting a certain standard of rational competence along the lines of RA, this standard is not especially high, such that a person can be intellectually virtuous while lacking many of the skills proper to RA.[15] This claim seems to me to be unmotivated. To be sure, a person who is minimally or less than fully intellectually virtuous might be deficient from the standpoint of RA. But the same can be said of the less-than-perfect critical thinker. Siegel acknowledges that being a critical thinker is a matter of degree (1993: 165). It follows that a person can be a (minimally or less than fully) critical thinker while still lacking some of the rational competence proper to RA. The important question is whether, say, a *maximally* intellectually virtuous person (i.e. one who possesses all the intellectual virtues to a maximal degree) might still be significantly deficient from the standpoint of RA. This seems dubious at best. Rather, given what we have seen of the close relationship between intellectual virtues and competent reasoning, a more plausible view is that a maximally intellectually virtuous agent would also be extremely (perhaps even perfectly) competent at the kind of reasoning required by RA. More precisely, a person who is maximally competent along the "judgment" and "skill" dimensions of all the intellectual virtues would not be significantly deficient along the RA dimension of critical thinking.

We are now in a position to draw several conclusions about the relationship between intellectual virtues and critical thinking understood in Siegel's terms. First, intellectual virtues at least partially comprise the CS component of critical thinking. Second, intellectual virtues involve a form of (second-order) rational judgment that in turn involves elements of the RA component of critical thinking. Third, intellectual virtues involve certain (first-order) virtue-specific skills or abilities that are also partly constituted by elements of RA. Regarding the latter two points, the idea is that the intellectual skills proper to RA are, as it were, "tools" required for the possession of certain core elements of an intellectual virtue. In this way, good thinking skills stand to intellectual virtues in much the same way that cognitive faculties like reason, vision, or introspection stand to intellectual virtues. In each case, the skills or capacities in question are among the tools or resources possessed by a virtuous epistemic agent.

The Aims of Education

In this final section, I examine the comparative suitability of intellectual virtues and critical thinking as educational ideals. My immediate aim is to rebut three recent arguments by Siegel (2016) for the claim that critical thinking is the superior ideal.[16]

The first argument is that educating for intellectual virtues is "educationally ambitious" in a way that educating for critical thinking is not. In mounting this argument, Siegel draws attention to my view (2015) that, in addition to the "judgment" and "skill" components discussed above, intellectual virtues also have an "affective" component. This view is akin to the familiar and plausible Aristotelian point that morally virtuous persons *enjoy* or take *pleasure* in morally virtuous activity. I argue that the same point applies in the case of intellectual virtues, that is, that an intellectually virtuous agent characteristically takes pleasure in her virtuous thinking and inquiry. Siegel replies:

> [D]o we really have to ensure that students take pleasure in the exercise of the virtues in order to have succeeded educationally? Supposing that Baehr is right about the necessity of the appropriate affect/attitude toward the exercise of the virtues in order to have them—she must take pleasure in their exercise—is the person who exercises the right dispositions out of duty rather than pleasure an educational failure?
>
> *(102–3)*

I have two main replies to this objection. First, educating for intellectual virtues as both Siegel and I are thinking of it is an educational *ideal*. Therefore, a student who, say, falls short of this ideal in some respects but closely approximates it in others would hardly be considered an "educational failure." Rather, a more relevant question is whether, from an ideal standpoint, we would like our students not only to become competent thinkers but also to learn to enjoy the learning process—to cultivate a "love of learning." Presumably the answer is "yes" (2013a). Second, in raising this objection, Siegel appears to have lost sight of just how much he packs into the CS component of critical thinking. As we saw above, this component is constituted by a "global disposition" that involves being "a certain sort of person" (8); it has "moral dimensions" including "character" and "values" (39); and its elements include various "rational virtues" (43), "love of reason," "love of truth," "rational passions," a "passionate drive for clarity, accuracy, and fair-mindedness" and for "listening sympathetically to opposing points of view" (39), and much more besides. To educate for critical thinking is (in part) to educate for these and many related qualities.[17] Educating for intellectual virtues, then, does not appear to be more ambitious than educating for critical thinking in Siegel's sense.

Siegel's second argument is that an educational approach aimed at critical thinking is the only one capable of showing proper respect for students:

> [Critical thinking understood as an educational ideal] is justified by our duty to treat students (and everyone else) with respect as persons. An education guided by the ideal of CT is the only one that so treats students, because it acknowledges, respects, and strives to foster their autonomy, independent judgment, and right to question, challenge, and demand reasons for what is taught (including CT itself).
>
> *(2016: 108)*

He continues:

> [I]f we are serious about treating students with respect, what they become and what dispositions and virtues they value, possess, and manifest is importantly *up to them*. While we strive to foster CT abilities and dispositions in our students, we also (if we are doing it right) invite them to evaluate for themselves the worthiness of these things and submit our arguments for that worthiness to their independent scrutiny and judgment.
>
> *(2016: 108)*

There are several problems with this objection. First, the kind of respect appealed to here involves a deep concern with students' intellectual autonomy. Yet intellectual autonomy is a central intellectual virtue that can and should be emphasized within any educational program aimed at fostering intellectual virtues (likewise for allied virtues like intellectual courage and tenacity). Second, it is no more (or less) plausible to think that students should be left to decide which traits of intellectual character are worth cultivating than it is which forms of reasoning are worth engaging in. Just as there may be a time and place for students to question the objectivity or efficacy of critical thinking, so might there be a time and place for them to question the merits of curiosity, intellectual honesty, carefulness, thoroughness, tenacity—even intellectual autonomy. However, in the same way that it would be a mistake to make it "optional" whether students leave our courses disposed to employ *modus ponens* rather than to "affirm the consequent," we should hardly be indifferent about whether they depart disposed to think or reason in ways that are honest vs. dishonest, careful vs. sloppy, open-minded vs. closed-minded, and so on. Third, respect for students' intellectual autonomy is not the only value that should govern our interactions with them. A good education will also help students learn to identify and acknowledge the *limitations* of their cognitive abilities and to *lean on the abilities of others* in the cognitive life. That is, it will also foster virtues like intellectual humility and intellectual trust. If, as Siegel suggests, an overriding concern with intellectual autonomy is essential to treating critical thinking as an educational ideal, this may be more of a liability than an asset.

Siegel's third argument is that treating intellectual virtues as an educational ideal is uniquely "philosophically daunting" because it requires dealing with a host of thorny philosophical issues about, for instance, the virtues' motivational structure, unity, and normative status (2016: 98). He contends that similar questions do not arise when conceiving of critical thinking as an educational ideal.[18]

However, once critical thinking is taken to involve the rich network of psychological states that Siegel ascribes to CS, it may in fact be subject to several of the worries just noted. Recall that on Siegel's view, CS consists of a "cluster" of "attitudes, dispositions, habits of mind, and character traits." (1988: 34). Siegel does not appear to be using these terms interchangeably.[19] Instead his view seems to be that CS is comprised of many different *types* of qualities. But what exactly these types are and how they are related to each other is far from obvious and is left unspecified by Siegel. Similarly, Siegel views CS as involving such virtue-relevant qualities as "intellectual honesty, justice to evidence, sympathetic and impartial consideration of interests, objectivity, and impartiality" (39). Here too it is difficult to see why gaining clarity about what these qualities amount to, how they overlap, where they derive their value, and so on, would be any less philosophically challenging than it is in the case of intellectual virtues. I contend that any appearance of a special problem for intellectual virtues in this area is due to the fact that the corresponding elements of CS have gone relatively unexplored by Siegel and other critical thinking theorists. Were these elements subjected to the kind of rigorous scrutiny that virtue epistemologists have devoted to intellectual virtues, similar questions and challenges would likely emerge.[20]

That said, a further response to Siegel's third objection suggests that it poses no real problem for thinking of intellectual virtues *or* critical thinking as educational ideals. Treating something as an educational ideal does not require working out a systematic philosophical theory of it. It is important, of course, that the goal be specified in enough detail that it can be intentionally and intelligently pursued and that its value be sufficiently evident to those involved in its pursuit (e.g. teachers and students). However, these conditions can be satisfied by proponents of either goal in the absence of answers to the sorts of thorny philosophical issues and questions identified by Siegel.

Conclusion

We have found that Siegel's arguments fail to demonstrate that critical thinking is a superior educational ideal compared with intellectual virtues. While I am not interested in trying to paint an opposite picture, one brief point in this direction is worth noting. Critical thinking, as conceived of by Siegel and others, is about the *assessment of reasons, evidence, and arguments* (1988: 30, 33–4, *passim*). As such, it addresses only one dimension of the cognitive life. While this dimension is broad and important, critical thinking thus conceived neglects other important intellectual activities—activities that are also important vis-à-vis the aims of education. In addition to wanting our students to become good reasoners, we also want them to become competent at imagining innovative solutions, entering into perspectives very different from their own, paying close attention, noticing important details, and formulating good questions. As we saw above, these are precisely the sorts of activities characteristic of intellectual virtues like creativity, open-mindedness, attentiveness, and curiosity. This suggests that the *scope* of intellectual virtues is broader than that of critical thinking—and broader in ways that matter from an educational standpoint.[21] Siegel could, of course, extend his account of critical thinking, such that it also covers these creative, imaginative, and observational aspects of cognition.[22] However, not only is such a move difficult to square with Siegel's claim that "reason assessment" is the defining activity of critical thinking, it would also threaten to make his account stipulative and artificial. In contrast with ordinary ways of thinking about "critical thinking," this move would seem to equate critical thinking with "good thinking" or "epistemically good mental activity." Accordingly, while there may be a way around the present worry, it would appear to come at a significant theoretical cost.[23]

Notes

1 For more on this movement, see (Riggs, 2008).
2 For more on this connection, see (Baehr, 2016a: Ch. 1).
3 Thus I am conceiving of intellectual virtues along "responsibilist" rather than "reliabilist" lines. For a representative example of the former, see (Zagzebski, 1996); for an example of the latter, see (Sosa, 2007). For more on the relationship between these approaches, see (Baehr, 2011: Chs. 1, 4).

4   See (Siegel, 1988: 5–6) and (Missimer, 1990).

5   See for example (Baehr, 2011: Chs. 1–2) and (2013a).

6   Siegel might balk at this conclusion in either of a couple of ways. First, he might argue that intellectual virtues are more *demanding* than the elements of CS, for example, by identifying the latter with mere *tendencies* or *inclinations* to engage in good thinking (see e.g. his 2016). However, this rather thin notion of CS is difficult to square with many of the very positive and robust descriptions Siegel offers in (1988) and elsewhere. It also appears to make his own view susceptible to some of the criticisms he raises against Robert Ennis's "skills plus tendencies" account of critical thinking (6–10). Second, Siegel might also object that thinking of intellectual virtues as partly or wholly constitutive of CS introduces "complications" that problematize critical thinking's status as an educational ideal (2016: 98). I address this worry later in the chapter.

7   See especially (2016: 101–3).

8   For a similar argument, see (Siegel, 2009: 29–31).

9   It is also difficult to reconcile with some of Siegel's other writings on this topic. For instance, in a paper titled "Not by Skill Alone: The Centrality of Character to Critical Thinking" (1993), he argues that if a person's reasoning process fails to manifest virtues like intellectual impartiality or patience, this "does tell us something about the quality of that process: a process of reasoning which fails to manifest impartiality is of lower quality than a comparable process which (to a greater extent) does" (1993: 164). This seems clearly to suggest that intellectually virtuous activity must meet a certain evaluative standard.

10 See Baehr (2011: Ch. 9).

11 See Roberts and Wood (2007: 305) for more on this point.

12 For more on this account of intellectual humility, see (Whitcomb *et al.*, 2015).

13 This holds provided that the activity in question is aimed at the truth to begin with. For more on this, see my (2013b) and (2011: Ch. 6).

14 I say "unlikely" only because of the possibility (however improbable or remote) that a person might have good reason to think that her intellectual activity is truth-conducive when in fact it isn't. But this kind of case needn't concern us here.

15 In (2016), Siegel briefly discusses the hypothetical case of "Maria" in support of something like this claim. Maria is "competent at taking another's point of view" and "so (to that extent at least) [has] the virtue of open-mindedness"; however, she is also "very bad or only minimally good at reason assessment" and so fails "to be competent with respect to the reason assessment component of CT" (107). However, we have just considered several reasons for thinking that a proper account of open-mindedness (or similar virtues) rules out cases of this sort—or, in any case, that they are possible only to the extent that the person in question is (merely) minimally or less than fully intellectually virtuous in the relevant respect (see immediately below).

16 My aim is not to give a full blown defense of educating for intellectual virtues—nor an account of the full range of objections that might be raised against such an approach. For a more thorough defense, see my (2013a and 2016b). Surprisingly, Siegel himself defends (1993) something like this approach against objections raised in (Missimer, 1990). He also defends (1999) the educational importance of "thinking dispositions," which on my view (though not on Siegel's) are deeply similar to intellectual virtues (here see Ritchhart, 2002, and my 2015).

17 See (Siegel, 1988: Ch. 2) and (2016: 96).

18 A closely related objection, also raised by Siegel, is that conceiving of intellectual character growth as an educational ideal requires an appeal to the controversial notion of *eudaimonia* or human flourishing (2016: 108). However, no such requirement exists. Several virtue epistemologists have developed accounts of the normative status or grounding of intellectual virtues that do not rely in any way on *eudaimonsitic* concepts. See, for example, (Zagzebski, 1996), (Montmarquet, 1993), (Battaly, 2015), and (Baehr, 2011).

19 See, for example, his (1988: 39) and (2016: 96).

20 Indeed, Siegel himself admits as much in (1993: 146). Missimer (1990: 145–6) makes a similar point. Further, where critical thinking theorists have gone further in elaborating on some of the details of CS (e.g. Paul, 1993), their discussions only prove the point in question (see esp. 262–4).

21 This is not to deny that, say, creativity often has a rational component; nor that critical thinking sometimes has an imaginative element. What it denies is that all (epistemically worthwhile) creativity activity is itself a mode or form of critical thinking.

22 Indeed, he endorses something like this broadening in (Bailin and Siegel 2003).

23 Many thanks to Lani Watson and Shane Ashton for several helpful conversations about the issues discussed herein. Thanks as well to members of the philosophy department at the University of Oklahoma for feedback on an earlier version of this paper. I am also grateful to Harvey Siegel for comments on a penultimate draft.

Bibliography

Baehr, J. (2011). *The Inquiring Mind: On Intellectual Virtues and Virtue Epistemology*. Oxford: Oxford University Press.

Baehr, J. (2013a). Educating for Intellectual Virtues: From Theory to Practice. *Journal of Philosophy of Education*, 47(2), pp. 248–262.

Baehr, J. (2013b). The Cognitive Demands of Intellectual Virtue. In H. Tim, and S. David, eds., *Knowledge, Virtue, and Action*, London: Routledge, pp. 99–118.

Baehr, J. (2015). Four Dimensions of an Intellectual Virtue. In M. Chienkuo, S. Michael, and S. Ernest, eds., *Moral and Intellectual Virtues in Western and Chinese Philosophy: The Turn toward Virtue*, New York: Routledge, pp. 86–98.

Baehr, J. (2016a). *Intellectual Virtues and Education: Essays in Applied Virtue Epistemology*. New York: Routledge.

Baehr, J. (2016b). Is Intellectual Character Growth a Realistic Educational Aim? *Journal of Moral Education*, 45(2), pp. 117–131.

Bailin, S., and Harvey S. (2003). Critical Thinking. In B. Nigel, S. Paul, S. Richard, and S. Paul, eds., *The Blackwell Guide to the Philosophy of Education*, Malden, MA: Blackwell, pp. 181–193.

Bailin, S., and Siegel, H. (2003). Critical Thinking. In N. Blake, P. Smeyers, R. Smith, and P. Standish, eds., *The Blackwell Guide to the Philosophy of Education*, London: Blackwell Publishing (pp. 181–193).

Battaly, H. (2015). *Virtue*. Cambridge: Polity Press.

Hare, W. (1979). *Open-Mindedness and Education*. Kingston: McGill-Queen's University Press.

Hare, W. (1985). *In Defence of Open-Mindedness*. Kingston: McGill-Queen's University Press.

Kotzee, B. (2016). Problems of Assessment in Educating for Intellectual Virtue. In B. Jason, ed., *Intellectual Virtues and Education: Essays in Applied Virtue Epistemology*, New York: Routledge, pp. 142–160.

Missimer, C. (1990). Perhaps by Skill Alone. *Informal Logic XII*, 3, pp. 145–153.

Montmarquet, J. (1993). *Epistemic Virtue and Doxastic Responsibility*. Lanham, MD: Rowman and Littlefield.

Paul, R. (1993). Critical Thinking, Moral Integrity, and Citizenship: Teaching for Intellectual Virtues. In R. Paul, and A. J. Binker, eds., *Critical Thinking: What Every Student Needs to Survive in a Rapidly Changing World*, Dillon Beach, CA: Foundation for Critical Thinking., pp. 255–267.

Riggs, W. (2008). The Value Turn in Epistemology. In V. F. Hendricks, and D. Pritchard, eds., *New Waves in Epistemology*, London: Palgrave Macmillan, pp. 300–323.

Ritchhart, R. (2002). *Intellectual Character: What It Is, Why It Matters, and How to Get It*. San Francisco: Jossey-Bass.

Roberts, R., and Wood, W. J. (2007). *Intellectual Virtues: An Essay in Regulative Epistemology*. Oxford: Oxford University Press.

Siegel, H. (1988). *Educating Reason: Rationality, Critical Thinking, and Education*. New York: Routledge.

Siegel, H. (1993). Not by Skill Alone: The Centrality of Character to Critical Thinking. *Informal Logical*, 15(3), pp. 163–177.

Siegel, H. (1997). *Rationality Redeemed? Further Dialogues on an Educational Ideal*. New York: Routledge.

Siegel, H. (1999). What (Good) Are Thinking Dispositions? *Educational Theory*, 49(2), pp. 207–221.

Siegel, H. (2003). Cultivating Reason. In C. Randall, ed., *A Companion to the Philosophy of Education*, Oxford: Blackwell, pp. 305–317.

Siegel, H. (2009). Open-mindedness, Critical Thinking, and Indoctrination: Homage to William Hare. *Paideusis*, 18(1), pp. 26–34.

Siegel, H. (2016). Critical Thinking and the Intellectual Virtues. In J. Baehr, ed., *Intellectual Virtues and Education: Essays in Applied Virtue Epistemology*, New York: Routledge, pp. 95–112.

Sosa, E. (2007). *A Virtue Epistemology: Apt Belief and Reflective Knowledge*. Oxford: Oxford University Press.

Whitcomb, D., Heather B., Jason B., and Daniel, H. (2015). Intellectual Humility: Owning Our Limitations. *Philosophy and Phenomenological Research*, DOI: 10.1111/phpr.12228.

Zagzebski, L. (1996). *Virtues of the Mind*. Cambridge: Cambridge University Press.

45

COMPUTATIONAL MODELS IN SOCIAL EPISTEMOLOGY

Igor Douven

In social epistemology, computational agent-based models have recently been much in the limelight. The present chapter describes the background of this development and pays special attention to arguably the most successful computational model in this context, the so-called Hegselmann–Krause model.

Introduction

Computational models, especially computational agent-based models, have become common tools for social science practitioners. These models have been used to study such diverse phenomena as migration dynamics, electoral behavior, fluctuations in housing demand, civil disobedience, racial segregation, the emergence of social norms, and the spread of epidemics. More generally, they have been used to investigate social phenomena that emerge from interactions among many individual agents.

Frequently the applications concern social phenomena too complex to be understood through purely analytical means. The best known model of this type is probably still Schelling's (1969) tipping model, which explains how racial segregation can persist in a society even if no members of that society have a strong preference for living among people of their own race.[1] While the specification of the model is exceedingly straightforward and compact—its core part consists of a set of simple rules for agents moving on a lattice they live on—mathematical analysis of the model has proven quite difficult and is still considered very much an open research question (Easley and Kleinberg 2010, p. 103). The same is true for many other computational models of social phenomena. In such cases, computer simulations tend to be essential for gaining a deeper understanding of the phenomena, and so serve more than merely illustrative or heuristic purposes (although they typically serve these purposes, too).

The use of computational models in social epistemology is a more recent development, but it has the same broad motivation as the use of computational models in the social sciences: the aim is to study epistemic phenomena that cannot be understood by focussing on agents outside their social context, or even by focussing on small groups of epistemically interacting agents, and that cannot fruitfully be investigated by exclusively analytical means.

In this chapter, we describe what led to this development, and we pay special attention to one specific model that, albeit simple in its most basic form, has proven to be extremely versatile and has been successfully applied to a number of different issues in social epistemology.

The Social Epistemology of Communities

For most of its history, the guiding model of epistemology has been that of a single cognizing subject, facing the world on her own. This model has proven useful, for instance, in studying the possibility of a priori knowledge, or that of perceptual justification, or the relation between inference and knowledge. But an epistemology focussing exclusively on this model will at best give an incomplete, and at worst a distorted, picture of human knowledge. As was forcefully argued in Goldman (1999), to pretend that we seek knowledge in complete isolation of others is to ignore crucial aspects of our epistemic lives. Much of what we know we owe to others, and a complete epistemology can only be obtained by also paying careful attention to our interactions with others and the concerted efforts we undertake as members of a community of truth-seekers. Our social embedding offers indispensable pathways to knowledge and justified belief.

Thus was born a new field: social epistemology. However, it is no exaggeration to say that, at least initially, the bulk of the work conducted in this new field concerned the topic of testimony, which typically involves situations in which the single thinker from the traditional model is confronted with one other thinker. Admittedly, there was also work on expertise, judgment aggregation, and peer disagreement, which occasionally considered situations involving more than two epistemically interacting agents. But insofar as groups of agents were discussed, these groups tended to be small. In fact, to the best of my knowledge, the only work in the early stages of social epistemology that looked at larger groups was centered on a model proposed in Lehrer and Wagner (1981), which now commonly goes by the name "Lehrer–Wagner model."

This model features a group of N agents, all of whom hold an opinion concerning the value x of some unspecified quantity X, with $x \in [0, 1]$. Also, each group member assigns a weight to all N members in the group, where the weight member i assigns to member j, w_{ij}, reflects the trust i invests in j's ability to correctly estimate the value of X. For each group member, the weights she assigns are in the unit interval, and together the weights sum to 1. A weight of 0 indicates no trust at all (the member being assigned that weight is basically seen as just guessing the value of X) and a weight of 1 indicates full trust. This yields an $N \times N$ matrix W of weights, with w_{ij} the entry in the i-th row and the j-th column of W. Let $P = \langle p_1, \ldots, p_N \rangle$ be the vector of estimates of X, with p_i being the estimate of agent i. Then Lehrer and Wagner prove that, under fairly weak conditions, there is a $P^* = \langle p_1^*, \ldots, p_N^* \rangle$, with $p_i^* = p_j^*$ for all i, j, such that $W^m P \to P^*$ as $m \to \infty$, where W^m indicates the operation of repeated multiplication of the matrix of weights; in other words, under rather weak assumptions, the group members come to agree on the value of X, at least in the limit, provided they iteratively take into account each others' weight assignments.[2]

Even granting that we can make our trust in others' capabilities numerically precise, the model has severe limitations. First, note that the Lehrer–Wagner model is only concerned with consensus formation. To be sure, that is a topic of great interest to social epistemologists. As will be seen below, however, there are formal models on the market that allow one to study, in addition to consensus formation, a whole range of other socio-epistemic phenomena. In light of this, it seems well advised to expend time and effort in exploring those models rather than in further developing the Lehrer–Wagner model.

Second, it is unclear whether the Lehrer–Wagner model has any psychological reality or indeed reflects the process of consensus formation as it occurs—or usually occurs, or even just sometimes occurs—in actuality. Nor do Lehrer and Wagner claim otherwise. Rather, the model is recommended as a rational method for reaching consensus when such consensus is unattainable by other means. But this does suggest that the Lehrer–Wagner model deserves no prominent place in social epistemology.[3]

Finally and most importantly, note that, with regard to real life, the Lehrer–Wagner model can still only be applied to medium-sized communities at best, given that all agents must know each other, and in fact must know each other more than superficially lest the assignment of weights will appear arbitrary, and the consensus reached will appear arbitrary as well.

And social epistemologists will want to investigate still larger communities, in which not all community members know each other, and even in which every member knows only a small fraction of the other members. Why? One straightforward answer is that we are part of such communities, and that we cannot assume a priori that any socio-epistemological questions that might arise out of this acknowledgement can be dealt with as well by concentrating on contexts involving only a relatively small number of epistemic agents. It is undeniable that our beliefs are not just shaped by those with whom we directly interact but also by the interactions that those with whom we interact have with others whom we may never meet. In turn, the beliefs of those others will be influenced by yet others, and so on, although at various junctures, the "others" may include ourselves or still further members of the community whose beliefs have been shaped, at least partly, and whether directly or indirectly, by ours.

This cobweb of direct and indirect mutual epistemic influences is especially manifest in modern science, where our views are formed in a myriad of ways, through our teachers, the papers and books we read, the talks we hear at conferences, the colleagues we meet in formal and informal settings, and so on. While nineteenth-century science was still "a gentlemanly hobby, where the interests and abilities of a single individual can have a profound impact"(Gribbin 2010, p. 359), at least since Kuhn (1962), it is somewhat of a commonplace that modern science can only be understood as an essentially social enterprise, involving groups of interacting agents who must be willing to circulate results and must be open to other manners of collaboration, if they are to stand a chance of making progress in their field. As is also clear, however, at the same time modern scientists are in competition with each other for recognition and financial resources. Some of the finer dynamics these interdependencies can give rise to, and the connection of this dynamics to questions concerning scientific progress, have been investigated by means of agent-based simulations, but the models used in this research all go far beyond what the Lehrer–Wagner model offers.[4]

There is a second reason for epistemologists to be interested in large communities of epistemic agents who interact with each other partly directly, partly indirectly. This reason is related to questions of social engineering, specifically, of how to organize a community, or even society as a whole, so that it can thrive. To give a simple example of this kind of engineering: if there is a surplus of general practitioners in the cities but a relative shortage of such practitioners in more rural areas, the government may look for ways to make it attractive for doctors to set up their practices in the countryside, to ensure that all citizens have ready access to primary health care. In our case, the focus is on ways to ensure that communities can thrive in epistemically relevant ways.

Computational agent-based models can be helpful here. In 2009, the editors of the journal *Nature* called for increased use of agent-based models in economics, arguing (among other things) that

> modellers seeking to make a real difference in the world should concentrate on the tangible, immediate questions that decision-makers actually worry about. A good example to follow is that of pandemic planning, in which simulations are already in widespread use to help officials decide when to close schools and other public gathering places, and how best to mount a vaccination campaign. The simulations alone cannot answer such questions, nor can they replace judgement. But by helping officials frame the problem, organize the available information and identify which factors matter, they can make judgements better informed.
>
> *(Editorial,* Nature *2009, 460, p. 667)*

Agent-based models have been used to explain observed patterns in the spread of pandemics (e.g., Ajelli et al. 2010), but they can also be used to try to predict the effects of possible responses to the outbreak of a pandemic, where they offer the advantages cited in the above passage, and that can make them an important decision support tool.

Governments not only want to protect their citizens as much as possible from rapidly spreading diseases, they also want citizens to be well-educated; they want the companies in their country to be strong in research and development so as to be competitive on the international market; they want their scientists to engage in cutting-edge and world-class research; they may want to foster collaborations between universities and the private sector; and so on. Governments can influence whether these and similar goals are achieved, at least to some extent, most obviously through the allocation of financial resources. To stimulate innovation, they may start a grants program for so-called high-risk, high-reward research (various countries have such programs); to stimulate international scientific cooperation, two or more countries may initiate a joint program to finance exchanges of their researchers (think, for instance, of the Marie Curie program of the European Commission); to stimulate research partnerships between universities and the private sector, they can create special funding schemes for projects requiring substantial input from both sides (such as the French ANR's current *Chaires industrielles* and *Institut Carnot* programs do).

But exactly how best to spend those resources in order to reach their goals regarding the level of education and science in their country is difficult if not impossible to say on an a priori basis. Just as computer simulations can help governments decide how to best respond to an emerging pandemic, they can help governments—and also non-governmental funding agencies—make decisions about how to best spend the available money to further their various ambitions with respect to science and education. These decisions ultimately concern normative epistemological questions, most notably questions of how to gain new knowledge and how to disseminate and optimally use existing knowledge.

To study such larger communities, then, social epistemologists have come to increasingly rely on computational agent-based models. In the next section, we look at what is unarguably the most popular model of this kind in social epistemology, the so-called Hegselmann–Krause (HK) model.

The Hegselmann–Krause Model

The HK model was first presented in Hegselmann and Krause (2002) and it was further developed in their (2005), (2006), and (2009). The model has attracted attention from diverse fields of research, including philosophy, mathematics, computer science, economics, and physics. Initially, uses of the model were mainly focussed on descriptive questions, most notably questions concerning when opinions in a community tend to polarize and when they tend to converge. However, in more recent work it has been applied to normative epistemological issues as well (see below). The HK model is by no means the only computational model that has featured in the social epistemology literature; see note 2 and below.[5] But, as noted, it is the most popular one, and for a good reason. The model is simple yet extremely versatile and flexible in that it can easily be extended to suit various philosophical needs and purposes. The following first describes the model as it was originally presented by Hegselmann and Krause and then looks at some extensions of that model and their applications in social epistemology.

In its most elementary form, all the HK model assumes are communities of agents trying to determine the value τ of some unspecified parameter; it is antecedently given that this value lies in the unit interval. Each agent proceeds by averaging, repeatedly, and simultaneously with the other agents, the opinions about τ of those agents who are within her so-called bounded confidence interval (BCI), where an agent is within another agent's BCI exactly if the absolute difference between their opinions about the value of τ does not exceed a given threshold value ε.[6]

For the most part, however, Hegselmann and Krause study a more sophisticated variant of this model, namely, one in which the agents also take into account evidence about τ. In this variant, the opinion of agent x_i after the $(u+1)$-st update is given by

$$x_i(u+1) = \alpha \frac{1}{|X_i(u)|} \sum_{j \in X_i(u)} x_j(u) + (1-\alpha)\tau. \tag{HK}$$

Here, $x_j(u)$ is the opinion of agent x_j after the u-th update,

$$X_i(u) \left\{ j : |x_i(u) - x_j(u)| \leq \varepsilon \right\}$$

is the set of agents within agent x_i's BCI after the u-th update, and $\alpha \in [0,1]$ determines the relative importance the agent gives to the social part of the updating process as compared to the evidential part. Note that the elementary version of the HK model, in which agents update only by averaging the opinions of the agents within their BCI, is the special instance of (HK) with $\alpha = 1$.

The above model assumes that the information the agents receive about τ is accurate. It also assumes that the agents' opinions about τ all weigh equally heavily in the updating process. As Douven and Riegler (2010) point out, both assumptions are rather unrealistic: in actuality, researchers have to cope with measurement errors and various other factors that cause data to be noisy, and the opinions of some members of the scientific community clearly count for more than those of others. To accommodate these observations, Douven and Riegler (2010) propose the following extension of (HK):

$$x_i(u+1) = \alpha \frac{\sum_{j \in X_i(u)} w_j x_j(u)}{\sum_{j \in X_i(u)} w_j} + (1-\alpha)(\tau + \text{rnd}(\zeta)), \tag{EHK}$$

where $w_j \geq 0$ represents the reputation of agent x_j, and $\text{rnd}(\zeta)$ returns a unique uniformly distributed random real number in the interval $[-\zeta, \zeta]$, with $\zeta \in [0,1]$, each time this function is invoked.[7]

Computer simulations using (EHK) have shown that communities whose agents receive noisy evidence still converge on τ, given any non-trivial value of α. However, communities of agents who give relatively more weight to the social aspect of the updating procedure (so who have higher values of α) tend to approach the value of τ more closely than communities who give more weight to the evidence, although in the latter communities, agents tend to get on average faster to a value that is at least moderately close to τ. Further simulations have shown that the assignment of reputation weights has only a small impact both on the average speed with which the opinions in a community converge to τ and on the average accuracy of the limit.

In Douven (2010), Douven and Riegler (2010), and De Langhe (2013a, 2013b), these and similar facts about the HK model or some of its straightforward extensions are brought to bear on the debate concerning peer disagreement (see, e.g., the papers in Antony, ed., 2007). For instance, Douven (2010) argues that there are no context-independent answers to the questions of whether, and to what degree, one should be willing to compromise with one's disagreeing peers: given that the decision to compromise can impact the speed and accuracy of one's convergence to the truth in different ways, it all depends on what one's contextually determined epistemic goal is, and specifically on whether that is better served by a rapid but imprecise convergence to the truth or rather by a close but relatively slower convergence. Other philosophical applications of the HK model in either of the above forms, or slights variants thereof, are to be found in Olsson's (2008) work on reliabilism and untruthful assertion, Douven and Kelp's (2011) work on truth approximation, and Gustafsson and Peterson's (2012) work on moral disagreements.[8]

Both (HK) and (EHK) concern agents whose belief states are, at any given point in time, exhaustively characterized by a single value. Riegler and Douven (2009) propose an extension of the HK model that allows agents to have richer belief states. In this extension, each agent's belief state is characterized by a complete theory about the world, where a theory can be thought of as consisting of a finite set of possible worlds: all those worlds that, as far as the agent's beliefs go, could be the actual one. Assuming some ordering of the worlds, a belief state can be represented by a bit string, where a 1-bit (0-bit) at the n-th location indicates that the i-th world in the ordering of worlds is epistemically possible (impossible) for the agent.

Belief revision again occurs by taking into account both the belief states of other agents in the model and new information about the world. And here, too, the belief states taken into account are only those that are not too far removed from the agent's own, which is again expressed by saying that they are within the agent's BCI, although now the BCI has a somewhat more complicated definition. The definition uses the so-called Hamming distance between bit strings, which for a given pair of bit strings is defined as the number of locations in which the strings differ. The BCI is then defined by placing a threshold value D on the distance, meaning that in updating, the agents take into account the belief state of another agent precisely if the Hamming distance between (the bit string representing) the agent's own theory and (the bit string representing) the other agent's theory is no greater than D.

To describe the update rule for this model, first consider the simplified case where there is no information coming from the world. In that case, the rule is a bitwise two-step operation consisting of averaging and rounding, in that order. In the averaging step, for each bit of the theory a straight average is taken of the corresponding bits of the agents in the agent's BCI. In the typical case, the result is a value in the unit interval rather than just a 0 or a 1. Then, in the rounding step, the agent's bit is updated either to 1 if the average is greater than $1/2$, or updated to 0 if the average is less than $1/2$; if the average is exactly equal to $1/2$, the bit is updated to a 1 or a 0 depending on the outcome of a coin flip.

To see how information about the world gets added, note that pieces of information can also be represented by bit strings, 1-bits indicating the worlds consistent with the information and 0-bits, the worlds ruled out by the information. Thus, in the update procedure, information can be treated the same ways as the agents in the BCI, where the relative weight given to the information—corresponding to the parameter setting of α in (HK) and (EHK)—is determined by how many copies of the bit string representing the information go into the averaging step, together with the bit strings representing the belief states of the agents within the BCI.

Riegler and Douven (2009) use this model to carry out a number of simulation experiments whose outcomes are pertinent again to the peer disagreement debate, where however now the peer disagreement may concern multiple issues at the same time.[9] Douven and Wenmackers (2017) tweak the model slightly by populating it with agents whose belief states are represented by vectors of probabilities: degrees to which they deem each world to be the actual one—rather than by bit strings which indicate, for each world, whether or not the agent deems it possible—and use the result to compare, along a number of epistemically important dimensions, updating via Bayes' rule with updating via some version of Inference to the Best Explanation (see Douven 2011), where the agents take into account both evidence directly about the world and each others' opinions. Finally, in a very similar model, Crosscombe and Lawry (2016) study the effect of agents having (partly) *vague* beliefs. The findings of their simulations add further support to the claim that agents who combine evidential updating and compromising with other agents end up having more accurate belief states than agents who rely only on evidential updating. Another interesting discovery reported in their paper is that agents starting out with vague beliefs end up with only crisp (i.e., non-vague) ones, given an intuitively plausible way of compromising on vague beliefs.

As mentioned, the HK model is not the only computational model on the market that has been used by social epistemologists. For such alternative models, see Zollman (2007), Zollman (2009), Zollman (2010), Zollman (2015), Semeshenko, Gordon, and Nadal (2008), Weisberg and Muldoon (2009), De Langhe and Greiff (2010), Muldoon and Weisberg (2011), Olsson (2011), Olsson and Vallinder (2013), De Langhe (2014a), (2014b), Muldoon et al. (2014), Muldoon, Lisciandra, and Hartmann (2014), and Vallinder and Olsson (2014). Most of these models can deal with much more complex interactions between agents than the HK model or its known extensions. However, because these other models are typically geared toward specific types of interactions, they are not as easily adapted to one's own purposes as the HK model is. Also, while one can get the HK model and its extensions up and running in most freely available languages —including NetLogo, Python, and R—with remarkably few lines of codes, the same cannot be said of many of the more elaborate simulation environments offered by the above-cited authors.

Summary

Computational agent-based models are among the standard research tools of many social scientists. There is reason to believe that they will become indispensable tools for social epistemologists as well. For, as argued above, social epistemologists should not be satisfied with studying the epistemic interactions among small numbers of agents, but should also consider large communities of epistemically interacting agents. However, the ways in which the epistemic interactions in such communities give rise to interesting social patterns can easily be too complex to be studied in sufficient depth through analytical methods.

This chapter has concentrated on a computational model that is increasingly popular in social epistemology, namely, the Hegselmann–Krause model. While it is simple, researchers have successfully used the model to illuminate both descriptive and normative socio-epistemological questions, including questions concerning consensus and dissensus formation in ways that have been empirically established but are formally not well understood, and questions of how best to change our beliefs or degrees of belief when we have access not only to direct evidence about the world but also to the beliefs or degrees of belief of other members of our community. Clearly, we are just at the beginning of the development, so with time, we should expect further useful computational models to become available to social epistemologists.[10]

Notes

1 See Muldoon, Smith, and Weisberg (2012) for a recent strengthening of Schelling's results.
2 See Lehrer and Wagner (1981) for mathematical details and also for a discussion of possible interpretations of the iteration process.
3 In fact, even the value of the Lehrer–Wagner model as a tool in the practice of group deliberation is dubitable. As Condon, Golden, and Wasil (2003) point out, the model is vulnerable to group members announcing weights and estimates of the value of the parameter at stake for strictly strategic reasons, in order to manipulate the outcome of the procedure.
4 See, for instance, Weisberg and Muldoon (2009), Zollman (2010), and De Langhe (2014a), (2014b).
5 Also, a number of models very similar to the HK model were independently developed by other researchers; see, e.g., Deffuant et al. (2000), Dittmer (2001), and Weisbuch et al. (2002).
6 In some of Hegselmann and Krause's studies, this value is allowed to vary among the agents, but here we consider only the kind of case in which all agents have the same threshold value.

7 It was previously seen as a major limitation of the Lehrer–Wagner model that it requires all agents to know each other. Note that, in effect, the HK model only requires that, at each update step, every agent knows those agents who are in his or her BCI. Riegler and Douven (2009) also present a version of the HK model in which the agents move on a two-dimensional grid and know only the opinions of their spatial neighbors on the grid.

8 Interestingly, Herzog and Hertwig's (2009) work on what they call "dialectical bootstrapping" suggests that the HK model may also be relevant to individualistic epistemology. They have shown experimentally that by generating two different opinions on a given issue—pretending to be a crowd of two, as it were—and then averaging those opinions, regarding the result as one's ultimate opinion on the issue, people are, under fairly general conditions, likely to increase the accuracy of their opinions. The idea of dialectical bootstrapping can be, and has been, generalized in various ways; see Herzog and Hertwig (2014).

9 For some analytical results about the model, see Wenmackers, Vanpoucke, and Douven (2012), (2014).

10 I am greatly indebted to Christopher von Bülow for valuable comments on a previous version.

References

Ajelli, M., Gonã§Alves, B., Balcan, D., Colizza, V., Hu, H., Ramasco, J. J., Merler, S., and Vespignani, A. (2010). Comparing large-scale computational approaches to epidemic modeling: Agent-based versus structured metapopulation models, *Infectious Diseases* 10(190), doi: 10.1186/1471-2334-10-190.

Anthony, L. (2007). *Philosophers without gods*. Oxford: Oxford University Press.

Condon, E., Golden, B., and Wasil, E. (2003). Visualizing group decisions in the analytic hierarchy process, *Computers and Operations Research* 30, pp. 1435–1445.

Crosscombe, M. and Lawry, J. (2016). A model of multi-agent consensus for vague and uncertain beliefs, *Adaptive Behavior*, in press.

De Langhe, R. (2013a). Peer disagreement under multiple epistemic constraints, *Synthese* 190, pp. 2547–2556.

De Langhe, R. (2013b). Mixing beliefs among interacting agents, *Advances in Complex Systems* 3, pp. 87–98.

De Langhe, R. (2014a). A comparison of two models of scientific progress, *Studies in History and Philosophy of Science* 46, pp. 94–99.

De Langhe, R. (2014b). A unified model of the division of cognitive labor, *Philosophy of Science* 81, pp. 444–459.

De Langhe, R. and Greiff, M. (2010). Standards and the distribution of cognitive labour: A model of the dynamics of scientific activity, *Logic Journal of the IGPL* 18, pp. 278–294.

Deffuant, G., Neau, D., Amblard, F., and Weisbuch, G. (2000). Mixing beliefs among interacting agents, *Advances in Complex Systems* 3, pp. 87–98.

Dittmer, J. C. (2001). Consensus formation under bounded confidence, *Nonlinear Analysis* 7, pp. 4615–4621.

Douven, I. (2010). Simulating peer disagreements, *Studies in History and Philosophy of Science* 41, pp. 148–157.

Douven, I. (2011). Abduction, in E. N. Zalta, ed., *Stanford encyclopedia of philosophy*. available at http://plato.stanford.edu/entries/abduction/.

Douven, I. and Riegler, A. (2010). Extending the Hegselmann–Krause model I, *Logic Journal of the IGPL* 18, pp. 323–335.

Douven, I. and Kelp, C. (2011). Truth approximation, social epistemology, and opinion dynamics, *Erkenntnis* 75, pp. 271–283.

Douven, I. and Wenmackers, S. (2017). Inference to the best explanation versus Bayes' rule in a social setting, *British Journal for the Philosophy of Science* 68, pp. 535–570.

Easley, D. and Kleinberg, J. (2010). *Networks, crowds, and markets*. Cambridge: Cambridge University Press.

Goldman, A. I. (1999). *Knowledge in a social world*. Oxford: Oxford University Press.

Gribbin, J. (2010). *Science: A history*. London: Penguin Books.

Gustafsson, J. E. and Peterson, M. (2012). A computer simulation of the argument from disagreement, *Synthese* 184, pp. 387–405.

Hegselmann, R. and Krause, U. (2002). Opinion dynamics and bounded confidence: Models, analysis, and simulations, *Journal of Artificial Societies and Social Simulation* 5, Available at http://jasss.soc.surrey.ac.uk/5/3/2.html.

Hegselmann, R. and Krause, U. (2005). Opinion dynamics driven by various ways of averaging, *Computational Economics* 25, pp. 381–405.

Hegselmann, R. and Krause, U. (2006). Truth and cognitive division of labor: First steps towards a computer aided social epistemology, *Journal of Artificial Societies and Social Simulation* 9, available at http://jasss.soc.surrey.ac.uk/9/3/10.html.

Hegselmann, R. and Krause, U. (2009). Deliberative exchange, truth, and cognitive division of labour: A low-resolution modeling approach, *Episteme* 6, pp. 130–144.

Herzog, S. M. and Hertwig, R. (2009). The wisdom of many in one mind: Improving individual judgments with dialectical bootstrapping, *Psychological Science* 20, pp. 231–237.

Herzog, S. M. and Hertwig, R. (2014). Harnessing the wisdom of the inner crowd, *Trends in Cognitive Sciences* 18, pp. 504–506.

Kuhn, T. S. (1962). *The structure of scientific revolutions*. Chicago: Chicago University Press.

Lehrer, K. and Wagner, C. (1981). *Rational consensus in science and society*. Dordrecht: Reidel.

Muldoon, R., Lisciandra, C., Colyvan, M., Martini, C., Sillari, G., and Sprenger, J. (2014). Disagreement behind the veil of ignorance, *Philosophical Studies* 170, pp. 377–394.

Muldoon, R., Lisciandra, C., and Hartmann, S. (2014). Why are there descriptive norms? Because we looked for them, *Synthese* 191, pp. 4409–4429.

Muldoon, R., Smith, T., and Weisberg, M. (2012). Segregation that no one seeks, *Philosophy of Science* 79, pp. 38–62.

Muldoon, R. and Weisberg, M. (2011). Robustness and idealization in models of cognitive labor, *Synthese* 183, pp. 161–174.

Olsson, E. J. (2008). Knowledge, truth, and bullshit: Reflections on Frankfurt, *Midwest Studies in Philosophy* 32, pp. 94–110.

Olsson, E. J. (2011). A simulation approach to veritistic social epistemology, *Episteme* 8, pp. 127–143.

Olsson, E. J. and Vallinder, A. (2013). Norms of assertion and communication in social networks, *Synthese* 190, pp. 2557–2571.

Riegler, A. and Douven, I. (2009). Extending the Hegselmann–Krause model III: From single beliefs to complex belief states, *Episteme* 6, pp. 145–163.

Schelling, T. C. (1969). Models of segregation, *American Economic Review* 59, pp. 488–493.

Semeshenko, V., Gordon, M. B., and Nadal, J.-P. (2008). Collective states in social systems with interacting learning agents, *Physica A: Statistical Mechanics and Its Applications* 387, pp. 4903–4916.

Vallinder, A. and Olsson, E. J. (2014). Trust and the value of overconfidence: A Bayesian perspective on social network communication, *Synthese* 191, pp. 1991–2007.

Weisberg, M. and Muldoon, R. (2009). Epistemic landscapes and the division of cognitive labor, *Philosophy of Science* 76, pp. 225–252.

Weisbuch, G., Deffuant, G., Amblard, F., and Nadal, J.-P. (2002). Meet, discuss and segregate, *Complexity* 7, pp. 55–63.

Wenmackers, S., Vanpoucke, D., and Douven, I. (2012). Probability of inconsistencies in theory revision, *European Physical Journal B* 85, pp. 1–15.

Wenmackers, S., Vanpoucke, D., and Douven, I. (2014). Rationality: A social-epistemology perspective, *Frontiers in Psychology* 5, doi: 10.3389/fpsyg.2014.0058.

Zollman, K. J. S. (2007). The communication structure of epistemic communities, *Philosophy of Science* 74, pp. 574–587.

Zollman, K. J. S. (2009). Optimal publishing strategies, *Episteme* 6, pp. 185–199.

Zollman, K. J. S. (2010). The epistemic benefit of transient diversity, *Erkenntnis* 6, pp. 17–35.

Zollman, K. J. S. (2015). Modeling the social consequences of testimonial norms, *Philosophical Studies* 172, pp. 2371–2383.

Further Reading

There is a special issue of the journal *Episteme* (issue 6 from 2009) that is entirely devoted to computational models in social epistemology. Worth reading are also various articles in two special issues of the journal *Synthese* about the role of simulations in science and the social epistemology of science (issue 3, vol. 169, 2009, and issue 1, vol. 180, 2011). Further relevant are many of the articles in *Scientific collaboration and collective knowledge*, edited by Thomas Boyer-Kassem, Conor Mayo-Wilson, and Michael Weisberg (Oxford University Press, 2017). For readers who would like to conduct agent-based simulations themselves, Richard Gaylord and Louis D'Andria's *Simulating society* (Springer, 1998) is still a good starting point. The book assumes the reader to have access to *Mathematica*, which is proprietary software (though at many universities available through a site license). However, the general modeling strategies shown in the book can be applied as well in languages such as R, Python, or Julia, all of which are open source and offer wonderful simulation environments.

46

EPISTEMOLOGY AND CLIMATE CHANGE

David Coady

Introduction

Referring to public and academic debate about climate change, Philip Kitcher has said that it is "an embarrassment that philosophers have not contributed more to this necessary conversation" (2010: 6). This is not entirely fair. There are philosophers who have made important contributions to this conversation, the vast majority of these contributions, however, come from a single area of philosophy: ethics.[1] This is unfortunate since public and academic debate about climate change is certainly not restricted in this way. Much of it (perhaps most of it) is about epistemic issues, rather than ethical issues.[2] In other words, it is about what we should believe and what we can know, rather than about what we should do or how we should live.[3] Epistemic questions are not only prominent in the public debate about climate change, they are also, in a clear sense, logically prior to the ethical questions. As Rousseau observed, "what one ought to do depends largely on what one ought to believe" (1782: Third Walk). For these reasons, it is clear that epistemologists *qua* epistemologists (and not merely in their capacity as global citizens) are obliged to contribute to the debate about climate change.

A handful of epistemologists have roused themselves to address this obligation. As will become clear in my discussion of them over the course of this chapter, there is a two-way relation between epistemology and the climate change debate. Not only does epistemology have an important contribution to make to the public debate about climate change, the public debate about climate change provides a useful case for testing some theoretical positions in epistemology.

The Political Patterning of the Debate

There is a clear and well documented connection between people's beliefs about climate change and their broader political views. This fact has been a recurring theme in the small literature on epistemology and climate change (e.g. John 2017 and Keller 2015). After citing some recent surveys in the US and the UK showing a strong correlation between people's views about climate change and their voting intentions, Stephen John suggests that there is something puzzling and unusual about this state of affairs.

> The political patterning of opinions on climate change differs from other politically patterned commitments – for example, opposition to gay marriage – in that it apparently

involves factual, rather than ethical, disagreement. In cases of factual disagreement, we typically think that discussants should defer to cognitive experts.

(John 2017)[4]

There are several assumptions apparent in the above passage that are worth noting.

First, the political patterning of opinions on climate change do not all involve factual, rather than ethical, disagreement. Many of these opinions concern fundamental disagreement about our obligations to people living in the developing world (see Singer 2002 and Coady and Corry 2013: 72–81), future generations (see Coady and Corry, 2013: 82–103), and our obligations to non-human animals and/or nature (Hassoun 2011). So, politically patterned disagreement over climate change is partly factual and partly ethical, and, as we shall shortly see, it is no easy matter to separate these components.

Second, insofar as the political patterning of opinions on climate change does involve factual disagreements, this does not make it particularly unusual. John presupposes that, in general, political commitment, and hence political disagreement, is fundamentally about ethics rather than facts, but that is not, in general, historically accurate. Republican voters in the United States, for example, were much more likely to believe in the effectiveness of nuclear deterrence, and this is clearly a factual issue. Even John's own example of a political commitment, opposition to gay marriage, is at least as much about factual disagreement as it is about ethical disagreement.[5]

Third, it is not at all clear, as John seems to presuppose, that deference to cognitive experts is something "we" think is particularly appropriate in cases of factual rather than ethical disagreement. The question of whether there is such a thing as ethical expertise is very controversial. I have argued (see Coady 2012: 51–55) against the existence of experts in ethics *as such*, but my argument does not imply that there is no such thing as experts (or cognitive experts) on the specific ethical issues raised by the problem of climate change.

Most western countries have some form of political duopoly.[6] That is they tend to be dominated by two rival camps (parties or coalitions), and political debate tends to be framed in terms of the debate between them. The climate change debate is no different. There is no uncontroversial way to name the two sides of the climate change debate. Indeed it often seems that to name the sides to the debate is, to some extent, to take a side.[7] Nonetheless, I will begin with some terminology that I hope is as neutral as possible. I call the following combination of beliefs "climate change orthodoxy":

1 The climate is changing; in particular average global temperatures are rising over the long term.
2 This change is largely caused by human activity.
3 This change is, on balance, a bad thing.
4 People are morally obliged individually and/or collectively[8] to mitigate this change.

(1) and (2) are purely factual beliefs, whereas (3) and (4) involve values as well as facts. Not everyone who believes (1) and (2) believes (3), and not everyone who believes (1), (2), and (3) believes (4).[9] I call anyone who doesn't believe one or more of (1) to (4) "a sceptic" or a "climate change sceptic".[10] This seems to conform reasonably well with ordinary usage. Certainly, it captures quite well the variety of views held by people who call themselves "sceptics". Some people in the orthodox camp, however, would object to my use of terminology, on the grounds that it is they who are the true sceptics, while their opponents, the "so-called sceptics", should more properly be called "denialists".[11] This rhetorical move reflects a widespread view in our culture that scepticism (or "scientific scepticism") is a good thing, a kind of intellectual

virtue that is central to the scientific method. This leads many people on both sides of the debate to claim the label "sceptic" for themselves.

The positive connotations of the terms "sceptic" and "scientific sceptic" have led to considerable confusion and unnecessary ill-will in the climate change debate. The pejorative connotations of the terms "denialist" and "scientific denialist" by many in the orthodox camp, to denote those who disagree with them, is even more unfortunate. Science denialism has been defined as the rejection of a "scientific consensus, often in favor of a radical and controversial point of view" (Scudellari 2010). It should be obvious that, at least on this understanding, there is nothing wrong with science denialism. On the contrary, it plays an important role in scientific progress. The rejection of the geocentric model of the universe, the rejection of phlogiston theory, and the rejection of phrenology were all instances of science denialism.

The negative connotations of the word "denialism" appear to originate in Freudian psychoanalysis, in which *denial* (also called *abnegation*) is a psychological mechanism involved in refusing to believe something one wishes were not true, even in the presence of overwhelming evidence that it is true. To call someone a "denialist" then is to imply that there is something pathological about his or her beliefs. The practice of pathologising of views one disagrees with is to be avoided in any serious debate, especially when it is a political debate, and the climate change debate is very much a political debate.[12]

It is probably best to avoid using the term "climate change denialist" altogether, but, if it is to be used, it should be reserved for those who *disbelieve* one or more of (1) to (4), above. So understood a denialist is a kind of sceptic. A climate change denialist does not *merely* not believe one or more of these propositions; he or she positively believes that one or more of them is false (i.e. he or she believes its negation).

Climate change sceptics are often portrayed by proponents of climate change orthodoxy as anti-science (i.e. they are science denialists), but many of them are, in fact, great fans of science (or at least that which they consider to be science). They merely, in some cases, have mistaken ideas about what science is. They are not entirely to blame for these mistakes, however, since these mistakes have been advanced as orthodoxies by a lot of scientists, as well as by a lot of philosophers, writing about science and the business of knowledge acquisition more generally. In the next two sections I will briefly discuss two of these mistakes.

Testimony and the Role of Trust in the Climate Change Debate

When people speak of "scepticism" or "scientific scepticism" as though it were an intellectual virtue, they usually have a particular form of scepticism in mind: scepticism about testimony (i.e. scepticism about the written or spoken assertions of others). The idea that we should be particularly sceptical of testimony is one that goes back to the origins of modern science. The motto of the Royal Society was (and still is) "Nullius in Verba", which may be translated as "Nothing on Testimony". John Locke, one of the most prominent spokesmen for the new science, gave voice to this form of scepticism in the following passage:

> I hope it will not be thought arrogance to say, that perhaps we should make greater progress in the discovery of rational and contemplative knowledge if we sought it in the fountain, in the consideration of things themselves, and made use rather of our own thoughts than other men's to find it: for I think we may as rationally hope to see with other men's eyes as to know by other men's understanding. ... The floating of other men's opinions in our brains makes us not one jot the more knowing, though they happen to be true. What in them was science is in us but opiniatrety.
>
> (Locke 1961/1690: 58)

As Simon Keller (2015: 224) points out, most people's opinions about climate change (especially their beliefs about the factual as opposed to the ethical issues) are heavily dependent on what others tell them. Locke's principle implies that most people's opinions about climate change are *just* opinions, not science and not genuine knowledge. Indeed, Keller seems to draw this conclusion when he concludes that because the debate is very much about whom to trust, climate change scepticism can be "subjectively rational" (Keller 2015: 229).

This may seem plausible, however a little reflection shows that it's not just the views of lay-people or non-scientists on this subject that are heavily dependent on the testimony of others, but everyone's. For example, no one arrived at the conclusion that average global temperatures have increased over the last century on their own. Rather, they reached this conclusion by relying on the testimony of thousands of people who have taken measurements and made calculations all around the world for a very long time.

Locke's position underestimates the extent to which scientific practitioners, and others working at the coal-face of knowledge acquisition, are reliant on testimony. This was true even in Locke's time[13]; it is much more so now, at the beginning of the twenty-first century, when human knowledge is much more extensive and (partly as a result) much more specialized. Cognitive labour is divided, to borrow Phillip Kitcher's (1990) phrase, in such a way that the general public is heavily reliant on what scientists tell them, and individual scientists are heavily reliant on what other scientists tell them.

George Monbiot, one of the most prominent public defenders of climate change orthodoxy, thinks that science is sending a contradictory message:

> The detail of modern science is incomprehensible to almost everyone, which means that we have to take what scientists say on trust. Yet science tells us to trust nothing, to believe only what can be demonstrated. This contradiction is fatal to public confidence.
>
> *(Monbiot 2010)*

There are two mistakes in this passage. First, the detail of modern science is not merely incomprehensible to *almost* everyone, it is incomprehensible to *absolutely* everyone. This is the case, not only if we consider science as a whole, but even if we restrict our attention to the practice of climate science. All the scientists on whom we rely for our opinions on climate change are themselves reliant on other scientists for their opinions on climate change (Coady and Corry 2013: 17–18).

This may make the problem Monbiot describes seem even worse, but fortunately he is wrong about something else; there is no contradiction between having an attitude of trust and believing only what can be demonstrated, because sometimes (indeed quite often) it can be demonstrated that we should be trusting, because some people are demonstrably trustworthy, at least in certain contexts and about certain subjects. If science really did tell us to trust nothing (or no one), then science would be giving us bad advice. But science doesn't tell us any such thing,[14] though many scientists (and philosophers) have unwisely said words to this effect.

Experts and Independence

We have seen that everyone is highly dependent on the testimony of others for their opinions about climate change. People (such as myself) who are not climate scientists and who believe the central factual claims of orthodox climate science are particularly dependent on the testimony of climate scientists for those beliefs. The main piece of supporting evidence (though not the only one) that we have is the fact that the overwhelming majority of climate scientists (presumably the experts on this subject) have testified that those factual claims are true (or at any rate, have testified to something which entails them).[15] Now some climate change sceptics doubt or deny that such a consensus (or near consensus) exists, but many, perhaps most of them, accept that it exists but deny that that the consensus constitutes genuine evidence for the rest of us of the factual claims in question.

What should we make of this? Once again there is a mistaken doctrine, which is widely accepted, in academic philosophy and our intellectual culture more broadly, that appears to support the climate change sceptic's position. This is the *independence principle*: that a consensus (or near consensus) of expert opinion is only evidentially significant to a non-expert if, and to the extent that, the parties to it have arrived at it independently of one another. Ben Almassi endorses the view in the following passage:

> Greater numbers should not lend more credence to a position unless one reasonably believes its individual adherents have come to their beliefs via somewhat independent processes. The appropriate weight is a function of the numbers of experts on each side and their relative epistemic independence as gauged by the listener.
>
> *(Almassi 2007: 378)*

Similarly, Adam Elga claims that the accumulation of testimony on one side of an issue "should move one only to the extent that one counts it as independent from opinions one has already taken into account" (Elga 2010: 177). He says that this view is "completely uncontroversial" and says that "every sensible view on disagreement should accommodate it".

If this were right, the consensus (or near consensus) of opinion amongst climate scientists about the reality of anthropogenic climate change would not be a good reason for the rest of us to accept it, since the scientists in question have palpably not converged on this conclusion independently of one another. The evidence on which climate science is based is too extensive, too varied in kind, and too widely distributed in space and time, for that to be possible.

Fortunately, for non-experts trying to work out whether to believe in anthropogenic climate change, the independence principle is false, and hence the fact that climate scientists are highly epistemically dependent on one another, and on earlier scientists, does not lessen the evidential significance of their consensus (or near consensus) for the rest of us.

To see this, it is helpful to make a distinction between *expertise* and *meta-expertise*. An expert is (roughly) someone who is unusually well-informed about a subject.[16] A meta-expert is (again roughly) someone who is unusually well-informed about who is unusually well-informed about it.[17] Although meta-expertise is distinguishable from first-order expertise conceptually, they overlap to a great extent in practice. Because experts typically work closely with other experts, they often have considerable meta-expertise as well as first order expertise, that is, they are often particularly good at identifying other experts in their field. They are, often, also good at recognizing which experts have greater expertise than themselves.

For this reason, experts need not arrive at their conclusions independently of one another in order to be justifiably confident of those conclusions. Their meta-expertise may allow them to recognize which experts are most likely to have correct opinions about a given issue, and come to share those opinions *for that reason*. When they do that, it is evidence, from a lay perspective, that the opinions in question are correct. So, for example, the fact that the vast majority of climate scientists accept the temperature records published by the National Ocean and Atmospheric Agency in the USA or the Hadley Climate Research Unit in the UK is evidence, from a lay perspective, that the scientists involved in producing this data are experts, and hence evidence of the reliability of the data.

Many prominent sceptics about anthropogenic climate change accept that there is a scientific consensus about the reality of anthropogenic climate change. However, they often seem remarkably unconcerned by it. William O'Keefe and Jeff Keueter (2010: 1) of the George C. Marshall Institute, for example, deny that non-experts should be influenced by this scientific consensus, on the grounds that "scientific history is replete with examples of consensus views that were flat out wrong". They are right about this, but scientific history is even more replete with examples of dissident views that were flat out wrong. The point is not that a scientific consensus cannot be wrong, but rather that where one exists, it is evidence, from the perspective of non-experts, of the truth of the consensus view.

Conclusion

I have argued that there are two epistemic errors underlying a great deal of climate change scepticism, particularly scepticism about the main factual claims of climate change orthodoxy. These errors are understandable because they have both acquired the status of conventional wisdom in our culture.

The first of these errors is scepticism about testimony: the view that testimony is in some way an inferior source of knowledge and/or justification (and perhaps not a source of knowledge or justification at all). If scepticism about testimony were right, that would entail that the confidence many of us have (including those of us who are climate scientists) about the reality of anthropogenic climate change, would be unjustified. However, scepticism about testimony is wrong. Testimony is a perfectly good way of acquiring knowledge and justifying our beliefs and there is nothing unscientific about acquiring beliefs through testimony.

The second of these errors is the independence principle. Many influential climate change sceptics think of science as the province of individual geniuses working in isolation from one another. Ian Plimer (2009: 14), for example, claims that most scientists are "anarchists" who accept no authority and who are indifferent to the opinions of others; he goes on to berate climate scientists at great length for their failure to live up to this ideal. But this was always a false ideal and its falsehood is particularly apparent in the case of contemporary climate science, which is, and needs to be, a highly interdisciplinary and collaborative enterprise in which all participants are highly dependent on those around them and on those who have gone before. This fact should not undermine the significance of the consensus climate scientists have reached.

Notes

1 Many of these contributions could be characterized as "political philosophy" as well as "ethics". They are about the ethical obligations of governments and international institutions.

2 Some of it is also about areas of philosophy other than ethics and epistemology. Some philosophers have considered the metaphysical issues raised by the climate change debate (Corry 2017) and some have considered the aesthetic issues raised by it (Brady 2014).

3 I have argued elsewhere (Coady 2012: 23–24) that strictly speaking epistemology is a branch of ethics. Nonetheless the distinction between ethics and epistemology is familiar enough and will be useful, so long as we bear in mind that when we distinguish them we are construing ethics narrowly as a subject concerned with "outward" actions, rather than "inner" actions (such as belief formation), or with moral virtues *rather than* intellectual virtues.

4 John goes on to argue that climate scientists represented in the Inter-governmental Panel on Climate Change (IPCC) have the relevant expertise and that, as a result, "regardless of their political commitments, non-experts should defer to the IPCC's testimony because the IPCC relies on the high epistemic standards which characterize scientific research" (John 2017).

5 Opponents of gay marriage tend to have a number of mistaken views about the causes of homosexuality and the behavior of homosexuals. They also often have views about the fate of homosexuals (and perhaps those who support their rights) in the after-life. I also think these are mistaken.

6 That is, they have two major parties or coalitions.

7 This is a common situation in highly politicised debates. For example, there seems to be no neutral way of defining the two sides to the abortion debate. One side often calls itself "pro-choice" and the other calls itself "pro-life", but these labels themselves are highly controversial.

8 Sinnott-Armstrong (2005) has argued that although we have no individual responsibility to reduce our own carbon footprint, our governments are obliged to force us to reduce our collective carbon footprint and that we have a collective responsibility to pressure our governments to do so.

9 Bjørn Lomborg (2001), for example, has argued that it is better to try to adapt to climate change than to mitigate it.

10 Clearly, there are in fact more than two sides to the climate change debate. There is disagreement amongst sceptics about which of the beliefs that constitute the orthodoxy they are skeptical of. There is also disagreement amongst the orthodox about precisely how rapidly the climate is changing, how much of it is due to human activity, how harmful its consequences are, and how to mitigate and who should be making the sacrifices required to mitigate it.

11 Authors who make this rhetorical move include Garvey (2008: 143–147); Garnaut (2011: 105–106); and Washington and Cook (2011).

12 The pathologizing of political dissent has a long and dark history. The practice of forcibly institutionalizing political dissidents in psychiatric hopticals in the Soviet Union is just one particularly extreme example (see Bloch and Reddaway 1978).

13 For example, in 1682 Edmund Halley noticed similarities between a comet he was observing and comets reported by earlier astronomers in 1531 and 1607. He inferred that they were all the same comet, and successfully predicted its return in 1758.

14 Of course, science itself doesn't really tell us anything, though scientific institutions and individual scientists do.

15 This seems clear from the fact that there is very little peer-reviewed literature challenging those factual claims (Oreskes and Conway 2010; Cook et al. 2013). Of course it is possible that some or all of the people publishing in peer-reviewed journals are not genuine experts and/or that genuine experts cannot get published in these journals. For more on this possibility see Coady and Corry (2013: 35–51).

16 For more detailed discussion of the precise definition of *expertise* see Coady (2012: 28–30).

17 I take the term "meta-expert" from Alvin Goldman (2001).

References

Almassi, B. (2007) Review of *The Philosophy of Expertise*. *Ethics: An International Journal of Social, Political, and Legal Philosophy* 117(2), pp. 377–381.

Bloch, S. and Reddaway, P. (1978) *Russia's Poltical Hospitals: Abuse of Psychiatry in the Soviet Union*, London: Futura.

Brady, E. (2014) Aesthetic Value, Ethics and Climate Change. *Environmental Values* 23, pp. 551–570.

Coady, D. (2012) *What to Believe Now: Applying Epistemology to Contemporary Issues*, Malden, MA: Wiley-Blackwell.

Coady, D. and Corry, R. (2013) *The Climate Change Debate: An Epistemic and Ethical Enquiry*, New York: Palgrave.

Cook, J., Nuccitelli, D., Green, S., Richardson, M., Winkler, B., Painting, R., Way, R., Jacobs, P., and Skuce, A. (2013) Quantifying the consensus on anthropogenic global warming in the scientific literature. *Environenental Research Letters* 8(2), pp. 1–7.

Corry, R. (2017) Did Climate Change Cause That? In: K-L. Rasmussen, K. Brownlee and D. Coady, eds., *A Companion to Applied Philosophy*, Chichester, UK: Wiley Blackwell, pp. 469–484.

Elga, A. (2010) How to Disagree about How to Disagree. In: R. Feldman and T. Warfield, eds., *Disagreement*, Oxford: Oxford University Press, pp. 175–186.

Garnaut, R. (2011) *The Garnaut Review 2011: Australia in the Global Response to Climate Change*, Cambridge: Cambridge University Press.

Garvey, J. (2008) *The Ethics of Climate Change: Right and Wrong in a Warming World*, London: Continuum.

Goldman, A. (2001) Experts: Which Ones Should You Trust? *Philosophy and Phenomenological Research* 63, pp. 85–110.

Hassoun, N. (2011) The Anthropocentric Advantage? Environmental Ethics and Climate Change Policy. *Critical Review of International Social and Political Philosophy* 14(2), pp. 235–257

John, S. (2017) From Social Values to P-Values: The Social Epistemology of the Intergovernmental Panel on Climate Change. *Journal of Applied Philosophy* 33(2), pp. 157–171.

Keller, S. (2015) Empathising With Scepticism About Climate Change. In: J. Moss, ed., *Climate Change and Justice*, Cambridge: Cambridge University Press, pp. 219–235.

Kitcher, P. (1990) The Division of Cognitive Labor. *Philosophy of Science* 87, pp. 5–22.

Kitcher, P. (2010) The Climate Change Debates. *Science*, Published online 27 May 2010. DOI:10.1126/science.1189312

Locke, J. (1690/1961) *An Essay Concerning Human Understanding*, ed. J. Youlton, London: Dent.

Lomborg, B. (2001) *The Sceptical Environmentalist: Measuring the Real State of the World*, Cambridge: Cambridge University Press.

Monbiot, G. (2010) The Trouble With Trusting Complex Science. *The Guardian*, March.

O'Keefe, W. and Kueter, J. (2010) *Clouding the Truth A Critique of Merchants of Doubt*, George C. Marshall Institute. www.marshall.org/pdf

Oreskes, N. and Conway, E. (2010) *Merchants of Doubt*. London: Bloomsbury Press.

Plimer, I. (2009) *Heaven and Earth: Global Warming and the Missing Science*. Ballan, Vic: Connor Court Publishing.

Rousseau, J. (1782/1980) *Reveries of a Solitary Walker*, London: Penguin.

Scudellari, M. (2010) State of Denial, *Nature Medicine* 16(3), pp. 248–249.

Singer, P. (2002) *One World: The Ethics of Globalisation*, Melbourne: The Text Publishing Company.

Sinnott-Armstrong, W. (2005) It's Not My Fault: Global Warming and Individual Moral Obligations. In: W. Sinnott-Armstrong and R. Howarth, eds., *Perspectives on Climate Change*, Bingley, UK: Emerald Group Publishng Limited, pp. 221–253.

Washington, H. and Cook, J. (2011) *Climate Change Denial: Heads in the Sand*, London: Routledge.

INDEX

Page numbers: Tables are given in **bold**; figures in *italics*; notes by [page number] 'n' [note number].